March 25–30, 2012
Potsdam, Germany

**Association for
Computing Machinery**

Advancing Computing as a Science & Profession

AOSD'12

Proceedings of the 11th Annual International Conference on
Aspect Oriented Software Development

Sponsored by:
ACM SIGPLAN and ACM SIGSOFT

Supported by:
AOSA

Association for Computing Machinery

Advancing Computing as a Science & Profession

The Association for Computing Machinery
2 Penn Plaza, Suite 701
New York, New York 10121-0701

ISBN: 978-1-4503-1092-5 (Digital)

ISBN: 978-1-4503-1741-2 (Print)

Additional copies may be ordered prepaid from:

ACM Order Department
PO Box 30777
New York, NY 10087-0777, USA

Phone: 1-800-342-6626 (USA and Canada)
+1-212-626-0500 (Global)
Fax: +1-212-944-1318
E-mail: acmhelp@acm.org
Hours of Operation: 8:30 am – 4:30 pm ET

Printed in the USA

MODULARITY: aosd.12–Chairs' Welcome

It is our great pleasure to welcome you to *Modularity: aosd.12,* the premiere international research conference on modularity in software and software-intensive systems. *Modularity: aosd.12* is the 11th annual international conference on *Aspect Oriented Software Development (AOSD),* and the first in which the conference committee will give an award for the most influential paper published in the Proceedings of the conference 10 years ago: in 2002.

This year's conference continues to broaden of the scope of the field to address all aspects of modularity, abstraction, and separation of concerns as they pertain to software, including new forms, uses, and analysis of modularity, along with the costs and benefits, and tradeoffs involved in their application. *Modularity* provides the international computer science research community and its many sub-disciplines (including software engineering, languages, and computer systems) with unique opportunities to come together to share and discuss perspectives, results, and visions with others interested in modularity as well as in the languages, development methods, architectures, algorithms, and other technologies organized around this fundamental concept.

The *Modularity: aosd.12* conference comprises two main events: Research Results and Modularity Visions. Both events invited full, scholarly papers of the highest quality on results and new ideas in areas that include but are not limited to complex systems, software design and engineering, programming languages, cyber-physical systems, and other areas across the whole system life cycle.

Papers submitted to the Research Results track were reviewed in accordance with the highest established standards of scientific rigor applied in peer review of putative research results. Reviewers assessed works in terms of research problem formulations, novelty and sophistication of proposed solutions, clarity and significance of hypotheses, proper design and execution of experimental or analytical assessments, sound interpretation of data, and correct characterization of work in relation to existing knowledge.

Papers submitted to the Modularity Visions track were reviewed in accordance with the highest established standards of scientific rigor applied in peer review of scientific research proposals. Reviewers assessed works in terms of research problem formulations, novelty and sophistication of proposed solutions, clarity and significance of hypotheses, compelling preliminary results, proposals for sound future experimental or analytical assessments and interpretation of data, and correct characterization of work in relation to existing knowledge.

The Results track attracted 79 submissions from across the world. Of these, 20 papers were accepted for publication, for a 25% acceptance rate. The program committee accepted papers in three rounds. In each round papers each paper was accepted, rejected, or (except in the last round) invited for revision and a second review. Five (5) papers were invited for revision and a second review, all of which were ultimately accepted. The Visions track reviewed 10 papers, one of which was referred from the Results track. Of these, three papers were accepted for publication for a 30% acceptance rate.

Our keynote and heart of technology speakers are Lars Bak, James O. Coplien, and Martin C. Rinard. Lars will report on implementing language-based virtual machines; Jim will talk about objects of the people, for the people, and by the people; and Martin will tell us what to do when things go wrong and how to recover in complex systems.

We wish to thank all members of our organizing and program committees and all co-reviewers.

We are looking forward to an interesting and inspiring *Modularity: aosd.12*.

Robert Hirschfeld
General Chair
Hasso-Plattner-Institut, Potsdam, Germany

Michael Haupt
Organizing Chair
Oracle Labs, Potsdam, Germany

Éric Tanter
Research Results Program Chair
Universidad de Chile, Chile

Kevin Sullivan
Modularity Visions Program Chair
University of Virginia, USA

Richard P. Gabriel
Heart of Technology Lectures Chair
IBM Research, USA

Table of Contents

Proceedings

Session 1: Features
Session Chair: David Lorenz *(The Open University of Israel)*

Session 2: Debugging
Session Chair: Wouter Joosen *(Katholieke Universiteit Leuven)*

Session 3: Languages
Session Chair: Mario Südholt *(École des Mines de Nantes)*

Session 4: Interference
Session Chair: Hidehiko Masuhara *(The University of Tokyo)*

Session 5: Empirical

Session Chair: Stefan Udo Hanenberg *(University of Duisburg-Essen)*

Session 6: Modularity in Systems Software

Session Chair: Michael Haupt *(Oracle Labs)*

Session 7: Implementing Languages

Session Chair: Eric Bodden *(Technische Universität Darmstadt)*

Session 8: Architecture and Design

Session Chair: Mira Mezini *(Technische Universität Darmstadt)*

MODULARITY: aosd.12–Organization

General Chair: Robert Hirschfeld *(Hasso-Plattner-Institut, University of Potsdam, Germany)*

Organizing Chair: Michael Haupt *(Oracle Labs, Potsdam, Germany)*

Program Chairs: Éric Tanter, Research Results Co-chair *(Universidad de Chile, Chile)*
Kevin J. Sullivan, Modularity Visions Co-chair *(University of Virginia, USA)*

Heart of Technology Lectures Chair: Richard P. Gabriel *(IBM Research, USA)*

Workshops Chairs: Sven Apel *(University of Passau, Germany)*
Bastian Steinert *(Hasso-Plattner-Institut, University of Potsdam, Germany)*

Demonstrations and BoFs Chairs: Carl Friedrich Bolz *(Heinrich-Heine-Universität Düsseldorf, Germany)*
Damien Cassou *(Inria Paris–Rocquencourt, France)*

Industry Chairs: Bogdan Franczyk *(Universität Leipzig, Germany)*
Andreas Polze *(Hasso-Plattner-Institut, University of Potsdam, Germany)*

Student Events Chairs: Hidehiko Masuhara *(The University of Tokyo, Japan)*
Michael Perscheid *(Hasso-Plattner-Institut, University of Potsdam, Germany)*

Publicity Chairs: Eric Bodden *(Technische Universität Darmstadt, Germany)*
Monica Pinto *(Universidad de Málaga, Spain)*

Student Volunteers Chairs: Ruzanna Chitchyan *(University of Leicester, UK)*
Jens Lincke *(Hasso-Plattner-Institut, University of Potsdam, Germany)*

Administrative Coordinator: Sabine Wagner *(Hasso-Plattner-Institut, University of Potsdam, Germany)*

Web Chair: Tobias Pape *(Hasso-Plattner-Institut, University of Potsdam, Germany)*

Design: Constanze Langer *(Institute of Industrial Design, Hochschule Magdeburg-Stendal, Germany)*

Steering Committee: Robert Baillargeon *(Panasonic Automotive Systems, USA)*
Paulo Borba *(Federal University of Pernambuco, Brazil)*
Shigeru Chiba *(Tokyo Institute of Technology, Japan)*
Thomas Cottenier *(UniqueSoft LLC, USA)*
Theo D'Hondt *(Vrije Universiteit Brussel, Belgium)*
Robert E. Filman *(USA)*
Richard Gabriel, **Vice Chair** *(IBM Research, USA)*
Michael Haupt, Secretary/Treasurer *(Oracle Labs, Potsdam, Germany)*
Robert Hirschfeld *(Hasso-Plattner-Institut, University of Potsdam, Germany)*
Uwe Hohenstein *(Siemens AG, Germany)*
Jean-Marc Jezequel *(Université de Rennes 1, France)*
Wouter Joosen *(Katholieke Universiteit Leuven, Belgium)*
Hidehiko Masuhara *(The University of Tokyo, Japan)*
Mira Mezini *(Technische Universität Darmstadt, Germany)*
Oege de Moor *(University of Oxford, UK)*
Ana Moreira *(Universidade Nova de Lisboa, Portugal)*
Oscar Nierstrasz *(University of Bern, Switzerland)*
Awais Rashid *(Lancaster University, UK)*
Mario Südholt, **Chair** *(École des Mines de Nantes, France)*
Kevin Sullivan *(University of Virginia, USA)*
Éric Tanter *(Universidad de Chile, Chile)*

Program Committee
Research Results: Jonathan Aldrich *(Carnegie Mellon University, USA)*
Sven Apel *(University of Passau, Germany)*
Eric Bodden *(Technische Universität Darmstadt, Germany)*
Paulo Borba *(Federal University of Pernambuco, Brazil)*
Shigeru Chiba *(Tokyo Institute of Technology, Japan)*
Yvonne Coady *(University of Victoria, Canada)*
Bruno De Fraine *(Vrije Universiteit Brussel, Belgium)*
Erik Ernst *(Aarhus University, Denmark)*
Patrick Eugster *(Purdue University, USA)*
Alessandro Garcia *(Pontifical Catholic University of Rio de Janeiro, Brazil)*
Stefan Hanenberg *(University of Duisburg-Essen, Germany)*
Michael Haupt *(Oracle Labs, Potsdam, Germany)*
Klaus Havelund *(Jet Propulsion Laboratory/NASA, USA)*
Wouter Joosen *(Katholieke Universiteit Leuven, Belgium)*
Gregor Kiczales *(University of British Columbia, Canada)*
Shriram Krishnamurthi *(Brown University, USA)*
Ralf Lämmel *(Universität Koblenz-Landau, Germany)*
Julia Lawall *(University of Copenhagen, Denmark)*
Karl Lieberherr *(Northeastern University, USA)*
David Lorenz *(Open University of Israel, Israel)*
Donna Malayeri *(Ecole Polytechnique Fédérale de Lausanne, Switzerland)*

MODULARITY: aosd.12–Sponsor & Supporters

Sponsor:

aosa
Aspect-Oriented Software
Association

In cooperation with:

acm SIGPLAN

SIGSOFT
SPECIAL INTEREST GROUP ON   SOFTWARE ENGINEERING

Supporters:

ORACLE®

SAP Innovation Center
Potsdam

Microsoft
Research

AO
AOSD-EUROPE
eu network of excellence

HPI Hasso
Plattner
Institut
IT Systems Engineering | Universität Potsdam

Separation of Concerns in Feature Modeling:
Support and Applications

Mathieu Acher

University of Namur
PReCISE Research Centre, Belgium
macher@fundp.ac.be

Philippe Collet
Philippe Lahire

Université Nice Sophia Antipolis,
France
{collet,lahire}@i3s.unice.fr

Robert B. France

Computer Science Department
Colorado State University, USA
france@cs.colostate.edu

Abstract

Feature models (FMs) are a popular formalism for describing the commonality and variability of software product lines (SPLs) in terms of features. SPL development increasingly involves manipulating many large FMs, and thus scalable modular techniques that support compositional development of complex SPLs are required. In this paper, we describe how a set of complementary operators (aggregate, merge, slice) provides practical support for separation of concerns in feature modeling. We show how the combination of these operators can assist in tedious and error prone tasks such as automated correction of FM anomalies, update and extraction of FM views, reconciliation of FMs and reasoning about properties of FMs. For each task, we report on practical applications in different domains. We also present a technique that can efficiently decompose FMs with thousands of features and report our experimental results.

Categories and Subject Descriptors   D.2.2 [*Software Engineering*]: Design Tools and Techniques

General Terms   Design, Languages, Theory

1. Introduction

The goal of software product line (SPL) engineering is to produce a family of related program variants for a domain [23]. SPL development starts with an analysis of the domain to identify commonalities and differences between the members of the product line. A common way is to describe variabilities of an SPL in terms of features which are domain abstractions relevant to stakeholders and are typically increments in program functionality [8]. A *Feature Model* (FM) is used to compactly define all features in an SPL and their valid combinations; it is basically an AND-OR graph with propositional constraints [12, 27, 32].

FMs are becoming increasingly large and complex. A contributing factor to their growing complexity is that FMs are being used not only to describe variability in software designs, but also variability in wider system contexts, at different times in the development and in different parts of the system structures [15, 19, 22, 24, 35]. As a result, the list of *concerns* that may be considered in an FM is very comprehensive [8, 34] ranging from hardware description [19], organizational structure [24], business or implementation details [22]. In practice, the concerns are related in a variety of ways and there can be hundreds of features whose legal combinations are governed by many and often complex rules. The automated extraction of FMs from large implemented software systems now produces very large FMs. As an extreme case, the variability model of Linux exhibits more than 6000 features [29].

It has been observed that maintaining a single large FM for the entire system may not be feasible [14, 23]. On the one hand, several FMs may be originally separated and combined: It is the case when one describes the variability of (sub-)systems that are by nature modular entities (e.g., software components or services [5]), when independent suppliers describe the variability of their different products in software supply chains [13, 16], or when a multiplicity of SPLs should be integrated [14, 15]. On the other hand, it can be the intention of an SPL practitioner to modularize the variability description of the system according to different criteria or concerns. It is the case when external variability is distinguished from internal variability [22, 23], when FMs are organized in layers [19], or when a simplified representation of an FM (a view) has been tailored for a specific stakeholder, role, task [17]. With FMs being increasingly complex, describing various concerns of an SPL and handled by several stakeholders (or even different organizations), managing them with a large number of features that are related in a variety of ways is intuitively a problem of *Separation of Concerns* (SoC) [9, 30]. First, composing support is needed to group and evolve a set of similar FMs, or

AOSD'12,   March 25 – 30, 2012, Potsdam, Germany.

to manage a set of inter-related FMs [2]. Second, some complementary decomposing support is as important to reason about local properties or to support multi-perspectives of a typically large FM [4]. Due to the complexity of FMs, SoC support should be soundly defined and automated as much as possible. In previous work, we designed a set of composition (insertion, merging, aggregation) [2] and decomposition (slice) [4] operators. Their semantic properties were precisely defined in terms of configuration set and feature hierarchy, and fully automated techniques were developed to synthesize FMs. Using these operators separately has practical but limited interests. In many scenarios and case studies, an SPL practitioner rather needs to combine both techniques and perform sequences of composition and decomposition, while reasoning about intermediate results.

In this paper, we show how the combined use of composition and decomposition operators forms a consistent and powerful support for SoC in feature modeling. We describe several novel applications of the operators, detailing the obtained benefits. These applications comprise *i)* the corrective capabilities of the operators themselves, *ii)* view extractions and updates on FMs, with the benefit of handling cross-tree constraints, *iii)* reconciling FMs that come from different stakeholders or organizations, and *iv)* reasoning about two kinds of variability to check important properties (realizability, usefulness) of an SPL. For each application, we report on practical use in different case studies. We revisit and implement some existing works with our operators and we report better results either in terms of capability or scalability. Furthermore, we present a technique that can efficiently decompose FMs with thousands of features and outperforms our previous implementation based on binary decision diagrams.

2. Background: Feature Models

FMs were first introduced in the FODA method [19], which also provided a graphical representation through Feature Diagrams. FMs are now widely adopted with support of formal semantics, reasoning techniques and tooling [8, 10, 12, 27]. An FM defines both a *hierarchy*, which structures features into levels of increasing detail, and some *variability* aspects expressed through several mechanisms. When decomposing a feature into subfeatures, the subfeatures may be *optional* or *mandatory* or may form *Xor* or *Or*-groups. In addition, any *propositional* constraints (e.g., implies or excludes) can be specified to express more complex dependencies between features. We consider that an FM is composed of a feature diagram coupled with a set of constraints expressed in propositional logic. Figure 1a shows an example of an FM. The feature diagram is depicted using a FODA-like graphical notation used throughout the paper.

The *hierarchy* of an FM is represented by a rooted tree $G = (\mathcal{F}, E, r)$ where $\mathcal{F}$ is a finite set of features and $E \subseteq \mathcal{F} \times \mathcal{F}$ is a finite set of edges (edges represent top-down hierarchical decomposition of features, i.e., parent-child relations between them) ; $r \in \mathcal{F}$ being the root feature.

An FM defines a set of valid feature *configurations*. A valid configuration is obtained by selecting features so that *i)* if a feature is selected, its parent is also selected; *ii)* if a parent is selected, all the mandatory subfeatures, exactly one subfeature in each of its Xor-groups, and at least one of its Or groups are selected; *iii)* propositional constraints hold. For example, in Figure 1a, { A, B, C, F, P, S, T, W } is a valid configuration, the features D and F cannot be selected at the same time and E cannot be selected without C due to the parent-child relation between E and C.

DEFINITION 1 (Configuration Semantics). *A configuration of an FM g is defined as a set of selected features. $[\![g]\!]$ denotes the set of valid configurations of the FM g and is thus a set of sets of features.*

FMs have been semantically related to propositional logic [12]. The set of configurations represented by an FM can be described by a propositional formula ϕ defined over a set of Boolean variables, where each variable corresponds to a feature (see Figure 1c for the formula corresponding to the FM of Figure 1a). The translation of FMs into logic representations allows one, as we will see in the next sections, to use reasoning techniques for automated FM analysis [10].

3. Composition and Decomposition Support

In previous work [2, 4], we designed a set of composition and decomposition *operators* that produce a new FM from one or more than one input FMs. We have defined the semantics of these operators in terms of:

configuration semantics We consider that the primary meaning of an FM, known as its configuration semantics, is a set of legal configurations – sets of selected features that respect the dependencies entailed by the diagram and the cross-tree constraints. We thus define the semantics of each operator in terms of the relationship between the configuration sets of the input FMs and the resulting FM.

feature hierarchy Another important property of an FM is the way features are organized – reflected in the feature hierarchy. We recall that two FMs can have identical configuration semantics, yet different hierarchies and thus ontological meaning [10, 29, 32]. As a result, we consider that the feature hierarchy should also be part of the semantics of the operators.

3.1 Aggregate

The *aggregate* operator supports cross-tree constraints between features so that separated FMs can be inter-related. The input FMs are aggregated under a synthetic root $synthetic_{ft}$ so that the root features of input FMs are child-mandatory features of $synthetic_{ft}$. In addition, the propositional constraints are added in the resulting FM. For example, the aggregate operator can be used to compose four FMs together with constraints (see Figure 5, page 6).

The properties of the aggregated FM heavily depends on the set of propositional constraints used during the aggre-

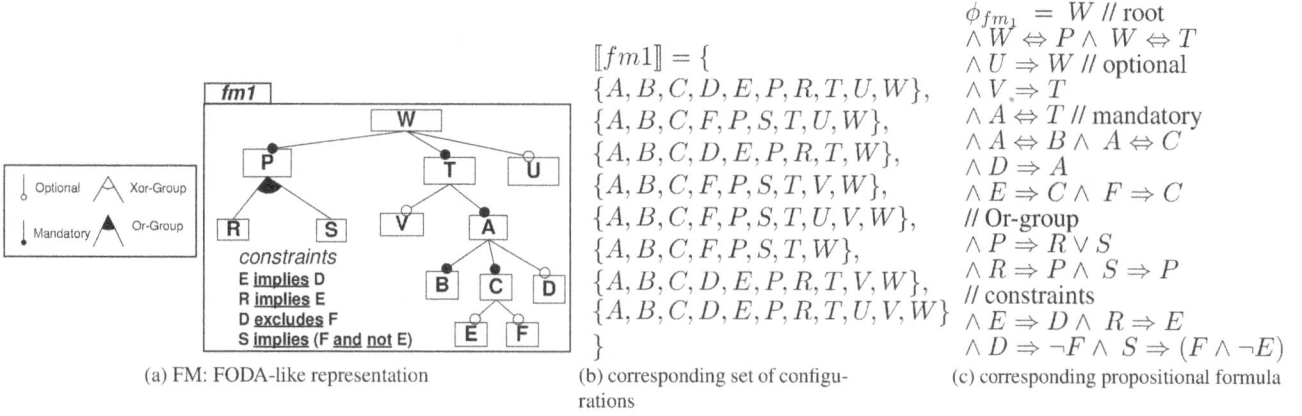

$\phi_{fm_1} = W$ // root
$\wedge\, W \Leftrightarrow P \wedge W \Leftrightarrow T$
$\wedge\, U \Rightarrow W$ // optional
$\wedge\, V \Rightarrow T$
$\wedge\, A \Leftrightarrow T$ // mandatory
$\wedge\, A \Leftrightarrow B \wedge A \Leftrightarrow C$
$\wedge\, D \Rightarrow A$
$\wedge\, E \Rightarrow C \wedge F \Rightarrow C$
// Or-group
$\wedge\, P \Rightarrow R \vee S$
$\wedge\, R \Rightarrow P \wedge S \Rightarrow P$
// constraints
$\wedge\, E \Rightarrow D \wedge R \Rightarrow E$
$\wedge\, D \Rightarrow \neg F \wedge S \Rightarrow (F \wedge \neg E)$

$[\![fm1]\!] = \{$
$\{A, B, C, D, E, P, R, T, U, W\},$
$\{A, B, C, F, P, S, T, U, W\},$
$\{A, B, C, D, E, P, R, T, W\},$
$\{A, B, C, F, P, S, T, V, W\},$
$\{A, B, C, F, P, S, T, U, V, W\},$
$\{A, B, C, F, P, S, T, W\},$
$\{A, B, C, D, E, P, R, T, V, W\},$
$\{A, B, C, D, E, P, R, T, U, V, W\}$
$\}$

(a) FM: FODA-like representation   (b) corresponding set of configurations   (c) corresponding propositional formula

Figure 1. FM, set of configurations and propositional logic encoding

gate. It may lead to situations where the aggregated FM does not represent any valid configuration or includes dead or core features (see Definition 2). We consider that the aggregate operator is purely syntactical. As we will see, other complementary techniques can be applied in case an SPL practitioner may want to simplify the aggregated FM or to reason about its properties.

3.2 Merge

The *merge* operator is dedicated to the composition of FMs that exhibit similar features (i.e., features with the same name). In this case, the merge operator can be used to *merge* the overlapping parts of the FMs and then to obtain an integrated FM. The merge uses name-based matching: two features match if and only if they have the same name.

Configuration Semantics. The properties of a merged FM produced by an application of the merge operator are formalized in terms of the sets of configurations of input FMs. Several modes are defined for the merge operator. We only describe here the modes that we will use in the remainder of the paper. The *intersection* mode is the most restrictive option: the merged FM, FM_r, expresses the common valid configurations of FM_1 and FM_2. The merge operator in the intersection mode is denoted as follows: $FM_1 \oplus_\cap FM_2 = Result$. The relationship between a merged FM *Result* in intersection mode and two input FMs FM_1 and FM_2 can be expressed as follows:

$$[\![FM_1]\!] \cap [\![FM_2]\!] = [\![Result]\!]$$

Another merge operator, called *diff*, is denoted as $FM_1 \oplus_\backslash FM_2 = Result$. The following defines the semantics of this operator:

$$[\![FM_1]\!] \backslash [\![FM_2]\!] = \{x \in [\![FM_1]\!] \mid x \not\models [\![FM_2]\!]\} = [\![Result]\!]$$

Hierarchy. Several FMs, with different hierarchies, can represent the same set of configurations [10, 29, 32]. So in particular several merged FMs can be produced and consistently represent the expected set of configurations while having different hierarchies. Intuitively, the more a parent-child relation occurs in the input FMs, the more an edge in the

merged hierarchy should be retained. The problem of choosing a hierarchy from amongst a set of hierarchies can be formulated as a minimum spanning tree problem (see details in [1]). An example of merge operation in intersection mode is given in Figure 8, page 7.

3.3 Slice Operator

The slice operator aims at simplifying or abstracting FMs by focusing on selected aspects of semantics. The overall idea behind FM slicing is similar to program slicing [36]. Program slicing techniques proceed in two steps: the subset of elements of interest (e.g., a set of variables of interest and a program location), called the slicing *criterion*, is first identified; then, a *slice* (e.g., a subset of the source code) is computed. In the context of FMs, we define the slicing criterion as a set of features considered to be pertinent by an SPL practitioner while the slice is a new FM.

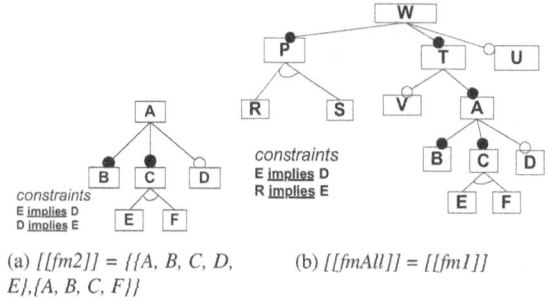

(a) $[\![fm2]\!] = \{\{A, B, C, D, E\}, \{A, B, C, F\}\}$ (b) $[\![fmAll]\!] = [\![fm1]\!]$

Figure 2. Two slice operations on fm1 (see Figure 1a)

Configuration Semantics. We define slicing as a unary operation on FM, denoted $\Pi_{\mathcal{F}_{slice}}(FM)$ where $\mathcal{F}_{slice} = \{ft_1, ft_2, ..., ft_n\} \subseteq \mathcal{F}$ is a set of features.

The result of the slicing operation is a new FM, FM_{slice}, such that: $[\![FM_{slice}]\!] = \{x \cap \mathcal{F}_{slice} \mid x \in [\![FM]\!]\}$ (called the *projected* set of configurations).

Hierarchy. Intuitively, the hierarchy of FM_{slice} is such that features are connected to their closest ancestor if their parent is not part of the slicing criterion. A formal definition can be found in [1]. Two examples of slice operation are given in Figure 2.

Case study	Concerns	Complexity
① Composing Multiple Variability Artifacts (domain: medical imaging, grid computing ; stakeholders: medical imaging/grid experts) [5]	the variability is described at different places of the workflow, describing various concerns of connected services	dozens of FMs (up to 30), hundreds of inter-related features (up to 400)
② Modeling Variability From Requirements to Runtime (domain: video surveillance (VS) systems ; stakeholders: VS expert, software engineer) [6]	the modeling of requirements and software variability is explicitly separated in two FMs, VSAR and PC	2 FMs, 77 features and 10^8 configurations in VSAR, 51 features and 10^6 configurations in PC, 39 constraints.
③ Management of Product Line and Software Variability (domain: any ; stakeholders: products manager, software engineer) [22]	two kinds of variability (software and product line) are specified and maintained in two separated FMs fm_{PL} and $fm_{software}$	2 FMs, 25 features in fm_{PL}, 11 features in $fm_{software}$, 13 constraints ;
④ Reverse Engineering FMs (domain: component and plugin based systems, stakeholder: software architect) [3]	multiple variability sources (including architect knowledge) are combined to construct semi-automatically an FM	92 features and 158 constraints ; the number of valid configurations varies from $\approx 10^{11}$ to $\approx 10^6$;

Figure 3. SoC in the case studies

Technique	Description	Operators	Application
Updating FM Views	several FM views are inter-related: The variability information is kept up-to-date in the different views, possibly by correcting some anomalies introduced by some constraints	aggregate, slice	①②③④
Supporting Multiple Perspectives	given an FM or a set of FMs, a stakeholder wants to focus only on a specific concern related to its expertises, role, task	aggregate, slice	①
Reconciling FMs	two (or more than two) FMs cannot be directly compared or merged: They are reconciled by removing unnecessary details	slice, merge	①④
Reasoning about Two Kinds of Variability	two FMs describing two variability concerns are inter-related: Reasoning techniques are applied to reason about their relationships	aggregate, slice, merge,	②③

Figure 4. SoC in feature modeling

4. Applying Separation of Concerns

Given these composition and decomposition mechanisms, we now argue that these operators, together with other reasoning and editing operators, form a consistent and powerful support for SoC in feature modeling.

Several usage scenarios can be envisaged:

- When an FM is decomposed into smaller FMs (using the slice operator), one may need to reason about the different sets of configurations or simply modify the smaller FMs. The composition operators can be applied afterwards to recompose the smaller FMs ;

- When some FMs are composed with constraints (using the aggregate operator), one may need to simplify, redecompose or check the satisfiability of the resulting composed FM ;

- Before merging two FMs, one may need to reconcile (or align) the two FMs in case the hierarchy and the vocabulary used in the two FMs differs ;

Beyond these simple examples, we now show that though the sole use of the composition / decomposition operators has practical interests, the area of applications grows when these operators are combined together[1].

The following sections will demonstrate either new capabilities in feature modeling or better scalability in representative scenarios of the field. Each presented technique has been validated on experimental or real-world case studies. Figure 4 gives an overview of the contribution. It charac-

terizes each technique, reports the operators involved in the realization of the technique as well as the practical use in case studies. The numbers correspond to the different case studies described in Figure 3, including the application domain, the stakeholders involved, the concerns considered as well as the complexity of FMs.

4.1 Corrective Capabilities

Manual or automatic creation of FMs may generate *anomalies* in them. Generally, these anomalies are regarded as a negative property of an FM since it can easily decrease its maintainability or understandability.

DEFINITION 2 (Dead and Core features). *A feature f of an FM is dead if it cannot be part of any of the valid configurations. A feature f of an FM is a core feature if it is part of all valid configurations.*

Error-free FMs. Benavides et al. identify different kinds of FM *anomalies* [10]: *i)* dead features (see Definition 2) ; *ii)* false optional features are core features (see Definition 2), despite not being modeled as mandatory ; *iii)* wrong feature group: For example, features may form an Or-group while being mutually exclusive (see features R and S in the FM of Figure 1a) ; *iv)* or redundancies [10] (e.g., cross-tree constraints may be redundant). Despite the need of automatic support for anomaly analysis in FMs, there is a lack of proposals that focus on producing *error-free* FMs, i.e., FMs that do not contain anomalies as the ones mentioned above.

A form of *corrective explanations* has been developed in [10]. It indicates changes (or edits) to be made in the original FM so that it does not contain anomalies anymore.

---

[1] The tooling and language support, **FAMILIAR**, is out of the scope of this paper. The interested reader can visit `https://nyx.unice.fr/projects/familiar/`

These changes are suggestions, usually once anomalies have been detected and explained, to be applied to the original FM. In this case, the set of configurations of the original FM may be altered (e.g., a dead feature may no longer be dead once changes have been applied). This approach is more appropriate for handling human *errors*, for example, when an SPL practitioner elaborates an FM and unintentionally introduces errors. On the contrary *automatic correction (or simplification)* aims at removing anomalies from the original FM while the set of configurations remains exactly the same. Our contribution here takes place in this category, as automatic correction pursues a different objective: anomalies are not necessary errors but an intentional, controlled and/or temporary properties of an FM, for example, when automatic operations are conducted on FMs. As we will see in the next section, it usually happens when two (or more than two) FMs are inter-related by constraints. In this case, features may become dead or core features.

Automatic simplification using the slice. The slicing implementation we propose ensures, by construction, that there is no dead feature, correctly detects core features (thereby false optional features) and avoids redundancy in the representation (e.g., we add an implies/excludes constraint only if it is not already induced by the FM) [4]. Hence, we guarantee that the sliced FM does not contain anomalies. As a result, the slice operator can be used as an automated technique to *correct anomalies* of FMs while preserving the original set of configurations and hierarchy. Moreover, the corrective modifications applied to the original FM can be detected and reported to an SPL practitioner. For example, the slice operation is performed on the FM of Figure 1a, $fm1$, using all features of $fm1$ as a slicing criterion. The resulting FM is $fmAll$ (see Figure 2b). Obviously the set of configurations represented by $fmAll$ is the same as the set of configurations represented by $fm1$, while their feature hierarchies are equal. We can notice that *i)* the features R and S form an Xor-group in $fmAll$ (and no longer form an Or-group as in $fm1$) ; *ii)* the features E and F form an Xor-group (and are no longer optional as in $fm1$) ; *iii)* some constraints are no longer present in $fmAll$ to avoid redundancy.

As an application, we directly used this correction technique to automatically remove anomalies in the randomly generated FMs that served as inputs for our experimentations (see Section 5.1 and 7). Both configuration sets and hierarchies were maintained while correcting anomalies.

4.2 Managing Different FM Views

We illustrate the need to manage several FMs, possibly interrelated, using an example in the medical imaging domain. In this domain, medical imaging services (e.g., algorithms) are assembled to form complex processing chains (also called workflows). Variability affects different concerns or *views* of a medical imaging service. In Figure 5, the service is described through different views: information about the deployment on the grid, internal algorithms, the supported communication protocols and the type of handled medical

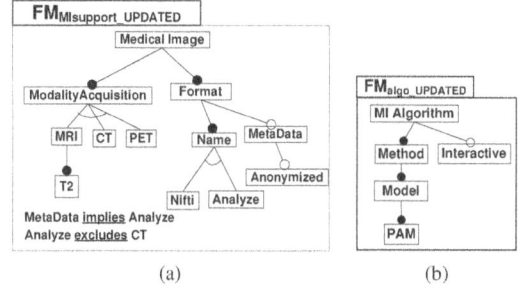

Figure 6. Updating FM views

images. As multiple sources of variation are present within a service, several FMs are used where each FM focuses on a specific view of a service. As shown in [5], these FMs can then be used to check consistency between composed services and to facilitate their coherent configurations.

4.2.1 Updating FM views

In practice, the different FM views of a service are not independent. The workflow designer has to add constraints to enforce interactions between the FM views. In our example, we consider the following constraints:

$MIService_{constraints} = \{$

(c1) $FM_{grid}.Kerberos \Rightarrow FM_{proto}.KDC$

(c2) $FM_{grid}.SSLAuth \Leftrightarrow FM_{proto}.SSL$

(c3) $FM_{MIsupport}.MRI \Rightarrow FM_{algo}.PAM$

(c4) $FM_{MIsupport}.CT \vee FM_{MIsupport}.SPEC$
$\Rightarrow FM_{algo}.BAM$

(c5) $FM_{MIsupport}.Anonymized$
$\Rightarrow FM_{proto}.HeaderEncoding$

(c6) $\neg FM_{grid}.GPU \vee \neg FM_{algo}.Interactive$

(c7) $FM_{algo}.Interactive \Rightarrow FM_{grid}..Linux$

(c8) $FM_{MIsupport}.DICOM$
$\Rightarrow FM_{proto}.Rotation \wedge FM_{proto}.PAM$

(c9) $FM_{algo}.Interactive \Rightarrow FM_{proto}.HeaderEncoding \}$

Determining the impact of these constraints on each FM view cannot be done manually or even automatically with current techniques and tools [10]. We rely on the corrective capabilities developed in Section 4.1 to perform the update of the different FM views.

Using the slice operator, it simply consists in *i)* aggregating the four feature models into a single one (*fmService*) with constraints mapped on it, *ii)* invoking *slice* four times producing as much sliced FMs, the slicing criterion being respectively the features of each of the four feature models. As a result, Figure 6a and Figure 6b correspond to the sliced FM with respectively the features of the FMs $FM_{MIsupport}$ and FM_{algo}. The two other FMs are not impacted by the constraints mapped on *fmService*.

4.2.2 Supporting multiple perspectives

On the same example, the slice operator can be used to extract other views (or *perspectives*) of a service. In Figure 7, we capture expertises related to security features or to the medical imaging domain. Two slice operations are applied and compute two FM views, stored into *fmViewMI*

5

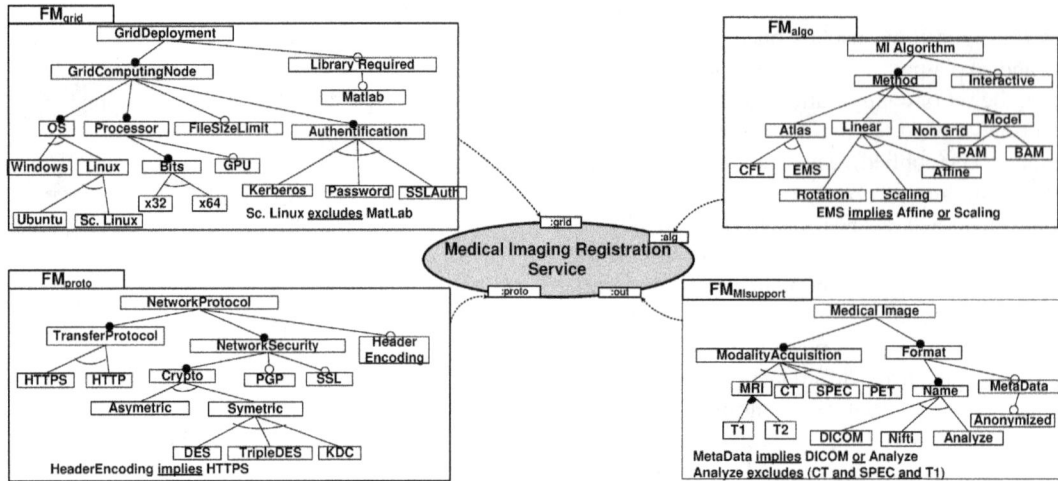

Figure 5. Variability and concerns within a medical imaging service

and *fmViewSecurity*. The slicing criterion used to compute *fmViewMI* (resp. *fmViewSecurity*) contains features from the FMs FM_{MI}, FM_{algo} and FM_{grid} (resp. FM_{MI}, FM_{proto} and FM_{grid}). The slice guarantees that all the interactions existing with other FM views are still enforced.

4.2.3 Practical applications

Reverse Engineering Architectural FMs. Besides the above application, the slicing technique was also extensively used in a tool-supported approach to reverse engineer software variability from an architectural perspective [3]. The proposed approach was evaluated when applied to FraSCAti, a large and highly configurable component and plugin-based system. Using the slicing technique an accurate view (i.e., an FM) of the software architecture was obtained. The idea was that the software architecture FM, originally produced by an extraction procedure, represents only an over approximation in terms of sets of valid configurations. Hence several sources of information were *combined*, namely software architecture, plugin dependencies and the correspondences between software elements and plugins. When combined through aggregation, slicing is used to update the view corresponding to the software architecture part. The aggregated FM resulting from the combination of different variability sources and the bidirectional mapping contains 92 features

and 158 cross-tree constraints (CTCR[2]=84%). The slicing technique significantly reduced the over approximation of the original architectural FM (from $\approx 10^{11}$ to $\approx 10^{6}$).

Variability in video surveillance. In the development of a video surveillance SPL, we represented the variability of the context and the variability of the software platform as two separated FMs [6]. 77 features and 10^8 configurations were present in the context FM while 51 features and 10^6 configurations were present in the software platform FM. The relationships between the two FMs were described as 39 rules (propositional constraints) relating features across models. Then, in line with specific requirements, we stepwise *specialized* the FM representing the context by removing some features, by modifying some feature groups, etc. After the specialization of the context FM, we needed to update the software platform FM. To do so, we aggregated the specialized context FM and the software platform FM together with rules. We used the slice operator on the aggregated FM by only including the set of features related to the software platform. We observed that from a specification of a context, the possible configurations in the software platform can be highly reduced. We applied the techniques on different scenarios: the average number of features to con-

---

[2] CTCR is the ratio of the number of features in the constraints to the number of features in the feature hierarchy.

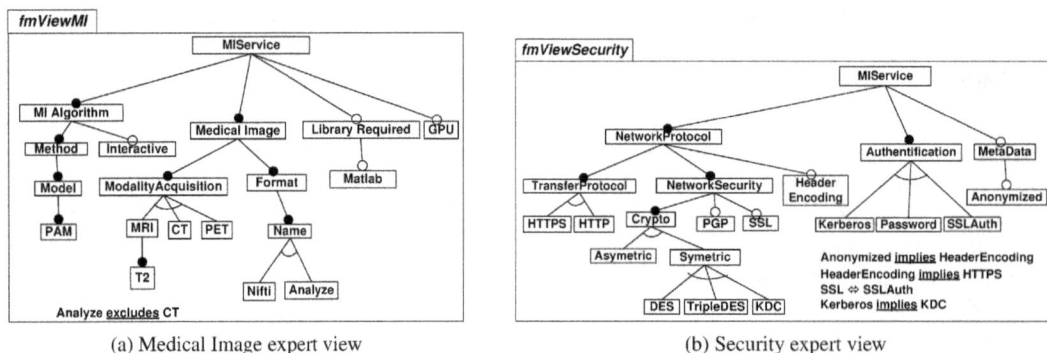

(a) Medical Image expert view

(b) Security expert view

Figure 7. Another decomposition strategy and set of FM views

sider in the software platform FM was less than 10^4 (instead of 10^6 configurations).

4.3 Reconciling Feature Models

When managing a set of FMs, the different stakeholders involved in the SPL development may have to put together very similar variability information but with a different structure. For example, in the medical imaging domain, different suppliers (scientists, research teams, companies, etc.) provide imaging services and may use different hierarchies, concepts, vocabulary, etc. when elaborating the FMs.

4.3.1 Technique and example

Let us consider two FMs, $fmMI1$ and $fmMI2$, in Figure 8. The two FMs differ. In particular, features Open, Proprietary, Niftil, Niftill are present in $fmMI1$ but not in $fmMI2$. Intuitively, more structure and details are modeled in $fmMI1$. As a result, a comparison (see Definition 3) or a merging (see Section 3.2) of the two FMs leads to counter intuitive results, i.e., the intersection of the two configuration sets is empty (see line 4 and 5 of the FAMILIAR script below). Looking at the two FMs, some configurations seem to correspond, for example, the valid configuration $\{MedicalImage, DICOM\}$ of $fmMI2$ with the configuration $\{MedicalImage, Open, DICOM\}$ of $fmMI1$. We thus need to *reconcile* (or align) the two FMs and allow an SPL practitioner to align in a coherent way information from $fmMI1$ and $fmMI2$.

DEFINITION 3 (Kind of edits and Comparison). *Let f and g be two FMs. f is a specialization of g if $[\![f]\!] \subset [\![g]\!]$. f is a generalization of g if $[\![g]\!] \subset [\![f]\!]$. f is a refactoring of g if $[\![g]\!] = [\![f]\!]$. f is an arbitrary edit of g if f is neither a specialization, a generalization nor a refactoring of g. A comparison computes the relationship between two FMs.*

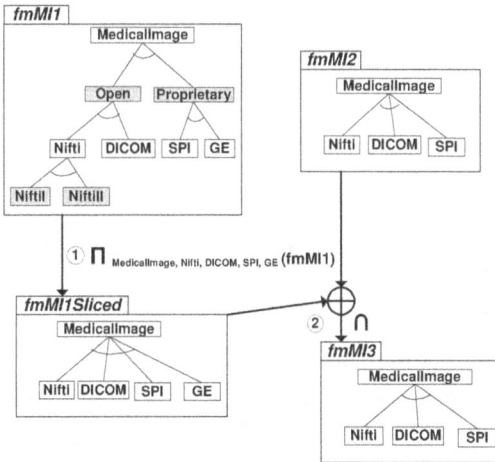

Figure 8. Slicing (①) to reconcile FMs and allow, e.g., comparison or merging (②)

Using the slice operator, we simply remove features of $fmMI1$ *i)* that structure the feature model (i.e., features Open, Proprietary) and *ii)* that can be abstracted by a single feature (i.e., Nifti abstracts features Niftil and Niftill). Then, the comparison can be computed or the merge operator can be used as in Figure 8.

4.3.2 Practical application

Besides the medical imaging domain, we also used the techniques described above for the reverse engineering of FraSCAti architectural FM. The architectural FM resulting from the automatic extraction (see Section 4.2.3) was compared with another architectural FM, this time manually designed by the software architect (SA) of FraSCAti. Unfortunately, the direct comparison yields to unexploitable results, mainly due to the difference of *granularity* (i.e., some features in one FM are not present in the other). Basic manual edits of FMs were unpractical as we needed to safely remove features involved in several constraints or that were in the middle of the hierarchy. The slicing operator was extensively applied to remove unnecessary details in both FMs. Once the FMs have been reconciled, the two FMs can be compared so that the differences between them can be identified. This encourages the SA to correct his initial model [3].

4.4 Reasoning about Two Kinds of Variability

In SPL engineering, two kinds of variability are usually distinguished [22, 23]: software (or internal) variability, hidden from customers, as opposed to product line (PL) (or external) variability, visible to them. Software variability and PL variability can be seen as two *concerns* of an SPL. Metzger et al. proposed a formal and concise approach for *separating* PL variability and software variability and enabling automatic analysis [22]. The two concerns are modeled as two FMs and inter-related by constraints. The authors mention several properties that should be checked when reasoning about the two kinds of variability. We now revisit here the approach defended in [22] and show how the operators can be combined to support SoC in this context.

4.4.1 Realized-by property

An important property of an SPL is *realizability*, i.e., whether the set of products that the PL management decides to offer is fully covered by the set of products that the software platform allows building. In Figure 9, we want to ensure that for each valid selection/deselection of features of fm_{PL} performed by a customer, there exists at least one corresponding software product described by $fm_{software}$. The PL variability is documented using fm_{PL}, the software variability is documented using another FM (see $fm_{software}$) and the two FMs are related through constraints (see map_{SoftPL}). Note that the mapping between features of fm_{PL} and $fm_{software}$ is not necessarily one-to-one. To this end we first reason about the relationship between $fm_{software}$ and fm_{PL}. We compute fm_G, the aggregation of fm_{PL} and $fm_{software}$ and add the constraints map_{SoftPL}.

In terms of FMs, the realizability property can be formally expressed ($\mathcal{F}_{PL}$ the set of features of fm_{PL}):

$$\forall cp \in [\![fm_{PL}]\!], cp \in [\![\Pi_{\mathcal{F}_{PL}}(fm_G)]\!] \tag{1}$$

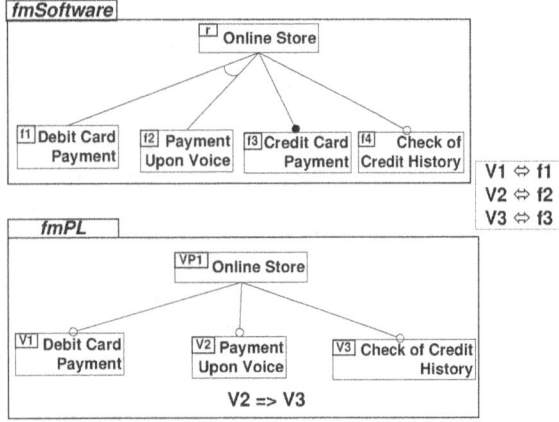

Figure 9. Software and PL Variability (adapted from [22])

Intuitively, if the restriction of the PL features to $[\![fm_G]\!]$ is equivalent to the original $[\![fm_{PL}]\!]$, the constraints map_{SoftPL} has no effect on the PL part of fm_G and thus the realizability property holds. Otherwise some products cannot be realized in the platform. Equation 1 implies to check if fm_{PL} is a refactoring (see Definition 3) of $\Pi_{\mathcal{F}_{PL}}(fm_G)$. Using the aggregate, slice and merge diff operators, we can automatically check this property. First, we slice the aggregated FM fm_G by only including $\mathcal{F}_{PL}$, the set of features of fm_{PL}. The slice produces a new FM, denoted $fm_{PL_{Prime}}$. Formally:
$$fm_{PL_{Prime}} = \Pi_{\mathcal{F}_{PL}}(fm_G)$$

Then, we compare the resulting FM, $fm_{PL_{Prime}}$, with the original PL model, fm_{PL}. If $fm_{PL_{Prime}}$ is not a refactoring of fm_{PL}, the realizability property is violated since some existing products of fm_{PL} are removed in $fm_{PL_{Prime}}$ and no product is added. Finally, we can compute the set of products that are in fm_{PL} but not in $fm_{PL_{Prime}}$ using the merge operator in *diff* mode. The merge operator produces fm_{PLDiff}.

Back to the example of Figure 9, we obtain that the realizability property does not hold and that three products proposed to customers cannot be realized by the platform:
$$[\![fm_{PL} \oplus_{\backslash} fm_{PL_{Prime}}]\!] = [\![fm_{PLDiff}]\!] = \{\{V1, V3, V2, VP1\}, \{V1, VP1\}, \{V3, VP1\}\}$$

Only the following two products can be realized:
$$[\![fm_{PL} \oplus_{\cap} fm_{PL_{Prime}}]\!] = [\![fm_{PLInter}]\!] = \{\{V1, V3, VP1\}, \{V2, V3, VP1\}\}$$

4.4.2 Non useful products

A product is useful if it is a possible realization of a PL member. As argued in [22], the list of non-useful products is a symptom of unused flexibility of the software platform. It can be on purpose, for example, justified by future marketing extensions. The usefulness property can be seen as the "symmetric" of the realized-by property. Formally, all products are useful if the following relation holds:
$$\forall cp \in [\![fm_{software}]\!], cp \in [\![\Pi_{\mathcal{F}_{software}}(fm_G)]\!]$$

Hence, similar techniques involving aggregate, slice and merge can be used to check the property.

4.4.3 Practical applications

Reasoning about two concerns. We apply the techniques using the larger example described in [22]. We successfully retrieved the same results, but our approach is more efficient since we do not enumerate configurations/products as they do. Moreover, high-level operators (slice, aggregate, compare, merge) facilitate the reasoning realization and offer a systematic solution for SPL practitioners when understanding and maintaining the two FMs. It should be noted that the technique for updating views (see Section 6) can be applied in such contexts, for example, to remove dead features in the PL or software model.

Reasoning about variability properties. In the development of video surveillance systems, a key issue is to ensure that, given a valid configuration of the context, a software configuration can always be obtained. This property is similar to the realized-by property and can be checked using the same techniques. We successfully scale for this case study, whereas it was clearly not the case with the enumerative technique proposed in [22].

5. Towards Scalable Technique to Separate Concerns

Central to the support for SoC in feature modeling is the ability to decompose (i.e., *slice*) FMs. All applications described in the previous section make extensive use of the slicing technique. It is thus crucial to provide a scalable implementation of the slice operator. A syntactical technique is not adequate, especially in the presence of cross-tree constraints. A technique based on the enumeration of configurations is not scalable, since the number of configurations is exponential to the number of features. To avoid these limitations, we developed a dedicated technique that consists in first computing the propositional formula representing the projected (see Section 3.3) set of configurations. The computation of the propositional formula is essential for *reasoning* about the projected set of configurations but also for *synthesizing* the FM. As detailed in [4], propositional logic techniques [12, 29] can be applied to construct an FM (including its hierarchy, variability information and cross-tree constraints) from the formula. In this section, we focus on the computation of the propositional formula. We report on the practical limits of an implementation based on binary decision diagrams (BDDs). We describe a symbolic technique that outperforms a BDD-based implementation and that can efficiently decompose FMs with thousands of features.

Propositional Formula Encoding. First, we describe the encoding of the projected set of configurations as propositional formula For a slicing $FM_{slice} = \Pi_{ft_1, ft_2, \ldots, ft_n}(FM)$, the propositional formula ϕ_{slice} corresponding to FM_{slice} can be defined as follows:
$$\phi_{slice} \equiv \exists\, ftx_1, ftx_2, \ldots ftx_{m'}\, \phi$$

where $ftx_1, ftx_2, \ldots ftx_{m'} \in (\mathcal{F} \setminus \mathcal{F}_{slice}) = \mathcal{F}_{removed}$.

Intuitively, all occurrences of features that are not present in any configuration of FM_{slice} are removed by existential quantification in ϕ. ϕ_{slice} is obtained from ϕ by *existentially quantifying out* variables in $\mathcal{F}_{removed}$.

DEFINITION 4 (Existential Quantification). *Let v be a Boolean variable occurring in ϕ. $\phi_{|v}$ (resp. $\phi_{|\bar{v}}$) is ϕ where variable v is assigned the value True (resp. False). Existential quantification is then defined as $\exists v \ \phi =_{def} \phi_{|v} \vee \phi_{|\bar{v}}$.*

5.1 BDD-based Implementation

In previous work [4], we rely on BDDs [11] to compute the propositional formula. A BDD is a compact representation of a Boolean function (e.g., a propositional formula). BDDs can be efficiently used to compute the propositional formula described above since computing the existential quantification can be performed in at most polynomial time with respect to the sizes of the BDDs involved [11]. Furthermore, BDDs can be used to synthesize an FM in polynomial time regarding the size of the BDD representing the input propositional formula [12]. A major drawback of BDDs is that finding an optimal variable ordering during BDD construction is NP-hard [11]. Some heuristics have been developed and successfully compile FMs to BDDs for a number of features up to 2000 [20].

The goal of our experiment was to determine the scalability of the BDD-based implementation w.r.t. the size of the input FMs (i.e., number of features) and the size of the slicing criterion (i.e., number of features to include). For the experiment, we reuse the heuristics (i.e., Pre-CL-MinSpan) developed in [20] to reduce the size of BDDs. For a first evaluation, we used several small and medium-sized FMs that were publicly available from SPLOT [21] repository as well as FMs from our case studies. We performed our experiments on more than 100 FMs, the bigger one having 290 features. We found that computing the slice is almost instantaneous in all cases. To go further, we randomly generated FMs with several hundreds of features. We varied *i)* the number of features, noted $\#features$, from 100 to 2000 features (the known practical limits of BDD) ; *ii)* $CTCR$ from 10% to 100%. We used the publicly available procedure described in [21] to randomly generate the FMs. In each generated model, each type of mandatory, optional, Xor and Or-groups was added with equal probability. For each FM, we randomly generated a slicing criterion. We varied the percentage of features to slice between 100% (no existential quantification is performed) and 1% (almost all features are existentially quantified). The main results show that:

- The synthesis of the feature diagram has practical limits (up to 800 features[3]). This limit also applies in our context. We observed that the slicing technique can scale even for an FM with 2000 features if the percentage of features to slice is $\leq 35\%$. The reason is that the size of a BDD will always be smaller or at least unchanged after existential quantification ;

---

[3] Janota et al. reported that the BDD-based algorithm proposed in [12] scales up only for FMs with 300/400 features [18], but did not use the heuristics proposed in [20]

- The primary limit of the BDD-based implementation lies in the difficulties to construct BDD from the original FM. In particular, the total number of features in the input FM should not be more than 2000 features, otherwise it is impossible to having a BDD-representation of the formula. It should be noted that whenever an FM can be represented as a BDD, ϕ_{slice} can be computed. Hence the encoding of ϕ_{slice} can scale up to 2000 features with a CTCR of 10, whatever the slicing criterion is ;

5.2 SAT-based Implementation

She et al. proposed techniques to reverse engineer very large FMs (i.e., with more than 5000 features) [29]. As shown above BDDs do not scale for this order of complexity and therefore the slicing operator cannot process such FMs. She et al. adapted their previous techniques and now rely on satisfiability (SAT) solvers (rather than BDDs as in [12]). They reported that the use of SAT solvers is significantly more scalable. Hence a SAT-based implementation of slicing is an interesting perspective that motivates our work.

We identify two main issues. First, the size of the formula exponentially increases when existential quantification is performed many times, i.e., the number of clauses doubles at each iteration. It may become an issue when the size of $\mathcal{F}_{removed}$ is important, even for small FMs. Second, SAT solvers require a formula to be in conjunctive normal form (CNF). It is straightforward to translate the propositional formula of an FM into CNF. However, when existential quantification is performed, the resulting formula is not in CNF (see Definition 4). To tackle the first issue, we substitue each feature of $\mathcal{F}_{removed}$ only in those clauses that contain the feature. More formally, let ft be a feature of $\mathcal{F}_{removed}$, ϕ a formula in CNF decomposed as follows:

$\phi = p(ft, \phi) \wedge c(ft, \phi)$ where $c(ft, \phi)$ denotes the conjunction of the clauses that do not contain the feature ft and $p(ft, \phi)$ denotes the conjunction of the clauses that do contain the feature ft. The existential quantification of ft in ϕ produces a new formula ϕ' defined as follows:

$\phi' = \phi_{|ft} \vee \phi_{|\bar{ft}} = (p(ft, \phi)_{|ft} \vee p(ft, \phi)_{\bar{ft}}) \wedge c(ft, \phi)$

Example. We consider $fm1$ of Figure 1a (see page 3). We slice $fm1$ using as slicing criterion all features except T and V (i.e., $\mathcal{F}_{removed} = \{T, V\}$). It should be noted that the existential quantification of T and V can performed in any order. In this example, we first perform the existential quantification of T, producing the following propositional formula: $\phi'_{fm_1} = ((W \Leftrightarrow True \wedge V \Rightarrow True \wedge A \Leftrightarrow True) \vee (W \Leftrightarrow False \wedge V \Rightarrow False \wedge A \Leftrightarrow False)) \wedge c(V, \phi) \wedge True \wedge \neg False$.

Then we iterate by performing the existential quantification of V in ϕ'_{fm_1}. We can observe that at each iteration the formula can be symbolically simplified in many ways. For instance, T cannot be evaluated to False in ϕ'_{fm_1} and therefore the disjunctive clause can be removed. We can also observe that $A \Leftrightarrow True \equiv True$ but we do not consider this kind of simplification since features included in the slicing criterion, like A, must not be removed. However we can simplify ϕ'_{fm_1} considering that $V \Rightarrow True \equiv True$ since $\vee$ is included in the slicing criterion. An additional optimisation, related to symbolic simplification, is the order in which the features are existentially quantified. Indeed, we observe that some features are likely to be simplified. We use an heuristic that existentially quantifies in priority features that are at the bottom of the feature hierarchy. To tackle the second issue, we transform the resulting propositional formula into CNF at each iteration (i.e., for each existential quantification of a feature ft). It should be noted that we only need to consider the transformation of $(p(ft, \phi)_{|ft} \vee p(ft, \phi)_{\bar{ft}})$ into CNF since $c(ft, \phi)$ is already in CNF.

Generated FMs. For the evaluation of the technique, we used the same FMs as with the experiments conducted for the BDD-based implementation. We also generated FMs with $2000 \geq \#features \geq 10000$ with the same parameters as previously described (10000 features is the practical limit admitted in the literature [10, 21, 32]). We first verified that the techniques described above are necessary since a naive substitution strategy that does not compute $c(ft, \phi)$ is not scalable (scalability issues are observed for $\#features \geq 50$). Using our technique, we found that: *i)* computing the propositional formula is almost instantaneous for all FMs of SPLOT (less than one second, whatever the size of the slicing criterion is); *ii)* the SAT-based implementation scales for $\#features \leq 10000$ whatever the size of the slicing criterion is; *iii)* the order in which the features are existentially quantified is of prior importance: we begin to observe scalability issues when quantifying first the features that are in top of the feature hierarchy for $\#features \geq 2000$; *iv)* for very large FMs ($\#features \geq 5000$), the computation time is inadequate for an interactive use of the slice operator (up to 20 minutes).

Real world FMs. As stated early, automated extraction techniques now produce very large FMs from existing software systems. We applied our technique to three independent systems relating to the operating system domain (Linux, eCos, and FreeBSD). Linux and eCos have FMs whereas FreeBSD has not. She et al. reverse engineer the propositional formula of FreeBSD and develop techniques to interactively specify the hierarchy [29]. For the experiment, we directly applied the slicing technique on the formula of FreeBSD. It should be noted that, in this specific case, we cannot use the heuristic mentioned above since we do not have access to the hierarchy of FreeBSD. We randomly generated the order in which features are existentially quantified. The technique succeeded almost instantaneously (FreeBSD has 1203 features). We also succeeded on eCos that has over 1200 features.

Finally, we applied our technique to the FM of Linux which exhibits 6300 features. Contrary to the results obtained from the two other operating systems or from the experimental study described above, we scaled only for less than 60% of features included in the slicing criterion (whereas this percentage drops to 1% in the other cases). In order to understand the reasons of this limitation, we need to compare the experimental conditions of the generated FMs with the properties of the Linux FM. The Linux model contains very small percentages of mandatory features (5%), grouped features (3%) – Linux features are mostly optional (92%). whereas in each generated model, each type of mandatory, optional, Xor and Or-groups was added with equal probability (25%). We can make the assumption that the slice operator is dependent on certain shapes of FMs, and/or certain kinds of constraints. We need to understand the impact of FM properties regarding the scalability of the slice operator. As future work, we plan to characterize more precisely the lack of scalability w.r.t. the Linux FM and develop new heuristics or specific techniques.

6. Comparison with Other Solutions

We now review existing approaches that have been developed to support SoC in FMs. We point out their relations to the SoC techniques that have been identified (see Figure 4) and illustrated by different case studies in Section 4. To this end, we rely on the numbers used in Figure 3, each corresponding to a case study. The general conclusion is that without the new capabilities brought by our solution (i.e., the *combined use of composition and decomposition operators*), some analysis and reasoning operations would not be made possible in the different case studies.

Composition. A few works consider some forms of composition for FMs and suggest the use of a merge operator [7, 15, 27, 28]. An in-depth comparison of implementation approaches is performed in [2]. Our proposal goes further since we clarified the semantics of the merge and showed that the merge alone is not sufficient to realize complex management tasks in the case studies ① and ③. It rather has to be combined with decomposition and reasoning mechanisms. Several approaches use several and interrelated FMs and views [15, 19, 22, 24, 35]. As shown, the aggregate operator combined with the slice can be used in such contexts to update the different views, to support multiple perspectives or to reason about properties of the FMs (see case studies ①, ②, ③ and ④). In [26], the authors tackled the problem of mapping problem-space features into solution-space features and proposed to use default logic. Our contributions rely on propositional logics and therefore are not applicable to this work. Thompson et al. proposed to specify a product family from n perspectives: one family-hierarchy per view such as software or hardware [31]. It is a form of SoC that is particularly needed in the case studies ① or ②. A set-theoretic foundation is proposed: it can be expressed and realized using FMs and the presented techniques.

Decomposition. Thüm et al. [32] presented an automated and scalable technique to characterize the kinds of edit between two FMs. An original property of the technique is that they distinguish abstract features from concrete features when reasoning. Abstract features are, in their work, nonleaf features. We consider this is the role of an SPL practitioner to explicitly determine which features are abstract (as shown in the example of Section 4.3, abstract features are not necessary non-leaf features). Our technique is thus more general and realize the vision of [27] that makes the distinction between features that are of interest per se (i.e., that will influence the final product) and others. As we have shown, reasoning about the relationship of two FMs (and thus using the comparison operator developed in [32]) is inappropriate until FMs are not reconciled (see case studies ① and ④). From our experience, tool supported techniques, such as the safe removal of a feature by slicing, are not desirable but mandatory (i.e., basic manual edits of FMs are not sufficient) in this context. Recently, Thüm et al. [33] extend the work described in [32] and propose to make abstract features explicit in FMs. They show how a propositional formula can be retrieved describing the set of distinct "program variants", corresponding to combination of concrete features. Interestingly, Thüm et al. plan to apply their techniques to SPL testing. We see this work as an application of the slicing technique where all features but abstract features are part of the slicing criterion. Our technique for computing the propositional formula is similar to the technique described in [33]. In addition we developed an heuristic that determines the order in which the features are existentially quantified. We also applied to very large FMs and reported scalability results. In the context of feature-based configuration, techniques have been proposed to separate the configuration process in different steps or stages [13]. Our work is complementary since we propose techniques to decompose FMs. Hubaux et al. provide view mechanisms to decompose a large FM [17]. However they do not propose a comprehensive solution when dealing with cross-tree constraints. Furthermore we have shown that the decomposition of FMs has several other interesting applications beyond the support of multiple perspectives (see case studies ①, ②, ③ and ④). Benavides et al. survey the literature of automated reasoning about FMs [10]. To the best of our knowledge, there is no existing work for *correcting* anomalies in FMs. Furthermore, existing approaches mentioned in [10] and discussed above either focus on composition or decomposition, but they do not try to combine the two mechanisms for supporting SoC in feature modeling. The *"tyranny of the dominant decomposition"* is a general issue for aspect-oriented approaches [30]. In [9], Batory et al. introduced multi-dimensional SoC where a dimension is a set of features addressing a particular concern. We can see a dimension as a slicing criterion. The approach of Batory et al. does not generate views but rather composes features along each dimension. It is thus complementary and can be used to produce parts of a system, being services (case study ①), components (case study ②) or plugins (case study ④). Rosenmüller et al. develop compositional support to manage different FMs, each focusing on a specific dimension [25]. They do not consider composition of FMs that introduce anomalies and do not propose automated decomposition (as need in all case studies).

7. Threats to Validity

Threats to external validity are conditions that limit our ability to generalize the results of our operators and experiment to industrial practice. Our first concern is whether generated FMs or Linux FM used in the experiments (see Section 5) are representative of industrial usage. Our second concern is whether the composition and decomposition operators are expressive and intuitive enough to support activities of SPL practitioners. As summarized by Figure 4 and Figure 3, the operators have been applied to different domains for different purposes and by different people (external to our team). Moreover we identify several works in the literature that can benefit from the techniques (see Section 6).

A first internal threat concerns the correctness of the operators implementation. In particular, the slice operator is supposed to guarantee that some semantic properties are preserved. Our implementation is currently checked by a comprehensive set of unit tests, complemented by cross-checked testing with other operations. For instance, we compared the formulas produced by the BDD-based and SAT-based implementation of the slice operator. We also manually verified a large number of slice examples. Besides we observed that randomly generated FMs may contain a lot of anomalies (e.g., dead features or wrong feature group). We used this opportunity to gain further confidence in our implementation and applied our slicing technique to automatically correct anomalies in generated FMs (see Section 4.1). We automatically checked that the original FM and the slice (i.e., corrected) FM were equivalent in terms of sets of configurations, that the slice FM did not contain any anomaly, and that the hierarchy conforms to the original FM.

8. Conclusion

In this paper, we described how a set of complementary operators (aggregate, merge, slice) can be used to provide a powerful support for SoC in feature modeling. We showed how the operators can assist in tedious and error prone tasks such as automated correction of FM anomalies, update and extraction of FM views, reconciliation of FMs or reasoning about properties of FMs. The operators bring new capabilities to the FM users for supporting SoC in feature modeling and when we revisited and reimplemented existing approaches with them, we observed a better scalability. Both these new capabilities and scalability results enabled us to apply SoC in feature modeling to different domains (medical imaging, video surveillance) and for different purposes (scientific workflow design, variability modeling of context and software platform, reverse engineering). We also developed a technique to implement the slice operator that scales up to FMs with 10000 features in certain conditions. As future work, we plan to study practical usage and applicability of the proposed techniques.

Acknowledgments. Dr. Acher's work is supported by the IAP Programme, the Belgian Science Policy under the MoVES project, the FNRS, and an FSR grant, co-funded by Marie-Curie actions of the European Commission.

References

[1] M. Acher. *Managing Multiple Feature Models: Foundations, Language and Applications*. PhD thesis, 2011.

[2] M. Acher, P. Collet, P. Lahire, and R. France. Comparing approaches to implement feature model composition. In *ECMFA'10*, volume 6138 of *LNCS*, pages 3–19, 2010.

[3] M. Acher, A. Cleve, P. Collet, P. Merle, L. Duchien, and P. Lahire. Reverse engineering architectural feature models. In *ECSA'11*, volume 6903 of *LNCS*, pages 220–235, 2011.

[4] M. Acher, P. Collet, P. Lahire, and R. France. Slicing feature models. In *ASE'11*, pages 424–427. IEEE, 2011.

[5] M. Acher, P. Collet, P. Lahire, A. Gaignard, R. France, and J. Montagnat. Composing multiple variability artifacts to assemble coherent workflows. *Software Quality Journal (Special issue on Quality Engineering for SPLs)*, 2011.

[6] M. Acher, P. Collet, P. Lahire, S. Moisan, and J.-P. Rigault. Modeling variability from requirements to runtime. In *ICECCS'11*, pages 77–86. IEEE, 2011.

[7] V. Alves, R. Gheyi, T. Massoni, U. Kulesza, P. Borba, and C. Lucena. Refactoring product lines. In *GPCE'06*, pages 201–210. ACM, 2006.

[8] S. Apel and C. Kästner. An overview of feature-oriented software development. *Journal of Object Technology (JOT)*, 8(5):49–84, July/August 2009.

[9] D. Batory, J. Liu, and J. N. Sarvela. Refinements and multi-dimensional separation of concerns. *SIGSOFT Softw. Eng. Notes*, 28:48–57, 2003.

[10] D. Benavides, S. Segura, and A. Ruiz-Cortes. Automated analysis of feature models 20 years later: a literature review. *Information Systems*, 35(6), 2010.

[11] K. S. Brace, R. L. Rudell, and R. E. Bryant. Efficient implementation of a bdd package. In *DAC '90: Design Automation Conference*, pages 40–45. ACM, 1990.

[12] K. Czarnecki and A. Wasowski. Feature diagrams and logics: There and back again. In *SPLC'07*, pages 23–34. IEEE, 2007.

[13] K. Czarnecki, S. Helsen, and U. Eisenecker. Staged configuration through specialization and multilevel configuration of feature models. *Software Process: Improvement and Practice*, 10(2):143–169, 2005.

[14] D. Dhungana, P. Grünbacher, R. Rabiser, and T. Neumayer. Structuring the modeling space and supporting evolution in software product line engineering. *Journal of Systems and Software*, 83(7):1108–1122, 2010.

[15] H. Hartmann and T. Trew. Using feature diagrams with context variability to model multiple product lines for software supply chains. In *SPLC'08*, pages 12–21. IEEE, 2008.

[16] H. Hartmann, T. Trew, and A. Matsinger. Supplier independent feature modelling. In *SPLC'09*, pages 191–200. IEEE, 2009.

[17] A. Hubaux, P. Heymans, P.-Y. Schobbens, D. Deridder, and E. Abbasi. Supporting multiple perspectives in feature-based configuration. *Software and Systems Modeling*, pages 1–23.

[18] M. Janota, V. Kuzina, and A. Wasowski. Model construction with external constraints: An interactive journey from semantics to syntax. In *MODELS'08*, volume 5301 of *LNCS*, pages 431–445, 2008.

[19] K. Kang, S. Kim, J. Lee, K. Kim, E. Shin, and M. Huh. Form: A feature-oriented reuse method with domain-specific reference architectures. *Annals of Software Engineering*, 5(1):143–168, 1998.

[20] M. Mendonca, A. Wasowski, K. Czarnecki, and D. Cowan. Efficient compilation techniques for large scale feature models. In *GPCE'08*, pages 13–22. ACM, 2008.

[21] M. Mendonca, A. Wąsowski, and K. Czarnecki. SAT-based analysis of feature models is easy. In *SPLC'09*, pages 231–240. IEEE, 2009.

[22] A. Metzger, K. Pohl, P. Heymans, P.-Y. Schobbens, and G. Saval. Disambiguating the documentation of variability in software product lines: A separation of concerns, formalization and automated analysis. In *RE'07*, pages 243–253, 2007.

[23] K. Pohl, G. Böckle, and F. J. van der Linden. *Software Product Line Engineering: Foundations, Principles and Techniques*. Springer-Verlag, 2005. ISBN 3540243720.

[24] M.-O. Reiser and M. Weber. Multi-level feature trees: A pragmatic approach to managing highly complex product families. *Requir. Eng.*, 12(2):57–75, 2007.

[25] M. Rosenmüller, N. Siegmund, T. Thüm, and G. Saake. Multidimensional variability modeling. In *VaMoS'11*, pages 11–20. ACM, 2011.

[26] F. Sanen, E. Truyen, and W. Joosen. Mapping problem-space to solution-space features: a feature interaction approach. In *GPCE '09*, pages 167–176. ACM, 2009.

[27] P.-Y. Schobbens, P. Heymans, J.-C. Trigaux, and Y. Bontemps. Generic semantics of feature diagrams. *Comput. Netw.*, 51(2):456–479, 2007.

[28] S. Segura, D. Benavides, A. Ruiz-Cortés, and P. Trinidad. Automated merging of feature models using graph transformations. In *GTTSE '07*, volume 5235 of *LNCS*, pages 489–505, 2008.

[29] S. She, R. Lotufo, T. Berger, A. Wasowski, and K. Czarnecki. Reverse engineering feature models. In *ICSE'11*, pages 461–470. ACM, 2011.

[30] P. Tarr, H. Ossher, W. Harrison, and S. M. Sutton, Jr. N degrees of separation: multi-dimensional separation of concerns. In *ICSE'99*, pages 107–119. ACM, 1999.

[31] J. M. Thompson and M. P. E. Heimdahl. Structuring product family requirements for n-dimensional and hierarchical product lines. *Requirements Engineering*, 8(1):42–54, 2003.

[32] T. Thüm, D. Batory, and C. Kästner. Reasoning about edits to feature models. In *ICSE'09*, pages 254–264. ACM, 2009.

[33] T. Thüm, C. Kästner, S. Erdweg, and N. Siegmund. Abstract features in feature modeling. In *SPLC'11*, pages 191–200. IEEE, Aug. 2011.

[34] T. T. Tun and P. Heymans. Concerns and their separation in feature diagram languages - an informal survey. In *International workshop SCALE@SPLC'09*, pages 107–110, 2009.

[35] T. T. Tun, Q. Boucher, A. Classen, A. Hubaux, and P. Heymans. Relating requirements and feature configurations: A systematic approach. In *SPLC'09*, pages 201–210. IEEE, 2009.

[36] M. Weiser. Program slicing. In *ICSE '81*, pages 439–449. IEEE, 1981.

Intraprocedural Dataflow Analysis for Software Product Lines

Claus Brabrand[1,2]   Márcio Ribeiro[2,3]   Társis Tolêdo[2]   Paulo Borba[2]

[1] IT University of Copenhagen, Rued Langgaards Vej 7, DK-2300, Copenhagen, Denmark
[2] Federal University of Pernambuco, Av. Prof. Luis Freire, 50.740-540, Recife, Brazil
[3] Federal University of Alagoas, Av. Lourival de Melo Mota, 57.072-970, Maceió, Brazil

{brabrand@itu.dk, {mmr3, twt, phmb}@cin.ufpe.br}

Abstract

Software product lines (SPLs) are commonly developed using annotative approaches such as conditional compilation that come with an inherent risk of constructing erroneous products. For this reason, it is essential to be able to analyze SPLs. However, as dataflow analysis techniques are not able to deal with SPLs, developers must generate and analyze all valid methods individually, which is expensive for non-trivial SPLs. In this paper, we demonstrate how to take *any* standard intraprocedural dataflow analysis and *automatically* turn it into a *feature-sensitive* dataflow analysis in three different ways. All are capable of analyzing *all* valid methods of an SPL without having to generate all of them explicitly. We have implemented all analyses as extensions of SOOT's intraprocedural dataflow analysis framework and experimentally evaluated their performance and memory characteristics on four qualitatively different SPLs. The results indicate that the feature-sensitive analyses are on average 5.6 times faster than the brute force approach on our SPLs, and that they have different time and space tradeoffs.

Categories and Subject Descriptors D.2.4 [*Software Engineering*]: Software/Program Verification; F.3.2 [*Theory of Computation*]: Semantics of Programming Languages — *Program Analysis*

General Terms Performance, Experimentation, Design

Keywords Dataflow Analysis, Software Product Lines.

1. Introduction

A software product line (SPL) is a set of software products that share common functionality and are generated from reusable assets. These assets specify common and variant behavior targeted at a specific set of products, usually bringing productivity and time-to-market improvements [7, 24]. Developers often implement variant behavior and associated features with conditional compilation constructs like `#ifdef` [1, 16], mixing common, optional, and even alternative and conflicting behavior in the same code asset. In these cases, assets are not valid programs or program elements in the underlying language. We can, however, use assets to generate valid programs by evaluating the conditional compilation constructs using preprocessing tools.

Since code assets might not be valid programs or program elements, existing standard dataflow analyses, which are for instance essential for supporting optimization [18] and maintenance [26] tasks, cannot be directly used to analyze code assets. To analyze an SPL using intraprocedural analysis, developers then have to generate all possible methods and separately analyze each one with conventional single-program dataflow analyses. In this case, generating and analyzing each method can be expensive for non-trivial SPLs. Consequently, interactive tools for single-program development might not be usable for SPL development because they rely on fast dataflow analyses and have to be able to quickly respond when the programmer performs tasks such as code refactoring [10]. Also, this is bad for maintenance tools [26] that help developers understand and manage dependencies between features.

To solve this problem and enable more efficient dataflow analysis of SPLs, we propose three approaches for taking any standard intraprocedural dataflow analysis and automatically lifting it into a corresponding *feature-sensitive* analysis that we can use to directly analyze code assets. The approaches analyze all configurations and thus avoid explicitly generating all possible methods of an SPL. Although we focus on SPLs developed with conditional compilation constructs, our results apply to other similar annotative variability mechanisms [16].

We evaluate our three *feature-sensitive* approaches (*consecutive*, *simultaneous*, and *shared simultaneous*) and compare them with a *brute force* intraprocedural approach that generates and analyzes all possible methods individually. We report on a number of performance and memory consumption experiments using two dataflow analyses (*definite assignments* and *reaching definitions* [23]) and four SPLs from different domains, with qualitatively different numbers of features, products, #ifdef statements, and other factors that might impact performance and memory usage results. We find that, for the analyses and SPLs used, when analyzing all configurations simultaneously (*simultaneous* approach), we reduce analysis time by a factor of up to more than eight times on SPLs with intensive feature usage (intensive #ifdef presence). For SPLs with low feature usage the *simultaneous* approach is only slightly faster than the brute force approach. In addition, the former consumes more memory when compared to the *shared simultaneous* approach, which shares values corresponding to configurations during the analysis.

We organize the rest of this paper as follows. Using a concrete example, Section 2 discusses and motivates the need for dataflow analysis of software product lines. Then, we introduce conditional compilation and feature models. After that, we briefly recall basic dataflow analysis concepts and present the main contributions of this paper:

- a *consecutive feature-sensitive* approach that analyzes all SPL configurations, one at a time and *simultaneous* and *shared simultaneous feature-sensitive* approaches that analyze all SPL configurations at the same time (Section 5);

- an *experimental prototype* implementation of the three above analyses; and

- *empirical evidence* of the superiority of our feature-sensitive approaches; in particular the *simultaneous* and *shared simultaneous* approaches, which are faster than the *consecutive* one, but use more memory (Section 6).

2. Motivating Example

To better illustrate the issues we are addressing in this paper, we now present a motivating example based on the Lampiro SPL.[1] Lampiro is an instant-messaging client developed in Java ME and its features are implemented using #ifdefs.

Figure 1 shows a code snippet extracted from Lampiro implemented in Java with the Antenna[2] preprocessor. As can be seen, if the GLIDER feature is *not* present (see the #if**n**def statement), the logo variable receives an image instantiated by the createImage method, so it is *initialized*. However, this variable is *uninitialized* if the GLIDER feature is *present* in the product. Such mistakes—and others like undeclared variables, unused variables, and null pointers— commonly occur when using conditional compilation. Indeed, despite their widespread usage to implement variabil-

---

[1] http://lampiro.bluendo.com/

[2] http://antenna.sourceforge.net/

```
Image logo;
...
//#ifndef GLIDER
...
logo = Image.createImage("/icons/lampiro_icon.png");
...
//#endif
...
UILabel uimg = new UILabel(logo);
```

Figure 1. Uninitialized variable when GLIDER is present.

ity in SPLs, #ifdefs pollute the code, lack separation of concerns, and make maintenance tasks harder [8, 20, 21, 27].

Thus, to maintain this kind of SPL, it is important to analyze its code and determine whether developers are introducing errors. For instance, consider the case where a developer is supposed to change the value of a variable that belongs to feature A. An analysis could be useful to warn of another feature, B, using the same variable just modified. Such feature dependency information is a signal to investigate feature B, to make sure that the modification did not introduce any problems in it. We proposed an idea to provide information about this kind of feature dependency [26]. This was our original motivation for adapting dataflow analysis for SPLs.

To capture these dependencies and consequently problems like uninitialized variables in SPLs, we need dataflow analyses to work on sets of SPL assets, like the ones using conditional compilation. However, programmers must resort to generating all possible methods and separately analyzing each one by using the conventional single-program dataflow analysis. Depending on the size of the SPL, this can be costly, which may be a problem for interactive tools that analyze SPL code, for example. As we shall see in Section 6, we are able to decrease such costs.

3. Conditional Compilation

In this section, we briefly introduce the #ifdef construction and *feature models*. We use a simplified ifdef construction the syntax of which is:

$$
\begin{array}{lll}
S & ::= & \text{"ifdef" "(" } \phi \text{ ")" } S \\
\phi & ::= & f \in \mathbb{F} \mid \neg \phi \mid \phi \wedge \phi
\end{array}
$$

S is a *Java Statement* and ϕ is a *propositional logic formula* over *feature names* where f is drawn from a finite alphabet of feature names, $\mathbb{F}$. We further eliminate #elif and #else branches by turning them into the normalized syntactic ifdef form listed in BNF above.

A *configuration*, $c \subseteq \mathbb{F}$, is a set of *enabled features*. A propositional logic formula, ϕ, gives rise to the *set of configurations*, $[\![\phi]\!] \subseteq 2^{\mathbb{F}}$, for which the formula is satisfied. For instance, given $\mathbb{F} = \{A, B, C\}$, the formula, $\phi = A \wedge (B \vee C)$ corresponds to the following set of configurations: $[\![A \wedge (B \vee C)]\!] = \{\{A, B\}, \{A, C\}, \{A, B, C\}\} \subseteq 2^{\mathbb{F}}$.

14

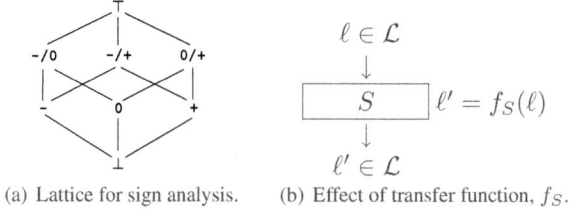

(a) Lattice for sign analysis.   (b) Effect of transfer function, f_S.

Figure 2. Lattice and transfer function.

To yield only valid configurations, sets of configurations are usually further restricted by a so-called *feature model* [13]. Conceptually, a feature model is just a propositional logic formula. Here is an example of a feature model with alphabet $\mathbb{F} = \{\texttt{Car}, \texttt{Air}, \texttt{Basic}, \texttt{Turbo}\}$:

$$\psi_{\text{FM}} = \texttt{Car} \wedge (\texttt{Basic} \leftrightarrow \neg\texttt{Turbo}) \wedge (\texttt{Air} \rightarrow \texttt{Turbo})$$

corresponding to the following set of *valid* configurations:

$$[\![\psi_{\text{FM}}]\!] = \{\{\texttt{Car}, \texttt{Basic}\}, \{\texttt{Car}, \texttt{Turbo}\}, \{\texttt{Car}, \texttt{Air}, \texttt{Turbo}\}\} \subseteq 2^{\mathbb{F}}$$

4. Dataflow Analysis

A Dataflow Analysis [18] is comprised of three constituents: 1) a *control-flow graph* (on which the analysis is performed); 2) a *lattice* (representing values of interest for the analysis); *and* 3) *transfer functions* (that simulate execution at compile-time). In the following, we briefly recall each of the constituents of the conventional (feature-oblivious) single-program dataflow analysis and how they may be combined to analyze an input program.

Control-Flow Graph: The *control-flow graph* (CFG) is the abstraction of an input program on which a dataflow analysis runs. A CFG is a directed graph where the nodes are the statements of the input program and the edges represent *flow of control* according to the semantics of the programming language. An analysis may be *intraprocedural* or *interprocedural*, depending on how functions are handled in the CFG. Here, we only consider intraprocedural analyses.

Lattice: The information calculated by a dataflow analysis is arranged in a *lattice*, $\mathcal{L} = (D, \sqsubseteq)$ where D is a set of elements and $\sqsubseteq$ is a *partial-order* on the elements [23]. Lattices are usually described diagrammatically using *Hasse Diagrams* which use the convention that $x \sqsubseteq y$ if and only if x is depicted *below* y in the diagram (according to the lines of the diagram). Figure 2(a) depicts such a diagram of a lattice for analyzing the sign of an integer. Each element of the lattice captures information of interest to the analysis; e.g., "+" represents the fact that a value is always *positive*, "0/+" that a value is always *zero-or-positive*. A lattice has two special elements; $\bot$ at the bottom of the lattice usually means *"not analyzed yet"* whereas $\top$ at the top of the lattice usually means *"analysis doesn't know"*. The partial order induces a *least upper bound* operator, $\sqcup$, on the lattice elements [23] which is used to *combine* information during the

analysis, when control-flows meet. For instance, $\bot \sqcup 0 = 0$, $0 \sqcup + = 0/+$, and $- \sqcup 0/+ = \top$.

Transfer Functions: Each statement, S, will have an associated *transfer function*, $f_S : \mathcal{L} \rightarrow \mathcal{L}$, which simulates the execution of S at compile-time (with respect to what is being analyzed). Figure 2(b) illustrates the effect of executing transfer function f_S. Lattice element, ℓ, flows into the statement node, the transfer function computes $\ell' = f_S(\ell)$, and the result, ℓ', flows out of the node. Here are the transfer functions for two assignment statements for analysing the sign of variable x using the sign lattice in Figure 2(a):

$$f_{\texttt{x=0}}(\ell) = 0 \qquad f_{\texttt{x++}}(\ell) = \begin{cases} \top & \ell \in \{-/+, -/0, \top\} \\ + & \ell \in \{0, +, 0/+\} \\ -/0 & \ell = - \\ \bot & \ell = \bot \end{cases}$$

The transfer function, $f_{\texttt{x=0}}$, is the constant zero function capturing the fact that x will always have the value *zero* after execution of the statement x=0. The transfer function, $f_{\texttt{x++}}$, simulates execution of x++; e.g., if x was *negative* ($\ell = -$) prior to execution, we know that its value after execution will always be *negative-or-zero* ($\ell' = -/0$). In order for a dataflow analysis to be well-defined, all transfer functions have to obey a *monotonicity* property [23].

Analysis: Figure 3 shows how to combine the control-flow graph, lattice, and transfer functions to perform dataflow analysis on a tiny example program.

First (cf. Figure 3(a)), a control-flow graph is built from the program and annotated with *program points* (which are the *entry* and *exit* points of the statement nodes). In our example, there are four such program points which we label with the letters a to d. Second (cf. Figure 3(b)), the annotated CFG is turned into a *whole-program transfer function*, $T : \mathcal{L}^4 \rightarrow \mathcal{L}^4$, which works on four copies of the lattice, $\mathcal{L}$, since we have four program points (a to d). The entry point, a, is assigned an initialization value which depends on the analysis (here, $a = \bot$). For each program point, we simulate the effect of the program using transfer functions (e.g., $b = f_{\texttt{x=0}}(a)$) and the least-upper bound operator for combining flows (e.g., $c = b \sqcup d$). Third (cf. Figure 3(c)), we use the Fixed-Point Theorem [23] to compute the fixed-point of the function, T, by computing $T^i(\bot)$ for increasing values of i (depicted in the columns of the figure), until nothing changes. As seen in Figure 3(c), we reach the fixed-point in five iterations (since $T^4(\bot) = T^5(\bot)$) and the least-fixed point, and hence the result of the analysis, is: $a = \bot, b = 0, c = 0/+, d = +$ (which is the unique least fixed-point of T). From this we can deduce that the value of the variable x is always *zero* at program point b, it is *zero-or-positive* at point c, and *positive* at point d. (Note that, in practice, the fixed-point computation is often performed using more efficient iteration strategies.)

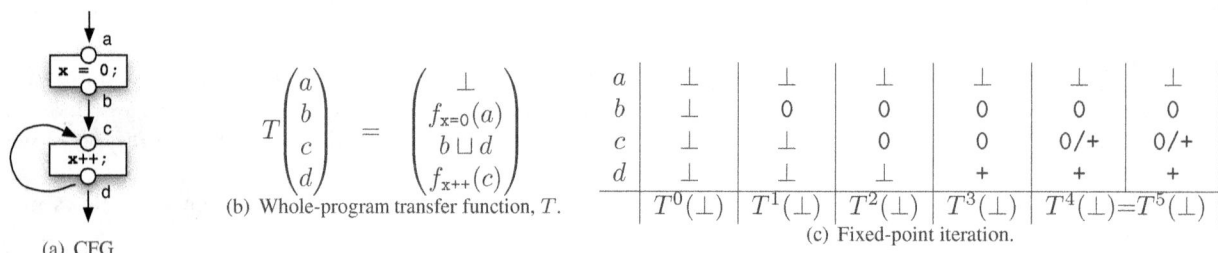

(a) CFG

$$T\begin{pmatrix} a \\ b \\ c \\ d \end{pmatrix} = \begin{pmatrix} \bot \\ f_{\text{x=0}}(a) \\ b \sqcup d \\ f_{\text{x++}}(c) \end{pmatrix}$$

(b) Whole-program transfer function, T.

a	$\bot$	$\bot$	$\bot$	$\bot$	$\bot$	$\bot$
b	$\bot$	0	0	0	0	0
c	$\bot$	$\bot$	0	0	0/+	0/+
d	$\bot$	$\bot$	$\bot$	+	+	+
	$T^0(\bot)$	$T^1(\bot)$	$T^2(\bot)$	$T^3(\bot)$	$T^4(\bot)=T^5(\bot)$	

(c) Fixed-point iteration.

Figure 3. Combining CFG, lattice, and transfer functions to perform dataflow analysis (as a fixed-point iteration).

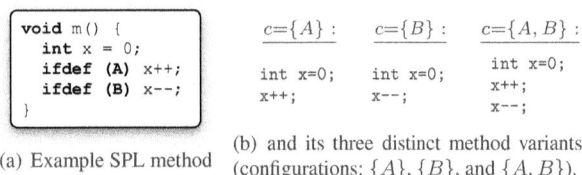

(a) Example SPL method

```
c={A} :        c={B} :        c={A,B} :

int x=0;       int x=0;       int x=0;
x++;           x--;           x++;
                              x--;
```

(b) and its three distinct method variants (configurations: $\{A\}$, $\{B\}$, and $\{A,B\}$).

Figure 4. A tiny example of an SPL method along with its three distinct method variants.

5. Dataflow Analyses for SPLs

In Section 2 we claimed that analyzing SPLs is important and that the naive brute force approach can be costly. In this section, we show how to take any feature-oblivious intraprocedural dataflow analysis and automatically turn it into a feature-sensitive analysis.

We present four different ways of performing intraprocedural dataflow analysis for software product lines (summarized in Figure 6). The four analyses calculate the same information, but in qualitatively different ways. To illustrate the principles, we use a deliberately simple example analysis; *sign analysis* of one variable, x, and use it to analyze an intentionally simple program (cf. Figure 4(a)) that increases and decreases a variable, depending on the features enabled.

The program uses features $\mathbb{F} = \{A, B\}$ and we assume it has a feature model $\psi_{\text{FM}} = A \vee B$ which translates into the following set of valid configurations: $[\![\psi_{\text{FM}}]\!] = \{\{A\}, \{B\}, \{A, B\}\}$.

$\mathcal{A}$1: Brute Force Analysis (Feature-Oblivious)

A software product line may be analyzed intraprocedurally by building *all* possible methods and analyzing them one by one using a conventional dataflow analysis as described in the previous section. A method with n features will give rise to 2^n possible end-product methods (minus those invalidated by the feature model). For our tiny example program that has two features, A and B, we have to build and analyze the *three* distinct methods as illustrated in Figure 4(b).

$\mathcal{A}$2: Consecutive Feature-Sensitive Analysis

We can avoid explicitly building all methods individually by making a dataflow analysis *feature-sensitive*. Now, we show how to take any single-program dataflow analysis and au-

tomatically turn it into a feature-sensitive analysis, capable of analyzing all possible method variants. Firstly, we consider the consecutive analysis, named this way because we analyze each of the possible configurations one at a time. We render it feature-sensitive by instrumenting the CFG with sufficient information for the transfer functions to know whether a given statement is to be executed or not in each configuration.

Control-Flow Graph: For each node in the CFG, we associate the *set of configurations*, $[\![\phi]\!]$, for which the node's corresponding statement is executed. We refer to this process as *CFG instrumentation*. Here is the instrumented CFG for our tiny method of Figure 4(a):

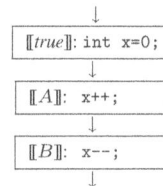

We label each node with "$[\![\phi]\!]: S$" where S is the statement and $[\![\phi]\!]$ is the configuration set associated with the statement. Unconditionally executed statements (e.g., `int x=0;`) are associated with the set of all configurations, $[\![true]\!]$. Statements that are nested inside several `ifdef`s will have the intersection of the configuration sets. For instance, statement S in "`ifdef` (ϕ_1) `ifdef` (ϕ_2) S" will be associated with the set of configurations $[\![\phi_1]\!] \cap [\![\phi_2]\!] \equiv [\![\phi_1 \wedge \phi_2]\!]$.

Lattice: Analyzing the configurations consecutively does not change the lattice, so the lattice of this feature-sensitive analysis is the same as that of the feature-oblivious analysis.

Transfer Functions: All we have to do in the feature-sensitive transfer function is use the associated configuration set, $[\![\phi]\!]$, to figure out whether or not to execute the feature-oblivious transfer function, f_S, in a given configuration, c; i.e., deciding $c \in [\![\phi]\!]$ (cf. Figure 6). Since the lifting only either applies the feature-oblivious transfer function or copies the lattice value, the lifted transfer function is also always monotone.

Analysis: In order to analyze a program using $\mathcal{A}$2, all we need to do is to combine the CFG, lattice, and transfer functions as explained in Section 4. Figure 5(b) shows the

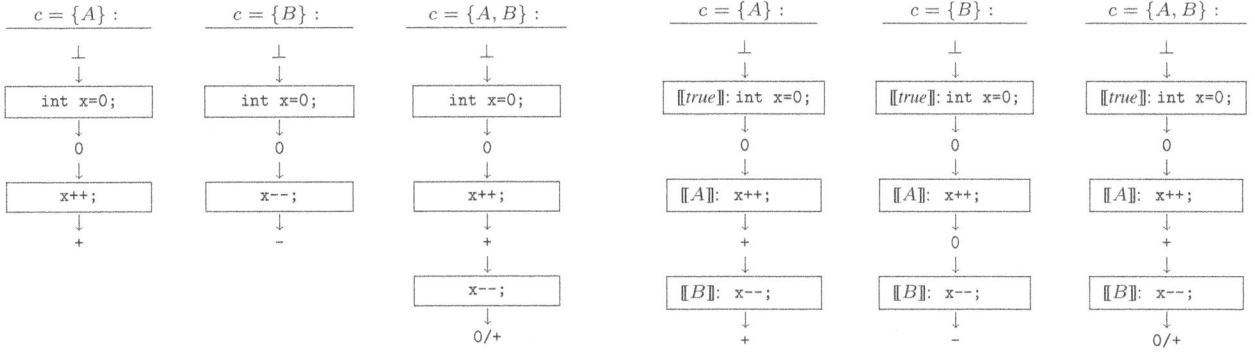

(a) Using the feature-oblivious analysis, $\mathcal{A}1$.

(b) Using the consecutive analysis, $\mathcal{A}2$.

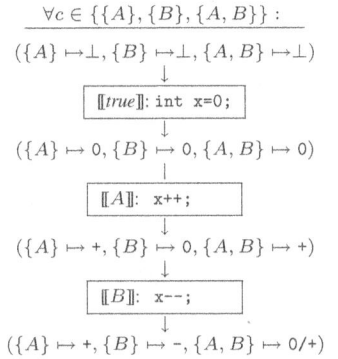

(c) Using the simultaneous analysis, $\mathcal{A}3$.

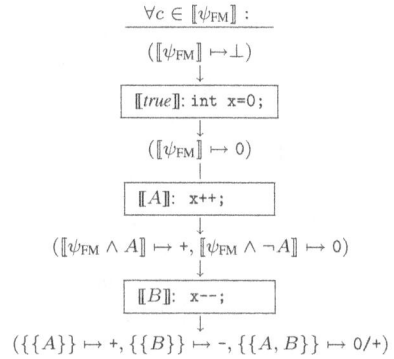

(d) Using the shared simultaneous analysis, $\mathcal{A}4$.

Figure 5. Results of using the four analyses on our tiny example program m (that increases and decreases variable, x).

result of analyzing the increase-decrease method using this consecutive feature-sensitive analysis. As can be seen, the consecutive feature-sensitive analysis needs one fixed-point computation for each configuration. $\mathcal{A}1$ and $\mathcal{A}2$ compute the same information (the same fixed-point solution); the only difference is whether the applicability of statements, $c \in [\![\phi]\!]$, is evaluated before or after compilation.

$\mathcal{A}3$: Simultaneous Feature-Sensitive Analysis

Another approach is to analyze all configurations *simultaneously* by using a *lifted* lattice that maintains one lattice element per valid configuration. As opposed to the consecutive analysis, the simultaneous analysis needs only *one* fixed-point computation. Again, this analysis will be *feature-sensitive* and it can also be automatically derived from the feature-oblivious analysis.

Control-Flow Graph: The CFG of $\mathcal{A}3$ is the same as that of $\mathcal{A}2$ as it already includes the necessary information for deciding whether or not to simulate execution of a conditional statement.

Lattice: As explained, we lift the feature-oblivious lattice, $\mathcal{L}$, such that it has one element per valid configuration:

$$\mathcal{L}_3 \quad = \quad [\![\psi_{\mathrm{FM}}]\!] \to \mathcal{L}$$

Note that whenever $\mathcal{L}$ is a lattice, then so is $[\![\psi_{\mathrm{FM}}]\!] \to \mathcal{L}$ (which is isomorphic to $\mathcal{L}^{|[\![\psi_{\mathrm{FM}}]\!]|}$). An example element of this lattice is:

$$(\{A\} \mapsto +, \{B\} \mapsto \text{-}, \{A,B\} \mapsto 0/+) \quad \in \quad [\![\psi_{\mathrm{FM}}]\!] \to \mathcal{L}$$

which corresponds to the information that: for configuration $\{A\}$, we know that the value of x is *positive* (+); for $\{B\}$, we know x is *negative* (-); and for $\{A,B\}$, we know it is *zero-or-positive* (0/+).

Transfer Functions: We *lift* the transfer functions correspondingly so they work on elements of the lifted lattice in a point-wise manner. The feature-oblivious transfer functions are applied only on the configurations for which the statement is executed. As an example, consider the statement "ifdef (A) x++;" where the effect of the lifted transfer function on the lattice element $(\{A\} \mapsto 0, \{B\} \mapsto 0, \{A,B\} \mapsto 0)$ is:

$$(\{A\} \mapsto 0, \{B\} \mapsto 0, \{A,B\} \mapsto 0)$$
$$\downarrow$$
$$\boxed{[\![A]\!]\colon \texttt{x++;}}$$
$$\downarrow$$
$$(\{A\} \mapsto +, \{B\} \mapsto 0, \{A,B\} \mapsto +)$$

17

The transfer function of the feature-oblivious analysis is applied to each of the configurations for which the ifdef formula A is satisfied. Since $[\![A]\!] = \{\{A\}, \{A, B\}\}$, this means that the function is applied to the lattice values of the configurations $\{A\}$ and $\{A, B\}$ with resulting value: $f_{\texttt{x++}}(0) = \texttt{+}$. The configuration $\{B\}$, on the other hand, does not satisfy the formula ($\{B\} \notin [\![A]\!]$), so its value is left unchanged with value 0. Figure 6 depicts and summarizes the effect of the lifted transfer function on the lifted lattice.

Since the feature-sensitive transfer function on $[\![\psi_{\text{FM}}]\!] \rightarrow \mathcal{L}$ only applies monotone transfer functions on $\mathcal{L}$ in a pointwise manner, it is itself monotone. This guarantees the existence of a unique and computable solution.

Analysis: Again, we simply combine the lifted CFG, lifted lattice, and lifted transfer functions to achieve our feature-sensitive simultaneous configuration analysis. Figure 5(c) shows the result of analyzing the increase-decrease method using the simultaneous feature-sensitive analysis. From this we can read off the information about the sign of the variable x at different program points, for each of the valid configurations. For instance, at the end of the program in configuration $\{B\}$, we can see that x is always *negative*. Compared to $\mathcal{A}2$, this analysis only has *one* fixed-point iteration and thus potentially saves the overhead involved. However, it requires the maximum number of fixed-point iterations that are performed in any configuration of $\mathcal{A}2$ in order to reach its fixed-point because of the pointwise lifted lattice. Again, it is fairly obvious that $\mathcal{A}2$ and $\mathcal{A}3$ compute the same information; the only difference being that $\mathcal{A}2$ does one fixed-point iteration per valid configuration whereas $\mathcal{A}3$ computes the same information in one iteration in a pointwise manner.

$\mathcal{A}4$: Shared Simultaneous Feature-Sensitive Analysis

Using the lifted lattice of the simultaneous analysis, it is possible to lazily share lattice values corresponding to configurations that are indistinguishable in the program being analyzed.

Control-Flow Graph: The CFG of $\mathcal{A}4$ is the same as that of $\mathcal{A}3$.

Lattice: To accomodate the sharing, the lifted lattice of $\mathcal{A}4$ will, instead of mapping configurations to base lattice values, map *sets of configurations* to base lattice values:

$$\mathcal{L}_4 \;=\; 2^{[\![\psi_{\text{FM}}]\!]} \hookrightarrow \mathcal{L}$$

This allows $\mathcal{A}4$ lattice values to *share* base lattice values for configurations that have not yet been distinguished by the analysis. For instance, the lifted lattice value of $\mathcal{A}3$, $(\{A\} \mapsto \ell, \{B\} \mapsto \ell, \{A, B\} \mapsto \ell)$, can now be represented by $([\![A \lor B]\!] \mapsto \ell)$ where the three configurations, $[\![A \lor B]\!] = \{\{A\}, \{B\}, \{A, B\}\}$, *share* the base lattice value, ℓ.

Transfer Functions: The transfer functions of $\mathcal{A}4$ work by lazily *splitting* sets of configurations, $[\![\psi]\!]$, in two disjoint parts, depending on the feature constraint, ϕ, attached with

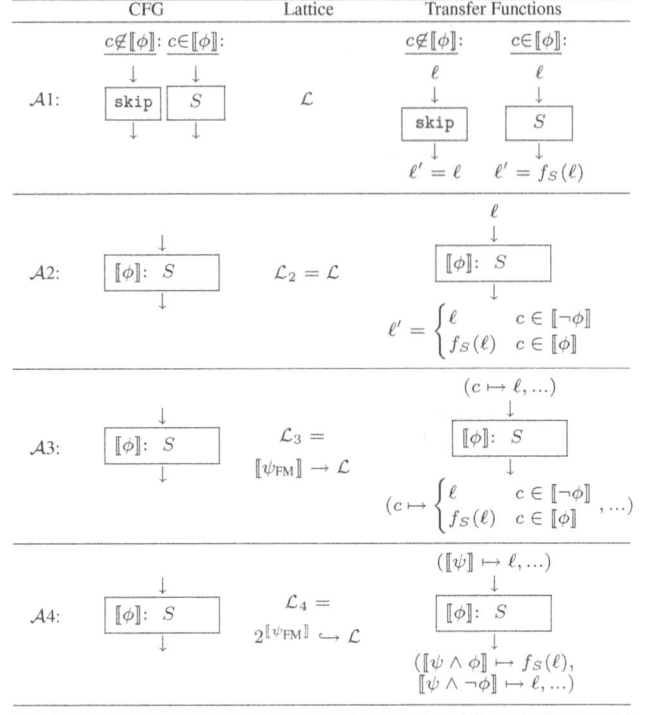

Figure 6. Summary of dataflow analyses for SPLs.

the statement in question: A set of configurations for which the transfer function should be applied, $[\![\psi \land \phi]\!]$; and a set of configurations for which the transfer function should not be applied, $[\![\psi \land \neg\phi]\!]$; i.e.:

$$
\begin{array}{c}
([\![\psi]\!] \mapsto \ell, \dots) \\
\downarrow \\
\boxed{[\![\phi]\!]: \quad S} \\
\downarrow \\
([\![\psi \land \phi]\!] \mapsto f_S(\ell), [\![\psi \land \neg\phi]\!] \mapsto \ell, \dots)
\end{array}
$$

Note that $[\![\psi \land \phi]\!] \cup [\![\psi \land \neg\phi]\!] = [\![(\psi \land \phi) \lor (\psi \land \neg\phi)]\!] = [\![\psi \land (\phi \lor \neg\phi)]\!] = [\![\psi \land true]\!] = [\![\psi]\!]$. In cases where $[\![\psi]\!]$ would be split into "nothing", $\emptyset$, and "everything", $[\![\psi]\!]$ (which happens whenever $\psi \land \phi \equiv false$ or $\psi \land \neg\phi \equiv false$), we eliminate the *false* constituents in order to ensure a canonical (minimal and finite) representation. It is also possible to join lattice values that are equal. However, this might compromise performance (in exchange for memory gains) due to the equality comparisons needed to determine if joins are possible.

Analysis: As always for the analysis, we simply combine the CFG, lattice, and transfer functions to achieve our shared simultaneous analysis. Figure 5(d) shows how this analysis will analyze our tiny program example from earlier. (For legibility, the last line of the figure is written with the expanded *sets of configurations* rather than with formula notation.) $\mathcal{A}3$ and $\mathcal{A}4$ compute the same information; $\mathcal{A}4$ just represents the same information more compactly using sharing.

$$\begin{aligned}
\mathrm{tasks}(\mathcal{A}1) &= \|[\![\psi_{\mathrm{FM}}]\!]\| \cdot \mathrm{compile} + \|[\![\psi_{\mathrm{FM}}]\!]\| \cdot \mathrm{analyze}_{\mathcal{A}1} \\
\mathrm{tasks}(\mathcal{A}2) &= \mathrm{compile} + \mathrm{instrument} + \|[\![\psi_{\mathrm{FM}}]\!]\| \cdot \mathrm{analyze}_{\mathcal{A}2} \\
\mathrm{tasks}(\mathcal{A}3) &= \mathrm{compile} + \mathrm{instrument} + \mathrm{analyze}_{\mathcal{A}3} \\
\mathrm{tasks}(\mathcal{A}4) &= \mathrm{compile} + \mathrm{instrument} + \mathrm{analyze}_{\mathcal{A}4}
\end{aligned}$$

Figure 7. Overall tasks performed by each of the analyses.

Other Analysis Approaches

A couple of variations of the feature-sensitive analyses are possible. One could retain the instrumented CFG calculated in $\mathcal{A}2$ and $\mathcal{A}3$, but then *specialize* [12] the CFG prior to analysis for every configuration by resolving all conditional statements relative to the current configuration. This approach would be a variation of $\mathcal{A}2$ with a higher cost due to CFG specialization, but which in turn saves by making membership decisions only once per CFG node. Another approach would be to transform `ifdefs` into normal `ifs` and turn feature names into static booleans [4, 25] which could then be resolved by techniques such as *partial evaluation* [12] prior to analysis. We do not explore this idea in the paper, but rather focus on the different ways of automatically transforming a feature-oblivious analysis into a feature-sensitive one, while staying within the framework of dataflow analysis.

Asymptotic complexity (TIME and SPACE)

We now consider and compare the asymptotic complexity of $\mathcal{A}2$, $\mathcal{A}3$, and $\mathcal{A}4$ in terms of first overall tasks, then performance, and finally memory consumption.

Total Time (including compilation): Figure 7 considers the overall tasks performed for each SPL method analyzed in each of the analyses. Apart from $\mathcal{A}3$ vs. $\mathcal{A}4$, they all differ substantially in the number of times each of the tasks are performed. Not surprisingly, $\mathcal{A}1$ needs to do a lot of (brute force) compilation. The rest require only one compilation, but pay the price of instrumentation to annotate the CFG with feature constraints. However, this is cheap in practice. $\mathcal{A}2$ performs the analysis (i.e., the fixed-point computation) for every valid configuration whereas $\mathcal{A}3$ and $\mathcal{A}4$ only do this once. We return to these considerations, in practice, when we discuss our experimental results (cf. Section 6).

Performance of Analyses (TIME): The asymptotic time complexity of the $\mathcal{A}2$ analysis is:

$$\mathrm{TIME}(\mathcal{A}2) = \mathcal{O}(\|[\![\psi_{\mathrm{FM}}]\!]\| \cdot |\mathcal{G}| \cdot T_2 \cdot h(\mathcal{L}_2))$$

where $|\mathcal{G}|$ is the size of the control-flow graph (which for the intraprocedural analysis is linear in the number of statements in the method analyzed, ignoring exceptions); T_2 is the execution time of a transfer function on the $\mathcal{L}_2$ lattice; and $h(\mathcal{L}_2)$ is the height of the $\mathcal{L}_2$ lattice. In total, we need to analyze $\|[\![\psi_{\mathrm{FM}}]\!]\|$ method variants. For each of these, we execute $\mathcal{O}(|\mathcal{G}|)$ different transfer functions, each of which

takes execution time, T_2, and can be executed a worst-case maximum of $h(\mathcal{L}_2)$ number of times.

Analogously, we can quantify the asymptotic time complexity of $\mathcal{A}3$:

$$\mathrm{TIME}(\mathcal{A}3) = \mathcal{O}(|\mathcal{G}| \cdot T_3 \cdot h(\mathcal{L}_3))$$

which is similar to $\mathcal{A}2$, except that we do not need to analyze $\|[\![\psi_{\mathrm{FM}}]\!]\|$ times and that the numbers are parameterized by the $\mathcal{A}3$ lattice and transfer functions. For the height of the lattice $\mathcal{L}_3$, we have:

$$\begin{aligned}
h(\mathcal{L}_3) &= h([\![\psi_{\mathrm{FM}}]\!] \to \mathcal{L}_2) &= h(\mathcal{L}_2^{\|[\![\psi_{\mathrm{FM}}]\!]\|}) \\
&= \sum_{c \in [\![\psi_{\mathrm{FM}}]\!]} h(\mathcal{L}_2) &= \|[\![\psi_{\mathrm{FM}}]\!]\| \cdot h(\mathcal{L}_2)
\end{aligned}$$

Note, however, that this is a purely theoretically worst case that does not naturally arise in practice because of the pointwise nature of $\mathcal{A}3$. Since all configurations are independent, the penalty for $\mathcal{A}3$ will not be the *sum*, but rather only the *maximum* number of fixed-point iterations of $\mathcal{A}2$. In practice, we have not observed any significant cost on behalf of $\mathcal{A}3$ from this effect, as we will see in Section 6. The remaining speed factor between $\mathcal{A}2$ and $\mathcal{A}3$ thus boils down to:

$$\mathcal{A}2 : \mathcal{A}3 \quad = \quad \|[\![\psi_{\mathrm{FM}}]\!]\| \cdot T_2 \; : \; T_3$$

In theory, we would not expect any difference in the speed of the two analyses; $\mathcal{A}2$ makes a sequence of n analyses and $\mathcal{A}3$ makes one analysis in which each step costs n. However, as we will see in Section 6, $\mathcal{A}3$ has better cache performance than $\mathcal{A}2$, since statement nodes only have to be retrieved and evaluated once per transfer function in $\mathcal{A}3$, instead of once per configuration as in $\mathcal{A}2$. Apart from data, also the fixed-point iteration code only runs once instead of once per configuration.

Memory Consumption of Analyses (SPACE): The asymptotic space complexity of the analyses $\mathcal{A}2$ and $\mathcal{A}3$ is simply proportional to the amount of data occupied by the lattice values:

$$\begin{aligned}
\mathrm{SPACE}(\mathcal{A}2) &= \mathcal{O}(|\mathcal{G}| \cdot log(|\mathcal{L}_2|)) \\
\mathrm{SPACE}(\mathcal{A}3) &= \mathcal{O}(|\mathcal{G}| \cdot log(|\mathcal{L}_3|))
\end{aligned}$$

Comparing the two, we can derive that:

$$\begin{aligned}
log(|\mathcal{L}_3|) &= log(|[\![\psi_{\mathrm{FM}}]\!] \to \mathcal{L}_2|) &= log(|\mathcal{L}_2^{\|[\![\psi_{\mathrm{FM}}]\!]\|}|) \\
&= log(|\mathcal{L}_2|^{\|[\![\psi_{\mathrm{FM}}]\!]\|}) &= \|[\![\psi_{\mathrm{FM}}]\!]\| \cdot log(|\mathcal{L}_2|)
\end{aligned}$$

which thus means that the difference is:

$$\mathrm{SPACE}(\mathcal{A}3) = \|[\![\psi_{\mathrm{FM}}]\!]\| \cdot \mathrm{SPACE}(\mathcal{A}2)$$

This relationship is also evident when comparing Figures 5(b) and 5(c). Although $\mathcal{A}3$ requires $n = \|[\![\psi_{\mathrm{FM}}]\!]\|$ times more memory to run, it is always possible to cut the $\mathcal{A}3$ lattice into k *slices* of n/k columns (i.e., analyze n/k number of configurations at a time). This provides a way of combining the time and space characteristics of $\mathcal{A}2$ and $\mathcal{A}3$ (and $\mathcal{A}4$).

Benchmark	LOC	$\vert \mathbb{F} \vert$	$\vert 2^{\mathbb{F}_{local}} \vert$	#methods	cc%
Graph PL	1,350	18	$2^9 = 512$	135 (964)	82%
MobileMedia08	5,700	14	$2^7 = 128$	285 (821)	45%
Lampiro	45,000	11	$2^2 = 4$	1,949 (1,980)	1.5%
BerkeleyDB	84,000	42	$2^8 = 256$	3,605 (7,446)	40%

Figure 8. Size metrics for our four SPL benchmarks.

6. Evaluation

We first present our study settings and then present our results in terms of total analysis time, performance, and memory consumption.

6.1 Study settings

To validate the ideas, we have implemented and evaluated the performance and memory characteristics of two ubiquitous intraprocedural dataflow analyses; namely *reaching definitions* and *definite assignments* (both of which are implemented using SOOT's interprocedural dataflow analysis framework for analyzing Java programs [28]).

We have subsequently lifted them into consecutive, simultaneous, and shared simultaneous feature-sensitive analyses for SPLs. Since we are using intraprocedural analyses which analyze one method at a time, we can use the *local* set of configurations, $\mathbb{F}_{local}$, local to each method which significantly reduces the size of the lattices we work with. However, instead of using the set of valid configurations, $[\![\psi_{FM}]\!]$, we use the set of all feature combinations, $2^{\mathbb{F}_{local}}$. Restricting to valid configurations only would make all feature-sensitive analyses faster.

We have chosen four qualitatively different SPL benchmarks, summarized in Figure 8. Graph PL (GPL) is a product line of small size with intensive feature usage [16] for desktop applications. MobileMedia08 is a product line of small size and moderate feature usage [9] for mobile applications for dealing with multi-media. Lampiro is a product line with low feature usage for instant-messaging clients [14]. Last but not least, BerkeleyDB is a product line for databases [16] of moderate feature usage. The table presented in Figure 8 summarizes: LOC, is the number of lines of code; $\vert \mathbb{F} \vert$, is the number of features in the SPL; $\vert 2^{\mathbb{F}_{local}} \vert$, is the maximum number of configurations of any one method in the SPL; #methods, is the number of methods (with the total number of different method variants, in parentheses); and cc%, is the percentage of methods with conditional compilation (ifdef) feature usage. Methods completely encompassed by ifdefs are also counted.

The histograms in Figure 9 illustrate the distribution of the number of configurations per method for each of the SPLs. MobileMedia08 (depicted in Figure 9(b)), for instance, has 157 methods without features, 78 methods with one feature (i.e., $2^1 * 78 = 156$ different method variants), 37 methods with two features (i.e., $2^2 * 37 = 148$ different method variants) etc, and one method with seven features (i.e., $2^7 * 1 = 128$ different method variants). The area

shown in the histograms is thus directly proportional to the number of method variants possible. As can be seen, the four benchmark SPLs have qualitatively different feature usage profiles.

Our analyses currently interface with CIDE (Colored IDE) [16] for retrieving the conditional compilation statements. CIDE is a tool that enables developers to annotate feature code using background colors rather than ifdefs directives, reducing code pollution and improving comprehensibility. Conceptually, CIDE uses a restricted form of ifdefs for which only conjunction of features is permitted.

Our analyses assume that each line never has two parts with different CIDE colorings (i.e., different formulae). This is a fair assumption as lines with multiple configurations could be accomodated by inserting appropriate line breaks.

We have executed the analyses on a 64-bit machine with a Intel® Core™ i7 920 CPU running at a 2.6 GHz frequency with 8 GB of memory and 8MB L2 cache on a Linux Ubuntu 2.6.32-30-generic operating system.

6.2 Results and Discussion

We now present the results[3] obtained from our empirical study. We first present and discuss our results pertaining to the total time, then the performance of the analysis only, and finally, memory consumption. All times given are averages over ten runs with the highest and lowest number removed.

Total Time (including compilation): Figure 10 plots the total time (including compilation) of the reaching definitions analysis on each of our four benchmarks. For the feature-oblivious brute force analysis, $\mathcal{A}1$, the total time is shown in black whereas the feature-sensitive analyses, $\mathcal{A}2$, $\mathcal{A}3$, and $\mathcal{A}4$, are plotted in dark gray, light gray, and white, respectively. All times comprise the tasks outlined in Figure 7. The compilation time given for $\mathcal{A}1$ is the average of the *slowest* configuration to compile ($c = 2^{\mathbb{F}}$) and the *fastest* configuration to compile ($c = \emptyset$) times the number of configurations to be compiled. We have to do this estimation because several configurations, although valid according to the feature model, generate code that does not compile. Also, since the CIDE API does not currently provide an efficient way of getting the color of a line, we omit the time of this calculation from the CFG instrumentation time.

We see that the feature-sensitive analyses, $\mathcal{A}2$, $\mathcal{A}3$, and $\mathcal{A}4$ are all faster than the brute-force approach, $\mathcal{A}1$, except on Lampiro where they are all fairly equal. If we take the best gain factors of the feature-sensitive analyses (Graph PL: 14; MobileMedia08: 4.8; Lampiro: 1.0; and BerkeleyDB: 2.6), for each benchmark, they give an average speed-up of 5.6 when compared to $\mathcal{A}1$. Continuing the comparison to $\mathcal{A}1$, $\mathcal{A}3$ (in general, the fastest) does the same analysis but takes 12% of the time on Graph PL, 21% on MobileMedia08, 105% on Lampiro, and 39%

---

[3] All results including equivalence proofs are available at: http://twiki.cin.ufpe.br/twiki/bin/view/SPG/EmergentAndDFA

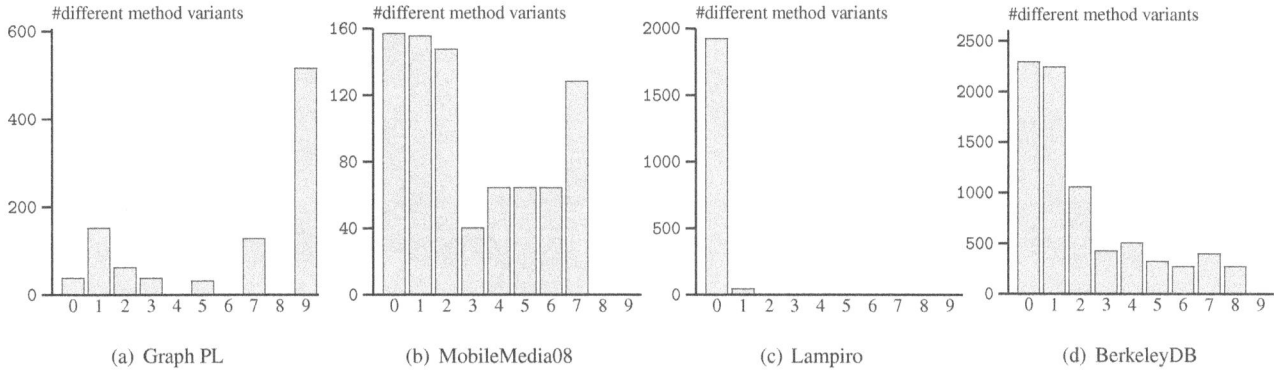

(a) Graph PL (b) MobileMedia08 (c) Lampiro (d) BerkeleyDB

Figure 9. Histogram showing the distribution of number of configurations per methods.

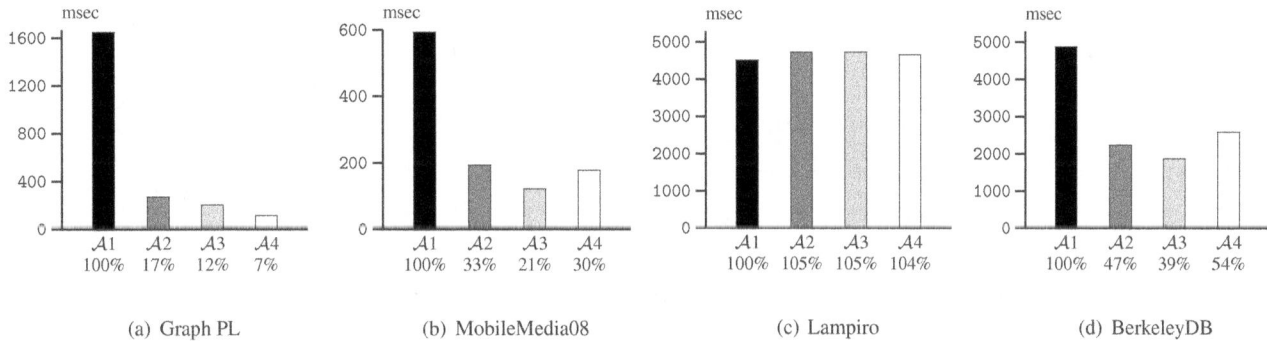

(a) Graph PL (b) MobileMedia08 (c) Lampiro (d) BerkeleyDB

Figure 10. The total time (including compilation) of RD: $\mathcal{A}1$ (black) vs. $\mathcal{A}2$ (dark gray) vs. $\mathcal{A}3$ (light gray) vs. $\mathcal{A}4$ (white).

on `BerkeleyDB` which translates into a gain factors of respectively: 8.3, 4.8, 1.0, and 2.6. So, $\mathcal{A}3$ is anywhere from slightly to slightly more than eight times faster than $\mathcal{A}1$.

The reason for this is *compilation overhead* that $\mathcal{A}1$ has to "pay" for each different method variant (see Figure 7). When considering $\mathcal{A}2$, $\mathcal{A}3$, and $\mathcal{A}4$, the *compilation* time is an overhead we only have to pay once, even if many analyses are performed. In the following, we will thus focus on the times of the analyses themselves without *compilation* time.

*Performance of Analyses (**TIME**):* Figure 11 plots the relative difference between the speed of the $\mathcal{A}2$, $\mathcal{A}3$, and $\mathcal{A}4$ feature-sensitive analyses (using reaching definitions). We observe that the $\mathcal{A}3$ is generally the fastest. Compared to $\mathcal{A}2$, it spends only 62% of the time on GPL, 46% on `MobileMedia08`, 100% on `Lampiro`, and 72% on `BerkeleyDB`. Figure 12 shows the numbers for the *definite assignments* analysis. Again, $\mathcal{A}3$ is, in general, the fastest. Compared to $\mathcal{A}2$, it spends only 47% of the time on GPL, 56% on `MobileMedia08`, and 199% on `Lampiro`, and 65% on `BerkeleyDB`. However, $\mathcal{A}4$ is fastest on GPL for both analyses because there are many sets of configurations that are indistinguishable by `#ifdefs`. In general, $\mathcal{A}4$ is slower than $\mathcal{A}3$ due to many comparisons it has to perform during the analyses to split sets of configurations.

The analysis time is virtually the same for all four analyses, $\mathcal{A}1$, $\mathcal{A}2$, $\mathcal{A}3$, and $\mathcal{A}4$ for `Lampiro`, except in Figure 12(c). This is because it has limited feature usage (only

1.5% of the methods have features and the average number of configurations per method is only 1.02), and thus most of the cost is the time of the analysis itself without any overhead from features. We take this as indication that the overhead of our approaches is almost nothing for SPLs with low feature usage and that it does not matter much which of the feature-sensitive analyses are used in such cases.

Recall that $\mathcal{A}3$ in principle has to do as many fixed-point iterations as are needed for the slowest converging configuration, unnecessarily reiterating already converged configurations. Our data, however, indicates that this is not a problem in practice. For example, in the reaching definitions analysis, $\mathcal{A}3$ only executes as little as 0.22% more unlifted transfer functions than $\mathcal{A}2$ on `BerkeleyDB`; only 0.05% more on GPL; and virtually 0% more on `Lampiro` and `MobileMedia08`.

As for caching, the first data column, *normal cache* of Figure 13, shows the relative difference between the number of cache misses in $\mathcal{A}2$ vs $\mathcal{A}3$. As expected, $\mathcal{A}2$ incurs quite a lot more cache misses than $\mathcal{A}3$, making the former comparatively slower since data has to be re-fetched on every configuration. To further substantiate this claim, we instrumented *both* $\mathcal{A}2$ and $\mathcal{A}3$ with instructions to fill up the L2 cache (traversing an 8MB array) prior to transfer function execution. The second data column, *full cache*, reveals that this indeed hurts $\mathcal{A}2$ more than $\mathcal{A}3$. We take this as evidence that $\mathcal{A}3$ has better cache properties than $\mathcal{A}2$.

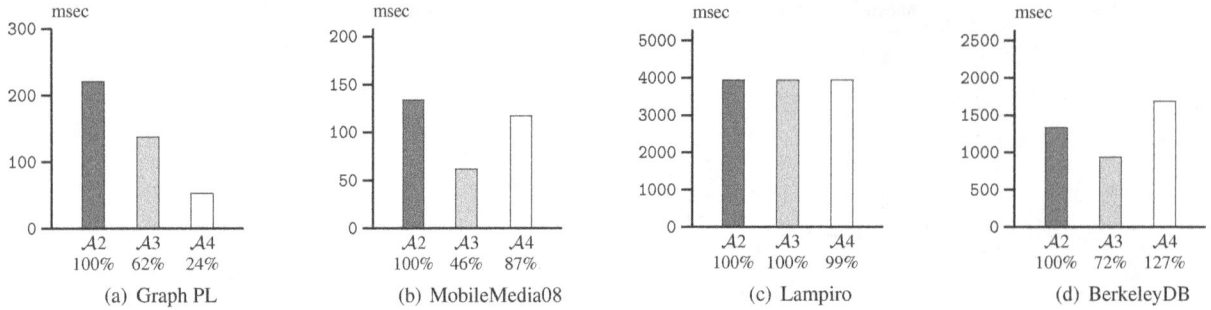

Figure 11. The analysis time of *reaching definitions*: $\mathcal{A}2$ (dark gray) vs. $\mathcal{A}3$ (light gray) vs. $\mathcal{A}4$ (white).

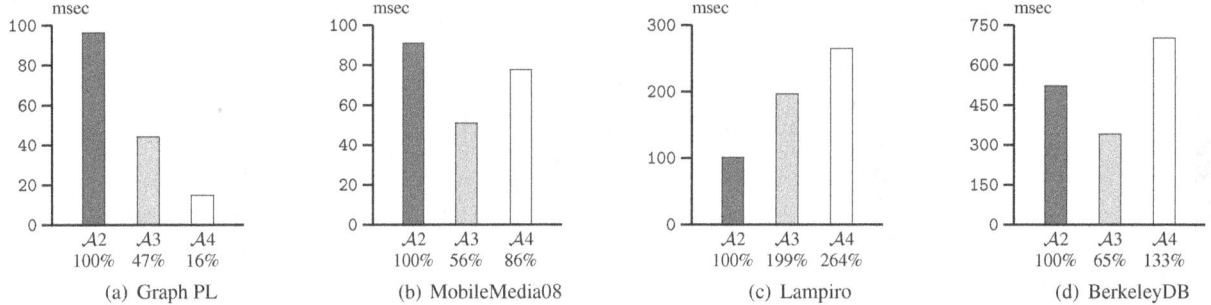

Figure 12. The analysis time of *definite assignments*: $\mathcal{A}2$ (dark gray) vs. $\mathcal{A}3$ (light gray) vs. $\mathcal{A}4$ (white).

Benchmark	$\mathcal{A}2 : \mathcal{A}3$ (normal cache)	$\mathcal{A}2 : \mathcal{A}3$ (full cache)
Graph PL	+ 4 %	+ 13 %
MobileMedia08	+ 36 %	+ 45 %
Lampiro	+ 12 %	+ 18 %
BerkeleyDB	+ 21 %	+ 29 %

Figure 13. Cache misses in $\mathcal{A}2$ vs $\mathcal{A}3$.

We thus have evidence that, in general, $\mathcal{A}3$ seems to be the fastest. If we average the speed ratio over the two analyses on the four benchmarks, $\mathcal{A}3$ outperforms $\mathcal{A}2$ in using only about 56% of the time to calculate the same information.

Memory Consumption of Analyses (SPACE): Figure 14 lists the space consumption by the maximum memory consuming method (wrt. $\mathcal{A}3$). Our experimental data confirms that $\mathcal{A}3$ requires almost $|2^{\mathbb{F}^{\text{local}}}|$ times more memory than $\mathcal{A}2$ since it has to keep all configurations in memory during its fixed-point computation. This does, however, not appear to be a problem in practice for intraprocedural analysis as it only needs to keep data for one method in memory at a time. Indeed, this has not been a problem on any of our four benchmarks. The shared analysis $\mathcal{A}4$ may reduce space usage anywhere between a factor of one to 15, depending on the SPL.

7. Related Work

Data-Flow Analysis: The idea of making dataflow analysis sensitive to statements that may or may not be executed is related to *path-sensitive* dataflow analysis. Such analyses compute different analysis information along different ex-

ecution paths aiming to improve precision by disregarding spurious information from infeasible paths [5] or to optimize frequently executed paths [2]. Earlier, disabling infeasible dead statements has been exploited to improve the precision of constant propagation [29] by essentially running a dead-code analysis capable of tagging statements as executable or non-executable during constant propagation analysis.

Predicated dataflow analysis [22] introduced the idea of using propositional logic predicates over runtime values to derive so-called *optimistic* dataflow values guarded by predicates. Such analyses are capable of producing multiple analysis versions and keeping them distinct during analysis much like our $\mathcal{A}3$ and $\mathcal{A}4$ analyses. However, their predicates are over dynamic state rather than SPL feature constraints for which everything is statically decidable.

The novelty in our paper is the application of the dataflow analysis framework to the domain of SPLs giving rise to the concept of *feature-sensitive* analyses that take conditionally compiled code and feature models into consideration so as to analyze not one program, but an entire SPL family of programs.

Analysis of SPLs: In SPLs, there are features whose presence or absence do not influence the test outcomes, which makes many feature combinations unnecessary for a particular test. This idea of selecting only relevant features for a given test case was proposed in a recent work [11]. It uses dataflow analysis to recover a list of features that are reachable from a given test case. The unreachable features are discarded, decreasing the number of combinations to test. In contrast, we defined and demonstrated how to au-

Benchmark	Max. memory consuming method	$|2^{\#local}|$	$\mathcal{A}2$	$\mathcal{A}3\ (\mathcal{A}2{:}\mathcal{A}3)$	$\mathcal{A}4\ (\mathcal{A}3{:}\mathcal{A}4)$
Graph PL	Vertex.display()	$2^9 = 512$	37 KB	9.9 MB (1:281)	1.4 MB (7.2:1)
MobileMedia08	MediaController.handleCommand()	$2^6 = 64$	93 KB	4.8 MB (1:53)	2.5 MB (1.9:1)
Lampiro	InfTree.clinit()	$2^0 = 1$	12 MB	12 MB (1:1)	12 MB (1:1)
BerkeleyDB	DbRunAction.main()	$2^7 = 128$	212 KB	20 MB (1:96)	1.3 MB (15:1)

Figure 14. Maximum memory consumption of lattice information during analysis ($\mathcal{A}2$ vs. $\mathcal{A}3$ vs. $\mathcal{A}4$).

tomatically make any conventional dataflow analysis able to analyze SPLs in a feature-sensitive way. Thus, our feature-sensitive idea might be used in such a work (testing). For example, it might further reduce the time spent figuring out which relevant feature combinations to test.

We recently proposed the concept of emergent interfaces [26]. These interfaces emerge on demand to give support for specific SPL maintenance and thus help developers understand and manage dependencies between features. Feature dependencies such as assigning a value to a variable used by another feature, have to be generated by feature-sensitive analyses. Thus, our present work may be used to generate emergent interfaces to support SPL maintenance. Our analyses are more efficient than the brute force approach, which is important to improve the performance during the computation of emergent interfaces.

Lifting for SPLs: Researchers already lifted automated analysis and processing such as for parsing [17], model checking [6], monitoring [19], type checking [3], and verification [4, 25]. Kaestner et al. [17] provides a variability-aware parser which is capable of parsing code without pre-processing it. The parser also performs instrumentation as we do, but on tokens, instead of statements. When the parser reaches a token instrumented with feature A, it splits into branches. Then, one parser assumes that feature A is selected and another assumes that A is not. So, the former consumes the token and the latter skips it. To avoid parsing tokens repeatedly (like a parenthesis instrumented with no feature), the branches are joined. This approach is similar to our shared simultaneous analysis $\mathcal{A}4$, where we lazily split sets of configurations. However, we do not perform join. On the one hand, we could join lattices of different configurations that are exactly the same in favor of memory usage. On the other hand, we would increase the performance overhead, since we need to verify the equality of lattices for each statement and potentially for many configurations.

Classen et al. [6] shows that behavioral models offer little means to relate different products and their respective behavioral descriptions. To minimize this limitation, they present a transition system to describe the combined behavior of an entire SPL. Additionally, they provide a model checking technique supported by a tool capable of verifying properties for all the products of an SPL once. Like our work, they claim that checking all product combinations at once instead of each product separately is faster. Their model checking algorithm was on average 3.5 times faster than verifying products separately.

Safe composition: Safe composition (SC) relates to the safe generation and verification of properties for SPL assets providing guarantees that the product derivation process generates products with properties that are obeyed [3, 15]. Safe composition may help in finding problems like undeclared variables. We complement safe composition, since when using our feature-sensitive idea, we are able to catch any errors expressible as a dataflow analysis (e.g., uninitialized variables and null pointers).

8. Conclusion

In this paper, we presented three approaches for taking any standard one-program dataflow analysis and automatically lifting it into a feature-sensitive analysis capable of analyzing all configurations of an SPL. To evaluate these approaches, we took two intraprocedural dataflow analyses and made them feature-sensitive. Experimental evaluation shows that the feature-sensitive approaches are faster than the naive brute-force approach. For SPLs with low feature usage, they are only slightly faster than the naive approach. For SPLs with high feature usage, the simultaneous feature-sensitive analysis ($\mathcal{A}3$), in particular, is up to more than eight times faster than the existing alternative ($\mathcal{A}1$).

We also conclude that our three approaches have different performance and memory consumption characteristics. The simultaneous feature-sensitive analysis ($\mathcal{A}3$) is, in general, the fastest. On the other hand, in terms of memory consumption, $\mathcal{A}4$ performs better than $\mathcal{A}3$. However, this does not show up as a problem in practice for intraprocedural analysis on the benchmarks we used.

Acknowledgments

We would like to thank CNPq, FACEPE, and National Institute of Science and Technology for Software Engineering (INES), for partially supporting this work. Also, we thank SPG[4] members for the fruitful discussions about this paper. We also thank Julia Lawall for the comments that helped to improve this paper.

References

[1] B. Adams, W. De Meuter, H. Tromp, and A. E. Hassan. Can we refactor conditional compilation into aspects? In *Proceedings of the 8th ACM international conference on Aspect-oriented software development (AOSD'09)*, pages 243–254, Charlottesville, Virginia, USA, 2009. ACM.

---

[4] http://www.cin.ufpe.br/spg

[2] G. Ammons and J. R. Larus. Improving data-flow analysis with path profiles. In *Programming Language Design and Implementation (PLDI'98)*, pages 72–84, Montreal, Canada, 1998.

[3] S. Apel, C. Kästner, A. Grösslinger, and C. Lengauer. Type safety for feature-oriented product lines. *Automated Software Engineering*, 17:251–300, September 2010.

[4] S. Apel, H. Speidel, P. Wendler, A. von Rhein, and D. Beyer. Detection of feature interactions using feature-aware verification. In *Proceedings of the 26th IEEE/ACM International Conference on Automated Software Engineering (ASE'11)*, Lawrence, USA, November 2011. IEEE Computer Society.

[5] T. Ball and S. K. Rajamani. Bebop: a path-sensitive interprocedural dataflow engine. In *PASTE'01*, pages 97–103, Snowbird, Utah, USA.

[6] A. Classen, P. Heymans, P.-Y. Schobbens, A. Legay, and J.-F. Raskin. Model checking lots of systems: efficient verification of temporal properties in software product lines. In *Proceedings of the 32nd ACM/IEEE International Conference on Software Engineering (ICSE '10)*, pages 335–344, Cape Town, South Africa, 2010. ACM.

[7] P. Clements and L. Northrop. *Software Product Lines: Practices and Patterns*. Addison-Wesley, 2001.

[8] M. D. Ernst, G. J. Badros, and D. Notkin. An empirical analysis of c preprocessor use. *IEEE Transactions on Software Engineering*, 28:1146–1170, December 2002.

[9] E. Figueiredo, N. Cacho, C. Sant'Anna, M. Monteiro, U. Kulesza, A. Garcia, S. Soares, F. Ferrari, S. Khan, F. C. Filho, and F. Dantas. Evolving software product lines with aspects: an empirical study on design stability. In *Proceedings of the 30th International Conference on Software Engineering (ICSE'08)*, pages 261–270, Leipzig, Germany, 2008. ACM.

[10] M. Fowler. *Refactoring: Improving the Design of Existing Code*. Addison-Wesley, 1999.

[11] C. Hwan, P. Kim, D. Batory, and S. Khurshid. Reducing combinatorics in testing product lines. In *Proceedings of the 10th International Conference on Aspect-oriented Software Development (AOSD'11)*, pages 57–68, Porto de Galinhas, Brazil, 2011. ACM.

[12] N. D. Jones, C. K. Gomard, and P. Sestoft. *Partial evaluation and automatic program generation*. Prentice-Hall, Inc., Upper Saddle River, NJ, USA, 1993.

[13] K. C. Kang, S. G. Cohen, J. A. Hess, W. E. Novak, and A. S. Peterson. Feature-Oriented Domain Analysis (FODA) feasibility study. Technical report, Carnegie-Mellon University Software Engineering Institute, November 1990.

[14] C. Kästner. *Virtual Separation of Concerns: Toward Preprocessors 2.0*. PhD thesis, University of Magdeburg, Germany, May 2010.

[15] C. Kästner and S. Apel. Type-checking software product lines - a formal approach. In *Proceedings of the 23rd IEEE/ACM International Conference on Automated Software Engineering (ASE'08)*, pages 258–267, L'Aquila, Italy, 2008.

[16] C. Kästner, S. Apel, and M. Kuhlemann. Granularity in software product lines. In *Proceedings of the 30th International Conference on Software Engineering (ICSE'08)*, pages 311–320, Leipzig, Germany, 2008. ACM.

[17] C. Kästner, P. G. Giarrusso, T. Rendel, S. Erdweg, K. Ostermann, and T. Berger. Variability-aware parsing in the presence of lexical macros and conditional compilation. In *Proceedings of the ACM International Conference on Object-Oriented Programming Systems Languages and Applications (OOPSLA'11)*, pages 805–824, Portland, OR, USA, 2011. ACM.

[18] G. A. Kildall. A unified approach to global program optimization. In *Proceedings of the 1st annual ACM symposium on Principles of programming languages (POPL'73)*, pages 194–206, Boston, Massachusetts, 1973. ACM.

[19] C. H. P. Kim, E. Bodden, D. Batory, and S. Khurshid. Reducing configurations to monitor in a software product line. In *1st International Conference on Runtime Verification (RV)*, volume 6418 of *LNCS*, Malta, November 2010. Springer.

[20] M. Krone and G. Snelting. On the inference of configuration structures from source code. In *Proceedings of the 16th International Conference on Software Engineering (ICSE'04)*, pages 49–57, Los Alamitos, CA, USA, 1994. IEEE Computer.

[21] J. Liebig, S. Apel, C. Lengauer, C. Kästner, and M. Schulze. An analysis of the variability in forty preprocessor-based software product lines. In *Proceedings of the 32nd ACM/IEEE International Conference on Software Engineering (ICSE'10)*, pages 105–114, Cape Town, South Africa, 2010. ACM.

[22] S. Moon, M. W. Hall, and B. R. Murphy. Predicated array data-flow analysis for run-time parallelization. In *Proceedings of the 12th International Conference on Supercomputing (ICS'98)*, pages 204–211, Melbourne, Australia, 1998. ACM.

[23] F. Nielson, H. R. Nielson, and C. Hankin. *Principles of Program Analysis*. Springer-Verlag, Secaucus, USA, 1999.

[24] K. Pohl, G. Böckle, and F. van der Linden. *Software Product Line Engineering: Foundations, Principles and Techniques*. Springer, 2005.

[25] H. Post and C. Sinz. Configuration lifting: Verification meets software configuration. In *Proceedings of the 23rd IEEE/ACM International Conference on Automated Software Engineering (ASE'08)*, pages 347–350, L'Aquila, Italy, 2008. IEEE Computer Society.

[26] M. Ribeiro, H. Pacheco, L. Teixeira, and P. Borba. Emergent feature modularization. In *Onward! 2010, affiliated with the 1st ACM SIGPLAN International Conference on Systems, Programming, Languages and Applications: Software for Humanity (SPLASH'10)*, pages 11–18, Reno, NV, USA, 2010.

[27] H. Spencer and G. Collyer. #ifdef considered harmful, or portability experience with C news. In *Proceedings of the Usenix Summer 1992 Technical Conference*, pages 185–198, Berkeley, CA, USA, June 1992. Usenix Association.

[28] R. Vallée-Rai, P. Co, E. Gagnon, L. Hendren, P. Lam, and V. Sundaresan. Soot - a java bytecode optimization framework. In *Proceedings of the 1999 conference of the Centre for Advanced Studies on Collaborative research (CASCON'99)*, pages 13–. IBM Press, 1999.

[29] M. N. Wegman and F. K. Zadeck. Constant propagation with conditional branches. *ACM Transactions on Programming Languages and Systems*, 13:181–210, April 1991.

Features and Object Capabilities

Reconciling Two Visions of Modularity

Salman Saghafi
WPI
salmans@cs.wpi.edu

Kathi Fisler
WPI
kfisler@cs.wpi.edu

Shriram Krishnamurthi
Brown University
sk@cs.brown.edu

Abstract

The prevalence of threats and attacks in modern systems demands programming techniques that help developers maintain security and privacy. In particular, frameworks for composing components written by multiple parties must enable the authors of each component to erect safeguards against intrusion by other components. Object-capability systems have been particularly prominent for enabling encapsulation in such contexts.

We describe the program structures dictated by object capabilities and compare these against those that ensue from feature-oriented programming. We argue that the scalability offered by the latter appears to clash with the precision of authority designation demanded by the former. In addition to presenting this position from first principles, we illustrate it with a case study. We then offer a vision of how this conflict might be reconciled, and discuss some of the issues that need to be considered in bridging this mismatch. Our findings suggest a significant avenue for research at the intersection of software engineering and security.

Categories and Subject Descriptors D.2.11 [*Software Architectures*]: Modules

General Terms Design, Languages, Security

Keywords Feature-oriented programming, object capabilities, modularity

1. Introduction

There are many competing visions of what constitutes the content of a module: phrases like "separation of concerns" still permit a wide variety of interpretations, as the past several decades of research demonstrates.

Given the increasing importance of security, privacy, and related properties, one useful criterion for decomposing systems into modules is to consider what impact the decomposition would have on enabling reasoning about these properties. In particular, when developers compose code written by multiple (perhaps mutually-untrusting) parties, there is a danger that code from one module might inadvertently or maliciously damage the behavior of another. Third-party composition takes place in many traditional component-based systems as well as newer platforms such as extensible Web browsers ("extensions"), client-side Web applications ("mashups"), and mobile phone operating systems ("apps").

Due to the dangers of unfettered code combination, platforms are moving towards circumscribing the set of system resources to which a component is given access, rather than letting the component get the full power of the user running it. This makes it possible to bound the damage that hostile or faulty modules can inflict. The mechanisms found in many of these systems either are, or resemble, *capabilities* [14]: e.g., when your mobile phone operating system lists a collection of system resources (location settings, local storage, etc.) that an application demands, your granting these privileges indicates you find this set of demands reasonable, and furthermore informs the operating system to not allow the application access to any other resources.

Capabilities have been a sideline in operating systems research for many years. Over time, they begat a particular form of programming mechanism called the *object capability* [17] (OCap), which uses programming language objects to represent capabilities. In an OCap framework, there are no global privileged resources—whether systems resources such as disks and networks, or program-defined ones such as confidential data structures. Instead, all access is provided through explicit granting of authority in the form of a capability object, whose methods represent operations on the privileged resource. This property is called the *absence of ambient authority* [16]; most programming languages violate it by providing static and global variables, through which they expose traditional systems resources (though in some languages, auxiliary mechanisms such as class-loaders can be used to obtain some degree of confinement). Run-time systems can also expose resources through the manufacture of object references; if this is disabled, the only way for one object to become aware of another is for the former to be given a reference to the latter. Objects can become aware of one another through a handful of mechanisms such as parameter-passing, lexical closure, inheritance, and so on. We abstract over these different mechanisms and (with slight abuse of standard OCaps language) refer to all these processes collectively as *introduction*. An object's net authority is thus the transitive closure of the (methods of the) capabilities to which it has been introduced.

Building on this linguistic foundation, OCap programmers expect modules to obey the *principle of least authority* (POLA) [21]. That is, a module must expect no more authority than it requires to accomplish its task. Because a module cannot obtain capabilities through other means (per the OCap assumptions), the user of the module can confidently bound what privileges it may use (and hence, potentially, abuse). OCaps are furthermore effective at thwarting *confused deputy* [7] attacks, because the capability is both a designator of an object and the authority to use it; attacks occur when these tasks are separated.

Curiously, though OCaps derive from a principle (POLA) usually associated with security, and their use addresses certain security problems, the reasoning that leads to OCaps is independent of security per se. Instead, POLA can be viewed as analogous to Parnas's principle of information hiding [18]: just as information hiding can be regarded as "need to know", Crockford labels POLA as handing out authority only on a "need to do" basis [17, page 72]. A module that demands more capabilities than its user expects is either being sloppy or mis-representing its purpose; in either case, a user should proceed with caution or reject the module.

In this paper, we examine how contemporary modularity methods interact with capability-based design, as embodied by POLA. Inherent to the notion of capability-style security (and indeed to most security mechanisms) is the ability to "draw boxes", and then argue how the content of the box cannot harm, or be harmed by, what lies outside it. Modern "boxes" include modularity methods such as aspect-oriented programming, feature-oriented programming, and other responses to weaknesses of traditional object-oriented programming. It is therefore instructive to consider how they fare in a POLA light.

From a POLA perspective, is easy to dismiss of many typical aspect-oriented programming mechanisms [10]. The point of weaving [11] is to run a program fragment in a context other than that in which it was defined. The woven program thus inherits the power of the location where it was injected. This directly violates the abstraction boundaries of the point of injection, and lets the aspect access capabilities that arguably were not granted to it explicitly (indeed, this is virtually the definition of a confused deputy attack!). Interfaces for aspect-orientation might help in this regard [1, 12, 13].

	if	printf	open-tcp	⋯
Interpreter		screen	network	
Type checker				
Pretty printer	screen	screen	screen	
⋯				

Figure 1. Features and capabilities in a suite of programming language tools

Feature-oriented programming [20] (FOP), in contrast, explicitly defines and composes "boxes". A feature is commonly regarded as a piece of system functionality that a user can identify. In FOP, the unit of modularity is the *feature*; each module implements, roughly, a feature, and the collection of modules corresponds to the features expected by the system's requirements. This alignment of modules with requirements makes it possible to easily customize an application by composing just those features that a particular user desires. Each composition then results in a different system, so FOP naturally leads to product-lines of systems. This connection to product lines underlies FOPs claims to support scalable software development [5].

2. An Inherent Conflict?

To concretize features and capabilities, consider a suite of tools that implement a programming language. Suppose each tool is a feature. Each tool must handle (as appropriate) each construct that exists in the language. Figure 1 shows the capabilities that would be needed across common language constructs and tools. For purposes of this paper, the key observations from this table are

- *Different features require different capabilities.* The pretty-printer only requires access to the screen; the interpreter needs both the screen and the network; the typechecker doesn't need any external resource.

- *Different tools require different capabilities across constructs.* The interpreter only needs write access to the screen to implement `printf`; that capability is irrelevant for the other constructs shown.

This table captures the essence of the different views of modularity between features and capabilities. FOP roughly views each row of this table as a module. As the cells within each row may require different capabilities, however, OCaps could demand finer-grained modules, perhaps as small-grained as individual cells. That FOP modularizes around rows as opposed to columns of the table is not relevant here (since different cells in the same column also have different capabilities). The point is that OCaps seeks a modular structure with strong access-control guarantees, FOP seeks a modular structure that enables large-scale, plug-and-play system construction, and these two would frame modules somewhat differently in this example.

Different Perspectives on Modularity Features and OCaps modularize systems differently because they view modularity as solving different problems. Features view modules as a way to enable flexible and scalable construction of families of products. OCaps view modules as a way to ensure that a composed program has no violations of least privilege. A key goal in FOP is to allow third parties to add new features to existing products without modifying existing code, while OCaps enable code from untrusting providers to compose without either party being able to infiltrate the other beyond the bounds specified in the interface. These goals are not identical, and indeed the FOP view is an expansive one while the OCap view is inherently untrusting.

Incompatibility Are these two styles compatible? Perhaps not: this example already illustrates a tension. To ensure least authority, the individual portions of the interpreter would each consume just the capabilities (including none) they require. However, that requires the client linking the features to deal with a potentially large number of small components. By packaging these up into a single component (namely the interpreter), the client linking the features gains scalability by having fewer and higher-level components to content with. In Batory's phrase [5], this packaging improves scalability. In return, however, the client must now grant all the capabilities to the interpreter as a whole and hope that it demultiplexes these properly without granting excess authority to any one fragment. Miller refers to this as the "nested platforms" problem [17, §22.1].

In short, just as in social structures, *scalability appears to demand delegation and diffusion of authority*. That is, while having lots of little components makes it possible to assign precisely the least authority to each one, this over-burdens the programmer who is responsible for linking them together. By "chunking" the linking, the programmer can deal with significantly fewer, higher-level pieces (the features); but these now require the aggregate of authority required by the components contained inside them. The programmer has to make an unsavory choice between an excessive number of modules with reasonable authority each or a reasonable number of modules with excessive authority each.

3. OCaps Discipline in a FOP System: A Case Study

Is this incompatbility a problem in practice? To gauge the extent to which FOP developers already follow an OCaps discipline, we studied an exemplary application built using FeatureHouse [2]. FeatureHouse is a cross-language framework for FOP; in FeatureHouse, program artifacts are represented as structured trees, and composition is the act of merging trees.

We hasten to note that the point of this section (and indeed of the whole paper) is not to study FeatureHouse in detail, but rather to ask how well existing programs already meet the POLA principle. If they do well, perhaps the theoretical

incompatibility is only that, and not a problem in practice. If they do poorly, however, there remains the open question of whether simple refactoring would address the problem, or whether the topic demands more foundational research.

3.1 Assessing Adherence to OCaps Discipline

We first present a simple classification we have found useful when evaluating FOP software for its adherence to OCaps. We classify each feature/capability pair thus:

- Required Capabilities: A capability c is required for a feature f (denoted $\text{Req}(f,c)$) if f is expected to receive c according to the program requirements.

- Given Capabilities: A capability c is given to feature f (denoted $\text{Given}(f,c)$) in a program if some part of f has capability c within the program's implementation.

- Used Capabilities: A capability c is used in feature f (denoted $\text{Used}(f,c)$) if some part of f actually uses c within the implementation.

Unlike given and used capabilities, which can be computed from the source code, required capabilities are hard to pinpoint: a program may have different implementation options, each of which depends on different capabilities. We choose to consider the maximal plausible requirements: this will make least-privilege violations out of given capabilities that have no plausible use in a feature.

The following table characterizes combinations of the labels relative to the goals of capability systems. We do not include the two combinations in which $\text{Used}(f,c)$ is true but $\text{Given}(f,c)$ is false because it is not possible for a system to use a capability that is not available to it.

Category	$\text{Req}(f,c)$	$\text{Given}(f,c)$	$\text{Used}(f,c)$
No error	false	false	false
No error	true	true	true
LPV	false	true	true/false
Diff Impl	true	true/false	false

Cases in which all labels have the same value do not flag any errors relative to capabilities. Least-privilege violations, denoted LPV in the table, arise when a feature has been given a capability that it does not plausibly need. Whether a feature uses an unrequired capability is not relevant: just because one implementation of a feature does not exploit an unnecessary capability, another implementation (perhaps by a third party) might. Cases in which a feature does not use a plausible capability are not necessarily errors, but indicate that a programmer may have found a different way to implement the system than envisioned in the requirements. In particular, a programmer might choose to virtualize the implementation (e.g., consuming a capability for the file system but actually using an in-memory store instead of the persistent store).

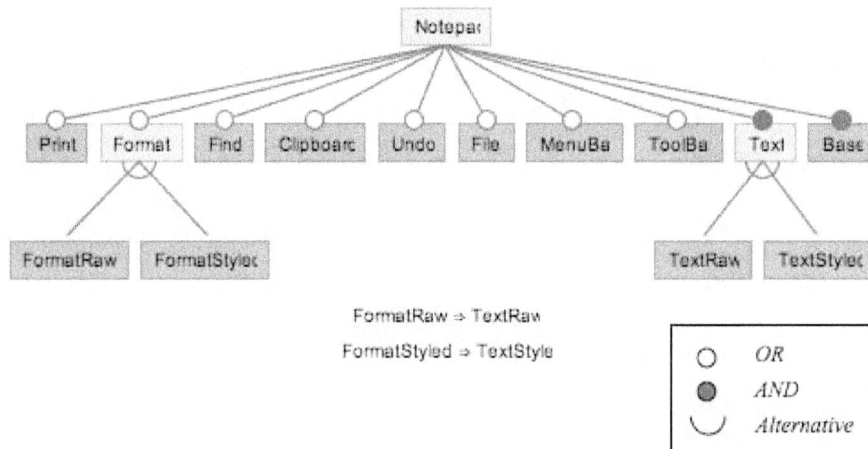

Figure 2. Feature model for the Notepad application. The propositional expressions in the picture shows that FormatRaw and FormatStyled depend on TextRaw and TextStyled respectively. Other dependencies between modules have been suppressed to keep the example small.

3.2 The Case Study

FeatureHouse presents 22 sample projects that have been written in a feature-oriented style in Java (it has additional projects written in other languages, such as Alloy, C, C#, Haskell, JavaCC and UML). We chose a Notepad application, which is both simple enough to immediately understand and rich enough to have interesting resources to protect. Though we studied the entire application, here we focus on a few representative features that illustrate our point.

Notepad implements a canonical note-taking application. Figure 2 shows a feature model of the entire Notepad product family. The primitive application offers a main window as a container for other components of the application. The application requires a Text feature, which provides a text area for editing (but not common file-menu operations). There are also numerous optional features. For this example, we will use features for a Clipboard (cut, copy, and paste), Find (search for text), and Undo. Features that we will not consider include text formatting, menubars, and toolbars.

Our goal is to identify whether Notepad has any least-privilege violations that trace back to its feature-oriented architecture. Recall the term *introduction* (Section 1) for the process by which one object comes to have a reference to another object. As Section 3.1 shows, least-privilege violations in a program arise from introductions that grant more access than necessary. Identifying the source and necessity of the introductions in a program is the first step to checking whether it maintains capability discipline.

For our sample features, we would expect that Find needs to read the contents of the text area and to highlight found terms. Clipboard needs to read, write, and delete from the text area. Undo will read and write to the text area. None of these features need access to each others' data structures, nor does the text area have need to know about these features.

At the implementation level, the Text feature adds a text area to the notepad, implemented as an instance of Java's `JTextPane` (a standard library class). The feature creates the area, adds it to the main application window, and endows it with a getter. The Text feature also creates an object that holds the callbacks associated with actions a user can take through the Notepad. The Find and Clipboard features add actions, but do not add to the notepad itself. The Undo feature adds an `UndoManager` (a standard Java library object) to the Notepad class rather than use the existing infrastructure for registering actions. For reference, Appendix A shows the portion of the source code for these features that is relevant for this paper (though a reader should be able to follow our arguments without reading the code).

Within this implementation, we find several least-privilege violations. Representative examples of these include:

- *Find has write access to the text area.* Find gets a reference to the text area so it can search the text, but is actually given all of the text area's methods. Under OCaps discipline, Find should have been given a reference to an object that provides only the search method that Find needs.

- *Undo has access to the Actions object,* even though it does not use it. This leakage arises from FeatureHouse's composition technique. Given an ordered list of features

  FeatureHouse Base Text Undo Find Clipboard

FeatureHouse creates a product by concatenating the contents of identically-named classes across the features. This approach makes all objects defined in one feature available to all other features in the same product. Since there are no class boundaries between features, even private variables in one feature are available to the others.

- *UndoAction has access to the entire Notepad*, even though it only needs access to the Notepad's `UndoManager` and one other specific field that the Undo feature itself added to the Notepad. This leakage arises from a poor architectural decision with the Notepad class. It could easily have been avoided by passing the two required fields rather than the entire Notepad object as arguments.

The first two problems lead to pervasive violation of least privilege. We manually analyzed the entire Notepad feature suite from Figure 2. To perform this analysis, we had to define the required capabilities, which we did by adhering closely to the principle of least privilege. Our analysis found 200 least-privilege violations that trace to the first issue and 373 that trace to the second. The third problem does not show up in required capabilities because the unnecessary object is of a class that is limited to the implementation and does not manifest in the requirements (which perhaps makes its availability even more insidious). Note that every violation is an opportunity for a feature implemented by a potentially untrusted third-party to obtain powers it should not have had.

We find it interesting that the Notepad features introduce relatively few methods of their own. Rather, they rely heavily on methods that are already part of existing Java classes (such as `JTextPane` and `UndoManager`). This is relevant to our discussion because it affects how we should think about required capabilities. We stated that Clipboard needs read and write access to the *text area*. In this implementation, however, Clipboard only uses existing read and write *methods* on the text area—it did not use the text area itself (other than as a route to these methods). Ideally, Notepad should introduce only these methods (or functions)—rather than the entire text area—to the Clipboard.

Wrapper objects are an effective way to limit visibility of existing methods. However, passing entire objects is easy; implementing wrappers is painstaking in Java because of the limitations of the nominal type system. As a result, programmers will be tempted to pass entire objects even if this approach leaks capabilities. The Notepad authors simply followed standard Java practices; unfortunately, those are not always consistent with OCaps discipline (and arguably, by extension, good modularity).

3.3 Feature-Aware Access Modifiers

Acknowledging that FOP may need to limit access to variables across features, some of the researchers behind FeatureHouse have proposed a set of access-modifiers unique to features [3]. In particular, they proposed the following modifiers (usable in the same places as standard Java public/private/etc modifiers):

- `feature`: limits access to the feature in which the variable is defined.
- `subsequent`: limits access to the feature containing the variable and all features composed subsequently (on the command line).
- `program`: the variable is available globally, as with the standard `public` modifier.

These modifiers would have limited value in limiting least privilege. Sometimes, one feature builds on another; these cases would require the `subsequent` modifier, which would leak data to any other features that happened to be included later in a composition. This approach also does little to address problems due to failure to wrap objects in more restricted interfaces.

3.4 Other Approaches to FOP

There are, of course, numerous other approaches to FOP, which are worth studying. We simply note that FOP as represented by tools like FeatureHouse appear to be somewhere in the middle of a spectrum in their ability to incorporate OCaps. Using annotative approaches [9] to FOP seems even less likely to be fruitful because of their invasiveness, which would enable feature code to obtain access to ambient capabilities just as with aspects.

While FeatureHouse separates features in its front-end language, its composition technique of syntactically merging code across feature boundaries is a distinct weakness with respect to preserving modular separation. As a result, even with well-designed interfaces, the resulting code still suffers from leakage of authority. However, the critique in our case study does not depend on this property (which is obvious, and might anyway be mitigated by using a different language such as Joe-E [15], a capability-safe version of Java).

Unlike FeatureHouse, AHEAD [4] (in "mixin", as opposed to "jampack" mode) does erect boundaries between features using subclassing. This in turn limits the scope of private variables to the feature in which they were defined. This obedience to source modularity, which is also found in other systems such as those of Prehofer [20] and Findler and Flatt [6], is an important step towards preventing unwanted comingling of code and hence the leakage of authority.

4. A Route Forward: Verified Demultiplexing

We repeat the main insight from earlier: scalability appears to demand delegation and diffusion of authority. To use FOP, a programmer is effectively forced to hand over a large set of capabilities to some features, expecting them to be redistributed internally using POLA.

This expectation should be captured by an appropriate interface specification that makes clear how the provided capabilities should be distributed internally, and furthermore (presumably) that the feature code in the interstices is itself not supposed to use any of them. The interface would take the form of access-control rules that dicate how sub-components receive capability objects, but might also include some integrity and information flow rules that dictate flows that are prohibited to avoid attacks through colluding sub-components. Writing such specifications somewhat diminishes the scalability benefits of features, but this appears an unavoidable trade-off, and hopefully these specifications do not need to be written very often.

Given such specifications, a good deal of research in language-based computer security deals with how one can actually enforce these expectations on bodies of code. Enriching a type system with this verification power, for instance, makes it easier to integrate such checking into the development cycle. By using languages or programming systems endowed with such verifiers, the composer of features can thus be confident that the demultiplexing of capabilities is happening in a trustworthy fashion, and that the use of features is not inhibiting the provision of security.

5. Perspective

This paper asks whether increments designed around user-identified functionality, which covers FOP and also aspects, are compatible with capability discipline. Capabilities enforce least privilege. Identifying idioms for programming simultaneously with feature-like constructs and security concerns such as least privilege is an important area for future research. In particular, our work to date raises the following observations and research questions:

- Formal modules, with checked and enforced interfaces, are critical to preventing least-privilege violations. The FOP community is actively debating whether features should be captured in formal modules [8]. Our observations demand that those who argue against formal interfaces explain how they can provide security guarantees without them, or why security guarantees do not apply in their context.

- One argument against features as modules is that features sometimes add very small amounts of code (a couple of lines). Formal interfaces on these "micromodules" can seem like overkill. Proponents of micromodules need to weigh the arguments in favor of these fragments against the corresponding leakage of authority.

- The alternative to preserving modularity in the composed system is to obtain its benefits through alternate means. For instance, it may be possible to devise type systems, static analyses, and so on that bless individual feature modules in such a way that even textual composition of such modules will not result in privilege leakage. It is worth noting that such textual analyses will effectively be implementing a modularity mechanism such as language-based sandboxing [19].

- We have argued that OCap discipline may be too rigid for features. If we relax that discipline, what other princi-

ples can provide design guidelines? One possibility is to incorporate threat modeling and align modules with trust boundaries. The correlation between feature boundaries and trust boundaries has not been studied in the literature, and appears to be a promising direction in the study of modularity.

It is also worth remembering that *least* privilege is itself a relative notion. It must be defined relative to purpose. For instance, an interface might require or provide more than the module's pure functionality seems to demand. These more expansive interfaces might support debugging, performance-tuning, future-proofing, etc. Are these violation of POLA? Not necessarily: it may just mean that the least privilege of the component amounts to more than just its current functionality. In other words, POLA is still a guideline open to multiple interpretations, and these interpretations will depend on the goals of various components.

In conclusion, with features and capabilities each targeting a real, pressing software concern, we cannot ignore the tension between them. We look forward to ongoing discussions about the tradeoffs between these approaches and techniques for making them interoperate.

Acknowledgments

This work is partially supported by the US National Science Foundation. We thank Mark S. Miller for many valuable conversations over the years. We are especially grateful to Kevin Sullivan for his shepherding of this paper. His detailed and thoughtful questions and comments greatly helped us clarify our presentation.

References

[1] ALDRICH, J. 2004. Open modules: Modular reasoning in aspect-oriented programming. In *Foundations of Aspect-Oriented Languages*. 7–18.

[2] APEL, S., KASTNER, C., AND LENGAUER, C. 2009. Featurehouse: Language-independent, automated software composition. In *Proceedings of the 31st International Conference on Software Engineering*. ICSE '09. IEEE Computer Society, Washington, DC, USA, 221–231.

[3] APEL, S., KOLESNIKOV, S., LIEBIG, J., KÄSTNER, C., KUHLEMANN, M., AND LEICH, T. 2010. Access control in feature-oriented programming. *Science of Computer Programming*.

[4] BATORY, D. 2004. Feature-oriented programming and the AHEAD tool suite. In *International Conference on Software Engineering*. 702–703.

[5] BATORY, D. S., SARVELA, J. N., AND RAUSCHMAYER, A. 2004. Scaling step-wise refinement. *IEEE Transactions on Software Engineering 30*, 6, 355–371.

[6] FINDLER, R. B. AND FLATT, M. 1998. Modular object-oriented programming with units and mixins. In *ACM SIGPLAN International Conference on Functional Programming*. 94–104.

[7] HARDY, N. 1988. The confused deputy (or why capabilities might have been invented). *ACM SIGOPS Operating Systems Review 22.*

[8] KÄSTNER, C., APEL, S., AND OSTERMANN, K. 2011. The road to feature modularity? In *Proceedings of the International Workshop on Feature-Oriented Software Development (FOSD).*

[9] KÄSTNER, C., APEL, S., THÜM, T., AND SAAKE, G. 2011. Type checking annotation-based product lines. *ACM Transactions on Software Engineering and Methodology (TOSEM).*

[10] KICZALES, G., HILSDALE, E., HUGUNIN, J., KERSTEN, M., PALM, J., AND GRISWOLD, W. 2001. An overview of AspectJ. In *European Conference on Object-Oriented Programming.* 327–353.

[11] KICZALES, G., LAMPING, J., MENDHEKAR, A., MAEDA, C., LOPES, C. V., LOINGTIER, J.-M., AND IRWIN, J. 1997. Aspect-oriented programming. In *European Conference on Object-Oriented Programming.* 220–242.

[12] KICZALES, G. AND MEZINI, M. 2005. Aspect-oriented programming and modular reasoning. In *International Conference on Software Engineering.* 49 58.

[13] KRISHNAMURTHI, S. AND FISLER, K. 2007. Foundations of incremental aspect model-checking. *ACM Transactions on Software Engineering and Methodology 16,* 2.

[14] LEVY, H. M. 1984. *Capability-Based Computer Systems.* Digital Equipment Corporation.

[15] METTLER, A., WAGNER, D., AND CLOSE, T. 2010. Joe-E: A security-oriented subset of Java. In *Network and Distributed System Security Symposium.*

[16] MILLER, M., YEE, K.-P., AND SHAPIRO, J. Capability myths demolished. Available online at http://srl.cs.jhu.edu/pubs/SRL2003-02.pdf. Last accessed Sept 23, 2011.

[17] MILLER, M. S. 2006. Robust composition: Towards a unified approach to access control and concurrency control. Ph.D. thesis, Johns Hopkins University.

[18] PARNAS, D. L. 1972. On the criteria to be used in decomposing systems into modules. *Communications of the ACM 15,* 12, 1053–1058.

[19] POLITZ, J. G., ELIOPOULOS, S. A., GUHA, A., AND KRISHNAMURTHI, S. 2011. ADsafety: Type-based verification of JavaScript sandboxing. In *USENIX Security Symposium.*

[20] PREHOFER, C. 1997. Feature-oriented programming: A fresh look at objects. In *ECOOP'97—Object-Oriented Programming, 11th European Conference,* M. Aksit and S. Matsuoka, Eds. Vol. 1241. Springer, Jyväskylä, Finland, 419–443.

[21] SALTZER, J. H. 1974. Protection and the control of information sharing in Multics. *Communications of the ACM 17,* 7.

```
                    ── Text/Base ──
class Notepad {
  public Actions actions = new Actions(this);
  private JTextPane textPane;

  public Notepad () {
    textPane = new JTextPane();
    getContentPane().add(textPane);
  }

  public JTextComponent getTextComponent() {
    return textPane;
  }
}

class Actions {
  Notepad n;

  public Actions(Notepad n) {
    this.n = n;
  }
}
```

Figure 3. Essence of the Text feature in FeatureHouse

```
                    ── Clipboard ──
class Actions {
  public void cut(){
    n.getTextComponent().cut();
  }

  public void copy(){
    n.getTextComponent().copy();
  }

  public void paste(){
    n.getTextComponent().paste();
  }
}
```

Figure 4. Essence of the Clipboard feature in FeatureHouse

A. Notepad Feature Code

This appendix presents fragments of the Notepad features that are relevant to our discussion of capabilities along with an example of how they appear in composition. Each feature consists of up to two class definitions. The Notepad class contains the structural elements of the notepad application (text areas, menu bars, etc); the Actions class contains methods for the callbacks that are executed when the user selects from menus, toolbars, or other GUI elements. Some features, such as Clipboard and Find, add new actions but no new structural elements.

The Text feature (Figure 3) creates a text area (line 6) and adds it to the main application window (line 7). It also adds a getter method for the private textPane variable (lines 10-12). This feature itself adds no actions; it merely connects a Notepad instance to an Actions class (lines 17-18).

```
1    class Actions {
2      public void find() {
3        findWord = JOptionPane.showInputDialog("Type the word to find");
4        findIndex = n.getTextComponent().getText().indexOf(findWord);
5        if (findIndex == -1) {
6          JOptionPane.showMessageDialog(null,"Word not found",...);
7        } else { selectFound(); }
8        ...
9      }
10
11     public void findNext() { ... }
12
13     private void selectFound() {
14       n.getTextComponent().select(findIndex, findIndex + findWord.length());
15     }
16   }
```

```
1    class Notepad {
2      UndoManager undo = new UndoManager();
3      UndoAction undoAction = new UndoAction(this);
4
5      public Notepad() {
6        getTextComponent().getDocument().addUndoableEditListener(... undo.addEdit() ...);
7      }
8    }
9
10   class UndoAction extends AbstractAction {
11     Notepad notepad;
12
13     public UndoAction(Notepad notepad){
14       this.notepad = notepad;
15     }
16
17     public void actionPerformed(ActionEvent e) {
18       notepad.undo.undo();
19     }
20   }
```

Figure 5. Essence of the Find and Undo features in FeatureHouse

Clipboard (Figure 4) introduces three actions—cut, copy and paste—that interact with the operating system's clipboard. Each action simply calls the relevant method of the text area object (lines 3, 7 and 11). The Find feature (Figure 5) adds two action methods (find and findnext) which execute when the user clicks on buttons that Find adds to the toolbar and menubar (these additions are not shown). The find method gets the search string from the user through a dialog box (line 3), then passes the search string to the text area's search methods (line 4). Find's actions use the selectFound method to highlight the strings found in the text area using the text area's methods (line 14).

Unlike the other features, Undo (Figure 5) defines its own action classes (UndoAction and RedoAction) rather than extend the existing Action class. It also adds an instance of

UndoManager, a standard Java class that manages undo/redo operations (line 2). When the user chooses to perform an undo/redo operation via the toolbar or the menubar, the undo/redo actions call the relevant methods of the undo manager instance to handle the operation (line 17).

Figure 6 shows the Notepad class that results from the composition of the Text and Undo features. The comments demark which portions of the class came from each of the features. The rest of the code has been omitted, as it does not add relevant detail to the example.

```
class Notepad
  //FROM TEXT-BASE
  public Actions actions = new Actions(this);
  private JTextPane textPane;
  //TEXT

  //FROM UNDO
  UndoManager undo = new UndoManager();
  UndoAction undoAction = new UndoAction(this);
  RedoAction redoAction = new RedoAction(this);
  //UNDO

  public Notepad  () {
    //FROM TEXT
    textPane = new JTextPane();
    getContentPane().add(textPane);
    //TEXT

    //FROM UNDO
    getTextComponent().getDocument().addUndoableEditListener(...);
    //UNDO
    ...
    }
  ...
}
```

Figure 6. The Notepad class composed from the Text and Undo features

Two-Way Traceability and Conflict Debugging for AspectLTL Programs *

Shahar Maoz

RWTH Aachen University, Germany

maoz@se-rwth.de

Yaniv Sa'ar

Weizmann Institute of Science, Israel

yaniv.saar@weizmann.ac.il

Abstract

Tracing program actions back to the concerns that have caused them and blaming specific code artifacts for concern interference are known challenges of AOP and related advanced modularity paradigms. In this work we address these challenges in the context of AspectLTL, a temporal-logic based language for the specification and implementation of crosscutting concerns, which has a composition and synthesis-based weaving process whose output is a correct-by-construction executable artifact. When a specification is realizable, we provide two-way traceability information that links each allowed or forbidden transition in the generated program with the aspects that have justified its presence or elimination. When a specification is unrealizable, we provide an interactive game proof that demonstrates conflicts that should be fixed. The techniques are implemented and demonstrated using running examples.

Categories and Subject Descriptors D.2.2 [*Software Engineering*]: Design Tools and Techniques; D.3.3 [*Programming Languages*]: Language Constructs and Features

General Terms Languages, Design

Keywords Aspect-oriented programming, linear temporal logic, synthesis

* This research was supported by The John von Neumann Minerva Center for the Development of Reactive Systems at the Weizmann Institute of Science. In addition, part of this research was funded by an Advanced Research Grant awarded to David Harel of the Weizmann Institute from the European Research Council (ERC) under the European Community's 7th Framework Programme (FP7/2007-2013). Finally, the first listed author acknowledges support from a postdoctoral Minerva Fellowship, funded by the German Federal Ministry for Education and Research.

1. Introduction

Separation of concerns at the source code level supports cleaner, modular designs, but may also make the traceability and debugging of the implementations more technically challenging. Thus, tracing program actions back to the concerns that have caused them and blaming specific code artifacts for concern interference are known challenges related to AOP and other advanced modularity paradigms.

AspectLTL [17] is a temporal-logic based language for the specification and implementation of crosscutting concerns in open reactive systems – discrete event systems that maintain ongoing interaction with their environment. An AspectLTL specification is made of a base system, given as a finite-state machine specified in SMV [23] format, and a set of LTL aspects, each of which is specified in a similar SMV-like format, containing a symbolic representation of the aspect's added behaviors (transitions) and a related LTL specification. The language has a composition and synthesis-based weaving process, based on GR(1) synthesis [19], whose output is a correct-by-construction executable artifact. An implementation of AspectLTL that produces a stand-alone Java controller was described in [17].

In this work we address the traceability and debugging challenges in the context of AspectLTL. When a specification is realizable, we provide two-way traceability information that links each allowed or forbidden transition in the generated program with the aspects that have justified its presence or elimination. When a specification is unrealizable, we provide an interactive game proof that demonstrates conflicts that should be fixed.

AspectLTL uses a declarative, symbolic programming style. For specifications that consist of several aspects and describe some possibly crosscutting concerns, traceability and debugging are *very different* than their counterparts in imperative programming languages. In particular, the presence or elimination of a behavior (i.e., a transition from one state to another) in the program, may be the result of the application of several, possibly overlapping, non-independent concerns. To support traceability, we use symbolic operations to check for intersections between the transitions that can or cannot be taken and the formulas defined in the LTL aspects. To support conflict debugging in unrealizable specifications we use the notion of counterstrategies [13]. By reversing the roles of the system and the environment in the synthesis game, we are able to generate a winning strategy for the environment. We use this strategy to produce a counter-implementation: an interactive program, whose runs show exactly how any generated system can be forced by an (adverse) environment to violate the specifications.

One may question the need for traceability and debugging for a language with a 'correct-by-construction' implementation: if the implementation is 'correct-by-construction', who needs debugging? Correctness, however, is relative to the specification: if the engineer writes a conflicting, unrealizable specification, no correct implementation can be generated. Instead, a conflict debugging technique should be used to prove unrealizability and point the engineer to conflicts in her specification. Thus, the 'correct-by-construction' implementation does not eliminate the need for debugging: it lifts debugging from the concrete implementation to the higher-level, declarative specification.

Further, one may question the need for traceability for realizable specifications: if the specification is realizable and the implementation is 'correct-by-construction', who needs traceability? Correctness of a realizable specification is, however, relative to the engineer's intention: when running the generated controller (the generated Java program) of a realizable specification, the engineer may experience some behavior she had not intended to be possible or miss some behavior she had intended to be performed. This means that although the specification is consistent, that is, mathematically, it is too permissive or too restrictive with regard to the engineer's intention. If the generated program does something that was not intended, the engineer can use traceability to check which part of the specification allows it. If the generated program does not do something that was intended, the engineer can use traceability to check which aspect has prevented it.

The new traceability and debugging techniques are implemented in the AspectLTL plug-in, available from our website [2], together with several running examples. We encourage the interested reader to try them out.

Finally, in a related line of research we are working on the addition of environment assumptions to AspectLTL syntax (in a dedicated LTLSPECENV section) and semantics (in the synthesis phase), thus taking full advantage of the expressive power of GR(1) [19]. In this paper, however, we chose to focus on the traceability and debugging techniques and limit most of the discussion to the AspectLTL fragment defined in [17], which does not contain environment assumptions. Nevertheless, where relevant, we mention assumptions in several places in the paper and discuss their possible effect on the traceability and debugging techniques.

Sect. 2 provides background on AspectLTL. Sect. 3 presents the running example we use. Sect. 4 defines and demonstrates traceability, Sect. 5 extends our example with additional aspects that are used in Sect. 6, which defines and demonstrates conflict debugging. Implementation and evaluation are presented in Sect. 7. Sect. 8 discusses related work and Sect. 9 concludes.

2. Preliminaries

2.1 An overview of AspectLTL

AspectLTL [17] is a language for the specification and implementation of crosscutting concerns, based on linear temporal logic (LTL) [20]. The aspects of AspectLTL, called LTL aspects, enable the declarative specification of expressive crosscutting concerns. These include the specification of safety properties, which may be used to prevent a base system from visiting 'bad states', the specification of liveness properties, which may be used to force a base system to visit 'good states' (infinitely often), and the addition of new behaviors to a base system, which is done by specifying the existence of new transitions and new states as necessary. To use the categorization by Katz [11], LTL aspects can specify spectative, regulative, and invasive aspects.

AspectLTL has a synthesis-based weaving process, whose output is a correct-by-construction executable artifact. Following a composition of the specified aspects with a base system, using symbolic disjunctive and conjunctive operations, we formulate the problem of correct weaving as a synthesis problem [21], essentially a game between the environment and the (augmented) base system. An algorithm based on [19] is used to solve the game, that is, to provide the augmented system with a winning strategy, if any.

If a winning strategy is found, it is presented as a deterministic, executable automaton, which represents an augmented base system whose behavior is guaranteed to adhere to the specified aspects, in all possible environments. If a winning strategy is not found, we know that it does not exist, that is, that no system exists which is based on the base system and can adhere to the specified LTL aspects in all environments. Thus, LTL aspect composition and synthesis is sound and complete.

An AspectLTL specification is made of a base system and a set of LTL aspects. The base is given as a finite-state machine specified in SMV [23] format. Each of the LTL aspects is specified in a similar SMV-like format, containing a symbolic representation of the aspect's added behaviors (transitions) and a related LTL specification.

AspectLTL is supported by an Eclipse plug-in, developed on top of JTLV [22], a framework for the development of verification algorithms, using BDD-based symbolic mechanisms. The plug-in is available from our website [2], with several examples and a programmer's guide. It includes support for editing and synthesizing AspectLTL programs, that is, it uses the results of the synthesis to generate an executable artifact in the form of stand-alone controller written in Java. As part of our work in the present paper, we have implemented the traceability and debugging features we describe and have integrated them into the plug-in.

A thorough and formal account of AspectLTL appears in [17]. Here we provide only the definitions that are required in the later parts of the paper.

2.2 Definitions (from [17])

We use the usual LTL notations (defined in [16, 20]), $\bigcirc$ (*next*), $\Diamond$ (*eventually*) and $\Box$ (*globally*), abbreviations of the Boolean connectives $\wedge$, $\rightarrow$ and $\leftrightarrow$, and the usual definitions for true and false.

A *discrete system* (DS) [12] is a symbolic representation of a transition system with finitely many states. Formally, a DS $\mathcal{D} = \langle \mathcal{V}, \theta, \rho \rangle$ consists of the following components:

- $\mathcal{V} = \{v_1, ..., v_n\}$: A finite set of Boolean variables. [1] A *state* s is an interpretation of $\mathcal{V}$, i.e., $s \in \Sigma_\mathcal{V}$.

- θ : The *initial condition*. This is an assertion over $\mathcal{V}$ characterizing all the initial states of the DS. A state is called *initial* if it satisfies θ.

- ρ . A *transition relation*. This is an assertion over the variables in $\mathcal{V} \cup \mathcal{V}'$, relating a state $s \in \Sigma_\mathcal{V}$ to its $\mathcal{D}$-successors $s' \in \Sigma_{\mathcal{V}'}$, i.e., $(s, s') \models \rho$.

We define a *run* of the DS $\mathcal{D}$ to be a maximal sequence of states $\sigma = s_0, s_1, \ldots$ satisfying (i) *initiality*, i.e., $s_0 \models \theta$, and (ii) *consecution*, i.e., for every $j \geq 0$, $(s_j, s_{j+1}) \models \rho$. A sequence σ is maximal if either σ is infinite or $\sigma = s_0, \ldots, s_k$ and s_k has no $\mathcal{D}$-successor, i.e., for all $s_{k+1} \in \Sigma$, $(s_k, s_{k+1}) \not\models \rho$. We say that a DS $\mathcal{D}$ *satisfies* a specification φ, denoted $\mathcal{D} \models \varphi$, if every run of $\mathcal{D}$ satisfies φ.

Given a subset of variables $\mathcal{X} \subseteq \mathcal{V}$, a DS $\mathcal{D}$ is *deterministic with respect to* $\mathcal{X}$, if (i) for all states $s, t \in \Sigma_\mathcal{V}$, if $s \models \theta$, $t \models \theta$, and both s and t have the same projection to the variables in $\mathcal{X}$, then $s = t$, and (ii) for all states $s, s', s'' \in \Sigma_\mathcal{V}$, if $(s, s') \models \rho$, $(s, s'') \models \rho$, and both s' and s'' have the same projection to the variables in $\mathcal{X}$, then $s' = s''$. Otherwise, $\mathcal{D}$ is called *non-deterministic*. Note that conventional programs (i.e., "real" programs) are deterministic with respect to their input variables.

Given a subset of variables $\mathcal{X} \subseteq \mathcal{V}$, a DS $\mathcal{D}$ is *complete with respect to* $\mathcal{X}$, if (i) for every assignment $s_\mathcal{X} \in \Sigma_\mathcal{X}$, there exists a state $s \in \Sigma_\mathcal{V}$ such that its projection to $\mathcal{X}$ is $s_\mathcal{X}$, and $s \models \theta$, and (ii) for all states $s \in \Sigma_\mathcal{V}$ and assignments $s'_\mathcal{X} \in \Sigma_\mathcal{X}$, there exists a state $s' \in \Sigma_\mathcal{V}$ such that its projection to $\mathcal{X}$ is $s'_\mathcal{X}$, and $(s, s') \models \rho$. A deterministic and complete discrete system is called a *controller*.

We are interested in *open* systems, that is, systems that interact with their environment. We model an open system by a discrete system whose variables are divided between environment controlled variables (inputs) and system controlled variables (outputs). A specification for an open system is in-

tended to hold for all possible environments. That is, to satisfy a specification, the system should guarantee that all its runs satisfy the specification, regardless of the environment's choice of assignments to input variables.

Given a specification, *realizability* amounts to checking whether there exists a controller that satisfies it. If the specification is realizable, then the construction of such a controller constitutes a solution for the *synthesis* problem. AspectLTL is based on the synthesis of LTL specifications that are written (or can be rewritten) in the form defined below.

DEFINITION 1.
Let $\mathcal{X}$ be a set of input variables, and $\mathcal{Y}$ be a set of output variables. We define the following fragment of LTL formulae[2] of the form

$$\varphi : \varphi_i \wedge \varphi_t \wedge \varphi_g \tag{1}$$

where

- *(i) φ_i is a Boolean formula which characterizes the initial states of the implementation.*

- *(ii) φ_t is a formula of the form $\bigwedge_{i \in I} \Box B_i$ where each B_i is a Boolean combination of variables from $\mathcal{X} \cup \mathcal{Y}$ and expressions of the form $\bigcirc v$ where $v \in \mathcal{X} \cup \mathcal{Y}$. φ_t characterizes the transition relation of the implementation.*

- *(iii) φ_g is a formula of the form $\bigwedge_{i \in I} \Box \Diamond B_i$ where each B_i is a Boolean formula. φ_g characterizes liveness requirements for the implementation.*

[19] presented an efficient polynomial time algorithm for the realizability and synthesis of specifications of the class of *Generalized Reactivity(1)* formulae (GR(1)). The GR(1) fragment contains formulas of the form defined in Equ. 1 and thus the solution presented in [19] is good for our needs.

DEFINITION 2 (Base system).
A base system is a discrete system $\mathcal{B} = \langle \mathcal{V}_B = \mathcal{V}_B^e \cup \mathcal{V}_B^s, \theta_B, \rho_B \rangle$ consisting of the following components:

- *$\mathcal{V}_B^e = \{u_1, ..., u_m\}$: A finite set of environment variables.*
- *$\mathcal{V}_B^s = \{v_1, ..., v_n\}$: A finite set of system variables.*
- *θ_B : An assertion over $\mathcal{V}_B$ characterizing the initial states of $\mathcal{B}$.*
- *ρ_B : An assertion over $\mathcal{V}_B \cup \mathcal{V}_B'$ characterizing the transition relation of $\mathcal{B}$.*

Note that we do not require a base system $\mathcal{B}$ to be deterministic (although our generated controller should be deterministic and complete with respect to $\mathcal{V}_B^e$). In cases where the base system represents a 'real' concrete implementation, it would indeed be deterministic. Supporting non-deterministic base systems is useful because it enables the use of abstractions.

DEFINITION 3 (LTL aspect).
An LTL aspect is a structure $A = \langle \mathcal{V}_A = \mathcal{V}_A^e \cup \mathcal{V}_A^s, \theta_A, \rho_A, \mathcal{L}_A^s \rangle$ consisting of the following components:

---

[1] In our work we use variables that range over any finite domain. These can be reduced to the Boolean variables used in the theoretical framework here.

[2] also known as the temporal semantics of *just discrete systems* (JDS) [12].

- $\mathcal{V}_A^e$: *A finite set of variables. $\mathcal{V}_A^e$ consists of environment variables that are defined at the base and used in the aspect, denoted by $\mathcal{V}_A^{e_{ext}}$, and of new environment variables introduced by the aspect, denoted by $\mathcal{V}_A^{e_{new}}$.*
- $\mathcal{V}_A^s$: *A finite set of variables. $\mathcal{V}_A^s$ consists of system variables defined at the base and are used in the aspect, denoted by $\mathcal{V}_A^{s_{ext}}$, and of new system variables introduced by the aspect, denoted by $\mathcal{V}_A^{s_{new}}$.*
- θ_A : *An assertion over $\mathcal{V}_A$ characterizing initial values added by A.*
- ρ_A : *An assertion over $\mathcal{V}_A \cup \mathcal{V}_A'$ characterizing transitions added by A.*
- $\mathcal{L}_A^s$: *The aspect's* LTL *specification given as a formula in the form of Equ. 1 (defined inside Defn. 1) over the variables in $\mathcal{V}_A$.*

Any or all the components may be empty. If $\mathcal{L}_A^s$ is not specified it is considered to be true.

DEFINITION 4 (AspectLTL specification).
An AspectLTL specification is a structure $\mathcal{S} = \langle \mathcal{B}, \mathcal{A} \rangle$ where $\mathcal{B}$ is a base system and $\mathcal{A} = \{A_1, A_2, .., A_k\}$ is a set of LTL *aspects.*

We omit obvious syntactic constraints, type checking, and name space issues, e.g., that for all $A_i \in \mathcal{A}$, the external variables of $\mathcal{V}_A^s$ are indeed defined by the base system, i.e., that $\mathcal{V}_A^{s_{ext}} \subseteq \mathcal{V}_B$, and that the domains of these variables, as defined in the aspects, are subdomains of the variables' domains as defined in the base.

DEFINITION 5 (AspectLTL implementation).
A discrete system $\mathcal{C} = \langle \mathcal{V}_C, \theta_C, \rho_C \rangle$ is an implementation of an AspectLTL specification $\mathcal{S} = \langle \mathcal{B}, \mathcal{A} \rangle$ iff the following hold:

- $\mathcal{V}_C = \mathcal{V}_B \cup \bigcup_{A \in \mathcal{A}} \mathcal{V}_A$
- *θ_C characterizes the set of initial states $\theta_B \vee \bigvee_{A \in \mathcal{A}} \theta_A$*
- *ρ_C is a subset of the transition relation satisfying $\rho_B \vee \bigvee_{A \in \mathcal{A}} \rho_A$*
- *$\mathcal{C}$ is deterministic with respect to $\mathcal{V}_B^e \cup \bigcup_{A \in \mathcal{A}} \mathcal{V}_A^e$*
- *Each run of $\mathcal{C}$ satisfies $\bigwedge_{A \in \mathcal{A}} \mathcal{L}_A^s$.*

Note that a specification defines no order between its aspects and indeed, the semantics of AspectLTL defined above is agnostic to aspect order.

DEFINITION 6 (AspectLTL realizability).
An AspectLTL specification is realizable iff it has an implementation.

3. A running example

Our running example is a printer management software, specified using a base and several aspects. The base describes a simple finite state machine over several system variables (state, setup, print) and a single environment

```
1   MODULE PrinterBase
2     VARENV -- environment variables (inputs)
3       newJob : boolean;
4     VAR  -- system variables
5       state : {ini,idle,work};
6       setup : {nil,warm,chk,done};
7       print : {nil,start,output,done};
8     ASSIGN
9       init(state) := ini;
10      init(setup) := nil;
11      init(print) := nil;
12
13      next(state) := case
14        state=ini & setup=done  : {ini,idle};
15        state=idle & newJob     : {idle,work};
16        state=work & print=done : {work,idle};
17        1                       : state;
18      esac;
19      next(setup) := case
20        state=ini & setup=nil   : warm;
21        state=ini & setup=warm  : {warm,chk};
22        state=ini & setup=chk   : {chk,done};
23        state!=ini              : nil;
24        1                       : setup;
25      esac;
26      next(print) := case
27        state=work & print=nil    : start;
28        state=work & print=start  : output;
29        state=work & print=output : done;
30        state=work & print=done   : nil;
31        1                         : print;
32      esac;
```

Listing 1. The code for the printer base system

controlled variable (newJob). Roughly, the printer starts in an ini state and following several steps can move to the idle state. Then, whenever a printing request is sent (the environment sets newJob), the system moves to work state, the request is printed (in several steps), and the system goes back to the idle state. The base serves as a blue print for the system to be. We show its code in List. 1.

Note that the base system is not deterministic. For example, when state=ini and setup=warm, it can either stay in setup=warm or move to setup=chk (representing 'check' phase) (line 21). As another example, when state=idle and the environment sets newJob, the system can move to work state or stay in state=idle. Such nondeterminism forms an abstraction for a set of states whose details are not yet specified. Still, the result of synthesis will be a concrete implementation, representing a deterministic controller.

Several features are defined on top of the base, and each is specified using a separate LTL aspect. We describe two of them here and leave two additional ones to Sect. 5.

The aspect PrinterCancelJob (List. 2) adds a cancel feature. Roughly, when the system is in state=work and the environment sets cancel to true (the user pressed the cancel button), the printer should immediately move to state=idle. More formally, this is specified in two parts. The TRANS section adds a transition to set the next

```
1   ASPECT PrinterCancelJob
2     VARENV
3       new cancel : boolean;
4     VAR
5       ext state : {idle, work};
6       ext setup : {nil};
7       ext print : {nil};
8     TRANS
9       cancel & next(state)=idle &
10      next(print)=nil & next(setup)=nil;
11    LTLSPEC
12      [] ((cancel & state=work)
13        -> next(state)=idle) &
14      [] ((cancel & state=work)
15        -> next(setup)=nil) &
16      [] ((cancel & state=work)
17        -> next(print)=nil);
```

Listing 2. The `PrinterCancelJob` LTL aspect

value of `state` to `idle` and of `setup` and `print` to `nil`. The `LTLSPEC` section is broken into three safety formulas: it must be globally true that immediately after `cancel & state=work` the system would satisfy `state=idle`, `setup=nil`, and `print=nil`. Thus, when `state=work` and `cancel` is true, this forces the system to follow the transition that was added in the `TRANS` section.

The aspect `PrinterGuarantees` (List. 3) forces the printer to (1) eventually complete its initialization and (2) eventually process jobs set by the environment. This is done by specifying liveness properties in the form of two response formulas: (1) globally, if `state=ini` then eventually `state=idle` and `setup=done`, and (2) globally, if `state=idle` and `newJob` is set, then eventually `state=work`. It could have been a better design to refactor these two guarantees into separate aspects (this would have no semantic consequences). We chose not to separate, so as to demonstrate that AspectLTL aspects can specify more than one liveness formula and that our traceability and debugging information is accurate: it points to specific formulas within the aspects.

Finally, the printer example is relatively small and simple. We use it to demonstrate two-way traceability and conflict

```
1   ASPECT PrinterGuarantees
2     VARENV
3       ext newJob : boolean;
4     VAR
5       ext state : {ini, idle, work};
6       ext setup : {done};
7     LTLSPEC
8       // guarantee to finish ini.
9       [] (state=ini
10        -> <> (state=idle & setup=done)) &
11      // guarantee to respond to newJob.
12      [] ((state=idle & newJob)
13        -> <> state=work);
```

Listing 3. The `PrinterGuarantees` LTL aspect

debugging, which are the focus of the paper. AspectLTL programs can be larger and much more complex.

4. Traceability

When an AspectLTL specification is realizable, traceability amounts to providing information that traces each allowed or forbidden transition in the resulting deterministic discrete system back to the aspects that have justified its presence or elimination. Below we formally define and demonstrate the concepts of positive and negative justifications and show how they are computed.

4.1 Positive justification

DEFINITION 7 (Positive justification).
Let $S = \langle \mathcal{B}, \mathcal{A} \rangle$ be an AspectLTL specification, let $\mathcal{C} = \langle \mathcal{V}_C, \theta_C, \rho_C \rangle$ be a DS that implements it, and let $t \in \rho_C$ be a transition in the implementation. We say that an aspect $A \in \mathcal{A}$ positively justifies t iff $t \models \rho_A$. We say that the base $\mathcal{B}$ positively justifies t iff $t \models \rho_B$. We denote the set of aspects (and base, if applicable) that positively justify t by $pos(t)$.

By definition of AspectLTL semantics, every transition in an implementation must be positively justified by the base or by at least one of the aspects, that is, $\forall t \in \rho_C, pos(t) \neq \emptyset$. A transition may be positively justified by several aspects.

For example, consider the specification $S = \langle PrinterBase, \{PrinterCancelJob, PrinterGuarantees\} \rangle$. When in state `state=idle & cancel`, the synthesized implementation includes the self transition to remain in `state=idle`. Computing positive justifications shows us that this transition is justified by the base `PrinterBase` as well as by the `PrinterCancelJob` aspect. As another example, when in `state=work`, the synthesized implementation includes the transition to `state=idle` even when `print!=done`. This transition, however, is justified only by the `PrinterCancelJob` aspect.

4.2 Negative justification

Negative justification is defined for transitions that cannot be part of the implementation. We distinguish two kinds, explicit and implicit. Explicit negative justification happens when a safety formula disallows a transition. Implicit negative justification happens when a transition is disallowed because it leads to a losing state, i.e., a state from which the system cannot win the synthesis game. Formally:

DEFINITION 8 (Negative justification).
Let $S = \langle \mathcal{B}, \mathcal{A} \rangle$ be an AspectLTL specification, let $\mathcal{C} = \langle \mathcal{V}_C, \theta_C, \rho_C \rangle$ be a DS that implements it, and let t be a transition from a state in the implementation to a losing state.

- *We say that t is explicitly negatively justified by the specification S iff (1) $t \models \rho_B \vee \bigvee_{A \in \mathcal{A}} \rho_A$ and (2) there exists $A \in \mathcal{A}$ such that $t \not\models \varphi_t$ where φ_t is the transition part (safety formula) of $\mathcal{L}_A^s$.*

- *We say that t is implicitly negatively justified by the specification $\mathcal{S}$ iff (1) $t \models \rho_B \vee \bigvee_{A \in \mathcal{A}} \rho_A$, (2) it is not explicitly negatively justified, and (3) it leads to a losing state, i.e., a state from which the system cannot guarantee to win the synthesis game (the environment can win).*

As an example, consider the specification $\mathcal{S} = \langle Printer\text{-}Base, \{PrinterCancelJob, PrinterGuarantees\} \rangle$. When `cancel` is set by the environment, the safety conjunct (lines 12-13) in `PrinterCancelJob` aspect LTLSPEC section, prevents `state=work` from staying in `state=work`, even if a `newJob` is set. Thus, this transition is explicitly negatively justified by `PrinterCancelJob`.

As another example, in the same specification, when a `newJob` is set in `state=idle`, the implementation cannot follow the transition that stays in `state=idle` (as allowed by `PrinterBase` at line 15) because this would lead to a losing state. For example if the environment chooses to reset the `newJob` and never set it again, the system will not be able to satisfy its response guarantee to eventually arrive to `state=work` (line 12-13 of `PrinterGuarantees`).

Note that not all transitions that are not in the implementation have to be negatively justified, explicitly or implicitly. Some such transitions may be not available in the implementation because they are not included in any of the transition relations defined by the base or the aspects, or because of choices made by the synthesis computation [19].

Finally, note that our definition of positive and negative justifications does not consider the possible effect of environment assumptions (see our remark at the end of Sect. 1). For example, in the presence of environment assumptions, additional traceability information that links the choice of transitions in the implementation to specific assumptions would be useful.

4.3 Computing two-way traceability

We compute positive justifications by iterating over the states of the implementation. For each transition from a state to a successor state, and for each of the TRANS sections of the aspects, we perform a single symbolic check to determine whether it is positively justified.

We compute explicit negative justifications by iterating over the states of the implementation. For each state in the implementation we identify the set of transitions that are allowed by the base or the TRANS sections of the aspects, but are blocked by safety formulas from some LTLSPEC sections. Computing implicit negative justifications is done by a similar symbolic operation, with respect to a 'safety formula' representing the set of transitions to all losing states (the symbolic representation of this set is a byproduct of the synthesis algorithm). To avoid exhaustive enumeration, we can either report the symbolic representation of each identified negative justification, or extract a witness.

Note that the traceability results point not only to the relevant aspects but also to their specific subformulas that partic-

```
1   ASPECT PrinterPause
2     VARENV
3       new pause : boolean; -- new input
4     VAR
5       ext print : {}; -- no value is assumed
6     TRANS
7       pause & print=next(print);
8     LTLSPEC
9       [] (pause -> print=next(print));
```

Listing 4. The `PrinterPause` LTL aspect

ipate in the justifications. We use the same results to provide traceability in the other way too: given a subformula from one of the aspects, we identify all transitions it has positively or negatively justified relative to a specific implementation. For example, our technique shows that the subformula in the TRANS section of the `PrinterCancelJob` aspect (lines 9-10), has positively justified many transitions in the implementation, e.g., a transition to `state=idle`, `print=nil`, and `setup=nil`, from many states where `state=work` & `cancel=true`, and from many states where `state=idle` & `cancel=true`.

All traceability results are collected so that they can be reported and presented in the plug-in UI (see Sect. 7).

5. Extending the example

We now present additional aspects that we will use in Sect. 6.

The aspect `PrinterPause` (List. 4) adds a pause printing feature: When the user presses the pause button, the printer should stop changing its print status. The aspect includes a new environment variable `pause`, representing the input from a pause button. It is defined in two parts: the TRANS section adds a transition to preserve the value of `print` when `pause` is true, and the LTLSPEC section specifies a safety formula, to force the system to pause in this case.

The aspect `PrinterInkManagement` (List. 5) adds ink related functionality: updating the ink cartridge state and disallowing printing when no ink is left. It defines two new variables (1) an environment variable `fillCartridge` and (2) a system variable `ink` representing the level of ink in the cartridge. The aspect constrains the initial value of the new `ink` variable and the related transitions: either `fillCartridge` is set and the ink level is correspondingly set to 7 (representing the maximal ink level), or the level of `ink` is decreased by one after `print=output`. Moreover, the aspect forbids the printer from printing when `ink=0` (there is no ink left), using a safety formula.

6. Conflict debugging

Some specifications are unrealizable: no implementation exists that can satisfy all their required guarantees in all environments. Deciding realizability, however, is not enough. We are interested in generating a proof that shows how an adverse environment can force the system to violate its specification and identify the conflicting aspects to blame. The

```
1   ASPECT PrinterInkManagement
2     VARENV
3       new fillCartridge : boolean;
4     VAR
5       ext print : {start, output};
6       new ink   : 0..7;
7     LTLSPEC
8       ink = 7 &
9       [] (next(ink) = case
10        fillCartridge       : 7;
11        ink>0 & print=output : ink - 1;
12        1                    : ink;
13       esac);
14    LTLSPEC
15      [] (! (ink=0 & print=start));
```

Listing 5. The `PrinterInkManagement` LTL aspect

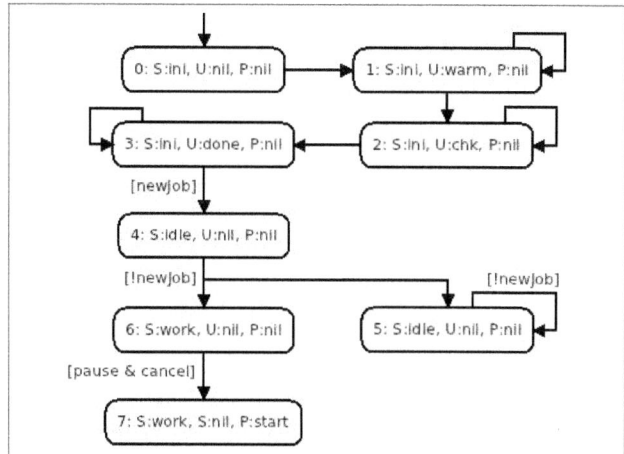

Figure 1. Debug information for Example I

proof we generate is interactive: it is an executable counter-implementation of the specification, which the engineer can not only manually statically analyze, but also 'play against'. The interactive, guided debugging session, illustrates to the engineer how, regardless of her choices, she will eventually end up violating one or more of the required specifications.

DEFINITION 9 (AspectLTL counter-implementation). *A discrete system* $C = \langle V_C, \theta_C, \rho_C \rangle$ *is a counter-implementation of an AspectLTL specification* $S = \langle B, A \rangle$ *iff the following hold:*

- $V_C = V_B \cup \bigcup_{A \in \mathcal{A}} V_A$
- θ_C *characterizes the set of initial states* $\theta_B \vee \bigvee_{A \in \mathcal{A}} \theta_A$
- ρ_C *is a subset of the transition relation satisfying* $\rho_B \vee \bigvee_{A \in \mathcal{A}} \rho_A$
- C *is deterministic with respect to* $V_B^s \cup \bigcup_{A \in \mathcal{A}} V_A^s$ *(i.e., the system variables rather than the environment variables as in Defn. 5)*
- *Each run of* C *satisfies* $\bigvee_{A \in \mathcal{A}} \neg \mathcal{L}_A^s$ *(i.e., falsifying one of the LTL specifications).*

LEMMA 1. *An AspectLTL specification is unrealizable iff it has a counter-implementation.*

The Lemma follows from the fact that the synthesis game is determined, that is, for every game instance there is a winning strategy for one of the players: either we can synthesize a controller or we can produce a counter-implementation.

The key to computing a counter-implementation is to set up a game with reversed roles. A solution to this game is an artifact representing an environment behavior that will eventually lead to violating the specification, no matter how the system will react. Such an artifact is a proof that the specification is unrealizable, as required.

Moreover, we accompany the counter-implementation with additional information. First, traceability information (as in the case of realizable specifications), which shows justifications to the transitions in the counter-implementation. Second, at each of the states in the counter-implementation,

we give pointers to the violated AspectLTL statements, i.e., to the specific liveness formulas, from the different aspects, that do not hold in the state. This information points to the exact aspects to blame.

We give two examples of unrealizable specifications with generated counter-implementations, as computed by the AspectLTL debugger.

6.1 Example I

As a first example, consider the AspectLTL specification $S = \langle PrinterBase, \{PrinterCancelJob, PrinterGuar-antees, PrinterPause\} \rangle$. Is this specification realizable?

Our debugging technique identifies that this specification is unrealizable and generates a short counter-implementation, as illustrated in the diagram shown in Fig. 1. In the diagram we use abbreviated notation: S for `state`, U for `setup`, P for `print`. To make it more readable we use an abstraction: in the states we show only the values of the system variables. The values of environment controlled variables (inputs) for the next state are shown on its incoming transition as guards. A transition without a guard means that it is taken for a value that the environment chose from its possible winning strategies (i.e., the actual input value chosen by the environment makes no difference in this case for our example of proving unrealizability). We now explain the counter-implementation in detail.

From states 0 to 3, the system is in `state=ini`. In these states, the system guarantee to eventually reach `state=idle` (as specified in the `PrinterGuarantees` aspect, lines 9-10 of List. 3) is not met, so the environment allows the system to stay in these states as long as it wishes (with self transitions); if the system chooses to stay there forever, it will 'lose the game', because this guarantee will not be satisfied.

In state 4, the environment sets `newJob` to `true` (the environment sends a new print job). Now the system has two choices: either to start working on the new printing job (have `state=work` in state 6) or remain in `state=idle` in state 5. Both alternatives are, however, not good.

41

If the system chooses to stay in state=idle, the environment immediately resets newJob to false: the system is forced to stay forever in state 5, where the 'response to new job' guarantee specified in the PrinterGuarantees aspect (lines 12-13 of List. 3) is not met. If the system chooses to start working on the new job, the environment blocks it by setting the cancel and pause inputs to true (pressing the cancel and pause buttons at the same time!). Now, in state 7, the system reaches a deadlock, caused by a conflict between the safety formulas from the PrinterCancelJob and PrinterPause aspects: the first requires that the next state will have print=nil (lines 16-17 of the PrinterCancelJob aspect), while the second requires that in the next state the value of print will stay the same (line 9 of the PrinterPause aspect), i.e., in this case, remain print=start.

6.2 Example II

As a second, somewhat more complex example, consider the AspectLTL specification $S = \langle PrinterBase, \{Printer\text{-}InkManagement, PrinterGuarantees, PrinterPause\}\rangle$. Is this specification realizable?

Our debugging technique identifies that this specification is unrealizable and generates a counter-implementation, as illustrated in the diagram shown in Fig. 2. Again we use abbreviated notation: S for state, U for setup, P for print, and I for ink. We now explain it in detail.

From states 0 to 3, as in the previous example, the system is in state=ini. In these states, the system guarantee to eventually reach state=idle (as specified in the PrinterGuarantees aspect, lines 9-10 of List. 3) is not met, so the environment allows the system to stay in these states as long as it wishes (with self transitions); if the system chooses to stay there forever, it will 'lose the game', because this guarantee will not be satisfied.

After reaching state 4, where the environment has sent a new printing job, the system needs to choose between two alternatives, either start working on the printing job (and move to state 6 where state=work) or stay in state=idle and move to state 5. Again, both alternatives are not good.

According to PrinterGuarantees, the new job set in state 4 requires that eventually state=work. If the system chooses not to start working immediately, the environment resets newJob and the system is forced to not reach state=work, forever, thus violating this guarantee. If the system chooses to start work immediately (and move to state 6), the run continues until the print job is done. As the environment tries to fail the system, it continues to set newJob whenever the system is back in state=idle, aiming to eventually reach a state where ink=0. Whenever newJob is set, the choice between working or staying in idle state is repeated (we do not show all repetitions in the diagram).

Finally, in state 17, there is no more ink, and the environment sets newJob for the last time. Again, if the system chooses not to handle this immediately and keep

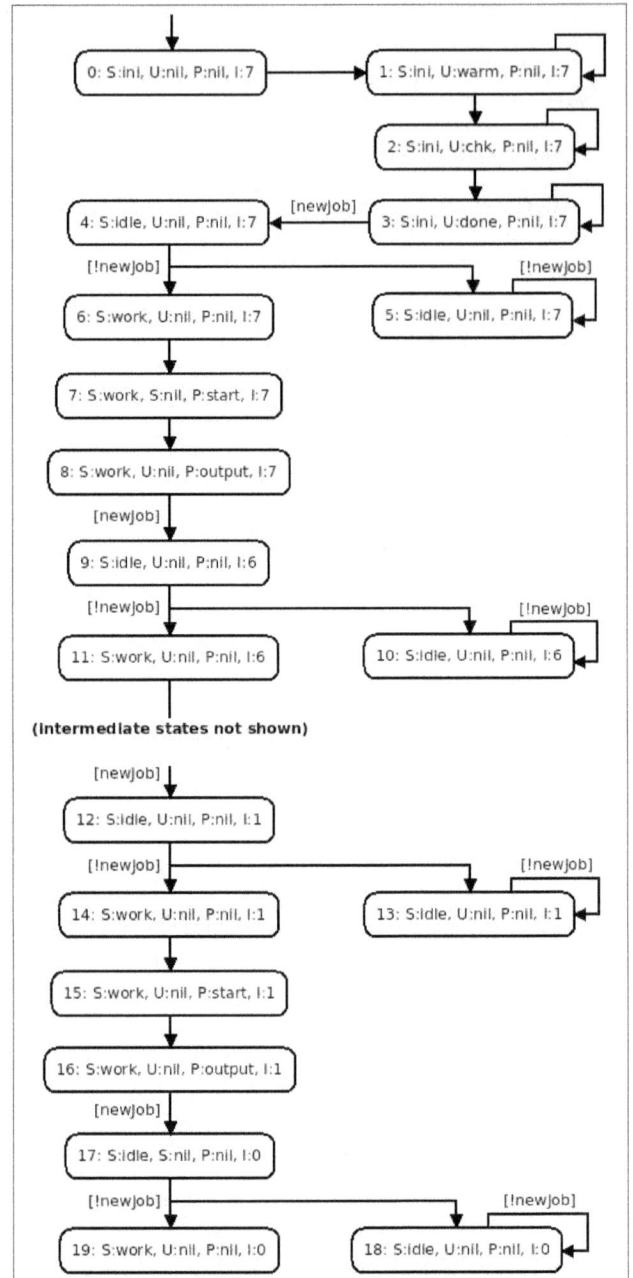

Figure 2. Debug information for Example II

state=idle, it is forced to stay in state 18 forever (the environment never sets newJob again) and thus lose the game by not satisfying the printing guarantee. If the system chooses to work on the job it moves to state 19 with state=work, the safety formula of line 15 in the PrinterInkManagement aspect prevents it from actually start printing (with print=start) and so it reaches a deadlock.

6.2.1 Unrealizable core

Interestingly, note that in this counter-implementation the environment did not 'use' the input pause, although the PrinterPause aspect is included in the specification. Indeed, the traceability information that we compute shows that the specifications of the `PrinterPause` aspect (the added transition and the safety formula) neither positively justified any of the transitions in the counter-implementation nor removed any negatively justified transitions that could have been defined as outgoing from the states in the counter-implementation. Thus, the traceability information shows that `PrinterPause` was not necessary in the proof for unrealizability: the combination of `PrinterInkManagement` and `PrinterGuarantees` is, by itself, unrealizable.

Our approach can identify such unnecessary aspects in the unrealizability proof, after a counter-implementation is computed. However, our current technique is not guaranteed to find a minimal unrealizable subset of the specification. This relates to the problem of finding an unrealizable core. See our discussion of future work in Sect. 9.

6.3 Computing a counter-implementation

Computing the counter-implementation is done by solving a Rabin game where the environment tries to falsify at least one of the system's guarantees, following the fixpoint algorithms described in [13, 18]. Roughly, the algorithm starts from the set of states from which the system has no valid possible successors. It then iterates 'backwards' by adding states from which the environment can either force the system to (1) reach previously found losing states, or (2) constantly violate one of the system's guarantees (each set of states where the guarantee is constantly violated, is computed using another nested fixpoint).

The fixpoint is reached when no additional losing states can be found. If there exists an environment initial choice for which all the system's initial choices are in the computed set, then the specification is unrealizable. A counter-implementation can be constructed from the intermediate values of the fixpoint computation (see [13, 19]), while pointing to the system's guarantee that the strategy is trying to falsify at each state of the counter-implementation. In the resulting counter-implementation, as presented to the user, each state is annotated with (1) the system's guarantee that the strategy is "currently" trying to falsify, and (2) the related traceability information as described in Sect. 4.

6.4 Environment assumptions

As mentioned at the end of Sect. 1, most of our discussion in this paper does not consider environment assumptions. In the context of conflict debugging, however, the presence of environment assumptions is significant: as assumptions limit the environment to certain behaviors, their addition may make a previously unrealizable specification realizable.

Consider the example presented in Sect. 6.1. Adding a simple assumption that 'prevents' the user from pressing the cancel and pause buttons at the same time, formally adding `[](!(pause & cancel))` as an assumption, renders the specification realizable. Indeed, in this case, the AspectLTL

plug-in successfully synthesizes a controller and generates an implementation.

Consider the example presented in Sect. 6.2. Adding a simple assumption, specifying that if the ink is empty, then a refill must occur in the following step, formally adding `[](ink=0 -> next(fillCartridge))` as an assumption, renders the specification realizable. As in the previous example, in this case, the AspectLTL plug-in successfully synthesizes a controller and generates an implementation.

Interestingly, however, note that the assumption we suggested to add to the first example, `[](!(pause & cancel))`, involves two environment variables that belong to different LTL aspects, `PrinterCancelJob` and `PrinterPause`! This assumption is thus not local to any of the aspects alone and its use may be viewed as violating the very idea of separation of concerns. We leave this for discussion in future work.

7. Implementation and Evaluation

We have implemented our ideas and integrated them into the AspectLTL plug-in. The implementation is based on the APIs of JTLV [22], a framework for the development of formal verification algorithms using BDD-based mechanism. The plug-in includes front-end editors with syntax highlighting for AspectLTL, on-the-fly parsing and quick fixes, outline, auto-completion, and views and markers to mark traceability information. The plug-in together with related documentation are available from our website [2]. All examples shown in this paper and mentioned in the evaluation below are available with the plug-in, so that all experiments can be reproduced. We encourage the interested reader to try them.

Fig. 3 shows a screen capture from the AspectLTL plug-in, displaying a tracing session of the specification $S = \langle PrinterBase, \{PrinterCancelJob, PrinterGuarantees\}\rangle$. Two aspects are shown in the main editor windows, with green markers highlighting subformulas that induce positive justifications and orange markers highlighting subformulas that induce explicit negative justifications. Note that the second safety formula of the aspect `PrinterCancelJob` is not marked, meaning that it does not induce any justifications. The tooltip over the orange marker relates to the third safety formula and presents the transitions that it negatively justifies, that is, it shows traceability from aspect specification to program behaviors. The complete list of justifications is shown in the lower right pane; clicking each item in the table leads to its related subformula in one of the aspects, that is, traceability from program behavior to the specification. The textual representation of the implemented controller is shown on the lower left (also annotated with per-state traceability information).

The plug-in supports a graph-based view of the implementation (or counter-implementation), similar to the graphs shown in Fig. 1 and Fig. 2. The graph unfolds dynamically, according to the engineer's choice of actions at each step.

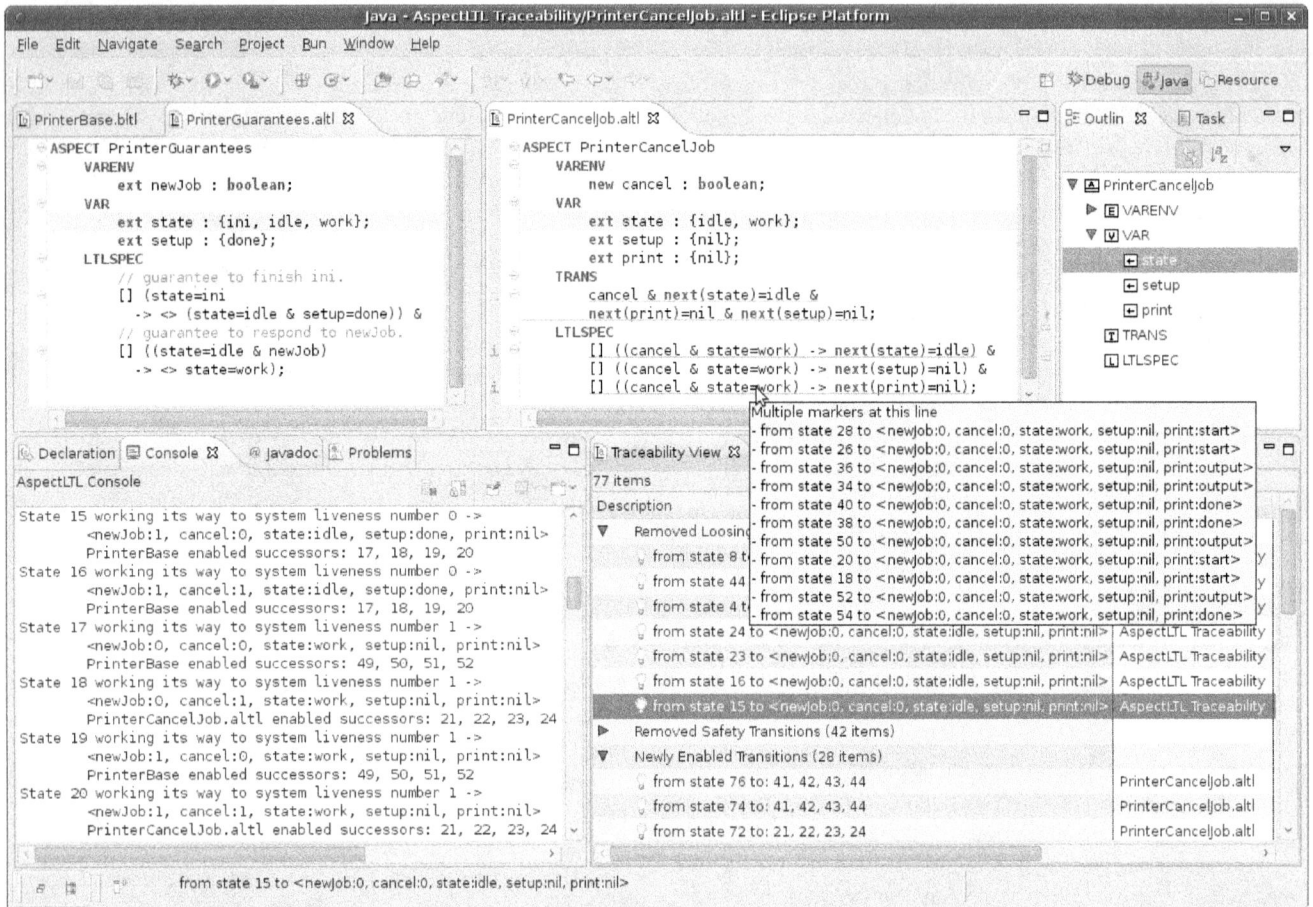

Figure 3. A screen capture of AspectLTL plug-in, displaying traceability information for the specification $\mathcal{S} = \langle PrinterBase, \{PrinterCancelJob, PrinterGuarantees\}\rangle$.

An example screenshot showing this graph is available from our website.

To emphasize the dynamic nature of AspectLTL debugging, a movie showing a typical debugging session that shows an execution of a generated, interactive counter-implementation program, is available from our website.

AspectLTL synthesis is based on GR(1) synthesis [19], whose complexity is cubic in number of states of the implementation, measured in symbolic steps. The symbolic algorithm allows it to scale well, at least up to medium size specifications [4]. While checking realizability / unrealizability is completely symbolic, the computation of a concrete implementation (or counter-implementation) requires the enumeration of states, which in some cases is much slower and does not scale well (specifically when dealing with data rather than control). Computing the additional traceability information is linear in the number of states and transitions in the implementation. The complexity of computing a counter-implementation is the same as that of synthesis.

To give a sense of the feasibility of AspectLTL synthesis, with and without traceability information, we report initial quantitative results from the performance of AspectLTL

realizability checking and implementation generation.[3] The experiments were performed on a regular computer, Intel Dual Core CPU, 2.4 GHz, with 4 GB RAM, running 64-bit Linux. Running times are reported in milliseconds.

Table 1 shows results of experiments on the Printer system and on two additional systems: ExamService, described in detail in [17], and Traffic, a two-cars race problem. These examples, and some additional ones, are available with the plug-in. For each system we report on several configurations. For each configuration we report on the number of aspects, the number of LTL specs (the total number of safety and liveness conjuncts) + the number of transition disjuncts, the state space of the specification, whether the specification was realizable or not, the time for checking realizability, the size of the implementation (or counter-implementation), the time for computing the implementation (or counter-implementation), and the additional time of computing traceability information. Additional performance

---

[3] We show the concrete performance results in order to give a general, rough idea about the feasibility of using AspectLTL. We have not made special efforts to optimize our implementation and do not consider the exact values shown to be important: optimizing the performance of AspectLTL synthesis is outside the scope of this paper.

Specification	# Aspects / # Specs (+ T)	State space	Realizable?	Deciding (ms)	Impl. size	Impl. gen. time (ms)	Traceab. time (ms)
PrinterBase weaved with: CancelJob (CJ), Guarantees (G), Pause (P), InkManagement (IM).							
CJ + G	2/5 (+1)	2^{12}	true	34	77	81	57
CJ + G + P	3/6 (+2)	2^{13}	false	34	9	48	2
CJ + G + P + IM	4/8 (+2)	2^{17}	false	62	9	88	5
CJ + G + IM	3/7 (+1)	2^{16}	false	53	43	75	27
ExamService weaved with: Tuition (T), AvailabilityBug (AB), Availability (A), FailuresLogging (FL), AllowQuitting (AQ), ExamProtection (EP), ExamCounter (EC).							
T + AB	2/2 (+1)	2^{10}	false	10	10	13	1
T + A + FL	3/3 (+1)	2^{12}	true	36	64	58	11
T + A + FL + AQ + EP	5/6 (+2)	2^{17}	true	34	272	240	81
T + A + AQ + EP + EC	5/8 (+3)	2^{18}	true	57	1760	7128	854
TrafficBase weaved with: Goal (G), Safety (S), Obstacle3 (O3), Obstacle4 (O4), ExtraSafety (ES), ReverseGear (RG).							
G + S	2/2 (+0)	2^{16}	true	65	31	68	8
G + S + ES + O3 + O4	5/6 (+0)	2^{16}	false	149	1	243	1
G + S + ES + O3 + O4 + RG	6/7 (+1)	2^{16}	true	455	37	459	9

Table 1. Results from running AspectLTL on several examples, checking realizability, generating an implementation (counter-implementation), and computing traceability information (see Sect. 7)

results are available in supporting materials [2]. The reported times do not include the marking in the eclipse UI.

The results suggest the following observations. First, checking for realizability is sometimes much faster and scales better than generating an implementation. Thus, we recommend the frequent use of realizability checking, without implementation generation (in the plug-in these features are intentionally separated). It is best if the engineer computes the implementation only when she wants to interactively execute the generated code, or when she finds that the specification is unrealizable. Second, the additional computation of traceability information is sometimes costly (proportional to the implementation size) but still does not carry a dramatic overhead on top of the implementation generation time. If it becomes too slow, one may allow to compute it on-demand for user-selected state/transition. Finally, overall, AspectLTL synthesis, with and without traceability information, seems to perform in acceptable time for all our examples. Larger examples may be slower and require the development of additional techniques, e.g., an incremental approach. We leave this for future work.

8. Related Work

We now discuss several related studies in the areas of traceability, feature interaction, and model-checking of aspects.

Borger et al. [3] present runtime, dynamic aspect traceability for AspectJ, by inspecting the stack to discover which pointcut causes a certain advice. Support for static traceability is provided, e.g., by AJDT [1], where in the source code view, the IDE shows which aspects (may) affect certain base artifacts and statements. In the context of AspectLTL, traceability is very different, in particular because the language is declarative and not imperative: the high-level motivation of relating aspect code artifacts with the concrete behavior

they induce is similar, but the setup and technologies used are completely different.

Checking the realizability of AspectLTL specifications and the debugging of unrealizable ones, are related to works that identify feature interactions or use model-checking to discover aspect interference. We mention some of the most relevant ones below.

Felty et al. [6] present the specification of features using LTL and a model-checking based method to automatically detect conflicts between features. Realizability is approximated by model-checking only a given scope: if a conflict is detected, it is a real conflict, and a counter example is provided. If no conflict is detected, the result is inconclusive, i.e., conflict detection is sound but incomplete. In contrast, our realizability checks are sound and complete. Moreover, when a specification is realizable, we provide a correct-by-construction implementation, which is not available in [6].

Many approaches specify features using state machines and consider feature interaction as part of their composition (see, e.g., [8, 9, 15]). To the best of our knowledge, none considers a symbolic, declarative representation like the one used in AspectLTL and most compositions are not sound and complete like AspectLTL synthesis. We could not find a description of traceability and debugging features similar to the ones presented in our work.

Katz and Katz [10] present incremental aspect interference analysis. The work models AspectJ-like aspects using an SMV-like format. Detection of various interferences is done using model checking. In case of conflict, a counter example is provided. Our work uses an SMV-like format to specify aspects. However, rather than using the specification for model checking, we use it as an input for synthesis. In case of unrealizability, we provide a counter-implementation.

Li et al. [15] present a methodology that views cross-cutting features as independent modules and verifies them against CTL properties as open systems. Features consists of state machines and composition is done by connecting them via transitions specified through interfaces. The work supports the detection of undesirable feature interactions. Support for traceability and debugging is not described.

In contrast, AspectLTL aspects are defined in a symbolic and declarative manner. Our method is fundamentally different: it not only solves the possible conflicts or interferences between the specified aspects (if indeed a solution to these conflicts exists) but also produces an executable correct-by-construction implementation. If a solution does not exist, we generate a counter-implementation, annotated with the traceability information that uncovers reasons for unrealizability.

9. Conclusion and Future Work

We presented two-way traceability and conflict debugging techniques for AspectLTL and demonstrated them on a running example. To support two-way traceability, we use symbolic operations that check for intersections between the transitions that can or cannot be taken and the formulas defined in the LTL aspects. To support debugging of unrealizable specifications we reverse the roles of the system and the environment in the synthesis game, and use the winning strategy of the environment to produce a counter-implementation, that is, an interactive program, whose runs show exactly how any generated system can be forced by an (adverse) environment to violate the specifications. We combine traceability and debugging to point at the aspects to blame. The techniques provide important support for the development of systems using AspectLTL, making its use more accessible and informative. The ideas are implemented in the AspectLTL plug-in, available from [2].

One future work direction deals with the computation of an unrealizable core. Given an unrealizable AspectLTL specification, an unrealizable core is a minimal unrealizable subset of the specification. An unrealizable core is useful in debugging, as it better identifies and isolates the causes of failures and enables the generation of smaller counter-implementations. Some recent works have considered the computation of unrealizable cores in the context of LTL (GR(1)) synthesis (see, e.g., [5]). However, computing an unrealizable core for AspectLTL specifications is particularly challenging due to the non-monotonic nature of the language: each aspect may not only restrict the possible behaviors (in its LTLSPEC sections) but also add new behaviors (in its TRANS sections). Another future work is to investigate how our approach to traceability and debugging can be applied to other aspect languages, e.g., AspectJ, using abstractions similar to the ones of [7, 14], or more generally, to other feature composition frameworks (e.g., [8, 9, 15]), where, we believe, similar two-way traceability and conflict debugging support could be very useful.

References

[1] AspectJ Development Tools. http://www.eclipse.org/ajdt/.

[2] AspectLTL website. http://aspectltl.ysaar.net/.

[3] W. D. Borger, B. Lagaisse, and W. Joosen. A generic and reflective debugging architecture to support runtime visibility and traceability of aspects. In *AOSD*, pages 173–184, 2009.

[4] J. R. Burch, E. M. Clarke, K. L. McMillan, D. L. Dill, and L. J. Hwang. Symbolic model checking: 10^{20} states and beyond. *Inf. Comput.*, 98(2):142–170, 1992.

[5] A. Cimatti, M. Roveri, V. Schuppan, and A. Tchaltsev. Diagnostic information for realizability. In *VMCAI*, 2008.

[6] A. P. Felty and K. S. Namjoshi. Feature specification and automated conflict detection. *ACM Trans. Softw. Eng. Methodol.*, 12(1):3–27, 2003.

[7] M. Goldman, E. Katz, and S. Katz. MAVEN: modular aspect verification and interference analysis. *Formal Methods in System Design*, 37(1):61–92, 2010.

[8] J. D. Hay and J. M. Atlee. Composing features and resolving interactions. In *SIGSOFT FSE*, pages 110–119, 2000.

[9] M. Jackson and P. Zave. Distributed feature composition: A virtual architecture for telecommunications services. *IEEE Trans. Software Eng.*, 24(10):831–847, 1998.

[10] E. Katz and S. Katz. Incremental analysis of interference among aspects. In *FOAL*, pages 29–38, 2008.

[11] S. Katz. Aspect categories and classes of temporal properties. In *T. Aspect-Oriented Softw. Dev. I*, pages 106–134, 2006.

[12] Y. Kesten and A. Pnueli. Verification by augmented finitary abstraction. *Inf. Comput.*, 163:203–243, 2000.

[13] R. Könighofer, G. Hofferek, and R. Bloem. Debugging formal specifications using simple counterstrategies. In *FMCAD*, pages 152–159, 2009.

[14] S. Krishnamurthi and K. Fisler. Foundations of incremental aspect model-checking. *ACM Trans. Softw. Eng. Methodol.*, 16(2), 2007.

[15] H. C. Li, S. Krishnamurthi, and K. Fisler. Verifying cross-cutting features as open systems. In *SIGSOFT FSE*, pages 89–98, 2002.

[16] Z. Manna and A. Pnueli. *The temporal logic of concurrent and reactive systems: specification.* 1992.

[17] S. Maoz and Y. Sa'ar. AspectLTL: An aspect langauge for LTL specifications. In *AOSD*, pages 19–30, 2011.

[18] N. Piterman and A. Pnueli. Faster solutions of rabin and streett games. In *LICS*, pages 275–284, 2006.

[19] N. Piterman, A. Pnueli, and Y. Sa'ar. Synthesis of Reactive(1) Designs. In *VMCAI*, pages 364–380, 2006.

[20] A. Pnueli. The temporal logic of programs. In *FOCS*, pages 46–57, 1977.

[21] A. Pnueli and R. Rosner. On the synthesis of a reactive module. In *POPL*, pages 179–190, 1989.

[22] A. Pnueli, Y. Sa'ar, and L. Zuck. JTLV: A framework for developing verification algorithms. In *CAV*, 2010.

[23] SMV model checker. http://www.cs.cmu.edu/~modelcheck/smv.html.

A Debug Interface for Debugging Multiple Domain Specific Aspect Languages *

Yoav Apter   David H. Lorenz   Oren Mishali

Open University of Israel,
1 University Rd., P.O.Box 808, Raanana 43107 Israel
yoav.ap@gmail.com,   {lorenz,omishali}@openu.ac.il

Abstract

Research in the area of multi-DSAL development has been mainly devoted to enabling the interoperability of multiple aspect mechanisms. Less attention has been given to making programming with multiple aspect languages practical. For domain specific aspect languages (DSALs) to be used in practice, there is a need for tools that make multi-DSAL development effective. This paper focuses on one such tool: a debugger. We define a multi-DSAL debug interface (MDDI) for inspecting the composition specification and the runtime state and behavior of applications written in multiple DSALs. To implement the interface, a multi-DSAL debug agent and special debug attributes are introduced into the weaving process. A concrete implementation of MDDI over the AWESOME aspect composition framework is presented. For validation we demonstrate a simple command line AWESOMEDEBUGGER that uses the debug interface.

Categories and Subject Descriptors   D.3.4 [*Programming Languages*]: Processors—Debuggers;   D.2.5 [*Software Engineering*]: Testing and Debugging—Debugging aids.

General Terms   Design, Languages.

Keywords   Aspect-Oriented Programming (AOP), Aspect-Oriented Software Engineering (AOSE), AspectJ, Awesome, Cool, Debugger, Domain Specific Languages (DSLs), Domain Specific Aspect Languages (DSALs), Validate.

---

* This research was supported in part by the *Israel Science Foundation (ISF)* under grant No. 926/08.

1.   Introduction

An aspect-oriented extension to a programming language is labeled *domain specific* (DSAL) when some (general purpose) expressiveness is surrendered for more (domain specific) conciseness in describing a specific crosscutting concern in the terminology of the domain. For example, COOL [12, 13] is a DSAL with high level constructs just for specifying declaratively the synchronization of threads in the program. To regain the lost expressiveness, DSALs are used with other DSALs and collectively with general purpose aspect languages.

The development of aspect-oriented software systems using multiple DSALs has gained attention in recent years (e.g., the DSAL workshop series in AOSD). This mode of development is denoted here as *multi-DSAL development* [1]. A major research effort in this area is to coordinate the collaborative operation of the *aspect mechanisms* [9] implementing the various DSALs. The research has led to the creation of *aspect composition frameworks*, e.g., Pluggable AOP [8], Reflex [20], Awesome [10], JAMI [6], Crosscutting Composition [4], and others.

Less research attention has been devoted to making the mode of multi-DSAL development practical. For DSALs to be used in practice, we need tools that make the actual development with multiple DSALs effective. This paper focuses on one such tool—the *debugger*.

1.1   Runtime State and Behavior

Modern debuggers provide by default standard facilities for examining the state and behavior of an application at runtime. However, when the object of debugging is a multi-DSAL application, additional unique investigation facilities are required from the debugger. For instance, when a breakpoint is placed on a *method-execution* join point, the developer should be able to examine the list of applied advice of *all* the aspect languages. Moreover, the developer needs to be able to distinguish between advice of different languages.

Today, debuggers are unaware of these requirements and do not provide such facilities. The only exception is the *aspect-oriented debugging architecture* (AODA) [2]. The

AODA debugger lets the developer investigate the application in terms of its AOP abstractions, namely, aspects, pointcuts, and advice. However, AODA is designed for a single aspect mechanism. When AODA is used to debug multi-DSAL applications, only ASPECTJ advice is listed during the debug process. Of course, the source code of the other aspect languages could be translated to ASPECTJ. However, even if such a translation occurs, the developer might be able to observe the whole list of advice, but they would all seem to belong to ASPECTJ. Moreover, source-to-source translation in general may introduce and expose synthetic join points that do not exist in the original source code, resulting in incorrect application behavior [11]. Hence, even AODA is not suited for multi-DSAL debugging.

1.2 Composition Specification

A multi-DSAL debugger should also provide the developer with the ability to reason about the *composition specification* [10, 14]. Composing multiple aspect mechanisms into a coherent weaver is a complex process that is facilitated by an aspect composition framework. In a typical composition process, the framework is provided with multiple aspect mechanisms, one for each aspect language. A *composition designer* then uses the framework to configure the interactions among the mechanisms, based on a particular composition specification. The specification may set, for instance, a specific order on advice of different aspect mechanisms that operate at the same join point. The composition framework produces as an output a single multi-DSAL weaver that behaves according to the specification.

It may be difficult for the composition designer to formulate in advance a complete composition specification that achieves the desired application behavior flawlessly. It may also be difficult to communicate the specification to the developer. Therefore, in addition to normal bugs whose cause lies in the application layer due to improper use of language constructs or incorrect application logic, composition bugs may exist due to an incorrect or misunderstood composition specification. Thus, the debugger should let the developer inspect the composition specification. Again, none of the debuggers currently supports this feature.

1.3 Contribution

This work presents a *Multi-DSAL Debug Interface* (MDDI). The interface comprises two sets of debug operations. The first set of operations can be used to examine the runtime state and behavior of a multi-DSAL application. The operations in this set enhance the debug features found in the AODA [2]. The second set of operations can be used to inspect the application from the composition specification point of view. The operations defined in this set are based on prior work that characterized abstract features of an aspect mechanism, and in particular, features of the composition of several mechanisms [9, 11]. These abstract features are materialized in terms of concrete debug operations in MDDI.

We provide an implementation of MDDI over a specific aspect composition framework called AWESOME [10]. We modified the AWESOME framework to produce a multi-DSAL weaver that is "debug aware." The weaver inserts into the woven files special debug attributes, which a debugger can access via MDDI to provide runtime state and behavior information and details about the composition specification.

Our scope of investigation for multi-DSAL development targets a dominant family of *reactive aspect mechanisms* [9]. This family includes the set of AOP languages known as *join point and advice*.

Outline. Section 2 presents an introductory example to concretely illustrate the problem and the solution. This example demonstrates use of MDDI to identify and locate the cause for a bug in a multi-DSAL application. Section 3 presents the debug operations in MDDI. In Section 4, a concrete implementation of the MDDI over the AWESOME framework is described. In Section 5, the debug interface is evaluated.

2. Motivating Example

To illustrate the issues involved in debugging a multi-DSAL application and to outline our solution, we first present a simple example. The application in our example comprises a base system, written in JAVA, with three concerns, each expressed in a different aspect language. ASPECTJ contributes tracing; COOL handles thread synchronization; and VALIDATE—a DSAL that we have defined ourselves—enforces validation of input parameters.

Recall that the source of bugs or surprising behavior in a multi-DSAL application is either erroneous implementation somewhere in the source code, or incorrect or misunderstood composition of the aspect mechanisms. In this section we provide an example for a bug of the latter sort. In the example, an unexpected behavior of the application is observed. We describe how the developer might utilize a multi-DSAL debug interface to: (1) identify a bug caused by an incorrect composition, and (2) understand the essence of the bug.

We provide as we go brief explanations that are necessary for understanding the part of the interface that is being discussed. A more complete specification of the debug interface is presented and explained in Sections 3 and 4.

2.1 A Multi-DSAL Application

Our running example is a multi-DSAL application, which is also multi-threaded. The base system is a JAVA class that implements a bounded stack. The class Stack (Listing 1) defines two public methods, push and pop, where an ArrayIndexOutOfBoundsException is thrown upon an attempt to pop objects off an empty stack or push objects onto a full stack.

In addition, three aspects are defined, each expressed in a different aspect language. Note that the term *aspect* is used here and throughout the paper in a broader meaning, and

```
1  public class Stack {
2    public Stack(int capacity) {
3      buf = new Object[capacity];
4    }
5    public void push(Object obj){
6      buf[ind] = obj;
7      ind++;
8    }
9    public Object pop() {
10     Object top = buf[ind-1];
11     buf[--ind] = null;
12     return top;
13   }
14   private Object[] buf;
15   private int ind = 0;
16 }
```

Listing 1. A stack implementation in JAVA

```
1  public aspect Tracer {
2    pointcut scope(): !cflow(within(Tracer));
3    before(): scope() {
4      out.println("before " + thisJoinPoint);
5    }
6    Object around(): scope() {
7      out.println("around " + thisJoinPoint);
8      return proceed();
9    }
10   after(): scope() {
11     out.println("after " + thisJoinPoint);
12   }
13 }
```

Listing 2. A tracing aspect in ASPECTJ

```
1  validator Stack {
2    validate Stack(int capacity):
3      $1 > 0;
4    validate push(Object obj):
5      string($1), email($1);
6  }
```

Listing 3. A validator in VALIDATE

```
1  coordinator Stack {
2    selfex {push, pop};
3    mutex {push, pop};
4    int len=0;
5    condition full=false, empty=true;
6    push: requires !full;
7    on_exit {
8      empty=false;
9      len++;
10     if (len==buf.length)
11       full=true;
12   }
13   pop: requires !empty;
14   on_entry { len--; }
15   on_exit {
16     full=false;
17     if (len==0)
18       empty=true;
19   }
20 }
```

Listing 4. A synchronization coordinator in COOL

refers to the language construct introduced by *any* aspect language to encapsulate a crosscutting concern. In ASPECTJ this construct is called *aspect*. COOL calls it *coordinator*, and in VALIDATE the aspect construct is denoted *validator*.

The first aspect is defined in ASPECTJ, a general purpose aspect language. The aspect enhances Stack with tracing facilities (Listing 2).

The second *coordinator* aspect (Listing 4) is written in COOL, an *off-the-shelf* DSAL that facilitates synchronization of JAVA methods. The coordinator enforces the following synchronization policy for each instance of Stack:

- neither push nor pop may be executed by more than one thread at a time (selfex declaration);

- push and pop are prohibited from being executed concurrently (mutex declaration);

- push may be called only if the stack is not full (condition full); and

- pop may be called only if the stack is not empty (condition empty).

The on_entry and on_exit clauses express the bookkeeping required to implement the last two items.

The third aspect language is called VALIDATE, a simple *in-house* DSAL that the developer defines. VALIDATE supports validation of input arguments passed to methods, constructors, and fields (field assignments). As a motivation for using such a language, consider a development team that is interested in involving domain experts in the implementation of the security concern of the system (one facet of security is input validation). Furthermore, assume that the domain experts are familiar with the Unix shell. To accommodate the

experts, VALIDATE takes on a syntax that resembles shell commands. The input validation of a particular program element, e.g., a method, is contained in a validation *command*. Within a command, $\$(i)$ is used to access the i'th input argument. In addition, a library of predicates exists for defining the validation criteria. Validation commands for one or more classes are grouped in a *validator* aspect.

In Listing 3, a validator for the Stack class is presented. It validates the constructor and the push method. The validator specifies that the constructor's first argument (the capacity of the stack) should be a positive integer. It also specifies that the element that is added to the stack via the push method should be a String object conforming to the format of an email address (string and email are predicates of the language).

2.2 A Multi-DSAL Debug Scenario

Consider the following scenario. During the development of our multi-DSAL application, it is tested and executed against different input sets. On one of the input sets, an unexpected behavior is observed: an exception is thrown from the push(Object) method indicating a validation error. This indicates that the VALIDATE aspect mechanism identified an invalid input argument. However, unexpectedly, the execution (of other threads) does not progress and it seems like the program is stuck. The developer initiates a debug session, ready to investigate the cause of the problem.

The exception was thrown from the push method, thus it becomes the natural suspect and a breakpoint is placed on the method entry. When the breakpoint is reached, the program suspends and waits for additional debugging commands. The developer first asks the multi-DSAL debugger for all the pieces of advice that were applied to this *method-execution* join point. The developer expects the advice of all the aspect mechanisms to be present, but discovers instead that the COOL advice seems to not have been applied. This is surprising, since the program explicitly specifies that push should be synchronized (Listing 4, lines 2-3).

Understanding the Composition   Generally, when debugging a multi-DSAL application, the basic guideline is to understand the feature interactions that are relevant to the portion of code under investigation. The developer should always look for the cause of the problem in the application code, but should also be open to the possibility that the unexpected behavior is a matter of a composition specification. In our case, it should be examined whether or not the unexpected absence of COOL advice originated from the composition. To find this out, the developer uses dedicated debug operations for inspecting the composition.

Join point granularity and join point visibility are two of several features that characterize a reactive aspect mechanism [11]. The join point granularity feature specifies what kinds of join point computations may be intercepted by the aspect mechanism. The granularity of ASPECTJ includes, for example, computations of kinds *method-call*, *method-execution*, *field-set*, etc. The join point visibility feature maps join point computations to actual join point instances. That is, each potential join point in the granularity is classified as either *visible* or *invisible*. For example, the visibility feature of ASPECTJ hides all the join points within the lexical scope of an if pointcut expression.

Based on these abstract features, MDDI defines concrete debug operations: *granularity* and *visibility*. These operations operate on code elements in a particular program. In the ASPECTJ language execution model, each dynamic join point has a corresponding static shadow in the bytecode of the program. Advice code may be inserted at these shadows to modify the behavior of the program [7]. Provided with a code element, e.g., a method, the granularity operation returns all the join point shadows in that method that a particular mechanism may *plausibly* advise. The visibility operation returns the join point shadows in the method that the mechanism may *actually* advise.

Returning to our example scenario, the developer requests from the debugger the join point shadows in push that are visible to COOL. Since COOL advice operate on methods, the *method-execution*(push) shadow is expected to be visible. However, the visibility operation returns an empty shadow set. This means that there are no join point shadows in push that are advisable by COOL. Just to make sure that the *method-execution*(push) shadow is visible to the other mechanisms, the developer asks the multi-DSAL debugger for the shadows in push that are visible to all the mechanisms. The operation returns the expected result: *field-get*(ind), *field-set*(buff), *field-get*(ind), *field-set*(ind), *method-execution*(push).

This means that these five join point shadows are weaving targets for ASPECTJ and VALIDATE. The developer concludes that it is not a coding error that causes the omission of the COOL advice. Rather, it is a design composition decision that prevents the advice from being applied. However, it is not yet clear whether this is caused by the granularity feature, i.e., that all *method-execution* join points are by definition not advisable by COOL, or by the visibility feature, which means that only certain join points of this kind are filtered out. Therefore, the developer asks the debugger for the granularity operation applied to push. An empty set is returned again, which improves somewhat the understanding: COOL may not intercept method executions at all.

Resolving the Bug   Armed with this knowledge, the developer can consult the composition designer to confirm that indeed the granularity of COOL includes join points of kind *method-call* (and not *method-execution*). The COOL mechanism defines two types of advice, lock and unlock, which are executed before and after the synchronized method, respectively. Thus, COOL's lock and unlock advice are inserted in the context of the *caller* method and not in the context of the *callee*.

The developer concludes that this particular organization of the advice is the cause for the bug. When a thread T_i calls push, the lock advice is executed first in the context of the caller. When T_i is allowed to execute push (hence acquiring the lock), the validate advice is executed in the context of the callee. If the argument to push is found to be invalid, an exception is thrown (like in our case). This exception causes the termination of T_i, but without releasing the lock. From there on, any other thread T_j which attempts to call push is blocked. Hence the program enters a deadlock.

The analysis implies that for the program to function properly, the validate advice should execute *before* the lock advice. Indeed one of the feature interactions that a composition designer should solve is so-called *emergent advice ordering* [11]. It is where the designer specifies an order between advice of different mechanisms. However, in our case the desired order cannot be set. An advice order can only be specified when the advice operate on the same join point. Here, lock advice will always execute before validate because a caller's *before* advice precedes any callee's advice. Therefore, it should be first specified that both lock and validate operate on the same join point (be it a *method-call* or a *method-execution*). This is done by modifying the granularity of COOL or that of VALIDATE. Then, the desired advice order should be set, i.e., that validate should occur before lock.

Note that the analysis also suggests that the COOL mechanism should be refined to release an acquired lock upon a thrown exception. Although such a refinement may solve the bug, the proposed solution is still more desirable, because a solution at the composition level is more robust and does not depend on a specific implementation approach.

3. Multi-DSAL Debug Operations

The multi-DSAL debug interface (MDDI) defines debug operations for inspecting a multi-DSAL application at runtime. In this section, the debug operations in MDDI are described in an abstract platform-independent terms. The description is organized in two parts: debug operations for examining the runtime state and behavior of a multi-DSAL application, and debug operations for inspecting the composition specification. In Section 4, the concrete implementation of MDDI for the AWESOME composition framework is presented.

3.1 Examining Runtime State and Behavior

Like a typical debugger, the debugging process of the multi-DSAL debugger is based on stopping the program at a certain breakpoint and then examining the runtime state and behavior using dedicated debug operations.

The AODA [2] defines an aspect-oriented breakpoint model with debug operations that support stopping at a join point shadow in three modes: before, after, and during the execution of the advice woven at that shadow. When a breakpoint is reached, AODA offers three debug operations for inspecting the list of advice:

1. **Inspection of woven advice.** This operation lists advice that are woven at a join point shadow. Note that a woven (applied) advice does not necessarily get executed, e.g., an advice associated with an `if` pointcut in ASPECTJ.

2. **Inspection of executing advice.** This operation lists advice that are currently executing on the stack. Note that several advice may be executing simultaneously, e.g., when an `around` advice calls `proceed` and, while it waits for the call to return, another `before` advice takes control.

3. **Inspection of past advice.** This operation lists advice that were already processed, indicating whether each advice on the list was actually executed or not.

The multi-DSAL debugger adjusts the AODA breakpoint model for debugging multi-DSAL applications. In comparison to the AODA, the multi-DSAL debugger displays the list of advice woven by *all* the aspect mechanisms. The multi-DSAL debugger indicates for each presented advice its originating aspect mechanism and the *type* of the advice. Each aspect mechanism defines its own advice types. ASPECTJ has three advice types, namely `before`, `after`, and `around`. COOL declares two advice types, `lock` and `unlock`, which are executed before and after the invocation of a synchronized method, respectively. The VALIDATE mechanism has a single advice type called `validate`, which is executed before the validated code element. Indicating the advice type and the originating mechanism may help the developer to get a clearer picture of the interactions involved.

Like the AODA, the multi-DSAL debugger produces *mirror objects* for the advice declared in the program. These are objects created during the debug process to reflect the state of corresponding objects in the debugged application [3, 16]. Each advice mirror is linked to the related source code. In ASPECTJ, the mapping is straightforward. Each advice mirror is simply mapped to the related advice construct in the source code. However, when DSALs are involved, this mapping is often implicit. For instance, the COOL advice types, `lock` and `unlock`, are concepts that are a part of the implementation model of COOL, but without an explicit representation in the source code. The COOL language designer should decide to which source code abstractions each advice type is mapped. For instance, a reasonable mapping is to associate a `lock` advice with operations defined in `mutex`, `selfex`, `requires`, and `on_entry` expressions (Listing 4). Therefore, the multi-DSAL debugger provides support for implicit source code mappings of this kind.

3.2 Inspecting the Composition Specification

The other part of MDDI includes operations for investigating the composition specification of a multi-DSAL weaver. These include *granularity* and *visibility* operations for investigating *which* join point shadows within a particular program element an aspect mechanism may affect. A third kind is *advisability* operations for determining *how* the aspect mechanism may affect those shadows.

Granularity Operations The join point granularity feature of an aspect mechanism $\mathcal{M}$, denoted $granularity(\mathcal{M})$, specifies in abstract terms the kinds of join point computations that the mechanism may intercept. For instance, $granularity(\text{COOL})$ includes computations of kind *method-invocation*. This indicates that COOL may affect the program only when methods are invoked. When the mechanism is implemented in the context of a specific environment, the granularity is normalized according to a shared join point scheme (in our case ASPECTJ). A *method-invocation* join point computation in COOL may be mapped to either a *method-call* or a *method-execution* join point in ASPECTJ. Both mapping options are reasonable normalization choices, yet, as illustrated in Section 2, the decision may change the collective behavior. Therefore, the mapping may be subjected to adjustments by the composition designer.

The granularity operation in MDDI is defined in relation to a particular code element in the program, such as a method, a class, or an aspect. The debug operation is of the form:

$$GRANULARITY_{\mathcal{M}} : \textit{Elements} \rightarrow P(\textit{Shadows})$$

Given a code element $\mathcal{C}$ and an aspect mechanism $\mathcal{M}$, the operation returns the join point shadows in $\mathcal{C}$ that are in the granularity of $\mathcal{M}$:

$$GRANULARITY_{\mathcal{M}}(\mathcal{C}) = \{\mathcal{S} \in \mathcal{C}$$
$$| \; shadow(\mathcal{S}) \wedge \mathcal{S}.kind \in granularity(\mathcal{M})\}$$

Note that the operation returns join point shadows, since it relates to code elements and not to the dynamic execution of the program.

As a usage example for this granularity operation, consider the method push defined in the Stack class (Listing 1, lines 5–8). The method includes five join point shadows: a *field-get* and a *field-set* in line 6, another *field-get* and *field-set* in line 7, and a *method-execution* shadow. The granularity operations of the different mechanisms evaluate to:

$$GRANULARITY_{\text{ASPECTJ}}(\texttt{push})$$
$$= \{\textit{field-get}(\texttt{ind}), \textit{field-set}(\texttt{buff}), \textit{field-get}(\texttt{ind}),$$
$$\textit{field-set}(\texttt{ind}), \textit{method-execution}(\texttt{push})\}$$

$$GRANULARITY_{\text{COOL}}(\texttt{push})$$
$$= \{\textit{method-execution}(\texttt{push})\}$$

$$GRANULARITY_{\text{VALIDATE}}(\texttt{push}) = \{\textit{field-set}(\texttt{buff}),$$
$$\textit{field-set}(\texttt{ind}), \textit{method-execution}(\texttt{push})\}$$

Note that the result returned by the COOL granularity operation reflects a change that was made to the composition in order to resolve the bug detected in Section 2. COOL and VALIDATE were reconfigured to operate on the same *method-execution* join points. The granularity of VALIDATE includes join point computations in which input validation makes sense, namely, computations of kinds *method-invocation* (mapped to *method-call* or to *method-execution*), *object-creation* (*constructor-execution*), and *field-assignment* (*field-set*).

Another unified operation, $GRANULARITY(\mathcal{C})$, returns the join point shadows in code element $\mathcal{C}$ that any of the mechanisms may affect. It is the union of all the mechanism-specific granularity features. In the case of push,

$$GRANULARITY(\texttt{push})$$
$$= GRANULARITY_{\text{ASPECTJ}}(\texttt{push})$$

However, should ASPECTJ be excluded from the composition, the resulted set would be different: the *field-get* shadows would not be included, since shadows of this kind are neither part of the granularity of COOL nor of VALIDATE.

Visibility Operations The join point visibility feature of an aspect mechanism classifies join points in the granularity as either *visible* or *invisible*. Invisible join points are not available for advising. The visibility operation in MDDI has the form:

$$VISIBILITY_{\mathcal{M}} : \quad Elements \quad \rightarrow \quad P(Shadows),$$

```
1  public aspect ConditionalTracer {
2    public static boolean trace = false;
3    before() : execution(* BoundedStack.pop())
4    && if(trace) {
5      System.out.println(thisJoinPoint);
6    }
7  }
```

Listing 5. A conditional tracer in ASPECTJ

where $VISIBILITY_{\mathcal{M}}(\mathcal{C})$ denotes the set of join point shadows in $\mathcal{C}$ that are visible to $\mathcal{M}$. A unified visibility operation, $VISIBILITY(\mathcal{C})$, returns the set of shadows in $\mathcal{C}$ that are visible to any of the aspect mechanisms. For a mechanism $\mathcal{M}$ and a code element $\mathcal{C}$, the following proposition holds:

$$VISIBILITY_{\mathcal{M}}(\mathcal{C}) \quad \subseteq \quad GRANULARITY_{\mathcal{M}}(\mathcal{C})$$

To illustrate the difference between granularity and visibility, consider a ConditionalTracer aspect in ASPECTJ (Listing 5). In ASPECTJ by design join point shadows within an if pointcut (line 4) are invisible. Therefore, whereas applying the ASPECTJ granularity operation on the aspect ConditionalTracer results in:

$$GRANULARITY_{\text{ASPECTJ}}(\texttt{ConditionalTracer})$$
$$= \{\textit{field-set}(\texttt{trace}), \textit{advice-execution}(\texttt{before}),$$
$$\textit{field-get}(\texttt{trace}), \textit{method-call}(\texttt{println}), \dots\},$$

the visibility operation returns:

$$VISIBILITY_{\text{ASPECTJ}}(\texttt{ConditionalTracer})$$
$$= \{\textit{field-set}(\texttt{trace}), \textit{advice-execution}(\texttt{before}),$$
$$\textit{method-call}(\texttt{println}), \dots\}.$$

Note that the *field-get*(trace) shadow, which corresponds to the read operation of the Boolean trace field in line 4, is in the granularity but not in the visibility.

Advisability Operations The join point advisability feature defines advising constraints for various types of join points, or even for specific join points [11]. Recall that each mechanism declares one or more advice types. For instance, ASPECTJ defines three types of advice: before, after, and around. By default, an aspect mechanism may apply any type of advice on a visible join point. However, in some cases the composition designer may be interested in restricting the potential effect of a particular aspect mechanism, that is, preventing advice of certain type from being applied at certain join points. For instance, it may be defined that ASPECTJ cannot declare an around advice at executions of COOL's lock and unlock advice. This may be essential in order to prevent ASPECTJ aspects from overriding COOL's synchronization logic.

$ADVISABILITY_{\mathcal{M}}$ lets the developer investigate how an aspect mechanism may affect a particular join point shadow in the program. The operation returns the advice types that the mechanism may apply at the shadow:

$$ADVISABILITY_{\mathcal{M}} : Shadows \rightarrow P(AdviceTypes)$$

Given an aspect mechanism $\mathcal{M}$ and a shadow $\mathcal{S}$, the advisability operation is defined by:

$$ADVISABILITY_{\mathcal{M}}(\mathcal{S}) = \{T \in \mathcal{M}$$
$$| adviceType(T) \wedge applicable(T, \mathcal{S})\}$$

Continuing the example, if $\mathcal{S}$ is $advice\text{-}execution(\texttt{lock})$ shadow in COOL, then its advisability in relation to ASPECTJ would be:

$$ADVISABILITY_{\text{ASPECTJ}}(advice\text{-}execution(\texttt{lock})) =$$
$$= \{\text{before}, \text{after}\}$$

This means that ASPECTJ may only apply `before` or `after` advice at a `lock` execution. Another unified advisability operation, $ADVISABILITY(\mathcal{S})$, returns the advice types that may be added by any aspect mechanism. In a configuration that includes ASPECTJ, COOL, and VALIDATE,

$$ADVISABILITY(advice\text{-}execution(\texttt{lock})) =$$
$$= ADVISABILITY_{\text{ASPECTJ}}(advice\text{-}execution(\texttt{lock}))$$

The same result is returned because *advice-execution* join points are not in the granularity of COOL nor of VALIDATE, hence by specification they cannot affect the join point.

4. MDDI Implementation

MDDI is implemented as a multi-DSAL extension to AJDI, a debug interace for aspect-oriented applications introduced in the AODA. AJDI itself is an extension to the Java Debug Interface (JDI). The implementation of MDDI requires debug information, which should be attached to the target multi-DSAL application. A common technique which we use is to add debug attributes to the class files of the application. We formulate the debug attributes that are needed for implementing the MDDI operations. For the operations that query the runtime state, we extend existing AODA debug attributes. For the composition specification operations, we define new debug attributes.

The debug attributes should be added to the class files of the application during the weaving process. In a multi-DSAL setup, the weaving process is controlled by an aspect composition framework. Since none of the existing frameworks handles debugging as part of its weaving process, we extend the AWESOME composition framework for that purpose.

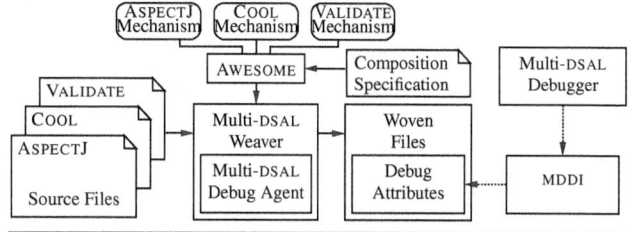

Figure 1. The multi-DSAL debugging process

The overall multi-DSAL debug process over AWESOME is illustrated in Figure 1. AWESOME is provided with multiple aspect mechanisms and with a composition specification, and outputs a single multi-DSAL weaver. AWESOME is customized such that the produced weaver is embedded with a multi-DSAL debug agent. The weaver is provided with an application written in multiple aspect languages, and during the weaving process the agent adds the dedicated debug attributes to the woven class files of the application. These attributes are then consumed by MDDI, which is utilized by the multi-DSAL debugger.

The embedded multi-DSAL debug agent is significantly different than that of AODA. In AODA, in order to add debug support for a particular aspect language, one must implement an appropriate debug agent. This is a difficult task since it requires to understand the structure of the debug attributes, as well as knowing how to embed them in the resulting class files. In contrast, the multi-DSAL debug agent that is added to AWESOME relieves the designer of the aspect mechanism from this tedious implementation task. Instead, the process of adding the debug attributes is handled by the agent. The information needed for producing the attributes that enable the composition operations is extracted by the agent from the composition specification. The information needed for the attributes of the state and behavior operations is fetched from dedicated interfaces that should be implemented by the developer of each mechanism.

In the rest of this section, we present the implementation of the debug operations for inspecting the composition specification, and for investigating the runtime state and behavior. For each kind of operation, we describe the corresponding MDDI elements, and the changes made to the AWESOME weaving process and to AJDI.

4.1 Composition Specification Operations

MDDI extends AJDI with several methods and types for inspecting the composition specification. The methods, listed here, realize the debug operations that were described in Section 3.

```
1  JoinPointComputation[] *.granularity();
2  JoinPointComputation[] *.granularity(Mechanism);
3  JoinPointComputation[] *.visibility();
4  JoinPointComputation[] *.visibility(Mechanism);
5  AdviceType[] JoinPointComputation.advisability();
6  AdviceType[] JoinPointComputation.advisability(Mechanism);
```

The methods let the debugger inspect the granularity, visibility, and advisability of the composition in relation to specific program elements. Each of the granularity or visibility methods (lines 1-4) is added to the AJDI elements `ClassType`, `Aspect`, and `Method`. The first granularity method (line 1) returns the granularity with respect to all aspect mechanisms. The second (line 2) returns the granularity in relation to a specific mechanism. The same applies to the visibility methods (lines 3-4). The advisability methods operate on a join point computation (shadow). The first method (line 5) returns all the advice types that may be applied at the shadow, of all aspect mechanisms. The second method (line 6) returns the advice types of a specific mechanism.

The implementation of the methods is facilitated by three debug attributes that are added to the woven class files of the multi-DSAL application during the weaving process: `GranularityAttribute`, `VisibilityAttribute`, and `AdvisabilityAttribute`.

GranularityAttribute During the extended AWESOME weaving process, the granularity of each method, class, or aspect, is calculated with respect to each aspect mechanism in the composition. The result is saved in a debug attribute (`GranularityAttribute`) that is attached to each corresponding code element in the woven class files. The following pseudo code shows the calculation of the granularity attribute for a method or a class element C in the base system:

```
1  GranularityAttribute att;
2  Shadow[] shadows = reify(C);
3  foreach s in shadows
4    att.append(s);
5    foreach mech in mechanisms
6      if( granularity(mech) includes s.kind )
7        att.append(mech);
8    endforeach
9    att.append(newline);
10 endforeach
```

The reify method in line 2 returns all the join point shadows in C. In line 4, the signature of each shadow is appended to the debug attribute (a debug attribute is simply a string that is later added to a class file). Afterward, we check for each of the mechanisms in the composition whether its granularity includes the kind of the current shadow (lines 5-6). If so, the name of the mechanism is written to the attribute (line 7). By that, we are able to tell, for each of the shadows in C, to which of the granularities of the different aspect mechanisms it belongs. We may also infer the shadows that do not belong to any granularity.

This calculation works for methods and classes in the base system. The calculation of the granularity attribute for aspects is slightly different. For an aspect A, the second line in the calculation is replaced by the line:

```
2  Shadow[] shadows = exposed_shadows(A);
```

An aspect language, in particular a domain-specific one, may operate in a higher level of abstraction. As a result,

some of the shadows of its aspects may be considered *internal*. It is the responsibility of the composition designer to decide which shadows in the aspects of each mechanism should be exposed for the use of others. For instance, a COOL coordinator reads and writes to local conditional and ordinary variables, and to fields of the coordinated object. Therefore, it is reasonable to expose in a coordinator the corresponding *field-get* and *field-set* shadows. However, the designer may decide not to expose the *constructor-execution* and *initialization* computations because they do not reflect COOL's visible operation process. Hence, the controlled `exposed_shadows` method is used instead of `reify`. The method returns all the shadows in the aspect A that the designer decided to expose.

VisibilityAttribute The calculation of the visibility attribute is similar to that of the granularity attribute. For a given program element, all its shadows are first retrieved (either by `reify` or by `exposed_shadows`). Then, for each shadow and aspect mechanism, it is checked whether or not the shadow is in the *visibility* of the mechanism.

The check is made against the composition specification, which is available during the AWESOME weaving process. The designer of each aspect mechanism defines the granularity, i.e., the kinds of join points that the mechanism may potentially affect. The designer also provides, for each join point kind in the granularity, a predicate that tells in which circumstances join points of this kind are not visible.

AdvisabilityAttribute This attribute indicates, for each code element to which it is attached, the advice types that may affect the visible join point shadows in the element. Each line in the attribute describes the advisability of a particular visible shadow. It holds the shadow's signature, and a list of the advice types that may be applied to it.

Also here, the calculation of the attribute is based on consulting the composition specification. The composition designer defines in the composition specification *advisability restrictions*. Each restriction consists of a join point kind, and a list of the disallowed advice types. For example, consider the following restriction:

advice-execution(validate)	aspectj.around

This restriction specifies that an ASPECTJ `around` advice cannot be applied at executions of a `validate` advice. The restriction prevents the `validate` advice from being overridden.

4.2 Runtime State and Behavior Operations

In this section we describe the modifications made in order to implement the part of MDDI that deals with the inspection of runtime state and behavior.

Extending the AspectAttribute An extended AODA debug attribute called `AspectAttribute` is attached to each class file that represents an aspect of any mechanism. This debug attribute includes general information about the aspect (e.g., the defining mechanism), and about the different advice that it defines (e.g., their type and source code locations). The attribute is generated by the multi-DSAL debug agent. For that, the agent queries each mechanism for information about its aspects via an extended AWESOME API, which is described next.

Extending the Awesome API In AWESOME, the interface IMechanism represents an abstract aspect mechanism. IMechanism is implemented by each of the concrete aspect mechanisms in the composition. We extended IMechanism with several methods needed by the multi-DSAL debug agent to retrieve structural information about aspects in the application. Examples of methods that were added are:

```
1 String getName();
2 boolean handledByMe(Aspect azpect);
3 List<IEffect> getEffects(Aspect azpect);
```

The debug agent, when producing an AspectAttribute for a particular aspect, first calls the handledByMe method of each mechanism for determining to which of them the aspect belongs. Then, information is retrieved from the relevant mechanism, e.g., the name of the mechanism (by calling getName), and the list of the effects (advice) that the mechanism may apply to program code (via method getEffects).

The interface IEffect is also extended:

```
1 AdviceType getType();
2 ISourceLocation[] getSourceLocations();
```

The first method returns the type of the advice. For example, it returns lock or unlock for a COOL advice. The second method returns the locations in the source code to which the advice is mapped. The method returns an array type since in some cases an advice may be mapped to several different locations in the source code (recall Section 3.1).

The author of each aspect mechanism must implement these methods to enable the creation of the debug attributes. However, the implementation effort is reasonable, since the data that the methods need is already required for the weaving process. In our multi-DSAL composition example, a total addition of 25 lines-of-code were needed for the ASPECTJ mechanism to be debuggable; for the COOL mechanism 35 new lines-of-code were added, and making VALIDATE debuggable required 30 lines-of-code.

5. Evaluation

To evaluate the MDDI implementation we built a simple, command line, AWESOMEDEBUGGER, capable of debugging multi-DSAL programs. We demonstrate the debugging process on the Stack example (Section 2).

5.1 Blame Assignment

In the example, an exception was thrown from the push method and then the program deadlocked. Here, we replay the debugging scenario of Section 2, and illustrate it concretely using the AWESOMEDEBUGGER.

We use the debugger to observe that COOL related advice are not applied at the push method. Next, we investigate whether the absence of the advice is a matter of the composition specification or not. We inspect the shadows in push that are visible to COOL:

```
(awdb) show visibilty COOL
[ID] [Joinpoint type] [Source location]
-------------------------------------------
```

An empty shadow set is displayed. We proceed to inspect the shadows in push that are visible to all the mechanisms:

```
(awdb) show visibility
[ID] [Joinpoint type] [Source location]
-------------------------------------------
0 Field Get Stack.java:6
1 Field Set Stack.java:6
2 Field Get Stack.java:7
3 Field Set Stack.java:7
4 Method Execution Stack.java:5
```

We then use the granularity operation to understand *why* the *method-execution* shadow is not visible to COOL:

```
(awdb) show granularity COOL
[ID] [Joinpoint type] [Source location]
-------------------------------------------
```

An empty set is displayed again. We conclude that the reason that COOL advice are missing is because the COOL mechanism was not designed to affect *method-execution* join point shadows. Once the cause for the bug is understood and we know whom to blame, we can report our findings to the composition designer. The fix is straightforward: the granularity of COOL is modified, and an appropriate advice order is set.

5.2 Debugging Foreign Advising

Foreign advising [11] refers to the case where an aspect of one mechanism advises join points in foreign aspects, i.e., aspects that belong to other mechanisms. The scope pointcut defined in the Tracer aspect (Listing 2) includes *advice-execution* join points contained in other foreign aspects, e.g., executions of COOL's lock and unlock advice. When applying an advice *around* join points in the scope, Tracer calls proceed (line 8). This is essential in order to resume the execution of the traced join points.

Consider a case where Tracer defines another advice that only monitors executions of COOL's unlock advice; and the call to proceed is mistakenly omitted. As a result, the unlock advice is not executed and thus the acquired lock is not released. The next thread that requests the lock is halted, and eventually the program may enter a deadlock.

When attaching the debugger to the deadlocked program we see the following stack trace in one of the halted threads:

```
(awdb) where
[0] Stack.pop Stack.java:13
[1] WriteReadThread.accessBuffer WriteReadThread.java:14
[2] BufferClientThread.run BufferClientThread.java:8
```

We further examine the advice that affect the execution of the pop method (in frame 0):

```
(awdb) show advice
[Aspect] [Location] [Type] [Skipped] [Mechanism]
-------------------------------------------
cool.StackCoord (2, 3, 13, 14) Lock 0 COOL
aspectj.Tracer (3) BEFORE 0 AJ
aspectj.Tracer (6) AROUND 0 AJ
aspectj.Tracer (10) AFTER 0 AJ
cool.StackCoord (2, 3, 15) Unlock 1 COOL
```

The Skipped column indicates whether an advice was executed or skipped ('0' means executed, '1' means skipped). We can see (in the last line) that the COOL unlock advice was skipped. We can either fix our around advice to always proceed, or change the composition specification so that COOL operations cannot be advised by an around advice.

5.3 Debugging Co-Advising

Co-advising [11] refers to the case where advice belonging to different mechanisms are applied at the same join point. Often, a specific advice order should be set or the program may behave unexpectedly. For instance, if ASPECTJ advice are allowed to execute before COOL's lock advice or after COOL's unlock advice, then the ASPECTJ advice may unsafely access program resources.

To illustrate such a situation, suppose we add a new top method to class Stack:

```
Object top() {
    return buf[ind-1];
}
```

Calling top from such an ASPECTJ advice can yield a wrong result or an ArrayIndexOutOfBoundsException, since the access of both buf and ind is not synchronized.

When examining the advice executed at top we get:

```
(awdb) show advice
[Aspect] [Location] [Type] [Skipped] [Mechanism]
-------------------------------------------
aspectj.Tracer (3) BEFORE 0 AJ
cool.StackCoord (2, 3, 13, 14) Lock 0 COOL
aspectj.Tracer (6) AROUND 0 AJ
cool.StackCoord (2, 3, 15) Unlock 0 COOL
aspectj.Tracer (10) AFTER 0 AJ
```

It may be inferred that the cause for the problem is an incorrect advice execution order that allows unsafe stack accesses. Hence we change the specification and set lock (unlock) to execute before (after) any ASPECTJ advice.

5.4 Debugging Advice Code

Another source for bugs is coding errors in the base program or in the aspects of the different DSALs. As an example, the coordinator in Listing 6 contains a simple bug: len is mistakenly decremented instead of being incremented (line 9). As a result, full is never set to true

```
1  coordinator Stack {
2    selfex {push, pop};
3    mutex {push, pop};
4    int len=0;
5    condition full=false, empty=true;
6    push: requires !full;
7    on_exit {
8      empty=false;
9      len--;
10     if (len==buf.length) full=true;
11   }
12   pop: requires !empty;
13   on_entry { len--; }
14   on_exit {
15     full=false;
16     if (len==0) empty=true;
17   }
18 }
```

Listing 6. Stack coordinator with a bug

(line 10). The requires condition in line 6 is thus always met, allowing new elements to always be added to the stack. However, buff has a limited capacity and an ArrayIndexOutOfBoundsException will eventually be thrown.

We suspect that the problem lies in some advice code. We begin with checking the advice applied at the push method:

```
(awdb) show advice
[Aspect] [Location] [Type] [Skipped] [Mechanism]
-------------------------------------------
validator.Stack (4) Validate 0 Validator
cool.StackCoord (2, 3, 6) Lock 0 COOL
aspectj.Tracer (3) BEFORE 0 AJ
aspectj.Tracer (6) AROUND 0 AJ
aspectj.Tracer (10) AFTER 0 AJ
cool.StackCoord (2, 3, 7) Unlock 0 COOL
```

The Location column links each advice to the corresponding source code (the numbers in parenthesis indicate the source lines relevant for each advice). The information helps in locating the specific advice code segments where the bug should be searched for. We check the code of each advice for errors, and eventually the bug is located in the on_exit declaration of the unlock advice.

6. Related Work

We first discuss works related to debugging of AOP programs. We then discuss the composition of multiple aspect mechanisms.

AOP debugging The debugging of AOP programs has been considered before. One approach is omniscient debugging [19]. Under this kind of debugger, a bytecode level trace is generated for the program execution. The trace includes synthetic code, woven advice, and other technology specific entities. Annotations on the trace indicate the origin of the bytecode, whether it is base code, residue or advice applications. While this kind of debugging can handle the execution of multiple aspects, it does not offer source level debugging, nor does it aid in solving problems that result from feature interactions between aspects or from the composition specification.

Another debugging approach used by Wicca [5] is providing a source-level representation of the woven source code. The representation is generated by a dynamic source weaver. However, even for the case of a single AOP language, this approach is limited, because the code presented is not the original source code written by the developer but the one generated by the source weaver. It also does not provide debugging in terms of source level abstractions, such as aspects and advice. In the case of a multi-DSAL program, a translation of the different source files to a common base language is required, which brings back the problems related to the composition of multiple aspect mechanisms [8].

Unlike Wicca, AODA [2] enables debugging that is aware of AOP source level abstractions, such as aspects and advice. It features a modular design that allows designing new debug agents to support different AOP languages. However, it does not address the unique problems presented by multi-DSAL programs. First, it does not provide a way for examining the composition specification. Second, it does not recognize AOP artifacts in the context of the original mechanisms, but only in a common base language abstraction (for example, when COOL coordinators are represented as ASPECTJ aspects). In addition, developing a new debug agent for a new mechanism is a difficult task, requiring implementation knowledge of AODA itself and how to add debug attributes to class files.

In comparison, our debugging infrastructure supports debugging multi-DSAL programs with source level abstractions in the context of each mechanism, including the inspection of the composition specification. We also provide a generic way to support debugging of new mechanisms without having to dive into the details of the debug attributes or class file structure.

Composition Frameworks Pluggable AOP [8] introduced the problem of aspect language extension compositions. The work presents a framework for third-party composition of arbitrary dynamic aspect mechanisms into an AOP interpreter.

AWESOME [10] is a composition framework that directly weaves DSAL code without an intermediate translation to a common base language. AWESOME provides a default composition specification. For example, by default aspects will advise a foreign aspect by advising only JAVA statements within its source code. AWESOME allows the composition designer to specify how to resolve feature interactions between aspect mechanisms in case the default specification is not the desired one. While AWESOME addresses the composition problem, it does not deal with the problem of debugging the woven multi-DSAL programs. The developer is required to use regular debugging tools, such as the JAVA debugger (jdb). However, such tools expose the synthetic

constructs of AWESOME and of the mechanisms, and they also do not provide debugging in terms of AOP source level abstractions.

A different approach for multi-DSAL composition is presented by Dinkelaker et al. [4]. They propose an architecture for embedded DSLs (EDSLs) that makes use of meta-object protocols and aspect-oriented concepts to support crosscutting composition of EDSLs. This enables writing modularized EDSL programs where each program addresses one concern. Their proposed architecture is implemented in Groovy, and like AWESOME, the architecture does not address the debugging problem at all, relying instead on the standard Groovy debugging tools.

7. Conclusion

In order for DSALs to be used in practice, multi-DSAL development has to be cost-effective. Cost effectiveness is a requirement that applies not only to the implementation of DSALs, but just as much to the effective use of these DSALs [15]. While significant progress has been made on the language implementation front, less attention has been given to making the development of applications with multiple DSALs practical.

Effective development of a multi-DSAL application requires appropriate tool support. One standard tool is a dedicated debugger. A multi-DSAL debugger should support the inspection of a running application in terms of the AOP abstractions introduced by the different DSALs, as well as their collaborative interaction. Additionally, the debugger should support inspection of the composition specification, since the composition of the various aspect mechanisms itself may be the source for unexpected behavior in the composed program.

In this paper the unique problems associated with debugging multi-DSAL applications were illustrated. A multi-DSAL debug interface (MDDI) was specified, and a corresponding implementation for the AWESOME composition framework was presented. The different implementation parts of MDDI include the formulation of dedicated debug attributes, and a generic multi-DSAL debug agent that is integrated into the AWESOME weaving process. MDDI consumes the debug attributes and offers a set of debug operations to be used by a multi-DSAL debugger. An AWESOMEDEBUGGER command line tool was implemented to validate the overall debug infrastructure. The tool was used to analyze the source of different bugs that may be found in multi-DSAL programs.

We have focused on the debugging of a dominant family of reactive aspect mechanisms known as join point and advice [9]. The multi-DSAL debug infrastructure was implemented for an ASPECTJ-based environment. Yet, a major portion of the implementation may be reused in other setups as well. For example, MDDI may be utilized in a JBoss AOP environment [18]. For that, one would need to implement a multi-DSAL debug agent that provides the defined debug information to MDDI. While the multi-DSAL debug agent in AWESOME is integrated into the weaver, the JBoss debug agent will be a remote agent included in the JBoss AOP runtime, similar to the approach taken in the AODA [2]. Debugging other non-reactive aspect mechanisms is a topic left for future work.

References

[1] Y. Apter, D. H. Lorenz, and O. Mishali. Toward debugging programs written in multiple domain specific aspect languages. In *Proceedings of the 6th AOSD Workshop on Domain-Specific Aspects Languages (DSAL'11)*, Porto de Galinhas, Brazil, 2011. ACM.

[2] W. D. Borger, B. Lagaisse, and W. Joosen. A generic and reflective debugging architecture to support runtime visibility and traceability of aspects. In *Proceedings of the 8th International Conference on Aspect-Oriented Software Development (AOSD'09)*, pages 173–184, Charlottesville, Virginia, USA, March 2009. ACM.

[3] G. Bracha and D. Ungar. Mirrors: Design principles for meta-level facilities of object-oriented programming languages. In *Proceedings of the 19th Annual ACM SIGPLAN Conference on Object-Oriented Programming Systems, Languages, and Applications (OOPSLA'04)*, pages 331–344, Vancouver, British Columbia, Canada, October 2004.

[4] T. Dinkelaker, M. Eichberg, and M. Mezini. An architecture for composing embedded domain-specific languages. In *Proceedings of the 9th International Conference on Aspect-Oriented Software Development (AOSD'10)*, pages 49–60, Rennes and Saint-Malo, France, 2010. ACM.

[5] M. Eaddy, A. Aho, W. Hu, P. McDonald, and J. Burger. Debugging aspect-enabled programs. In *Proceedings of the 6th International Symposium on Software Composition (SC'07)*, number 4829 in Lecture Notes in Computer Science, pages 200–215. Springer Verlag, 2007.

[6] W. Havinga, L. Bergmans, and M. Akşit. Prototyping and composing aspect languages: using an aspect interpreter framework. In *Proceedings of the 22nd European Conference on Object-Oriented Programming (ECOOP'08)*, number 5142 in Lecture Notes in Computer Science, pages 180–206, Paphos, Cyprus, July 2008. Springer Verlag.

[7] E. Hilsdale and J. Hugunin. Advice weaving in AspectJ. In *Proceedings of the 3rd International Conference on Aspect-Oriented Software Development (AOSD'04)*, pages 26–35, Lancaster, UK, March 2004. ACM.

[8] S. Kojarski and D. H. Lorenz. Pluggable AOP: Designing aspect mechanisms for third-party composition. In *Proceedings of the 20th Annual ACM SIGPLAN Conference on Object-Oriented Programming Systems, Languages, and Applications (OOPSLA'05)*, pages 247–263, San Diego, CA, USA, October 2005. ACM Press.

[9] S. Kojarski and D. H. Lorenz. Modeling aspect mechanisms: A top-down approach. In *Proceedings of the 28th International Conference on Software Engineering (ICSE'06)*, pages 212–221, Shanghai, China, May 2006. ACM Press.

[10] S. Kojarski and D. H. Lorenz. Awesome: An aspect co-weaving system for composing multiple aspect-oriented extensions. In OOPSLA'07 [17], pages 515–534.

[11] S. Kojarski and D. H. Lorenz. Identifying feature interaction in aspect-oriented frameworks. In *Proceedings of the 29th International Conference on Software Engineering (ICSE'07)*, pages 147–157, Minneapolis, MN, May 2007. IEEE Computer Society.

[12] C. V. Lopes. *D: A Language Framework for Distributed Programming*. PhD thesis, Northeastern University, 1997.

[13] C. V. Lopes and G. Kiczales. D: A language framework for distributed programming. Technical Report SPL97-010, Xerox PARC, Palo Alto, CA, USA, Feb. 1997.

[14] D. H. Lorenz and O. Mishali. Spectackle: Toward a specification-based DSAL composition process. In *Proceedings of the 7th AOSD Workshop on Domain-Specific Aspects Languages (DSAL'12)*, Potsdam, Germany, March 2012. ACM.

[15] D. H. Lorenz and B. Rosenan. Cedalion: A language for language oriented programming. In *Proceedings of the 26th Annual ACM SIGPLAN Conference on Object-Oriented Programming Systems, Languages, and Applications (OOPSLA'11)*, pages 733–752, Portland, Oregon, USA, October 2011. ACM.

[16] D. H. Lorenz and J. Vlissides. Pluggable reflection: Decoupling meta-interface and implementation. In *Proceedings of the 25th International Conference on Software Engineering (ICSE'03)*, pages 3–13, Portland, Oregon, May 2003. IEEE Computer Society.

[17] *Proceedings of the 22nd Annual ACM SIGPLAN Conference on Object-Oriented Programming Systems, Languages, and Applications (OOPSLA'07)*, Montreal, Canada, October 2007. ACM Press.

[18] R. Pawlak, J.-P. Retaillé, and L. Seinturier. *Foundations of AOP for J2EE Development*. APress, 2005.

[19] G. Pothier, Éric Tanter, and J. Piquer. Scalable omniscient debugging. In OOPSLA'07 [17], pages 535–552.

[20] É. Tanter. Aspects of composition in the Reflex AOP kernel. In *Proceedings of the 5th International Symposium on Software Composition (SC'06)*, number 4089 in Lecture Notes in Computer Science, pages 98–113, Vienna, Austria, March 2006. Springer Verlag.

A Fine-Grained Debugger for Aspect-Oriented Programming

Haihan Yin, Christoph Bockisch, Mehmet Akşit

Software Engineering group, University of Twente, 7500 AE Enschede, the Netherlands
{h.yin, c.m.bockisch, m.aksit}@cs.utwente.nl

Abstract

To increase modularity, aspect-oriented programming provides a mechanism based on implicit invocation: An aspect can influence runtime behavior of other modules without the need that these modules refer to the aspect. Recent studies show that a significant part of reported bugs in aspect-oriented programs are caused exactly by this implicitness. These bugs are difficult to detect because aspect-oriented source code elements and their locations are transformed or even lost after compilation. We investigate four dedicated fault models and identify ten tasks that a debugger should be able to perform for detecting aspect-orientation-specific faults. We show that existing debuggers are not powerful enough to support all identified tasks because the aspect-oriented abstractions are lost after compilation.

This paper describes the design and implementation of a debugger for aspect-oriented languages using a dedicated intermediate representation preserving the abstraction level of aspect-oriented source code. We define a debugging model which is aware of aspect-oriented concepts. Based on the model, we implement a user interface with functionalities supporting the identified tasks, like visualizing pointcut evaluation and program composition.

Categories and Subject Descriptors   D.2.5 [*Testing and Debugging*]: Debugging aids;   D.3.2 [*Language Classifications*]: Very high-level languages

General Terms   Language, Design

Keywords   Debugger, AOP, visualization, advanced-dispatching, fine-grained intermediate representation

1. Introduction

Aspect-oriented programming (AOP) allows programmers to modularize concerns which would be crosscutting in object-oriented programs into separate *aspect*s. An aspect can define functionality *and* when it must be executed, i.e., other modules do not have to explicitly call this functionality. Due to this implicitness, it is not always obvious where and in which ways aspects apply during the program execution. A recent study carried out by Ferrari et al. [12] focuses on the fault-proneness in evolving aspect-oriented programs. They investigated the aspect-oriented (AO) versions of three medium-sized applications. It shows that 42 out of 104 reported AOP-related faults were due to the lack of awareness of interactions between aspects and other modules.

For locating faults in aspect-oriented programs, a programmer can inspect the source code and browse static relationships. This is supported by tools like the AspectJ Development Tools (AJDT)[1] and Asbro [17]. To detect a fault in this way, programmers are required to inspect multiple files and mentally construct the dynamic program composition, which is a tedious and time-consuming task. Furthermore, connections between aspects and other modules are often based on runtime states which cannot be presented by static tools. Debuggers are, thus, needed for inspecting to the runtime state to help programmers understanding the program behavior and eventually finding a fault.

Aspect-oriented languages are nowadays compiled to the intermediate representation (IR) of an established non-AO language; this usually entails transforming code already provided in that IR [3], a compilation strategy often called *weaving*. A typical example is AspectJ which is compiled to Java bytecode.

Because of that approach, it is possible to use a debugger existing for the underlying non-AO language, like the Java debugger in the case of AspectJ. But a consequence of that weaving approach is that the aspect-oriented source code is compiled to an IR whose abstractions reflect the module concepts of the so-called base language, but not those of the AOP language. Therefore, what is inspected in the described approach is actually the woven and transformed code instead of the source code.

Several research works discuss AOP debuggers to provide information closer to the source code, such as the composite source code in Wicca [11], the aspect-aware break-

---

[1] See http://www.eclipse.org/ajdt/.

point model in AODA [10], or the identified AOP activities in TOD [18]. Nevertheless, all of these debuggers use only the woven IR of the underlying language. AOP-specific abstractions, such as aspect-precedence declarations, and their locations in the source code are partially or even entirely lost after compilation.

While, e.g., the AspectJ language provides runtime-visible annotations that can represent all aspect-oriented source constructs, these annotations are not suitable to alleviate the above mentioned limitations. Also in the presence of these annotations, bytecode is woven and it is not always possible to retrieve the annotations that have influenced certain instructions during debugging.

In this paper, we introduce our concept and implementation of a dedicated debugger for AO programs which is able to support locating all types of dynamic AO-related faults identified in previous research like the one by Ferrari, mentioned above. Our debugger is aware of aspect-oriented concepts and presents runtime states in terms of source level abstractions, e.g., pointcuts and advices. It allows programmers to perform various tasks specific to debugging aspect-oriented constructs. Examples of such tasks are inspecting an aspect-aware call stack, locating AO constructs in source code, excluding AO definitions at runtime, etc. Our debugger is integrated into Eclipse and provides visualizations illustrating, e.g., pointcut evaluation and advice composition.

2. Problem Analysis and Requirements

Recently fault models for AOP languages have been researched with the target to systematically generate tests which execute all potentially faulting program elements. We can use the results of these studies to derive the capabilities required from a debugger to locate all faults in a program related to (dynamic) features of aspect-orientation. In the following subsections, we summarize the work on AO fault models, discuss tasks required to localize the faults, evaluate the capabilities of existing debuggers and formulate requirements for a debugger with full support for AOP.

2.1 AOP Fault Models

We have investigated four fault models proposed in the literature and summarize them in table 1. In our study, we exclude faults related to static features like inter-type declarations because the static code inspection tools offered by modern development tools like the AJDT are already sufficient for localizing these faults. The first column shows the fault model by Alexander et al. [1] which contains examples of AOP-specific faults, like incorrect pointcut strength. Ceccato et al. [16] extend this model with three types concerning exceptional control flow and inter-type declarations (ITD). Ferrari et al. [13] proposed a fault model, presented in the second column, reflecting where a fault originates, i.e., in pointcuts, advices, ITDs or the base program. Column three shows the fault model of Baekken [4] which follows a simi-

lar approach; he focuses on AspectJ [15] programs and systematically considers its syntactic elements as potential fault origins. In the last column, we define a category name summarizing the fault kinds described in literature and presented in the same row.

2.2 Detecting faults

When a programmer encounters an error during the execution of an AspectJ program, this can be caused by a faults in one of the categories presented in the previous sub-section. But the observed error does not yet tell the programmer what the actual fault is. To figure this out, a debugger should be applied. In the following, we discuss tasks to be provided by an ideal debugger for identifying a fault in each of the fault categories. We tag these tasks in the format "**T#**".

If a pointcut-advice definition is faulty, the programmer needs to (**T1**) set a breakpoint at the join point[2], rerun the program, analyze program states, and eventually (**T2**) locate faulty constructs.

2.2.1 Detecting pointcut-related faults

If the programmer finds out that an advice is unexpectedly executed or not executed, she knows that the pointcut evaluated to the wrong value at one join point. To understand the exact cause why the pointcut matches or fails to match, the programmer needs to further (**T3**) evaluate sub-expressions of this pointcut and to check the structure of the pointcut. As the right-most column in table 1 shows, possible causes are *incorrect pointcut composition*, *incorrect pattern*, *incorrect designator*, or *incorrect context*.

Incorrect pointcut composition First, the programmer can consider the correctness of the pointcut structure which may include references to named pointcuts and composition operators. To inspect the actual pointcut expression that is evaluated, pointcut references must be (**T4**) substituted with their definition. To check the composition operators &&, ||, and !, the programmer needs to (**T3**) determine the evaluation result of sub-expressions, perform further evaluations on them and check whether the structure violates the intention.

Incorrect pattern From the above inspection, it may turn out that a pointcut designator like **call** or **get**, which defines a pattern matching a signature, is wrong. Patterns are composed of sub-patterns; thus, the programmer needs to (**T5**) evaluate each sub-pattern to find the actual fault. As an example, consider the AspectJ pattern $*$ Customer.payFor($*$); it matches any method named payFor in the Customer class that takes one argument with any type and returns any type. When debugging the evaluation of that pattern at a join point with the signature **void** Customer.payFor(**int**, **boolean**), a programmer should be able to determine that the parameters sub-pattern causes the pattern to fail.

---

[2] In this paper, we use the term *join point* to refer to a code location (often also called join-point shadow) and to its execution.

Alexander et al. (extended by Ceccato et al.)	Ferrari et al.	Baekken	Category
	Advice bound to incorrect pointcut	Incorrect or missing composition operator Inappropriate or missing pointcut reference	**Incorrect pointcut composition**
Incorrect strength in pointcut patterns	Incorrect matching based on exception throwing patterns Base program does not offer required join points	Incorrect method/ constructor/ field/ type/ modifier/ identifier/ parameter/ annotation pattern	**Incorrect pattern**
	Incorrect use of primitive pointcut designators	Mixed up pointcuts method call and execution, object construction and initialization, cflow and cflowbelow, this and target	**Incorrect designator**
	Incorrect matching based on dynamic values and events	Incorrect arguments to pointcuts this/ target/ args/ cflow/ cflowbelow/ if/ within/ withincode	**Incorrect context**
Incorrect aspect precedence	Incorrect advice-type specification	Incorrect advice type	**Incorrect composition control**
Incorrect changes in control dependencies Incorrect changes in exceptional control flow (extended)	Incorrect control or data flow due to execution of the original join point Infinite loops resulting from interactions among advices	Incorrect or missing position of proceed Incorrect arguments to proceed	**Incorrect flow change**
Failure to establish expected postconditions Failure to preserve state invariants	Incorrect advice logic, violating invariants and failing to establish expected postconditions		**Violated requirements**

Table 1. A systematic fault model for aspect-oriented programs

Incorrect designator The programmer may also encircle the fault in a pointcut designator specifying a dynamic condition instead of a pattern, like *target* constraining the type of a runtime value, or *cflow* specifying the currently executing methods. Then the programmer needs to (**T6**) check the runtime values on which the evaluation of that pointcut designator depends; or she must (**T7**) inspect the current control flow, i.e., the join points which are currently executing on the stack.

Incorrect context When a pointcut designator depends on a runtime value and the evaluation result is unexpected, the programmer needs to (**T6**) inspect the context value to which the designator refers and (**T3**) evaluate the restriction on this value specified by the pointcut designator. As an example, consider the pointcut sub-expression target(Customer); the callee object is required to be an instance of the type Customer. The programmer must be able to inspect the value and type of the callee object to determine if the pointcut is specified wrongly or the program uses the wrong object.

2.2.2 Detecting advice-related faults

An error can also occur when an advice is neither missing nor redundant at a join point but the advice does not behave as expected. Possible faults leading to such an error are *incorrect program composition*, *incorrect flow change* and *violated requirements*.

Incorrect program composition There are three types of composition control in AspectJ influencing the execution order of advices at shared join points: advice-type specification, precedence declaration and lexical order. Advice-type specification, e.g., the keywords before or after, define the order between advices relative to the join point. Precedence declaration (declare precedence) defines the partial order between different aspects. The precedence of advice defined in the same aspect is determined by their lexical order.

To detect this type of fault, a programmer needs to (**T8**) inspect how programs are composed at a join point, be able to (**T9**) reason about the composition controls affecting that composition, and (**T2**) locate the definition of the composition controls.

Incorrect flow change The execution of an advice at a join point may alter the control flow or the data flow at that join point. Take the around advice as an example: It can skip the join point execution or modify runtime values from the dynamic context of the join point by invoking *proceed*.

To determine which advice is responsible for the wrong control or data flow, the programmer needs to (**T7**) inspect the stack of executing join points including (**T8**) the composition of advices applicable at each join point. To observe data flow, she needs to (**T6**) inspect the runtime values.

Violated requirements   Advice may also violate requirements, like post conditions or state invariants, of the modules they apply to. To localize such faults, the programmer may need to (**T6**) inspect runtime values. Another technique often used for localizing faults is to run the program with one or more modules disabled; if the error disappears, the fault most likely lies in the disabled module. To be able to apply this technique, the programmer must be allowed to (**T10**) disable single pointcut-advice, ideally at runtime.[3]

2.3   State-of-the-art

Table 2 summarizes the required debugging tasks identified in the previous sub-sections and gives them short names. In the following we discuss how these tasks are supported by the traditional Java Debugger and by AOP debuggers proposed in the literature.

Tag	Task Name
T1	Setting AO breakpoints
T2	Locating AO constructs
T3	Evaluating pointcut sub-expressions
T4	Flattening pointcut references
T5	Evaluating pattern sub-expressions
T6	Inspecting runtime values
T7	Inspecting AO-conforming stack traces
T8	Inspecting program compositions
T9	Inspecting precedence dependencies
T10	Excluding and adding AO definitions

Table 2. Tasks that an ideal AOP debugger should perform

The Java debugger is the most commonly used tool for debugging AspectJ programs which are compiled to pure Java bytecode. Some elements of the aspect definition are partially evaluated during compilation and drive a series of code transformations applied to the aspect and non-aspect modules. Thus, there is no one-to-one mapping between elements in the source code and in the bytecode; because of this and due to limitations of the Java bytecode format, the contained debugging information is not sufficient to store source location information about all aspect-oriented elements that are compiled. Thus, tasks are either only partially supported (T1, T6, T7) or not at all (T2, T3, T4, T5, T8, T9, T10). For example, the stack trace (T7) becomes misleading when it

involves the execution of advices. A stack frame representing the execution of an advice indicates that this execution is invoked by the method represented by the previous frame. However, this method does not contain this invocation but the advice is implicitly triggered by a pointcut defined in another piece of code.

The *Aspect Oriented Debugging Architecture* (AODA) by De Borger et al. [10] is built based on a debugging interface which restores some source-level abstractions from the bytecode. Entities comprising the debugging interface model many AspectJ concepts, such as join points, advices, etc. The debugging interface allows to query advices applied on a join point, the stack trace with advice execution history, and so on. Besides, the AODA contains an aspect-aware breakpoint model which allows programmers to set a breakpoint to aspect-related operations like the instantiation of an aspect. However, their model is not fine-grained enough; it lacks entities which cannot be represented in a non-AO IR like patterns, precedence declarations. Thus, tasks T2, T3, T6 are partially supported and T5, T9 are not supported by AODA. Due to the compile-time weaving strategy fostered by AODA, it is impossible to exclude AO definitions at runtime (T10).

Wicca [11] is a dynamic AOP system for C# applications that performs source weaving at runtime. For debugging purposes, the woven source code can be inspected, e.g., for checking if programs are correctly composed. Wicca also allows to enable/disable aspects at runtime. Though Wicca fully supports T8, T10, it poorly supports our other identified tasks because it debugs the woven code. Although the presented C# source code is more easy to understand than woven bytecode which is available in other systems, it does not contain the AO source-level abstractions anymore.

Pothier and Tanter [18] implemented an AO debugger based on an open source omniscient Java debugger called *TOD*. TOD records all events that occur during the execution of a program and the complete history can be inspected and queried offline after the execution. Programmers can choose to present all, part or none of the aspect activities carried out during runtime. It can show the execution history of join points related to particular AO elements, e.g., where a pointcut matched or did not match. However, the granularity of such elements in TOD is as coarse as in the other presented approaches for debugging woven code. Therefore, only T1, T2, T6, T7, T8 are partially supported in TOD.

2.4   Requirements for an AOP Debugger

Based on the above observations and discussions, we formulate requirements for a dynamic debugger dedicated to aspect-oriented programs. In the following three sections, we describe how we achieve each of these.

- An intermediate representation must be provided that preserves all AO constructs found in the source code as well as their source location.

---

[3] Dynamic (de-)activation of aspects or advice bears the risk to leave the aspect in a wrong state, e.g., when join points at which the aspect performs an initialization have already passed. But often aspects are less complex and being able to (de-)activate them at runtime is an efficient debugging technique—it must be used with caution, though.

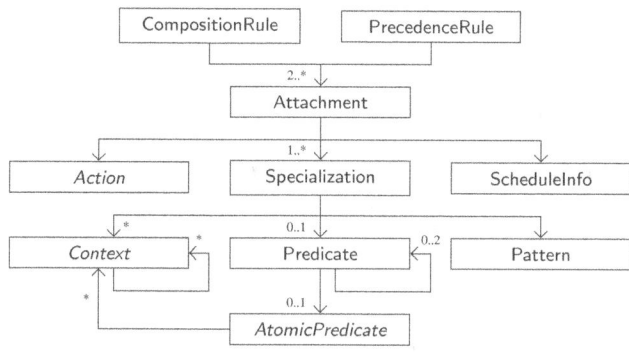

Figure 1. The LIAM meta-model of advanced dispatching

- A fine-grained debugging interface must be provided to allow observation of and interaction with the execution at the granularity of AO abstractions.

- The debugging infrastructure should be integrated with an integrated development environment (IDE) to provide a dedicated user interface on which all tasks listed in table 2 can be performed.

3. Debugging Information

We choose to base the implementation of the debugger on our previous work, a generic implementation architecture of so-called advanced-dispatching (AD) languages which includes AOP languages. One of the main components of this *ALIA4J* architecture[4] [7] is a meta-model of AD declarations, called *LIAM*[5]. When implementing, e.g., AspectJ in ALIA4J, an advanced-dispatching declaration corresponds to a pointcut-advice definition. A model instantiating the LIAM meta-model is an intermediate representation (IR) of the AO program elements.

For our debugger, we have extended LIAM to store detailed source-location information with every element in the IR. Since ALIA4J keeps the IR as first-class objects at runtime, it can be accessed by our debugger to observe the program execution in an AO-specific way. This fact as well as the declarative and fine-grained nature of LIAM facilitate the support for all identified debugging tasks.

3.1 Aspect-Oriented Intermediate Representation

The meta-model, LIAM, itself defines *categories* of concepts and how these concepts relate, e.g., a dispatch may be ruled by *atomic predicates* which depend on values in the dynamic *context* of the dispatch. LIAM has to be *refined* with the concrete language concepts like the **cflow** or **target** pointcut designators.

Figure 1 shows the meta-entities of LIAM, discussed in detail by Bockisch et al. [6, 7], which capture the core

---

The Advanced-dispatching Language Implementation Architecture for Java. See http://www.alia4j.org.

[4] The Advanced-dispatching Language Implementation Architecture for Java. See http://www.alia4j.org.

[5] The Language-Independent Advanced-dispatching Meta-model. See http://www.alia4j.org/alia4j-liam/.

concepts underlying the various dispatching mechanisms. The meta-entities *Action*, *AtomicPredicate* and *Context* can be refined to concrete concepts; we provide refinements for several languages, including AspectJ [7].

An *Attachment* corresponds to a unit of dispatch declaration, roughly corresponding to a pointcut-advice pair in AspectJ. *Action* specifies functionality that may be executed as the result of dispatch (e.g., the body of an advice). *Specialization* defines static and dynamic properties of state on which dispatch depends. *Pattern* specifies syntactic and lexical properties of the dispatch site. *Predicate* and *Atomic Predicate* entities model conditions on the dynamic state a dispatch depends on. *Context* entities model access to values like the called object or argument values. The *Schedule Information* models the time relative to a join point when the action should be executed, i.e., before, after or around. Finally, *Precedence Rule* models partial ordering of actions and *Composition Rule* models the applicability of actions at a shared join point; for example, overriding can be expressed by this.

3.2 XML-based LIAM model

Figure 2 shows the life cycle of the debugging information related to AO features in our approach. Following the bold directed lines, AO-specific information is first written in the source code of aspects and then compiled into a separate XML file containing serialized LIAM-based declarations. At runtime, the XML file is deserialized and the program is executed taking the aspect definitions into account.

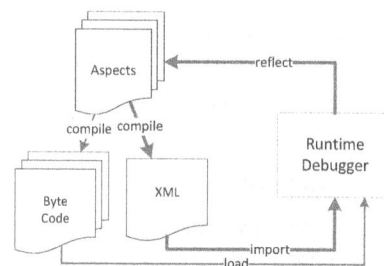

Figure 2. Debugging information life cycle

This approach requires a specific compiler to generate the IR. In the context of this paper, we just elaborate on our implementation of an AspectJ compiler based on the *abc* compiler [3]. As an example of the compilation, consider the AspectJ code in listing 1. After compilation, it is transformed into an *Attachment* XML element presented in listing 2.

There is a many-to-many relationship between source language constructs and LIAM entities. For example in listing 1 the pointcut designator **target**(b) is transformed to two LIAM entities because it plays two roles: It specifies a dynamic condition under which the pointcut matches a join point (represented by the *AtomicPredicate* in lines 4–13, listing 2), as well as a value that is exposed to associated advice (represented by the *Context* in lines 14–17). The pointcut designator, and thus also the atomic predicate, additionally depends on the declaration of the formal advice parameter Base b: The callee object must be an instance of type Base. Thus, the atomic predicate is influenced by two locations in the source code which both are stored in our IR, as shown on lines 5–6 and 10–11 in listing 2.

With our intermediate representation presented above, we support the task *locating constructs* (**T2**) presented in section 2.3.

```
1 aspect Azpect {
2   before(Base b) : call(∗ Base.foo()) && target(b) { ... }
3 }
```

Listing 1. An aspect example in AspectJ

```
1  <attachment>
2    <specialization>
3      <pattern> ... </pattern>
4      <atomicPredicate type="InstanceofPredicate">
5        <requiredTypeName file="Azpect.aj" line="2"
6          column="9" endLine="2" endColumn="13">
7          test.Base
8        </requiredTypeName>
9        <context type="CalleeContext"
10         file="Azpect.aj" line="2" column="25"
11         endLine="2" endColumn="50">
12       </context>
13     </atomicPredicate>
14     <context type="CalleeContext"
15       file="Azpect.aj" line="2" column="25"
16       endLine="2" endColumn="50">
17     </context>
18   </specialization>
19   <action> ... </action>
20   <scheduleInfo> ... </scheduleInfo>
21 </attachment>
```

Listing 2. XML-based AO intermediate representation

4. Infrastructure of the AOP debugger

Extending figure 2, the overall structure of our debugger is presented in the figure 3. It consists of a debuggee side and a debugger side; both sides communicate via the *Java Platform Debugger Architecture* (JPDA)[6] and the Advanced-Dispatching language Debugging Wire Protocol (ADDWP). The debuggee-side virtual machine runs the debuggee program and sends debugging data and events via the two channels. Our user interface (debugger side) presents this information and provides controls to the programmer to interact with the debuggee. These controls are implemented by using the Java Debug Interface (JDI) and the Advanced-Dispatching Debug Interface (ADDI). As our debug interface is based on ALIA4J's meta-model of advanced dispatching, we reuse that terminology in our infrastructure. Nevertheless, our goal is to support aspect-oriented programs and our case study is based on AspectJ.

---

[6] See   http://java.sun.com/javase/technologies/core/toolsapis/jpda/.

The ADDWP is implemented as two agents running on the debugger and debuggee sides respectively. It has a similar structure and working mechanism as the JDWP but sends and receives AD-specific information. The following subsections describe the execution environment and the ADDI in detail. The UI is explained in the next section.

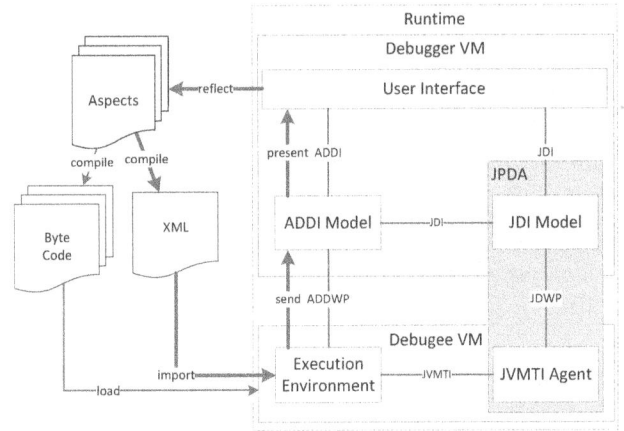

Figure 3. The architecture of our AOP debugger

4.1 Debuggee Side

In the ALIA4J approach, the execution environment is an extension to the Java Virtual Machine (JVM). The extension allows deploying and undeploying LIAM dispatch declarations and derives an *execution strategy* per call site that considers all dispatch declarations present in the program.

The execution strategy consists of the so-called dispatch function (for details see Sewe et al. [19]) that characterizes which actions should be executed as the result of the dispatch in a given program state. This function is represented as a binary decision diagram (BDD) [8], where the inner nodes are the atomic predicates used in the predicate definitions and the leaf nodes are labeled with the actions to be executed. For each possible result of dispatch, the BDD has one leaf node, representing an alternative result of the dispatch, i.e., which actions to execute and in which order.

Our current implementation of the debugger is based on the ALIA4J NOIRIn execution environment [7], which is implemented as a Java 6 agent intercepting the execution of the base program to perform the dispatch. NOIRIn can integrate with any standard Java 6 JVM, therefore our approach does not require using a custom virtual machine.

4.2 Advanced-Dispatching Debug Interface

The Advanced-Dispatching Debug Interface (ADDI) is the debugger-side interface of the debugging infrastructure. It provides various functionalities to perform the tasks identified in section 2.3, which it implements in collaboration with the debuggee virtual machine. A simplified UML class diagram of ADDI is presented in figure 4.

The Java Debug Interface (JDI) provides mirrors for every runtime entity in a Java program, like objects, classes,

Breakpoint
+int hitCount()
+boolean enabled()

ADPointcutBreakpoint
+String expression()

ILocatable
+Location location()

ADEvaluator
+String evaluatePointcut(String)

PredicateMirror

SpecializationMirror
+PatternMirror pattern()
+PredicateMirror predicate()
+ContextMirror[] contexts()

DispatchFrameMirror
+CallContextMirror callContext()
+JoinPointMirror joinPoint()
+ActionOrderElementMirror actionsToPerform()

JoinPointMirror
+VertexMirror dispatchStrategy()

AtomicPredicateMirror
+boolean isSatisfied()

PrecedenceRuleMirror
+int type()

PatternMirror
+boolean match(String)

ActionOrderElementMirror
+AttachedActionMirror[] before()
+AttachedActionMirror[] after()
+AttachedActionMirror around()
+ActionOrderElementMirror inner()

AttachedActionMirror
+ContextMirror[] contexts()
+ActionMirror action()
+ScheduleInfoMirror scheduleInfo()
+AttachmentMirror attachment()

ActionMirror

AttachmentMirror
+ActionMirror action()
+SpecializationMirror[] specializations()
+ScheduleInfoMirror scheduleInfo()
+PrecedenceRule precedes(AttachmentMirror)
+void deploy()
+void undeploy()

MethodPatternMirror

ModifiersPatternMirror
+boolean match(String)

TypePatternMirror
+boolean match(String)

ClassTypePatternMirror
+boolean match(String)

NamePatternMirror
+boolean match(String)

ParametersPatternMirror
+boolean match(String)

ExceptionsPatternMirror
+boolean match(String)

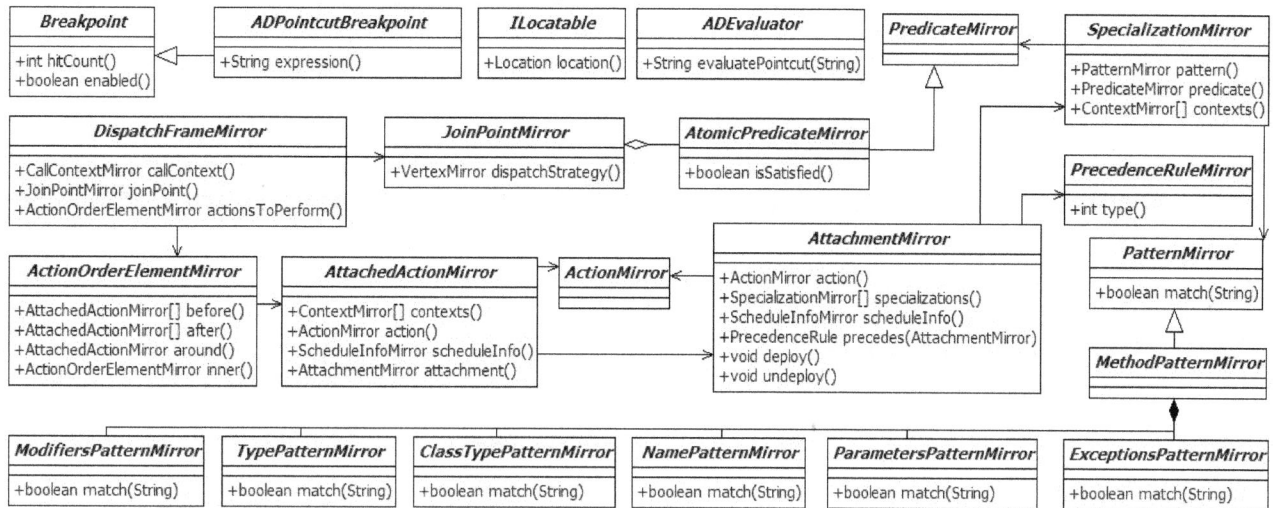

Figure 4. A simplified UML class diagram of the Advanced-Dispatching Debug Interface

or threads. The ADDI extends the JDI by additionally providing mirrors for the LIAM entities which exist in the debuggee virtual machine and which represent the pointcut-advice definitions. Since LIAM entities are plain Java objects, the ADDI mirrors are implemented by aggregating the JDI mirrors of those objects.

ADDI's breakpoints do not wrap existing Java breakpoints. When a breakpoint is set, the debugger-side sends the breakpoint information to the execution environment at the debuggee side. The execution environment registers a breakpoint event according to the received information. When a registered breakpoint event occurs, the execution environment sends the JDI command for suspending the virtual machine. Below, we discuss the top-level mirrors of the ADDI:

ADPointcutBreakpoint provides the interface for setting breakpoint by utilizing pointcut expressions (**T1**).

ILocatable is an interface for locating entities. In our implementation of ADDI, subclasses of ActionMirror, AtomicPredicateMirror, PatternMirror, AttachmentMirror, DispatchFrameMirror, and PrecedenceRuleMirror implement this interface. Therefore, corresponding constructs can be located in the source code at runtime (**T2**).

ADEvaluator can perform evaluation on given pointcut expressions or sub-expressions (**T3**). It takes strings as input, sends them to the back-end. The back-end compiler compiles received strings into LIAM entities, evaluates their value according to the current program state and returns the result to the debugger side. If the expression is syntactically incorrect, an error message is returned.

DispatchFrameMirror reifies a stack frame containing the execution strategy at a join point (**T7**). It provides inspection of the call context (**T6**) and of the program composition (**T8**) at the current join point.

AtomicPredicateMirror performs evaluations to pointcut sub-expressions (**T3**).

ActionOrderElementMirror reifies the program composition (**T8**). It consists of four parts, namely *before*, *after*, *around*, and *inner*. The before, around, and after parts point to advice (respectively the action representing the join point operation) which are sequentially executed at a join point. The inner part refers to the actions to be executed when the around advice performs the proceed operation.

AttachmentMirror first provides access to the three parts of an attachment declaration (corresponding to a pointcut-advice): action, specialization (corresponding to the pointcut) and schedule information. Second, it can be activated or deactivated at runtime (**T10**).

PrecedenceRuleMirror represents ordering relations between attachments (**T9**). This includes precedence defined in AspectJ through the **declare precedence** statement, through the **before**, **after** or **around** keywords, and through the lexical order of advice definitions.

SpecializationMirror reifies static and dynamic sub-expressions of pointcuts which are decomposed into a pattern, a predicate, and contexts.[7] Referenced named pointcuts are resolved and inlined in the specialization (**T4**).

PatternMirror can be used to perform evaluations to patterns used in pointcuts. As illustrated by the example of method patterns in figure 4, patterns consist of smaller sub-patterns which are separate entities in ADDI and can be evaluated respectively (**T5**).

---

[7] See Bockisch et al. [5] for a detailed discussion of how to transform any AspectJ pointcut to our data structure.

5. User Interface

The front-end of our debugger is integrated into the Eclipse IDE, although any IDE with a comparable infrastructure would also be applicable. Our AOP debugger extends the Eclipse Java debugger with additional user interfaces. These are Eclipse views specific to visualizing and interacting with ALIA4J's representation of pointcut-advice in order to support the tasks discussed in section 2. The developed debugger provides three new views, namely the *Join Point* view, the *Attachments* view, and the *Pattern Evaluation* view.

Throughout this section, we illustrate the functionality of our debugger by means of the example AspectJ program shown in listing 3 and listing 4. There are four advices (on line 5, 8, 12, and 15, listing 4) declared in Azpect. Suppose the program is currently suspended at line 16 of listing 4. We introduce each view in this scenario in the following subsections.

```
1  package test;
2  public class Base {
3      private int someField;
4      public static void main(String [] args) {
5          Base b = new Base();
6          b.normalMethod();
7      }
8      public void normalMethod() {
9          advicedMethod();
10     }
11     public void advicedMethod() {
12         someField = 1;
13     }
14 }
```

Listing 3. An example base program

```
1  package aspects;
2  import test.Base;
3  public aspect Azpect {
4      pointcut base() : call(* Base.advicedMethod());
5      before() : base() && target(Base) {
6          System.out.println("before−target");
7      }
8      Object around() : base() {
9          proceed();
10         return null;
11     }
12     before() : base() && !target(Base) {
13         System.out.println("before−!target");
14     }
15     after() : set(* Base.someField) {
16         System.out.println("after−set");
17     }
18 }
```

Listing 4. An example aspect

5.1 Join Point View

The *Join Point* view is the central view of the debugger showing runtime information about the join point at which the debuggee is currently suspended. A snapshot of the Join Point view is given in figure 5.

Structure of the Join Point View The view has several parts to allow the programmer interacting with the debuggee. The top left panel displays the stack of join points that are currently executed when the debuggee is intercepted. For each such join point, the signature and the source location of the corresponding join-point shadow are presented (**T7**).

The bottom left panel gives a graphical representation of the execution strategy for the join point selected in the top left panel (**T8**). Each label represents an action that has been executed, is executing, or will be executed at this join point. In figure 5, it displays one composition with two sequential actions which are a field assignment and an advice execution. In AspectJ, advices do not have names. Therefore, we choose to use the name of the aspect and the line number where an advice is defined to uniquely identify the advice, like Azpect.after@line15(). The label with green (highlighted) background indicates that the action it represents is currently executing.

The top right panel of the Join Point view uses a tree viewer to show all context values needed to evaluate the join point's execution strategy and exposed to the actions (**T6**). The bottom right panel gives a string description of the item currently selected in the tree view.

Graphical Representation of Dispatch The graphical representation of a join point visualizes the execution strategy applied by the ALIA4J execution environment and allows navigating to the corresponding definitions in the source code. For illustration consider that the second frame is selected in the example. Figure 6 shows the join point visualization for this case.

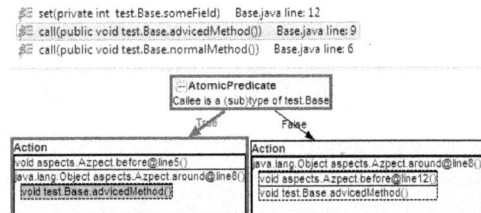

Figure 6. A graphical representation of dispatch

This graphical representation consists of an *AtomicPredicate* testing whether the callee object at this call site is an instance of test.Base and two *Action* nodes with different program compositions according to the evaluation result of the *AtomicPredicate* (**T3**). The blue (bold) path indicates the evaluation result of the atomic predicates and the composition of actions to be performed at the current join point. The highlighted *Action* node first performs Azpect.before@line5() and then Azpect.around@line8(); when the latter proceeds, Base.advicedMethod() is executed. The dashed box surrounding Base.advicedMethod() visualizes the fact that the surrounding action may not execute *proceed* and thus may leave out the execution of this action. Double-clicking on a label representing an atomic predicate or an action reveals the corresponding source location (**T2**).

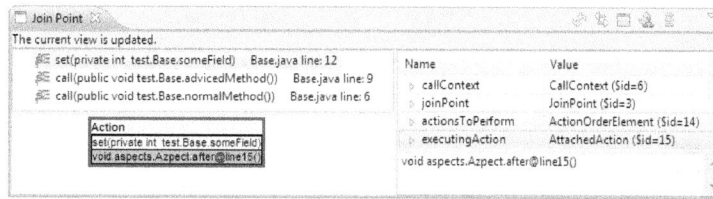

Figure 5. A snapshot of the Join Point view

If more complex pointcuts apply to this join point, i.e., more atomic predicates are evaluated, the size and complexity of the BDD may grow significantly. To reduce the presented information the "-" icon in labels representing atomic predicates can be clicked to collapse subtrees. Furthermore a more compact tabular representation of the execution strategy is available as detailed in the following.

Textual Representation of Dispatch By clicking the "Table" button on the toolbar, the bottom left part is switched to a table, as shown in figure 7. This table contains several pieces of information to support **T3** and **T8**: First it lists all actions that are potentially applicable at this join point, i.e., the standard join point action (Base.advicedMethod()) and all advice whose pointcut statically matches the join point.

Figure 7. A textual representation of dispatch

Second, for all actions whose pointcut dynamically matches the join point, the execution sequence as well as nesting levels (for *around* actions) are shown. For example, "2.1" for Base.advicedMethod() means that this action is executed as the first action when the second action from the level above (advice Azpect.around@line8 numbered with 2) performs *proceed*. Similar to the graph representation, the currently executing action is highlighted with green background. For those actions whose pattern statically matched, but where the dispatch function determined that they are not applicable at this call, the table shows an 'X' in the order column.

Third, the table shows the results of all atomic predicates of pointcuts that are evaluated at this join point. Compared to the graphical representation, the table does not show the process of evaluation and other possible program compositions.

Visualization of Precedence Dependencies To reason about the composition of advices at a join point (**T9**), the precedence relationships between the advices are visualized. To illustrate how the visualization of precedence dependencies works, we use three additional aspects which are shown in listing 5. Both aspects, PrecedingAzpect and PrecededAzpect, declare a **before** advice. The aspect IrrelevantAzpect defines the precedence between PrecedingAzpect and PrecededAzpect.

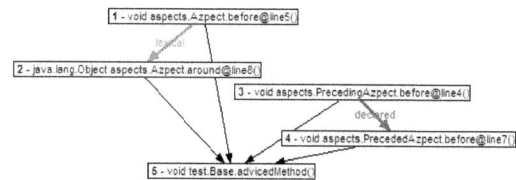

Figure 8. The graphical representation of precedence dependencies

```
1   package aspects;
2   import test.Base;
3   aspect PrecedingAzpect {
4       before() : call(* Base.advicedMethod()) { ... }
5   }
6   aspect PrecededAzpect {
7       before() : call(* Base.advicedMethod()) { ... }
8   }
9   aspect IrrelevantAzpect {
10      declare precedence : PrecedingAzpect, PrecededAzpect;
11  }
```

Listing 5. Aspect illustrating precedence dependencies

Consider that the execution is suspended at the call to advicedMethod() at line 9, listing 3. By clicking the "Precedence" button on the toolbar of the Join Point view, the graph panel changes to a representation of the precedence dependencies as shown in figure 8.

Labels representing actions are numbered and connected by directed lines. The direction of a connection indicates the precedence between two actions. We use the numbers as substitute for action names in the following paragraph; for example, "action 1" represents Azpect.before@line5().

There are three types of connection representing precedence declared in different ways: Precedence may be declared explicitly by means of the **declare precedence** statement, visualized by a bold blue (dark) connection labeled with "declared"; it may be defined by the *lexical order* of advice definitions in the same aspect, visualized by a bold gray (light) connection labeled with "lexical"; or it may be determined by the kind of action (i.e., **before**, **after**, **around** advice or the join point action), visualized by a thin black connection without label.

Explicitly declared precedence has a source location, like line 10 in listing 5. The corresponding source location can be highlighted when the connection is double-clicked (**T2**). An example of precedence declaration by means of lexical order is shown in listing 4: Action 1 is declared on line 5 and,

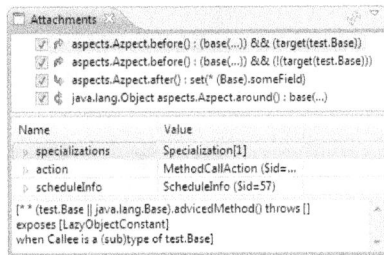

Figure 9. A snapshot of the Attachments view

Figure 10. A snapshot of the Pattern Evaluation view

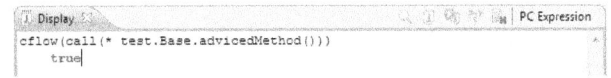

Figure 11. The extended Display view for evaluating point-cut expressions

thus, precedes action 2 defined on line 8. The precedence between any two actions without a connection is random, such as action 1 and action 3.

5.2 Attachments View

In order to dynamically deploy and undeploy attachments during runtime, the *Attachments* view is provided. A snapshot of the *Attachments* view is given in figure 9. The top panel shows a textual representation of all attachments that are defined in the executing program together with a checkbox indicating whether the attachment is currently deployed or not. Unchecking or checking one of the items will lead to undeployment or deployment of the corresponding attachment in the debugged program (**T10**). The bottom parts presents details of the selected attachment.

In figure 9, the first attachment, representing the *before* advice declared on line 5 in listing 4, is selected. This advice has a pointcut containing a reference to another pointcut declared on line 4. The *specialization* of the selected attachment describes the related pointcut in the bottom panel and the referred pointcut is inlined in the description (**T4**).

5.3 Pattern Evaluation View

To debug patterns used in pointcuts, we visualize the pattern evaluation at the granularity of sub-patterns specified for the separate parts of the join-point signature. Since patterns that do not match at a join point are not shown in the Join Point view, this functionality is accessible through the Attachments view which contains all pointcut-advice definitions in the program.

For illustration suppose we select the third frame representing the call to method test.Base.normalMethod() in figure 5. We find that the before advice declared on line 5 in listing 4 does not appear in the execution strategy. That means the pattern used in the before advice is unsatisfied. To evaluate the method signature against the pattern, we use the item representing the before advice in the *Attachment* view. Then, an evaluation result of each sub-pattern is presented in the *Pattern Evaluation* view as shown in figure 10. It gives the evaluation results for each sub-pattern (**T5**).

5.4 Setting Pointcut Breakpoint and Evaluating Pointcut Expression

Except three newly added views, we also extend two existing views in Eclipse. We extend the *Breakpoints* view to allow specifying pointcut expressions in order to set pointcut breakpoints (**T1**).

The pointcut evaluation provided in the *Join point* view shows only expressions existing in the source code. The programmer is unable to test a new pointcut expression unless she modifies and reruns the program. To provide more flexibility in evaluating pointcut expressions (**T3**), we extend the *Display* view. For example, suppose the second frame shown in figure 5 is selected, the programmer evaluates the expression **cflow(call(∗ test.Base.advicedMethod()))**. The result is shown in figure 11.

6. Related Work

The related work basically falls into two parts which are debuggers for AOP languages and other development tools for AOP languages. In the following subsections we present tools in these categories and discuss them according to the requirements listed in this paper.

6.1 Debuggers for Aspect-Oriented Languages

We discussed the state-of-the-art AOP debuggers in section 2.3. The evaluation is summarized in table 3 showing that tasks T5 and T9 are not supported at all by any of these debuggers; for tasks T2, T3 and T6 only partial support is provided by the related approaches. The reason for these limitations is the approach that all previous debuggers share: They debug woven code which lost some of the aspect-oriented abstractions. In contrast, our approach introduces an intermediate representation that preserves all source-level abstractions and thus allows observing and interacting with the execution of the debuggee in terms of these abstractions.

6.2 Development tools for aspect-oriented languages

AO-specific information provided by tools or systems are not only provided in online debuggers. Static tools can be

Tag	Task Name	Our debugger	JDB	AODA	Wicca	TOD
T1	Setting AO breakpoints	√	○	√		○
T2	Locating AO constructs	√		○		○
T3	Evaluating pointcut sub-expressions	√		○		
T4	Flattening pointcut references	√		√		
T5	Evaluating pattern sub-expressions	√				
T6	Inspecting runtime values	√	○	○		○
T7	Inspecting AO-conforming stack traces	√	○	√		○
T8	Inspecting program compositions	√		√	√	○
T9	Inspecting precedence dependencies	√				
T10	Excluding and adding AO definitions	√			√	

Table 3. Comparison between different AOP debuggers from the perspective of supporting the identified tasks

used as auxiliary approaches to understand program behavior or structure during debugging.

Common IDE tools for AOP languages, like the AspectJ Development Tools (AJDT)[8], CaesarJ [2] Development Tools (CJDT)[9], JAsCo [20] Development Tools (JAsCoDT)[10] etc., require using the Java debugger. Thus, abstractions inspected during debugging are Java abstractions resulting from the weaving compilation. They provide additional, static features decreasing the effort in understanding and coding corresponding programs. For example, AJDT provides the *Aspect Visualiser* to find places affected by an aspect. JAsCoDT has an *Introspector* which displays the connectors found within the system.

For the ObjectTeams programming language an Eclipse-based IDE exists that enhances the standard JDT Java debugger [14]. The enhancement filters call frames that belong to infrastructural code and adapts the placement of breakpoints. The step-into debugger action is aware of "callin bindings" which correspond to advice in AOP. The ObjectTeams Development Tools (OTDT) provide a view for showing the active and inactive "Teams", their form of aspect declarations, allowing to dynamically enable and disable Teams, similar to the Attachments view of our debugger. While these enhancements hide the details of generated code from programmers, it still falls short in providing additional language-specific functionality.

Some work has been performed on enhancing the visualization of the structure of AO programs. Pfeiffer and Gurd [17] introduced a treemap-based visualization, called *Asbro*. Asbro uses colored and nested rectangles to present the hierarchy as well as the crosscutting structure. It is especially effective in navigating large-scale AO programs. Coelho and Murphy [9] implemented *ActiveAspect* which can present a subset of the crosscutting structure at the right time, thus decreasing the complexity of information to be analyzed. These systems aid language users to comprehend programs by simplifying the presentation of the crosscutting structure. Our debugger more concentrates on dynamic information, especially for pointcut and pattern evaluation, and program composition.

7. Conclusions and Future Work

In this paper we have investigated four fault models for aspect-oriented programming (AOP) languages and categorized AOP faults related to dynamic features into seven fault categories. To detect all kinds of dynamic AOP faults, we identified ten tasks that an ideal AOP debugger should be able to perform.

To enable these tasks, the debugging infrastructure must use an intermediate representation of the program to debug which preserves all source-level abstractions. This is necessary to let the programmer inspect and influence the execution of all aspect-oriented program elements in the source code. It must be possible to add source-location information to elements in the IR to be able to localize their source definition during a debugging session. Therefore, we have based our prototype on our previous work which provides such an intermediate representation for languages with advanced-dispatching (AD) which is a generalization of aspect-oriented programming (AOP). We transform aspect-oriented (AO) information into AD models and store them in an XML file after compilation. The stored information is available to the debugger by means of the Advanced-Dispatching Debug Interface (ADDI), which allows observing the program executions in terms of AO abstractions. Based on the ADDI, we implemented a user interface in terms of three new and two extended Eclipse views.

According to the identified AOP debugging tasks which we generalized from commonly identified AOP faults in the literature, our debugger is the first approach to fully provide the following features.

1. It visualizes all evaluation results of pointcut sub-expressions at a join point, and it represents the constraints de-

[8] See http://www.eclipse.org/ajdt/.

[9] See http://caesarj.org.

[10] See http://ssel.vub.ac.be/jasco/index.html.

fined in the AOP program that lead to a specific composition.

2. It performs evaluations on pointcut and pattern sub-expressions.

3. All elements that rule the execution at a join point are shown by the visual debugger and the source code defining them can be located.

4. The runtime stack is enhanced to present join points as well as all applicable advice at once.

5. It visualizes the declarations leading to a program composition at a join point.

6. It shows all advices defined in the program and allows deploying and undeploying them at runtime.

While our requirements for the debugger are based on a taxonomy of faults in aspect-oriented programs, we believe that our approach can be generalized to the concept of advanced dispatching. In our work we did not consciously applied any constraints specific to aspect-oriented programming languages. Therefore we expect that this work can be easily extended to support other advanced-dispatching programming languages supported by the ALIA4J architecture, like predicate dispatching or domain-specific languages.

Besides studying the applicability of our approach to other programming language paradigms, we will extend our user interface with advanced support for simplifying recurring tasks. Furthermore, we will investigate supporting debugging in ALIA4J's optimizing execution environments.

Acknowledgments

This work is partly funded by the Chinese Scholarship Council (CSC Scholarship No.2008613009).

References

[1] R. T. Alexander, J. M. Bieman, and A. A. Andrews. Towards the systematic testing of aspect-oriented programs. Technical report, 2004.

[2] I. Aracic, V. Gasiunas, M. Mezini, and K. Ostermann. An overview of CaesarJ. 3880:135–173, 2006.

[3] P. Avgustinov, A. S. Christensen, L. Hendren, S. Kuzins, J. Lhoták, O. Lhoták, O. de Moor, D. Sereni, G. Sittampalam, and J. Tibble. abc: an extensible aspectj compiler. In *Proceedings of the 4th AOSD*, pages 87–98, New York, NY, USA, 2005. ACM.

[4] J. S. Baekken. *A fault model for pointcuts and advice in AspectJ programs*. Master's thesis, School of Electronical Engineering and Computer Science, Washington State University, 2006.

[5] C. Bockisch, M. Haupt, M. Mezini, and R. Mitschke. Envelope-based weaving for faster aspect compilers. In *NODe/GSEM*, volume 69 of *LNI*, pages 3–18. GI, 2005.

[6] C. Bockisch, S. Malakuti, M. Akşit, and S. Katz. Making aspects natural: events and composition. In *Proceedings of the 10th AOSD*, pages 285–300, New York, NY, USA, 2011. ACM.

[7] C. Bockisch, A. Sewe, M. Mezini, and M. Akşit. An overview of alia4j: an execution model for advanced-dispatching languages. In *Proceedings of the 49th TOOLS*, pages 131–146, Berlin, Heidelberg, 2011. Springer-Verlag.

[8] R. E. Bryant. Graph-based algorithms for boolean function manipulation. *IEEE Trans. Comput.*, 35:677–691, August 1986.

[9] W. Coelho and G. C. Murphy. Presenting crosscutting structure with active models. In *Proceedings of the 5th AOSD*, pages 158–168, New York, NY, USA, 2006. ACM.

[10] W. De Borger, B. Lagaisse, and W. Joosen. A generic and reflective debugging architecture to support runtime visibility and traceability of aspects. In *Proceedings of the 8th AOSD*, pages 173–184, New York, NY, USA, 2009. ACM.

[11] M. Eaddy, A. Aho, W. Hu, P. McDonald, and J. Burger. Debugging aspect-enabled programs. In *Proceedings of the 6th international conference on SC*, pages 200–215, Berlin, Heidelberg, 2007. Springer-Verlag.

[12] F. Ferrari, R. Burrows, O. Lemos, A. Garcia, E. Figueiredo, N. Cacho, F. Lopes, N. Temudo, L. Silva, S. Soares, A. Rashid, P. Masiero, T. Batista, and J. Maldonado. An exploratory study of fault-proneness in evolving aspect-oriented programs. In *Proceedings of the 32nd ICSE - Volume 1*, pages 65–74, New York, NY, USA, 2010. ACM.

[13] F. C. Ferrari, J. C. Maldonado, and A. Rashid. Mutation testing for aspect-oriented programs. In *Proceedings of the 2008 ICST*, pages 52–61, Washington, DC, USA, 2008. IEEE Computer Society.

[14] S. Herrmann, C. Hundt, M. Mosconi, C. Pfeiffer, and J. Wloka. Das object teams development tooling. *Softwaretechnik-Trends*, 26(4):42–43, 2006.

[15] G. Kiczales, E. Hilsdale, J. Hugunin, M. Kersten, J. Palm, and W. G. Griswold. An overview of aspectj. In *Proceedings of the 15th ECOOP*, pages 327–353, London, UK, UK, 2001. Springer-Verlag.

[16] F. M. Ceccato, P. Tonella. Is aop code easier to test than oop code? In *In Workshop on Testing Aspect-Oriented Programs*, 2005.

[17] J. Pfeiffer and J. R. Gurd. Visualisation-based tool support for the development of aspect-oriented programs. In *Proceedings of the 5th AOSD*, pages 146–157, New York, NY, USA, 2006. ACM.

[18] G. Pothier and E. Tanter. Extending omniscient debugging to support aspect-oriented programming. In *Proceedings of SAC*, pages 266–270, New York, NY, USA, 2008. ACM.

[19] A. Sewe, C. Bockisch, and M. Mezini. Redundancy-free residual dispatch: using ordered binary decision diagrams for efficient dispatch. In *Proceedings of the 7th workshop on FOAL*, pages 1–7, New York, NY, USA, 2008. ACM.

[20] D. Suvée, W. Vanderperren, and V. Jonckers. Jasco: an aspect-oriented approach tailored for component based software development. In *Proceedings of the 2nd AOSD*, pages 21–29, New York, NY, USA, 2003. ACM.

A Monadic Interpretation of
Execution Levels and Exceptions for AOP

Nicolas Tabareau

INRIA
École des Mines de Nantes, France

Abstract

Aspect-Oriented Programming (AOP) started fifteen years
ago with the remark that modularization of so-called crosscutting functionalities is a fundamental problem for the engineering of large-scale applications. Originating at Xerox
PARC, this observation has sparked the development of a
new style of programming features that is gradually gaining traction. However, theoretical foundations of AOP have
been much less studied than its applicability. This paper proposes to put a bridge between AOP and the notion of 2-
category to enhance the conceptual understanding of AOP.
Starting from the connection between the λ-calculus and
the theory of categories, we provide an internal language
for 2-categories and show how it can be used to define the
first categorical semantics for a realistic functional AOP language, called MinAML. We then take advantage of this new
categorical framework to introduce the notion of computational 2-monads for AOP. We illustrate their conceptual
power by defining a 2-monad for Éric Tanter's execution
levels—which constitutes the first algebraic semantics for
execution levels—and then introducing the first exception
monad transformer specific to AOP that gives rise to a non-
flat semantics for exceptions by taking levels into account.

Categories and Subject Descriptors D.3.1 [*Formal Definitions and Theory*]: semantics; F.3.2 [*Semantics of Programming Languages*]: Algebraic approaches to semantics

1. Introduction

Aspect-Oriented Programming (AOP) [13] promotes better
separation of concerns in software systems by introducing
aspects for the modular implementation of crosscutting concerns. Much of the research on aspect-oriented programming
has focused on applying aspects in various problem domains
and on integration of aspects into full-scale programming
languages such as Java. However, aspects are very powerful and the development of a weaving mechanism becomes
rapidly a very complex task. While some research efforts
[5, 10, 25, 26] have made significant progress on understanding some of the semantic issues involved, the algebraic
explanation of aspect features has never reached the beauty
and simplicity of the connection between the λ-calculus and
Cartesian closed categories that provided a categorical foundation for functional programming.

Giving a precise meaning to aspects in AOP is a fairly
tangled task because the definition of a single piece of code
can have a very rich interaction with the rest of the program, whose effect can come up at anytime during the execution. The main purpose of this paper is to formalize this
interaction—in particular for two recent sophisticated weaving definitions of aspects and base computation: (1) execution levels [24] that enable to stratify the computation space
in order to prevent from basic infinite recursion; (2) execution levels with exceptions [6] that enable to avoid unexpected catching of exceptions in this stratified space.

More precisely, we propose to put a bridge between
(weaving-based approach to) AOP and the notion of 2-
category. Starting from the connection between the λ-
calculus and category theory [15], we propose to see an
aspect as a 2-cell, that is as a morphism between morphisms.
In the programming language point of view, this means that
an aspect can be seen as a program which transforms the
execution of other programs. In this perspective, a weaving algorithm that defines the interaction of a collection of
aspects with a given program will be understood as the computation of a normal form in the underlying 2-category of
interest. Thus, an algorithm that is usually defined by hand
and described coarsely in AOP systems becomes here a basic notion of rewriting theory. This fact will be made explicit
by presenting *the first categorical semantics* for a thin functional AOP language called MinAML—semantics obtained
by translating of a program written in this language into a
term of the λ_2-calculus. Then, we show that program evalu-

ation corresponds exactly to normal form computation in the 2-category induced by the λ_2-term. Note that MinAML has a simple AOP semantics were aspects can only substitute globally one function for another. Richer pointcut quantifications can be introduced by considering a richer typing systems, for instance by adding sum types for conditionals or recursive types for fixpoints. We do not consider such extension in this paper.

To capture the more complex weaving of aspects provided by execution levels, we define an extension of the standard notion of computational monads [20] to aspectual computation. Such 2-monads are given by a 2-dimensional version of the categorical definition of monads. Using monads for AOP enables to give *the first algebraic semantics for execution levels*. Indeed, it appears that execution levels can be understood as normal aspectual computation in presence of a specialization of the state 2-monad that stratifies the computation space. Formally, we extend MinAML with execution levels, MinAML$_{EL}$, and show that evaluation in MinAML$_{EL}$ corresponds to normal form computation in the λ_2-calculus extended with this new 2-monad. We finally show that execution levels with exceptions can be understood as aspectual computation in presence of a stratified version of the exception monad transformer, thus defining *the first exception monad transformer specific to AOP*. The use of such algebraic semantics should allow to import directly equational reasoning induced by the 2-monad at the language level. We believe that this line of work should turn out to be very fruitful for proving program equivalence in presence of aspects.

2. Aspect-Oriented Programming in the light of 2-categories and 2-monads

λ-calculus and Cartesian closed categories. Category theory and programming languages are closely related. It is now folklore that the typed λ-calculus is the internal language of Cartesian closed categories. Recall that a *category* $\mathcal{C}$ is a class of objects equipped with a class $\mathcal{C}(A, B)$ of morphisms between any two objects A and B of $\mathcal{C}$. Going one dimension higher, a 2-category $\mathcal{C}$ is basically a category in which the class $\mathcal{C}(A, B)$ of morphisms between any two objects A and B is itself a category. In other words, a 2-category is a category in which there exists morphisms

$$f : A \to B$$

between objects , and also morphisms

$$\alpha : f \Rightarrow g$$

between morphisms. The morphisms $f : A \to B$ are called *1-cells* and the morphisms $\alpha : f \Rightarrow g$ are called *2-cells*.

In the computer science point of view, objects of the category correspond to types in the typed λ-calculus and morphisms between objects A and B of the category correspond to λ-terms of type B with (exactly) one free variable of type

A. The composition of morphisms corresponds to substitution, a notion that is at the heart of β-reduction—the fundamental rule of the λ-calculus.

This interpretation of the λ-calculus started in the early 80's from the work of John Lambek and Philip Scott [15, 16]. Soon later, Robert Seely proposed a 2-categorical interpretation of the λ-calculus [22] where β-reduction constructs 2-cells between terms and their β-reduced versions. This perspective is in line with the thought that 2-cells can be seen as rewriting rules between morphisms (or terms). This idea has been pushed further by Barnaby Hilken in [8] where he developed a 2-dimensional λ-calculus that corresponds to the free 2-category with lax exponentials.

Seely's interpretation shows how typed λ-calculus can naturally be viewed as a 2-category. In this paper, we define an advised λ-calculus extending the typed λ-calculus with 2-dimensional primitives that enable to describe any 2-cell of a Cartesian closed 2-category. Those additional primitives construct a kind of 2-dimensional terms that we will (by extension) call aspects. The resulting language, called λ_2-calculus, defines an internal language for Cartesian closed 2-category and will be the base of our explanation of aspects in AOP.

AOP and 2-categories. The keystone of this paper is to consider aspects in AOP as 2-cells in a 2-category just as functions (more precisely λ-terms) are interpreted as morphisms in a category. But this simple idea raises interesting and difficult issues: (i) What are the 2-dimensional notions of β-reduction and variables? (ii) How to describe vertical and horizontal composition of a 2-category in the language of typed λ-calculi? Interestingly, while developing an internal language for Cartesian closed 2-categories [23], the author has discovered that Tom Hirschowitz was independently working on the same structure in his study of higher-order rewriting [9]. This should not appear as a surprise because higher-order rewriting and program transformation are closely related. In this paper, we present the calculus in the style of [9] because we found the presentation more elegant and the connection to Cartesian closed 2-categories more precise but the resulting calculus in [9] and in [23] are identical.

Given the λ_2-calculus, it becomes simpler to describe the interaction of an aspect with the rest of a program. Indeed, the 2-dimensional constructors of the λ_2-calculus enable to faithfully describe all situations in which an aspect can be applied to a given program.

Of course, existing AOP languages do not look like the λ_2-calculus so we show how programs of a simple functional language with aspects—introduced by David Walker and colleagues in [25] and called MinAML—can be translated into the λ_2-calculus. As claimed at the beginning of the paper, the semantics of such programs is provided by a *weaving* algorithm that corresponds to the computation of a normal form in the underlying 2-category.

Note that the work of Kovalyov [14] on modeling aspects by category theory is in accordance with the school of category theory for software design [1]. In this paper, category theory is used as a foundational model for programming languages, which is a completely different line of work.

Using monads in AOP. A very interesting and fruitful use of the correspondence between λ-calculi and categories has been to express computational effects—such as side-effects, exceptions or non-determinism—using the categorical notion of monad, leading to computational monads of Eugenio Moggi [20]. This notion of monad has since been used in functional programming, with Haskell as a spearhead, to accommodate *pure* programs with effects. Namely, given a computational monad T, programs of pure type A are seen as *values* of type A while programs of type TA are seen as *computations* of type A.

Exploiting our connection between λ_2-calculi and 2-categories, we can define a notion of computational 2-monads for AOP as a 2-categorical version of computational monads to extend programs and aspects with effects. We can in particular extend most of existing monads to 2-monads in order to add the corresponding effect in the λ_2-calculus. But most interestingly, this new point of view leads us to the definition of an original 2-monad corresponding to *execution levels*, a notion quite specific to AOP, and a new exception 2-monad transformer that give rise to *execution level with exception*.

Note that monads have already been considered in the setting of AOP. They have been the basis for an analysis of the weaving process [17, 19]. More closely to our work, monads have been used to define effective advices [21]. In this work, advices are encoded as open functions in Haskell and weaving corresponds to the application of a fixpoint combinator on open functions. Our work is more general as we propose to define 2-monads at the top of any functional language with aspects— eg. AspectScheme[7]—without the short-hand of defining advices as open functions.

A monad for execution levels. Execution levels have been proposed by Éric Tanter [24] to structure program computations into *levels*. This stratification enables to prevent infinite recursion and unwanted interference between aspects when aspectual computation is visible to all aspects—including themselves. The standard behaviour is that computation happening at level n produces join points observable by aspects deployed at level $n + 1$ only. This means that an aspect can not see its own join points anymore.

Interestingly, we can define a computational 2-monad for execution levels by

$$\mathbf{EL}(A) \quad = \quad \mathrm{Nat} \to (A \times \mathrm{Nat}) \qquad (1)$$

that corresponds to a particular case of the so-called *state monad* for $S = \mathrm{Nat}$. For that 2-monad, a value is a simple computation oblivious of the current level of execution,

whereas a computation from A to B has type (after uncurrying)

$$A \times \mathrm{Nat} \to B \times \mathrm{Nat}$$

and can thus adapt its behaviour to the level and even change the current level of execution.

The idea is that the notion of execution level introduced in [24] can be translated directly in the calculus induced by $\mathbf{EL}$, where execution levels are managed abstractly through the monadic interpretation. For instance, **up** and **down** operations of type $\mathbf{EL}(\mathbf{Unit})$ can be defined using the successor and predecessor functions on Nat. This corresponds to level shifting operators defined in [24].

Mixing exceptions and execution levels monads. As it is the case for traditional functional programming language, we can define also define 2-monad transformers, and in particular the exception 2-monad transformer that transform a 2-monad T into a 2-monad

$$T_{\mathrm{EX}}A \quad = \quad T(A + \mathbb{E}) \qquad (2)$$

where $\mathbb{E}$ is a set of exceptions. It appears that—when combined with the execution-level 2-monad—the induced notion of exception is *flat* in the sense that they are oblivious of the current level. This means that an aspect can typically catch an exception raised by the base computation and reciprocally, which is in particular what happens in AspectJ. In a recent paper, Ismael Figueroa and Éric Tanter [6] have proposed a calculus where exceptions and execution levels can be mixed in such a way that the basic behavior is the following: an aspect only sees exceptions that have been raised at its level. The default behavior of an advice is thus to catch none of the exceptions raised by the base computation.

At the end of this paper, we show that this calculus with exception can be obtained by combining the execution-level 2-monad $\mathbf{EL}$ with a modified version of the exception 2-monad transformer that takes levels into account.

Plan of the paper. We introduce (§3) the language of Cartesian closed 2-categories, define (§4) the λ_2-calculus, an extension of the λ-calculus with 2-dimensional primitives and present a canonical weaving algorithm based on the computation of a normal form in the underlying 2-category. We then recall a functional AOP language called MinAML (§5), define a translation into the λ_2-calculus and show that weaving in MinAML corresponds to weaving of the translated program in the λ_2-calculus. Finally, we introduce the notion of 2-monad for AOP and use it to define a 2-monad for execution level (§6) and a specialisation of the exception 2-monad transformer (§7) that gives rise to execution levels with exception as introduced in [6].

3. Cartesian Closed 2-Categories in a Nutshell

In this section, we introduce Cartesian closed 2-categories. They are the basis of our conceptual understanding of AOP and we try consequently to explain each construction (2-categories, Cartesian product and closure) in terms of AOP notions. Nevertheless, the reader not comfortable with category theory can skip this section and understand the rest of the paper only in terms of programming language principles.

3.1 A glance at 2-categories

2-categories [11] can be viewed as categories enriched over **Cat**, the category of categories (for more details about enriched category theory, see the monograph of Max Kelly [12]). This means that a 2-category is a category for which the set of morphisms between two objects is itself a category. More concretely, a 2-category $\mathcal{C}$ has a class of objects (also called 0-cells), usually noted $A, B, \ldots$, a class of morphisms (also called 1-cells) between objects, usually noted $f : A \to B$ and a class of morphisms between morphisms (also called 2-cells), usually noted

$$\alpha : (f \Rightarrow g) :: A \to B$$

(or simply $\alpha : f \Rightarrow g$ no confusion is possible). A 2-cell $\alpha : (f \Rightarrow g) :: A \to B$ is generally diagrammatically represented as a 2-dimensional arrow between the 1-dimensional arrows f and g

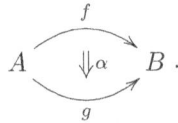

0- and 1-cells form a category called the underlying category of $\mathcal{C}$ – with identity on A denoted by id_A and composition of morphisms f and g denoted by $g \circ f$. 2-cells may be composed "horizontally" and "vertically". We write

$$\beta \circ \alpha : f' \circ f \Rightarrow g' \circ g$$

for the horizontal composite of two 2-cells $\alpha : f \Rightarrow g$ and $\beta : f' \Rightarrow g'$, represented diagrammatically as

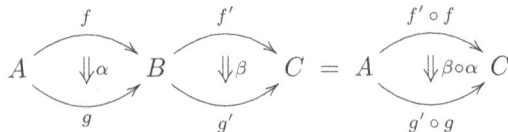

and we write

$$\alpha * \beta : f \Rightarrow h$$

for the vertical composite of two 2-cells $\alpha : f \Rightarrow g$ and $\beta : g \Rightarrow h$, represented diagrammatically as

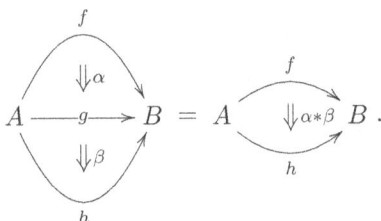

From an AOP point of view, horizontal composition corresponds to functional application and vertical composition corresponds to composition of aspects.

The vertical and horizontal composition laws are required to define categories—they are associative and there are identities

$$1_f : f \Rightarrow f$$

for each 1-cell $f : A \to B$. The identity for the horizontal composition is given by 1_{id_A}, and one requires that

$$1_{g \circ f} = 1_g \circ 1_f.$$

Note that the horizontal composition is extended to a composition between a 2-cell α and a 1-cell f by implicitly regarding the 1-cell f as the identity 2-cell 1_f.

There is one remaining law of compatibility between the horizontal and the vertical composition. This law, called the *interchange law*, guarantees that the two ways of reading the (labelled pasting) diagram

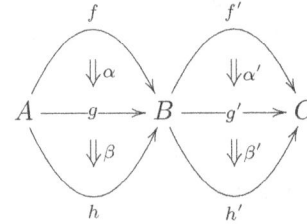

are equal—which means that

$$(\alpha' * \beta') \circ (\alpha * \beta) = (\alpha' \circ \alpha) * (\beta' \circ \beta).$$

Putting on the AOP hat, this property guarantees that application and composition of advices do commute. This means that we can still reason modularly in presence of aspects.

The different associativity, unit and interchange laws guarantee a fundamental property of 2-categories: *each labelled pasting diagram has a unique composite*. From an AOP point of view, this means that the application of a piece of advice (without side effect) at one point of a program must not perturb the application of other advices at other points of the same program. We will see in Sections 6 and 7 how to allow effectful aspects using 2-monads.

To state precisely the connection between Cartesian closed 2-categories and the λ_2-calculus, we need to introduce the standard notions of functors and natural transformations in a 2-dimensional setting.

There is a canonical notion of morphisms between 2-categories, called *2-functor*. Just as a 2-category is a **Cat**-category, a 2-functor consists of a functor enriched over **Cat**. In other words, a 2-functor from $\mathcal{C}$ to $\mathcal{D}$ is a map from i-cells to i-cells (i being 0,1 and 2) that preserves all the structure of a 2-category on the nose. In particular, each 2-functor defines a functor between the underlying categories. As it is the case for functors between categories, there is a notion of *2-natural transformation* transformations between two 2-functors that enables to relate one 2-functor to another.

3.2 Cartesian closed 2-categories

We now present the notion of Cartesian product and closure in a 2-categories that corresponds to the existence of product and functions in functional programming.

A 2-category $\mathcal{C}$ is said to be Cartesian when every pair of objects A_1 and A_2 is equipped with two projection morphisms

$$\pi_1 : A_1 \times A_2 \to A_1 \qquad \pi_2 : A_1 \times A_2 \to A_2.$$

satisfying the following universal property: for every pair of 2-cells

$$\alpha_1 : f_1 \Rightarrow g_1 : X \to A_1 \qquad \alpha_2 : f_2 \Rightarrow g_2 : X \to A_2$$

there exists a unique 2-cells

$$\langle \alpha_1, \alpha_2 \rangle : \langle f_1, f_2 \rangle \Rightarrow \langle g_1, g_2 \rangle : X \to A_1 \times A_2$$

satisfying the two equalities (where i is either 1 or 2)

$$\pi_i \circ \langle \alpha_1, \alpha_2 \rangle = \alpha_i.$$

We also require that $\mathcal{C}$ has a particular object 1, called the *terminal* object, such that there exists a unique 1-cell $\mathbf{skip}_A : A \to 1$ and $1_{\mathbf{skip}_A} : \mathbf{skip}_A \Rightarrow \mathbf{skip}_A$ is the unique 2-cell of that type. The underlying category of a Cartesian 2-category is also Cartesian.

From an AOP point of view, the object 1 corresponds to the type **Unit** and the unique 1-cell of that type is the constant term **skip**. Then, the unique aspect on **skip** is the identity aspect.

A Cartesian 2-category $\mathcal{C}$ is *closed* when it is equipped with a family of functors $\Lambda_{A,B,C} : \mathcal{C}(A \times B, C) \to \mathcal{C}(B, C^A)$ and a family of morphisms $\mathrm{eval}_{A,B} = A \times B^A \to B$ such that

$$\mathrm{eval} \circ (1_A \times \Lambda(\alpha)) = \alpha \quad \text{and} \quad \Lambda(\mathrm{eval} \circ (1_A \times \beta)) = \beta$$

for every 2-cell

$$\alpha : f \Rightarrow g : A \times B \to C \quad \text{and} \quad \beta : f' \Rightarrow g' : B \to C^A.$$

Again, we remark that the underlying category of a Cartesian closed 2-category is also Cartesian closed.

4. The λ_2-calculus

In this section, we present the λ_2-calculus—independently studied by Tom Hirschowitz in [9]—and connected to the notion of 2-λ calculi in the sense of Barnaby Hilken [8]. We adopt Hirschowitz presentation of the calculus has we found it more elegant and concise than our previous version. Sections 4.1–4.3 are a synthesis of [9]; more detailed definitions and proofs can be found there. We then focus at the end of this section on the connection to AOP through an abstract definition of the weaving algorithm.

4.1 2-dimensional signatures

A *2-dimensional signature* Σ consists in a set of base types Σ_0, a set of constant terms $(X_1, \Sigma_1 : X_1 \to \mathbf{L}_0(\Sigma_0))$ indexed by types constructed over Σ_0 and a set of aspects $(X_2, \Sigma_2 : X_2 \to \mathbf{L}_1(\Sigma_1)_{\parallel})$ indexed over parallel terms (having the same type) constructed over Σ_1. The set of types $\mathbf{L}_0(\Sigma_0)$ is generated from element S of Σ_0, the unit type, product and arrow types:

$$A ::= S \mid \mathbf{Unit} \mid A \times A \mid A \to A$$

where S is any element of Σ_0. The set of parallel terms $\mathbf{L}_1(\Sigma_1)_{\parallel}$ is constituted by closed terms (modulo β-η) of the same type obtained from Σ_1 and the 1-dimensional typing rules of Figure 1 corresponding to the traditional λ-calculus.

4.2 λ_2-calculus and permutation equivalence.

Given a 2-signature Σ, we consider the λ_2-calculus $\mathbf{L}(\Sigma)$ whose types are $\mathbf{L}_0(\Sigma_0)$, terms are $\mathbf{L}_1(\Sigma_1)$ and aspects are constructed over Σ_2 using the 2-dimensional typing rules of Figure 1. The typing judgment

$$\Gamma \vdash \alpha : (t \Rightarrow t') :: A$$

says that the aspect α transforms the term t (modulo β-η) of type $\Gamma \vdash A$ into the term t' (modulo β-η) of type $\Gamma \vdash A$; where Γ is a context constituted of a list of a variable and a type, with no variable appearing more than once. All constructions for pairing, abstraction and horizontal composition are extended to aspects and there is a notion of vertical composition $\alpha * \beta$ which corresponds to sequential composition of α and β.

To reflect the structure of Cartesian closed categories, the simply typed λ-calculus is equipped with a notion of equivalence over terms that deals with products and with the closure using the so-called β and η-equivalences. The λ_2-calculus follows the same design principles but is far more bureaucratic. This is not surprising because the notion of Cartesian closed 2-categories requires many diagram commutations that must be captured by equivalences in the calculus. The confluence of such complex equivalences is handled with the use of *permutation equivalences* developed by Sander Bruggink in his study of higher-order rewriting [3]. For instance, the associativity of the vertical composition is reflected by the equivalence

$$\frac{\Gamma \vdash \alpha_i : (t_i \Rightarrow t_{i+1}) :: A \qquad i \in \{1, 2, 3\}}{\Gamma \vdash (\alpha_1 * \alpha_2) * \alpha_3 \equiv \alpha_1 * (\alpha_2 * \alpha_3) : (t_1 \Rightarrow t_4) :: A}$$

In the same way, the interchange law is captured by the equivalence

$$\frac{\Gamma \vdash \alpha : (u_1 \Rightarrow u_2) :: A \quad \Gamma \vdash \beta : (t_1 \Rightarrow t_2) :: A \to B}{\Gamma \vdash (\beta \circ \alpha) * (\beta' \circ \alpha') \equiv (\beta * \beta') \circ (\alpha * \alpha')}$$
$$: (t_1(u_1) \Rightarrow t_3(u_3)) :: B$$

with the second premises:
$$\Gamma \vdash \alpha' : (u_2 \Rightarrow u_3) :: A \quad \Gamma \vdash \beta' : (t_2 \Rightarrow t_3) :: A \to B$$

1-DIMENSIONAL TYPING RULES.

CONSTANT
$$\frac{\Sigma_1(f) = A}{\Gamma \vdash f : A}$$

VARIABLE
$$\frac{}{\Gamma, x : A, \Delta \vdash x : A}$$

ABSTRACTION
$$\frac{\Gamma, x : A \vdash t : B}{\Gamma \vdash \lambda x.\, t : A \to B}$$

APPLICATION
$$\frac{\Gamma \vdash t : A \to B \qquad \Gamma \vdash u : A}{\Gamma \vdash t(u) : B}$$

BOTTOM
$$\frac{}{\Gamma \vdash \mathbf{skip} : \mathbf{Unit}}$$

PAIRING
$$\frac{\Gamma \vdash t : A \qquad \Gamma \vdash t' : B}{\Gamma \vdash \langle t, t' \rangle : A \times B}$$

PROJECTION
$$\frac{}{\Gamma \vdash \pi_i^{A_1, A_2} : A_1 \times A_2 \to A_i}$$

2-DIMENSIONAL TYPING RULES.

2-CONSTANT
$$\frac{\Sigma_2(\alpha) = (f \Rightarrow g) :: A}{\Gamma \vdash \alpha : (f \Rightarrow g) :: A}$$

2-IDENTITY
$$\frac{\Gamma \vdash t : A}{\Gamma \vdash t : (t \Rightarrow t) :: A}$$

2-PAIRING
$$\frac{\Gamma \vdash \alpha : (t \Rightarrow t') :: A \qquad \Gamma \vdash \beta : (u \Rightarrow u') :: B}{\Gamma \vdash \langle \alpha, \beta \rangle : (\langle t, u \rangle \Rightarrow \langle t', u' \rangle) :: A \times B}$$

2-ABSTRACTION
$$\frac{\Gamma, x : A \vdash \alpha : (t \Rightarrow t') :: B}{\Gamma \vdash \lambda x.\, \alpha : (\lambda x.\, t \Rightarrow \lambda x.\, t') :: A \to B}$$

2-APPLICATION
$$\frac{\Gamma \vdash \beta : (t \Rightarrow t') :: A \to B \qquad \Gamma \vdash \alpha : (u \Rightarrow u') :: A}{\Gamma \vdash \beta \circ \alpha : (t(u) \Rightarrow t'(u')) :: B}$$

VERTICAL-COMPOSITION
$$\frac{\Gamma \vdash \alpha : (t_1 \Rightarrow t_2) :: A \qquad \Gamma \vdash \beta : (t_2 \Rightarrow t_3) :: A}{\Gamma \vdash \alpha * \beta : (t_1 \Rightarrow t_3) :: A}$$

Figure 1. Typing rules of the λ_2-calculus

The complete set of permutations equivalences can be found in [9]. The only equivalence that is not a direct translation of the corresponding categorical structure is the β-equivalence

$$\frac{\Gamma, x : A \vdash \alpha : (t_1 \Rightarrow t_2) :: B \qquad \Gamma \vdash \beta : (u_1 \Rightarrow u_2) :: A}{\Gamma \vdash (\lambda x.\, \alpha) \circ \beta \equiv \alpha[\beta/x]}$$

which requires to define a 2-dimensional notion of substitution. Although very intuitive, the definition appears to be a bit technical because it somehow reflects the two equivalent order of composition in the interchange law. As it is not important for our technical development on AOP, we do not present the definition here and refer the interested reader to [9] for details.

4.3 Cartesian closed 2-categories and the λ_2-calculus

The definition above leaves a lot of freedom. There are many λ_2-calculus. Namely, given a 2-signature Σ, the λ_2-calculus constructed on this 2-signature corresponds to the free Cartesian closed 2-category generated by this signature, as stated by the following proposition.

PROPOSITION 1. *The construction* **L** *that computes a λ_2-calculus from a 2-signature induces a functor* **C** *from the category* **2-Sig** *of 2-signatures and signature-preserving morphisms to the category* **2-CCC** *of Cartesian closed 2-categories and strictly structure preserving 2-functors. This*

functor is the left component of the adjunction

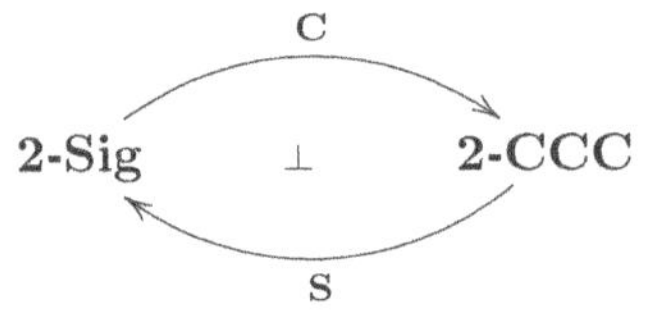

This means that λ_2-calculi correspond exactly to Cartesian closed 2-categories where no additional equality has been added to structural equalities.

4.4 Weaving in the λ_2-calculus

Using the correspondence between the λ_2-calculus and Cartesian closed 2-categories, we can now define a weaving algorithm in terms of categorical rewriting.

As sketched in the introduction, given a term $t(x) : B$ of a λ_2-calculus $\mathbf{L}(\Sigma)$ where x is of type A, we will consider all the possible interactions of aspects defined in $\mathbf{L}(\Sigma)$ with $t(x)$ by considering the category $\mathbf{C}(\Sigma)(A, B)$. This category contains all aspects that transform terms of type $A \to B$ and so the execution of an aspect corresponds to the application of a morphism in that category. The result of the weaving algorithm is thus given by *all* normal forms of the image of $t(x)$ in that category.

More precisely, the set of woven terms is defined as

$$\mathbf{weave}(t(x)) = \{(t'(x), \alpha) \mid (x, t(x)) \xrightarrow{\alpha} (x, t'(x))$$
is a maximal reduction in the category $\mathbf{C}(\Sigma)(A, B)\}$.

Of course, such a normal form has no reason to be unique or even to exist. The purpose of specific AOP languages is often to provide more advanced definitions of aspects that guarantee the uniqueness and sometimes the existence of such a normal form so that the set **weave**$(t(x))$ is a singleton for every term $t(x)$.

Uniqueness of the normal form.   Observe that all the work on *aspect composition* can be understood as a way to combine aspects while conserving uniqueness of the definition of the woven program. Indeed, uniqueness of the normal form corresponds to *determinism* of the weaving algorithm, which is most of the time a property required by a programmer.

For example, when multiple advices can be applied at the same join point, precedence orders are defined in AspectJ, based on the order in which definitions of advices syntactically appear in the code. Those orders, even often opaque, enables a programmer to keep track of which aspect should be applied at a given time.

More algebraic approaches have been proposed (see e.g. [18]) were explicit operators for advices and aspects composition have been introduced.

Existence of a normal form.   The absence of a normal form is often understood as a *circularity* in the application of aspects. This problem is difficult to overcome and can arise even in simple programs. For instance, the work of Éric Tanter on execution levels (reunderstood in Section 6 using 2-monad) is precisely a way to introduce a hierarchy in the application of aspects and thus to avoid basic circular definition. Other lines of work have proposed to restricted the power of advices (for example using a typing system [4]) in order to guarantee that the execution of the program is not critically perturbed.

Weaving on an example.   Suppose that we have defined an aspect

$$\alpha : sqrt \Rightarrow sqrt \circ abs$$

which rewrites all calls to a square root function to ensure that inputs are non-negative. The effect of α on the program

$$p = \lambda x.\, sqrt(sqrt(x))$$

will be described by the composed 2-cell

$$\beta = \lambda x.\, \alpha \circ \alpha \circ x : p \Rightarrow p'$$

that transforms the program p into the program

$$p' = \lambda x.\, sqrt(abs(sqrt(abs(x)))).$$

The aspect β is automatically generated from the aspect α and constructors of the λ_2-calculus. Note that one could argue that this violates one of the primary design goals of AOP, which is to allow separation of cross-cutting concerns. Indeed, each aspect is monomorphic in the sense that the aspect β in the example above is specific to the program p. It could seem unfortunate because an important goal of

AOP languages is that the aspect may be oblivious to the target program – in 2-categorical/λ-calculus terms what seems needed is naturality/parametricity in the scaffolding. However, this is not the point of view adopted in the λ_2-calculus. The idea is that a single definition of an aspect will generate all the possible interactions of this aspect with any program.

5. MinAML

This section shows that the weaving process of a concrete AOP language called MinAML can be understood through a translation into the λ_2-calculus.

MinAML is a version (without conditionals and `before` and `after` advice) of the language introduced in [25] to give one of the first AOP language with a formal semantics. The absence of `before` and `after` advice is unimportant because they can both be encoded with an `around` advice. But the main difference between the original MinAML is that we do not address here the question of scoping of aspects. This scoping mechanism is orthogonal to the question addressed in this paper and would introduce unnecessary complications in definition of the associated λ_2-calculus and of the weaving mechanism. Indeed, the definition of the underlying 2-category associated to a program in MinAML, as well as the corresponding rewriting system, would have to evolve with the change of scope. We have thus decided to omit this mechanism in the definition of the language and work with a global scope.

5.1 Syntax

MinAML is an extension of the λ-calculus with products in two steps. The first extension is usual: we introduce declaration names that can be used to define names for terms of the language with the `let` constructor

$$\texttt{let } f = e.$$

We suppose given a set of declaration names, noted $f, g, \ldots$

The second extension is the introduction of aspects with the constructor

$$\texttt{around } f(x) = e$$

which indicates that at execution, the application of the function f with argument x is replaced by the term e. Using the terminology standard AOP terminology, the term $f(x)$ defines the *pointcut* of the aspect and the term e defines its *advice*.

When declaring advices, the programmer can choose either to replace f entirely or to perform some computations interleaved with one (or more) execution of f (possibly with new arguments) using the keyword `proceed`. When multiple aspects intercept the same function f, one must define on order in the weaving mechanism. For simplicity, we have decided to choose the order of declaration in the program.

The grammar of MinAML is fully described in Figure 2. A program p is constituted by a list of declarations d_s, a list of aspects a_s and a term e. The fact that there is only a global

types	A	$::=$	$S \mid \mathbf{Unit} \mid A \times B \mid A \to B$
values	v	$::=$	$\mathbf{skip} \mid \lambda x.\, e$
expr.	e	$::=$	$v \mid x \mid \mathtt{proceed} \mid e(e)$

aspects	a_s	$::=$	$[\,] \mid [\mathtt{around}\ f(x) = e] \cdot a_s$
declarations	d_s	$::=$	$[\,] \mid [\mathtt{let}\ f = e] \cdot d_s$
programs	p	$::=$	$d_s \cdot a_s \cdot e$

Figure 2. The grammar of the MinAML

scope for aspects in our calculus is enforced by the stratified structure of a program. The term $[\,]$ stands for the empty list, $[h]$ stands for the singleton list with element h and $l \cdot l'$ denotes the concatenation of lists.

5.2 A simple example

Let us now express in this language the example developed in Section 4—of an aspect that ensures that all calls to the *sqrt* function are performed with non-negative values. The following program of MinAML (where we use some usual primitives on integers) defines such an aspect and run *sqrt* on the negative value -4.

$$\mathbb{P} = [\mathtt{let}\ sqrt = \lambda x.\, \sqrt{x},\ \mathtt{let}\ abs = \lambda x.\, |x|] \cdot$$
$$[\mathtt{around}\ sqrt(x) = \mathtt{proceed}(abs(x))] \cdot$$
$$[sqrt(-4)]$$

5.3 Typing

The typing rules for $MinAML$ can be found in [25]. We only present rules for binding and aspects.

Programs are typed in the presence of a context $\Gamma; \Delta$. Γ stipulates the type of variables and Δ stipulates the type of declaration names. This dichotomy enables to force free variables appearing in the definition of a piece of advice to be associated with declaration names only.

Rule BINDING for the $\mathtt{let}$ binder requires that the open variables appearing in t are related to declaration names.

BINDING
$$\frac{;\Delta \vdash e : A \quad ;\Delta, f : A \vdash p : B \quad (f \notin \Delta)}{;\Delta \vdash \mathtt{let}\ f = e; p : B}$$

In Rule AROUND,

AROUND
$$x : A; \Delta, f : A \to A' \vdash e[f/\mathtt{proceed}] : A'$$
$$\frac{;\Delta, f : A \to A' \vdash p : B}{;\Delta, f : A \to A' \vdash \mathtt{around}\ f(x) = e; p : B}$$

one assume that a declaration name f of type $A \to A'$ is already defined in Δ and check that t (where every occurrence of $\mathtt{proceed}$ is replaced by f) has type A' assuming that the argument x of $f(x)$ has type A and is the only variable in the environment Γ. In that case, the program $\mathtt{around}\ f(x) = t; p$ is given the same type as the program p.

It is important that declaration names can only be bound to terms defined on declaration names. In this way, aspects in MinAML are not able to intercept terms with free variables in the same way as constant aspects in λ_2-calculus cannot be defined between open terms.

5.4 Operational semantics.

In [25], the semantics of MinAML is given by a translation into a more basic AOP language. We define here a direct and equivalent operational semantics of MinAML using a reduction relation $\rightharpoonup$ which described a call-by-value small step semantics between configurations of the form $\langle d_s, a_s, e \rangle$. This small step reduction is described by

$$\langle d_s, a_s, E(f) \rangle \quad \rightharpoonup \quad \langle d_s, a_s, E(\mathrm{Weave}(a_s, f, d_s)) \rangle$$
$$\langle d_s, a_s, E((\lambda x.e)(v)) \rangle \quad \rightharpoonup \quad \langle d_s, a_s, E(e[v/x]) \rangle$$

where E is an evaluation context (i.e. an expression with a hole) and $\mathrm{Weave}(a_s, f, d_s)$ is the weaving function

$$\mathrm{Weave}([\mathtt{around}\ f(x) = e] \cdot a_s, f, d_s) =$$
$$e[\mathrm{Weave}(a_s, f, d_s)/\mathtt{proceed}]$$
$$\mathrm{Weave}([\mathtt{around}\ f'(x) = e] \cdot a_s, f, d_s) =$$
$$\mathrm{Weave}(a_s, f, d_s) \qquad (f \neq f')$$
$$\mathrm{Weave}([\,], f, d_s \cdot [\mathtt{let}\ f = e] \cdot d_s') = e$$

The application of a bound name f to a value v is first woven with respect to the list of aspects a_s (in their apparition order) and, when their is no more aspects in the list, each call to $\mathtt{proceed}$ is replaced by the term bound to f.

5.5 A translation into the pure λ_2-calculus

We now present the translation of a typed program

$$p = d_s \cdot a_s \cdot e$$

into the λ_2-calculus. More precisely, we will define a λ_2-calculus $\mathbf{L}_p$ based on declarations present in d_s and aspects present in a_s and a translation $[\![e]\!]$ of the term e, see Figure 3. The construction of the 2-signature Σ_p of $\mathbf{L}_p$—presented in Figure 3 in Ocaml style—goes in two steps:

(a) we produce a list of aspects $[\![a_s]\!]$ and a mapping γ from declaration names in d_s to integers (Figure 3-a). Because a declaration name f can be intercepted by more than one aspect, we introduce a fresh declaration name f_i each time we translate an aspect whose pointcut relies on f. That is, the ith aspect $\mathtt{around}\ f(x) = t$ that intercept f will thus be translated into the constant aspect

$$a_{f_i} : f_i \Rightarrow \lambda x.\, [\![t[f_{i+1}/\mathtt{proceed}]]\!]$$

that intercepts f_i and proceeds with f_{i+1}. In this way, we construct a sequence of declaration names that drives the list of aspects that can intercept applications of the function f.

$$\Sigma_p = (\{S, \mathbf{Unit}\}, \{f_i \mid f \in d_s \text{ and } 1 \le i \le \gamma(f)\}, [\![a_s]\!] \cdot [\![d_s]\!])$$
$$[\![e]\!] = e[f_1/f] \quad \text{(for all } f \text{ occurring in } e)$$

(a)
```
let trans_asp(a,b) = match (a,b) with
    | ((γ,A),(around f(x) = t)) -> (γ[f ↦ γ(f) + 1],
        A·[ a_{f_γ(f)} : f_{γ(f)} ⇒ λx. [[t[f_{γ(f)+1}/proceed]]]])
in (γ,[[a_s]]) = fold_l(trans_asp,(let γ x = 1,[]),a_s)
```

(b)
```
let trans_eq(d) = match d with
    | let f = t -> [a_f : f_{γ(f)} ⇒ [[t]]]
in [[d_s]] = map trans_eq d_s
```

Figure 3. Translation of MinAML into the λ_2-calculus

(b) we define a list of aspects $[\![ds]\!]$ (Figure 3-b) by translating each declaration $\mathtt{let}\ f = t$ into the constant aspect $a_f : f_{\gamma(f)} \Rightarrow [\![t]\!]$.

For example, the 2-signature $\Sigma_{\mathbb{P}}$ corresponding to $\mathbb{P}$ is given by the constant terms

$$sqrt_1, sqrt_2, abs_1$$

and by the three aspects

$$
\begin{aligned}
a_1 &: \quad sqrt_1 \Rightarrow \lambda x.\ sqrt_2(abs_1(x)) \\
a_2 &: \quad sqrt_2 \Rightarrow \lambda x.\ \sqrt{x} \\
a_3 &: \quad abs_1 \Rightarrow \lambda x.\ |x|
\end{aligned}
$$

5.6 Weaving in MinAML

Once the λ_2-calculus $\mathbf{L}_p$ has been generated, the weaving algorithm is defined as in Section 4.4. Namely, we compute the normal form (if it exists) in the corresponding category—observe that the ordering of advices guarantees that there is at most one normal form. The correction of this interpretation is stated by the following proposition.

PROPOSITION 2 (Translation of MinAML). *Given a program $d_s \cdot a_s \cdot e$ of type A, the configuration $\langle d_s, a_s, e \rangle$ reduces to $\langle d_s, a_s, v \rangle$ for some value v of type A if and only if*

$$\mathbf{weave}([\![e]\!]) = \{[\![v]\!]\}.$$

5.7 Weaving on a simple example

Let us now explain the behavior of the weaving algorithm on the simple example $\mathbb{P}$. The computation can be described by the following sequence of reduction (where some extra β-reduction has been performed to make the reading easier):

$$
\begin{array}{ccc}
sqrt_1(-4) & \xrightarrow{a_1 \circ \mathbb{I}(-4)} & sqrt_2(abs_1(-4)) \\
& \xrightarrow{a_2 \circ \mathbb{I}(abs_1(-4))} & \sqrt{abs_1(-4)} \\
& \xrightarrow{\mathbb{I}(\sqrt{-}) \circ a_3 \circ \mathbb{I}(-4)} & \sqrt{|-4|} = 2
\end{array}
$$

REMARK 1. *In the rest of this paper, we suppose that our calculus (and the corresponding 2-category) is equipped with a proper notion of natural numbers of type Nat (with equality, successor $(\mathrm{Succ}(n))$, predecessor $(\mathrm{Pred}(n))$ and conditionals (which corresponds to coproducts at the 2-categorical level) written as 'if e then e_1 else e_2'. We use standard primitives on integers and if-then-else constructor in the expected way.*

6. The Execution-Level Monad

In this section, we introduce a 2-dimensional version of Moggi's *computational monads*. To illustrate this new powerful tool for AOP, we extend MinAML with Tanter's execution levels and show that this new calculus can be translated in the λ_2-calculus extended with the execution-level 2-monad **EL**.

6.1 Computational 2-monads

A (strict) *2-monad* [2] can be seen as a monad in the 2-category of 2-categories, 2-functors and 2-natural transformations. In its Kleisli presentation, a 2-monad T on a 2-category $\mathcal{C}$ is a 2-functor from $\mathcal{C}$ to $\mathcal{C}$ equipped with a 2-natural transformation $\eta_A : A \to TA$ and a transformation $*$ that transports every 2-cell $\alpha : (f \Rightarrow g) :: A \to TB$ into the 2-cell $\alpha^* : (f^* \Rightarrow g^*) :: TA \to TB$ satisfying

- $\eta_A^* = \mathrm{id}_{TA}$
- $\alpha^* \circ \eta_A = \alpha \quad$ for $\alpha : (f \Rightarrow g) :: A \to TB$
- $\beta^* \circ \alpha^* = (\beta^* \circ \alpha)^* \quad$ for $\alpha : (f \Rightarrow g) :: A \to TB$ and $\beta : (g \Rightarrow h) :: B \to TC$

For compatibility with products in Cartesian closed 2-categories, we define a *computational 2-monad* as a strict 2-monad equipped with a strength

$$A \times TB \xrightarrow{t_{A,B}} T(A \times B)$$

subject to usual identity and associativity laws.

EXAMPLE 1. *Most of usual computational monads can be extended to the 2-dimensional setting, in particular:*

- **side-effect** *: $TA = S \Rightarrow (A \times S)$, where S is the set of states*
- **exceptions** *: $TA = A + \mathbb{E}$, where $\mathbb{E}$ is the set of exceptions*

This 2-categorical machinery justifies the following notion of computational 2-monad for AOP as a metalanguage for the λ_2-calculus. For the simplicity of the development, we will forget about the underlying *Kleisli interpretation* in the Kleisli 2-category induced by the 2-monad and only present the results from a programming language point of view.

A *computational 2-monad* on the λ_2-calculus consists in:

- A function T that associates a computational type TA to any type A.

- A lifted aspect

$$[\alpha]_T$$

of type $([e]_T \Rightarrow [e']_T) :: TA$ for any aspect α of type $(e \Rightarrow e') :: A$. The idea is that $[e]_T$ is the computation that simply returns the value e and $[\alpha]_T$ is an aspect between two such computations. This corresponds to the unit of the 2-monad.

- A let-binder

$$\mathtt{let}_T\ x \Leftarrow \alpha\ \mathtt{in}\ \beta$$

of type $((\mathtt{let}_T\ x \Leftarrow e_1\ \mathtt{in}\ e_2) \Rightarrow (\mathtt{let}_x\ e_1' \Leftarrow e_2'\ \mathtt{in}\ )) :: TB$ for α of type $(e_1 \Rightarrow e_1') :: TA$ and β of type $(e_2 \Rightarrow e_2') :: TB$ assuming that x has type A. The idea is that $\mathtt{let}_T\ x \Leftarrow e_1\ \mathtt{in}\ e_2$ is a computation that evaluates e_1 first and binds the result to x in e_2 and $\mathtt{let}_T\ x \Leftarrow \alpha\ \mathtt{in}\ \beta$ is an aspect between two such computations. This corresponds to the composition $\beta^* \circ \alpha$ in the Kleisli 2-category.

- A function

$$\mathtt{run}_{T,A} : TA \to A$$

that runs a computation of type A and returns its result.

Those new constructions are subject to equality that mimics the commutative diagram in the categorical setting (see [20] for details). Depending on the considered 2-monad, there can be new constructors in the language that enable to handle the computation effect. For instance, for the state 2-monad, there are functions $\mathtt{lookup}$ and $\mathtt{update}$ that respectively returns and updates the current state. In the case of the exception 2-monad, there are $\mathtt{raise}$ and $\mathtt{handle}$ constructors that respectively raises and catches an exception.

6.2 MinAML$_{\mathrm{EL}}$: MinAML with execution level

We now extend MinAML with a notion of execution levels as defined in [24]. As explained in introduction, the idea behind execution levels is to enhance computation with an integer that represents the *current level* of execution. This level is then used to make join points produced by computation happening at level n observable by aspects deployed at level $n + 1$. Note that in the original paper, the deployment of aspects is entirely dynamic, whereas the deployment in MinAML is static. This is not an issue because the management of execution levels in MinAML can still be dynamic. This shows by the way that a dynamic deployment of aspects is not required to have a proper notion of dynamic execution levels.

MinAML$_{\mathrm{EL}}$ is an extension of MinAML with four new constructors

$$e ::= \ldots \mid \mathtt{up}(e) \mid \mathtt{down}(e) \mid \mathtt{in\_up}(e) \mid \mathtt{in\_down}(e)$$

where $\mathtt{in\_up}(e)$ and $\mathtt{in\_down}(e)$ are only here to define the operational semantics and are not user-visible. The typing system is extended straightforwardly to those new constructors.

Operational semantics of MinAML$_{\mathrm{EL}}$ is defined between configurations of the form $\langle l, d_s, a_s, e \rangle$, where l is the current level of execution. Because the deployment of aspects is static, we can simplify the semantics. By default an aspect is always deployed at level 1 and deployment at a higher level l must be explicitly express by the user using

$$\mathtt{around}\ (l, f(x)) = e.$$

The small step semantics is extended accordingly

$$\langle l, d_s, a_s, E(\mathtt{up}(e)) \rangle \rightharpoonup \langle \mathtt{Succ}(l), d_s, a_s, E(\mathtt{in\_up}(e)) \rangle$$
$$\langle l, d_s, a_s, E(\mathtt{in\_up}(v)) \rangle \rightharpoonup \langle \mathtt{Pred}(l), d_s, a_s, E(v) \rangle$$
$$\langle l, d_s, a_s, E(\mathtt{down}(e)) \rangle \rightharpoonup \langle \mathtt{Pred}(l), d_s, a_s, E(\mathtt{in\_down}(e)) \rangle$$
$$\langle l, d_s, a_s, E(\mathtt{in\_down}(v)) \rangle \rightharpoonup \langle \mathtt{Succ}(l), d_s, a_s, E(v) \rangle$$
$$\langle l, d_s, a_s, E(f(v)) \rangle \rightharpoonup$$
$$\langle l, d_s, a_s, E(\mathtt{up}(\mathrm{Weave}(a_s, (\mathtt{Succ}(l), f), d_s))) \rangle$$

where $\mathrm{Weave}(a_s, (l, f), d_s)$ is extended as

$$\mathrm{Weave}([\mathtt{around}\ (l, f(x)) = e] \cdot a_s, (l, f), d_s) =$$
$$e[\mathrm{Weave}(a_s, (l, f), d_s)/\mathtt{proceed}]$$
$$\mathrm{Weave}([\mathtt{around}\ (l', f'(x)) = e] \cdot a_s, (l, f), d_s) =$$
$$\mathrm{Weave}(a_s, (l, f), d_s) \quad (f \neq f'\ \text{or}\ l \neq l')$$

The reduction of $\mathtt{up}(e)$ increases the level and places the marker $\mathtt{in\_up}$ in the execution context. When the nested expression is reduced to a value, this marker is disposed while decreasing the level back (and dually for $\mathtt{down}(e)$ and $\mathtt{in\_down}(e)$). The weaver is a modified version of the weaver of Section 5.4 where the level at which the join point as been emitted is checked to match the level of deployment of the aspect.

Note that the only difference with execution levels defined by Éric Tanter is the absence of level-capturing functions. They could be easily added to MinAML$_{\mathrm{EL}}$ but their translation in the monadic language would require non-canonical constructors whose definitions have been left for future work.

6.3 The execution-level monad

It is possible to define a 2-monad on the λ_2-calculus in order to recover execution levels and interpret MinAML$_{\mathrm{EL}}$. As explained in introduction, **EL** (defined in Equation (1)) is a restriction of the state 2-monad where the state only contains information on the current level. The lifting, let-binder and run function are given by

$$[\alpha]_{\mathbf{EL}} = \lambda n.\ (\alpha, n)$$
$$\mathtt{let}_{\mathbf{EL}}\ x \Leftarrow \alpha\ \mathtt{in}\ \beta = \lambda n.\ \mathtt{let}\ (a, n') \Leftarrow \alpha \circ n\ \mathtt{in}$$
$$(\beta \circ a) \circ n'$$
$$\mathtt{run}_{\mathbf{EL}, A}\ c = c(0)$$

and we can define three operations specific to the execution-level 2-monad that respectively returns, upgrades or downgrades the current level:

$$
\begin{aligned}
lookup: &\quad \mathbf{EL}(\mathbb{N}\mathrm{at}) &=&\quad \lambda n.\,(n,n) \\
up: &\quad \mathbf{EL}(\mathrm{Unit}) &=&\quad \lambda n.\,(\mathbf{skip}, \mathrm{Succ}(n)) \\
down: &\quad \mathbf{EL}(\mathrm{Unit}) &=&\quad \lambda n.\,(\mathbf{skip}, \mathrm{Pred}(n))
\end{aligned}
$$

6.4 Interpreting MinAML$_{\mathrm{EL}}$ using the execution-level monad

We now translate MinAML$_{\mathrm{EL}}$ into the λ_2-calculus extended with $\mathbf{EL}$. The structure of the translation is the same as the translation of MinAML given in Figure 3, the only differences take place in the definition of $[\![e]\!]_{\mathbf{EL}}$ and the translation of $\texttt{around}\ (l, f(x)) = e$. The translation of a term of MinAML is given by lifting and the translation of applications is given by the let-binder

$$
\begin{aligned}
[\![e]\!]_{\mathbf{EL}} &= [[e]]_{\mathbf{EL}} &&(e \in \mathrm{MinAML}) \\
[\![e_2(e_1)]\!]_{\mathbf{EL}} &= \mathtt{let}_{\mathbf{EL}}\ x \Leftarrow [\![e_1]\!]_{\mathbf{EL}}\ \mathtt{in}\ [\![e_2]\!]_{\mathbf{EL}}(x)
\end{aligned}
$$

The translation of up- and down-lifters is given by

$$
\begin{aligned}
[\![\texttt{in\_up}(e)]\!]_{\mathbf{EL}} &= \mathtt{let}_{\mathbf{EL}}\ a \Leftarrow [\![e]\!]_{\mathbf{EL}}\ \mathtt{in} \\
&\qquad \mathtt{let}_{\mathbf{EL}}\ () \Leftarrow down\ \mathtt{in}\ [a]_{\mathbf{EL}} \\
[\![\texttt{up}(e)]\!]_{\mathbf{EL}} &= \mathtt{let}_{\mathbf{EL}}\ () \Leftarrow up\ \mathtt{in}\ [\![\texttt{in\_up}(e)]\!]_{\mathbf{EL}}
\end{aligned}
$$

and dually for $\texttt{in\_down}(e)$ and $\texttt{down}(e)$. It remains to define the constant aspect associated to $\texttt{around}\ (l, f(x)) = e$,

$$
\begin{aligned}
a_{f_i}: f_i \Rightarrow\ &\mathtt{let}_{\mathbf{EL}}\ n \Leftarrow lookup\ \mathtt{in} \\
&\mathtt{if}\ (l == n)\ \mathtt{then}\ (\lambda x.\ [\![t[f_{i+1}/\mathtt{proceed}]]\!]_{\mathbf{EL}}) \\
&\qquad \mathtt{else}\ f_{i+1}
\end{aligned}
$$

Prop 2 can be extended to MinAML$_{\mathrm{EL}}$.

PROPOSITION 3 (Translation of MinAML$_{\mathrm{EL}}$). *Given a program $d_s \cdot a_s \cdot e$ of MinAML$_{\mathrm{EL}}$ of type A, the configuration $\langle 0, d_s, a_s, e\rangle$ reduces to $\langle 0, d_s, a_s, v\rangle$ for some value v of type A if and only if*

$$
\mathbf{weave}(\mathtt{run}_{\mathbf{EL},A}\ [\![e]\!]_{\mathbf{EL}}) = \{\mathtt{run}_{\mathbf{EL},A}\ [\![v]\!]_{\mathbf{EL}}\}.
$$

7. The Execution-Level-with-Exception Monad

The usual management of exceptions in AOP (e.g. in AspectJ) is *flat* in the sense that an advice can typically catch an exception raised by the base computation and conversely. Starting from this observation, Ismael Figueroa and Éric Tanter have proposed to take levels into account when raising exceptions [6]. In this section, we present an extension MinAML$_{\mathrm{EL}}$ with exceptions sensitive to execution levels and show that this extension can be seen as the use of a particular exception 2-monad transformer.

7.1 MinAML$_{\mathrm{EL}}$ with exceptions

We extend MinAML$_{\mathrm{EL}}$ with three new constructors

$$e ::= \ldots \mid \mathtt{raise}\ ex \mid \mathtt{raise}_l\ ex \mid \mathtt{try}\ e\ \mathtt{with}\ e$$

where ex belongs to a special set $\mathbb{E}$ of exceptions and $\mathtt{raise}_l$ is not user-visible. The typing system is defined in a standard way and the small step reduction is extended as

$$
\begin{aligned}
\langle l, d_s, a_s, E(\mathtt{raise}\ ex)\rangle &\rightharpoonup \langle l, d_s, a_s, E(\mathtt{raise}_l\ ex)\rangle \\
\langle l, d_s, a_s, E(\mathtt{try}\ v\ \mathtt{with}\ e)\rangle &\rightharpoonup \langle l, d_s, a_s, E(v)\rangle \\
\langle l, d_s, a_s, E(\mathtt{try}\ (\mathtt{raise}_l)\ ex\ \mathtt{with}\ e)\rangle &\rightharpoonup \langle l, d_s, E(e(ex))\rangle \\
\langle l, d_s, a_s, E(\mathtt{try}\ (\mathtt{raise}_{l'}\ ex)\ \mathtt{with}\ e)\rangle &\rightharpoonup \\
\langle l, d_s, E(\mathtt{raise}_{l'}\ ex)\rangle &\qquad (l \neq l')
\end{aligned}
$$

7.2 The execution-level-with-exception monad transformer

If we apply the traditional exception 2-monad transformer (as defined in Equation (2)) to the execution-level 2-monad, we end up with a *flat* notion of exception that is oblivious to the current level. As in AspectJ, such a flat notion is not convenient because it typically allows advices to intercept exceptions raised by the base computation. To recover the semantics of MinAML$_{\mathrm{EL}}$ with exception, we need to define a 2-monad transformer

$$T_{\mathbf{EX}}\ A \quad = \quad T(A + (\mathbb{E} \times \mathrm{Nat}))$$

for any 2-monad T. This 2-monad transformer generates a notion of exceptions at the top of T that enables to attach an integer to an exception. In the case of the execution-level monad, we will use this integer to store the level at which the exception has been raised. $T_{\mathbf{EX}}$ is defined as (specific constructors of T are lifted straightforwardly)

$$
\begin{aligned}
[\alpha]_{T_{\mathbf{EX}}} &= [in_L\alpha]_T \\
\mathtt{let}_{T_{\mathbf{EX}}}\ x \Leftarrow \alpha\ \mathtt{in}\ \beta &= \mathtt{let}_T\ u \Leftarrow \alpha\ \mathtt{in}\ \mathtt{case}\ u\ \mathtt{of} \\
&\qquad a \Rightarrow \beta \circ a \mid e \Rightarrow [in_R e]_T \\
\mathtt{run}_{T_{\mathbf{EX}},A}\ c &= \mathtt{case}\ (\mathtt{run}_{T,A}\ c)\ \mathtt{of}\ a \Rightarrow a
\end{aligned}
$$

and we can define the two classical operations specific to the raiser and the handler:

$$
\begin{aligned}
raise_A &: (\mathbb{E} \times \mathrm{Nat}) \rightarrow T_{\mathbf{EX}}\ A \\
raise_A\ (e, n) &= [in_R\ (e, n)]_T \\
handle_A &: T_{\mathbf{EX}}\ A \rightarrow ((\mathbb{E} \times \mathrm{Nat}) \rightarrow T_{\mathbf{EX}}\ A) \rightarrow \mathbf{EX}\ A \\
handle_A\ c\ f &= \mathtt{let}_T\ u \Leftarrow c\ \mathtt{in}\ \mathtt{case}\ u\ \mathtt{of} \\
&\qquad a \Rightarrow [a]_{T_{\mathbf{EX}}} \mid e \Rightarrow f(e)
\end{aligned}
$$

7.3 Interpreting MinAML$_{\mathrm{EL}}$ with exceptions using the execution-level-with-exception monad

We now show how to interpret MinAML$_{\mathrm{EL}}$ with exceptions in the λ_2-calculus on the 2-monad $\mathbf{EL}_{\mathbf{EX}}$. The translation is the same as in Section 6, it just remains to lift the translation for terms of MinAML$_{\mathrm{EL}}$

$$
\begin{aligned}
[\![e]\!]_{\mathbf{EX}} &= \mathtt{let}_{\mathbf{EL}}\ x \Leftarrow [\![e_1]\!]_{\mathbf{EL}}\ \mathtt{in}\ [x]_{\mathbf{EX}} \\
[\![e_2(e_1)]\!]_{\mathbf{EX}} &= \mathtt{let}_{\mathbf{EX}}\ x \Leftarrow [\![e_1]\!]_{\mathbf{EX}}\ \mathtt{in}\ [\![e_2]\!]_{\mathbf{EX}}(x)
\end{aligned}
$$

and translate the raiser and the handler

$$[\![\texttt{raise } e]\!]_{\textbf{EX}} = \texttt{let}_{\textbf{EL}_{\textbf{EX}}}\ n \Leftarrow lookup \texttt{ in } raise_A(e, n)$$

$$[\![\texttt{try } c \texttt{ with } f]\!]_{\textbf{EL}} = handle_A\ c\ \tilde{f}$$

with $\tilde{f} = \lambda(e, n).\ \texttt{let}_{\textbf{EL}_{\textbf{EX}}}\ l \Leftarrow lookup \texttt{ in}$
$\qquad\qquad \texttt{if } (l == n) \texttt{ then } [\![f]\!]_{\textbf{EX}}(e) \texttt{ else } raise_A\ (e, n)$

Prop. 3 can be extended to $\text{MinAML}_{\text{EL}}$ with exceptions.

PROPOSITION 4 (Translation of $\text{MinAML}_{\text{EL}}$). *Given a program $d_s \cdot a_s \cdot e$ of $MinAML_{EL}$ with exception of type A, the configuration $\langle 0, d_s, a_s, e \rangle$ reduces to $\langle 0, d_s, a_s, v \rangle$ for some value v of type A if and only if*

$$\textbf{weave}(\texttt{run}_{\textbf{EL}_{\textbf{EX}}, A}\ [\![e]\!]_{\textbf{EX}}) = \{\texttt{run}_{\textbf{EL}_{\textbf{EX}}, A}\ [\![v]\!]_{\textbf{EX}}\}.$$

8. Conclusion

The keystone of this paper is to approach AOP (and more generally type-preserving program transformation) from a category-theoretic perspective, in order to complement the software engineering approach. We believe that this approach could have substantial benefit at the level of conceptual understanding of what AOP actually is. More precisely, we identify (Cartesian closed) 2-categories as a suitable setting in which programs can be seen as 1-cells and aspects can be seen as 2-cells. To make this analogy precise, we present an internal language for Cartesian closed 2-categories called the λ_2-calculus—a 2-dimensional extension of the traditional λ-calculus. We formulate a notion of weaving inside the λ_2-calculus and demonstrate the applicability of our construction by translating a more realistic functional AOP language called MinAML into the λ_2-calculus. This translation enables to interpret a program of MinAML in a Cartesian closed 2-category and to define the weaving algorithm as the computation of a normal form in a rewriting system based on that 2-category. Finally, we introduce the notion of 2-monads for AOP, which are the direct extension of computational monads used in functional programming. We illustrate the conceptual power of 2-monads by defining an execution-level 2-monad that corresponds to Tanter's *execution levels* and a new exception monad transformer that give rise to *execution level with exception*.

Acknowledgments The author thanks Tom Hirschowitz and Éric Tanter for valuable discussions.

References

[1] D. Batory, M. Azanza, and J. Saraiva. The objects and arrows of computational design. In *Model Driven Engineering Languages and Systems*, volume 5301 of *LNCS*, pages 1–20. Springer Berlin / Heidelberg, 2008.

[2] R. Blackwell, G. Kelly, and A. Power. Two-dimensional monad theory. *Journal of Pure and Applied Algebra*, 59(1):1–41, 1989.

[3] S. Bruggink. *Equivalence of Reductions in Higher-Order Rewriting*. PhD thesis, Utrecht University, 2008.

[4] D. Dantas and D. Walker. Harmless advice. In *Proceedings of POPL*, volume 41, page 396, 2006.

[5] B. De Fraine, E. Ernst, and M. Südholt. Essential aop: the a calculus. *Proceedings of ECOOP*, pages 101–125, 2010.

[6] I. Figueroa and É. Tanter. A semantics for execution levels with exceptions. In *Proceedings of FOAL*, 2011.

[7] I. Figueroa, E. Tanter, and N. Tabareau. A Practical Monadic Aspect Weaver. *Proceedings of FOAL*, 2012.

[8] B. Hilken. Towards a proof theory of rewriting: the simply typed 2λ-calculus. *Theoretical Computer Science*, 170(1-2):407–444, 1996.

[9] T. Hirschowitz. Cartesian closed 2-categories and permutation equivalence in higher-order rewriting. submitted.

[10] R. Jagadeesan, A. Jeffrey, and J. Riely. A calculus of untyped aspect-oriented programs. In *Proceedings of ECOOP*, 2003.

[11] G. Kelly and R. Street. Review of the elements of 2-categories. In *Category Seminar*, pages 75–103. Springer, 1974.

[12] M. Kelly. *Basic Concepts of Enriched Category Theory*, volume 64 of *Lecture Notes in Mathematics*. Cambridge University Press, 1982.

[13] G. Kiczales, J. Lamping, A. Mendhekar, C. Maeda, C. Lopes, J. Loingtier, and J. Irwin. Aspect-Oriented Programming. In *Proceedings of ECOOP*, volume 1241. Springer-Verlag, 1997.

[14] S. Kovalyov. Modeling Aspects by Category Theory. *Proceedings of FOAL*, page 63, 2010.

[15] J. Lambek. Cartesian closed categories and typed lambda-calculi. In *13th Spring School on Combinators and Functional Programming Languages*, page 175. Springer-Verlag, 1985.

[16] J. Lambek and P. Scott. *Introduction to higher order categorical logic*. Cambridge University Press, 1988.

[17] R. Lämmel. Adding Superimposition To a Language Semantics. In *FOAL'03*, Mar. 2003.

[18] R. Lopez-Herrejon, D. Batory, and C. Lengauer. A disciplined approach to aspect composition. In *Proceedings of PEPM*, page 77. ACM, 2006.

[19] W. D. Meuter. Monads as a theoretical foundation for aop. In *AOP position paper at ECOOP*, 1997.

[20] E. Moggi. Notions of computation and monads. *Information and Computation*, 93:55–92, 1991.

[21] B. C. d. S. Oliveira, T. Schrijvers, and W. R. Cook. Effectiveadvice: disciplined advice with explicit effects. In *Proceedings of AOSD*, 2010.

[22] R. Seely. Modelling computations: a 2-categorical framework. In *Proceedings of LICS*, pages 65–71, 1987.

[23] N. Tabareau. Aspect oriented programming: a language for 2-categories. In *Proceedings of FOAL 2011*, 2011.

[24] É. Tanter. Execution levels for aspect-oriented programming. In *Proceedings of AOSD*, 2010.

[25] D. Walker, S. Zdancewic, and J. Ligatti. A theory of aspects. In *Proceedings of ICFP*, volume 38, pages 127–139, 2003.

[26] M. Wand, G. Kiczales, and C. Dutchyn. A semantics for advice and dynamic join points in aspect-oriented programming. *ACM TOPLAS*, 26(5):890–910, 2004.

Adaptable Generic Programming with Required Type Specifications and Package Templates

Eyvind W. Axelsen   Stein Krogdahl

Department of Informatics, University of Oslo, Norway

{eyvinda, steinkr}@ifi.uio.no

Abstract

The aim of this work is to provide better support for adaption and refinement of generic code. This type of flexibility is desirable in order to fully reap the potential of generic programming. Our proposal for an improved mechanism is an extension to the previously published *Package Templates* (PT) mechanism, which is designed for development of reusable modules that can be adapted to their specific purpose when used in a program. The PT mechanism relies on compile-time specialization, and supports separate type checking and type-safe composition of modules. The extension to PT presented here is called *required types*, and can be seen as an enhanced form of type parameters, allowing them the same flexibility as other elements of the PT mechanism. We implement a subset of the *Boost Graph Library* in order to exemplify, validate, and compare our approach to other options.

Categories and Subject Descriptors   D.2.13 [*Software Engineering*]: Reusable Software; D.3.3 [*Programming Languages*]: Language Constructs and Features—Modules, packages

General Terms   Languages, Design

Keywords   Generic Programming, Reuse, Templates

1. Introduction

When developing libraries or other software components meant for widespread reuse, it is vital to minimize assumptions on the client code. On the other hand, it is equally important to be able to express a sufficient set of requirements for the clients of the library so that it can be written in a type-safe manner that yields efficient code. Furthermore, it is important that a client can refine and adapt the library to the problem at hand.

Many languages, such as e.g. Java, C#, C++, Scala, and Haskell, support constructs for *generic programming* in order to better facilitate the development of reusable libraries. The degree to which each language supports such constructs varies, and an excellent overview that compares several languages with respect to support for generic programming can be found in [11].

There are several definitions of what generic programming actually entails (or should entail), but perhaps a more fruitful angle is to consider what it is that we are trying to achieve with such mechanisms. In that respect, Jazayeri et. al [15, page 2] state the following:

> "The goal of generic programming is to express algorithms and data structures in a *broadly adaptable*, interoperable form that allows their direct use in software construction" [emphasis ours].

We agree, to a large extent, with this quote, even if it may be deemed a bit wide in scope. The adaptability part of the goal is in our opinion very important, and in this paper we will describe a mechanism that we think in many cases can represent both an improvement and a simplification with respect to adaptable generic programming compared to contemporary approaches.

The mechanism is an extension of the Package Template (PT) mechanism [3, 16]. We will in the following refer to the previously published variant as *basic PT*, or just PT when the variant is obvious from the context. Basic PT allows type safe renaming, merging, and refinement in the form of static additions and overrides that are orthogonal to ordinary inheritance. It thus differs from typical virtual class-based [17] mechanisms in that composition and refinement (beyond ordinary OO constructs) is reified at compile-time only, yielding a simpler type system.

Seeking to also attain the goal presented above for *generic*, potentially *heavily parameterized*, libraries, we incorporate a notion of *required type specifications* in the PT mechanism, and we label this variant PT*r*. The approach is inspired by suggestions to use virtual types as an alternative approach to generic parameterization in Java [27], and enables utilization of basic PT's inherent capabilities for adaption also for generic concepts and constraints. PT*r* supports multi-type concepts, associated types, and nominal and structural generic bounds. Retroactive modeling and adaption through renaming, merging and additions are thus also supported, without sacrificing type safety, performance, or dynamic dispatch.

To demonstrate and validate our approach, we have implemented a small yet non-trivial subset of the Boost Graph Library [25], which employs a rather advanced usage of generics. The subset is the same as that described and implemented by [11], and we will compare and contrast the implementation made possible with *PTr* with those of [11]. The implementation and a prototype compiler can be downloaded from `http://swat.project.ifi.uio.no/software`.

The main contribution of this paper is thus to present PT*r* as an approach to creating flexible generic libraries, and to demonstrate through a non-trivial example its benefits and tradeoffs.

The rest of this paper is organized as follows: Section 2 presents necessary background material and introduces basic PT (2.1), and the Generic Graph Library (2.2) through a discussion on criteria for generic constructs in general and the goals of our mechanism in particular. Sections 3 and 4 contain a description of the proposed addition of required types to PT, and an overview of how PT*r* fulfills most of the criteria presented in Section 2.2, respectively. Related work is treated in Section 5, and Section 6 concludes this paper.

2. Background

2.1 A Brief Overview of the Basic PT Mechanism

In this section we give a general overview of the basic PT mechanism. The concepts of the mechanism are not in themselves tied to any particular object-oriented language, but the examples will be presented in a Java-like syntax. The interested reader is referred to [3, 16] for a more thorough exposition.

A package template looks much like a regular Java package, but we will use a syntax where curly braces enclose the contents of both templates and regular packages, e.g.:

```
template T<R> { // R is not discussed here, see Sec. 3
  class A { ... }
  class B extends A { ... } }
```

In contrast to for instance templates in C++, package templates can be type checked independently of their potential usage(s).

A template is instantiated at compile time with an `inst` statement. Such an instantiation will create a local copy of the template classes, potentially with specified modifications, within the instantiating package or template. An example of this is shown below:

```
package P {
  inst T with A => C, B => D;
  class C adds { ... }
  class D adds { ... } // D extends C since B extends A
}
```

Here, a unique instance of the contents of the package template T will be created and imported into the package P. In its simplest form, the `inst` statement just names the template to be instantiated, e.g. "inst T". However, modifications can also be made to the template classes upon instantiation, such as:

- Elements of the template may be renamed. This is done in the `with`-clause of the `inst`-statement, and is only shown for class names above (A is renamed to C and B is renamed to D). For renaming of class attributes another arrow is used (`->`). Note that all renaming in PT is done based on the name bindings from the semantic analysis.

- In each instantiation the classes in the template may be given additions: fields and methods may be added and virtual methods may be overridden. This is done in `adds`-clauses as shown for C and D.

An important property of PT is that everything in the instantiated template that was typed with classes from this template (A and B) is updated to instead refer to the corresponding names of the addition classes (C and D) at the time of instantiation. Any sub/super-type relations within the template are preserved in the package where it is instantiated. Note that templates can also be instantiated in other templates.

Classes from different template instantiations may be *merged* to form one new class. Syntactically, merging is obtained by renaming classes from two or more template instantiations to the same name, and they thereby end up as one class. The new class gets all the attributes of the instantiated classes, together with the attributes of the common addition class. Consider the simple example below:

```
template T { class A { int i; A m1(A a) { ... } } }
template U {
  abstract class B { int j; abstract B m2(B b); }
}
```

Consider now the following usage of these templates:

```
inst T with A => MergeAB;
inst U with B => MergeAB;
class MergeAB adds {
    int k;
    MergeAB m2(MergeAB ab) { return ab.m1(this); }
}
```

These instantiations result in a class MergeAB, that contains the integer variables i, j and k, and the methods m1 and m2. Note how the abstract method m2 from B is implemented in the adds clause, and furthermore how both m1 and m2 now have signatures of the form MergeAB → MergeAB.

Merging classes in this manner might obviously lead to name clashes; such conflicts must be resolved through renaming.

2.2 The Generic Graph Library and Evaluation of Generic Support

For the purpose of demonstrating and validating the generic programming constructs added to PT in this paper, we have implemented a small yet non-trivial subset of the Boost Graph Library (BGL) [25], revolving around a set of algorithms using variants of breadth-first search, including Prim's minimum spanning tree, Dijkstra's shortest paths, Johnson's shortest paths, and Bellman & Ford's shortest paths algorithms. The implemented subset is the same as that of [11].

In the implementations from [11], emphasis is put on expressing minimal requirements for each algorithm. These have internal (acyclic) dependencies, e.g. Johnson's algorithm depends on Dijkstra's algorithm.

The graph itself is represented in terms of *concepts*. The term concept is in [11] used to mean a set of requirements consisting of required operations (methods) and data type constraints. A type (or a set of types) is said to *model* a concept if it (they) fulfill(s) these requirements. In a Java-like language, concepts are typically realized as interfaces[1], and classes implementing such an interface thus model the corresponding concept. The following main concepts of the graph library are in Java implemented as interfaces:

- VertexListGraph: provides an iterator yielding all vertices in the graph in an unspecified order.

- EdgeListGraph: provides an iterator yielding all edges in the graph in an unspecified order.

- IncidenceGraph: provides an iterator yielding the directed edges going out of a given vertex.

These concepts are used by the algorithms to express constraints on their input parameters. For convenience, concepts that are combinations of the aforementioned ones are introduced, e.g. the VertexList-AndIncidenceGraph concept which is an interface that extends both the interfaces representing the Vertex-ListGraph concept and the IncidenceGraph concept. Additionally, the different algorithms require various data structures for coloring, ordering, etc., realized as

e.g. property maps, queues, etc. These structures are supplied explicitly as parameters to each algorithm.

Several languages were studied in [11], and subsequently evaluated based on their support for generic programming constructs. Table 1 shows an overview of the rating for C++ and Java from that paper, plus an additional column for Scala, the latter taken from [22]. The different categories in the table are described in Table 2A, taken from [11]. An extended evaluation, including PTr, will be presented in Section 4.

While the original study included several other languages as well, we focus on Java and C++, and in addition we include Scala. C++ is interesting because its generic capabilities rely heavily on its templating mechanism, and it is in this language that the Boost Graph Library has its native implementation. However, C++ templates differ drastically from the templates of PT, most notably in the sense that PT templates are declarationally complete semantic units that can be type checked independently of their usage. As can be seen from the table, while much can be achieved in C++ due to its flexibility with regards to template definition, we only get limited compiler support.[2] Java is obviously interesting because the lacking points for Java in the table is the situation that we wish to ameliorate with PTr, and PT is designed as an extension to Java-like languages. Scala is a rather advanced JVM language that also addresses many of the weaknesses of Java with regards to generic programming, and as such it is an interesting language with which to compare and contrast our mechanism.

A partial goal for this paper can thus be summarized as *to bring some of the flexibility of C++ generic template programming to Java with PTr, while retaining compiler support, static safety, and relative simplicity.*

However, if we look back to the goal from [15] presented in the introduction, we argue that the criteria from [11] do not adequately encompass requirements for writing algorithms and data structures that are *broadly adaptable*. For instance: How can a constraint for a generic parameter be adapted to match existing code? How can a constraint be refined by subsequent users? How can a concept be adapted to allow modeling by existing data structures, or vice versa?

In order to cover these usage scenarios, we introduce two new criteria related to adaptability, presented in Table 2B. Thus, another part of our goal with this paper is *to satisfy the adaptability criteria for generic programming.*

Scores for Scala. In [22], Oliviera et al. discuss the criteria from Table 2A in context of the Scala language.

---

[1] See [22] for an alternative approach based on the Concept pattern.

[2] Note, however, that Java-style generics can be emulated in C++, with compiler support, through use of for instance the Boost Library's BOOST_STATIC_ASSERT.

	C++	Java	Scala
Multi-type concepts	*	○	●
Multiple constraints	*	●	●
Associated type access	●	◐	●
Constraints on assoc. types	*	◐	●
Retroactive modeling	*	○	●
Type aliases	●	○	●
Separate compilation	○	●	●
Implicit argument deduction	●	●	●

Table 1. *The table shows the level of support for generic programming constructs for C++, Java, and Scala. The table criteria and the support levels for the former two are taken directly from [11, page 147]. A black circle indicates full support, a half-filled circle indicates partial support and a white circle indicates poor or no support at all. For C++, a rating of '*' means that the feature is not explicitly supported by the language, but the permissiveness of the language allows one to program as if it were supported, though sans compiler support.*

In their treatment, Scala receives the *full support* verdict on all points, as shown in Table 1. One could thus think that there is little room for making improvements with PTr. However, we have found that, at least with respect to an implementation of the generic graph library, Scala still leaves a few things to be desired with respect to these criteria. Furthermore, as we shall see, PTr takes quite a different approach to generics compared to Scala. Also note that [22] changes the scores for Java, but we have kept them in their original form from [11]. We refer to the discussion of the individual criteria in Section 4 for details.

3. Required Type Specifications in PTr

Basic PT [3, 16] allows templates to have generic type parameters in much the same way as ordinary Java classes can, e.g. as in

```
template T<R> { ... }
```

The parameters may be constrained, either through a nominal inheritance specification (akin to Java generics) or through a structural requirements specification, e.g.:

```
template T1<R extends Runnable> { ... }
template T2<R extends { void run(); }> { ... }
```

While this provides the ability to let the template classes be collectively parameterized, which in itself can be very useful, the approach has certain limitations. To begin with, the parameter R in the examples above does not naturally lend itself to the kind of modification that are allowed for basic PT classes, e.g. renaming of attributes, merging etc. Since the parameter is part of the template specification, it could be natural

(or even necessary) to adapt the parameter specification along with other adaptions of the template. Furthermore, neither the name R nor the requirement it poses is *propagated* to other templates that instantiate T, T1, or T2. As we will see examples of below, and as was demonstrated in [11], this is a real issue for the implementation of larger libraries as it often leads to unnecessary code duplication. Also, as a consequence of the lack of propagation, there is no straightforward way to refine constraints without cumbersome and error-prone repetition of code.

With basic PT, class declarations in a package template can, as we have seen in Section 2.1, be adapted in several ways. It seems like a natural step forward to provide the same degree of flexibility for parameterization of templates. Thus, this can be seen as making the generic constraints of a template *first class entities* of the template, in the same way that classes and interfaces are. In the rest of this section, we will look at how PTr provides this feature.

Required types as first-class template declarations. The syntax for required types in PTr is summarized in Figure 1. A basic specification requiring an unconstrained type, i.e. any Java class or interface, to be supplied can be expressed as follows:

```
template T1 { required type R { } }
```

An actual parameter for R can be supplied to T1 when instantiating the template, by utilizing the <= arrow. To e.g. supply String for R in T1, the following instantiation could be used (within another template or package, see separate paragraph on that below):

```
inst T1 with R <= String;
```

At this point we see an important difference between required types in PTr and type parameters as found in e.g. Java, Scala or C#with regards to their scope: Required types are at the same lexical level as class declarations, and can thus naturally constrain a *set* of classes. This is to some extent similar to abstract types and nested classes within an outer class in e.g. Scala, but it is important to note that required types in PTr (and package templates as a whole) is a compile-time construct only. Thus, after instantiation of the template in a package, there will be no inner abstract types (and thus no full family polymorphism [8] nor path-dependent types). This amounts to a simpler type system, and is as such comparable to the flattening property of traits [23].

A required type R can be constrained by both structural and nominal specifications; below we see an example of the former:

```
template T2 { required type R { void run(); } }
```

Given an instantiation that supplies an actual type for a required type R with a structural constraint, such

	Criterion	Definition
A)	Multi-type concepts	Multiple types can be simultaneously constrained.
	Multiple constraints	More than one constraint can be placed on a type parameter.
	Associated type access	Types can be mapped to other types within the context of a generic func.
	Constraints on associated types	Concepts may include constraints on associated types.
	Retroactive modeling	New modeling relationships can be added after a type has been defined.
	Type aliases	A mechanism for creating shorter names for types is provided.
	Separate compilation	Generic functions can be type checked and compiled independent of calls to them.
	Implicit argument deduction	The arguments for the type parameters of a generic function can be deduced and do not need to be explicitly provided by the programmer.
B)	Retroactive concept adaption	Concepts can be adapted after their initial definition. If the concept spans multiple types, a single adaption may affect several types.
	Retroactive constraint adaption	Constraints for generic parameters can be adapted and refined after their initial definition to better match existing code.

Table 2. *A) The different criteria for evaluation of support for generic constructs in programming languages, taken directly from [11, page 147]. B) Additional criteria for evaluation of support for adaptable generic programming. We discuss these criteria in further detail in Section 4.*

as "inst T2 with R <= Runnable", the compiler will check that the supplied type structurally conforms to the specification given by R. Conformance entails that all the required methods (and constructors if they are present, see below) must have an *exact* match (save for parameter names) in the supplied type. Covariant or contravariant signatures are not allowed; allowing this would not be type safe (e.g. when merging). Thus, for required types with only methods, the conformance relation for required types is equivalent to the <# matching relation of the $\mathcal{LOOM}$ language [5].

If the signature check succeeds, the compiler will *replace* all occurrences of R (based on the semantic analysis) in the instantiated template with the supplied type; in the example instantiation in the paragraph above, references to the type R will be replaced by references to the type java.lang.Runnable. The actual declaration of the required type R will be removed. Thus, for every class in the template, a version specific to this instantiation, with the given parameterization, is created. Note that, as opposed to in e.g. Scala, there is never a need for runtime reflection when dealing with structural constraints, since the actual type always will be known at *compile-time*.

Bounds for required types can be specified nominally as well as structurally. Taking the example from above, we can express that R must be a nominal subtype of e.g. the Runnable interface:

```
template T3 { required type R extends Runnable { } }
```

Thus, when supplying an actual type A for R in an instantiation of T3, it must explicitly implement or extend the Runnable interface (or A might be the Runnable interface itself).

Nominal and structural subtyping can also be mixed in a declaration of a required type. To demand an explicit, nominal, implementation of Runnable, and furthermore that a method stop must be present, we can easily express this as follows:

```
template T4 {
    required type R extends Runnable { void stop(); }
}
```

Classes and interfaces. Java generics do not allow the use of primitive types (though Scala does), and we do not in this work intend to lift that restriction. However, it is still important in some cases to be able to explicitly constrain a required type to be either an interface or a class.[3]

As can be seen from the syntactical overview in Figure 1, such constraints can be imposed by declaring a required type explicitly as either a required interface or a required class. Declaring requirements in this way puts further constraints on the required types; e.g. the ability to have constructors and fields are only available to required classes.

Thus, the term *required type* is overloaded in this paper, and is used both in the inclusive sense to refer to the syntactical and semantical constructs of required *types*, required *classes* and required *interfaces*, and, on the other hand, in the narrow sense to *only* refer to required *types*. When this distinction is important, we will be explicit about this; otherwise, the inclusive sense is implied.

Instantiation and concretization As mentioned above, upon instantiation of a template, the programmer may

---
[3] An example of a similar construct in a mainstream OO language is the where R : class constraints of C#.

required-spec	::=	required [<r-type> | <r-class> | <r-interface>]
r-type	::=	`type` <identifier> [adds] [<extends-clause>] { <r-type-body>* }
r-interface	::=	`interface` <identifier> [adds] [<extends-clause>] { <r-type-body>* }
r-class	::=	`class` <identifier> [adds] [<implements-clause>] [<extends-clause>] { <r-class-body>* }
r-type-body	::=	<method-signature>
r-class-body	::=	<constructor-signature> | <field-signature> | <method-signature>

Figure 1. *Syntax for required types. Non-terminals are written within <angled brackets>, and optional symbols are delimited by [square brackets]. A vertical line (|) signifies alternatives, and a star (*) signifies zero or more repetitions of a symbol. Terminal symbols are written with a* `monospace` *font. Productions left out (for the sake of brevity), such as e.g. the* extends-*clause, are to be understood as syntactically equal to their pure Java equivalents.*

choose to supply an actual concrete type for a required type R that satisfies the constraints of R. We will refer to this as a *concretization* of the required type.

A template can be instantiated in other templates and in packages. When a template T is instantiated in another template U, it is not mandatory to concretize the required types of T. Any required types in T that are not concretized upon instantiation in U will be propagated to U, and will thus become required types of U.

On the other hand, when a template T is instantiated in a package P, every (remaining) required type must be given a concretization. The concrete types may be classes or interfaces from instantiated templates (including the template containing the required type), or from other ordinary Java packages.

Sometimes, it can be nice to provide sensible default concretizations for required types, to alleviate the burden of always having to concretize every (remaining) required type when a template is instantiated in a package. For a mechanism like PTr, where a number of required types can be gathered in one template, a way to specify such defaults would indeed be helpful. A default concrete type or implementation could explicitly be given in the declaration of a required type. Another option for simple cases is to choose a default concretization from the bound of the required type. We are still studying how this can best be done, but for simple cases, the prototype compiler currently resorts to the latter approach.

Subtype hierarchies. Table 3 shows the relationships that are supported between required types, required interfaces, required classes, classes, and interfaces, for the `extends` and `implements` relations, respectively.

An extends or implements relationship between two required types does not in itself form a hierarchy. Rather, it puts forth a requirement for a hierarchy, i.e. a constraint that actual supplied types must (transitively/reflexively) fulfill.

Constructor definitions. Although it was not explicitly treated in [11], a seemingly common issue with type parameters is that you might want to create ob-

extends	RT	RI	RC	I	C
RT			✓		
RI	✓	✓		✓	
RC			✓		
I	✓	✓		✓	
C				✓	✓

implements	RT	RI	RC	I	C
RT					
RI	✓		✓		✓
RC					
I	✓		✓		✓
C					

Table 3. *Support for the* `extends` *and* `implements` *relations between required types (RT), required interfaces (RI), required classes (RC), ordinary (template) interfaces (I) and ordinary (template) classes (C). The table is supposed to be read from the top row and down and to the left. I.e.,* RC extends RT *is a legal relationship, while the converse* RT extends RC *is not.*

jects of the actual types. In Java and Scala, however, this is disallowed, so even if you have a method or a class parameterized by a type T, you cannot say "new T()".[4] C# is a bit more expressive, and allows the developer to constrain the type parameter by adding a "where T: new()" constraint, requiring the actual type to have a parameterless constructor. Other kinds of constructor requirements cannot be expressed.

When utilizing `required classes`, constructor requirements can quite naturally be handled simply by adding the necessary required constructor signatures to the class. These requirements can subsequently be structurally matched with the actual constructors of the class supplied upon instantiation. An example is shown below:

```
template T { required class E { E(int value); } ... }
```

---

[4] You can, however, in some cases create an object of a generic type T using reflection. Furthermore, in Scala, you can utilize implicit factories for similar results.

Inside classes in the template T above, or in classes from other templates or packages that instantiate T, statements such as "new E(42)" can safely be used.

Note that required constructors can *only* be defined for required *classes*, and not for required interfaces or plain required types.

For a required class RC that has a nominal subtyping requirement with bound B, where B is a class with accessible constructors, the required class must still structurally specify constructor requirements explicitly if "new RC(...)" is to be allowed. This is because a Java subclass in general needs not implement the same constructors as its superclass.

Refinement through additions. A required type in PTr can be given additions in the same way as classes and interfaces can in basic PT, through an adds clause. This can be used to refine constraints in subsequent instantiations. Consider a template T defined as follows:

```
template T { required type R { void run(); } }
```

In another template U that instantiates T, R can be refined by adding nominal or structural constraints. An example that does both is shown below:

```
template U {
  inst T;
  required type R adds implements Runnable {void stop();}
}
```

Here, R is *refined* in U, and further constrained to both nominally implement the Runnable interface and to implement a parameterless stop() method that returns void.

Merging. With basic PT, classes (or interfaces) from different template instantiations can be merged to form one new class. The details of the merge mechanism are beyond the scope of this article, the interested reader is referred to [3] for a more thorough exposition.

In PTr, required types can be merged in the same way that ordinary template classes and interfaces can. As for ordinary merges, different *kinds* of types cannot be "cross merged" with each other. I.e. a required interface can only be merged with other required interfaces, required classes only with other required classes, and required types only with other required types. The main difference from ordinary class or interface merging lies in the handling of conflicts. If, in the merge of two required types, there are equal signatures stemming from each of the types, this is not considered a conflict. Rather, the two signatures are merged into one in the resulting required type. If a given pair of equal signatures should indeed be kept separate, the developer may explicitly rename one or both of them in the instantiation. Merging required types where more than one has a nominal bound that is a class is considered a compile time error.

	C++	Java	Scala	PTr
Multi-type concepts	*	○	●	●
Multiple constraints	*	●	●	●
Associated type access	●	◐	●	●
Constr. on assoc. types	*	◐	●	●
Retroactive modeling	*	○	●	●
Type aliases	●	○	●	○
Separate compilation	○	●	●	◐
Implicit arg. deduction	●	○	●	●
Retroact. concept adapt.	○	○	◐	●
Retroact. constr. adapt.	○	○	◐	●

Table 4. *Support for adaptive generic programming in C++, Java, Scala, and PTr.*

Through merging of required types from different instantiations, the developer is able to express equality constraints across template instances, by explicitly declaring that two previously distinct required types are to be considered the same in the context of the current package or template. In contrast to an ordinary equality constraint, a merge also alleviates the need to provide the same parameter twice, making for more succinct code.

4. Fulfilling the Generic Programming Criteria

In this section, we discuss how and to what extent PTr fulfills the requirements listed in Table 2, as shown in Table 4. For brevity, we will not discuss scores that PTr "inherits" directly from Java.

Multi-type concepts. The essence of supporting multi-type concepts lies in the ability to simultaneously constrain more than one type. In PTr, constraints can be specified by required types within templates, to which several other (required) types of a multi-type concept can refer, and thus be simultaneously constrained. An example of this from our implementation of the generic graph library is shown below:

```
template GraphConcepts {
 required type Vertex { }
 required type Edge { Vertex source(); Vertex target();}
 required type EdgeIter extends Iterator<Edge> { }
 required type OutEdgeIter extends Iterator<Edge> { }
 required type VertexIter extends Iterator<Vertex> { }
 required interface IncidenceGraph {
   OutEdgeIter out_edges(Vertex v);
   int out_degree(Vertex v); }
 ...
}
```

As we can see from the code, the Edge, VertexIter, and IncidenceGraph types are all constrained by the (same) Vertex type, and the EdgeIter and OutEdgeIter types are constrained by the Edge type. Furthermore, we here see an example of traditional Java type pa-

89

rameterization (of the `java.util.Iterator<T>` interface) combined with PT*r*'s required types. Note that this template can be instantiated by relying on default concretization, as discussed briefly in Section 3, so that we might e.g. only explicitly concretize `Vertex` and `Edge`, and let the compiler concretize the remaining required types to their bounds. Note also that a concept can be composed from other concepts, each of which might span one or more types, by instantiating templates representing other concepts. Thus, with PT*r* one can express sub-concepts that are themselves comprised of other sub-concepts and/or types, and reuse and/or refine the constraints from these.

Multi-type concepts in Scala are typically implemented through use of the *Concept pattern* [22], parameterized with multiple type parameters. Applying this pattern thus implies creating separate concept classes (or singleton objects) that implement/model the concept interface/trait. Using Scala's `implicit` definitions this can in many cases make for a quite elegant solution. However, for the graph library functionality we found that having multiple multi-type concepts, implemented through the Concept pattern and constrained by the same associated/abstract types, quickly led to a rather complex solution.

Also in Java, multi-type concepts can be expressed through the Concept pattern, but this approach may quickly become cumbersome due to the fact that concept implementations must be referred to explicitly. The score for Java from [11] in Table 4 is instead based on a nominal subtyping approach.

Associated type access. Access to associated types is a property that allows code to refer to types that are associated with a generic concept. For instance, the general `Graph` concept has associated types `Edge` and `Vertex`. If the concept is expressed in a package template, and associated generic types as required types, one can simply refer directly (without any additional qualification) to the required types `Edge` and `Vertex`. These required types will be replaced by the actual types upon instantiation, at the latest in a package. Thus, associated type access comes "for free" with PT*r*.

In languages like Java, associated types are typically represented by generic parameters, and this quickly leads to verbose definitions. As an example, contrast the Java definition skeleton in Figure 2 of the breadth first search algorithm from [11] with the Scala and PT*r* versions directly below it.

Note how in the PT*r* version, the only parameterization that is necessary for the algorithm is to specify the `ColorMap` type, which is not in itself an associated type of the graph concept. The associated (required) type `Vertex` can be accessed directly (even though its actual type has not been supplied yet).

```
// Java version:
class breadth_first_search {
 public static <Vertex,
  Edge extends GraphEdge<Vertex>,
  VertexIterator extends Iterator<Vertex>,
  OutEdgeIterator extends Iterator<Edge>,
  ColorMap extends ReadWritePropertyMap<Vertex, Integer>>
  void go(VertexListAndIncidenceGraph<
        Vertex,Edge,VertexIterator, OutEdgeIterator> g,
     Vertex s, Visitor vis, ColorMap color) {
    ...
    graph_search.go(g,s,vis,color, ...);
} }

// Scala version
object breadth_first_search {
 def go[Graph <: VertexListAndIncidenceGraph,
    ColorMap <: ReadWritePropertyMap
        {type Key = Graph#Vertex; type Value = Int}]
       (g: Graph, s:Graph#Vertex, vis: Visitor,
        color: ColorMap ){
    ...
    graph_search.go(g, s, vis, color, ...);
} }

// PTr version:
inst GraphConceps;
class breadth_first_search {
 public static <ColorMap extends
    ReadWritePropertyMap<Vertex, Integer>>
  void go(VertexListAndIncidenceGraph g, Vertex s,
     Visitor vis, ColorMap color) {
    ...
    graph_search.go(g,s,vis,color, ...);
} }
```

Figure 2. *Associated type access in Java, Scala and PTr*

In Scala, an associated type is typically implemented as an abstract type within a class or a trait. Access to such a type is achieved through the type projection construct, e.g. `Graph#Vertex`. For the Scala code above, a parameter for the graph type is thus needed to access the `Vertex` type. Also note that neither the Java nor the Scala versions are parameterized on the `Visitor` concept, as this is not an associated type of the graph concept. For PT*r*, on the other hand, the `Visitor` concept is realized as a required type, and parameterization is thus available without any additional overhead.

A limitation that made implementing graph library functionality a little harder and less natural in Scala was the fact that you cannot use an abstract type as the type of a parameter to a method in another abstract type [21, sec. 3.2.7].

The example presented in Figure 2 is closely related to the issue of *constraint propagation*. We notice in that example that the PT*r* version does not need to mention the constraints for generic types it does not itself directly utilize, whereas the Java version must repeat the constrains for `VertexIterator`, `EdgeIterator`, etc. The example below shows how this can lead to complexity in even very simple cases:

```
// Java version:
interface VertexListAndIncidenceAndEdgeListGraph<
    Vertex,
    Edge extends GraphEdge<Vertex>,
    VertexIterator extends java.util.Iterator<Vertex>,
    OutEdgeIterator extends java.util.Iterator<Edge>,
    EdgeIterator extends java.util.Iterator<Edge>>
  extends
    VertexListAndIncidenceGraph<Vertex,Edge,
        VertexIterator,OutEdgeIterator>,
    EdgeListGraph<Vertex,Edge,EdgeIterator> {}

// PTr version:
required interface VertexListAndIncidenceAndEdgeListGraph
 extends VertexListAndIncidenceGraph,EdgeListGraph {}
```

The interface above, in either version, defines nothing more than a composition (through inheritance) of existing interfaces, and does as such not introduce any associated types or requirements on its own. The PT*r* version can be written in a much more succinct manner because there is no need to repeat the associated types as they are *propagated automatically upon instantiation*, and can thus be accessed without resorting to additional generic type parameters.

For Scala, the definition of `VertexListAndIncidenceAndEdgeListGraph` would be similar to the PT*r* version, but its constituents would in each of their definitions have to repeat the constraints for vertices and edges (and the concept could not itself be an associated type, due to the limitation mentioned above).

Constraints on associated types. There are several kinds of constraints that can be useful for associated types. A common form of constraints is that of an equality constraint, i.e. the requirement that an associated type of two other types must be the same. In a template with required types, this can easily be achieved in PT*r* by referring to the same requirement in both of the types. For associated types that were previously unrelated, one can express that they should in a given context be the same by merging the corresponding required types; the new required type will represent the union of the original ones.

Another typical form of constraints are in the form of sub/super relationships. With PT*r*, this can be expressed directly, with e.g. declarations of the form "required interface I extends J {...}". If J is itself a required interface, the actual type supplied for I is constrained to be a subtype of the actual type supplied for J.

Basic PT (and thus also PT*r*) amends the problem inherent to Java (and Scala) generics where it is not possible, due to type erasure, to constrain a generic type to two different parameterizations of the same generic interface (or trait). PT allows multiple instantiations (and thus also parameterizations) of a single template.

Retroactive modeling. In C++, retroactive modeling is implicitly supported since the compiler does not check the constraints put forth by templated concepts. Hence, any type can be said to model a concept without any prior reference to the concept itself, as long as the type provides the (implicitly) required operations.

In Java, there is no direct support for retroactively saying that a given class models (implements) a given concept (interface), short of changing its source code. However, a work-around might be the Concept pattern, though this is somewhat awkward to use since concepts must explicitly be passed around.

As Java, Scala supports retroactive modeling through the use of the Concept pattern, but `implicit` declarations make the use of concepts much more convenient and natural to the programmer in Scala.

Existing Scala libraries can be extended (or rather, appear to be extended) through the "library pimping" approach [20], in order to support retroactive modeling. However, this approach is typically based on implicit runtime creation of new objects, which might lead to subtle bugs e.g. when references to such objects are passed around. There is, in our opinion, a significant difference between retroactively adjusting the model (as PT*r* can do), and annotating the model with conversions to and from the modeled concepts.

With PT*r*, classes from templates can model new concepts through being merged with other classes that model the concept, or by having interface implementation declarations added by an adds part. The possibility for name changes makes it easier to let existing code retroactively model new interfaces. A small example sketch is shown below, where a concept M is realized by the interface M. The template T contains a class C, that implements the desired functionality in a method mx, however, it does not explicitly implement M:

```
interface M { void m(); }
template T { class C { void mx() { ... } } }
```

With PT*r*, we can retroactively define the implements-relation between M and an instance of C, as follows:

```
// rename method "mx" to "m":
inst T with C => C ( mx() -> m );
// add the interface implementation decl:
class C adds implements M { }
```

Type aliases. Type aliases are supported by C++ and Scala (and other languages) as a way to make long type names shorter, and are as such especially useful when dealing with heavily parameterized code. However, it has not been our goal to support this in our work with PT*r*, and the level of support is thus the same as for plain Java. Even so, PT*r* does alleviate this issue to a certain extent, since the parameterized types can be fixed at the time of instantiation, and need thus not be repeated for subsequent uses.

Separate compilation. This criterion includes both separate type checking and compilation into independent units. Java and Scala support both parts of the criterion, while the templates of C++ supports neither. The former part is fulfilled by PT*r*, since every template can be separately type checked independently of subsequent usage. The latter part is not supported by the current prototype compiler, which produces separate code for each instantiation (a heterogenous implementation). However, we have previously experimented with how a homogenous implementation can be made for an extended JVM, with special instructions e.g. for invoking methods in adapted template classes. Such an approach does, in contrast to the current heterogenous compile-time specialization scheme, come with some runtime performance overhead (which is also incidentally true for Scala's implicit definitions and Java's runtime casts due to erasure).

Retroactive concept adaption. As one of the additional two criteria we added in order to support the programming of adaptable generic libraries, retroactive concept adaption is the ability to unintrusively (i.e. without making changes to the original source code) make certain changes to a concept after its initial definition. These changes include renaming of methods and of the concept itself, and changes to the types returned by or accepted as parameters to the operations (methods) of the concept. Such changes can be important in order to provide a better match for existing code, or in order to better reflect the domain of the problems that the program is supposed to solve. Name changes may seem like a trivial modification to any program, but influential development methodologies like domain-driven design (see e.g. [9]), as well as research into naming conventions and intended semantics (see e.g. [13]), put emphasis on the importance of proper naming. Neither Java nor C++ supports the retroactive adaption of concepts, and developers are hence relegated to either make do with the concept as they were originally defined, make wrappers around them, or duplicate code. In Scala, concepts can, to a certain extent, be retroactively adapted through the use of implicit declarations and inheritance.

For PT*r*, retroactive adaption is one of the main motivating goals for the mechanism, and adaption of concepts (defined as interfaces, required interfaces or abstract base classes) as well as their potential implementations can be expressed as part of an instantiation of a template. The fact that each instantiation results in a new set of classes is the main reason for PT*r*'s flexibility with regards to name changes.

Beyond name changes, a concept in PT*r* might be refined by adding new operation signatures through the use of adds clauses (for both concept definitions and

implementations). The PT*r* approach supports overloads and (single) dynamic dispatch of added operations, in contrast to mechanisms such as extension methods in C# or the Concept pattern through implicits in Scala, which rely on static dispatch.

Retroactive constraint adaption. Constraints form a significant part of the interface to a generic library, and hence if retroactive modeling and adaption are deemed important, the possibility for retroactive adaption of constraints should be of equal importance.

In Java, constraints cannot be adapted short of changing the source code or creating wrappers that refine the original constraint. Scala supports refinement of constraints expressed as abstract types through subtyping, but the original constraint cannot be adapted.

With PT*r*, constraints in form of required types can be adapted in several ways. To begin with, their names can be changed, along with the names of method signatures within them. Changing the name of a required type might be useful when a type is not supplied at instantiation, and a default interface definition is subsequently created by the compiler. Changing the names of method signatures is useful in order to adapt the generic library to existing code, when one is unable or unwilling to change the latter. Below is an example of a small library for representing cities and roads, encapsulated in a package named Geography.

```
package Geography {
  class City { String name; int population; ... }
  class Road {
    private City from, to;
    City getFrom() { return from; }
    void setFrom(City c) { from = c; }
    City getTo() { return to; }
    void setTo(City c) { to = c; }
} }
```

It would be nice to be able to apply the algorithms from the generic graph library, like e.g. Dijkstra's shortest paths, to cities and roads from the Geography package. In our implementation, the Algorithms template contains the desired functionality, and it will in turn instantiate the GraphConcepts template, which contains the requirement for a Vertex class and an Edge class, and corresponding constraints. The requirements will be propagated to the instantiating package. Thus, we can use the instantiation below to adapt the generic constraints to our Geography package:

```
inst Algorithms with Vertex <= City,
    Edge (source() -> getFrom, target() -> getTo) <= Road;
```

With this approach, we can apply all the algorithms from the generic graph library to the classes from the Geography package.

A constraint may also be adapted in PT*r* by providing an addition that refines the constraint, typically in a narrowing fashion. For instance, to further constrain the `Vertex` type to include a `getName` method, we can utilize the following code in a template:

```
inst GraphConcepts;
required type Vertex adds { String getName(); }
```

It is important to note that such modifications are local to the current instantiation, and do not propagate globally to other potential instantiations of the `GraphConcepts` template in other parts of the program. Thus, retroactive constraint adaption can in PT*r* be done in a controlled and unintrusive manner.

Aside: code complexity comparison. The Java implementation from [11] has 760 lines of code[5], while the corresponding PT*r* implementation has 691 lines. However, this includes a lot of imperative code that is identical in the two versions. To approach an understanding of the relative complexity in terms of parameterizations and constraints, we have tried to count these in a reasonable way. In both versions we have counted all elements that occur within angle brackets `<...>`, and all elements that occur as subtype bounds for generic constraints. In addition, we have counted all required types and explicit concretizations of such for PT*r*. The count is 542 occurrences for Java and 325 for PT*r*, i.e. a reduction of about 40%. We think that this can have a significant impact on the comprehensibility and maintainability of the code.

5. Related Work

Virtual classes originated with the BETA language [17, 18], and has subsequently inspired a host of other languages and mechanisms, such as e.g. gbeta [7], Caesar [1], J& [19], and Newspeak [4]. These mechanisms support a certain degree of parameterization based on overrides (or *refinements*) of the virtual types, typically contained within ordinary classes. An important advantage of the virtual type approach over type parameterization as found e.g. in Java is the automatic propagation of constraints.

In [26], Thorup argues for the inclusion of virtual types in Java as an alternative to classes with type parameters. In this proposal, Java classes can contain bounded `typedef`s, that can be used to define generic classes that abstract over an open set of types. A problem with this approach is that static type safety is reduced, and every class could now potentially be subject to runtime exceptions due to covariant subtyping. With PT*r*, this kind of typing issues are not problematic since actual types *substitute* all occurrences of references to required types at *compile-time*.

A subsequent paper [27] presents an approach that combines virtual types (in a type safe variant [6]) with structural subtyping. This gives three "dimensions" of subtyping: the ordinary subclass variant, covariance in the generic parameter, and binding of the generic parameter to its bound. This allows virtual types to be used in many situations where parameterized types traditionally have been considered a better option. We have not discussed the issue of subtyping of parameterized classes to any extent in this paper, but it seems clear that if subtype relations between different parameterizations of the same class are required, PT*r* is not the ideal tool, since every instantiation results in a new, independent, set of classes (though template classes can implement common external interfaces).

Both [26] and [27] provide adequate support for associated types of concepts, however, as opposed to in PT*r*, multi-type concepts are not as easily expressed.

In [14], the authors introduce explicit support for associated types and constraint propagation in C# with a mechanism resembling virtual classes. However, an important distinction from prototypical virtual classes is that nested types are not specific for each object of an outer class. Like PT*r*, they support assignment of pre-existing types to the associated (virtual) type definitions. Constraint propagation is automatic, as for PT*r*, but limited to the confines of singular class hierarchies.

Neither of the virtual type-based mechanisms support retroactive adaption of concepts or constraints in a manner resembling PT*r*.

Scala [21] has been discussed in some detail in this paper, however, there are some additional points that should be addressed. We have mentioned that the static nature of our mechanism facilitates a simpler type system, and arguably also a simpler conceptual model. However, this has some obvious drawbacks, most notably that full family polymorphism [8] and dependent types are not supported (since we do not allow creating instances of templates at runtime). Furthermore, Scala supports several advanced features that PT*r* does not, such as e.g. higher-ordered types, pattern matching and implicits.

JavaGI [28] is an extension to Java inspired by Haskell's type classes. It supports retroactive modeling through explicit implementation declarations. *Multi-headed interfaces* provide support for multi-type concepts in a natural way, exemplified by the Observer pattern [10]; a corresponding implementation in PT could be a template with types for each role, an example can be found in [2]. JavaGI does not fully support retroactive adaption.

The $\mathcal{G}$ language [24] compiles to C++ and contains explicit support for generic concepts and models, and supports all the criteria listed in Table 2A. Like PT*r* it supports modular type checking, and also separate compilation, but not the criteria from Table 2B.

---

[5] Counted with the CLOC tool: `http://cloc.sourceforge.net/`

Partly building on the work on $\mathcal{G}$, ConceptC++ [12] supports explicit concept definitions and constrained function and class templates. Retroactive modeling is achieved through concept maps, and in general the criteria from Table 2A are well supported, though type checking is not fully modular due to their support for concept-based overloading, which PT*r* does not fully support. A goal for ConceptC++ was to form the basis for the inclusion of concepts in the new C++0x standard. However, the current version of the standard excludes concept support.[6] To our knowledge, neither ConceptC++ nor C++0x fully supports the criteria in Table 2B.

6. Concluding Remarks

The package template (PT) mechanism extended with required type specifications yields a, to the best of the authors' knowledge, rather novel blend of support for parameterization and retroactive modeling and adaption through compile-time specialization with separate type checking. We refer to this variant of PT as PT*r*.

We have shown that PT*r* applied to a mainstream OO language like Java supports almost all of the criteria put forth by [11], as well as additional criteria identified in this paper for adaptability of generic code. Furthermore, early investigations suggest that PT*r* can provide a significant reduction of duplicated code in generic Java libraries, and in some cases provide a simpler solution compared to other mechanisms aiming at similar problems, such as virtual class- or abstract type-based mechanisms.

Acknowledgments

This work has been done within the context of the SWAT project (NFR grant 167172/V30). We thank the reviewers for helpful comments on previous versions of this paper, and Steinar Kaldager and Daniel Rødskog for dedicated work on the PT(*r*) compiler.

References

[1] I. Aracic, V. Gasiunas, M. Mezini, and K. Ostermann. An overview of CaesarJ. In *Trans. AOSD I*, volume 3880 of *LNCS*, pages 135–173. Springer Berlin / Heidelberg, 2006.

[2] E. W. Axelsen, F. Sørensen, and S. Krogdahl. A reusable observer pattern implementation using package templates. In *ACP4IS '09*, pages 37–42, New York, NY, USA, 2009. ACM.

[3] E. W. Axelsen, F. Sørensen, S. Krogdahl, and B. Møller-Pedersen. Challenges in the design of the package template mechanism. *Transactions on Aspect-Oriented Programming*, 2012. To appear, available now from http://swat.project.ifi.uio.no/.

[4] G. Bracha, P. von der Ahé, V. Bykov, Y. Kashai, W. Maddox, and E. Miranda. Modules as objects in newspeak. In T. D'Hondt, editor, *ECOOP 2010*, LNCS. Springer, 2010.

[5] K. B. Bruce, L. Petersen, and A. Fiech. Subtyping is not a good match for object-oriented programming languages. In *ECOOP '97*, 1997.

[6] M. T. Computer and M. Torgersen. Virtual types are statically safe. In *Proc. FOAL '98*, 1998.

[7] E. Ernst. gbeta - a language with virtual attributes, block structure, and propagating, dynamic inheritance, 1999.

[8] E. Ernst. Family polymorphism. In J. L. Knudsen, editor, *ECOOP*, volume 2072 of *LNCS*. Springer, 2001.

[9] E. Evans. *Domain-Driven Design: Tacking Complexity In the Heart of Software*. Addison-Wesley Longman Publishing Co., Inc., Boston, MA, USA, 2003. ISBN 0321125215.

[10] E. Gamma, R. Helm, R. Johnson, and J. Vlissides. *Design Patterns -Elements of Reusable Object-Oriented Software*. Addison-Wesley, 1994.

[11] R. Garcia, J. Jarvi, A. Lumsdaine, J. Siek, and J. Willcock. An extended comparative study of language support for generic programming. *J. Funct. Program.*, 17:145–205, March 2007.

[12] D. Gregor, J. Järvi, J. Siek, B. Stroustrup, G. Dos Reis, and A. Lumsdaine. Concepts: linguistic support for generic programming in C++. In *Proc. OOPSLA '06*, pages 291–310, New York, NY, USA, 2006. ACM.

[13] E. Høst and B. Østvold. Debugging method names. In S. Drossopoulou, editor, *ECOOP 2009*, volume 5653, pages 294–317. Springer Berlin / Heidelberg, 2009.

[14] J. Järvi, J. Willcock, and A. Lumsdaine. Associated types and constraint propagation for mainstream object-oriented generics. OOPSLA '05, pages 1–19, New York, NY, USA, 2005. ACM.

[15] M. Jazayeri, R. Loos, and D. Musser. Generic Programming - Report from Dagstuhl Seminar. Technical report, 1998.

[16] S. Krogdahl, B. Møller-Pedersen, and F. Sørensen. Exploring the use of package templates for flexible re-use of collections of related classes. *Journal of Object Technology*, 8(7):59–85, 2009.

[17] O. L. Madsen and B. Møller-Pedersen. Virtual classes: a powerful mechanism in object-oriented programming. In *OOPSLA '89*, New York, NY, USA, 1989. ACM.

[18] O. L. Madsen, B. Møller-Pedersen, and K. Nygaard. *Object-oriented programming in the BETA programming language*. ACM Press/Addison-Wesley, New York, NY, USA, 1993.

[19] N. Nystrom, X. Qi, and A. C. Myers. J&: nested intersection for scalable software composition. In *OOPSLA '06*, pages 21–36, New York, NY, USA, 2006. ACM. ISBN 1-59593-348-4.

[20] M. Odersky. Pimp my library, 2006. URL http://www.artima.com/weblogs/viewpost.jsp?thread=179766.

[21] M. Odersky. The scala language spec. version 2.9 – draft, 2011.

[22] B. C. Oliveira, A. Moors, and M. Odersky. Type classes as objects and implicits. In *Proc. OOPSLA 2010*, pages 341–360, New York, NY, USA, 2010. ACM. ISBN 978-1-4503-0203-6.

[23] N. Schärli, S. Ducasse, O. Nierstrasz, and A. Black. Traits: Composable units of behavior. In *ECOOP 2003*, volume 2743 of *LNCS*, pages 327–339. Springer Berlin / Heidelberg, 2003.

[24] J. G. Siek and A. Lumsdaine. A language for generic programming in the large. *Science of Computer Programming*, 76(5):423 – 465, 2008. ISSN 0167-6423.

[25] J. G. Siek, L.-Q. Lee, and A. Lumsdaine. *The Boost Graph Library: User Guide and Reference Manual (C++ In-Depth Series)*. Addison-Wesley Professional, Dec. 2001. ISBN 0201729148.

[26] K. K. Thorup. Genericity in java with virtual types. In *In Proceedings ECOOP '97*, pages 444–471. Springer-Verlag, 1997.

[27] K. K. Thorup and M. Torgersen. Unifying genericity - combining the benefits of virtual types and parameterized classes. ECOOP '99, pages 186–204, London, UK, 1999. Springer-Verlag.

[28] S. Wehr, R. Lämmel, and P. Thiemann. JavaGI: Generalized Interfaces for Java. In *ECOOP 2007, Proceedings*, LNCS. Springer-Verlag, July 2007.

---

[6] See e.g. http://drdobbs.com/architecture-and-design/218600111?pgno=3

Do We Really Need to Extend Syntax for Advanced Modularity?

Shigeru Chiba[1]

Tokyo Institute of Technology

chiba@acm.org

Michihiro Horie[2]

Tokyo Institute of Technology

horie@csg.is.titech.ac.jp

Kei Kanazawa

Tokyo Institute of Technology

kanazawa@csg.is.titech.ac.jp

Fuminobu Takeyama

Tokyo Institute of Technology

f_takeyama@csg.is.titech.ac.jp

Yuuki Teramoto

Tokyo Institute of Technology

teramoto@csg.is.titech.ac.jp

Abstract

For every new language construct (or abstraction), we have been always developing new syntax. Is this a right approach? In this paper, we propose that, if we develop a new language construct for advanced modularity, we should consider the use of *dynamic text* for designing the construct. We mention that language constructs designed with only syntactic extensions (*i.e.* static text) are not satisfactory in aspect oriented programming. Then we present our two prototype systems to demonstrate language constructs designed with dynamic text. One is synchronous copy and paste and the other is a virtual-file editor named *Kide*. We show how they enable aspect-oriented programming in plain Java.

Categories and Subject Descriptors D.3.3 [*Programming Languages*]: Language Constructs and Features

General Terms Languages, Design

Keywords Modularity, aspect-oriented programming, dynamic text.

1. Introduction

Providing linguistic mechanisms for modularization is one of the primary concerns of programming language design. A recent trend in such mechanisms is aspect orientation. A number of language constructs for the aspect-orientation mechanisms have been proposed, for example, at a series of AOSD conferences. The most popular one is an *aspect*

---

[1] Also, The University of Tokyo and JST CREST.

[2] Currently, IBM Research – Tokyo.

in AspectJ [12], which consists of pointcut definitions and advice declarations.

An aspect in AspectJ is expressed with a syntactic extension to Java as other language constructs for aspect orientation in Java. This is natural; whenever we invent a new language construct (or abstraction), we have been developing a new syntactic extension. The question we discuss in this paper is "Is this a right approach?"

A significant role of language constructs for modularity is to visually present module structures of programs. Traditional syntactic extensions lexically present the structures and thus they have a limitation in the presentation. Since a program is a one-dimensional array of characters, they can only present hierarchical or nested structures without abstract reasoning such as tracing references through symbolic names. This limitation was not a serious problem until crosscutting concerns are widely recognized.

Some code snippets implementing a crosscutting concern often relate to other secondary concerns. Thus, in an ideal presentation, developers should be able to easily comprehend that those code snippets are included in more than one modules if we follow the principle that every concern is implemented by a different dedicated module. Unfortunately, such an ideal presentation is not available through source code in aspect-oriented languages like AspectJ. Using tool supports like AJDT [18] is mandatory to obtain such an ideal presentation. This problem is also known as obliviousness [5], that is, a developer cannot see which aspect is woven into a class when she is working on that class and not reading the source code of the aspect.

To overcome this problem, we propose using not only static text but also *dynamic* text to design a language construct for modularity. Dynamic text automatically changes its shape depending on the contexts. It enables to express more complex module structures of programs, such as crosscutting structures, than hierarchical ones. The resulting language might be categorized into visual languages, which require tool supports for editing a program, but its programs still consist of only a (dynamically changing) character string. Since tool supports like AJDT are almost mandatory in today's software development, considering tool supports at language design is a natural approach.

In the paper, we present two prototype systems based on this idea. One is synchronous copy and paste and the other is a virtual-file editor named *Kide*. Although the essential ideas behind these two systems are not very unique or novel, we developed these systems to demonstrate the design of language constructs with dynamic text. We show new linguistic extensions to Java for aspect-oriented programming although we do not extend the syntax of Java. Some readers might think that our extensions are not language constructs but just new tool supports because of no syntactic extensions. However, our extensions are integrated into the language and hence they are not genuine tool supports, which are optional when programming.

In the rest of the paper, Section 2 mentions the aims of modularization and a brief introduction of aspect orientation. Then it presents limitations of syntactic extensions. Section 3 describes our idea and presents synchronous copy and paste. Then Section 4 presents Kide. Section 5 discusses related work and Section 6 concludes this paper.

2. Language design for aspect orientation

Modularization is a significant issue in modern programing language design. It has at least four aims: code reuse, information hiding [16], composability, and grouping related code.

Here, *code reuse* is to run the same code snippet at different sites in a program. In other words, it is to avoid code duplication as much as possible. Since a program often contains a number of code snippets that are not identical but alike, most modularization mechanisms enable the reuse in that case by some generic expressions such as parametrization.

Information hiding is to hide the knowledge of design decisions on code snippets included in a module. Only the limited knowledge is visible through its interface from the outside. Implementation details are normally invisible.

Composability allows composing a complete program of arbitrarily selected modules with little or no modification of the module code. For example, a procedure is a minimal form of module and it can be added into a program *as is* without modification. Only the caller-site code in the program must be modified to explicitly invoke it. When the procedure is replaced with another, the code at the caller site must be modified since the name of the called procedure changes. However, the definitions of the old and new procedures are not modified at all.

Finally, *grouping related code* is to increase the spacial locality of code snippets belonging to the same concern. This enables independent development of every group of code, which is a module. This also helps developers efficiently

Listing 1. DisplayUpdate aspect

```
1  aspect DisplayUpdate {
2    pointcut change(Shape s):
3      execution(void Shape+.set*(..)) && this(s);
4
5    after(Shape s): change(s) {
6      s.display().repaint(s);
7    }
8  }
```

maintain a program. Reasoning about the behavior of the program on a specific concern is made easier since developers do not have to read an entire program when they want to understand that behavior.

Aspect orientation

Aspect orientation is a modularization technique of a recent trend. It was invented to modularize a *crosscutting* concern. Under the existence of crosscutting concerns, some code snippets in a program belong to multiple concerns. Hence, existing modularization mechanisms are not satisfactory with respect to the criterion of *grouping related code*.

An example of crosscutting concern is a security concern. Suppose that there is a database of academic papers and every access to the database must be checked to confirm that the access is permitted. The code snippets to check this obviously belong to the security concern. On the other hand, they also belong to other application-level concerns, for example, to generate a web page showing a list of papers presented at some past AOSD conference, or to process an HTTP request for registering a new paper in the database.

Since these concerns are functional, some readers might not think that the security-check code belongs to them as well as the security concern, which is non-functional. However, when developers discuss the user interface of obtaining a web page listing papers at a specified AOSD conference, they will want to consider when the security-check code is executed; at the very beginning when the user visits this web site? just before submitting a database query? Except for small applications, the security-check code is not transparent or independent of the code belonging to a functional concern, such as generating a web page.

AspectJ

AspectJ [12] is a programming language designed for addressing the modularity problem of crosscutting concerns. It provides three language constructs such as aspects, pointcut, and advice, and it provides syntactic extensions to Java for them.

An aspect in AspectJ is a main module for implementing a crosscutting concern. Listing 1 is a famous example of aspect, which is an aspect-oriented implementation of Observer pattern [6]. This aspect is part of the implementation

Listing 2. Line class

```
1  class Line extends Shape {
2    int angle, len;
3    void setPos(int nx, int ny) {x = nx; y = ny;}
4    void setLength(int nlen) { len = nlen; }
5    void setAngle(int a) { angle = a; }
6    int getLength() { return len; }
7  }
```

of a figure editor and its concern is to notify a Display object to repaint a window whenever a figure is manipulated by the user and thereby its field is set to a new value. We assume that a figure is represented by Line objects, Rectangle objects, and so forth and Shape is their super class. Listing 2 is an example of Line class.

The DisplayUpdate aspect contains one pointcut change and one advice (with no name). The change pointcut (line 2-3) specifies join points, which are the execution points when a method with a name starting with set (here, * represents a wild card) is invoked on an instance of Shape or its subclass. For example, the join points will include the time when a setLength method on a Line object is invoked. The change pointcut takes a parameter s that is bound to the object on that a set* method is invoked. The body of the advice (line 5-7) in the DisplayUpdate aspect is at line 6 and it is implicitly invoked just after the join points specified by the change pointcut since the advice declaration starts with a keyword after. While executing the advice body, the parameter s is bound by the change pointcut to the object on that the set* method is invoked.

The resulting behavior by the aspect is equivalent to object-oriented code shown in Listing 3 although the object-oriented code is inferior to the AspectJ code with respect to composability. Note that in Listing 3 a call to the advice method in the DisplayUpdate class has been inserted at the end of every method in the Line class. Where the method calls are inserted corresponds to the join points specified by the change pointcut in Listing 1. Since those method-call expressions are embedded in the Line class, decoupling the DisplayUpdate class from the Line class needs code modification to remove those call expressions in the Line class. In AspectJ, decoupling the DisplayUpdate aspect does not need modifying the Line class. The DisplayUpdate aspect can be removed from the rest of the program by just deleting or moving to elsewhere its source file in the source tree.

Modularization in AspectJ

AspectJ improves modularity with respect to crosscutting concerns. As for code reuse, AspectJ eliminates redundant method calls in the Line class, which are necessary to invoke the advice method in the DisplayUpdate class in the object-oriented code in Listing 3. Information hiding is preserved as in the object-oriented code since the logic of how to repaint a

Listing 3. An object-orientated equivalence

```
1   class DisplayUpdate {
2     static void advice(Shape s) {
3       s.display().repaint(s);
4     }
5   }
6
7   class Line extends Shape {
8     int angle, len;
9     void setPos(int nx, int ny) {
10      x = nx; y = ny; DisplayUpdate.advice(this);
11    }
12    void setLength(int nlen) {
13      len = nlen; DisplayUpdate.advice(this);
14    }
15    void setAngle(int a) {
16      angle = a; DisplayUpdate.advice(this);
17    }
18    int getLength() { return len; }
19  }
20
21  // other subclasses of Shape are not shown.
```

window is hidden in the advice of the DisplayUpdate aspect. Composability is improved against the object-oriented code since the developers do not have to modify the program when the functionality of the DisplayUpdate aspect is added to the program or when it is removed. They do not have to modify the Line class or other subclasses of Shape.

However, the program in AspectJ is less satisfactory with respect to grouping related code. Listing 1 collects all the code snippets related to the concern of updating a display. On the other hand, the Line class in Listing 2 does not contain all the code related to the Line concern. The Line class in Listing 3 contains a method call to advice. The call to advice belongs primarily to the display-update concern but also to the concern of the Line figure. Since the AspectJ developers do not easily recognize that a call to set* method in Line causes update on a display, they are recommended to use tool supports by an integrated development environment (IDE), such as AJDT [18]. AJDT graphically shows on a source code editor that the advice in DisplayUpdate is invoked after the execution of set* methods in the Line class. The syntactic extension to Java alone does not fully express the modularity introduced by the new language construct, an aspect.

Another problem is that code duplication increases in AspectJ if an advice body needs local contexts different for each join point. Suppose that we want to call the repaint method at line 6 in Listing 1 only when an attribute of the Shape object is changed so that flicker noise will be reduced. Since it is different for every join point how to check whether an attribute is changed, the aspect will have multiple advice

Listing 4. Another DisplayUpdate aspect

```
1  aspect DisplayUpdate {
2    void around(Line line, int x, int y):
3        execution(void Line.setPos(int,int))
4        && this(line) && args(x, y) {
5      if (line.x != x || line.y != y) {
6        proceed(line, x, y);
7        line.display().repaint(line);
8      }
9    }
10
11   void around(Line line, int len):
12       execution(void Line.setLength(int))
13       && this(line) && args(len) {
14     if (line.len != len) {
15       proceed(line, len);
16       line.display().repaint(line);
17     }
18   }
19
20   void around(Line line, int angle):
21       execution(void Line.setAngle(int))
22       && this(line) && args(angle) {
23     if (line.angle != angle) {
24       proceed(line, angle);
25       line.display().repaint(line);
26     }
27   }
28
29   // advice bodies for other subclasses
30   //      :
31 }
```

bodies for each method and subclass as we show in Listing 4. The first advice (line 2-9) is for the setPos method in the Line class while the second advice (line 11-18) is for the setLength method and the third one (line 20-27) is for the the setAngle method. They compare the argument(s) with the value(s) of the corresponding attribute(s) and, if they are different, execute the original method body by proceed and call the repaint method. Although Listing 4 does not show, the aspect will also have an advice body for every method in the other subclasses of Shape. Since the difference is only the condition of the if statement, those number of advice bodies are similar to each other and hence redundant with respect to code duplication.

3. Language constructs designed with dynamic text

Our observation is that the problem mentioned in the previous section is due to using only a *static* syntactic extension for designing a new language construct for modularity. The use of a static syntactic extension is natural since program-

ming languages have been "languages" in that programs are expressed in the form of one-dimensional simple character array. However, this design approach implies a limitation; software development in AspectJ premises tool supports by IDEs with respect to grouping related code.

Our idea is to use not only static text but also dynamic text for expressing a new language construct for modularity. Dynamic text automatically changes its shape while editing and browsing. We borrowed this concept from an interactive web page, in which its contents dynamically change in accordance with the user's input by, for example, embedded JavaScript code. A language using dynamic text is a variation of visual language but it is still a traditional text-based language since visual icons or fancy graphics are not used. Our proposal is that the text that may dynamically change could be considered as a building block when designing a new language construct. Thus we still design a syntactic extension although the syntax deals with not only static but dynamic text.

To further investigate this idea, we have developed two preliminary systems. We present the first one in the rest of this section and the other one in the next section. By using these systems, we illustrate language constructs with dynamic text to extend plain Java for aspect-oriented programming.

3.1 Synchronous copy and paste

"Copy and Paste" is an easiest way to reuse a code snippet. On most source-code editors, developers can *copy* a selected text into an internal memory ("the clipboard") and then *paste* it at a different position. Although this practice is easy to learn and thus it is popular with novice developers, it is known as bad one with respect to code reuse since it degrades the maintainability of programs. After finishing the paste action, a new copy of the code snippet inserted by that action is independent of the original copy of that code snippet. If a developer wants to modify text in the code snippet, she has to edit the two copies of the code snippet at the same time.

To decrease the negative impact of the original copy and paste on maintainability while keeping its intuitiveness, we propose a new mechanism named *synchronous copy and paste*. We also implemented its prototype on Eclipse IDE (Figure 1). Our idea is simple; a pasted copy of text is automatically updated when the original copy is modified by a developer, and vice versa. If there are multiple pasted copies, all the copies (including the original) are updated when one of them is modified. In Figure 1, the code snippets highlighted in green in editor panes are synchronously updated. The proposed mechanism also provides a small window (called "View" on Eclipse) that shows which group of copies of text synchronously update each other. This small window is called *the concerns view* of the synchronous copy and paste. Developers can name every group of copies syn-

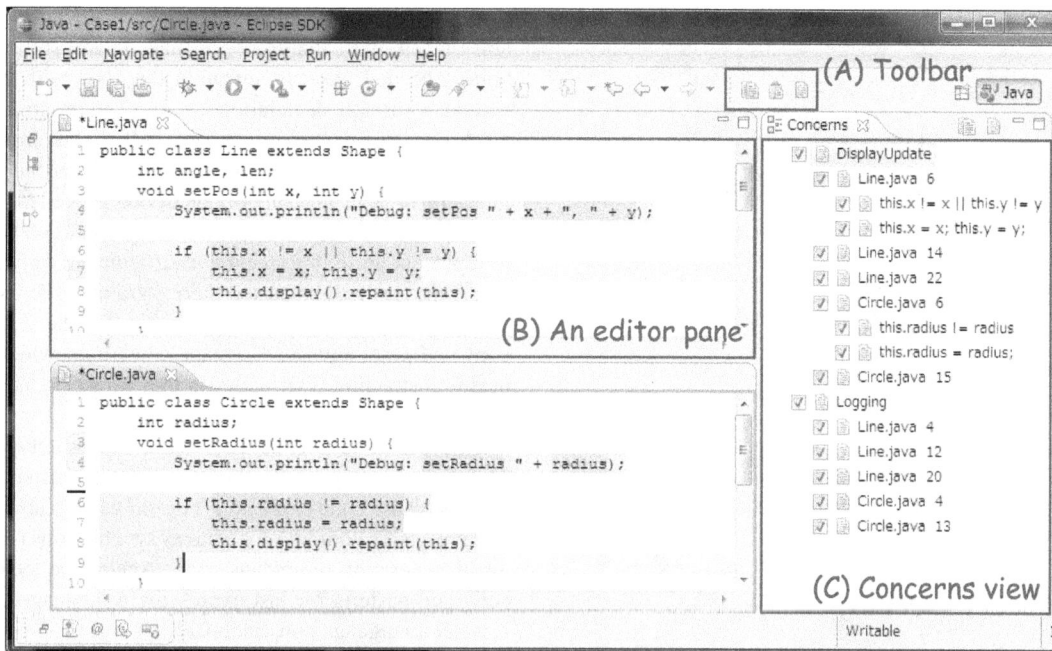

Figure 1. The synchronous copy and paste on Eclipse IDE

chronously updated so that they can easily identify it in the concerns view.

3.2 Procedure abstraction

The synchronous copy and paste is a simple approach to introduce dynamic text into a programming language. It can be used to express a language construct. For example, the expression of procedures can be redesigned with this mechanism. We first present this example to demonstrate our idea although the new design is much worse than typical design of procedure with static text. In Listing 3, the advice method is used as a procedure. Let us rewrite this procedure with our proposed mechanism. We would first modify the setPos method in the Line class into the following:

```
void setPos(int nx, int ny) {
  x = nx; y = ny;
  this.display().repaint(this);
}
```

The method call would be inlined. Then, for the setLength method, we would copy the inlined code and paste it in the setLength method by the proposed mechanism:

```
void setLength(int nlen) {
  len = nlen;
  this.display().repaint(this);
}
```

Since the pasted code is synchronized, if we change it to, for example,

```
void setLength(int nlen) {
  len = nlen;
  for (Display d: this.display()) {
    d.repaint(this);}
}
```

then the body of setPos is also updated (Figure 2). Once the code is "copied," it is listed in the concerns view and the developers can give it an appropriate name to easily identify. This name corresponds to a procedure name. Since the concerns view lists all the code snippets copied before (this information is saved as part of the project), when the developers want to reuse one of those code snippets, they can select its name in the concerns view and paste it at an appropriate place. This corresponds to write a procedure-call expression there.

The proposed mechanism can express a procedure with parameters. Developers can make "holes" in a copied code snippet so that the text in the holes will not be synchronized. The holes are highlighted in magenta in Figure 1. The holes correspond to procedure parameters. If a code snippet has multiple holes, it is possible to synchronize some of the holes and keep them holding the same text. For example, suppose that the two green text-regions in the following code are pasted copies of the same code snippet:

```
int mhp = q.getMaximumHeight();
q.setHeight(mhp < h ? mhp : h);
if (q == null) { return; }
int mhq = q.getMaximumHeight();
q.setHeight(mhq < h ? mhq : h);
```

```
void setPos(int nx, int ny) {                (1)
    x = nx; y = ny;
    this.display().repaint(this);
}

void setLength(int nlen) {
    len = nlen;
    this.display().repaint(this);
}
    void setPos(int nx, int ny) {             (2)
        x = nx; y = ny;
        for (Display d: this.display()) {
            d.
    }

    void setLength(int nlen) {
        len = nlen;
        for (Display d: this.display()) {
            d.|
    }
        void setPos(int nx, int ny) {         (3)
            x = nx; y = ny;
            for (Display d: this.display()) {
                d.repaint(this);}
        }

        void setLength(int nlen) {
            len = nlen;
            for (Display d: this.display()) {
                d.repaint(this);}
        }
```

Figure 2. Synchronously updated code snippets are like inlined procedure bodies.

The boxes represent the holes. In the upper green text region, three boxes of mhp and two boxes of p are holes. They are synchronously updated, respectively. This is similar to a macro function in the C language. Note that the text in the boxes is given at every pasted place; different text can be given to (every copy of) the same box at a different place. In the lower green text region, three red boxes hold mhq and two blue boxes hold q instead of mhp and p.

The new design of procedure using the synchronous copy and paste provides acceptable ability with respect to code reuse, composability, and grouping related code. Code reuse is easy; pasting code is a simple and intuitive action. Composition is as simple as traditional procedures with static text. Since the code snippets synchronized with each other are listed in the concerns view, developers can easily identify a group of related code snippets. However, the new design of procedure does not provide information hiding since the pasted code is directly inlined. The details of the code is not hidden at all. To address this problem, the proposed mechanism should be able to fold the pasted text into short text, such as its name, so that it will look like a procedure-call expression. We have not implemented this on our prototype system yet.

Some readers might wonder how to declare local variables when using the proposed mechanism. If a local variable is needed, we can surround the code with braces {} and put a variable declaration into it.[3] The proposed mechanism, however, cannot prevent the pasted code from accessing variables in an outer block. Furthermore, the proposed mechanism does not support recursive procedure calls. To do that, we must introduce something like "delayed paste" to represent an infinite recursive structure. It only indicates that some text will be pasted there on demand (conceptually at runtime). Note that our claim is not that the synchronous copy and paste replaces language constructs, which provide useful abstraction. Our claim is that it can be used for the expression of such language constructs.

Another issue is code size. Since our prototype naively implements the synchronous copy and paste, too many pasting may cause code explosion. This drawback, however, will be reduced if a compiler recognizes synchronous pasting and avoid generating redundant code. Again, the synchronous copy and paste is for just expressing a language construct. It is not a language construct itself.

3.3 Aspects

The synchronous copy and paste can be used in normal Java for expressing an aspect, which is a primary language construct in aspect-oriented programming. We next demonstrate it by rewriting the aspect in Listing 1. To implement this modularity in AspectJ, we start with the object-oriented code in Listing 3. Since this code contains several method calls to advice and those calls are redundant, we use the synchronous copy and paste so that all the call expressions to advice will be synchronized for updates. This improves the code reuse in Listing 3. Information hiding by the after advice in Listing 1 (line 6) is achieved by the advice method in the DisplayUpdate class in Listing 3 (line 3).

Although the obliviousness property [5] by AspectJ is not provided, composability is also improved than the original Listing 3, which has the problem mentioned in the previous section. In the original Listing 3, every method call to advice must be manually deleted when the DisplayUpdate class is decoupled from the Line class and other subclasses of Shape. Now it is easier to delete all the method calls all at once (or change them to empty expressions) since they are synchronously updated. Restoring the deleted method calls in the Line class is also easy since the synchronized code snippets remain as blanks after the method calls are deleted.

The synchronous copy and paste also improves grouping related code. Since the concerns view presents where the method calls to advice are pasted in the program, developers can see at a glance the overview of where all the code snippets of the display-update concern are. This is similar to

---

[3] Java does not allow variable declarations with the same name as a variable declared in an outer block. Hence this approach does not provide equivalent ability in Java to local variables within a procedure.

the information available from the DisplayUpdate aspect in Listing 1, that is, about the code related to the display-update concern.

Furthermore, unlike in AspectJ, developers can also see the entire code of the Line concern, which includes the method calls to advice. Since the method calls to advice belong to both concerns, showing this fact with traditional language constructs with static text is difficult. If only static text is used, every code snippet must belong to a single lexical module such as a source file. Otherwise, it would make extra code duplication. Dynamic text provides better flexibility to the language design as we showed above with the synchronous copy and paste.

The aspect in Listing 1 can be rewritten in another approach. This is preferable for addressing the problem of AspectJ shown in Listing 4 in the previous section. This problem was that code duplication increases if an advice body needs local contexts different for each join point. In fact, the DisplayUpdate aspect in Listing 4 has a number of similar advice bodies for every join point. Since the differences are only the condition part of the if statement, those advice bodies are somewhat redundant.

This redundancy is minimized if we use the synchronous copy and paste. See a normal Java program in Figure 3, where the advice bodies in Listing 4 are inlined in each corresponding method. Although this naive program may look problematic with respect to modularity, the synchronous copy and paste reduces this modularity problem. Suppose that the entire body of every method is synchronized for updates but the condition part of the if statement and the first statement of the then block are "holes," which are not synchronized. This text synchronization works as a macro function and hence improves code reuse.

Furthermore, the synchronous copy and paste provides the concerns view, which presents the same information that the pointcut in the AspectJ aspect in Listing 4 provides. It gives a view of the code snippets implementing the display-update concern as that AspectJ aspect does. The developers can easily see two views of group of related code: one is an editor pane of Line.java for the Line concern (and other shape concerns) and the other is the concerns view in Figure 4 for the display-update concern. Note that code snippets are shared by both views. In AspectJ, since the if statement and the call expression to repaint, such as line 4 and 6 in Figure 3, are contained only in the aspect in Listing 4, the entire overview of the code belonging to the Line concern is difficult to see without an appropriate tool support. Moreover, the concern view in Figure 4 presents the text in every "hole". This corresponds to arguments passed to an advice body in AspectJ although an aspect in AspectJ abstracts formal parameters from them. To obtain the information available in the concerns view, AspectJ developers must read the class declaration where the aspect is woven.

Figure 3. An aspect-oriented Line class in Java

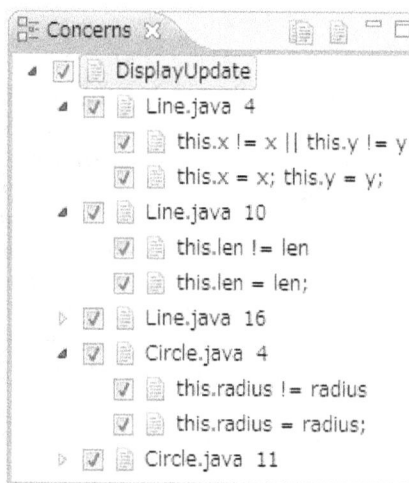

Figure 4. The concerns view for the synchronous copy and paste

4. Kide

We next show another prototype system for using dynamic text. We developed this system named *Kide* for investigating our idea of using dynamic text for modularizing a crosscutting concern (Figure 5). It is a plug-in for Eclipse IDE.

As we mentioned in Section 2, AspectJ assumes that every code snippet belongs to a single concern. An aspect in AspectJ is designed for moving a code snippet from an irrelevant class, where otherwise the code snippet would be placed, to an appropriate aspect, a special module provided

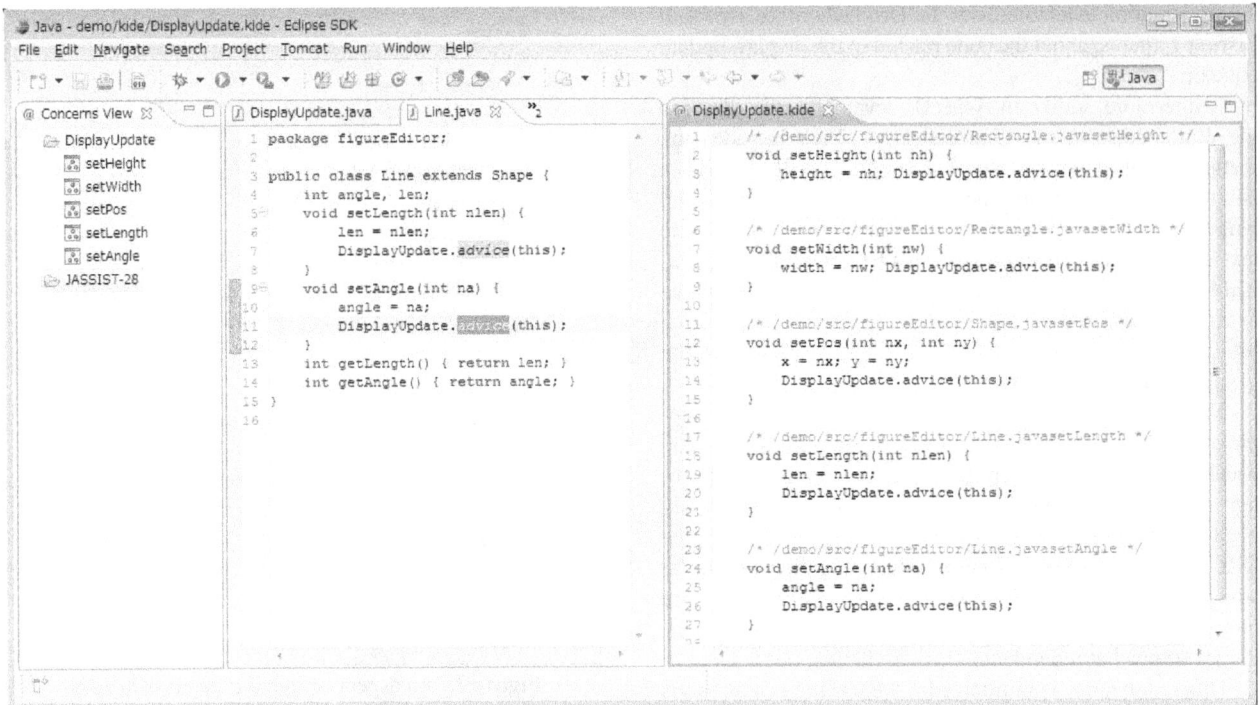

Figure 5. Showing the DisplayUpdate concern by Kide

by AspectJ as well as a class, if that code snippet is for a crosscutting concern. However, such code snippets often belong to not only the crosscutting concern but also other non-crosscutting concerns. Since an aspect in AspectJ is based on static text, it cannot directly show that the other concerns also need those code snippets; some extra tool supports are required to know the fact. For example, the method call to repaint at the line 6 in Listing 1 belongs to not only the display-update concern implemented by the aspect, but also the concerns of the Line class and other subclasses of Shape.

Kide allows developers to make a virtual source file that contains code snippets taken from other source files in Java. Hence one code snippet can be contained in multiple source files (one physical source file and multiple virtual source files). Since all the copies of a code snippet are shared, editing it in one source file is immediately reflected on other source files. In the current implementation of Kide, only a constructor, field, and method declaration can be collected into a virtual source file. Collecting part of a method body is not allowed. A virtual source file is saved as part of a project; once making it, it is always available until developers explicitly delete it.

Kide provides a support mechanism for selecting method declarations to be collected. While developers can manually select method declarations one by one, they can also select several method declarations at once. Kide currently allows selecting all the methods overriding a specific method or all

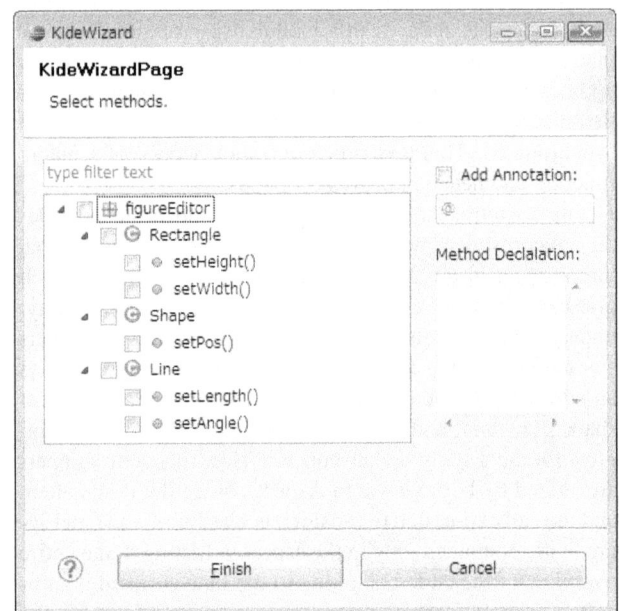

Figure 6. A wizard of Kide for selecting methods shown together

the methods calling a specific method through wizard-like user interface (Figure 6). It is also possible to further screen the methods by hand after selecting by the wizard.

The virtual source files specified by developers are listed in a small window named *the concerns view*. Developers must give an appropriate name to a virtual source file. For every virtual source file, the concerns view presents its name and the names of the methods, fields, and/or constructors collected in that file. If developers open a virtual source file in the concerns view, a source code editor is launched and then they can edit that file. In a virtual source file, every method (and field, constructor) has a comment indicating the physical source file of its origin. The order of listing those methods can be changed by developers. The editor of a virtual source file allows developers to insert the same text at the beginning of all the method bodies collected in that source file or just before all the return statements contained in the methods (if no return statement, at the end of the method bodies).

Aspect orientation by Kide

Kide can be used to do aspect-oriented programming in Java without syntactic extensions. A virtual source file can be used as a module containing methods and fields related to a crosscutting concern. Since code snippets for a crosscutting concern often belong to other (non-crosscutting) concerns, Kide provides better modularity than AspectJ with respect to grouping related code. A code snippet can be contained in multiple source files and thus developers can browse and edit at a glance in one source file all the code snippets for a particular concern.

For example, when developers are working on the Line concern, they can open and edit a file Line.java, which contains the Line class shown in Listing 3 and thus all the code snippets related to the Line-figure concern. Note that, although calls to the advice method (line 10, 13, and 16) belong to the display-update concern, they also belong to the Line concern since they are part of the behavior of Line objects. When developers are interested in the display-update concern, they can make a virtual source file DisplayUpdate and collect into this file all setter methods in subclasses of Shape, such as setPos and setLength. A getter method, such as getLength, is not collected into the virtual file. Then developers can see all the methods related to the display-update concern by opening that virtual file.

Crosscutting over documentation

A virtual source file in Kide can contain not only Java code but also plain text taken from a separate text file. Like a method declaration, developers can select a text block surrounded by XML tags and put it in a virtual source file.

This helps literate programming [13] since it allows mixing code and text in one file. In practice, it is useful for bug tracking during software maintenance. When a development team receives a bug report, they investigate the bug, discuss how to fix it, implement the fix, and finally check the new code into the source code repository. This activity is often managed by a bug tracking system, which records a chat log among developers and the revision numbers of the related source files before/after the fix. When a similar bug is reported later, developers refer to this recorded chat log and understand how the source files are changed for fixing the original bug.

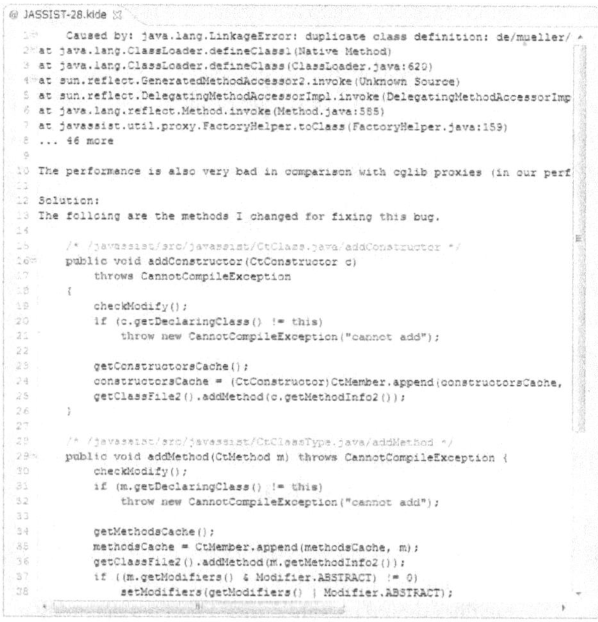
JASSIST-28.kide

```
    Caused by: java.lang.LinkageError: duplicate class definition: de/mueller/
at java.lang.ClassLoader.defineClass1(Native Method)
at java.lang.ClassLoader.defineClass(ClassLoader.java:620)
at sun.reflect.GeneratedMethodAccessor2.invoke(Unknown Source)
at sun.reflect.DelegatingMethodAccessorImpl.invoke(DelegatingMethodAccessorImp
at java.lang.reflect.Method.invoke(Method.java:585)
at javassist.util.proxy.FactoryHelper.toClass(FactoryHelper.java:159)
... 46 more

The performance is also very bad in comparison with cglib proxies (in our perf

Solution:
The follcing are the methods I changed for fixing this bug.

    /* /javassist/src/javassist/CtClass.java/addConstructor */
    public void addConstructor(CtConstructor c)
        throws CannotCompileException
    {
        checkModify();
        if (c.getDeclaringClass() != this)
            throw new CannotCompileException("cannot add");

        getConstructorsCache();
        constructorsCache = (CtConstructor)CtMember.append(constructorsCache,
        getClassFile2().addMethod(c.getMethodInfo2());
    }

    /* /javassist/src/javassist/CtClassType.java/addMethod */
    public void addMethod(CtMethod m) throws CannotCompileException {
        checkModify();
        if (m.getDeclaringClass() != this)
            throw new CannotCompileException("cannot add");

        getMethodsCache();
        methodsCache = CtMember.append(methodsCache, m);
        getClassFile2().addMethod(m.getMethodInfo2());
        if ((m.getModifiers() & Modifier.ABSTRACT) != 0)
            setModifiers(getModifiers() | Modifier.ABSTRACT);
```

Figure 7. A bug report written by Kide

Kide helps developers write a detailed report of how they fixed a bug for future reference. Kide makes it easy to write a documentation quoting several method declarations from source files. We demonstrate this idea by using a bug report for Javassist [2], which is a Java bytecode engineering library widely used by a number of software including commercial products such as Red Hat JBoss AS. One day, the development team received a bug report that pointed out that the software consumes too much memory.[4] The team found that the bug is not memory leak but decided to introduce a mechanism to reduce memory consumption. Then they implemented a prune method, which discards unnecessary information of a specified class file. This method is invoked when a class file is loaded by the Java virtual machine. The implementation of the prune method involves several support methods in different classes. Furthermore, since after calling the prune method, part of the Javassist functionality on the class is not available, the development team had to modify several methods so that they would check at runtime that the prune method is not called yet. A method call to checkModify was inserted at the beginning of every method that accesses the information discarded by the prune method. After the prune method is called, the checkModify method

[4] https://issues.jboss.org/browse/JASSIST-28

throws a runtime exception to notify that the functionality of Javassist is not available.

If Kide were available, the development team could write a virtual source file that includes the original bug report, the description of how to change the source code for it, and the implementations of the prune method and its support methods. The methods calling the checkModify method could be included in that documentation since they are part of the *pruning* concern (Figure 7). Both code and documentation crosscutting over a number of classes and files are collected into a single file. The resulting file will be useful for future bug fixes and maintenance.

5. Related work

There have been a number of mechanisms similar to the synchronous copy and paste or Kide. Our main contribution is to propose the use of those mechanisms for designing a language construct for advanced modularity. Those mechanisms should not be supplementary tool supports provided by IDEs but they should be tightly integrated into a language.

Code clone

Simultaneous editing [15] and Linked Editing [19] are the most direct related work of the synchronous copy and paste. Both were developed for managing duplicated code or code clone. They allow developers to edit distinct code regions simultaneously as they do with the synchronous copy and paste. Simultaneous editing provides a generalization mechanism so that the system automatically generalizes developers' editing actions to apply other code regions. Like our synchronous copy and paste, a motivation of the study of Linked Editing is to overcome limitations of the language constructs with static text with respect to duplicated code.

However, either simultaneous editing or Linked Editing does not provide the correspondent to the concerns view of the synchronous copy and paste. The concerns view is significant since the design focus of the synchronous copy and paste is on modularity instead of code duplication whereas Linked Editing is a tool mainly for managing code duplication than modularity as pointed out in [9]. Furthermore, the user interface when dealing with more than two code regions synchronously updated together would be inefficient without the concerns view. Giving a name to a group of code regions synchronously updated is also important for modularity. This ability is also provided by the concerns view.

The idea of synchronous updates of copy-and-paste induced code clone is also found in other systems. For example, CReN [8] is a tool for detecting code clones and maintaining clone evolution by synchronous updates. It enables automated consistent renaming of program elements such as variables in synchronized code clones. The main focus of those systems, however, is on automated maintenance of code clones. It is not on providing better views of programs with respect to modularity.

Aspect orientation

In the contexts of aspect-oriented programming, several tool supports have been proposed for providing multiple views of programs for developers. Mylar [11] (now Eclipse Mylyn) monitors developers' editing actions and automatically detect a group of related source files. This group corresponds to a concern that the developer was working on during a certain period. For example, when the developer is working on fixing a bug, Mylar records a group of files that the developer opens and edits for that work. Mylar uses the information of this group for presenting only interested elements in windows such as a package explorer and an outline view. It filters out unnecessary source files and program elements by using that information. A difference from our work is that Mylar is a support tool and it deals with temporal concerns whereas our work deals with concerns on program structures. Furthermore, unlike Kide, a source code editor of Mylar does not dynamically change the expression of a program according to the developer's current concern.

Fluid AOP [7] is an IDE for aspect-oriented programming (AOP). Like our work, the goal of Fluid AOP is to overcome limitations of language constructs designed with static text. Fluid AOP still uses AspectJ-like syntax but also utilizes dynamic text. It simultaneously provides different views of a program independently of actual source files. A difference is that Fluid AOP uses AspectJ-like pointcut definitions for specifying module structures whereas our work does not introduce extra syntactic extensions to Java; our developers do not have to learn the pointcut language. They can specify module structures by copy-and-paste actions or wizard-based user interface. Furthermore, unlike Kide, Fluid AOP cannot deal with documentation.

A fluid source code view [3] is an source code editor in which, when the developer clicks a method-call expression, the declaration of that called method is superimposed on that method-call expression. This reduces navigation efforts of the developer. Although a fluid source code view can present the declarations of multiple methods in a single editor pane, the methods presented together must have caller-callee relations. In Kide, it is possible to present the declarations of arbitrary selected methods in a single editor pane.

Other systems

CIDE [10] is an Eclipse-based tool for decomposing applications into features. Developers can mark a code snippet with a color of the feature that the code snippet belongs to. After coloring, developers can easily include/exclude the code snippets belonging to a specific feature as they can do with a preprocessor directive #ifdef. CIDE also provides a navigation panel similar to our concerns view. The difference is that CIDE does not present a view of virtual source file including all the program elements related to a specific feature. It can change the expression of a program only within an actual source file. On the other hand, a virtual source file of

Kide can collect all program elements from different source files. Kide is better designed for dealing with crosscutting concerns.

Code Bubbles [1] is an IDE in which developers can make a small editor pane for a method and freely place it on the screen. The small editor is called *a bubble*. With bubbles, developers can see and work with a complete working set of related code-snippets. Although the Code Bubbles IDE does not provide a wizard-based support tool, which Kide provides, to collect methods related to a specific concern, a set of bubbles could be used as a replacement of a virtual source file in Kide. However, Kide gives developers a uniform view of group of related code snippets, which is a source file, whichever the code snippets are collected from other various source files or a single physical source file. A source file is a traditional metaphor of module.

Cedalion [14] supports projectional editing. It allows programmers to directly edit an abstract syntax tree through a human-readable textual view of that tree. Since the textual view is a projection of the tree, it can contain special symbols and be displayed with different fonts and unorthodox layout. The edit-time MOP [4] also enables extended presentation of source programs. These systems share a similar idea with our proposal but their primary focus is on internal domain-specific languages.

The idea of virtual source files in Kide is also found in Desert [17]. Desert is an IDE in which developers can create a virtual file to make navigation among code snippets efficient. Desert can generate a virtual file that contains code snippets including compilation errors or matching a given search pattern. Our contribution is that we pointed out that virtual source files are useful abstraction for crosscutting modularity.

6. Conclusion

In this paper, we presented limitations of syntactic extensions for new language constructs for modularity, specifically, aspect orientation. Then we proposed using dynamic text when designing new language constructs. To demonstrate this idea, we presented the synchronous copy and paste and Kide. We illustrated concrete examples of language constructs with dynamic text as aspect-oriented programming extensions to Java without modifying the original syntax. Although there have been a number of similar linguistic mechanisms like ours, our main contribution is that we showed that designing language constructs with dynamic text is useful for aspect oriented programming. Another message is that language designers should consider tool supports as not optional features but integrated part of programming language design.

Acknowledgments

This work has been strongly influenced by our joint work on universal AOP with Awais Rashid, Ruzanna Chitchyan, and Phil Greenwood. We would also like to thank Eric Tanter, Romain Robbes, and the members of the PLEIAD group for their insightful comments.

References

[1] A. Bragdon, S. P. Reiss, R. Zeleznik, S. Karumuri, W. Cheung, J. Kaplan, C. Coleman, F. Adeputra, and J. J. LaViola, Jr. Code bubbles: Rethinking the user interface paradigm of integrated development environments. In *Proc. of the 32nd ACM/IEEE Int'l Conf. on Software Engineering (ICSE '10)*, pages 455–464. ACM, 2010.

[2] S. Chiba. Load-time structural reflection in Java. In *ECOOP 2000*, LNCS 1850, pages 313–336. Springer-Verlag, 2000.

[3] M. Desmond, M.-A. Storey, and C. Exton. Fluid source code views. In *14th IEEE Int'l Conf. on Program Comprehension (ICPC'06)*, pages 260–263. IEEE, 2006.

[4] A. D. Eisenberg and G. Kiczales. Expressive programs through presentation extension. In *Proc. of 6th Int'l Conf. on Aspect-Oriented Software Development (AOSD 2007)*, pages 73–84. ACM, 2007.

[5] R. E. Filman and D. P. Friedman. Aspect-oriented programming is quantification and obliviousness. In R. E. Filman, T. Elrad, S. Clarke, and M. Akşit, editors, *Aspect-Oriented Software Development*, pages 21–35. Addison-Wesley, 2005.

[6] E. Gamma, R. Helm, R. Johnson, and J. Vlissides. *Design Patterns*. Addison-Wesley, 1994.

[7] T. Hon and G. Kiczales. Fluid aop join point models. In *Proc. of ACM OOPSLA*, pages 712–713. ACM, 2006.

[8] D. Hou, F. Jacob, and P. Jablonski. Exploring the design space of proactive tool support for copy-and-paste programming. In *Proc. of the 2009 Conf. of the Center for Advanced Studies on Collaborative Research (CASCON '09)*, pages 188–202. ACM, 2009.

[9] C. J. Kapser and M. W. Godfrey. "cloning considered harmful" considered harmful: patterns of cloning in software. *Empirical Software Engineering*, 13(6):645–692, 2008.

[10] C. Kästner, S. Apel, and M. Kuhlemann. Granularity in software product lines. In *Proc. of the 30th Int'l Conf. on Software Engineering (ICSE '08)*, pages 311–320. ACM, 2008.

[11] M. Kersten and G. C. Murphy. Mylar: a degree-of-interest model for ides. In *Proc. of the 4th Int'l Conf. on Aspect-Oriented Software Development (AOSD '05)*, pages 159–168. ACM, 2005.

[12] G. Kiczales, E. Hilsdale, J. Hugunin, M. Kersten, J. Palm, and W. G. Griswold. An overview of AspectJ. In *ECOOP 2001 – Object-Oriented Programming*, LNCS 2072, pages 327–353. Springer, 2001.

[13] D. E. Knuth. Literate programming. *The Computer Journal*, 27(2):97–111, 1984.

[14] D. H. Lorenz and B. Rosenan. Cedalion: a language for language oriented programming. In *Proc. of ACM OOPSLA*, pages 733–752. ACM, 2011.

[15] R. C. Miller and B. A. Myers. Interactive simultaneous editing of multiple text regions. In *Proc. of the General Track:*

2002 USENIX Annual Technical Conference, pages 161–174. USENIX Association, 2001.

[16] D. L. Parnas. On the criteria to be used in decomposing systems into modules. *Commun. ACM*, 15:1053–1058, December 1972.

[17] S. P. Reiss. Simplifying data integration: The design of the desert software development environment. In *Proc. on Int'l Conf. on Software Engineering (ICSE '96)*, pages 398–407. IEEE, 1996.

[18] The Eclipse Foundation. AspectJ development tools (ajdt). http://www.eclipse.org/ajdt.

[19] M. Toomim, A. Begel, and S. Graham. Managing duplicated code with linked editing. In *2004 IEEE Symposium on Visual Languages and Human Centric Computing*, pages 173 –180, 2004.

A Closer Look at Aspect Interference and Cooperation

Cynthia Disenfeld   Shmuel Katz

Department of Computer Science
Technion - Israel Institute of Technology
{cdisenfe,katz}@cs.technion.ac.il

Abstract

In this work we consider specification and compositional verification for interference detection when several aspects are woven together under joint-weaving semantics without recursion. In this semantics, whenever a joinpoint of an aspect is reached, the corresponding advice is begun even if the joinpoint is inside the advice of other aspects. This captures most of the possible aspect interference cases in AspectJ. Moreover, the given technique is used to capture cooperation among aspects, which enhances modularity. The extended specification and proof obligations should provide insight to the possible interactions among aspects in a reusable library.

Categories and Subject Descriptors   D.2.1 [*Software Engineering*]: Requirements/Specifications; D.2.4 [*Software Engineering*]: Software/Program Verification—Correctness proofs, Model checking

General Terms   Languages, Verification

Keywords   Aspects, Joint-Weaving, Verification, Composition, Cooperation, Interference

1. Introduction

Aspects capture problems that may crosscut the application, such as logging, persistence, exception management, and others. Weaving several aspects within an application may lead to *interference*: given a set of aspects, each aspect on its own behaves as expected but when considering all aspects woven together the expected behavior is no longer achieved.

In this work, we extend existing results on interference detection, to treat the basic *joint-weaving* semantics seen in AspectJ. In joint-weaving semantics, whenever a joinpoint of an aspect is reached, the corresponding advice is begun even if the joinpoint is inside the advice of other aspects.

```
aspect Auth
before() : doTrans()
    Usr u = requestUsr()
    Pwd p = requestPwd()
    authenticated = usrPwdExist(u,p)

aspect SaveCookie
after (Usr u, Pwd p) returning (boolean success):
    call(* usrPwdExist(..)) && args(u,p)
    if (success) saveCookie(u,p)

aspect EncryptPwd
Pwd around(): call(requestPwd())
    Pwd p = proceed()
    return encrypt(p)
```

Figure 1. Aspects `Auth`, `SaveCookie` and `EncryptPwd`

The program listing in Figure 1 shows AspectJ-style aspects to authenticate transactions on a website (`Auth`), to save a cookie on authentication success (`SaveCookie`), and to encrypt passwords (`EncryptPwd`), where the latter two are activated within the advice code of the first.

Note that `SaveCookie` does not affect the behavior of `Auth`. However `EncryptPwd` may cause an existing user and password not to be found anymore by `Auth` (because the password is now encrypted by the time the check is done). This interference is caused from the execution of `EncryptPwd` within `Auth`. In this paper, we will consider a precise representation of aspect specifications which allow using formal verification techniques to detect such interference.

If `EncryptPwd` assumes that every password satisfies some necessary constraints (such as a minimum number of characters, combination of letters, numbers and symbols), then another aspect may collaborate in order to guarantee that the assumptions of `EncryptPwd` hold. Such aspect collaboration will also be considered.

A restricted procedure for detecting interference among aspects using model checking is presented in MAVEN [8]. This method assumes that there are no joinpoints inside advice and is valid for *sequential weaving*, where the advice of an aspect is woven into the system at the joinpoints available so far, and then another aspect can be woven. (In addition, [8] considers simple cases in which joint weaving is equivalent to sequential weaving.)

We will analyze and present a compositional verification and interference detection technique for the case in which aspects may have new joinpoints within the advice of other aspects and that is valid for joint-weaving semantics. As explained in the following section, the verification technique is based on model checking state machines derived from AspectJ code. The method to be presented is for at most weakly-invasive aspects [12], that is they may return to a different state of the underlying system as long as the state was already reachable from some other execution. This assumption is in order to make notation simpler, but the same ideas can be applied for the general case, as explained at the begining of Section 5. We also assume that there is no recursion, i.e. an aspect is never executed under its own execution flow, not even indirectly.

The method predicates that aspects can be given a generalized assume-guarantee specification, where the underlying system and environment are assumed to satisfy the aspect's assumption, and the augmented system with the aspect should satisfy its guarantee. This form of specification allows building a library of verified aspects where possible interference has been analyzed in advance. Then, this library may be used in any system that satisfies the properties that the aspects assume, and the guarantees of the aspects hold without the need to perform any additional checks.

This work provides the following main contributions:

- understanding the problems that arise when considering joint-weaving semantics instead of sequential weaving. By giving examples it will be shown how existing mechanisms that rely on sequential weaving do not always detect interference when the joint-weaving model is used.

- treating joint weaving by distinguishing between *global* and *local* guarantees. When aspects may add joinpoints of other aspects, some aspects may not be aware of all the matching joinpoints in the state machine model of aspect weaving. Hence, global guarantees express properties that should hold even when not all aspects are aware of all joinpoints, and local guarantees express what is expected at those joinpoints of which the aspect is aware.

- treating aspects that contain joinpoints of other aspects by adding an *internal assumption* to the specification of every aspect A. The *internal assumption* of A represents what every other aspect B to be executed within the execution of A must satisfy.

    Some default internal assumption sorts are presented, e.g. when inserted aspects are assumed to satisfy an invariant; however they are not restrictive and any such assumption can be treated.

    Being aware of the need for internal assumptions when writing aspect specifications promotes a better understanding of the system, even when not applying formal verification techniques: aspect interactions, dependencies

and cooperation requirements are conveyed by the internal assumptions.

- providing a compositional verification technique to verify non-interference in a set of aspects that may add new joinpoints of other aspects under joint weaving semantics. This technique takes into account the particular internal assumption, since certain defaults may lead to simpler checks.

    Given a library of aspects, they must be checked only once, and then for any system which satisfies the necessary aspect assumptions, the system augmented with the aspects is already proven to satisfy all aspect guarantees.

    Adding a new aspect to a library implies checking this aspect against all the other aspects in the library, but the proofs already done are still valid and used in the new proof of interference-freedom.

- extending the compositional verification technique for considering aspect cooperation.

    The correctness proof of collaborative aspects yields aspect dependencies, and also allows incrementally verifying as the system is being built - the assumptions of an aspect A are considered to hold, and then the necessary assistant aspects can be developed and verified to satisfy the assumptions of A.

The next section gives background on aspects, temporal logic, weaving semantics and the previous work on aspect verification that is extended here. Sections 3 and 4 describe the technique for detecting interference, including aspect specification and verification. The soundness proof is given in Section 5. Section 6 discusses cooperation. The technique applied to removed joinpoints is considered in Section 7. Section 8 presents related work and we conclude in Section 9.

2. Background

2.1 Aspects

Aspects allow describing crosscutting concerns of a system by defining in which states (*joinpoints*) a certain response should be woven, and what the response consists of (*advice*). *Pointcut descriptors* describe the joinpoints where the response should be woven. Each *advice* consists of the code to be executed when the pointcut is matched. In this work, we consider aspect advices given by state machines. Even though the examples are given in AspectJ, as mentioned before we assume the use of tools such as [5] that can transform code to state machines automatically. Creating such a finite-state model from Java code is a non-trivial task, and generally requires abstracting data domains and system states. Often, a careful abstraction can guarantee that if the specification holds for the abstracted model it also holds for the original version. Weaving an aspect A to a system S is then a state machine transformation, where for each state s in S

that represents a joinpoint of A the next states of s are now the entry points to the aspect execution. When A returns, it returns to a state representing the program point where it should go (if no exceptions were thrown) and the variable contents according to the changes that A has applied.

Aspects can be categorized according to the semantic transformation they make to the underlying system [12]:

Spectative aspects gather information, but do not change control flow or the values of the variables non-local to the aspect.

Regulative aspects may change the control flow, but do not change the values of non-local variables.

Weakly-Invasive aspects may also change the values of the variables, as long as the returning state was already reachable in the underlying system.

Strongly-Invasive aspects are allowed to change the contents of the variables even when returning to states that were not originally reachable in the underlying system.

2.2 Temporal logic

Temporal logic allows expressing properties related to time formally. In particular, we work with linear temporal logic, which expresses for every computation path what must be satisfied. We will use propositional logic operators together with linear temporal logic (LTL) formulas. The operators available in LTL are

- $\mathbf{X}\varphi$: next φ. The next state must satisfy φ.

- $\mathbf{G}\varphi$: always φ. Every state in the future must satisfy φ.

- $\mathbf{F}\varphi$: eventually φ. There exists a state in the future that must satisfy φ.

- $\psi\mathbf{U}\varphi$: ψ until φ. Every state must satisfy ψ until φ holds.

- $\psi\mathbf{W}\varphi$: ψ weak-until φ. Equivalent to $(\mathbf{G}\psi) \vee (\psi\mathbf{U}\varphi)$

2.3 Weaving semantics

In this work we extend the ideas of interference detection in the sequential weaving model to the joint-weaving model.

The notation $S + A$ indicates the system S with A *woven into* it. A is aware of its joinpoints in S already, so $S + A$ results in the system where A is executed at all its joinpoints. However, in the sequential weaving $(S + A) + B$, B is woven into $S + A$, but if B has joinpoints of A, they are not recognized and the advice of A is not woven at those points.

In the sequential weaving model each aspect is woven to the system in a certain order, e.g. given the aspects A, B where there is no precedence defined among the aspects, the possible results are $(S + A) + B$ or $(S + B) + A$. Note that in both cases added joinpoints may not be recognized by the first woven aspect.

In the joint-weaving model, aspects may add or remove joinpoints of other aspects without restrictions, and all joinpoints are recognized. $S + (A, B)$ is used to denote this se-

mantic model, which corresponds to the semantics of AspectJ.

2.4 Previous work

In MAVEN [8], every weakly-invasive aspect has to satisfy its specification (P, R), where P is the assumption and R the guarantee. A sequence of aspects $\{A_1, \ldots, A_n\}$ woven sequentially in this order is said to be interference-free if and only if whenever all assumptions are satisfied, and the aspects in the set are woven in that order, then all of the guarantees will be satisfied:

$$S \vDash \bigwedge_{i=1}^{n} P_{A_i} \Rightarrow ((S + A_1) + \ldots) + A_n \vDash \bigwedge_{i=1}^{n} R_{A_i}$$

In order to satisfy non-interference, every pair of aspects A, B is shown to satisfy two rules:

KP$_{\mathbf{AB}}$: For any system S that satisfies $P_A \wedge P_B$, the assumptions of both A and B, when A is woven into S the obtained system $(S + A)$ must preserve the assumption of B: $S \vDash P_A \wedge P_B \Rightarrow S + A \vDash P_B$.

KR$_{\mathbf{AB}}$: For any system S that satisfies the guarantee of A (R_A) and the assumption of B (P_B), when B is woven into S the obtained system $(S + B)$ must preserve the guarantee of A: $S \vDash R_A \wedge P_B \Rightarrow S + B \vDash R_A$.

In proving these properties, the state machine of the assumption (the tableau of the LTL formula) is used to represent all base programs satisfying the conjunction on the left hand side of the implication, and the appropriate aspect is woven to the state machine to yield a state machine that should satisfy the formula on the right hand side of the implication.

The rules are sufficient to guarantee correctness and non-interference only if (1) A cannot interfere with B's assumption while advice of B is executing (2) B cannot interfere with A's guarantee while A is executing, and (3) B does not in itself add new joinpoints of A. None of these conditions are true in our new general setting.

3. Specification

In this section we will consider the aspects given in Figure 1 to understand the specification method. Intuitively, `Auth` is correct if when woven to any system, every time it reaches a before `doTrans` joinpoint, eventually `Auth` returns where the value of `authenticated` is true if and only if the user and password exist in the system. This field can be used later to allow or not different actions on the transaction, for instance when not authenticated, the user may read but not write to the database.

The aspect `SaveCookie` is correct if when woven to any system, every time after the method `usrPwdExist` is completed and the user and password indeed exist, then a cookie is saved.

Finally, `EncryptPwd` guarantees that when woven, the aspect encrypts the password obtained by `requestPwd()`.

In the temporal logic representations of the specifications, for any aspect A, P_A represents the assumption on the underlying system and R_A expresses the guarantee of the augmented system when the aspect is woven. The formal specifications of the aspects are:

`Auth`:
$$P_{\texttt{Auth}} = \texttt{true}$$
$$R_{\texttt{Auth}} = \mathbf{G}(doTrans_{before} \Rightarrow$$
$$\quad (\mathbf{F}(usrRequested \wedge usr = U_0) \wedge$$
$$\quad \mathbf{F}(pwdRequested \wedge pwd = P_0) \wedge$$
$$\quad \mathbf{F}(ret_{\texttt{Auth}} \wedge authed \Leftrightarrow usrPwdInDB(U_0, P_0))))$$

`SaveCookie`:
$$P_{\texttt{SaveCookie}} = \texttt{true}$$
$$R_{\texttt{SaveCookie}} = \mathbf{G}((call\_usrPwdExist_{after} \wedge Success)$$
$$\quad \Rightarrow \mathbf{F}\, cookieSaved)$$

`EncryptPwd`:
$$P_{\texttt{EncryptPwd}} = \texttt{true}$$
$$R_{\texttt{EncryptPwd}} = \mathbf{G}(call\_reqPwd \Rightarrow \mathbf{F}\, pwdEncrypted)$$

The atomic propositions used for the aspects in Figure 1 are: $doTrans_{before}$, $call\_usrPwdExist_{after}$, $call\_reqPwd$ for every state which matches the respective aspect joinpoints, $ret_{\texttt{Auth}}$ to represent the return states of `Auth`, $authed$ represents the truth value of `authenticated` which may be used elsewhere in the system, the atomic proposition $usrPwdInDB$ indicates that the user and password exist in the database, $Success$ represents the returned Boolean value of the call to the method `usrPwdExist()`, and $cookieSaved$ represents that a cookie has been saved. Finally, $pwdEncrypted$ indicates that the password has been encrypted.

In the guarantee of `Auth`, U_0 and P_0 represent the input values, and can be thought of as bound to a universal quantifier. This can be expressed in propositional temporal logic by substituting each user and password pair (the domain is finite).

Note that for all three aspects, the guarantee has the form $\mathbf{G}(\text{pointcut} \Rightarrow \text{expected behavior})$. We will use this below to identify local and global guarantees.

4. Interference detection

4.1 Extended Specifications

If we attempt to apply the original rules to these aspects, problems arise. For example, although there is in fact no interference between `Auth` and `SaveCookie`, when the rule $KR_{\texttt{SaveCookie,Auth}}$ is checked, it will fail because it does not consider that `SaveCookie` will actually be executed at its new joinpoint added within `Auth`.

To treat the three conditions listed at the end of Section 2.4 that no longer hold (and thus are sources of inconsistency), we extend the specification of an aspect to include a distinction between global guarantees and local ones, and add an internal assumption.

Thus, we now consider guarantees of the form: $R = (RL, RG)$, where RL represents the local guarantee, a property that must be satisfied at each joinpoint, and RG a global guarantee, a global property not connected to being at a joinpoint.

The local guarantee can express properties both for each advice that starts executing because the current joinpoint matches the pointcut descriptor, or properties that should hold each time an advice of A has finished executing. Then, for an aspect A, RL is the conjunction of formulas of the form:

$\mathbf{G}(ptc_A \Rightarrow \varphi)$: Every time the pointcut of A is matched, φ should hold. Note that φ is not necessary a state property, but rather a temporal logic formula. φ is a formula expressing what A's execution guarantees.

In particular, guarantees of the form $\mathbf{G}(ret_A \Rightarrow \phi)$ expressing what is expected at the end of each execution of A can be translated to $\mathbf{G}(ptc_A \implies (\neg ret_A \mathbf{W} (ret_A \wedge \phi)))$ which has the form presented before: $(\varphi \equiv \neg ret_A \mathbf{W} (ret_A \wedge \phi))$.

This separation of the guarantee will be helpful in our verification, because each part is treated differently.

However, we still need to consider the difficulty that even if an aspect B does not interfere when activated before or after an aspect A, it might interfere *during* A's execution. To handle this, the specification is further extended to include internal assumptions that describe for each aspect A what is expected of aspects to be executed during A.

Thus, the specification of an aspect A now consists of:

external assumption of A **(PE_A):** The assumption about the system where A is to be woven. Equivalent to the previous P_A.

internal assumption of A **(PI_A):** The assumption on aspects to be executed during A.

local guarantee of A **(RL_A):** The guarantee of A true at each of its joinpoints.

global guarantee of A **(RG_A):** The part of the guarantee that must be satisfied even when A is not aware of all its joinpoints.

P_A is now defined as (PE_A, PI_A) and R_A is (RL_A, RG_A). An aspect specification is given by (P_A, R_A).

4.2 Partial Guarantee

In this section, we present the solution to the problem presented in Section 4.1.

In the given example the check of $KR_{\texttt{SaveCookie,Auth}}$ fails because there exist joinpoints of `SaveCookie` in $S + $ `Auth` that `SaveCookie` is not *aware* of (in particular, the one inside `Auth`).

In our extended aspect specification, we distinguished between the global guarantees and the local ones: those that express what must be satisfied at every place the advice is executed. In our verification technique we consider only part of the joinpoints of A, but show that this is sufficient to guarantee correctness under full joint-weaving semantics.

In the model, we assume that weaving an aspect A to a system S adds a label aw_A to those states in S where A is aware of the joinpoint.

We now proceed to define a *partial guarantee* to express what must be satisfied when there are aspects not aware of every joinpoint. These do not follow the joint-weaving semantics, but are possible under sequential weaving.

Definition 1. *Let* $RL_A = \bigwedge \psi_i$. *For each* ψ_i *we define* $\widetilde{\psi_i} = \mathbf{G}((ptc_A \wedge aw_A) \Rightarrow \varphi)$. *Then the partial local guarantee of A is given by* $\widetilde{RL_A} = \bigwedge \widetilde{\psi_i}$.

$\widetilde{RL_A}$ is based on the local guarantee but including the atomic proposition that identifies whether an aspect is aware of a joinpoint, so it will be satisfied even when there are unaware joinpoints. When all aspects are aware of all their joinpoints, the original local guarantee is satisfied.

Definition 2. *The partial guarantee of A denoted* $\widetilde{R_A}$ *is given by* $(\widetilde{RL_A}, RG_A)$.

Note that for any system S, $S \vDash R_A \Rightarrow S \vDash \widetilde{R_A}$.

Moreover, if $S \vDash \widetilde{R_A}$ and A is aware of all its joinpoints in S, then $S \vDash R_A$.

Now, if the aspects of Figure 1 are checked taking the partial guarantee of SaveCookie ($\widetilde{R}_{\text{SaveCookie}}$) as in equation (1), every check is satisfied proving non-interference.

$$\widetilde{RL}_{\text{SaveCookie}} = \mathbf{G}((call\_usrPwdExist_{after} \wedge$$
$$ret\_val = Success \wedge aw_{\text{SaveCookie}}) \Rightarrow$$
$$(Success = true \Rightarrow \mathbf{F}\ cookieSaved)) \quad (1)$$

However, this change in the rules is by itself unsound for joint-weaving semantics: when the aspects of Figure 1 are considered and checked against the partial guarantees, then every pairwise assertion is satisfied, returning that the set of aspects is apparently interference-free even though there is interference between EncryptPwd and Auth.

4.3 Augmented aspects

In order to present the full technique for verifying non-interference, the internal assumption must be considered, as seen in the following definition:

Definition 3. *An aspect A is* augmented *(noted as* A^{+PI}*) if and only if it has the internal assumption model woven into* A.

The augmented aspect is built by adding for each state that could be a joinpoint, a transition to the state machine that represents the internal assumption, and transitions from the final states of the internal assumption state machine to corresponding states of the aspect.

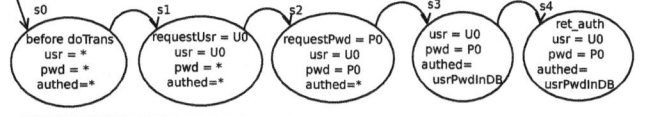

Figure 2. Auth model

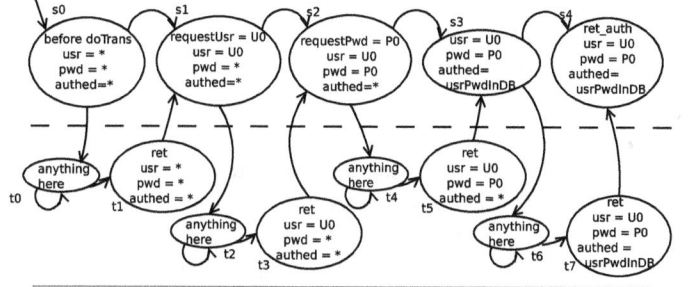

Figure 3. Auth^{+PI} model

Example. A reasonable internal assumption for the aspect Auth in Figure 1 is for any inserted aspect to return without any exception thrown to the execution and preserve the values of the variables usr, pwd and authenticated. Hence, the aspect and the augmented version of the aspect are presented in Figures 2 and 3, respectively. Note that * in the figures represents some arbitrary initial value, different for each field.

The states $s_0, \ldots, s_4$ appear both in the aspect model and in the augmented model of the aspect.

In the augmented aspect, there is a transition from the state s_0 to the states t_0 and then t_1. This means that if an aspect is inserted at this point of Auth then the aspect can do anything (t_0) as long as eventually when reaching a returning state (t_1) the values of usr, pwd and authenticated are preserved, and hence it then executes the statement Usr u = requestUsr() of Auth (in state s_1).

It is assumed in this example that the fairness constraints are defined in order to avoid paths which stay infinitely in an "anything here" state.

Note that the augmented version of the aspect captures as well the assumption on aspects which share joinpoints, hence, shared-joinpoints interference is also covered by this compositional verification technique. In particular in the example, t_0 and t_1 represent the assumption of any aspect that may respond at the joinpoint before doTrans() and might be executed before the first statement of the aspect Auth.

4.4 Formal verification

In this section a modular verification technique to guarantee non-interference is presented, considering the extended specification with partial guarantees and internal assumptions.

First, the definition of non-interference for joint-weaving, based on that in [8], is presented.

Definition 4. *Let Aspects* $= \{A_1, \ldots, A_n\}$ *be a set of aspects. Let* (P_i, R_i) *be the specification of each aspect* A_i. *Then the set Aspects is said to be* interference-free *if and only if* $OK_{Aspects}$ *holds.*

$$OK_{Aspects} \triangleq S \vDash \bigwedge_{i=1}^{n} P_i \Rightarrow S + (A_1, \ldots, A_n) \vDash \bigwedge_{i=1}^{n} R_i$$

$OK_{Aspects}$ *expresses that weaving all aspects together with the joint-weaving model into any system* S *that satisfies the assumptions, satisfies the expected guarantees.*

In [8] aspects were assumed not to add joinpoints of other aspects and hence the internal assumption was not necessary. The verification technique for each aspect on its own under the new specification simply incorporates the internal assumption by using the augmented aspect. Let A be the aspect to be verified and let (P_A, R_A) be A's specification. Then, A is correct with respect to its specification if and only if $S \vDash PE_A \Rightarrow S + A^{+PI_A} \vDash R_A$. This formula expresses that for every system S that satisfies the external assumption of A, when A is woven into S (with all its possible inserted aspects that satisfy the internal assumption) the resulting system satisfies both the local and global guarantees of R_A. Instead of verifying the aspect under the assumption that it is the only one, we verify it under the assumption (PI) that any other aspects maintain its correctness with respect to its specification.

When several aspects are jointly woven into a system S, all of them correct with respect to their specification, we intend to guarantee non-interference.

In order to achieve this, a set of rules is presented. If a library of aspects satisfies all the rules, then the library is interference-free, otherwise there may be interference.

The rules that aspects must satisfy in order to guarantee non-interference are now presented:

1. The aspect is correct by itself (OK_A^+):

$$S \vDash PE_A \Rightarrow S + A^{+PI_A} \vDash R_A$$

   As explained above, this rule guarantees aspect correctness with respect to its specification. Given that the external assumption holds, the system obtained from weaving the aspect and all possibly inserted aspects must satisfy the local and global guarantees.

2. Considering A as the aspect currently being verified, and B any other aspect, the rules to detect interference are:

KPI_{AB}^+: $S \vDash \widetilde{R}_A \wedge PE_B \Rightarrow S + B^{+PI_B} \vDash PI_A$

   This rule expresses that every aspect must satisfy the internal assumptions of other aspects.

KPE_{AB}^+: $S \vDash PE_A \wedge PE_B \Rightarrow S + A^{+PI_A} \vDash PE_B$

   This rule expresses that when weaving A augmented to a system where the external assumption of another aspect B holds, this assumption should be preserved.

KR_{AB}^+: $S \vDash \widetilde{R}_A \wedge PE_B \Rightarrow S + B^{+PI_B} \vDash \widetilde{R}_A$

   This rule expresses that when an aspect A has already been woven, weaving another aspect B preserves the partial guarantee of A (even if it adds new joinpoints of A).

In order to guarantee non-interference, rules KPI_{AB}^+, KPE_{AB}^+ and KR_{AB}^+ must be satisfied by every pair of aspects.

In the next sections we explain in more detail each rule.

4.4.1 KPI_{AB}^+

As mentioned above, rule KPI_{AB}^+ expresses that every aspect must satisfy the internal assumptions of other aspects.

The internal assumption of an aspect A determines what is expected of aspects that execute during A.

The general form of the internal assumption is (ρ, φ) where ρ is a propositional logic formula describing joinpoints and φ is a temporal logic formula describing restrictions on the behavior of the possible aspects executed at those joinpoints.

Example (Trans). An aspect A may initiate a transaction and do some actions, and then close the transaction. We want to avoid that during the execution of the transaction any possibly woven aspect B may perform commit for that transaction. Then the internal assumption of A is defined as: any advice B to be executed at any state within the transaction of A should never perform commit until the return point is reached.

Such an internal assumption is given by the pair (ρ, φ) where $\rho : inTrans$ and $\varphi : \mathbf{G}\neg commit$.

Definition 5. *An augmented aspect* B^{+PI} *satisfies* A's *internal assumption* (ρ, φ) *if and only if: for every execution* π *of* B *that starts from a state in* A *which satisfies* ρ *and matches* B's *pointcut descriptor,* π *satisfies* φ.

Example. In Example (Trans), $B^{+PI} \vDash PI_A$ with $PI_A = (\rho, \varphi)$ as presented above if and only if for every joinpoint of B in A where A is in a transaction, B^{+PI} satisfies $\mathbf{G}\neg commit$.

Internal Assumption Defaults There are *default internal assumptions* that can be defined. Typical examples are:

$PI_A = NoAspect$: If the guarantee of the aspect A is sensitive to next state assertions (X) or real time constraints, PI_A may assume that no aspect is woven during A's execution.

$PI_A = Spectative$: It may be assumed from the environment that any aspect to be woven during the execution of A is spectative.

$PI_A = ReturningValuesPreserved(V)$: Perhaps, any woven aspect B may change things as long as when returning to the execution flow of A the values of a certain set of variables (V) remain as they were before executing

```
aspect LogDB: after call(send(msg))
  beforeStartTrans()
  startTrans()
  getTable(Log)−>newRecord()
  getTable(Log)−>setField(msgField, msg)
  getTable(Log)−>setField(dateField, today)
  commit()
```

Figure 4. Internal assumption example

B. This is the internal assumption needed to preserve the values of usr, pwd and authenticated in Auth.

$PI_A = Invariant (I)$: Any aspect to be executed during A may need to satisfy a certain invariant I at every state.

$PI_A = ReturnsOK$: It can be assumed that every aspect executed within A terminates without throwing exceptions.

$PI_A = NoMandatoryProceed$: It can be assumed that by default all around advices have the proceed statement, but if aspects are allowed to be inserted into A without having to satisfy this condition (and hence possibly removing joinpoints), it can be identified by $NoMandatoryProceed$. This internal assumption differs from the previous ones in that instead of restricting the possible aspects, it allows more behaviors. The idea is that in most cases around advices still have *proceed*, and with this PI the particular cases in which there is no *proceed* are considered.

Internal assumptions can be combined by overriding $\oplus$, conjunction $\wedge$ or disjunction $\vee$ of PI assumptions. Thus, combining a $ReturningValuesPreserved$ assumption with an internal assumption (ρ, φ) may look like: $PI = ReturningValuesPreserved(V) \circledast (\rho, \varphi)$ where $\circledast \in \{\oplus, \wedge, \vee\}$.

Example. In Figure 4, the aspect $LogDB$ exhibits the use of an internal assumption as explained above. In this case:

$$PI_{LogDB} = ReturningValuesPreserved(msg) \wedge$$
$$(inTrans, \mathbf{G} \neg commit)$$

expresses that any other aspect B to be executed during $LogDB$ while in a transaction should not commit that transaction. The intersection of assumptions guarantees that as well every advice to be woven preserves the value of msg.

Checking that an aspect satisfies the internal assumptions of another aspect may involve model checking or syntactic checks, depending on the internal assumption.

Now, we present the satisfiability conditions of default internal assumptions.

Definition 6. *An augmented aspect B^{+PI} satisfies the default internal assumptions of A (PI_A) - noted as $B^{+PI} \models PI_A$ - if one of the following conditions hold:*

1. There are no joinpoints of B in A.

2. *If $PI_A = Spectative$ and there is a joinpoint of B in A, then all the possible augmented executions of B from joinpoints of A are spectative. In terms of temporal logic: $B^{+PI} \models \mathbf{G}(V = V_0)$ where V are all the variables that are not local to B and V_0 represents their original values before B is executed.*

3. *If $PI_A = ReturningValuesPreserved(V)$ and there is a joinpoint of B in A, then all possible augmented executions of B from joinpoints of A preserve the values of the variables in V at the returning state. In terms of temporal logic: $B^{+PI} \models \mathbf{G}(ret_B \Rightarrow V = V_0)$.*

4. *If $PI_A = Invariant (I)$ and there is a joinpoint of B in A, then all possible augmented executions of B from joinpoints of A satisfy the invariant at every state. In terms of temporal logic: $B^{+PI} \models \mathbf{G}I$.*

5. *If $PI_A = ReturnsOK$ and there is a joinpoint of B in A, then all possible augmented executions of B from joinpoints of A reach a returning state without throwing any exception. In terms of temporal logic: $B^{+PI} \models \mathbf{F}(ret_B \wedge \neg exception\_thrown)$.*

6. *If $NoMandatoryProceed \notin PI_A$ and there is a joinpoint of an around advice B in A, then B should have a proceed statement for every execution path in the augmented model of B starting from joinpoints of A.*

Example. Considering the program listing in Figure 1 and the rule KPI_{AB}^+: the augmented version of EncryptPwd should satisfy the internal assumptions of Auth to prove that these aspects do not interfere. The specifications of the aspects are now extended to include the following internal assumptions:

Auth:
$PI_{\text{Auth}} = ReturnsOK \wedge$
$ReturningValuesPreserved(usr, pwd, authed)$
EncryptPwd:
$PI_{\text{EncryptPwd}} = Spectative$

The actual interference will be detected in this example when evaluating $KPI_{\text{Auth,EncryptPwd}}^+$: In this case EncryptPwd does not satisfy the internal assumption of Auth of preserving the value of the password.

4.4.2 KPE_{AB}^+ and KR_{AB}^+

Rules KPE_{AB}^+ and KR_{AB}^+ are the extensions of the rules described in 2.4, now considering possibly inserted aspects and partial guarantees.

Rule KPE_{AB}^+ expresses that when weaving A augmented to a system where the external assumption of another aspect B holds, this assumption should be preserved.

Rule KR_{AB}^+ expresses that when an aspect A has already been woven, weaving another aspect B preserves the partial guarantee of A.

Moreover, given that the conditions for checking KPI_{AB}^+ and KR_{AB}^+ are the same, in certain cases both rules can be considered together. However, in several situations the model is smaller when checking both properties separately. Note that even though the rules only imply that the partial guarantee is preserved, eventually all aspects will be aware of all their joinpoints, hence the partial guarantee will imply the guarantee.

4.5 Steps for each aspect added

If a set of aspects $\{A_1, \ldots, A_{n-1}\}$ has been proven to be correct with respect to their specification and without interference, when adding a new aspect A_n with specification $((PE_n, PI_n), (RL_n, RG_n))$, then the following properties should be checked:

1. Check that $OK_{A_n}^+$ holds.

2. Check that $KPI_{A_i A_n}^+$, $KPI_{A_n A_i}^+$, $KPE_{A_i A_n}^+$, $KPE_{A_n A_i}^+$, $KR_{A_i A_n}^+$, and $KR_{A_n A_i}^+$ are satisfied for all $1 \leq i \leq n-1$.

When building a library of n aspects we must do: n checks for the OK^+ rule, n^2 for each of the rules KPI^+, KPE^+ and KR^+. In several cases checking KPI^+ does not require model checking but perhaps uses static/syntactic analysis to detect joinpoints, check whether an aspect B satisfies an invariant or B is spectative. All these checks are done as the library is constructed and then a set of interference-free aspects can be used for any system that satisfies all aspect assumptions.

5. Justifying the rules

5.1 Assumptions

In this paper we treat weakly-invasive aspects [12], where control is returned after an advice execution to a state which existed in some execution of the original system. In [10], verification is shown for strongly-invasive aspects, by adding an assumption U about the base system states previously unreachable that now can occur in the woven system after aspect advice completes. A relatively complex modular verification technique is given that treats sequential weaving without joinpoints in advice. The treatment here can also be applied to that technique, both for each aspect on its own and for the rules to detect interference.

We also assume that the aspects treated are never activated under their own execution flow, i.e. there is no recursion. Allowing recursion introduces the problem of analyzing termination and liveness properties possibly affected.

These assumptions can often be checked by already existing techniques. In [3], dataflow techniques were presented to detect aspect categories. To guarantee no recursion a dependency graph can be built and analyzed to check that no aspect depends on itself.

5.2 Soundness proof

We now show the soundness of the rules in order to guarantee non-interference of a set of aspects that satisfies the necessary conditions.

First we prove how the augmented versions of the aspects satisfy the partial guarantees when their preconditions initially hold. Secondly we show that this also holds for the original aspects and the full guarantee when considering joint-weaving semantics and all aspects are woven.

Lemma 1. *Let* $\{A_1, \ldots, A_n\}$ *be a set of aspects such that for all of them the previous checks have been applied and all assertions have been proven to hold. Then, for any system S such that $S \models \bigwedge_{i=1}^{n} PE_i$, S with all the augmented aspects woven satisfies their partial guarantees, i.e.*

$$S + \left(A_1^{+PI}, \ldots, A_n^{+PI}\right) \models \bigwedge_{i=1}^{n} \widetilde{R}_i$$

Proof. By induction on the number of aspects in the set.

- Base case: When adding one aspect A to the system S which satisfies PE_A, from OK_A^+, $S + A^{+PI_A} \models R_A$. Then in particular, $S + A^{+PI_A} \models \widetilde{R}_A$

- Inductive step: We assume by inductive hypothesis that for any system S such that $S \models \bigwedge_{i=1}^{n-1} PE_i$, then $S + \left(A_1^{+PI}, \ldots, A_{n-1}^{+PI}\right) \models \bigwedge_{i=1}^{n-1} \widetilde{R}_i$ and we want to see that for any system S such that $S \models \bigwedge_{i=1}^{n} PE_i$, then $S + \left(A_1^{+PI}, \ldots, A_n^{+PI}\right) \models \bigwedge_{i=1}^{n} \widetilde{R}_i$.
  Given that $S \models \bigwedge_{i=1}^{n} PE_i$, then in particular, $S \models \bigwedge_{i=1}^{n-1} PE_i$ and by the inductive hypothesis

$$S + \left(A_1^{+PI}, \ldots, A_{n-1}^{+PI}\right) \models \bigwedge_{i=1}^{n-1} \widetilde{R}_i$$

First, we need to see that A_n's assumption still holds. From $KP_{A_i A_n}^+$ the assumption of A_n is preserved as other aspects are woven to the system. Hence, $S + \left(A_1^{+PI}, \ldots, A_{n-1}^{+PI}\right) \models PE_n$.
Then, when weaving A_n^{+PI} to $S + \left(A_1^{+PI}, \ldots, A_{n-1}^{+PI}\right)$, the conjunction $\bigwedge_{i=1}^{n-1} \widetilde{R}_i$ is preserved from $KR_{A_n A_i}^+$ and for those places where the A_n is woven in the execution of an aspect A_i, the correctness is preserved from $KPI_{A_i A_n}^+$ and $OK_{A_i}^+$: the paths added by A_n are already considered in A_i^{+PI} and satisfy the corresponding $\widetilde{R}_i$.
Weaving A_n may add joinpoints of already woven aspects, but these paths are already considered in the augmented version of A_n, and due to KPI_{A_n, A_i}^+ and $OK_{A_n}^+$ the guarantee of A_n is also preserved.
Therefore $S + \left(A_1^{+PI}, \ldots, A_n^{+PI}\right) \models \bigwedge_{i=1}^{n} \widetilde{R}_i$.

$\square$

The lemma shows that if all the conditions hold then weaving all the augmented versions of the aspects is interference-free. The next theorem uses this lemma in order to prove that if we have established that all the augmented versions of the aspects are interference-free then, in particular, there is no interference when considering the resulting system with the (not augmented) aspects woven.

Theorem 1. *Let $\{A_1, \ldots, A_n\}$ be a set of aspects such that for all of them the previous checks have been applied and all assertions have been proven to hold. Then $\{A_1, \ldots, A_n\}$ is interference-free. That is, for any system S such that $S \vDash \bigwedge_{i=1}^{n} PE_i$, then S with all the aspects woven satisfies their guarantees, i.e.*

$$S + (A_1, \ldots, A_n) \vDash \bigwedge_{i=1}^{n} R_i$$

Proof. From Lemma 1, for any system S such that $S \vDash \bigwedge_{i=1}^{n} PE_i$ it holds that

$$S + \left(A_1^{+PI}, \ldots, A_n^{+PI}\right) \vDash \bigwedge_{i=1}^{n} \widetilde{R}_i$$

In particular, $S^+_{Aspects} = S + \left(A_1^{+PI}, \ldots, A_n^{+PI}\right)$ is an over-approximation of $S_{Aspects} = S + (A_1, \ldots, A_n)$. That is, every path in $S_{Aspects}$ is a path in $S^+_{Aspects}$. Given that all R_i are formulas in LTL, $S^+_{Aspects} \vDash \bigwedge_{i=1}^{n} \widetilde{R}_i \Rightarrow S_{Aspects} \vDash \bigwedge_{i=1}^{n} \widetilde{R}_i$. Moreover, given that all aspects are already woven, then all aspects are aware of all their joinpoints, and hence: $S_{Aspects} \vDash \bigwedge_{i=1}^{n} \widetilde{R}_i \Rightarrow S_{Aspects} \vDash \bigwedge_{i=1}^{n} R_i$ $\qquad\square$

Theorem 1 shows that this procedure is sound under the given assumptions. However, it is not complete. In particular, modularity affects completeness: there could be sets of aspects which are interference-free but this cannot be shown with the assumptions and guarantees defined. That is, there may be two aspects A and B, both correct with respect to their specification and when woven together there is no interference, but the rules fail because the assumption or guarantee are not preserved in an intermediate state of building the augmented model.

The main advantages of this interference detection process is that it is modular, it provides flexibility to different external and internal assumptions, and is also used to prove the correctness and non-interference of collaborative aspects (described in the next section).

6. Cooperation

Cooperation is tightly related to modularity: an aspect A may assume the existence of an aspect B that takes care of certain functionality and then A can be shown to be correct.

6.1 Examples of cooperation

Following, two examples are presented to show different types of cooperation.

Example (Encrypt). The aspect `EncryptPwd` that encrypts the password being sent from a registration form may assume the existence of another aspect (`CheckPwd`) that only allows sending passwords that satisfy some criteria, e.g. that the password includes a combination of numbers, lowercase and uppercase letters.

`CheckPwd:`
$PE_{\texttt{CheckPwd}} = \texttt{true}$
$R_{\texttt{CheckPwd}} = \mathbf{G}\,(to\_be\_sent \Rightarrow correct)$
`EncryptPwd:`
$PE_{\texttt{EncryptPwd}} = \mathbf{G}\,(to\_be\_sent \Rightarrow correct)$
$R_{\texttt{EncryptPwd}} = \mathbf{G}(to\_be\_sent \Rightarrow \mathbf{F}\,(sent \wedge encrypted))$

It is obvious that not necessarily every system satisfies the assumption of `EncryptPwd`, but if `CheckPwd` is also woven, and satisfies its specification, then the assumption of `EncryptPwd` holds.

Example (Copy). An aspect (Copy) saves the objects of a certain class when necessary, trying initially to save them to a database and cooperating with another aspect (`CopyToFile`) when copying to the database fails. `CopyToFile` copies objects to an xml file. Either way, the objects are guaranteed to be saved.

`Copy:`
$PE_{\texttt{Copy}} = \texttt{true}$
$PI_{\texttt{Copy}} = EXISTS\_ASPECT$
$\qquad \mathbf{G}((call(DB.saveObject) \wedge DBerror) \Rightarrow$
$\qquad\qquad \mathbf{F}\,savedObjectToFile)$
$R_{\texttt{Copy}} = \mathbf{G}(objectChanged \Rightarrow$
$\qquad \mathbf{F}\,(savedObjectToDB \vee savedObjectToFile))$
`CopyToFile:`
$PE_{\texttt{CopyToFile}} = \texttt{true}$
$PI_{\texttt{CopyToFile}} = Spectative$
$R_{\texttt{CopyToFile}} = \mathbf{G}((objectChanged \wedge$
$\qquad \mathbf{F}((call(DB.saveObject) \wedge DBerror)))$
$\qquad\qquad \Rightarrow \mathbf{F}\,savedObjectToFile)$

$EXISTS\_ASPECT$ represents the assumption that there **must** be an aspect satisfying the internal assumption.

The specification of Copy guarantees that when an object is changed, it is eventually copied, either to the database or to a file. Copy assumes ($PI_{\texttt{Copy}}$) the existence of an aspect that saves the object to a file if there is an error when trying to save an object to the database.

The specification of `CopyToFile` does in fact guarantee this.

In the first example one aspect helps establish the external assumption of another, while in the second, it helps to establish the internal assumption.

6.2 Formal verification of cooperation

The idea is that if there exists an order in which the joint-weaving model can be built such that all preconditions are eventually satisfied and there is no interference, then the whole system can be woven together under joint-weaving semantics and the set of aspects is interference-free.

Definition 7. *An aspect A is* augmented considering cooperation, *if it is augmented and it includes only the paths where the expected $EXISTS\_ASPECT$ assumptions are woven.*

115

Example. In the augmented version of `Copy`, all paths include the cooperation assumption of an aspect that on error saves to a file.

Definition 8. *A set of aspects* $\{A_1, \ldots, A_n\}$ *is cooperation inductive if they can be arranged in a sequence* $A_{i_1}, A_{i_2}, \ldots, A_{i_n}$ *such that for all* k, $1 \le k < n$

$$S \models PE_{i_k} \Rightarrow S + A_{i_k}^{+PI} \models PE_{i_{k+1}} \qquad (2)$$

Equation (2) expresses that when the assumption of A_{i_k} *holds, then when weaving the augmented model of* A_{i_k}, *the assumption of* $A_{i_{k+1}}$ *holds.*

Given a set of aspects, finding an cooperation inductive sequence of the aspects is a necessary condition in order to prove correctness and interference-freedom, otherwise an aspect assumption may not hold, and hence weaving it does not imply its guarantee.

This sequence is not to indicate an order in which aspects are woven or executed, but in order to guarantee that eventually all aspect's assumptions will be satisfied, and hence the aspects can be woven and their guarantees will hold.

The proof of soundness of the method consists of three parts:

1. Proving that weaving the augmented version of the first $k-1$ aspects leads to the assumptions of the kth aspect to hold (by induction on the length of a cooperation inductive sequence of aspects).

2. Use the previous proof in order check that when all the augmented aspects are woven then their partial guarantees are proven to hold (by induction on the length of an cooperation inductive sequence of aspects).

3. Finally, given that all the augmented aspects are woven and their partial guarantees hold, it can be proven that when all aspects are woven (not augmented), their guarantees do in fact hold.

The proofs mentioned in 1 and 2 are very similar to the proof of Lemma 1. The proof mentioned in item 3 follows the same logic as in Theorem 1.

Example. Considering the previous examples, now the correctness of both `EncryptPwd` in Example ($Encrypt$) and `Copy` in Example ($Copy$) can be shown.

In Example ($Encrypt$), it is enough to consider $A_{i_1} = A_{\texttt{CheckPwd}}$ and $A_{i_2} = A_{\texttt{EncryptPwd}}$.

In Example ($Copy$), the expected internal assumption is woven to build the augmented version of the aspect `Copy` and then `CopyToFile` is shown to satisfy the internal assumption.

Note that by means of the cooperation proofs, and a subset of aspects that is intended to be woven in an application, the necessary cooperative aspects are found, either by those that are found before in the sequence of assumptions, or that are forced to exist by the keyword $EXISTS\_ASPECT$.

```
aspect Req&EncrPwd
after returning: enterUsr()
  enterPwd()
  encryptDES()

aspect DESSave
after returning: encryptDES()
  savePwd()

aspect AESEncr
void around: encryptDES()
  encryptAES()
```

Figure 5. Removed joinpoints

7. Removing Joinpoints

In this section, we show that the extended specification and verification also handle the removal of joinpoints of one aspect by another.

Example. In Figure 5 we show an example with removed joinpoints. It is easy to see that the aspect `AESEncr` removes joinpoints of `DESSave`. DES and AES are encryption algorithms.

In a system in which initially the DES encryption algorithm was used, the specification of the aspects could be given by:

`Req&EncrPwd:`
$PE_{\texttt{Req\&EncrPwd}} = \textbf{true}$
$PI_{\texttt{Req\&EncrPwd}} = EXISTS\_ASPECT$
   $\mathbf{G}(encryptedDES \Rightarrow \mathbf{F}savePwd)$
$R_{\texttt{Req\&EncrPwd}} = \mathbf{G}(enterUsr_{after} \Rightarrow$
   $\mathbf{F}(enterPwd \wedge \mathbf{F}(encryptedPwd \wedge \mathbf{F}savePwd)))$

`DESSave:`
$PE_{\texttt{DESSave}} = \textbf{true}$
$PI_{\texttt{DESSave}} = Spectative$
$R_{\texttt{DESSave}} = \mathbf{G}(encryptedDES \Rightarrow \mathbf{F}savePwd)$

`AESEncr:`
$PE_{\texttt{AESEncr}} = \textbf{true}$
$PI_{\texttt{AESEncr}} = Spectative$
$R_{\texttt{AESEncr}} = \mathbf{G}(call\_encryptDES$
   $\Rightarrow \mathbf{X}((\mathbf{G} \neg encryptedDES) \wedge \mathbf{F}(encryptedAES)))$

That is, `Req&EncrPwd` takes care of requesting a password and calling the encryption algorithm and assumes the existence of `DESSave`, an aspect that guarantees that eventually the encrypted password is saved. It is possible to see the cooperation in the assertion $PI_{\texttt{Req\&EncrPwd}}$. For now, we concentrate on the guarantee that the password must be saved (not necessarily encrypted).

However, due to a security problem, it is decided to create an aspect such that around every call to DES it uses now the AES encryption algorithm. The guarantee of `AESEncr` indicates that every time `encryptDES()` is called, it guarantees that no password is encrypted using DES ($\mathbf{G} \neg encryptedDES$), but now every call to encrypt the password is replaced by `encryptAES()`. Then, when the aspect `AESEncr` is checked with other aspects to detect interference, given that `AESEncr` has no proceed and $NoMandatoryProceed \notin PI_{\texttt{Req\&EncrPwd}}$ the rule $KPI^+_{\texttt{Req\&EncrPwd,AESEncr}}$ is not satisfied.

This interference causes that the joinpoint of the call to `encryptDES()` is removed, and hence the password is no longer saved.

Note that even if $NoMandatoryProceed$ did belong to the definition of $PI_{\texttt{Req\&EncrPwd}}$, then when checking $OK^+_{\texttt{Req\&EncrPwd}}$ the problem would have been detected, as there would be paths in $\texttt{Req\&EncrPwd}^{+PI}$ where the call to the encryption would not be reachable and hence, the password would not be saved.

Thus, in both cases there is interference, and the interference-freedom checks, as expected, do not succeed.

The cooperation among `Req&EncrPwd` and `DESSave` shows our technique with removed joinpoints, but this example serves also to get a better understanding of interference detection. We now consider the following, perhaps more natural, specification of `Req&EncrPwd`:

$$PE_{\texttt{Req\&EncrPwd}} = \texttt{true}$$
$$PI_{\texttt{Req\&EncrPwd}} = ReturningValuesPreserved(pwd)$$
$$R_{\texttt{Req\&EncrPwd}} = \mathbf{G}(enterUsr_{after}$$
$$\Rightarrow \mathbf{F}(enterPwd \wedge \mathbf{F}encryptDES))$$

If the set of aspects is checked for interference, the rule $KPI^+_{\texttt{Req\&EncrPwd,AESEncr}}$ fails again because of the absence of $NoMandatoryProceed$ in $PI_{\texttt{Req\&EncrPwd}}$. Detecting interference in this case is correct given that around advices without `proceed()` may cause the password not to be encrypted.

Furthermore, if $NoMandatoryProceed$ belonged to $PI_{\texttt{Req\&EncrPwd}}$, the rule $OK^+_{\texttt{Req\&EncrPwd}}$ would fail as it would no longer be guaranteed that after each joinpoint the password is eventually entered and encrypted.

8. Related work

Advice specification composition has been considered in [4], where aspects that may change the effective specification are called *assistants*. However, only method invocation joinpoints are considered and obliviousness is affected - accepted aspects must be specified in the specification, and dynamic context is not considered.

Besides MAVEN [8, 9], other previous work [1, 6, 7, 13, 15] has treated estricted forms of syntactic and/or semantic interference, considering in some cases disjoint joinpoints and in others shared ones.

Shared joinpoints interference has been considered in [11]. By answering some questions given in natural language regarding the expected behavior, an automatic extended version of the specification is built, and then, MAVEN can be used to detect interference. However, the method does not work for joint-weaving semantics.

The work in [14] discusses modular reasoning in aspect oriented programming. The concept of *aspect-aware interfaces* extends object and aspect interfaces to include global knowledge. In our work, we represent this global knowledge using specification: what is expected of the system and other cross-cutting concerns. These specifications serve to characterize each aspect without giving details of its implementation, and the technique presented allows checking aspect correctness, and non-interference even before the underlying system is completely programmed.

Aspects may be woven at joinpoints exposed by a module's signature in [2], and other joinpoints within the module are ignored. This affects obliviousness (a module must expose the places where an aspect may be woven in its signature) and does not consider joinpoints internal to a module.

In [13] the idea of internal assumptions is represented by Hoare-logic assertions that cross-cutting concerns must satisfy. This approach describes the acceptable state changes. In our approach we show that a general temporal logic formula or some syntactic check is satisfied instead of considering only a Hoare logic assertion where advice is woven and returns.

The work in [15] works with interfaces in temporal logic (CTL in their case), covers removed joinpoints due to the absence of proceed, but assumes that any advice restores the stack to the same state it had before the advice execution, not covering weakly-invasive aspects in general. To capture cascading advice, the states at which advice might apply must have an accurate interface. Knowing which are the states and what advice might apply affects obliviousness. This might also be a problem in our approach, especially for cooperation.

In [6] unification conflicts are detected, which may yield false positives when considering the problem of detecting semantic aspect interference.

In [17], aspect dependencies are found using as a base Reaching Definitions Data-flow Analysis [16]. These dependencies do not necessarily lead to semantic interference, possibly yielding false positives (i.e., it only detects cases of suspected interference), and the summary transfer functions imply analyzing a particular underlying system, instead of considering the aspects as an independent library.

9. Conclusions

Systems that work under the aspect paradigm usually include more than one aspect. It is important to check both that each aspect satisfies its specification and that the interaction of aspects does not lead to interference.

Existing work did not capture important cases of aspect composition and cooperation under joint-weaving semantics. Here, we have extended the verification technique to detect interference under joint-weaving semantics when aspects may insert or remove joinpoints of other aspects as long as this does not create a recursive call stack to a certain aspect.

The assumption part of an aspect A's specification should now consider both assumptions of the system to which A is woven, and the aspects that may be woven in the execution of A. This gives a better understanding of an aspect: its specification now characterizes the environment where the aspect executes correctly.

We have presented a set of possible default internal assumptions as well as the possibility to define special internal assumptions, identifying the joinpoints and the temporal logic formulas that woven aspects must satisfy.

Moreover, adding aspect internal assumptions to aspect specification allows building a modular proof of non-interference among a set of aspects. The proof can be built once - when the library is built - and when interference-freedom is established, the aspects may be used for any system guaranteeing the necessary external assumptions.

The guarantee of the specification is now divided into local and global guarantee in order to represent global properties and properties related to the places where advice is woven. This separation aids in characterizing the proof obligations under joint-weaving semantics.

This same technique, considering internal assumptions and partial guarantees, allows extending the techniques to prove the correctness of cooperative aspects, both in the case an aspect is needed to satisfy the external assumptions of another one, or when the internal assumption of an aspect A forces an aspect to exist in order to guarantee A's correctness.

This verification technique exposes aspect interactions, dependencies and cooperation that can help AOP developers gain a deeper insight into the system under development.

References

[1] M. Aksit, A. Rensink, and T. Staijen. A graph-transformation-based simulation approach for analysing aspect interference on shared join points. In *Proceedings of the 8th ACM international conference on Aspect-oriented software development*, AOSD '09, pages 39–50, New York, NY, USA, 2009. ACM.

[2] J. Aldrich. Open modules: A proposal for modular reasoning in aspect-oriented programming. In *In Workshop on foundations of aspect-oriented languages*, pages 7–18, 2004.

[3] Y. Alperin-Tsimerman and S. Katz. Dataflow analysis for properties of aspect systems. In *Proceedings of 5th Haifa Verification Conference, LNCS 6405*, 2009.

[4] C. Clifton and G. T. Leavens. Observers and assistants: A proposal for modular aspect-oriented reasoning. In *In FOAL Workshop*, 2002.

[5] J. C. Corbett, M. B. Dwyer, J. Hatcliff, S. Laubach, C. S. Păsăreanu, Robby, and H. Zheng. Bandera: extracting finite-state models from java source code. In *Proceedings of the 22nd international conference on Software engineering*, ICSE '00, pages 439–448, New York, NY, USA, 2000. ACM.

[6] R. Douence, P. Fradet, and M. Südholt. A framework for the detection and resolution of aspect interactions. In *Proceedings of the 1st ACM SIGPLAN/SIGSOFT conference on Generative Programming and Component Engineering*, GPCE '02, pages 173–188, London, UK, 2002. Springer-Verlag.

[7] P. E. A. Durr, T. Staijen, L. M. J. Bergmans, and M. Akşit. Reasoning about semantic conflicts between aspects. Technical Report TR-CTIT-05-73, Centre for Telematics and Information Technology University of Twente, Enschede, September 2005.

[8] M. Goldman, E. Katz, and S. Katz. Maven: modular aspect verification and interference analysis. *Form. Methods Syst. Des.*, 37:61–92, November 2010.

[9] E. Katz and S. Katz. Incremental analysis of interference among aspects. In *Proceedings of the 7th workshop on Foundations of aspect-oriented languages*, FOAL '08, pages 29–38, New York, NY, USA, 2008. ACM.

[10] E. Katz and S. Katz. Modular verification of strongly invasive aspects: summary. In *Proceedings of the 2009 workshop on Foundations of aspect-oriented languages*, FOAL '09, pages 7–12, New York, NY, USA, 2009. ACM.

[11] E. Katz and S. Katz. User queries for specification refinement treating shared aspect join points. SEFM '10, pages 73–82, Washington, DC, USA, 2010. IEEE Computer Society.

[12] S. Katz. Aspect categories and classes of temporal properties. *T. Aspect-Oriented Software Development I*, pages 106–134, 2006.

[13] R. Khatchadourian, J. Dovland, and N. Soundarajan. Enforcing behavioral constraints in evolving aspect-oriented programs. In *Proceedings of the 7th workshop on Foundations of aspect-oriented languages*, FOAL '08, pages 19–28, New York, NY, USA, 2008. ACM.

[14] G. Kiczales and M. Mezini. Aspect-oriented programming and modular reasoning. In *Proceedings of the 27th international conference on Software engineering*, ICSE '05, pages 49–58, New York, NY, USA, 2005. ACM.

[15] S. Krishnamurthi and K. Fisler. Foundations of incremental aspect model-checking. *ACM Trans. Softw. Eng. Methodol.*, 16, April 2007.

[16] F. Nielson, H. R. Nielson, and C. Hankin. *Principles of Program Analysis*. Springer-Verlag New York, Inc., Secaucus, NJ, USA, 1999.

[17] N. Weston, F. Taiani, and A. Rashid. Interaction analysis for fault-tolerance in aspect-oriented programming. In *In Proc. Workshop on Methods, Models, and Tools for Fault Tolerance*, pages 95–102, 2007.

Management of Feature Interactions with Transactional Regions

Thomas Cottenier

UniqueSoft, LLC

thomas.cottenier@uniquesoft.com

Aswin van den Berg

UniqueSoft, LLC

aswin.vandenberg@uniquesoft.com

Thomas Weigert

Missouri University of S&T

weigert@mst.edu

Abstract

This paper presents a modeling language to modularize the features of a system using orthogonal regions and to manage the interactions between these features. Orthogonal regions are a language construct to structure a state machine into a set of semi-independent behaviors. We introduce two concepts to manage the interactions between regions. First, we present a notion of interface between regions which captures the essence of their interactions. Second, we introduce a transactional composition operator to synchronize the regions and check the interaction for non-determinism and termination. The approach is evaluated by comparing a monolithic legacy implementation of a telecommunication component to two refactored implementations. Our results show that transactional region composition can achieves independence between the implementations of the features of the system and that it improves the cohesion of the regions, compared to classic regions.

Categories and Subject Descriptors D.3.3 [**Programming Languages**]: Language Constructs and Features – *classes and objects, modules, packages.*

General Terms Design, Languages

Keywords feature interaction, statecharts, modularity

1. Introduction

Systems that are decomposed into features take the form S = F1 + F2 + F3 where each Fi is a feature module and + denotes a feature composition operation. Structuring a system by feature requires implementing each feature into a separate module. Ideally, this module implements a cohesive piece of functionality that can be understood, implemented and tested independently of the other features so that different development teams can focus on different features of the system. Isolating the implementation of the

different features also provides the flexibility of delivering different variants of a system by assembling different combinations of feature modules. However, this assembly requires a thorough understanding of the interactions between features. A feature interaction occurs when one feature modifies the way another feature contributes to the overall behavior of the system. The feature interaction problem is known to be a difficult problem of general importance [1]. The approach presented in this paper is most directly applicable to distributed systems where components interact asynchronously. We believe however that it is relevant to all systems that need to be decomposed into a set of semi-independent features for modularity or flexibility purposes.

Our goal is to allow a feature of a system to be understood and implemented independently of other features. In this paper, we present a modeling language that supports the modularization of features using orthogonal regions. Orthogonal regions are a language construct to structure state diagrams into a set of semi-independent behaviors [2]. Orthogonal regions have been widely adopted in state machine based formalisms such as the UML. When system features are modularized using regions, the feature interactions take the form of interactions between regions. These region interactions need to be understood and managed to avoid conflicts and inconsistencies. In most cases, synchronization entities such as additional states and transitions have to be added to the regions to coordinate their execution.

When the number of regions in the system grows, the interactions between regions can become very hard to maintain. Our language therefore introduces a concept of interface between regions. Such an interface concisely captures the essence of the interaction and avoids direct dependencies between regions that implement different features.

Nevertheless, the coordination of the regions still requires synchronization. The core behavior of each region becomes tangled with synchronization behavior. The introduction of states whose purpose is to coordinate with the interface region is a source of errors and can easily lead to deadlocks. In order to address these issues, our modeling language introduces a transactional composition operator that simplifies the synchronization of regions and whose semantics detects deadlocks.

We evaluate interface regions and transactional composition by comparing size, coupling and diffusion metrics for three versions of an industrial telecommunication component. The first version was developed as a monolithic state machine by a third party. The second and third versions were obtained by refactoring the monolithic version for maintenance purposes. The second version uses regions to modularize the features of the system. The third version uses interfaces between regions and transactional composition semantics. Our results show that interface regions and transactional composition improve the quality of the system and support the management of the interactions between the system features.

The paper is organized as follows. Section 2 introduces the case study and describes the features of the system. Section 3 introduces orthogonal regions and presents the operational semantics of our modeling language. Section 4 discusses interactions between regions and interface regions and details the syntax and semantics of the transactional composition operator. Section 5 presents the experiment setting. Section 6 discusses the metrics used to evaluate the system and presents the results of our study in terms of size, coupling and complexity. Section 7 presents related work and Section 8 concludes this paper.

2. Case Study: Cellular Network

2.1 Cellular Network

The component used in the case study is a base station controller (BSC) of a cellular network. A mobile subscriber (MS) communicates with the network through a set of base stations (BTS), which are controlled by a BSC. Each base station provides coverage over a cell of the network. Adjacent base stations are grouped into paging groups. Data packets flow from the network to a base station through a series of routers (RTR) controlled by the BSC. The subscriber context is maintained in a database (CTXT). The communication between the network and the mobile subscriber is secured by an authentication protocol (AK). The BSC monitors network incoming data for a mobile subscriber through a proxy router (PROXY). The behavior of the system can be described according to two complementary decompositions: a feature-based decomposition and a scenario-based decomposition.

2.2 Base Station Controller Features

The behavior of the base station controller can be decomposed into the following features:
1. Lease Management (LSM): tracks which component of is currently handling the session with the MS.
2. Context Management (CX): handles the download and upload of context information between BTS and BSC
3. Authentication Keys (AK): handles the synchronization of the authentication keys between BTS and BSC.
4. Idle Mode Management (IMM): tracks when the subscriber enters or exits idle mode.
5. Handover (HO): handles the transfer of a session from a serving BTS to a target BTS.

6. Paging Control (PC): performs paging when inbound traffic is detected for a MS in idle model.
7. Proxy Monitoring (PY): monitors traffic intended for a MS when the MS is in idle mode
8. Router Control (RR): updates the routing tables when a handover is performed. The system supports three types of routing: nomadic (NRR), simple IP (SRR) and mobile IP router control (MRR).

2.3 Base Station Controller Scenarios

The requirements of the system are described using basic scenarios. Each scenario describes how the BSC responds to an input. These scenarios are organized as follows:
1. Lease Request (LREQ): a BTS requests control over a session or renews a session.
2. Lease Release Request (LREL): the subscriber enters idle mode and the BTS releases control over the lease
3. Idle Mode Request (IMREQ): the MS requests to enter idle mode.
4. Exit Idle Mode Request (XIM): the MS requests to exit idle mode.
5. Power Down Indication (PDIND): the subscriber device is powering down.
6. Context Download Request (CXDLD): a base station requests a copy of the subscriber context.
7. Reentry Complete Indication (REIND): a handover was successfully performed.
8. Location Update Request (LUREQ): a subscriber in idle mode has moved to a new paging group.
9. MIP Request and Verify (MIPRV): sent by the MS to maintain a mobile IP session with the network.

3. Orthogonal Regions

3.1 Introduction

We use orthogonal regions to modularize the implementation of the system features. Figure 1 presents a state machine composed of four regions, represented using the statechart notation. Each region implements a different feature of the cellular network component. The *LSM* region implements the lease management feature. The *IMM* region implements the idle mode management feature. The *PY* region implements the proxy monitoring region and the *RTR* region controls a router.

Each region is composed of a set of states and a set of transitions between these states. Transitions are executed in response to stimuli, which can be external events or internal events. The trigger of a transition is expressed using a logical expression over the occurrence of events. The execution of a transition corresponds to the execution of the actions of the transition. These actions are defined using statements and expressions. Transitions can also be guarded by logical expressions over the state of other regions. The guard *[IMM::ACT]* on the *LSM* transition triggered by the signal *LEASE_REQ* indicates that the transition is only enabled when the *IMM* region is in the state *ACT*.

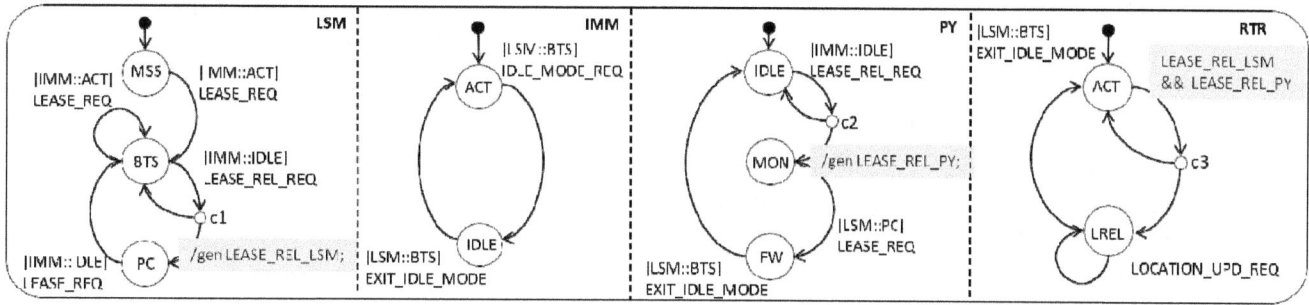

Figure 2. A state machine composed of 4 regions that implement different features of a telecom component.

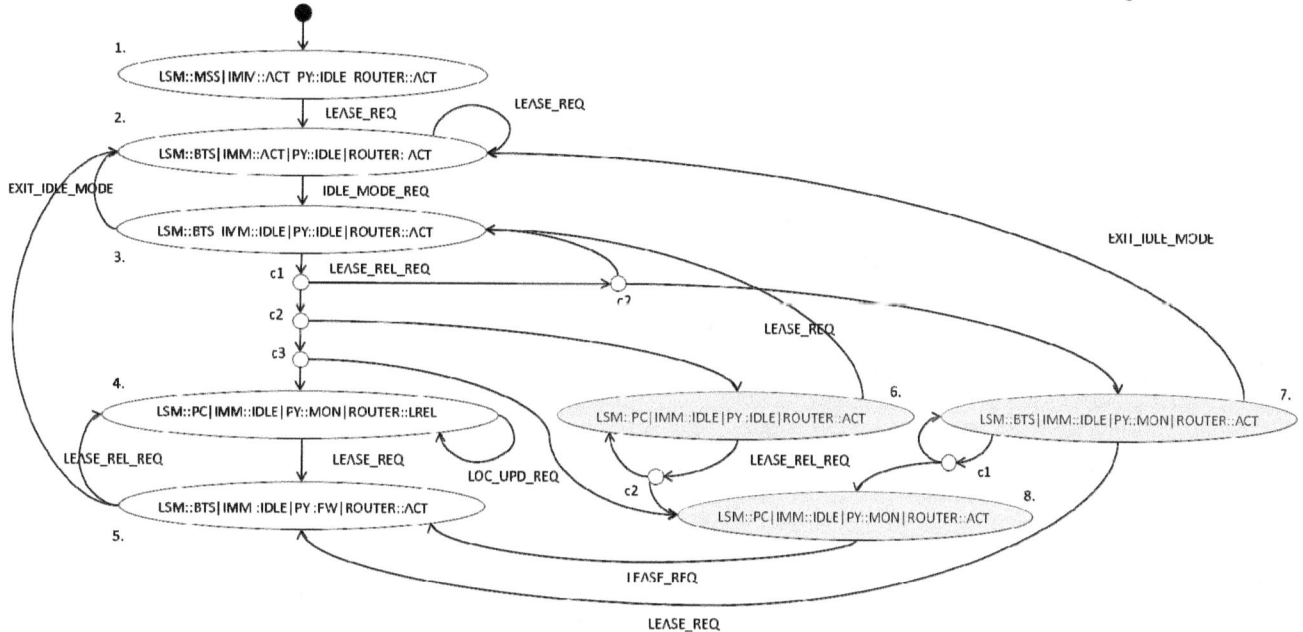

Figure 1. State machine obtained by flattening the 4 regions into a single region.

In Figure 1, the transition from state *BTS* to state *PC* in the *LSM* region is triggered when the external signal *LEASE_REL_REQ* is received by the state machine and the *IMM* region is in the *IDLE* state. The transition evaluates a conditional expression $c1$ and executes the corresponding decision branch. Depending on the conditional, the transition either generates the internal event *LEASE_REL_LSM* (using the *gen* keyword) and steps into the *PC* state or it steps back into the *BTS* state. The *LEASE_REL_LSM* internal event triggers the transition from *ACT* to *LREL* in the *RTR* region if and only if the *LEASE_REL_PY* internal signal is generated during the same step of execution as indicated using the conjunction in the trigger of the transition.

Figure 2 shows a state diagram composed of a single region that was obtained by weaving together the regions of Figure 1. The states of the state machine of Figure 2 correspond to the reachable combination of the states of the regions. Such a combination is called a configuration. A state machine that consists of multiple regions executes according to steps between state configurations. A step corresponds to the execution of a set of enabled transitions from different regions.

In the example of Figure 1, the external signal *LEASE_REL_REQ* triggers a series of steps in the configuration *(BTS, IDLE, IDLE, ACT)*. The first step simultaneously executes the transition from *BTS* to *PC* in the *LSM* region and the transition from *IDLE* to *MON* in the *PY* region. Depending on the evaluation of the conditionals, the state machine steps into the configurations *(BTS, IDLE, MON, ACT)*, *(PC, IDLE, IDLE, ACT)*, *(PC, IDLE, MON, ACT)* or back into *(BTS, IDLE, IDLE, ACT)*. In case both events *LEASE_REL_LSM* and *LEASE_REL_PY*.are generated in the first step, a second step is triggered, which consist of the execution of the *ACT* to *LREL* transition in the *RTR* region. The state machine then reaches a quiescent state, where it has nothing left to executed The series of steps that are executed in response to the external event *LEASE_REL_REQ* until the state machine reaches a quiescent state is called a macro-step. The corresponding configurations are called macro-configurations. In the woven state machine of Figure 2, only the macro-configurations are represented as states.

The semantics of step execution are further detailed in the next section.

3.2 Operational Semantics or Regions

The semantics used in this paper are close to the semantics of classic statecharts as implemented in the Statemate tool [3]. Our approach follows the following guiding principles:

1. Determinism: Our semantics do not allow non-determinism to avoid differences of behavior between simulation and execution of the generated code on the target platform.
2. No shared variables: Our semantics do not allow the sharing of variables between regions. The sharing of variables between regions violates encapsulation and is a cause of non-determinism. Transitions that access the same variable in the same step can cause race conditions.
3. Causality: Internal events are only sensed in the step that follows the step in which they are generated. They do not persist after the following step.
4. Asynchrony: External signals received by the state machine are queued in a buffer. The state machine fetches a signal from the queue and executes until it reaches a quiescent state, after which it fetches the next signal from the queue. Timeout events are treated as external events and put in the same queue as external signals.

The semantics of our language make it more appropriate for distributed systems such as telecom systems rather than embedded real-time systems. However, the concepts presented in this paper are applicable to other statechart variants or other concurrent programming formalisms. To simplify this discussion, we do not consider hierarchy, state entry and exit actions or history. We do not discuss static reactions, spontaneous transitions or transition priorities.

Listing 1 defines the semantics of the state machine execution in Lisp pseudo-code. It is assumed that a data structure *sm* containing the topology of the state machine is available. A state machine executes steps until it terminates. Each step takes as input a status, which consists of a configuration and a set of events and produces a new status. The execution of a step consists of computing the set of enabled transitions for each region based on the current status, followed by the execution of the enabled transitions. If the set of events is empty, the state machine enters a quiescent state after which it fetches a new event from the queue.

The set of enabled transitions is computed by matching the trigger and the guards of each outgoing transition with respect to the current configuration and set of events. The set of triggers and guards are first normalized in the disjunctive normal form so that each element in the list is a conjunct of guards or triggers. The matching functions evaluate whether the set of events matches the expression of the trigger and whether the configuration matches the expression of the guards. The guard and trigger logical expression support conjunction, disjunction and negation. Conjunction of events means that all events are generated during the same step, as events only persist for a single step.

The execution of a step consists of executing all the enabled transitions. Each transition execution updates the status of the step by adding the events generated during the transition execution to the set of events and by updating the configuration based on the next state of the transition. The configuration is updated by replacing the region's previous state by the new state.

```
(defstruct status
           configuration events termination)
(defun execute-statemachine (sm)
 (let (status)
  (while (status.configuration != stop)
   (set status (execute-step sm status)))))
(defun execute-step (sm status)
 (when (status.events = ())
  (let ((event (pop-event-from-queue sm)))
   (when event
    (push event status.events))))
 (if (status.events != ())
  (let ((trs (get-enabled-transitions sm
                                 status)))
   (set status.events ())
   (set status (execute-transitions sm trs
                                 status)))
  else
   status))
(defun execute-transitions (sm trs status)
 (let ((ustatus status))
  (dolist (tr trs)
   (set ustatus (execute-transition sm tr
                                 ustatus)))
  (set status ustatus)))
(defun execute-transition (tr sm status)
 (set tr (bind-parameters-to-actuals tr status))
 (let (a)
  (while (set a (get-next-action a tr))
   (when (is-gen-action a)
    (push a.event status.events))
   (when (is-nextstate-action a)
    (set status.configuration
     (update-configuration sm
       status.configuration (get-nextstate a)))
   (when (is-stop-action a)
    (set status.configuration stop))
   (execute a)))
  status)
```

Listing 1. Statemachine execution semantics

```
(defun get-enabled-transitions (sm status)
 (let (enabled-transitions)
  (dolist (r sm.regions)
   (set enabled-transitions
    (append enabled-transitions
     (get-enabled-transition r sm status))))))
(defun get-enabled-transition (r sm status)
 (let (enabled-transitions)
  (dolist (tr (outgoing-transitions r
                          status.configuration))
   (dolist (g tr.guards)
    (when (match-guard g status.configuration)
     (dolist trig in tr.triggers
      (when (match-trigger (trig, status.events))
       (push tr enabled-transitions))))))
  enabled-transitions))
```

Listing 2. Computation of the set of enabled transitions

3.3 Checker Semantics

The state machine checker computes the set of macro-configurations of the system and detects problems with the region composition such as deadlocks. The checker algorithm can also be used to statically compose the regions into a single region by weaving together the actions of the region transitions, as illustrated in Figure 2.

The checker algorithm of Listing 3 performs a depth-first traversal on the reachable configurations by iterating over all possible external inputs and paths.

```
(defvar *macro-configs* ())

(defun check-statemachine (sm
 (let (status)
  (traverse-statemachine sm status)))

(defun traverse-statemachine (sm status)
 (if (status.events = ())
  (when (not (find status.configuration
                   *macro-configs*))
   (push status.configuration *macro-configs*)
   (dolist (s *signals*)
    (push s status.events)
    (compute-step sm status))
  else
   (compute-step sm status)))

(defun compute-step (sm status)
 (let (new-statuses)
  (dolist (r sm.regions)
   (let ((tr (get-enabled-transition r sm
                                     status)))
    (when tr
     (set new-statuses (append new-statuses
           (collect-reachable-statuses r
                         (list status) tr)))))
  (dolist (st new-statuses)
   (traverse-statemachine sm st))))

(defun collect-reachable-statuses (r statuses tr)
 (dolist (a tr.actions)
  (when (is-gen-action a)
   (let (event (get-signal a))
    (dolist (st statuses)
     (when (not st.termination)
      (push event st.events)))))
  (when (is-nextstate-action a)
   (dolist (st statuses)
    (when (not st.termination )
     (set st.configuration
       (update-configuration st.configuration
                            (get-nextstate a)))
     (set st.termination t))))
  (when (is-stop-action a)
   (dolist (st statuses)
    (when (not st.termination)
     (set st.configuration stop)
     (set st.termination t))))
  (when (is-decision-action a)
   (let ((branches (get-decision-branches a))
         (continuation (get-continuation tr a))
    (dolist (br branches)
     (set br.actions (append br.actions
                            continuation.actions))
     (set statuses (append statuses
       (collect-reachable-statuses r statuses br))))))
```

Listing 3. Checker traversal of the state machine

The checker algorithm is exponential with respect to the number of paths and regions. In our experience, the exponential complexity has not proven to be a problem as systems are usually composed of a small set of coarse-grained regions. Hierarchy can also be used to reduce the number of regions if needed.

During the state machine traversal, configurations for which the set of internal events is empty are marked as macro-configuration. The algorithm then considers all possible external inputs (stored in *signals*) to drive the traversal further recursively. For each status, the algorithm collects all the statuses that are reachable trough the next step.

If the new statuses correspond to transient configurations, the next steps are computed. Otherwise, the configuration is a macro-configuration and the algorithm performs the next traversal. Conditional branches are expanded so that the algorithm can cover all possible combinations of target configurations and sets of generated events. In practice, the transitions are first normalized and caching is used to avoid the exponential blow up due to branching. The checker algorithm can detect the following situations:

1. Non-determinism exists in the system when the number of enabled transitions is larger than one within a region:
   ```
   (when ((length enabled-transitions) > 1)
    (error "found non-determinism"))
   ```

2. A deadlock occurs when a macro-configuration does not have enabled-transitions for any external signal:
   ```
   (dolist (mc *macro-configs*)
    (let ((trs ()))
     (dolist (s *signals)
      (let ((status (make-status mc s)))
       (set trs (append trs
                 (get-enabled-transitions sm status))
     (when (trs = ())
      (error "found deadlock")))
   ```

3. An internal event is generated in one step but not consumed by a trigger. The event is lost. This can be detected by adding the following code to compute-step:
   ```
   (let ((triggers ())
         (trs (get-enabled-transitions sm status)))
    (dolist (tr trs)
     (set triggers (append triggers tr.triggers)))
    (dolist (ev status.events)
     (when (not (find ev triggers))
      (warning "internal event ev is lost"))))
   ```

4. Managing Region Interactions

4.1 Region Interactions

The composition of Figure 1 generates macro-configurations that are inconsistent with the requirements. The configurations 6, 7 and 8 in Figure 2 violate the system consistency invariants. In our case study, releasing the lease consists of three tasks:

1. The lease management region checks if the request originates from the BTS that is currently holding the lease. If the request is valid, the region releases the lease to the paging controller (state *PC*).

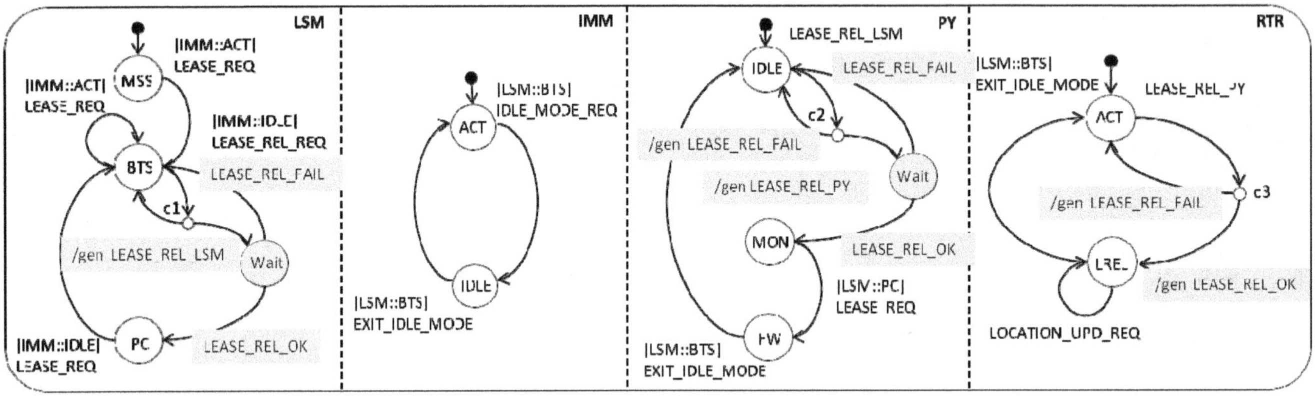

Figure 3. Interactions between the regions of a state machine

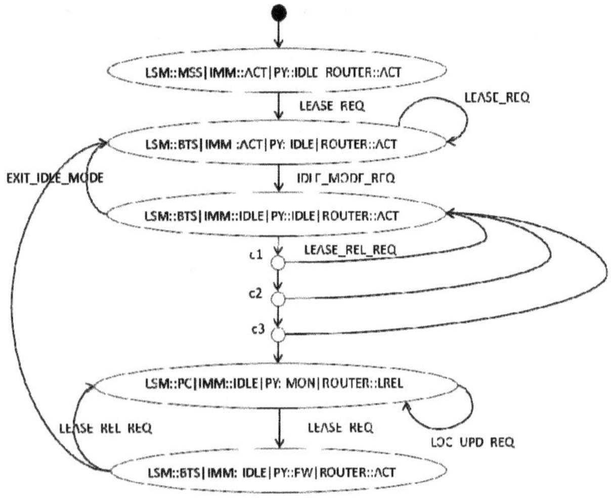

Figure 4. Flattened state machine generated from Figure 3

2. The proxy region is responsible for monitoring inbound traffic when the lease is released. If the request succeeds, the proxy region enters the monitoring state *MON*.

3. The router region needs to update the routing tables by sending an ARP request. If the ARP is sent successfully, the router region enters the *LREL* state.

Each of these tasks can be described and implemented independently of the other tasks. However, when the regions are composed with each other, the combinations of the branches in the different regions lead to inconsistent states. In configuration 6, the lease was released in the *LSM* region, but the proxy component failed to start monitoring the network. Inbound data will not trigger the paging procedure. In configuration 7, the proxy is monitoring the network traffic for inbound traffic, but the lease release operation failed in the *LSM* region. Incoming traffic will unnecessarily trigger the paging procedure. In configuration 8, the lease has been released and the proxy is monitoring the network. However, the routing table was not updated, and inbound traffic will not be received by the MS.

The composition requires synchronization to prevent inconsistencies. Figure 3 shows a version of the system where the region synchronization logic was modified to avoid inconsistent configurations. Figure 4 presents the

resulting woven state machine which shows that the undesirable configurations are not reachable anymore.

In the solution of Figure 3, an order of execution between the participating regions was selected. The lease management region first determines whether it is able to process the request. If so, it propagates the request to the proxy region and enters a waiting state. The proxy region evaluates its conditional expression. If successful, it propagates the request to the router region and enters a waiting state. Otherwise, it notifies the lease management region. The router region sends back an acknowledgment if the request is successful or a failure signal if it fails. If successful, the *LSM*, *PY* and *RTR* regions will step into *(PC, MON, LREL)*. If unsuccessful, they will step back into *(BTS, IDL, ACT)*. The undesirable configurations are not reachable. However, the solution is not satisfactory with respect to:

1. Information hiding. The data carried by the signals is propagated from region to region. Each region has access to the entire payload of the signal

2. Coupling. The synchronization signals tightly couple the regions to each other. Adding a region to the interactions will require changes to the implementations of the other participant regions.

3. Cohesion. A synchronization state was introduced in two regions. These states do not correspond to logical states of the feature implemented by the region. Logic that was previously implemented in a single transition is now split over three transitions.

4. Termination. The synchronization structure requires that a *LEASE_REL_OK* or *LEASE_REL_FAIL* internal event is always generated in one of the steps that follow the regions entering a wait state or the system will enter a partial deadlock (one region enters a deadlock, while the others continue execution). It is the developer's responsibility to detect and prevent these situations.

4.2 Interface Regions

We introduce a design pattern to address the information hiding and coupling issues with the solution presented in Figure 3. The pattern uses an interface region *IF* to mediate between the interacting regions.

```
region IF {                      region LSM {                     region PY {                       region RTR {
 forstate S {                      forstate BTS {                   forstate IDL {                    forstate ACT {
  [LSM::BTS && IMM::IDL             input LEASE_REL_LSM(a){          input LEASE_REL_PY(b){            input LEASE_REL_RTR(c){
  && PY::IDL  && RTR::ACT]           if (c1) {                       if (c2) {                         if (c3) {
  input LEASE_REL_REQ(lr){            gen LEASE_REL_LSM_OK();          gen LEASE_REL_PY_OK();            gen LEASE_REL_RTR_OK();
   gen LEASE_REL_LSM(lr.a);         } else {                         } else {                          } else {
   gen LEASE_REL_PY( lr.b);         gen LEASE_REL_LSM_FAIL();         gen LEASE_REL_PY_FAIL();           gen LEASE_REL_RTR_FAIL();
   gen LEASE_REL_RTR(lr.c);         }                                }                                 }
   nextstate Wait; } }             nextstate Wait; } }              nextstate Wait; } }               nextstate Wait; } }
 forstate Wait {                  forstate Wait {                  forstate Wait {                   forstate Wait {
  input LEASE_REL_COMMIT(){         input LEASE_REL_COMMIT(){        input LEASE_REL_COMMIT(){         input LEASE_REL_COMMIT(){
   output LEASE_REL_RSP(OK);         nextstate PC; }                 nextstate MON; }                  nextstate MON; }
   nextstate S; }                  input LEASE_REL_ABORT() {        input LEASE_REL_ABORT() {         input LEASE_REL_ABORT() {
  input LEASE_REL_ABORT() {          nextstate BTS; } } .. }          nextstate IDL; } } .. }           nextstate IDL; } } .. }
   output LEASE_REL_RSP(ER);
   nextstate S; } } ... }

 gen LEASE_REL_COMMIT() when LEASE_REL_LSM_OK()   && LEASE_REL_PY_OK()   && LEASE_REL_RTR_OK();
 gen LEASE_REL_ABORT()  when LEASE_REL_LSM_FAIL() || LEASE_REL_PY_FAIL() || LEASE_REL_RTR_FAIL();
```

Listing 4. The lease release transition using an interface region

Listing 4 shows a textual representation of the lease release transitions in the *IF*, *LSM*, *PY* and *RTR* regions. The *IF* region interacts with the 3 other regions. However, The *LSM*, *PY* and *RTR* regions do not interact directly with each other. Listing 4 produces the same set of configurations as the state machine of Figure 3.

The *LSM*, *PY* and *RTR* implementation regions follow the same structure as the *IF* interface region. All regions include a synchronization state *Wait*, which separates the step that evaluates the conditionals from the step that executes the outcome of the transition. The interface region propagates the request to all participating implementation region, passing only the data that they need to proceed with the execution. Next, the implementation regions execute their decision step. The regions produce internal signals that indicate the outcome of the local decision phase. Finally, all regions execute the same global outcome.

The outcomes are defined using *gen* statements: if all three *OK* events are generated in the same step, the *COMMIT* outcomes will be executed in each region. If one of the *FAIL* events is generated, the *ABORT* outcome is executed. Gen statements are implemented through textual substitution of the triggers corresponding to the left hand side of the gen statement by the expression on its right hand side.

Listing 4 shows the general case where each regions produces different types of events. It is however not required that each region contributes to the mapping function of the *gen* statement or that they produce distinct types of events. The solution has the following advantages:

1. Information hiding. The interface region only propagates the parameters that are required by each region. Regions do not have access to data they do not need.
2. Coupling. The implementation regions do not interact or dependent on each other directly. All dependencies are between the interface regions and the implementation regions.

However, interface regions do not address the cohesion and termination issues highlighted in Section 4.1.

4.3 Transactional Regions

The management of region interactions is complicated by the termination issue. The function that maps local events to the different possible outcomes of the interaction needs to be deterministic and free of deadlocks. The set of outcomes needs to be complete: one of the outcomes must always be selected before the end of the macro-step. The synchronization states should never be part of a macro-configuration. This property cannot be checked automatically as the checker has no way of distinguishing synchronization states from other states. This constraint complicates maintenance and refinement of the system. During maintenance tasks, branches can be introduced in the regions that mistakenly omit to trigger decision events.

We therefore introduce a language construct to distinguish between state and transitions that correspond to macro-steps and states and transitions whose primary purpose is synchronization. Listing 5 shows how the *IF* and *LSM* regions are synchronized using the transaction construct. A transaction is a statement that has a name and a set of outcomes. In the example of Listing 5, the transaction *lrel* spans over the regions *IF* and *LSM*. The outcomes of the transactions are captured by a set of transitions with complementary triggers. The transaction can only complete in two ways: *LEASE_REL_COMMIT* is generated or *LEASE_REL_ABORT* is generated, based on the mapping function of the transaction expressed using a *gen* statement.

```
region IF {                       region LSM {
 forstate S {                      forstate BTS {
  [LSM::BTS]                        input LEASE_REL_LSM(a){
  input LEASE_REL_REQ(lr){          if (c1) {
   gen LEASE_REL_LSM(lr.a);          gen LEASE_REL_LSM_OK; }
   transaction lrel {               else {
    input LEASE_REL_COMMIT{          gen LEASE_REL_LSM_FAIL;}
     output LEASE_REL_RSP1;          transaction lrel {
     nextstate S; }                   input LEASE_REL_COMMIT{
   input LEASE_REL_ABORT {            nextstate PC; }
     output LEASE_REL_RSP2;           input LEASE_REL_ABORT {
     nextstate S; } } ... }           nextstate BTS; } }..}

 gen LEASE_REL_COMMIT() when LEASE_REL_LSM_OK();
 gen LEASE_REL_ABORT()  when LEASE_REL_LSM_FAIL();
```

Listing 5. Transaction between *IF* and *LSM*

A transaction contains a set of outcomes. An outcome has the same syntax as the input part of a *forstate*, except that it cannot be guarded. Transactions with the same name in different regions need to have the same set of triggers for their outcomes. Transactions have the following properties:

1. Determinism. There should not exist a status for which the number of enabled outcomes is larger than 1.
2. Termination. One of the outcomes of a transaction is always executed before the completion of the macro-step in which the transaction started.

Transactions are implemented by translating the transaction statements into synchronization states, and by translating the outcomes into transitions. The algorithm to perform the translation is as follows. In each region:

1. Move the declarations used in the outcomes but declared in the context of the transition to the scope of the region and rename the declarations and references.
2. Generate a new synchronization state based on the name of the transaction, and annotate it as a generated synchronization state.
3. Replace the transaction statement by a *nextstate* action that steps into the synchronization state.
4. Generate a *forstate* for the synchronization state and add the outcomes of the transaction as input parts of the *forstate*.

This transformation is performed before running the checker. As the transaction outcomes are implemented as transitions, the checker automatically ensures that the outcomes are deterministic. The termination property is enforced by running the following code after the execution of the checker:

```
(dolist (mc *macro-configs*)
  (when (contains-synchronization-state mc)
    (error "synch state in macro-configuration")))
```

The check enforces that a synchronization state is never part of a macro-configuration. Its incoming transitions and outgoing transitions are always executed in the same macro-step. The transactional composition construct has the following advantages:

1. Cohesion. Actions that are executed during the same macro-step are syntactically located in the same transition. The notation avoids the need to introduce states whose purpose is to coordinate with other regions.
2. Termination. The semantics of transactions automatically detect partial deadlocks that would not be reported otherwise.

5. Case Study: Implementation

We evaluate the transactional composition by comparing three implementations of an industrial telecommunication component using modularity metrics. The first version of the system is a monolithic implementation. The second version uses classic regions to encapsulate the features of the system. The third version uses interface regions and transactional region composition.

5.1 Monolithic Implementation

The monolithic implementation was performed by a third party using a commercial modeling tool. The state machine is composed of a single region of 3 states: *Init*, *Idle*, and *Active*, corresponding to the idle mode feature. The states of the other features are encoded using flags. The model is structured according to the basic scenarios described in Section 2.3. The modeling tool used did not support regions or another mechanism to modularize features. The features described in Section 2.2 are therefore not modularized.

A typical transition in the monolithic implementation is represented in Listing 6. The actions corresponding to the different features have been annotated with a color code that corresponds to different features. The transition checks and updates the state of the LSM feature using the *itsLeaseState* flag at lines 3, 16 and 32. The state of the proxy feature is encoded using the *g_proxyEnabledFlag* at lines 20, 24, 36, 41, 45, 48 and 53. The state of the router feature is encoded using *the g_simIpSs* at line 9, the *g_MipFlag* at line 11 and the flags passed to the *sendFaARP* function at lines 14 and 30.

The transition has a complex control flow based on conditional expression over the return values of operations and flags that encode the state of the features. The implementations of the features are clearly tangled. It is hard to determine that the transition always sends a location update response back to the BTS. The router feature is not modularized and the three versions of the router feature are implemented within the transition.

5.2 Region-Based Implementation

The region-based implementation implements the same behavior as the monolithic implementation using regions. It was obtained through successive refactoring of the monolithic implementation. Each feature is implemented as a separate region. The states of the features are encoded using symbolic states rather than flags. The interactions between the regions are managed as in Figure 3. For each scenario that cuts across multiple regions, an order of execution was selected between the regions. Each region attempts to execute the request. If successful, it propagates the request to the next region and enters a synchronization state. Eventually, all regions handle the request successfully or a failure signal is generated.

5.3 Transactional Implementation

The transaction-based implementation was obtained by further refactoring of the region-based implementation. It uses interface regions to decouple the regions from each other and transactional composition to manage the synchronization between regions. Listing 7 shows the transitions of the interface, lease management, proxy and router regions that interact to implement the lease release request.

```
1.forstate Idle {
2. input M_LSM_MSS_LEASE_RELEASE_REQ(hdr_in, lrel) {
3.  if (itsLeaseState == BTS) {
4.   if (Ignore23bitAndCompare(lrel.BSId, g_BSID)) {
5.    switch (lrel.ReasonCode) {
6.     case Lease_Hold_Timer_expiration : {
7.      g_rc = sendProxyMonitorDataInd(lrel.SsIp);
8.      if (g_rc == MOB_OK) {
9.       switch (g_simIpSs) {
10.       case false : {
11.        if (g_MipFlag == MIP) {
12.         g_rc = sendFaLLC(); }
13.        else {
14.         g_rc = sendFaARP(ARP_WAIT_ONE); }
15.        if (g_rc == MOB_OK) {
16.         itsLeaseState = PC;
17.         if (! timeStampIsOld(lrel.TimeStamp)) {
18.          g_timestamp = lrel.TimeStamp; }
19.         reset (T_LEASE_DURATION());
20.         g_proxyEnabledFlag = true;
21.         sendLeaseReleaseResponse(g_MacAddr, OK); }
22.         nextstate -;
23.        else {
24.         g_proxyEnabledFlag = false;
25.         sendLeaseReleaseResponse(g_MacAddr, FAIL);
26.         nextstate -; } }
27.       case true : {
28.        g_rc = checkVlanIdInUseAndRouterIp();
29.        if (g_rc == MOB_OK) {
30.         g_rc = sendFaARP(ARP_RSP_WAIT);
31.         if (g_rc == MOB_OK) {
32.          itsLeaseState = PC;
33.          if (! timeStampIsOld(lrel.TimeStamp)) {
34.           g_timestamp = lrel.TimeStamp; }
35.          reset (T_LEASE_DURATION());
36.          g_proxyEnabledFlag = true;
37.          sendLeaseReleaseResponse(g_MacAddr, OK); }
38.          nextstate -; }
39.         else {
40.        sendLeaseReleaseResponse(lrel.MacAddress,FAIL);
41.         sendProxyIdleModeRelease();
42.         stop; } }
43.        else {
44.        sendLeaseReleaseResponse(lrel.MacAddress,FAIL);
45.         sendProxyIdleModeRelease();
46.         stop; } } }
47.      else {
48.       g_proxyEnabledFlag = false;
49.       sendLeaseReleaseResponse(g_MacAddr, FAIL);
50.       nextstate -; } }
51.     case Idle_Mode_System_Timer_Expiration_at_BS : {
52.      sendLeaseReleaseResponse(lrel.MacAddress,FAIL);
53.      sendProxyIdleModeRelease();
54.      stop; } }
55.    else {
56.     sendLeaseReleaseResponse(lrel.MacAddress, FAIL);
57.     nextstate -; } }
58. else {
59.  sendLeaseReleaseResponse(lrel.MacAddress, FAIL);
60.  nextstate -; } } }
```

Listing 6. Lease Release - Monolithic implementation

First, the *IF* interface region defines the preconditions for processing the lease release request based on the state of the participant regions. Second, the request is propagated to the participant regions. Finally, the interface region sends back a response to the environment based on the outcome of the transaction. The region *IF* declares the outcomes of the transaction in terms of two types of exceptions: *LEASE_RELEASE_FAIL* and *LEASE_RELEASE_EXIT*. *LEASE_RELEASE_PROCEED* is executed when the *LEASE_RELEASE_OK* signal is generated and none of the exceptions are generated in the same step. The exception outcomes cover the cases where one exception is generated

```
1.  gen LEASE_RELEASE_PROCEED() when  LEASE_RELEASE_OK()
2.     && ! LEASE_RELEASE_FAIL && ! LEASE_RELEASE_EXIT;
3.  region IF {
4.   forstate Idle {
5.   [LSM::BTS && PROXY::Idle && ROUTER::Idle]
6.    input M_LSM_MSS_LEASE_RELEASE_REQ(hdr_in, lrel) {
7.     gen LEASE_RELEASE_LSM (lrel.BSId, lrel.ReasonCode,..
8.     gen LEASE_RELEASE_PROXY (lrel.SsIp);
9.     gen LEASE_RELEASE_ROUTER ();
10.    transaction lrelease {
11.     input LEASE_RELEASE_PROCEED() {
12.      sendLeaseReleaseResponse(lrel.MacAddress, OK);
13.      nextstate Idle; }
14.     input LEASE_RELEASE_FAIL()&& !LEASE_RELEASE_EXIT {
15.      sendLeaseReleaseResponse(lrel.MacAddress, FAIL);
16.      nextstate Idle; }
17.     input LEASE_RELEASE_EXIT() {
18.      sendLeaseReleaseResponse(lrel.MacAddress, FAIL);
19.      nextstate Idle; } }
20.    [! (LSM::BTS && PROXY::Idle && ROUTER::Idle)]
21.    input M_LSM_MSS_LEASE_RELEASE_REQ(hdr_in, lrel) {
22.     sendLeaseReleaseResponse(lrel.MacAddress, FAIL);
23.     nextstate Idle;   } } } }
24.  region LSM {
25.   forstate BTS {
26.    input LEASE_RELEASE_LSM(BSId, ReasonCode,TimeStamp){
27.     if (Ignore23bitAndCompare(BSId, g_BSID)) {
28.      switch (lrel.ReasonCode) {
29.       case Lease_Hold_Timer_expiration : {
30.        gen LEASE_RELEASE_OK (); }
31.       case Idle_Mode_System_Timer_Expiration_at_BS : {
32.        gen LEASE_RELEASE_EXIT (); }
33.      else {
34.       gen LEASE_RELEASE_FAIL(); }
35.      transaction lrelease {
36.       input LEASE_RELEASE_PROCEED () {
37.        if (! timeStampIsOld(lrel.TimeStamp)) {
38.         g_timestamp = lrel.TimeStamp; }
39.        reset (T_LEASE_DURATION());
40.        nextstate PC; }
41.       input LEASE_RELEASE_FAIL() && !LEASE_RELEASE_EXIT{
42.        nextstate BTS; }
43.       input LEASE_RELEASE_EXIT () {
44.        stop; } } } }.. }
45.  region PROXY {
46.   forstate Idle {
47.    input LEASE_RELEASE_PROXY (SsIp) {
48.     g_rc = sendProxyMonitorDataInd(lrel.SsIp);
49.     if (g_rc != MOB_OK) {
50.      gen LEASE_RELEASE_FAIL(); }
51.     transaction lrelease {
52.      input LEASE_RELEASE_PROCEED() {
53.       nextstate MON; }
54.      input LEASE_RELEASE_FAIL() && !LEASE_RELEASE_EXIT{
55.       nextstate Idle; }
56.      input LEASE_RELEASE_EXIT() {
57.       sendProxyIdleModeRelease();
58.       nextstate Idle; } } } } .. }
59.  region SIP_ROUTER {
60.   forstate Idle {
61.    input LEASE_RELEASE_ROUTER () {
62.     g_rc = checkVlanIdInUseAndRouterIp();
63.     if (g_rc == MOB_OK) {
64.      g_rc = sendFaARP(ARP_RSP_WAIT);
65.      if (g_rc != MOB_OK) {
66.       gen LEASE_RELEASE_EXIT(); } }
67.     else {
68.      gen LEASE_RELEASE_EXIT(); }
69.     transaction lrelease {
70.      input LEASE_RELEASE_PROCEED() {
71.       nextstate LRPL; }
72.      input LEASE_RELEASE_FAIL || LEASE_RELEASE_EXIT {
73.       nextstate Idle; } } } } .. }
```

Listing 7. Lease Release - Transactional implementation

but not the other and the case where both are generated in the same step.

6 Case Study Results

6.1 Metrics

The metrics used to evaluate the approach include:

- Lines of code of an entity or a feature of the system.
- Number of transitions and number of states of a region
- Coupling between transitions: the coupling index between transition i and transition j is 1 when transitions i and j access a shared variable or interact through an internal signal or a guard, 0 otherwise.
- Concern diffusion over transitions: the diffusion index between concern i and transition j is 1 if the transition implements part of concern i, 0 otherwise. The diffusion of a concern is the sum of its diffusion index with all transitions, divided by the number of transitions. It reflects the amount of scattering of its implementation.

6.2 Results

Table 1 compares the size of the 3 implementation in terms of lines of code (LOC), number of regions, number of states and number of transitions. All three implementations are about the same size in terms of lines of code. The region-based implementation is slightly smaller, due to the elimination of replication through the modularization of the features. This reduction is partly compensated by the additional structure of the new regions, states and transitions defined in the system. The transactional implementation is slightly larger is size, due to the interface region.

The region-based implementation contains many more states and transitions than the monolithic one. This is due to two factors. First, most of the basic scenarios introduce transitions in multiple regions. Second, the interactions between regions introduce many synchronization states. The synchronization causes behavior that is logically executed during the same macro-step to be split over multiple transitions.

The transactional implementation eliminates the waiting states and allows the behavior of one macro-step to be syntactically represented as a single cohesive transition. Compared to the region-based implementation, the transactions eliminate 45 states and 54 transitions. The transactional implementation is more structured than the monolithic one, but avoids the scattering of behavior over a large number of transitions by maintaining behavior that is executed in the same macro-step in the same transition. The transactional implementation is more cohesive than the region-based implementation.

	LOC	Regions	States	Transitions
Monolithic	2709	1	3	30
Region-based	2679	10	76	122
Transactional	2739	11	32	81

Table 1. Size of the three implementations

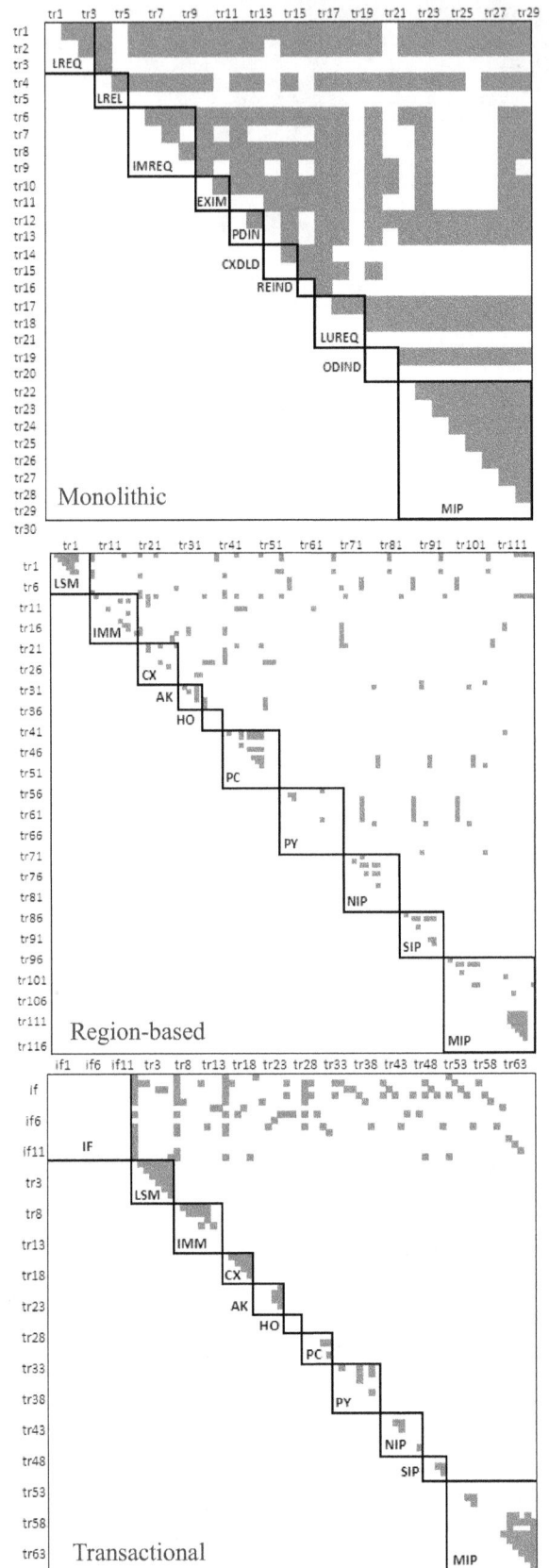

Figure 5. DSM's for the 3 implementations

	av.diff scenario	max.diff scenario	av.diff features	max.diff features
Monolithic	5.3%	6.7%	28.7%	60.0%
Region-based	6.8%	22.3%	10.0%	19.0%
Transactional	6.3%	16.2%	8.2%	18.5%

Table 2. Diffusion of the scenarios and features

Figure 5 compares the design structure matrices (DSM) [4] for the three implementations. The axes correspond to transitions of the state machine. The value of a matrix entry represents the coupling index between these transitions. The transitions are grouped according to the basic scenarios or the region they are part of by boxes along the diagonal.

The DSM of the monolithic implementation shows that the transitions that implement a scenario are tightly coupled with transitions that implement other scenarios. The scenarios cannot be implemented independently of each other.

The DSM for the region-based implementation is much sparser than the monolithic matrix, due to the large number of additional synchronization transitions. The number of coupling dependencies between regions is relatively smaller than the coupling dependencies between basic scenarios. However, there are still an important number of dependencies between regions, corresponding to guards and internal signal dependencies.

Finally, the DSM for the transactional implementation is denser than the region-based DSM, due to elimination of synchronization states. The DSM does not contain dependencies between the regions that implement the features of the system. All dependencies are concentrated on the interface region, at the top of the matrix.

Table 2 shows the average and maximum diffusions for the scenarios and the features of the three implementations of the system. A diffusion value of 5% means that the implementation of a scenario or a feature spreads over 5% of the transitions of the state machine. The average value indicates the average diffusion for all concerns. The maximum value indicates the diffusion of the concern that has the highest diffusion.

The results of Table 2 indicate that the implementations of the features are less scattered in the region-based and transactional implementations than in the monolithic implementation. The modularization of the features increases the diffusion of the scenarios, but in an acceptable manner. Compared to the region-based implementation, the transactional implementation reduces the diffusion of both the scenarios and the features. This is due to the transactional composition, which eliminate synchronization transitions.

6.3 Discussion

Our case study presents an example of a system that can be decomposed and understood in two complementary manners. When the basic scenarios are used as the primary decomposition, the reaction of the system to an external event is easy to understand: all the conditions to evaluate and actions to be performed are located in the body of one or two transitions. However, these scenarios cannot be implemented independently as they interact in complex ways trough shared variables and flags. The solution is also more rigid, as the features implemented by the system are scattered all over the transitions that implement the scenarios.

Feature-based decomposition increases flexibility. Different versions of the system that support different combinations of features can be delivered. In the case study, the isolation of the simple, nomadic and mobile IP router features allowed us to reduce the memory footprint of a session by 15%, by only loading the features required by the subscriber. The solution also gains in modularity, as the features can be implemented independently of each other using an interface region.

However, the interactions between the features can be hard to manage. The transactional composition semantics alleviate this problem by requiring that all features that interact within a basic-scenario share a common set of outcomes. The composition semantics ensure that synchronization problems within transactions will be detected.

The decomposition into features also makes the basic reaction of the system to an external event harder to understand. The actions executed in response to an event are scattered over the different regions. Yet, the reaction of the system can be understood in terms of a sequence of transactions in the interface region. The transactions provide a high-level, yet precise, view of the execution of each basic scenario and its possible outcomes.

The semantics of the transactional composition are more complex then the semantics used to perform a scenario-based decomposition. However, the transactional composition does not need to be understood by all developers. One of the main objectives of the decomposition by feature is to allow each feature to be implemented, tested and maintained by a different team. The team implementing a feature only needs to know about the outcomes defined in the interface region. It is then the role of the integration team to understand the interactions between the features and define the guards and the mapping between the events generated locally and the global outcomes.

The use of interface regions and transactions does not preclude the use of classic synchronization mechanisms. The decision to isolate features into regions and use interface regions should be guided by the need to enable the independent activation of a feature or the need to enable the independent development of the feature.

7 Related Work

Transactional region composition can be seen as a form of symmetric AOP [6]. Each region provides a view of the behavior of the system, seen from the perspective of a feature. Interface regions define design rules [4] or crosscutting interfaces [7]. They define the preconditions, triggers and post-conditions for transitions of the participating regions. Transactions define an interface that cuts across the decomposition into features, and enables the system to support a decomposition into features and a decomposition into scenarios simultaneously.

In [8], Mussbacher considers the modularization and management of features within scenarios. The main decomposition is defined using scenarios but the language provides support to modularize features. Our approach uses features as the primary decomposition while providing language support to capture the essence of scenarios using transactions.

The work presented in this paper builds on a large body of research in the area of Aspect-Oriented Modeling [9]. In [10], Elrad identifies the similarities between aspect-oriented compositions and orthogonal regions and proposes to model aspect-oriented composition using internal signals between orthogonal regions. In [11], Mahoney proposes a notation to decouple regions by extracting internal signals from statecharts using an aspect-oriented notation. Zhang [12] introduces an aspect-oriented notation to modularize crosscutting concerns across different regions of UML state machines. Protocol modeling [13] proposes a semantic for the orthogonal composition of behaviors using a state machine-based notation based on CSP. Neither of these approaches achieves complete independence between the regions. The AOM approaches use small examples to illustrate the proposed syntax and do not address the issue of scalability and maintenance of large systems. Neither of the proposed approaches is evaluated quantitatively.

8   Conclusions

We show through an industrial case study that orthogonal regions can be used to modularize the features of a complex system. However, the interactions between the features of the system require a large amount of synchronization between the regions. The synchronization tightly couples the regions to each other and reduces the cohesion of each region. We therefore introduce a notion of interface region that decouples the regions from each other. We also introduce a transactional composition operator that reduces the diffusion of behavior caused by synchronization and facilitates the detection and management of feature interactions. We evaluate the approach by comparing a monolithic implementation of a real-world telecom system to a region-based implementation and a transactional implementation using size, coupling and diffusion metrics. Our results show that the transactional implementation is more modular and more cohesive than the monolithic and region-based implementations and that it supports the independent implementation and deployment of features.

References

[1]   Bouma, L.G., Griffeth, N. and Kimbler, N. 2000. Feature Interactions in Telecommunications Systems. Computer Networks 32:4.

[2]   Harel, D. 1987. Statecharts: A visual formalism for complex systems, Science of Computer Programming, Volume 8, Issue 3. 231-274.

[3]   Harel, D. and Naamad, A. 1996. The STATEMATE Semantics of Statecharts, ACM Transactions on Software Engineering and Methodology (TOSEM), Volume 5, Issue 4. 293-333.

[4]   Baldwin, C. and Clark, K. 2000. Design Rules vol I, The Power of Modularity. MIT Press.

[5]   Garcia, A et al. 2005. Modularizing design patterns with aspects: a quantitative study. In Proceedings of the 4th international conference on Aspect-oriented software development, Chicago, USA. 3-14.

[6]   Tarr, P., Ossher, H., Harrison, W. and Sutton, S. 1999. N Degrees of Separation: Multi-Dimensional Separation of Concerns. In proceedings of the 21st international conference on Software engineering. Los Angeles, USA. 107-119.

[7]   Kiczales, G. and Mezini, 2005. M. Aspect-oriented programming and modular reasoning. In proceedings of the 27th international conference on software engineering, St Louis, USA. 49-58.

[8]   Mussbacher, G., Amyot, D., Weigert, T. and Cottenier, T. 2009. Feature Interactions in Aspect-Oriented Scenario Models. In proceedings of the 10th International Conference on Feature Interactions in Software and Communication Systems, Lisbon, Portugal. 75-90.

[9]   Kienzle J. et al. Report of the 14th International Workshop on Aspect-Oriented Modeling. In Models in Software Engineering, LNCS 6002, 98-103.

[10] Elrad, T., Aldawud, O. and Bader, A. 2002. Aspect-Oriented Modeling: Bridging the Gap between Implementation and Design. In proceedings of the 1st conference on Generative Programming and Component Engineering, Pittsburgh, USA, LNCS 2487. 189-201.

[11] Mahoney, M., Bader, A., Aldawud, O. and Elrad, T.: 2004. Using Aspects to Abstract and Modularize Statecharts. The 5th Aspect-Oriented Modeling Workshop in Conjunction with the UML 2004 conference. Lisbon, Portugal.

[12] Zhang, G., Hölzl, M. and Knapp, A. 2007. Enhancing UML State Machines with Aspects. In proceedings of the 10th International Conference on Model Driven Engineering Languages and Systems. Nashville, USA. LNCS 4735. 529-543.

[13] McNeile, A. and Roubtsova, E. 2010. Aspect-Oriented Development Using Protocol Modeling. In A Common Case Study for Aspect-Oriented Modeling Approaches, Transactions on Aspect Oriented Software Development, Volume 7. LNCS 6210. 115-150.

Method Shelters: Avoiding Conflicts among Class Extensions Caused by Local Rebinding

Shumpei Akai   Shigeru Chiba

Tokyo Institute of Technology, Japan

akai@csg.is.titech.ac.jp   chiba@acm.org

Abstract

A class extension, also known as open classes, allows programmers to modify existing classes and thus it is supported by several programming languages. However, class extensions imply a risk that they supply different definitions for the same method and those definitions conflict with each other. Several module systems have been proposed to address these conflicts. One approach lexically restricts the scope of class extensions but they do not allow us to change the behavior of methods called indirectly. Another approach is to make only class extensions explicitly imported effective while preserving the local rebinding property, which allows us to change the behavior of indirectly called methods. However, this approach causes conflicts if potentially conflicting class extensions are imported together. To address this problem, we propose a new module system named *method shelters*. A method shelter confines a scope of class extensions while preserving the local rebinding property. Hidden class extensions in a method shelter are not visible from the outside. We implemented a prototype of the proposed module system in Ruby. This paper illustrates several examples of the use of method shelters and also shows the results of benchmarks on our prototype.

Categories and Subject Descriptors   D.3.3 [*Programming Languages*]: Language Constructs and Features

General Terms   Languages, Design

Keywords   Module, Class extension, Open class.

1. Introduction

Extending existing classes by redefining methods or adding new methods, known as *class extensions*, *open classes* [11] or *revisers* [6], is an important feature for object-oriented programming languages to get better expressiveness. This feature is found in several languages: Smalltalk [8], CLOS [4], Objective-C, Ruby [14] and aspect-oriented languages including AspectJ [10] (as inter-type declarations). In Ruby and especially in Ruby on Rails [13], which is a popular web application framework for Ruby, class extensions are widely used to make the code simpler. Class extensions are used for three major aims: (1) adding convenient methods to core classes, (2) traversing trees without the Visitor pattern, and (3) redefining or adding methods to existing classes (*monkey patching*).

However class extensions also cause a problem; methods added by different libraries may conflict. If library $L1$ and $L2$ required by the same application program define methods with the same name for the same class and they have different behavior, they may crash the program. In Ruby's culture, libraries often modify core-classes and classes in other libraries required by them. Avoiding conflicts among method (re)definitions has been a serious issue.

To address this problem, several mechanisms such as selector namespaces [17], Classboxes [2, 3] and Ruby's Refinements have been proposed. They introduce modules to confine class extensions. Selector namespaces and Refinements allow changing the behavior of methods only in a specific lexical scope, but they cannot change the behavior of methods indirectly called. Classboxes allows us to change the behavior of indirectly called methods (called the *local rebinding* property). Classboxes are useful to create a customized version of an existing library, for example, to create the Swing library from the AWT library of Java. The change is confined within a classbox but not effective out of the classbox. However, it is not possible to address conflicts when a classbox imports other classboxes and they provide conflicting class extensions.

We introduce a new module system named *method shelters* to avoid conflicts among class extensions while addressing the limitations of the previous proposals. A method shelter is a module for restricting a scope of method definitions. By appropriately controlling a scope of every method (re)definitions, programmers can avoid unanticipated conflicts. A method shelter provides:

AOSD'12,   March 25-30, 2012, Potsdam, Germany.
Copyright © 2012 ACM 978-1-4503-1092-5/12/03...$10.00

1. a scope of method definitions,

2. the ability to import methods defined in other method shelters,

3. the ability to redefine a method defined in an imported method shelter,

4. the ability to protect methods from redefinition and

5. no ambiguity with respect to method lookup.

The main contributions of this paper are: (i) the model of method shelters, (ii) the lookup algorithm written in Scheme and (iii) a proof-of-concept implementation for Ruby with performance benchmarks. According to our benchmarks, overheads due to method shelters are acceptable and one benchmark showed that method shelters may even improve execution performance.

In the rest of this paper, Section 2 presents motivating examples and the problem in the existing systems. In Section 3 we illustrate the model and lookup algorithm of method shelters. Section 4 shows our proof-of-concept implementation on the Ruby virtual machine. In Section 5 we show that method shelters and our implementation can be used to avoid conflicts among class extensions. In Section 6 we discuss the performance of method shelters. Section 7 describes related work. Section 8 concludes this paper.

2. Motivation: class extensions and method conflict

Subclassing and inheritance are popular techniques to extend a program in object-oriented programming languages. Subclassing allows programmers to create a new class with different behavior while partly reusing the implementation of its super class. However it cannot redefine an existing class. Class extensions and open classes are proposals to enable that. They are useful when programmers want to reuse a *whole* program (or framework) and partly customize it to build new software as we mentioned in Section 2.1 of [6].

2.1 Usage of class extensions

Class extensions are frequently used in Ruby[14]. For example, a number of use cases are found in Ruby on Rails[13]. We below show typical usage of class extensions in Ruby.

Convenient methods Class extensions are used to add convenient methods to core classes: Integer, String, Array and so on. For example, in Ruby on Rails, a suite of bytes methods are added to Numeric class, which is a super class of Integer and Float classes. The method call "n.kilobytes" (where n is a number) returns $n \times 1024$ and "n.megabytes" returns $n \times 1024^2$. These bytes methods are useful when writing a program that handles file sizes. Programmers' intentions will be clear.

Another example is sum method. Ruby on Rails also adds sum method to Enumerable module, which is a mixin [5] module for list-like classes. This method computes the sum of elements in an Enumerable object. This method is simple and useful although the Ruby's standard library does not provide it. By using class extensions, third party libraries such as Ruby on Rails can easily add convenient methods.

Operator redefinition In Ruby, several operators, such as +, -, * and /, are normal methods. Thus anyone can redefine them.

Division of integers in Ruby returns an integer by default, for example, 1/2 returns 0. On the other hand, the Ruby's standard library mathn redefines it. Once you load this library, division of integers returns a rational. 1/2 returns a Rational object that represents $\frac{1}{2}$. This library makes it possible to describe mathematical expressions with normal notations.

Tree traversal Class extensions simplify tree traversal. If you naively write traversal code separately from tree-node classes, the code includes runtime type checking and it must be modified when a new node class is added. Although the code following the Visitor pattern is more extensible, all node classes must have methods for the Visitor pattern in advance. The Visitor pattern is not applicable to a tree if the node classes do not conform the Visitor pattern or they are not modifiable since a third-party library provides them.

If class extensions are available, you can add methods for traversal to node classes on demand. For example, suppose that a tree consists of Integer and Array and you want to sum up every integer elements in a tree. You only have to write the following code

```
1   class Integer
2     def sum_tree
3       self
4     end
5   end
6
7   class Array
8     def sum_tree
9       result=0
10      for child in self
11        result += child.sum_tree
12      end
13      result
14    end
15  end
```

The Visitor pattern is not required to traverse trees if you have class extensions. The code including runtime type checking is not needed.

Serialization libraries for Ruby often use this technique. For example, a JSON [7] library for Ruby adds to_json method to core classes, such as Integer, String, Array and Hash. A JSON serializer uses this method to traverse a tree made by core classes and dump a JSON file.

Monkey patching When a third-party library has a bug, class extensions allow programmers to patch and fix it. A method that includes a bug can be replaced with a correct implementation of that method. Programmers do not have to directly modify the source code of the library. This technique is known as *monkey patching*.

2.2 A problem: method conflicts

Redefinition of a method by a class extension is visible from all classes. If more than one libraries redefine a method with the same name in the same class, those redefinitions conflict with each other. In Ruby, if there are multiple definitions, only the definition loaded last is made effective. Thus, which method definition is executed when the method is called depends on the order of loading classes and libraries. A library including class extensions implies a risk that it crashes other libraries calling the methods that those class extensions redefines.

This is a real problem in Ruby. If you load mathn library, all integer division results in a rational number. However, almost all programs in Ruby expect it results in an integer. Except writing small scripts, programmers have to treat this library with special care.

Library developers can avoid method conflicts to a certain degree by introducing a naming convention. If all method names include a unique prefix or suffix, a risk of conflicts is decreased against other libraries. This approach avoids conflicts of added methods but it is not suitable for method redefinition. Moreover, this approach may degrade the usability of a library.

2.3 Classboxes and Ruby's Refinements

To address the problem of conflicting method definitions, several module systems have been proposed. *Classboxes*[3] and *Classbox/J*[2] provide a module named a *classbox*. Classboxes allow programmers to write class extensions to modify a library while not affecting other application programs using that library. A classbox can import a class from another classbox and it can redefine a method of the imported class. The redefinition is visible from not only that importing classbox but also the methods of the classes imported by that classbox. Hence a classbox can override the behavior of its imported classbox; this property is called *local rebinding* in the literature.

Although a classbox hides method definitions from the outside[1], it exposes them to classboxes importing it. Thus, if a classbox imports classes from other classboxes and those classes contain conflicting method definitions, the problem occurs. Figure 1 shows an example of the problem. *CB0* is a classbox that provides Integer class and its div method returning an integer. Classbox *CB1* provides List class with avg method. To calculate an average, *CB1* imports Integer class from *CB0* and redefines div method to return a rational number. Since avg method calls div method internally, it returns an average of elements by a rational number. *CB2* imports List from *CB1* to calculate an average, and imports

---

[1] As far as we know, the original design of classboxes does not provide a mechanism for communicating between a class box and its outside. A whole application program has to run in a classbox.

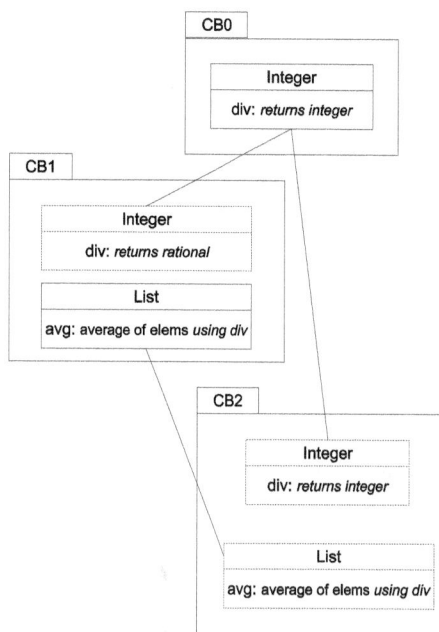

Figure 1. A problem in classboxes

Integer from *CB0* to perform *integer* division. Although the programmer of *CB2* does not know *CB1* internally modifies Integer class, she will expect that avg method returns a rational number. However, Integer from *CB0* overwrites the whole Integer class including the definition of div method due to the local rebinding property. Thus, in *CB2*, avg returns not a rational but an integer number since the two definitions of div conflict in *CB2* and the conflict resolution does not fit the programmer's anticipation.

To address the problem of conflicting method definitions, another approach named *Refinements* were proposed for Ruby in the *ruby-core* mailing list. Refinements make class extensions effective only when the (re)defined methods are directly called within a specific lexical scope. Figure 2 shows a sample code for Refinements. A block starting with refine (line 2) defines class extensions. In the example, the / operator for Fixnum is redefined to return a rational number. Then, the using declaration makes class extensions effective within the current lexical scope. For example, using at line 10 makes the class extensions in MathN effective and hence a call to the / operator at line 12 executes the definition in MathN instead of one in the standard library. However, the class extension in MathN is effective only within the lexical scope from line 9 to 14. If foo method at line 11 calls another method out of this scope and it calls the / operator, then the definition in MathN is not executed. Refinements do not preserve the local rebinding property.

3. Method Shelters

We propose a new module system called *method shelters* to address conflicts among class extensions. Our idea is to

```
1   module MathN
2     refine Fixnum do
3       def /(other)
4         Rational(self,other)
5       end
6     end
7   end
8
9   class Foo
10    using MathN
11    def foo()
12      p(1 / 2)
13    end
14  end
15
16  f = Foo.new
17  f.foo # prints "(1/2)"
18  p(1 / 2) # prints "0"
```

Figure 2. Example of Ruby's *Refinements*

make some class extensions effective only within the module defining them and ones imported by that module. We also protect some class extensions from accidental overriding by outer modules, which directly/indirectly import that module. Thus, if programmers carefully control the scope of class extensions, unexpected conflicts among class extensions are avoidable.

We designed method shelters to provide the local rebinding property but make conflicts avoidable to a certain degree. On the other hand, the refinements of Ruby does not provide the local rebinding property. Classboxes provide it but may cause conflicts among class extensions if multiple versions of class extensions are used in an importing chain.

3.1 Overview

A method shelter, which is a unit of our module system, consists of two *chambers*: an *exposed* chamber and a *hidden* chamber. A chamber contains *import* declarations and method definitions. An import declaration imports another method shelter. A method definition may define a new method added to an existing class and it may redefine an existing method in an existing class.

Figure 3 shows a code sample in Ruby. It is a solution of the problem mentioned in Figure 1. In the code in Figure 3, three method shelters CoreShelter, AverageShelter, and ClientShelter are defined. CoreShelter has an Integer#div method in its exposed chamber. CoreShelter is imported by ClientShelter in its exposed chamber. Importing another method shelter in an exposed chamber is called *exposedly importing*.

If only exposed chambers are used, method shelters are similar to classboxes. The local rebinding property is preserved. The methods in exposed chambers are executed as if they all were in the exposed chamber of the outermost or root method shelter, which exposedly imports their method shelters directly or indirectly. If there are multiple definitions of

```
1   shelter :CoreShelter do
2     class Integer
3       def div(x)
4         # <returns integer result>
5       end
6     end
7   end
8
9   shelter :AverageShelter do
10    class Array
11      def avg
12        s = self.sum
13        return s.div(self.size) # rational version is called
14      end
15    end
16
17    hide
18    import :CoreShelter
19    class Integer
20      def div(x)
21        # <returns rational result>
22      end
23    end
24  end
25
26  shelter :ClientShelter do
27    import :Core
28    import :AverageShelter
29    def calc
30      [1,2,3,4].avg # returns "(5/2)"
31      5.div(2) # returns "2"
32    end
33  end
```

Figure 3. Code sample (a solution of the problem in Figure 1)

the same method m, the method definition of the outermost method shelter S is selected, and other method definitions of m in method shelters imported from S are overridden. Thus, if a method calls another method in the same method shelter, the call selects and executes a different definition of that method in an outer method shelter. Programmers must consider that a method in an exposed chamber may be redefined by another method shelter importing it.

On the other hand, method definitions in a hidden chamber are not visible from the outside. Furthermore, they are never redefined by another method shelter importing them. In Figure 3, AverageShelter has a hidden chamber (below line 17), which contains another Integer#div method. It is visible within AverageShelter but not from ClientShelter, which imports AverageShelter. Thus a call to div at line 31 in ClientShelter never selects the definition in AverageShelter whereas a call to div at line 13 in the exposed chamber of AverageShelter selects the definition at line 20 in the hidden chamber of AverageShelter. The problem in Figure 1 does not happen. However, hidden chambers have trade-off. A method defined in a hidden chamber cannot be redefined even if it has a bug and the user wants to fix it by monkey patching. The concept of exposed and hidden chambers are

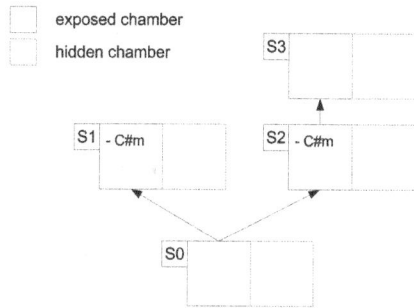

Figure 4. Ambiguous methods in a method shelter

similar to public/private methods in OOP languages. However method shelters are orthogonal to the public/private access control. We decided to use exposed and hidden as keywords to avoid misunderstanding.

Importing another method shelter in a hidden chamber is called *hiddenly* importing. The methods imported in a hidden chamber are visible only within the method shelter importing them, both its exposed and imported chambers. Note that those methods are imported only from an exposed chamber since methods in a hidden chamber are not visible from the outside. The methods imported in the hidden chamber of a method shelter S are not visible from other method shelters importing S.

The local rebinding property is preserved in a method shelter hiddenly imported. A method imported in a hidden chamber may be redefined in that hidden chamber. A hidden chamber is used to import and redefine several classes freely for local use only.

Our method-shelter system does not allow ambiguity with respect to method lookup. For example, in Figure 4, a method shelter S0 imports S1 and S2. Since both S1 and S2 have a method named m in C class, a call to C#m in the method shelter S0 is ambiguous and hence raises an error. It was possible to design the system so that such ambiguity can be implicitly resolved by introducing some precedence rules, for example, the last imported method shelter has the highest precedence. However, we did not adopt such implicit ambiguity resolution since we believe it will confuse programmers.

Global methods. We call methods (re)defined not within a method shelter *global methods*. A method in a method shelter can call a global method. Our module system considers that all global methods are contained in some anonymous method shelter. This method shelter is implicitly exposedly-imported by the method shelter that contains a caller method to a global method. Thus, the global methods can call methods in the exposed chamber where the caller method is defined. A redefinition of a method in that chamber is also effective when a global method calls it. On the other hand, the methods in the hidden chambers of the caller's method shelter are not visible from the global methods. If a global

method calls another global method, these two methods can access the same shelters. For example, if a global method m0 is called from a method in a shelter S and m0 calls a global method m1, then m1 can call the same set of methods in the exposed chamber of S that m0 can call.

Entry point. Since a method in a method shelter is not visible from the outside, we need a special mechanism to call it at the beginning. In other words, we have to jump into a method shelter from normal execution contexts. We call that method shelter *an entry point*, which is the outermost method shelter in the import chain. An appropriate strategy depends on the base language:

- define a main function or method in a method shelter if the base language has it. The method shelter containing a main function is an entry point. A main function is a function that is first executed when a program starts.

- define a special code block specifying a method shelter. The code block is executed as if it existed within that method shelter. The entry point is that method shelter. Our ruby prototype adopts this strategy since Ruby does not have a main function like other scripting languages.

Note that in our programming model, every library, framework and application program is in a separate method shelter. The method shelter of an application program imports other method shelters of libraries and frameworks. Hence, having an entry point is natural.

3.2 Lookup semantics

In this section, we present the semantics of method shelters by showing its method lookup algorithm.

3.2.1 Method shelter tree

Method shelters can be imported from other method shelters. Hence the import relation among shelters constructs a directed graph. For the sake of presentation, we first transform this graph into a tree. We will use this tree to describe where we start looking up a method. This transformation is also used in our implementation in Section 4 for performance reason.

Figure 5 shows an example, where method shelter A imports B and C, and B imports C. We do not have to distinguish a type of importing, exposedly or hiddenly, in this transformation. If a method shelter (C in the example) is imported by multiple different method shelters, the node of that imported method shelter C is duplicated and the importing method shelters B and A import a different node of C (Figure 6). The resulting graph after this transformation is a tree, where every (node of a) method shelter is imported by at most one method shelter, that is, every node has at most one parent. We use this property of the tree for describing the algorithm of method lookup. Although this transformation does not work if import relations make a cycle, method shel-

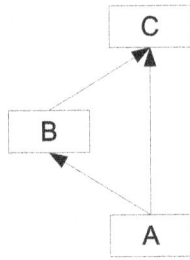

Figure 5. An example of an import graph of method shelters

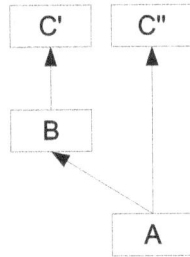

Figure 6. A method shelter tree reconstructed from Figure 5

```
1  (define (lookup context class methodname)
2    (let ((method (lookup-method-of-class context class
                      methodname)))
3      (cond
4        (method method)
5        ((superclass class) (lookup context (superclass class)
                              methodname))
6        (else (error "no␣method␣error" class name)))))
7
8  (define (lookup-method-of-class context class methodname)
9    (let ((hidden-method (lookup-hidden context class
                            methodname)))
10     (if hidden-method
11         hidden-method
12         (let* ((source-chamber (find-source-chamber context))
13                (source-node (node-of-chamber source-))
14                (exposed-method
15                  (if (is-exposed? chamber)
16                      (lookup-exposed source-node class
                                        methodname)
17                      (lookup-hidden source-node class
                                        methodname))))
18           (if exposed-method
19               exposed-method
20               (lookup-global node class name))))))))
```

Figure 7. Method lookup functions of method shelters

```
1  (define (hidden-imported? node)
2    <Is the given node is hidden-imported from parent?>)
3  (define (exposed-imported? node)
4    <Is the given node is exposed-imported from parent>)
5
6  (define (find-source-chamber node)
7    (cond
8      ((not (parent-node node)) (list node 'exposed))
9      ((hidden-imported? node) (list (parent-node node) 'hidden))
10     ((exposed-imported? node) (find-source-chamber (
                                   parent-node node)))
11   ))
```

Figure 8. Definition of source-node and source-chamber

ters prohibit cyclic importing. If cyclic importing is detected, this graph-to-tree transformation raises an error.

Our semantics currently supposes that method shelters are immutable. If importing relations of method shelters are changed at run time, a method shelter tree should be reconstructed.

3.2.2 The lookup algorithm

We show the algorithm for looking up a method in a method shelter. Figure 7 lists the algorithm written in Scheme. lookup is the main function. It takes three arguments: *context*, *methodname* and *class*. *methodname* and *class* are the name of a called method and the class of the receiver object. *context* is a node in the tree of method shelters mentioned above. It indicates the method shelter that contains the caller method, which is currently running and attempts to call the method on the receiver object. The result of the method lookup depends on where the caller method is located.

lookup first tries to find a method in a given *class* by calling lookup-method-of-class. If a method is not found there, then lookup tries to find a method in the super class. Note that Ruby adopts single inheritance. lookup and lookup-method-of-class return a pair of the found method and the tree node of the method shelter containing that method, which will be implicitly passed to the found method for further method lookup.

lookup-method-of-class looks up a method in method shelters. First, it looks up the hidden chamber of the given method shelter node. If the method is found in that chamber, the found method is returned. If not found, it tries to look up a method again in the subtree rooted at the *source chamber*.

Methods in the given shelter's exposed-side are looked up from the source chamber. The root chamber or hidden chambers which imports the given node can be the source chamber. The one nearest to the given shelter is selected as the source chamber. Figure 8 shows the find-source-chamber function that computes the the source chamber.

Figure 9 shows an example. Suppose that $S0$ exposedly imports $S1$, $S1$ exposedly imports $S2$, and $S1$ also hiddenly imports $S3$. Then the source chamber of $S0$, $S1$ and $S2$ is the exposed chamber of $S0$. Note that $S0$ is the method shelter at the entry point. The source chamber of $S3$ is the hidden chamber of $S1$ since $S3$ is hiddenly imported.

Figure 10 shows the definitions of lookup-exposed, lookup-hidden, and lookup-global functions used in lookup-method-of-class. lookup-exposed first searches the exposed chamber of the given node. If a method is found, the function returns

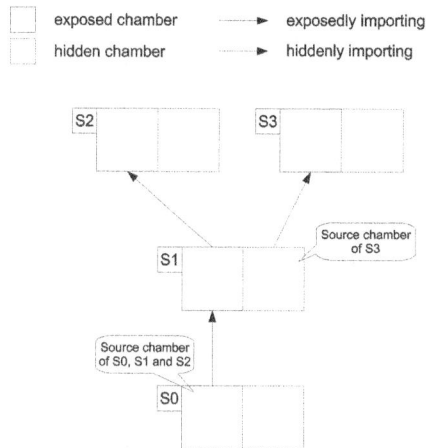

Figure 9. An example of source-node and source-chamber

```
1   (define (lookup−exposed node class name)
2    (if (exposed−method−table−exists? node class name)
3        (list node
4              (exposed−method−table−get node class name))
5        (filter−methods class name
6          (map (lambda (e) (lookup−exposed e class name))
7               (exposedly−importings node)))))
8
9   (define (lookup−hidden node class name)
10   (if (hidden−method−table−exists? node class name)
11       (list node
12             (hidden−method−table−get node class name))
13       (filter−methods class name
14         (map (lambda (e) (lookup−exposed e class name))
15              (hiddenly−importings node)))))
16
17  (define (lookup−global node class name)
18   (if (global−method−table−exists? class name)
19      (list <a node which is exposely imported by the given node>
20           (global−method−table−get table name))
21     #f))
```

Figure 10. Definition of lookup-exposed and lookup-hidden

a pair of the given node and the found method body. Otherwise, the function recursively calls itself on all the nodes of the subtree rooted at the given node although the nodes hiddenly imported are excluded from the search space. Then the function makes a list of the values returned by the recursive calls. The list is processed by filter-methods, which returns an element if the list contains only one element. filter-methods raises an error if the list contains multiple elements since the method to look up is ambiguous. lookup-hidden is similar. It first searches the hidden chamber of the given node and then the subtree rooted at the given node. It searches only the nodes exposely imported by the given node directly or indirectly. Finally, lookup-global searches the global method table. If it finds a method, it returns a pair of a method-shelter node and the body of the method found. This method-shelter node represents a method shelter that corresponds to the global method table and it is directly imported by the node given to lookup-global.

4. A proof-of-concept implementation

We made a proof-of-concept implementation [2] of method shelters in Ruby since Ruby already has a class extensions feature and its source code is publicly available. We modified the virtual machine of Ruby 1.9.2.

Since Ruby has already powerful expressiveness, we decided not to extend Ruby's syntax. The syntax of method shelters is based on Ruby's syntax. Figure 11 shows a sample code for illustrating method shelters' syntax. Although shelter looks like a keyword, it is a method name. "shelter" method takes shelter's name and a block. ":S2" represents a symbol S2. "do ... end" represents a block. The methods defined in the block are contained in the method shelter. By default, those methods belong to an exposed chamber. On the other hand, the methods defined after a call to hide method

(at line 15) belong to a hidden chamber. To import another method shelter, call import method. Its argument is a method shelter's name. If import method is called after hide method, the imported shelter is hiddenly imported and hence belongs to a hidden chamber.

The method shelter at the entry point is specified by shelter_eval method. For example, the line 24 and 25 in Figure 11 is executed within the contexts of the method shelter S0.

4.1 Implementation details

When a shelter method is called, we create a shelter object. A shelter object consists of five members: its name, a list of exposely imported shelters, a list of hiddenly-imported shelters, an exposed method table and a hidden method table. When a method is defined in a method shelter, its method name is converted to a unique name. The mapping between the original method name and the converted one is recorded in the shelter object's method table. At method lookup, the table of converted method names is searched first.

As mentioned in Section 3.2, the method lookup algorithm needs a current node in a method-shelter tree representing import relations. To maintain a current node, we added a new member to the stack frame of the Ruby VM. When shelter_eval method is called, a method shelter tree is constructed from the specified method shelter and the root node of the tree is set to the stack frame of the block.

4.2 Optimization

We implemented a few optimization techniques for method shelters to improve execution performance. First, we added a method cache to every node of a method-shelter tree. It records a mapping from a pair of a class name and a method

---

[2] The source code is available at
http://github.com/flexfrank/ruby_with_method_shelters

```
1  shelter :S2 do
2    class Integer
3      def inc(n)
4        self + n
5      end
6    end
7  end
8
9  shelter :S1 do
10   class Integer
11     def inc10
12       self.inc(10)
13     end
14   end
15   hide
16   import :S2
17 end
18
19 shelter :S0 do
20   import :S1
21 end
22
23 shelter_eval :S0 do
24   p(1.inc10) # prints 11
25   p(1.inc(1)) # error: method is not found
26 end
```

Figure 11. The syntax of method shelters

```
1  shelter :ActiveSupportNumericTime do
2    class Numeric
3      # ** snip **
4
5      def days
6        ActiveSupport::Duration.new(self * 24.hours, [[:days, self]])
7      end
8      alias :day :days
9
10     # ** snip **
11   end
12 end
```

Figure 12. The time-related methods we defined in a method shelter

```
1  shelter :DateControllerShelter do
2    class DateController < ApplicationController
3      def days_ago
4        @text=params[:id].to_i.days.ago
5      end
6    end
7
8    hide
9    import :ActiveSupportNumericTime
10 end
```

Figure 13. A client code of Ruby on Rails

name to a pair of a method entry and the tree node where the method is found. A method entry is a primitive data structure for calling a method in the Ruby VM. A cache entry is updated at method lookup. This cache reduces the overhead of method lookup in particular when an import chain is long.

Since method shelters change the algorithm of method lookup, we also modified the implementation of the inline cache of the Ruby VM. The modified implementation records a current node of a method-shelter tree.

4.3 Compatibility

Our implementation keeps the compatibility with the original Ruby. A normal Ruby program written without method shelters can run on our modified Ruby interpreter. Although we added an additional member to a stack frame of the Ruby VM, this member for maintaining a current node of a method shelter tree is set to NULL at initialization. If the current node is NULL, the method lookup uses the original algorithm for Ruby.

5. Applications

We below illustrate several examples of the use of method shelters.

5.1 Convenient methods in Ruby on Rails

The first example is Ruby on Rails. The ActiveSupport library, which is part of Ruby on Rails, provides a number of convenient methods for Ruby's core classes. Among those methods, we moved time-related methods in the Numeric class into a method shelter. ActiveSupport adds minutes, hour and days methods to Numeric class. These methods return Duration objects representing time. They simplify writing code for calculating time. For example,

```
10.minutes.ago
```

returns Time object representing the time 10 minutes before the current time.

We can move the definitions of these methods into a method shelter. Figure 12 is a code snippet of the method shelter containing these methods. Figure 13 shows a controller class for Ruby on Rails. Like a servlet in Java, it is executed when a corresponding web page is accessed by a web browser. This controller class is in a method shelter, which hiddenly imports ActiveSupportNumericTime. Thus, days method in Figure 12 is available only in this controller class whereas it is not in the rest of the program. Note that days method is not visible even in method shelters importing the method shelter in Figure 13. To call days, method shelters must import ActiveSupportNumericTime again within the method shelters.

5.2 Operator redefinition

We mentioned a problem of conflicting redefinition of the "/" operator in Section 2.3. The sketch of the solution with method shelters was already presented in Figure 3.

Figure 14 shows a realistic version of the code in Figure 3. In Ruby, numbers are represented by Fixnum objects and "/"

```
1   shelter :MathNShelter do
2     class Fixnum # fixed size integer in Ruby
3       def /(x)
4         Rational(self,x)
5       end
6     end
7   end
8
9   shelter :AverageShelter do
10    class Array
11      def avg
12        sum = self.inject(0){|r,i|r+i}
13        sum / self.size
14      end
15    end
16    hide
17    import :MathNShelter
18  end
19
20  shelter :ClientShelter do
21    import :AverageShelter
22
23    def calc
24      p([1,2,3,4,5,6,7,8,9,10].avg) # prints "(11/2)"
25      p(55/10) # prints 5
26    end
27  end
28
29  shelter_eval :ClientShelter do
30    calc
31  end
```

Figure 14. The code that redefines "/" methods in method shelters

method is defined in this class. Since the original division method "/" of Fixnum is built in, this code does not include CoreShelter shown in Figure 3. The "/" method is redefined in MathNShelter instead of AverageShelter. This simulates Ruby's "mathn" library, which is a separate library providing the redefined "/" method.

Since MathNShelter is hiddenly imported by a method shelter AverageShelter, avg method in Array returns a rational value. The "/" operator at line 13 executes the definition in MathNShelter method shelter. A method shelter ClientShelter can safely import AverageShelter and call avg method without being aware of MathNShelter. Note that since Fixnum is a class in the standard library, calc method can execute the "/" operator at line 25 without explicitly importing Fixnum class. The "/" operator here returns an integer.

Since Ruby is a scripting language, the lines from 28 to 30 compose the code running first when this program is invoked. This "main function" is executed in ClientShelter method shelter.

5.3 Protecting optimized methods

The Ruby VM optimizes several special methods including arithmetic operators. When one of the special methods is called and it is not redefined by the users, the VM directly

performs its operation instead of executing that method. The VM manages for every operator a flag indicating whether or not the special methods are redefined. The receiver class is not considered for a reason of performance trade-off. Thus, if "+" operator for Integer is redefined by the users, the VM recognizes all "+" operators including one for Float are also redefined and makes them unoptimized. Redefining a single special method may cause serious performance overhead.

If such a special method is redefined in a method shelter, the VM can directly perform the optimized operation when it is out of that method shelter. Our implementation of method shelters manages the flags per method shelter. Hence, if a method shelter S redefines a special method in a hidden chamber, that redefinition is not visible from other method shelters importing S and the VM performs optimized operations for special methods in these method shelters. Otherwise, if a method shelter S_1 redefines a special method in an exposed chamber and another method shelter S_2 hiddenly imports S_1 for reusing the redefinition, then the redefinition is not visible from method shelters importing S_2, which are ones indirectly importing S_1. The VM performs optimized operations in these method shelters.

5.4 Private instance variables

In Ruby, private instance variables are not available. A method shelter can be used to define private instance variables visible only within the method shelter.

Figure 15 shows the code for defining getter and setter methods for accessing an instance variable with a newly generated unique name. When shelter_accessor method is called, accessor methods with the given name are defined. Note that in Ruby an instance variable is automatically created when it is first used. The code in Figure 15 does not use method shelters but the reflection capability of Ruby. get_var_name_for_current_shelter returns a unique name for the given name and the caller's method shelter. If the name and the shelter are same it returns the same variable name.

Figure 16 shows the client code. Two method shelters S0 and S1 add accessor methods to Object class. Although both the names of the added instance variables are counter, they access different instance variables. The methods defined by a call to shelter_accessor in different method shelters are distinct.

6. Performance

In this section, we discuss the performance of our prototype implementation of method shelters. Our implementation is based on Ruby 1.9.2 [3]. We compare it with the original implementation of Ruby 1.9.2. We ran our benchmark programs on Mac OS X 10.6 with 2.54GHz Intel Core 2 Duo processor and 4GB memory.

---

[3] The revision number of Ruby's subversion repository is 30579

```
1  class Module
2    def shelter_accessor(name)
3      define_method name do
4        ivname= get_var_name_for_current_shelter(name)
5        self.instance_variable_get(ivname)
6      end
7
8      define_method (name.to_s+"=").to_sym do|val|
9        ivname= get_var_name_for_current_shelter(name)
10       self.instance_variable_set(ivname,val)
11     end
12   end
13 end
```

Figure 15. The code for defining getter and setter methods to access a private instance variable

```
1  shelter :S0 do
2    class Object
3      shelter_accessor :counter
4    end
5  end
6  shelter :S1 do
7    class Object
8      shelter_accessor :counter
9    end
10 end
11
12 o=Object.new
13 shelter_eval :S0 do
14   o.counter=0
15   p o.counter #prints 0
16 end
17 shelter_eval :S1 do
18   p o.counter #prints nil
19   o.counter=1
20   p o.counter #prints 1
21 end
22 shelter_eval :S0 do
23   p o.counter #prints 0
24 end
```

Figure 16. The client code using accessor methods to a private instance variable

6.1 Micro benchmark

First, to measure an overhead of method lookup, we ran a program that calls a method with an empty body. The benchmark program calls an empty method 10,000,000 times. We prepared five environments: the original Ruby VM, our modified VM without method shelters, our VM with one method shelter and our VM with five method shelters imported. The benchmark code with five method shelters is shown in Figure 17. We ran the benchmark programs 1,000 times on each environment.

Table 1 shows the results. When method shelters are not used, our VM runs 10% slower than the original VM. This is because our VM must check whether a method shelter is passed or not on method lookup. When one method shelter

```
1  shelter :S0 do
2    def a
3    end
4  end
5  shelter :S1 do import :S0 end
6  shelter :S2 do import :S1 end
7  shelter :S3 do import :S2 end
8  shelter :S4 do import :S3 end
9
10 shelter_eval :S4 do
11   10000000.times do
12     a
13   end
14 end
```

Figure 17. The benchmark program that calls an empty method under five method shelters

	Avg. time (s)	SD[4]
On the original VM	1.430	0.010
On our VM without method shelters	1.575	0.018
With 1 method shelter	1.476	0.013
With 5 method shelters	1.493	0.018

Table 1. Execution time of empty method (1,000 tries)

	Avg. time (s)	SD
On the original VM	1.000	0.005
On our VM without method shelters	1.141	0.004
With 1 method shelter	1.180	0.036
With 5 method shelters	1.192	0.049

Table 2. Execution time of fib(33) (1,000 trials)

is used, the overhead is about 3%. Method shelters make method lookup faster, this is due to method caches that we added. When five method shelters are used, it works with comparative speed to one method shelter. This result is also due to the caches.

We also measured execution time of the Fibonacci function under the same environments as above. Table 2 lists the results. In this case the overhead of our VM is about 14% and with method shelters is 18% to 19%.

6.2 tDiary

To measure the performance of method shelters on a real application, we applied method shelters to *tDiary* [15], a web-based diary system written in Ruby. We used tDiary 3.0.1 for this benchmark. tDiary 3.0.1 redefines three methods in String class: to_a, each and method_missing. We redefined these three methods in a method shelter and ran the main code of tDiary in a method shelter importing it. We ran tDiary on Apache 2.2.17 with CGI and measured response time

---
[4] standard deviation

140

	Avg. time (ms)	SD
On the original VM	704	7.1
On our VM without method shelters	704	6.6
With method shelters	627	6.5

Table 3. Response time of tDiary (300 trials)

by ApacheBench. For comparison, we used three versions of tDiaries: tDiary without method shelters on the original Ruby VM, without method shelters on our Ruby VM and with method shelters on our Ruby VM. We accessed the top page of each diary 300 times.

Table 3 lists the results. This results show that our modified VM does not impact performance of existing applications when method shelters are not used. It also indicates method shelters improve the execution speed. This is due to Ruby VM's optimizations that we mentioned in Section 5.3. method_missing, which we confined into a method shelter, is the one of special methods. method_missing is a hook method that is called when an undefined method is called. If method_missing is not redefined, the VM can skip a call to it since the default definition is empty. In this benchmark, we redefined method_missing for String in a method shelter. Hence this redefinition does not affect the performance of the code out of that method shelter. On the other hand, tDiary running on the original Ruby VM gets performance penalties due to the redefinition of method_missing. This is why method shelters improved the execution performance of this benchmark test.

6.3 Ruby on Rails

We applied method shelters to Ruby on Rails in Section 5.1. We measured the performance of a Ruby on Rails application with method shelters. Figure 18 is a benchmark program we used. index method is an action method, which calculates time and accesses a database once. We used SQLite 3.6.12 for a database engine. The version of Ruby on Rails is 3.0.7. We ran this application on WEBrick, a web server written in Ruby. We requested the action 1,000 times through ApacheBench and measured response time.

Table 4 lists the results in *development environment*. In this environment, user-defined application classes are reloaded per request. In this case, method shelters made the execution performance about 50% slower. Table 5 lists the results in *production environment*, in which application classes are not reloaded per request. In this environment, the overhead is less than 4%. This difference between two environments result from the hit ratio of method caches. In the development environment, whenever classes are reloaded, the VM invalidates method caches for method shelters. This implies serious performance penalties.

Table 6 lists the hit ratio of method caches in method shelters after warming-up. In the production environment, over 90% and 100% of lookups hit inline method cache.

```
1  class TestController < ApplicationController
2    def index
3      @text="#{(1.day.ago + 1.day)}"
4      @accesses=Access.order("id desc").limit(10).find_all.to_a.
         inspect
5    end
6  end
```

Figure 18. The benchmark program for Ruby on Rail

	Avg. time (ms)	SD
On the original VM	53.131	14.7
On our VM without method shelters	53.341	14.7
With method shelters	78.871	16.2

Table 4. Response time of Rails application (1,000 trials, development env.)

	Avg. time (ms)	SD
On the original VM	10.865	7.7
On our VM without method shelters	11.049	7.8
With method shelters	11.296	7.7

Table 5. Response time of Rails application (1,000 trials, production env.)

	development	production
Inline cache hit (%)	58.35	92.55
Total cache hit (%)	74.0	100.0

Table 6. Cache hit ratios of Rails application (1,000 trials, production env.)

In the development environment, less than 75% hit inline caches. This result indicates that method shelter is not so slow when method caches are appropriately filled.

7. Related work

We have already mentioned several related languages and mechanisms. This section presents other related work.

Java class loader. Since every Java class loader makes a separate name space, a different class loader can load a differently declared class with the same name. However, an instance of that class cannot be passed into the name spaces constructed by other class loaders while method shelters allow exchanging any instance among shelters.

Selector Namespaces. The concept of *selector namespaces* was introduced by Modular Smalltalk [17]. Selector namespaces allow scoped class extensions hence method conflicts can be resolved to a certain degree. However, they do not preserve the local rebinding property. In selector namespaces, you can add new methods to existing classes but cannot redefine existing methods.

Open Classes. *MultiJava* [11] introduces *open classes* and *multiple dispatch* into Java. Open classes allow you to add new methods to existing classes although redefining a method is not allowed. The added methods are available only within a compilation unit that explicitly imports them. Here, a compilation unit is a module lexically specified.

Context-oriented programming. *Context-oriented programming* languages [9] allows multiple definitions of a method for the same class. Which definitions are executed at a method call depends on the runtime contexts. On the other hand, in method shelters, it depends on not the runtime contexts but the static contexts, which are static relations among modules with respect to importing. Although we could make these relations dynamically changeable according to the runtime contexts, that is not necessarily required.

Open modules. Since aspect-oriented programming (AOP) also allows class extensions, several approaches proposed in the contexts of AOP are included in the related work. For example, *Open modules* [1, 12] are modules for AOP; they expose only selected join points to the outside. Other join points are hidden in the modules. The exposed join points correspond to method definitions, which are newly added to existing classes, in an exposed chamber while the hidden join points correspond to ones in a hidden chamber. However, open modules do not control the visibility of advices, which correspond to method redefinitions, which modify an existing method, in method shelters.

Type classes. Type classes [16] in functional programming languages also provide a way to add methods or generic functions to existing types. Although type classes help extension of software, they do not support local rebinding property. Method shelters target programming languages with a construct supporting it.

8. Conclusion

We propose method shelters to address conflicts among class extensions. Each method shelter consists of exposed and hidden chambers. While methods defined in an exposed chamber are visible from method shelters that import it, methods in a hidden chamber are visible only from the same method shelter. We provide hidden chambers for defining class extensions only for internal use. Hence, if programmers carefully put class extensions in an appropriate chamber, unanticipated conflicts will be avoidable. When updating a method, programmers must preserve the backward compatibility if the method is in an exposed chamber. If programmers want to keep freedom for future updates, methods must be in a hidden chamber and other method shelters internally used must be hiddenly imported in a hidden chamber.

We presented the lookup algorithm for method shelters and showed a prototype implementation of method shelters

on the Ruby virtual machine. According to our benchmarks, general overheads due to method shelters are acceptable. Furthermore, one benchmark revealed that method shelters may even help performance optimization and boost the execution speed.

References

[1] J. Aldrich. Open modules: Modular reasoning about advice. In *ECOOP '05*, pages 144–168, 2005.

[2] A. Bergel, S. Ducasse, and O. Nierstrasz. Classbox/j: controlling the scope of change in java. In *OOPSLA '05*, pages 177–189. ACM, 2005.

[3] A. Bergel, S. Ducasse, O. Nierstrasz, and R. Wuyts. Classboxes: Controlling visibility of class extensions. In *Computer Languages, Systems and Structures*, 2005.

[4] D. G. Bobrow, L. G. DeMichiel, R. P. Gabriel, S. E. Keene, G. Kiczales, and D. A. Moon. Common lisp object system specification. *SIGPLAN Not.*, 23:1–142, September 1988.

[5] G. Bracha and W. Cook. Mixin-based inheritance. In *OOPSLA/ECOOP '90*, pages 303–311. ACM, 1990.

[6] S. Chiba, A. Igarashi, and S. Zakirov. Mostly modular compilation of crosscutting concerns by contextual predicate dispatch. In *OOPSLA '10*, pages 539–554. ACM, 2010.

[7] D. Crockford. The application/json Media Type for JavaScript Object Notation (JSON). RFC 4627 (Informational), July 2006. URL http://www.ietf.org/rfc/rfc4627.txt.

[8] A. Goldberg and D. Robson. *Smalltalk-80: the language and its implementation*. Addison-Wesley Longman Publishing Co., Inc., Boston, MA, USA, 1983.

[9] R. Hirschfeld, P. Costanza, and O. Nierstrasz. Context-oriented programming. *Journal of Object Technology*, 7(3): 125–151, March-April 2008.

[10] G. Kiczales, E. Hilsdale, J. Hugunin, M. Kersten, J. Palm, and W. G. Griswold. An overview of aspectj. In *ECOOP '01*, pages 327–353. Springer-Verlag, 2001.

[11] T. Millstein, M. Reay, and C. Chambers. Relaxed multijava: balancing extensibility and modular typechecking. In *OOPSLA '03*, pages 224–240. ACM, 2003.

[12] N. Ongkingco, P. Avgustinov, J. Tibble, L. Hendren, O. de Moor, and G. Sittampalam. Adding open modules to aspectj. In *AOSD '06*, pages 39–50. ACM, 2006.

[13] Rails core team. Ruby on rails. http://rubyonrails.org/, 2011.

[14] Ruby community. Ruby programming language. http://www.ruby-lang.org/, 2011.

[15] tDiary.org. tDiary. http://sourceforge.net/projects/tdiary/, 2011.

[16] P. Wadler and S. Blott. How to make ad-hoc polymorphism less ad hoc. In *POPL '89*, pages 60–76. ACM, 1989.

[17] A. Wirfs-Brock and B. Wilkerson. A overview of modular smalltalk. In *OOPSLA '88*, pages 123–134. ACM, 1988.

An Exploratory Study of the Design Impact of Language Features for Aspect-oriented Interfaces

Robert Dyer   Hridesh Rajan

Iowa State University
{rdyer,hridesh}@iastate.edu

Yuanfang Cai

Drexel University
yfcai@cs.drexel.edu

Abstract

A variety of language features to modularize crosscutting concerns have recently been discussed, e.g. open modules, annotation-based pointcuts, explicit join points, and quantified-typed events. All of these ideas are essentially a form of aspect-oriented interface between object-oriented and crosscutting modules, but the representation of this interface differs. While previous works have studied maintenance of AO programs versus OO programs, an empirical comparison of different AO interfaces to each other to investigate their benefits has not been performed. The main contribution of this work is a rigorous empirical study that evaluates the effectiveness of these proposals for AO interfaces towards software maintenance by applying them to 35 different releases of a software product line called Mobile-Media and 50 different releases of a web application called Health Watcher. Our comparative analysis using quantitative metrics proposed by Chidamber and Kemerer shows the strengths and weaknesses of these AO interface proposals. Our change impact analysis shows the design stability provided by each of these recent proposals for AO interfaces.

Categories and Subject Descriptors   D.3.3 [*Programming Languages*]: Language Constructs and Features — Control structures

General Terms   Design, Human Factors, Languages

Keywords   aspect-oriented, implicit invocation, empirical study, AO interfaces, annotations, events, open modules

1. Introduction

There has been a large body of recent case studies on the software engineering (SE) benefits of aspect-orientation [7, 8, 12, 13, 16]. These works compute standard SE metrics such as coupling and cohesion and compare aspect-oriented (AO) designs to object-oriented (OO) designs or use the metrics to determine stability and fault-proneness of the systems. However, most of these works focus on comparing AspectJ [15] to Java and do not compare different AO interfaces with each other, leaving developers to wonder about the benefits of one proposal over others.

This work fills that gap. It studies and compares different proposals for aspect-oriented interfaces to study how they impact code changes. For this, we consider a software product line for handling multimedia on mobile devices, called MobileMedia [8] and a web-based health application, called Health Watcher [16, 20]. Similar to previous in-depth analyses by Figueiredo *et al.* [8] and Greenwood *et al.* [11], we present metrics such as coupling and cohesion as well as an analysis of the change propagation across releases. However, unlike those studies we consider not only OO and pattern-based pointcuts (PCD) but also three other proposals for AO interfaces: open modules [1] (OM), annotation-based pointcuts [13] (@PCD), and quantified, typed events [19] (EVT).

Results and Contributions   There were several interesting results to come out of our case study. First, the annotation-based pointcut and quantified, typed event approaches showed several benefits, in terms of change impact, over the standard pattern-based pointcut approach.

- The @PCD releases have 18% fewer changed pointcuts than the PCD releases, due to a lack of fragile pointcuts.

- The total number of changed event types in MobileMedia is 74% fewer than the total number of changed pointcuts.

Second, the PCD and @PCD releases showed benefit over EVT for certain design rules.

- For the EVT releases, we had to be aware of and manually maintain design rules related to encapsulating entire types (e.g. to make an entire class synchronized). The PCD, @PCD, and OM releases used pointcuts to automatically maintain such design rules.

- Such design rules show cases where patterns do not exhibit fragile pointcut behavior, as the pointcuts are expected to capture all methods in the advised types.

Additionally, the EVT releases showed some benefit over the @PCD releases due to its ability to uniformly access context information when announcing events.

In summary, the key contributions of the case study performed in this work are:

- The first rigorous study of different language features for four different AO interfaces on substantial case studies.

- A suite of tools to automate measuring change propagation for PCD, OM, @PCD, and EVT. This automation reduces the chance for errors in our empirical study.

- A new set of 21 MobileMedia and 30 Health Watcher releases using @PCD, OM, and EVT interfaces.

- A change propagation analysis, that shows the stability gained from designs using annotation-based pointcuts and quantified, typed events in the face of fragile pointcuts [8, 19, 22].

Next we describe some prior studies on AO interfaces. In Section 3 we introduce the studied language designs. We then present our case study in Sections 4–7. Then we conclude with discussion in Section 8 and future work.

2. Related Work

Language Feature Comparison Studies Figueiredo *et al.* [8] studied the effects of evolving software product lines (SPLs) using aspects. Similar to our study, they measure change propagation and a set of standard metrics (such as coupling and cohesion). Their study showed some of the pros and cons to using AO language features when compared to OO features. For example, their study showed that changes affecting core features (such as changing a mandatory feature into an optional feature) are not well suited for AO. However, their study was limited to only one AO interface (pattern-based pointcuts) and as such does not generalize to other AO interfaces.

Hoffman and Eugster [12] studied the coupling, cohesion and separation of concerns for several projects with implementations in Java, AspectJ, and explicit join points (EJPs). Their study focused solely on implementing exception handling with each AO interface. Similar to our study, their study examines software engineering metrics and compares each AO interface against each other. Our study however looks at a total of 4 AO interfaces and multiple types of crosscutting behavior (instead of just exception handling) in two distinct systems with a total of 68 AO releases.

Kiczales and Mezini [13] studied seven different AO interfaces for improving separation of concerns in AspectJ-like languages. These included standard method calls, explicit join points using annotation-based pointcuts and implicit pattern-based pointcuts. They analyze each mechanism based on locality, explicit/implicit and ease of evolution and then provide guidelines on when each mechanism should be used in practice. Our work is similar in the sense that we an-

alyze several language interfaces. Their work uses a simple example for comparison while our work examines 7 releases of the MobileMedia [8] software product line and 10 releases of the Health Watcher [11, 20] web application.

Maintenance Studies Ferrari *et al.* [7] studied several SPLs to determine the possible language features that led to faults in those systems. Their results show that obliviousness was a key cause of faults in those systems and that pattern-based pointcuts are not necessarily the main cause of faults in AO designs. Their study focused on determining the cause of faults in AO systems while our study examines the effects of several AO interfaces on software maintenance.

Kulesza *et al.* [16] investigated the effect of AO interfaces on software maintenance by measuring standard software engineering metrics. They measured separation of concerns, coupling, cohesion, and size and concluded that in the presence of widely-scoped design changes, the AO designs exhibited superior stability and reusability compared to OO designs. In their study, they look at 2 releases of the Health Watcher application. Our study on the other hand examines 10 releases of Health Watcher and 7 releases of MobileMedia, giving us more variability to examine and allowing us to analyze the effects of varying types of interfaces added to a system. Their work also focuses solely on pattern-based pointcuts, whereas we consider several AO interfaces.

3. Background

In this section, we give an overview of each studied AO interface using an example based on a pattern occurring frequently in one of our case study candidates, MobileMedia.

Let us consider the class `FileScreen` shown in Figure 1. This class represents a screen presented to a user for manipulating a file. When the `saveCommand` is requested, the class saves the data to the specified file name. When the `deleteCommand` is requested, the file is deleted. The screen is shown on a `display`, which can be updated to show different screens.

An example requirement for such a class is to consistently display error messages to the user. There may be multiple screens that deal with I/O and all such screens should consistently handle errors that occur during that I/O by showing the I/O error screen. Note that in some cases, the designers have decided no error should be displayed (for example, when deleting a file and it was deleted by another user between the time of request and handling of the command).

3.1 Using Pattern-Based Pointcuts

The aspect `ExceptionHandler` shown in Figure 1 (lines 12–21) implements the requirement to consistently handle all exceptions using pattern-based pointcuts. This aspect contains an around advice (lines 15–20), which when triggered will properly handle the exception. The named pointcut `savepc` (lines 13–14) matches the execution of the method `save`, which had to be created in order to have a join point capable of being advised by the aspect. This is an example of quantification failure [24]. Note the advice uses the `display` variable, which is not exposed as context in the pointcut and is instead accessed indirectly through available context (the receiver object, `screen`).

```
1  @interface FileSaveEvent { }
2  class FileScreen {
3    Display display;

5    void handleCommand (Command c) {
6      if (c == saveCommand) { save (); }
7      else if (c == deleteCommand) { .. }
8    }
9    @FileSaveEvent
10   void save () { /* open the file and save data */ }
11 }
12 aspect ExceptionHandler {
13   pointcut savepc(FileScreen screen):
14   execution(* FileScreen.save ()) && this(screen) {
15   around(FileScreen screen): savepc(screen) {
16     try { proceed (); }
17     catch (FileNotFoundException e) {
18       screen.display.ShowFileError (e);
19     }
20   }
21 }
```

Figure 1. An example usage of pattern-based pointcuts [15]

3.2 Using Quantified, Typed Events

Quantified, typed events [19] allow programmers to declare named event types. An event type declaration p has a return type, a name, and zero or more context variable declarations. These context declarations specify the types and names of reflective information communicated between announcement of events of type p and handler methods. These declarations are independent from the modules that announce or handle these events. The event types thus provide an interface that completely decouples subjects and observers. An example event type declaration is shown in Figure 2 (line 1). The **event** `FileSaveEvent` declares that events of this type make one piece of context available: the `display`.

```
1  void event FileSaveEvent { Display display; }
2  class FileScreen {
3    Display display;

5    void handleCommand (Command c) {
6      if (c == saveCommand) {
7        announce FileSaveEvent(display) {
8          // open the file and save data
9        }
10     } else if (c == deleteCommand) { .. }
11   }
12 }
13 class ExceptionHandler {
14   void handler(FileSaveEvent next) {
15     try { next.invoke(); }
16     catch (FileNotFoundException e) {
17       next.display().ShowFileError (e);
18     }
19   }
20   when FileSaveEvent do handler;
21 }
```

Figure 2. An example usage of quantified, typed events [19]

The class `FileScreen` declares and announces an event of type `FileSaveEvent` using an announce expression (lines 7–9). Arbitrary blocks can be declared as the body of an announce expression, which avoids quantification failure. The event type `FileSaveEvent` declares one context variable, thus the **announce** expression binds the field `display` to the context variable named `display` (line 7).

Finally, the names of **event** declarations can be utilized for quantification in a binding declaration. A binding declaration, binding in short, associates a handler method to a set of events identified by an event type. The binding (line 20) says to run the method **handler** when events of type `FileSaveEvent` are announced. This allows quantifying over all announcements of `FileSaveEvent` with a succinct binding declaration, without depending on the modules that announce events. Use of event names in bindings simplifies them and avoids coupling observers with subjects.

Each handler method takes an event closure as the first argument. An *event closure* [19] contains code needed to run other applicable handlers and the original event's code. An event closure is run by an **invoke** expression. The **invoke** expression in the implementation of the handler method (line 15) causes other applicable handlers and the original event's code to run before handling any exceptions.

3.3 Using Annotation-based Pointcuts

When using pattern-based pointcuts, the code being advised by aspects is completely oblivious to those aspects. One approach that sacrifices some obliviousness, which is quite similar looking to quantified, typed events, is to mark each advised join point with an annotation [13]. The aspects then match based on that annotation.

For example, consider the code shown in Figure 1. The gray portions of the code represent what was changed from the pattern-based implementation. An annotation `FileSaveEvent` was created (line 1) and then used to mark the advised join point method `save` (line 10). The pointcut for the aspect (line 14) was modified to become **execution**(@FileSaveEvent * *(..)) and match based on that annotation instead of matching against the string representation of the method name.

3.4 Using Open Modules

Open modules [1] declare which join points are exposed to aspects via a module definition. This puts the burden onto the module maintainer to maintain relationships between join points in the base code and pointcuts matching those points.

Ongkingco *et al.* [17] proposed an extended version of open modules and an implementation for AspectJ [15]. We use their implementation's syntax for this example. Figure 3 is an example module for our exception handling requirement. The figure omits the class `FileScreen` and aspect `ExceptionHandler`, as they are identical to Figure 1.

The module `ExHandle` (lines 3–7) for the class `FileScreen` (Figure 1, line 4) exposes one named join

```
1 /* class FileScreen and aspect ExceptionHandler
2    same as in Figure 1. */
3 module ExHandle {
4   class FileScreen;
5   expose :
6      ExceptionHandler.savepc(FileScreen);
7 }
```

Figure 3. Exception handling with open modules [1, 17]

point in that class: the pointcut `savepc` defined in the aspect `ExceptionHandler` (Figure 1, line 6). The module states that the aspect is allowed to match this join point. If the signature of the pointcut changes in the aspect, the maintainer of the module would be required to update the module definition as well.

4. Case Study Overview

To evaluate the proposed AO interfaces studied here, we examined them in the context of two applications: an existing software product-line application called MobileMedia [8] and an existing web application called Health Watcher [11, 20]. Thus, both cases are already vetted.

This section describes our experimental setup, the technique used to generate new releases of the studied applications and the tools developed and used for the study.

4.1 Experimental Setup

In order to perform this case study, we created a total of 51 modified releases of the MobileMedia and Health Watcher applications, modified 2 compilers to automatically compute various software engineering metrics and created a tool for automatically measuring change propagation. All artifacts and tools are available for download[1]. An important advantage of these tools was that they removed the manual, and often error-prone, steps from our empirical study. In this section, we describe each tool in detail.

4.1.1 New Code Artifacts

The OO and pattern-based pointcut code artifacts for this study were re-used from previous work [8, 11, 20]. Since the artifacts using annotation-based pointcuts, open modules and quantified, typed events did not previously exist for either application, we created them. When creating these artifacts, *our objective was to keep other variables such as design strategy constant between all versions and only change the crosscutting feature.*

For example, starting with release 4 of the Health Watcher releases for AspectJ, an observer pattern aspect library was used. This library was re-used in the annotation-based pointcut, open modules and Ptolemy releases despite the fact that Ptolemy's quantified, typed events actually make this library unnecessary (the events implement the observer pattern directly, so no library is needed). Removing this library how-

---
[1] **Tools/artifacts download:**
http://ptolemy.cs.iastate.edu/design-study/

ever would change the base and aspect components in the system and introduce extra variables into the analysis. Leaving it in place meant the only difference between the Ptolemy and other releases was the quantification mechanism used for implementing crosscutting behavior.

Creating Annotation-based Pointcut Releases   Using the pattern-based pointcut releases as a starting point, we implemented all 7 releases of MobileMedia and all 10 releases of Health Watcher using an annotation-based pointcut syntax [13]. We modified each pointcut in every aspect to match based on a new annotation and for each join point in the base code which matched the original pointcut, we annotated the method with the new annotation. The names of the annotations were chosen based on properties of the code, following the guidelines of Kiczales and Mezini [13]. The results were verified by comparing the weaving logs produced by the standard AspectJ compiler (ajc) for both the original pattern-based pointcut releases and the new annotation-based pointcut releases.

Creating Open Module Releases   To study the effect of open modules [1], we implemented all 7 MobileMedia and all 10 Health Watcher releases using the AspectJ-based implementation of open modules [17]. Starting with the first release, we made a copy of the pattern-based pointcut release and then created module definitions.

For each subsequent release, we copied the pattern-based pointcut release and then copied and updated the module definition(s) from the previous open modules release. Modules were updated to reflect changes in the base code and, where appropriate, new modules were added. Modules were created to follow the package structure of the system, following the recommendation of Ongkingco *et al.* [17].

Creating Quantified, Typed Event Releases   For each quantified, typed event [19] release we started with the pattern-based pointcut release as a template, creating one handler class for each aspect. For each advice body in an aspect, a new handler method was added to the handler class. Event types were created and event announcement added to emulate the pattern-based pointcut-advice semantics.

Note that since the initial work on Ptolemy [19], the language has been extended to include support for inter-type declarations. The syntax is identical to that of AspectJ and the implementation was directly borrowed from the ABC AspectJ compiler [2] and added to the Ptolemy compiler, as the research version of the Ptolemy compiler is also based on the JastAdd [5] extensible compiler framework.

4.1.2 Automation of Empirical Evaluation

Evaluating the benefits of the studied designs using standard software engineering metrics and change propagation by hand can be tedious and error-prone. To solve this problem, we built several tools to automatically measure these metrics and allow for consistency. These included several modified compilers and tools for measuring change propagation. Our tool support builds on the open-source ABC [2] AspectJ compiler. The ABC compiler was used for two reasons: it has a JastAdd [5] extensible frontend available which simplifies extensions and it contains support for the only known implementation of open modules. The use of ABC was also driven by the fact that the research version of the Ptolemy compiler is also JastAdd-based and our tool extensions could be re-used for both compilers (giving us automated tool support for every studied language design).

Measuring Change Propagation To measure change propagation, a JastAdd module was created to serialize the parsed AST into an XML format. Since every compiler used in our study is based on the JastAdd extensible compiler, the new functionality was shared as a reusable module between these compilers. This also ensured that change propagation measurement was done consistently.

A separate tool was created that takes two of these XML files as input, representing two versions of the same code tree, and compares the two trees to determine which components are new, were removed, or have changed. We considered a renamed component (including moving it to another package) as a change (instead of a remove and an add) and manually identified such renames in a separate XML file to aid the tool.

The tool is capable of determining changes at the granularity of classes, aspects, event types, annotations, and pointcuts. The results were then manually verified against diffs of the MobileMedia code releases for Java and AspectJ to ensure the accuracy of the tool.

Measuring Software Engineering Metrics To measure the metrics suite proposed by Chidamber and Kemerer [4] for coupling and cohesion, we created another JastAdd module which measures and reports these metrics. This module was shared and used in each compiler in our study.

Chidamber and Kemerer propose that a component is coupled to another component if it accesses a field or calls a method from the other component. They also propose a class is cohesive if the operations of the class operate on similar attributes of the class.

We used the previous results from Figueiredo *et al.* [8] as a guide for our implementation, comparing the values for the OO and pattern-based pointcut MobileMedia releases to their previously published results. No extension was necessary for the annotation-based pointcuts, as the existing OO and pattern-based pointcut metrics apply directly. The metrics suite was extended to support open modules and quantified, typed events in a straight-forward manner, similar to the pattern-based pointcut extensions.

For open modules releases, modules are treated like classes and join point exposures treated similar to an aspect pointcut. For quantified, typed events, event type declarations are treated like a class with context access considered

a field of the event type. Announcing an event is treated like a method call.

4.2 Threats to Validity

In this section we discuss internal and external threats to the validity of our case study.

4.2.1 Internal Validity

To reduce the risk of bias when selecting languages for study, we first decided the focus of the study to be examining the effect of AO interfaces for minimizing pointcut fragility and change propagation. Then we categorized existing AO interfaces by how they achieve quantification.

In the first category, quantification is controlled solely by aspects and pattern-based pointcuts was the most relevant choice in this category as it is used in industry and also highly researched. In the second category, quantification is controlled solely by the base code. In this category, there were two candidates: aspect-aware interfaces [14] and open modules [1]. We picked open modules because an implementation was available for it. In the third category, quantification is controlled by an intermediary between base components and aspects. There were several candidates: XPIs [24], annotation-based pointcuts, implicit invocation with implicit announcements [21] and quantified, typed events [19]. We picked quantified, typed events due to our familiarity with its compiler infrastructure and also picked annotation-based pointcuts as the language was not developed by the authors and compiler support was readily available.

The code artifacts created for this study were the Mobile-Media and Health Watcher (releases for annotation-based pointcuts (@PCD), open modules (OM), and quantified, typed events (EVT). To reduce the risks associated with creating these artifacts, we attempted to keep other variables constant (such as design strategy used) and only vary the quantification mechanism used.

We reduced the risk associated with creating the EVT, @PCD, and OM releases by first basing them off the existing pattern-based pointcut releases (which were not created by any of the authors). Next, we used recommendations by experts in each respective language in their published work [13, 17, 19] to modify the pattern-based pointcut releases and create the releases for the new AO interfaces.

For example, we followed the guidelines given by the implementers of the open modules implementation used to create one module definition for each package [17]. We also followed a naming scheme proposed by Kiczales and Mezini [13] when generating annotations for the @PCD releases, which was shown to offer design stability.

4.2.2 External Validity

The main concern regarding external validity that we identified is the studied systems may not faithfully represent software in industry. This risk is reduced since the applications are implemented in both Java and AspectJ, which is a representative approach in the AO domain. Further, MobileMedia is a software-product line comprised of 8 releases based on industry-strength technologies for mobile systems, such as the Java Mobile Information Device Profile (MIDP) and Mobile Media API (MMAPI). Additionally, this system has been studied extensively [7–9, 11].

Similarly, Health Watcher is a real-world application used for reporting health complaints. This system uses several industrial strength technologies/techniques, such as persistence mechanisms, remote invocation (RMI), concurrency, JDBC, etc.

5. Case Study: MobileMedia

This section contains our first studied project, a software product-line application called MobileMedia [8]. MobileMedia is an extension of MobilePhoto [25], which was developed to study the effect of AO designs on software product lines (SPL). MobileMedia is an SPL for applications that manipulate photos, music, and videos on mobile devices. MobileMedia extends MobilePhoto to add new mandatory, optional and alternative features.

5.1 Change Propagation Analysis

A key benefit of a modular software design is in its ability to hide design decisions that are likely to change [18]. Thus, we consider the number of changed components as a result of a changed design decision to be an important comparator for a software design. To quantify this, similar to Figueiredo *et al.* [8], we measured the number of added, removed, and changed components in each system for each release.

5.1.1 Component Changes

The changes to base components are shown in Figure 4. This table includes the pure Java releases (OO), pattern-based pointcut releases (PCD), annotation-based pointcut releases (@PCD), open modules releases (OM), and the quantified, typed event releases (EVT). This table considers Java classes and interfaces, aspects, and open modules.

Note that the declarations of annotations and event types are not included in the counts for this table, as they are measured separately and considered in the next section to give a direct comparison to pointcuts.

Components Added   For all releases, new components added in the pattern-based pointcut (PCD) releases were also added to the annotation-based pointcut (@PCD), open modules (OM), and quantified, typed event (EVT) releases. Note that the @PCD values are identical to the PCD values.

In R2, R6, R7, and R8, the number of added components differs for the open modules (OM) releases compared to PCD (marked in bold) due to the addition of modules in each of those releases. All aspects and base components in the OM releases are identical to the PCD releases.

In R4, the releases with pointcuts (PCD, @PCD, and OM) added an aspect that only handles precedence. This

		R2	R3	R4	R5	R6	R7	R8	Total
	OO	9	1	0	5	7	10	6	38
	OM	17	2	3	6	11	17	22	78
Added	PCD	13	2	3	6	8	14	16	62
	@PCD	13	2	3	6	8	14	16	62
	EVT	13	2	2	6	8	14	16	61
	Differences to PCD marked in BOLD blue								
	OO	0	0	0	0	0	1	1	2
	OM	1	0	0	0	0	1	0	2
Removed	PCD	1	0	0	0	0	1	0	2
	@PCD	1	0	0	0	0	1	0	2
	EVT	1	0	0	0	0	1	0	2
	OO	5	8	5	8	6	19	17	68
	OM	5	14	6	13	6	34	26	104
Changed	PCD	5	10	2	10	5	27	18	77
	@PCD	5	8	2	11	7	27	20	80
	EVT	5	9	1	8	5	25	20	73

(Left side label: *Components*)

Figure 4. Base components change propagation in MobileMedia for each release

aspect was not added in the quantified, typed event release, as precedence in that release is controlled by the order of registering handler classes. This registration occurs inside the main class.

Components Removed   In all 7 changed releases (R2–R8), the AO releases all have the same components removed. In R2, the PCD release removed a class `BaseThread` and in R8 the OO release removed the class `SplashScreen`. Since we did not implement either of the OO or PCD releases, we simply mimicked these changes in the @PCD, OM, and EVT releases.

Components Changed   The difference between the components changed for the pattern-based pointcuts (PCD) and open modules (OM) releases is due entirely to changes in the modules, as once again all aspects and base components in the OM releases are identical to the PCD releases. Starting with R3, each release modified modules from the prior release due to changes in the aspects.

In R3, the PCD release changes two more components (`UtilAspectEH` and `ControllerAspectEH`) than the @PCD release due to the fragility of the pointcuts in those components. However, in R5, R6, and R8 the @PCD releases change more base components than the PCD releases, despite avoiding the fragile pointcut problem with existing pointcuts. This is due to the need to annotate the base code with new annotations.

The difference in changes for R3 between @PCD and EVT was due to a changed event type requiring a change in the signature of the handler method.

For R4 however, the difference in values represents two important differences in the AO interfaces. First, the changed component in EVT was due to adding a precedence declaration to a handler (in @PCD this was a new aspect, not a changed aspect). Second, the two changed components in PCD and @PCD were from refactoring base code to expose join points. EVT did not need to perform such refactorings as it allows arbitrary statements as event announcements.

Of the remaining 7 changes that occurred in @PCD and not EVT, 3 were due to updating the precedence aspect, 1 was due to exposing join points and the remaining 3 were from changes in context (which for EVT shows up as changes in the event types).

5.1.2 Quantification Mechanism Changes

The change propagation results are shown in Figure 5. The table lists the number of pointcuts added, changed, or removed for the open modules (OM), annotation-based pointcut (@PCD), and pattern-based pointcut (PCD) releases. The number of annotations added, changed or removed are shown for the @PCD releases and the number of event types added, changed, or removed are shown for the EVT releases.

	Pointcuts	R2	R3	R4	R5	R6	R7	R8	Total
Add	OM	87	19	18	6	21	53	58	262
	PCD	64	12	13	4	15	39	43	190
	@PCD	64	12	13	4	15	39	43	190
Remove	Differences to PCD marked in BOLD blue								
	OM	0	0	0	0	2	12	11	25
	PCD	0	0	0	0	1	6	8	15
	@PCD	0	0	0	0	1	6	8	15
Change	OM	0	10	0	29	2	104	9	154
	PCD	0	9	0	18	2	74	4	107
	@PCD	0	4	0	13	2	65	4	88

	Events/Anns	R2	R3	R4	R5	R6	R7	R8	Total
Add	@PCD	24	7	1	2	6	11	5	56
	EVT	16	4	0	2	6	5	3	36
Rem	Differences to EVT marked in BOLD red								
	@PCD	0	0	0	0	1	0	0	1
	EVT	0	0	0	0	0	0	0	0
Ch	@PCD	0	1	0	0	0	0	0	1
	EVT	0	2	0	1	0	12	1	16

Figure 5. AO interfaces change propagation in MobileMedia for each release

Pointcuts The pointcuts added, removed, and changed were measured for all releases with pointcuts (PCD, @PCD, and OM) and there are two sets of comparisons to note. First, the OM releases have more pointcuts added and changed in almost every release (marked in bold) when compared to the PCD releases. This is due to the additional pointcuts contained in the module definitions.

The second comparison is between the PCD and @PCD releases. In three releases, the @PCD releases have fewer changed pointcuts. This occurred due to the gained stability from using the annotation-matching pointcut syntax. In total, the @PCD releases have almost 18% fewer changed pointcuts compared to the PCD releases.

Annotations and Events The annotations for the @PCD releases and the event types for the EVT releases are similar in that both mark join points in the base code for aspect code to advise. The change propagation of these two mechanisms

is also similar. The differences between them (marked in bold) occur for several reasons.

The event types in EVT contain typed context declarations, while annotations do not contain any context. As such, when types in the base code (used as context) change, any event type referencing those types must also be updated. This is why the annotations have no changes in any @PCD release (the change in R3 was a renamed annotation) and the EVT releases have several changes.

In R2, the difference in the number of added event types and annotations is due to EVT's lack of quantification failure. For example, the @PCD release had to create an annotation to mark a join point for use in a `within` pointcut due to quantification failure. The EVT release was also able to re-use more event types than the @PCD release, saving the addition of 7 event types.

Pointcuts vs Annotations/Events In R7 a mandatory feature was turned into two alternative features, leading to changes in the base components which propagated to the event types and event handlers for the EVT release. 10 of the 12 resulting event type changes were due to the renaming of base components passed as context in those events types. Consider on the other hand the PCD release which required changing 38 of the 74 pointcuts due to the fragility of those pointcuts.

In R8, several new alternate features were added to the system. The EVT release was able to re-use several existing event types, leading to the addition of only 3 new event types. Similarly, the @PCD release only required the addition of 5 new annotations. The PCD release however required adding 43 new pointcuts to the system.

In general, note that the total number of added event types and annotations are 81% and 70% fewer, respectively, than the total number of added pointcuts for PCD releases. Also note that the total number of changed event types is 85% fewer than the total number of changed pointcuts in the PCD releases and 82% fewer than the total pointcuts changed in the @PCD releases.

5.1.3 Summary

In summary, for some releases quantified, typed events showed an improved ability to withstand changes in components. In particular, for releases where significant refactoring in the base components took place, the EVT designs were able to reduce the impact of these changes in the base code from the handlers. Additionally,

- the total number of added event types and annotations are less than a third the number of pointcuts added in the PCD releases, showing that event types and annotations are re-used by multiple pointcuts,

- the total number of changed event types is 85% fewer than the total number of changed pointcuts in the PCD releases and 82% fewer than the total pointcuts changed in the @PCD releases,

- the @PCD releases have almost 18% fewer changed pointcuts compared to the PCD releases due to the lack of fragile pointcuts, and
- the EVT and @PCD releases were both able to efficiently re-use events/annotations leading to fewer additions in releases adding alternate features.

5.2 Software Engineering Metrics

As previously discussed, the main difference between most AO interfaces and quantified, typed events is that the dependency between components that announce events is explicitly stated using announce expressions that name event types. With most AO interfaces, this dependency is implicitly defined by the language semantics. Explicitly naming event types or annotations introduces coupling. The main goal of this section is to study the change in coupling between components. In order to perform this evaluation, we used a subset of the metrics suite proposed by Chidamber and Kemerer [4], Fenton and Pfleeger [6], and subsequently refined by Garcia et al. [8, 10].

		R2	R3	R4	R5	R6	R7	R8
CBC	OO	32	40	40	65	80	103	131
	OM	35	50	59	94	121	159	217
	PCD	35	50	59	94	121	159	217
	@PCD	82	106	122	161	200	255	332
	EVT	74	100	120	159	203	271	371
LCOO	OO	123	194	224	241	296	311	365
	OM	147	244	266	259	369	502	534
	PCD	147	244	266	259	369	502	534
	@PCD	147	244	266	259	369	502	534
	EVT	123	162	171	257	365	426	539

Figure 6. Coupling and Cohesion for MobileMedia

Coupling Coupling between components (CBC) [4] is a measurement of coupling. A component is coupled to another component if it accesses a field or calls a method on it. Figure 6 shows the results of our measurements.

The @PCD and EVT releases all have upwards of twice as much explicit coupling in the system compared to the PCD and OM releases. This is due to the explicit marking of join points (with annotations and event type announcements). However, realize that the added coupling is not coupling between aspects and base code but rather aspects to event types and base code to event types. Thus, this coupling only creates a maintenance issue if an event type changes (such as in R7).

Cohesion Lack of cohesion in operations [4] (LCOO) is a measurement of cohesion of the classes in the system, based on how similar operations use attributes of the class. If methods of a class operate on the same attributes, the class is said to be cohesive and has a lower LCOO value. LCOO for all releases was measured and is shown in Figure 6. Note that the PCD, @PCD, and OM releases all have the same values due to having the same methods/fields in classes and ITDs/advice in aspects.

In general, quantified, typed events have more cohesion (indicated by lower LCOO) than the pointcut-based approaches. This is mostly due to the lack of needing to refactor the base code to expose join points to the aspect code. Such refactored code often only works on a small sub-set of the fields in the class, making the class less cohesive.

		R2	R3	R4	R5	R6	R7	R8
LOC	OO	1159	1314	1363	1555	2051	2523	3016
	OM	1337	1570	1700	1928	2474	3207	3999
	PCD	1276	1494	1613	1834	2364	3068	3806
	@PCD	1452	1723	1852	2094	2664	3461	4257
	EVT	1427	1669	1781	2050	2646	3398	4254
NOC	OO	24	25	25	30	37	46	51
	OM	31	33	36	42	53	69	91
	PCD	27	29	32	38	46	59	75
	@PCD	51	60	64	72	85	109	130
	EVT	47	53	56	64	78	96	115
NOA	OO	62	71	74	75	106	132	165
	OM	82	99	108	112	149	187	237
	PCD	62	72	76	77	110	139	177
	@PCD	62	72	76	77	110	139	177
	EVT	71	92	96	101	144	175	217
NOO	OO	124	140	143	160	200	239	271
	OM	143	169	179	197	247	308	369
	PCD	143	169	179	197	247	308	369
	@PCD	143	169	179	197	247	308	369
	EVT	142	167	177	196	245	302	378

Figure 7. The measured size metrics for MobileMedia

Size Metrics Figure 7 shows the number of components (NOC) and total lines of code (LOC) for each release. The number of components includes classes and interfaces for all releases. For the PCD, @PCD, and OM releases it also includes aspects. For OM it includes modules, @PCD includes annotations and EVT includes event types.

Lines of code were measured using a tool[2] that ignores comment and whitespace lines. All other lines were included and every component from NOC was included.

Number of operations (NOO) was measured as the total number of methods in classes, introduced methods in aspects, advice bodies in aspects and handler methods in event handlers. Number of attributes (NOA) was measured as the total number of fields in classes or aspects (including intertype declared fields) and the number of context variables in quantified, typed events.

As one would expect from creating so many events and annotations, the lines of code and number of components is higher for both @PCD and EVT. The number of attributes is also higher for EVT due to counting event type context variables as attributes.

Summary In summary, our results show the total coupling is higher in the annotation-based pointcut and quantified, typed event releases due to the interface added between base components and aspects. The increased coupling is a tradeoff for the stability gained by the interface between aspect and base code, as the previous section clearly demonstrates.

---

[2] Retrieved from: http://reasoning.com/downloads.html

6. Case Study: Health Watcher

This section contains our second studied project, a web-based application called Health Watcher [11, 16, 20]. Health Watcher is an application for users to file health complaints. The system was initially developed in 2001 and has undergone 9 releases to add new features and fix previous bugs.

6.1 Change Propagation Analysis

As stated in the previous case study, we consider the number of changed components as a result of a change in a design decision to be an important comparator for a software design. This section performs our analysis on Health Watcher.

6.1.1 Component Changes

The changes to base components are shown in Figure 8. This table includes the Java releases (OO), pattern-based pointcut releases (PCD), annotation-based pointcut releases (@PCD), open modules releases (OM), and the quantified, typed event releases (EVT). This table considers Java classes/interfaces, aspects, and open modules.

		R1	R2	R3	R4	R5	R6	R7	R8	R9	R10	Total
	OO	88	4	12	2	3	4	4	4	12	5	138
	OM	106	12	16	4	0	4	4	2	12	6	166
Added	PCD	101	11	16	3	0	4	4	2	12	6	159
	@PCD	101	11	16	3	0	4	4	2	12	6	159
	EVT	100	10	16	3	0	4	4	2	12	6	157
		Differences to PCD marked in BOLD blue										
	OO	0	0	0	0	1	0	0	0	0	2	3
	OM	0	0	0	0	0	0	0	0	0	1	1
Removed	PCD	0	0	0	0	0	0	0	0	0	1	1
	@PCD	0	0	0	0	0	0	0	0	0	1	1
	EVT	0	0	0	0	0	0	0	0	0	1	1
	OO	0	22	6	15	16	2	27	3	23	48	162
	OM	0	27	9	9	1	3	27	5	23	55	159
Changed	PCD	0	25	8	7	1	2	27	3	22	52	147
	@PCD	0	26	8	29	1	2	27	3	23	55	174
	EVT	0	26	8	32	1	2	27	3	23	54	176

Figure 8. Base components change propagation in Health Watcher for each release

Components Added   For all releases, new components added in the pattern-based pointcut (PCD) releases were also added to the annotation-based pointcut (@PCD), open modules (OM), and quantified, typed event (EVT) releases. Note that the @PCD values are identical to the PCD values (as annotations are considered separately in Figure 9).

In R1, R2, and R4, the number of added components differs for the open modules (OM) releases compared to PCD (marked in bold) due to the addition of modules in each of those releases. All aspects and base components in the OM releases are identical to the PCD releases.

In R1, an aspect that only contains a declare parents statement was not added in the EVT release. This statement failed to compile with the abc based intertype declarations implementation. Instead, we manually modified the base classes to add the Serializable interface to the 2 types. This

particular aspect did not change in the PCD releases, thus our work-around did not cause problems in later EVT releases.

In R2, the releases with pointcuts (PCD, @PCD, and OM) added an aspect that only handles precedence. This aspect was not added in the quantified, typed event release, as precedence in that release is controlled by the order of registering handler classes. This registration occurs inside the main class or using annotations in the handler classes.

Components Removed   Similar to MobileMedia, in all 9 changed Health Watcher releases (R2–R10), the AO releases all have the same components removed.

Components Changed   Unlike MobileMedia where the difference between the components changed for the pattern-based pointcuts (PCD) and open modules (OM) releases was due entirely to changes in the modules, in Health Watcher some of the aspects also were modified in order to give anonymous pointcuts names (for the modules to reference).

Also unlike MobileMedia, the components changed for @PCD and EVT are more in Health Watcher for R4 than the PCD release due to needing to add annotations and event announcements in base code. This was because fewer base components changed in the PCD release but over 20 had to be modified to add annotations and event announcement.

6.1.2 Quantification Mechanism Changes

The change propagation results in terms of modularization techniques are shown in Figure 9. The table lists the number of pointcuts added, changed, or removed for the open modules (OM), annotation-based pointcut (@PCD), and pattern-based pointcut (PCD) releases. The number of annotations added, changed or removed are shown for the @PCD releases. It also lists the number of event types added, changed, or removed for EVT.

Pointcuts   Again, the pointcuts added, removed, and changed were measured for all releases with pointcuts (PCD, @PCD, and OM). Once again, the OM releases have more pointcuts added and changed compared to the PCD releases, as the module definitions also contain named pointcuts.

Unlike the MobileMedia case study, Health Watcher had relatively stable pointcuts. As such, the only benefit observed in the @PCD releases occurred in R2, where 3 fewer pointcuts were changed.

Annotations and Events   Unlike the MobileMedia case study, annotations and event types in Health Watcher perform roughly the same in all releases, with the exception of R3. In this release, there were several (4) events that had to be duplicated: once with a void return type and once with a non-void return type. This was due to the advice being applied to multiple methods (with differing return types). The PCD releases simply marked all methods with the same annotation and the aspect was able to advise them all, without regard to the return type. This problem also accounts for the extra events in R1 and R2.

Pointcuts		R1	R2	R3	R4	R5	R6	R7	R8	R9	R10	Total
Add	OM	57	16	36	16	0	0	0	6	0	30	161
	PCD	28	11	12	10	0	0	0	6	0	20	87
	@PCD	28	11	12	10	0	0	0	6	0	20	87
	Differences to PCD marked in BOLD blue											
Remove	OM	0	0	0	0	0	0	0	6	6	0	12
	PCD	0	0	0	0	0	0	0	4	4	0	8
	@PCD	0	0	0	0	0	0	0	4	4	0	8
Change	OM	0	4	0	0	0	0	1	2	6	3	16
	PCD	0	4	0	0	0	0	1	0	5	3	13
	@PCD	0	1	0	0	0	0	1	0	5	3	10

Events/Anns		R1	R2	R3	R4	R5	R6	R7	R8	R9	R10	Total
Add	@PCD	13	2	2	4	0	0	0	1	0	0	28
	EVT	14	4	9	5	0	0	0	0	0	10	42
	Differences to EVT marked in BOLD red											
Rem	@PCD	0	0	0	0	0	0	0	0	0	0	0
	EVT	0	0	0	0	0	0	0	0	0	0	0
Ch	@PCD	0	0	0	0	0	0	0	0	0	0	0
	EVT	0	1	0	0	0	0	0	0	0	0	1

Figure 9. AO interfaces change propagation in Health Watcher for each release

Pointcuts vs Annotations/Events In general, note that the total number of added event types and annotations are 52% and 68% fewer, respectively, than the total number of added pointcuts for PCD releases. This result is similar to the MobileMedia results.

6.1.3 Summary

In summary, the Health Watcher case study showed similar results to the MobileMedia case study. The noticeable differences between the studies were due to the fact that the Health Watcher study tended to simply add new aspects and avoid changing existing aspects and base code as much as possible while the MobileMedia study made significant modifications (in order to change mandatory features into optional ones).

6.2 Software Engineering Metrics

The software engineering metrics for Health Watcher followed the same trends as for Mobile Media and thus were omitted for space reasons.

7. Key Observations

We observed several key benefits to the studied designs. These benefits are described in detail in this section.

7.1 Inter-Type Declarations

A static feature of AspectJ that allows adding fields/methods to other classes is inter-type declarations (ITDs) [15]. This feature was recently added to the Ptolemy language (with the same syntax as AspectJ) and thus available for all studied AO interfaces.

In MobileMedia, ITDs are used mostly for two purposes: to add additional data (fields) to existing types (and manipu-

late that new data) and to provide alternate implementations of features. ITDs first show up in R3 and are heavily used in later releases which contain alternate features. For example in R8, ITDs are defined in 12 out of the 22 aspects (54%).

In Health Watcher, ITDs are used to add methods for timestamping complaints, starting the remote server for RMI and to implement a singleton pattern. In the system, a total of 3 out of 26 aspects (11.5%) contain ITDs.

7.2 Declare Parents

Similar to ITDs, type hierarchies in the base components can be extended in a modular manner using AspectJ's *declare parents*. This feature seems well suited to help handle alternate features in a system, but was not heavily used by the current design of the MobileMedia product-line.

In MobileMedia, only R8 contains declare parents statements to extend two type hierarchies by adding a new superclass to the base components. For the PCD, @PCD, and OM releases these effects were modular. For the EVT releases, the base components had to be modified (due to a compiler bug) and these changes were non-modular, but not invasive.

In Health Watcher, declare parents statements appear in 6 out of 26 (23%) aspects. The statements are used in several places to place marker interfaces onto a set of types, which are then advised by the pointcut patterns. This was a useful pattern in this system and while Ptolemy supports declare parents statements, the lack of a pattern form of quantification meant that these marker interfaces were not useful in those releases.

7.3 Quantification Support

Quantified, typed events give the programmer the ability to add event announcement for any arbitrary statement in the base components. The pattern and annotation-based pointcut approaches can only advise join points available in the provided pointcut language, such as method executions or calls. This often results in what Sullivan *et al.* called quantification failure [24] and is caused by incompleteness in the language's event model. Quantification failure occurs when the event model does not implicitly announce some kinds of events and hence does not provide pointcut definitions that select such events [24].

In MobileMedia, we observed several instances of quantification failure. For example, in R2 the aspects needed to advise a *while* loop and similarly in R3 the aspects needed to advise a *for* loop. To accommodate this, all pointcut-based releases (PCD, @PCD, OM) refactor the base components, for example moving these loops into newly added methods. By R8, a total of 5 refactorings were made to expose join points. This accounts for approximately 5% of the advised join points. The EVT releases did not suffer from this problem and thus these refactorings were not necessary.

In Health Watcher, we observed a different form of quantification failure. However, this time the failure was in the EVT releases and related to the handling of design rules that encapsulate entire types. As previously mentioned, the PCD releases used declare parents statements to add marker interfaces to several types. The aspects then used pattern pointcuts to target all method executions in sub-types of that marker interface. This was used for things such as making all methods in a class synchronized. Figure 10 shows the implementation for this design rule in PCD, which uses the marker interface SynchronizedClasses on two types and around advice to wrap the execution of all methods in those types in a **synchronized** statement.

```
1 private interface SynchronizedClasses {};
2 declare parents: EmployeeRepositoryArray ||
3   ComplaintRepositoryArray implements SynchronizedClasses;
4 Object around(Object o): this(o) &&
5     execution(* SynchronizedClasses+.*(..)) {
6   synchronized(o) { return proceed(o); }
7 }
```

Figure 10. Pattern-based pointcut version of a design rule to encapsulate 2 types and make all their methods synchronized

For the EVT releases, we had to manually track this design rule across the releases. This meant that if the types involved added new methods we would need to remember the design rule and ensure those new methods also announced the proper event. For the Health Watcher example, this maintenance scenario did not occur (as the types involved did not evolve across releases) but it is important to note that we still had to be aware of the design rules and check them in each release - something the PCD releases did not require.

7.4 Fragile Pointcut Problem

As mentioned by Figueiredo *et al.* [8], the pattern-based pointcut releases of MobileMedia suffer from a fragile pointcut problem [8, 19, 22]. This could be observed in R7, where a mandatory feature PHOTO is generalized into two alternative features PHOTO or MUSIC. This required modifying many pointcuts previously relying on an implicit matching of signatures in the base components.

The renaming of the base components itself is not a problem in the EVT releases and in fact requires no modification of events or handlers; the handlers will match on the event type which remains unchanged. If the event type is renamed (for example, to remain consistently named to the base components) then all handlers and events for that event type must be updated accordingly. The key difference in these two scenarios is that in the PCD case, the developer must be aware of which pointcuts matched the given join point (which can be aided with tools such as AJDT) while in the EVT case, the compiler will specify type errors for every publisher and subscriber for that event type, eliminating fragile pointcuts.

Since @PCD releases are structurally similar to the EVT releases, they also benefited from a lack of fragile pointcuts. Similarly, the OM releases also benefited from a lack of fragile pointcuts.

Fragile pointcuts were observed in releases 3, 5, and 7. In total, 19 out of the 107 pointcuts changed (18%) across all releases were due to fragile pointcuts. This problem has already been demonstrated in small examples, however, its appearance in PCD releases of MobileMedia presents real evidence that it could affect maintenance of PCD systems. The ability of EVT, @PCD, and OM to mitigate these risks shows that such problems, when they occur in practice, can be solved using these different AO interfaces.

7.5 Access to Context Information

AspectJ provides means to access context information from advised join points [15]. The type of information available to advice however is limited by the language, such as the receiver object, method arguments, etc. In MobileMedia and Health Watcher, there were several instances where this lack of flexible availability to context added complexity to the system. For example, the exception handling aspects needed access to a field in the controller class being advised. Thus, the field needed marked public, a getter method added, or the aspect marked as privileged. Either way, the aspect becomes coupled to the interface of the advised class. This was a problem for all pointcut-based releases (PCD, @PCD, OM).

This was also a key difference between the @PCD and EVT releases. While the @PCD releases provided similar benefits in terms of preventing fragile pointcuts, in terms of context exposure the annotations were not a sufficiently expressive quantification mechanism when compared to EVT.

8. Discussion

It is important to note that our measurements of the open module releases are all based on the AspectJ-based implementation of open modules [17] (which to our knowledge is the only open modules implementation available). Thus, some of the measured differences we see are due not necessarily to open modules as an AO interface but instead due to this specific implementation.

The use of named pointcuts in this implementation required copying the full pointcut signature to the module definition. This has the effect of requiring updating two locations (the original pointcut definition and the module) if that signature changes. The pointcut signatures change any time the exposed context types changed. Any difference in the number of changed pointcuts between the PCD and OM releases of Figure 5 and Figure 9 are a result of this problem.

Specifically, for MobileMedia this was a large problem in two releases (5 and 7) as a number of base components were renamed. This renaming caused multiple pointcuts to change and that effect was duplicated in the module definitions. This problem does not necessarily manifest itself in Open Modules, as originally defined by Aldrich but is an artifact of this specific implementation.

9. Conclusion and Future Work

Finding a good separation of concerns is an important problem. It is vital for improving the reliability and evolution of software systems. New modularization techniques enable improved separation of concerns. Their invention and refinement is thus equally important for maintaining intellectual control on the growing complexity of software systems. Pattern-based [15] and annotation-based [13] pointcuts, open modules [1, 17], and quantified, typed events [19] are examples of such modularization mechanisms.

In this paper, we presented a rigorous evaluation of these AO interfaces on two already well-substantiated case studies [8, 20]. The results of our change propagation and analysis using standard design metrics [4, 6, 10] show that annotation-based pointcuts and quantified, typed events help limit the impact of change, at the cost of increased explicit coupling. This coupling however is generally not a problem as it is to interface-like entities (annotations and event types), not between base components and/or aspects.

Despite the similarites, quantified, typed events have several benefits over annotation-based pointcuts. Event types are flexible and do not suffer from quantification failure. Additionally, the uniform access to context information avoided the need to break encapsulation by exposing fields to make them available to the aspects.

In the future we plan to perform a net options value analysis [3, 23] to investigate the trade-off between the higher coupling of the annotation-based pointcut and quantified, typed event releases and the stability provided by their interfaces between aspect and base code.

Acknowledgments This work was supported in part by the NSF grant CCF-10-17334. Mehdi Bagherzadeh and Youssef Hanna provided useful comments and discussion.

References

[1] J. Aldrich. Open Modules: Modular reasoning about advice. In *ECOOP '05*, pages 144–168, 2005.

[2] P. Avgustinov, A. S. Christensen, L. Hendren, S. Kuzins, J. Lhotak, O. Lhotak, O. de Moor, D. Sereni, G. Sittampalam, and J. Tibble. abc: an extensible AspectJ compiler. In *AOSD*, pages 87–98, 2005.

[3] C. Y. Baldwin and K. B. Clark. *Design Rules, Vol. 1: The Power of Modularity*. MIT Press, 2000.

[4] S. R. Chidamber and C. F. Kemerer. A metrics suite for object oriented design. *IEEE TSE*, 20(6):476–493, 1994.

[5] T. Ekman and G. Hedin. The JastAdd system — modular extensible compiler construction. *Sci. Comput. Program.*, 69 (1-3):14–26, 2007.

[6] N. E. Fenton and S. L. Pfleeger. *Software Metrics: A Rigorous and Practical Approach*. Course Technology, 1998.

[7] F. Ferrari, R. Burrows, O. Lemos, A. Garcia, E. Figueiredo, N. Cacho, F. Lopes, N. Temudo, L. Silva, S. Soares, A. Rashid, P. Masiero, T. Batista, and J. Maldonado. An exploratory study of fault-proneness in evolving aspect-oriented programs. In *ICSE'10*, pages 65–74, 2010.

[8] E. Figueiredo, N. Cacho, C. Sant'Anna, M. Monteiro, U. Kulesza, A. Garcia, S. Soares, F. Ferrari, S. Khan, F. Cas-

tor Filho, and F. Dantas. Evolving software product lines with aspects: an empirical study on design stability. In *ICSE*, 2008.

[9] F. C. Filho, N. Cacho, E. Figueiredo, R. Maranhão, A. Garcia, and C. M. F. Rubira. Exceptions and aspects: The devil is in the details. In *FSE*, 2006.

[10] A. Garcia, C. Sant'Anna, E. Figueiredo, U. Kulesza, C. Lucena, and A. von Staa. Modularizing design patterns with aspects: a quantitative study. In *AOSD*, pages 3–14, 2005.

[11] P. Greenwood, T. T. Bartolomei, E. Figueiredo, M. Dósea, A. F. Garcia, N. Cacho, C. Sant'Anna, S. Soares, P. Borba, U. Kulesza, and A. Rashid. On the impact of aspectual decompositions on design stability: An empirical study. In *ECOOP*, pages 176–200, 2007.

[12] K. J. Hoffman and P. Eugster. Towards reusable components with aspects: an empirical study on modularity and obliviousness. In *30th International Conference on Software Engineering (ICSE)*, pages 91–100, 2008.

[13] G. Kiczales and M. Mezini. Separation of concerns with procedures, annotations, advice and pointcuts. In *ECOOP '05*, pages 195–213, 2005.

[14] G. Kiczales and M. Mezini. Aspect-oriented programming and modular reasoning. In *27th international conference on Software engineering (ICSE)*, pages 49–58, 2005.

[15] G. Kiczales, E. Hilsdale, J. Hugunin, M. Kersten, J. Palm, and W. G. Griswold. An overview of AspectJ. In *ECOOP*, 2001.

[16] U. Kulesza, C. Sant'Anna, A. Garcia, R. Coelho, A. von Staa, and C. Lucena. Quantifying the effects of aspect-oriented programming: A maintenance study. In *International Conference on Software Maintenance (ICSM)*, pages 223–233, 2006.

[17] N. Ongkingco, P. Avgustinov, J. Tibble, L. Hendren, O. de Moor, and G. Sittampalam. Adding Open Modules to AspectJ. In *AOSD '06*, pages 39–50, 2006.

[18] D. L. Parnas. On the criteria to be used in decomposing systems into modules. *Communications of the ACM*, 15(12): 1053–8, December 1972.

[19] H. Rajan and G. T. Leavens. Ptolemy: A language with quantified, typed events. In *ECOOP*, 2008.

[20] S. Soares, E. Laureano, and P. Borba. Implementing distribution and persistence aspects with AspectJ. In *17th conference on Object-oriented programming, systems, languages, and applications (OOPSLA)*, pages 174–190, 2002.

[21] F. Steimann, T. Pawlitzki, S. Apel, and C. Kastner. Types and modularity for implicit invocation with implicit announcement. *TOSEM '10*, 20(1), 2007.

[22] M. Störzer and C. Koppen. PCDiff: Attacking the fragile pointcut problem. In *European Interactive Workshop on Aspects in Software*, September 2004.

[23] K. J. Sullivan, W. G. Griswold, Y. Cai, and B. Hallen. The structure and value of modularity in software design. In *ESEC/FSE*, 2001.

[24] K. J. Sullivan, W. G. Griswold, H. Rajan, Y. Song, Y. Cai, M. Shonle, and N. Tewari. Modular aspect-oriented design with XPIs. *ACM TOSEM*, 20(2), 2009.

[25] T. Young. Using AspectJ to build a software product line for mobile devices. Master's thesis, UBC, 2005.

Comprehensively Evaluating Conformance Error Rates of Applying Aspect State Machines

Shaukat Ali

Certus Software V&V Center, Simula
Research Laboratory
P.O. Box 134, 1325, Lysaker, Norway
Department of Informatics, University of
Oslo, Oslo, Norway
shaukat@simula.no

Tao Yue

Certus Software V&V Center, Simula
Research Laboratory
P.O. Box 134, 1325, Lysaker, Norway
tao@simula.no

Zafar I. Malik

Academy of Educational Planning and
Management,
Ministry of Education, Islamabad, Pakistan
zafarimalik@acm.org

Abstract

Aspect Oriented Modeling (AOM) aims to provide enhanced separation of concerns during the design phase and proclaims many benefits (e.g., easier model evolution, reduced modeling effort, and reduced modeling errors) over traditional modeling paradigms such as object-oriented modeling. However, empirical evaluations of these benefits is severely lacking in the AOM community. In this paper, we empirically evaluate one of the AOM profiles: AspectSM, via a controlled experiment to assess if it can help in reducing modeling errors (referred as conformance errors in this paper), which is one of the benefits offered by AOM. AspectSM is a UML profile, which is developed to support automated state-based robustness testing. With AspectSM, crosscutting behaviors are modeled as aspect state machines using the stereotypes defined in AspectSM. We evaluate the conformance error rates of applying AspectSM from various perspectives by conducting four activities: 1) identifying modeling defects, 2) comprehending state machines, 3) modeling state machines, and 4) weaving aspect state machines into base state machines. For most of these activities, experimental results show that the error rates while performing these four activities using AspectSM are significantly lower than standard UML state machine modeling approaches.

Categories and Subject Descriptors D.2.2 [**Design Tools and Techniques**] State diagrams, Object-oriented design methods G.3 [**Probability and Statistics**] Experimental Design

General Terms Measurement, Design, Reliability, and Experimentation

Keywords Aspect-oriented Modeling, Controlled Experiment, Modeling Errors, UML State machines

1. Introduction

Aspects are increasingly being used in various software development phases such as requirements, analysis, design, development and testing. Aspect-oriented paradigm aims to provide enhanced Separation of Concerns (SoC) and hence yield several potential benefits such as enhanced modularization, easier evolution, increased reusability, understandability, and applicability. Aspect-Oriented Modeling (AOM) is a research stream in this field and aims to support SoC during design

modeling and it also claims similar benefits. However, there is very little empirical evidence of such benefits. Empirical studies are required to support these benefits about AOM and better understand its limitations.

While modeling behavior of industrial systems, such as using UML state machines, it is important to not only model nominal behavior but also robustness behavior which describes how the system should react to abnormal environmental conditions. It is needed to support, for example, model-based robustness testing of embedded or communication systems, which is the aim of the AspectSM profile [1]. It was developed to support model-based robustness testing of video conference system of Cisco, Norway [1]. However the approach is general enough to be used for other embedded or communication systems. Using AspectSM, crosscutting behavior can be modeled as aspect state machines, in order to facilitate the use of AOM for the purpose of SoC and therefore increase the readability, understandability, and applicability.

Motivated by this, we report a controlled experiment to comprehensively check whether AspectSM can help achieve lower error rates when performing the following four modeling activities: 1) identifying seeded defects, 2) comprehending state machines, 3) modeling crosscutting behaviors, and 4) weaving crosscutting behaviors (modeled as aspect state machines) to their corresponding base state machines. AspectSM is compared with standard UML state machines when crosscutting behavior is modeled using different modeling approaches. The controlled experiment was conducted with 25 fully trained, graduate students taking a graduate course in "Advanced Software Architecture" at the University Institute of Information Technology (UIIT) at the Pir Mehr Ali Shah Arid Agriculture University, Rawalpindi, Pakistan.

Results of the experiment showed that AspectSM has significantly lower error rates in terms of identifying modeling defects than the standard UML state machine modeling approach. Regarding comprehensibility, we observed that standard UML state machines with hierarchy achieved significantly lower error rates than aspect state machines. For the activity of modeling crosscutting behaviors, we found that aspect state machines have significantly lower error rates than standard UML state machines. Finally, we observed that for weaving aspect state machines, conformance error rate is on average less than 30%.

The rest of the paper is organized as follows: Section 2 describes the necessary background to understand the rest of the paper. Section 3 provides details on our experiment planning, and Section 4 reports on results and discussions. Section 5 presents possible threats to validity and Section 6 compares existing, related experiments in Aspect-oriented Programming (AOP) to our experiment. Finally, we conclude our paper in Section 7.

2. Background

In this section, we provide a brief reminder of UML state machines and an overview of aspect state machines in AspectSM, the AOM mechanism being evaluated in our controlled experiment.

2.1 UML State Machines

UML state machines enable modeling the dynamic behavior of a class, subsystem, or system. State machines in general are extensively used to model a variety of systems such as communication [2] and control systems [3]. Due to the ability of state machines to capture rich and detailed information, they have been used for automatic code generation [4] and the automated generation of test cases [5-7]. UML state machines provide many advanced features such as concurrency and hierarchy, which aim at supporting large-scale modeling. Concurrency enables the modeling of concurrent behavior whereas state hierarchies capture commonalities among states. A submachine state in a state machine functions like a simple state, but is referring to another state machine. A submachine can be reused in more than one state machine and may refer to other submachines [8]. They can therefore help reduce the structural complexity of state machines. State machines developed using the hierarchical features of UML will be referred to as hierarchical state machines in this paper and the ones developed without using submachine states, with only basic features of UML state machines, will be referred as flat state machines.

2.2 Aspect State Machines

AspectSM is a UML profile described in [1], which supports the modeling of a system robustness behavior, which is very common type of crosscutting behavior in many types of systems. An example of a robustness behavior for a communication system is related to how the system should react, in various states, in the presence of high packet loss. The system should be able to recover lost packets and continue to behave normally in a degraded mode. In the worst case, the system should go back to the most recent state and not simply crash or show inappropriate behavior. In a control system, one needs to model, for example, how the system should react, in various states, when a sensor breaks down. Though AspectSM was originally defined to support scalable, model-based, robustness testing, including test case and oracle generation, a fundamental question is whether it is easier to model crosscutting concerns such as robustness with AOM in general, and AspectSM in particular, than simply relying

on UML state machines to do it all. In AspectSM, the core functionality of a system is modeled as one or more standard UML state machines (called base state machines). Crosscutting behavior of the system (e.g., robustness behavior) is modeled as aspect state machines using the AspectSM profile. State machines developed using this profile will be referred as aspect state machines. A weaver [1] then automatically weaves aspect state machines into base state machine to obtain a complete model, that can for example be used for testing purposes. The AspectSM profile specifies stereotypes for all features of AOM, in which the concepts of Aspect, Joinpoint, Pointcut, Advice, and Introduction [9] are the most important ones. Below, we briefly describe these concepts along with how they are represented in the profile. Figure 1 shows the metamodel representing and relating these concepts. The complete discussion of the AspectSM profile can be found in [1]. We can see from that description that proper modeling requires the modeler to master AOM concepts and mentally determine the end result of weaving; an exercise that cannot be taken for granted and be a priori considered easier than directly modeling crosscutting concerns in a state machine. Investigating the benefits of AspectSM, and more generally AOM, is the main purpose of our experiment.

2.2.1 Main Concepts in AspectSM

Aspect This concept describes a crosscutting concern, e.g., the robustness behavior of a system in the presence of failures in its environment (e.g., network failures in communication systems). Using the AspectSM profile, we model each aspect as a UML 2.0 state machine augmented with stereotypes and attributes.

Joinpoint A Joinpoint is a model element selected by a *Pointcut* (defined next) where an *Advice* or *Introduction* (additional behavior) can be applied [9]. In the context of UML, all modeling elements in UML can be possibly joinpoints. In UML state machines, joinpoints can be, for example, *State*, *Activity*, *Constraint*, *Transition*, *Behavior*, *Trigger*, and *Event*.

Pointcut A *Pointcut* selects one or more joinpoints, where *Advice* or *Introduction* can be applied. A *Pointcut* can have at most one *Before* advice, one *Around* advice and one *After* advice. In the AspectSM profile, all pointcuts are expressed with the Object Constraint Language (OCL) [8] on the UML 2.0 metamodel [8]. We decided to use the OCL to query joinpoints because the OCL is the standard way to write constraints and queries on UML models and can therefore be used to query jointpoints in UML state machines. Also, several OCL evaluators are currently available that can be used to evaluate OCL expressions such as the IBM OCL evaluator [10], OCLE 2.0 [11], and EyeOCL [12]. Furthermore, writing pointcuts as OCL expressions does not require the modeler to learn a notation that is not part of the UML

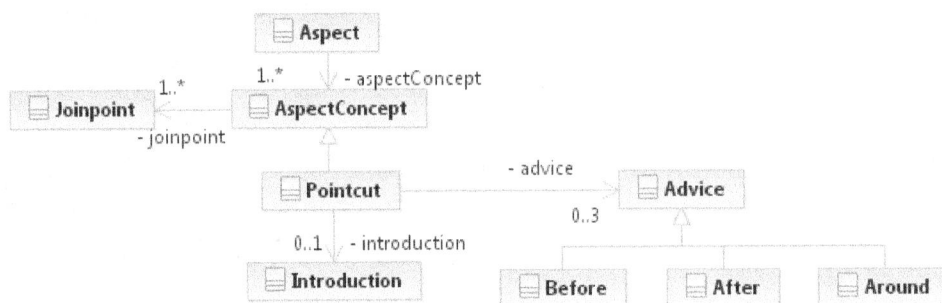

Figure 1. Conceptual domain model of the AspectSM profile

standard. In the literature, several alternatives are proposed to write pointcuts [13-17] but all of them either rely on languages (mostly based on wildcard characters to select joinpoints, for instance, '*' to select all joinpoints) or diagrammatic notations which are not standard, thus forcing modelers to learn and apply new notations or languages. Using the OCL, we can write precise pointcuts to select jointpoints with similar properties. We do so by selecting modeling elements (jointpoints) based on the properties of UML metaclasses. This further gives us the flexibility to specify precise pointcuts as any condition defined based on some or all of the properties of a UML metaclass, e.g., a pointcut on the *Transition* metaclass, selecting a subset of transitions in a base state machine, which have triggers of type *CallEvent* and do not have any guard.

Advice An *Advice* is one of the crosscutting behaviors of the Aspect. The *Advice* is attached to Joinpoint(s) selected by the *Pointcut*. In correspondence to AspectJ [18] concepts, an *Advice* can be of type *Before*, *After*, or *Around*. A *Before* advice is applied before Joinpoint(s), an *After* advice is applied after Joinpoint(s), whereas an *Around* advice replaces Joinpoint(s). For example, introducing guards on a set of transitions of a state machine is an example of a *Before* advice on transitions (*Joinpoint*).

Introduction An *Introduction* is similar to the inter-type declaration concept in AspectJ [18]. Using *Introduction* in our context, new modeling elements (e.g., state or transition) can be introduced into a UML state machine.

2.2.2 Example of applying AspectSM

In this section, we present an example of the application of AspectSM. An aspect state machine modeling crosscutting behavior *EmergencyStop* is shown in Figure 2. This UML state machine is stereotyped as <<Aspect>>, which means that it is an aspect state machine. The <<Aspect>> stereotype has two attributes: *name* and *baseStateMachine*, whose values are shown in the note labeled as '1' in Figure 2. The name attribute contains the name of the aspect (*EmergencyStop* in this example), whereas the *baseStateMachine* attribute holds the name of the base state machine, on which this aspect will be woven, which is *ElevatorControl* provided in [19] in this example.

The aspect state machine consists of two states: *SelectedStates* and *ElevatorStopped*. *SelectedStates* is stereotyped as <<Pointcut>>, which means that this state selects states from the base state machine. There are two attributes of <<Pointcut>>, whose values are shown in the note labeled as '2' in Figure 2. The

name attribute indicates the name of the pointcut and type denotes the type of the pointcut, which is *All* in this case meaning that we are selecting all states of the base state machine. In AspectSM, different types of pointcuts can defined, a complete list of other types of pointcuts is presented in [1]. All the model elements stereotyped as <<Introduction>> (one state, two transitions) will be newly introduced elements in the base state machine during weaving. This aspect introduces the *ElevatorStopped* state in the base state machine, and selects all states of the base state machines and introduces transitions from them to *ElevatorStopped* with trigger *EmergencyStopButtonPressed*. In addition this aspect introduces transitions from *ElevatorStopped* to all the states selected by *SelectedStates* with trigger *EmergencyStopButtonReleased*.

3. Experiment Planning

This section discusses planning of the experiment based on the experiment reporting template defined by Wohlin et al. [20].

3.1 Goal, Research Questions and Hypotheses

The objective of our experiment is to assess the AspectSM profile with respect to the modeling errors made by the subjects while performing different modeling activities. Modeling errors are assessed from four perspectives corresponding to four activities of applying AspectSM: 1) errors made while inspecting state machines to identify seeded defects, 2) errors made while comprehending state machines via answering a comprehension questionnaire, 3) errors made while designing state machines, and 4) errors made while weaving an aspect state machine into its base state machine.

Based on the above-mentioned objectives of our experiment, we defined the following research questions:
RQ1: Does the use of AspectSM reduce errors while inspecting aspect state machines (against their specifications) to identify defects, when compared to hierarchical and flat state machines?

We compare aspect state machines with two different types of state machines capturing crosscutting behavior: hierarchical and flat state machines for this activity. None of the expected differences between them can a priori be certain to be in a specific direction. This therefore leads to the definition of two-tailed hypotheses.

H^1_0: *Error rate in inspecting aspect state machines to detect defects is the same as hierarchical state machines.*

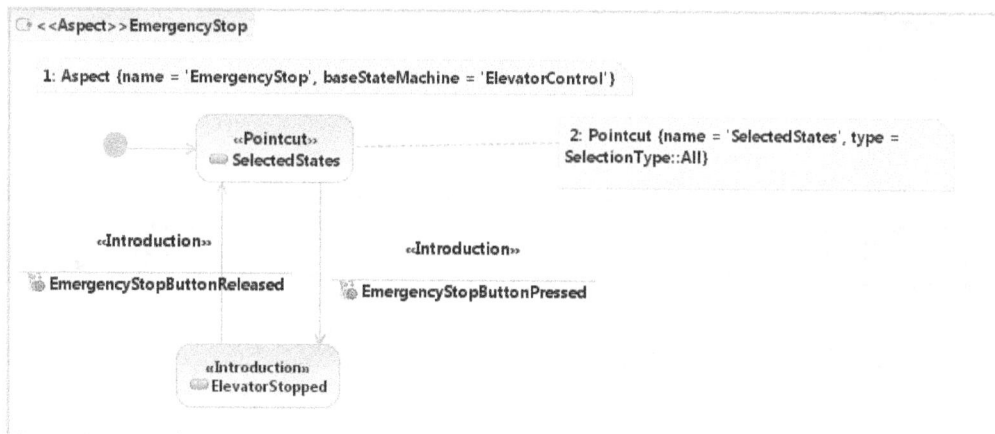

Figure 2. An aspect state machine for crosscutting behavior EmergencyStop

H^2_0: *Error rate in inspecting aspect state machines to detect defects is the same as flat state machines.*

RQ2: Does the use of AspectSM reduce errors in comprehending aspect state machines when compared to hierarchical and flat state machines?

Similar to the previous research question, we compare the comprehensibility of AspectSM with the two different types of state machines capturing crosscutting behavior (hierarchical and flat state machines) based on the scores to answer a comprehension questionnaire. We defined the following two-tailed null hypotheses accordingly.

H^3_0: *The error rate in comprehending aspect state machines is the same as hierarchical state machines.*

H^4_0: *The error rate in comprehending aspect state machines is the same as flat state machines.*

RQ 3: Does the use of AspectSM reduce conformance errors of designing aspect state machines with respect to reference state machines, when compared to flat state machines and/or hierarchical state machines?

We evaluate AspectSM from the perspective of how well it can support the activity of modeling crosscutting behaviors by measuring conformance error rates of aspect state machines against their reference state machines. We further calculate conformance error rates of using flat state machines and/or hierarchical state machines to model the same crosscutting behaviors against their respective reference state machines. Finally, we compare the conformance error rates of aspect state machines with the conformance error rates of the flat and/or hierarchical state machines for the same crosscutting behaviors. Since the differences in results can be in either direction, we defined a two tailed null hypothesis as follows:

H^5_0: *Conformance error of aspect state machines is the same as flat/hierarchical state machines.*

RQ 4: To which extent do the woven state machines derived by subjects conform to the reference state machines automatically produced by our weaver?

This question calculates the errors made by the subjects to weave aspect state machines into their corresponding base state machine for the purpose of evaluating how well the subjects can understand the aspect state machines through this weaving activity. In our previous work [1], we developed a weaver for AspectSM, which automatically weaves aspect state machines into base state machines and produces a woven state machine. To answer this research question, we compared woven state

machines developed by a subject with the woven state machines automatically produced by our weaver.

3.2 Experiment Subjects

Our controlled experiment was conducted at the Pir Mehr Ali Shah Arid Agriculture University, Rawalpindi, Pakistan. The subjects in the experiment are 25 graduate students taking a graduate course in 'Advanced Software Architecture' at the University Institute of Information Technology (UIIT). Our motivation was to find a group of subjects with adequate background that could be trained to use our AOM approach over a short period of time. Most practitioners have very little knowledge of AOP and even less of AOM. Ensuring they have the required background is also difficult. This is why we relied on a group of mature graduate students.

The course is offered in the Master of Science program. The students in this degree already hold a Bachelor in Computer Science or Information Technology and have already been exposed to the UML notation and extensions in the form of UML profiles. On average, each student went through five development and two modeling courses. Eighteen students (out of twenty-five) have used the UML notation for their final year projects before the experiment was conducted. Twenty students gained experience in development work in IT companies or as teaching staff in computer science.

The subjects were free to choose to participate or not into the experiment and were told their choice would have no effect on their course grades.

3.3 Material

In this section, we provide the material we used to conduct the experiment.

3.3.1 Case Study Systems

Two case study systems were used for the experiment: elevator control system (ECS) and automated teller machine (ATM). Detailed description of ECS/ATM and the crosscutting behaviors used in the experiment is presented in [21]. The complexity of the state machines in terms of numbers of model elements of the two case study systems is shown in Table 1. Below, we provide a brief but necessary discussion of these two case study systems.

Elevator Control System The first system used for the experiment is an elevator control system (ECS) that controls movements of an elevator in a building. For our experiment, we extended the specification of the elevator given in [19] with two additional crosscutting behaviors so that the AspectSM profile could be used to model them. These two crosscutting behaviors are:

Emergency call behavior (Call) The behavior of an elevator, when an emergency call is made.

Table 1. Complexity of the state machines

Case Study	Crosscutting Behavior	ASM				HSM			FSM		
		#S	#T	#P	Total	#S	#T	Total	#S	#T	Total
ECS	Emergency Call	16	18	1	35	17	21	38	15	27	42
	Emergency Stop	14	17	1	32	14	17	31	13	23	36
ATM	Cancel Transaction	7	15	2	24	-	-	-	6	15	21
	Network Failure	8	16	2	26	-	-	-	7	22	29
	Power Failure	8	15	2	25	-	-	-	7	21	28
ATM	Cancel Transaction	-	-	-	-	-	-	-	6	15	21
	Network Failure	-	-	-	-	-	-	-	7	22	29
	Power Failure	-	-	-	-	-	-	-	7	21	28

ASM = Aspect State Machine, HSM = Hierarchical State Machine, FSM = Flat State Machine
#S = Number of states, #T = Number of transitions, #P = Number of pointcuts

Emergency stop behavior (Stop) the behavior of an elevator, when the emergency stop button is pressed.

Automated Teller Machine The second system used for the experiment is the popular automated teller machine (ATM) system from [19].

"A bank has several (ATMs), which are geographically distributed and connected via a wide area network to a central server. Each ATM machine has a card reader, a cash dispenser, a keyboard/display, and a receipt printer. By using the ATM machine, a customer can withdraw cash from either a checking or a saving account, query the balance of an account, or transfer funds from one account to another. A transaction is initiated when a customer inserts an ATM card into the card reader. Encoded on the magnetic strip on the back of the card is recognized, the system validates the ATM card to determine that the expiration date has not passed, that the user-entered PIN matches the PIN maintained by the system, and that the card is not lost or stolen. The customer is allowed three attempts to enter the correct PIN; the card is confiscated if the third attempt fails."

The following crosscutting behaviors were defined for ATM.

Cancel Transaction A customer may cancel a transaction at any time except when the ATM is closed down or not idle. Whenever a cancel request is made, the transaction is terminated and then the card is ejected.

Network Failure An important robustness behavior of ATM is the behavior in the presence of network failure. Whenever network connection fails during the operation of ATM except when it is closed down, it saves the current transaction in its local memory and then tries to recover the network connection. If the network connection is established, the saved transaction is loaded and ATM continues the transaction. Otherwise, it will simply be closed down.

Power Failure Another robustness behavior of ATM is that in the case of power failure it starts its Uninterruptable Power Supply (UPS) and continues the operation.

3.3.2 Design Defect Classification

To answer RQ1 (Section 3.1), the experiment subjects were asked to identify defects seeded in state machines through checking the conformance of the state machines against their corresponding specifications (Section 3.4).

To systematically inspect state machines for various types of defects, a classification of different types of design defects is required. The classification we used in the experiment is given below and was adapted from Binder's book [6]. It was provided to the subjects of the experiment as part of the answer sheet (Section 3.3.5) to systematically collect their answers.

Incorrect Transition (IT) A transition that comes from or leads to a wrong state or the transition has wrong guard, trigger, and/or events.

Missing Transition (MT) According to the specification of a state machine, there is a transition missing.

Extra Transition (ET) A transition is subsumed by another transition in a state machine. Such a transition is redundant in the sense that removing it still keeps the state machine in conformance to its specification.

Missing State (MS) A state that should be modeled in a state machine according to its specification but is missing.

Incorrect State (IS) A state is incorrect if it has a wrong state invariant, do, entry and/or exit activities.

Extra State (ES) A state is subsumed by another state. This state is considered as an extra state in the sense that removing it still keeps the state machine in conformance to its specification.

3.3.3 Seeded Defects

It is important to note that to answer RQ1, we were interested in studying errors made by the subjects while inspecting crosscutting behaviors to detect defects; therefore we seeded defects only in the crosscutting behaviors. Different types of defects were selected after we carefully examined the base and aspect state machines and identified possible independent defects. This resulted in three types of defects for the first crosscutting behavior (Call): missing transition (MT), incorrect transition (IT), and incorrect state (IS), and a missing transition (MT) for the second crosscutting behavior (Stop). Table 2 shows the distribution of these defects that were seeded in the compared state machines.

Because aspects model crosscutting behavior, it is expected that one defect in an aspect often corresponds to several defects in the corresponding hierarchical state machine. Similarly, because hierarchical states factor out common behavior, one defect in a hierarchical state machine often leads to several defects in its corresponding flat state machine. As a result, different numbers of defects were seeded in the three state machines in order to conceptually correspond to equivalent defects.

Table 2. Distribution of seeded defects in state machines

Approach	Call			Stop
	MT	IT	IS	MT
Aspect	1	1	1	1
Hierarchical	4	2	1	1
Flat	11	9	1	10

3.3.4 Comprehension Questionnaire

For RQ2, we want to evaluate how error prone it is to comprehend various types of state machines. To this effect, a comprehension questionnaire was designed to evaluate, in a repeatable and objective way, the extent to which a subject can understand the state machines. For example, questions concern what scenario is triggered when an event happens in a certain state. The subjects were asked the same ten questions on two crosscutting behaviors together for all three types of state machines. The subjects had to answer each question by inspecting the state machines assigned to them and error scores were computed by accounting for partially correct answers. For example, if the answer to a question entailed to list four transitions, then wrongly pointing out each transition contributed 0.25 to the full mark of the question.

3.3.5 Answer Sheets

There were four answer sheets developed for the experiment. The first answer sheet (for RQ1) was developed to collect information about classes of defects that were identified by each subject, the number of defects in each class, and the location of identified defects. A table was provided to subjects for each crosscutting behavior. The rows of the table were labeled with each defect class, whereas the columns featured two pieces of information about defects: number of defects identified in each class and location of each identified defect. The second answer sheet (for RQ2) was designed to collect answers to the comprehension questionnaire. The third answer sheet (for RQ3) was developed to collect answers for two groups modeling crosscutting behaviors:

Table 3. Design of the experiment

Round	Task	Task Type	Case Study	Crosscutting behavior	Group 1		Group 2		Group 3	
					Approach	Data points	Approach	Data points	Approach	Data points
1	R1T1	Identify Defects	ECS	Emergency call	ASM	8	HSM	8	FSM	9
				Emergency stop	ASM	8	HSM	8	FSM	9
	R1T2	Comprehend state machines		Emergency call and stop	FSM	9	ASM	8	HSM	8
2	R2T1	Model crosscutting behaviors	ATM	Cancel transaction	ASM	10	FSM	10	-	-
				Network failure	ASM	10	FSM	10	-	-
				Power failure	ASM	10	FSM	10	-	-
3	R3T1	Weave crosscutting behaviors	ATM	Cancel transaction	-	15	-	-	-	-
				Network failure	-	15	-	-	-	-
				Power failure	-	15	-	-	-	-

ASM: Aspect state machine, FSM: Flat state machine, and HSM: Hierarchical state machine
R1T1: Round 1 Task 1, R1T2: Round 1 Task 2, R2T1: Round 2 Task 1, and R3T1: Round 3 Task 1

one for the group using standard UML state machines to directly model crosscutting behaviors on the base state machine and the second for the group modeling crosscutting behaviors using aspect state machines. The answer sheet was designed so that subjects can provide their solution one after another and provide time required to model each crosscutting behavior. The fourth answer sheet (for RQ4) was developed to collect woven state machines from subjects. The answer sheet contained a base state machine and three aspect state machines corresponding to the three crosscutting behaviors (Section 3.3) of the ATM system. The answer sheet was designed such that the subjects can provide their solutions one after another and provide time they spent to weave each aspect state machine into the base state machine.

3.4 Design

The design of our experiment is summarized in Table 3. Our experiment design consists of three rounds. For the first round, we divided the subjects into three groups: Group1, Group2, and Group 3. Given the number of subjects, this led respectively to 8, 8, and 9 subjects in each group. In the first round, there were two tasks. In each task, each group was given a different type of state machines (Aspect, Hierarchical, or Flat). During the training sessions (Section 3.6), each subject was equally trained to understand all three different types of state machines. The subjects were also given a modeling assignment, after the training sessions, for them to practice before the actual experiment tasks. This assignment was marked by the first author of this paper and grades were used to form blocks (i.e., groups of students of equivalent skills). The experiment groups were then formed through randomization and blocking to obtain three comparable groups with similar proportions of students from each skill block.

As shown in Table 3, for R1T1 (Round 1 Task 2), each group was asked to sequentially identify defects in the state machines modeling two crosscutting behaviors: Emergency call and Emergency stop. Group 1 was given state machines modeled using AspectSM. The subjects in Group 1 were given one base state machine and one aspect state machine (ASM) modeling Emergency Call and one ASM for the Emergency Stop crosscutting behavior. Group 2 was given one hierarchical state machine (HSM) for Emergency Call and one HSM for Emergency Stop. Similarly, Group 3 was given one flat state machine (FSM) for Emergency Call and one FSM for Emergency Stop. Seeded defects for each type of state machines (Aspect, Hierarchical, and Flat) are presented in Table 2. For R1T1, we used a between-subjects design, which offers several advantages. First, a between-subjects design counterbalances learning effects since each subject is exposed to just one type of treatment (e.g.,

the Aspect approach) and one task (e.g., one crosscutting behavior) and thus the performance of subjects is not influenced with the experience gained while working with other treatments with the same crosscutting behavior. Second, between-subjects design counterbalances fatigued effect, which is common while working with several treatments for many tasks.

In R1T2, the three groups divided for R1T1 were rotated for pedagogical reasons so that each group can experience difference types of state machines. For example, Group 1 in R1T2 was given flat state machines instead of the aspect state machines which is the case in R1T1.

In R2T1, the subjects were divided into two groups: one group (the FSM group) was asked to use flat state machines to design crosscutting behavior and the other (the ASM group) was asked to apply ASM. Both groups were asked to model the same set of crosscutting behaviors, based on the same base state machine specifying the core behavior of the ATM system. The ASM group was asked to model crosscutting behaviors as aspect state machines, whereas the FSM group was asked to model crosscutting behaviors directly on the base state machine. Notice that in this round, 20 subjects participated in the experiment; therefore we have 10 subjects per group. Again in this round, we used a between-subjects design because of the same reasons as we discussed previously.

In R3T1, there was just one group of subjects and they were asked to sequentially perform three tasks by weaving one aspect state machine at a time and provide the time they spent to each weaving activity. The three tasks were to weave the following three aspect state machines: Cancel transaction, Network failure, and Power failure. A brief description of these aspect state machines is provided in Section 3.3.1. In this round, 15 subjects participated in the experiment.

Note that in Table 3 for different rounds, different number of subjects participated. This is due to the reason that each round was conducted on a separate day and some subjects couldn't participate, for instance, due to practical reasons such as clashes with courses and exams.

3.5 Dependent Variables

Error Rate in Identifying Defects (ERID) This variable calculates the percentage of seeded defects not identified by a subject and is calculated as:

Number of unidentified defects by a subject / Total number of seeded defects

Error rate of answering comprehension questionnaire (ERC) This calculates the error rate of answering the comprehension questionnaire and is calculated as:

Sum of the scores of the wrong answers of the questions / Total number of questions (i.e. 10)

In the formula above, the score for each answer was calculated based on the marking procedure discussed in Section 3.3.4 and 10 is the total number of the questions in the questionnaire.

Conformance error of state machine (CERSM) This variable measures the conformance error of a subject's state machine by comparing it with a reference state machine. It is determined by the conformance error of states and transitions-two main modeling elements of a state machine. Note that, since we have two sets of results with respect to two different treatments (for R2T1): flat state machines and aspect state machines, two sets of measures were designed to evaluate the completeness of two different types of state machines derived by the subjects given different treatments.

The formula for *CERT* (i.e., conformance error in transitions) shown in Table 4, calculates the conformance error of a subject's state machine by looking at the transitions of the subject's solution with the reference solution (this holds for each group) that do not match. Matching of transitions is determined by looking at whether the source and target states of a transition match to the source and target states of any transition in the reference model. Three model elements constituting a transition (i.e., guard, trigger, and effect) are further assessed to evaluate the conformance error of a transition. Matching of the trigger, guard, and effect of a transition is determined whether their names are the same or similar to the corresponding elements of the matched transition in the reference state machine. The conformance error of a transition is calculated based on the proportion of the trigger, guard, and effect of the transition that do not match with the reference solution. For instance, if only the guard and trigger of a transition do not match with a transition in the reference solution, then this means that the transition conformance error is 66% (2/3) to the reference transition. In other words, 33% (1/3) of modeling elements of the transition are missing. For flat state machines, we compare only the guard, trigger, and effect of a transition; while for aspect state machines, in addition we also check whether required stereotypes are applied to transitions. This is so because AspectSM requires applying stereotypes on states and transitions in aspect state machines (Section 2.2). For each transition k in a subject's solution, we check if its guard, trigger, or effect is missing with respect to the matched transition in the reference solution (Table 5). For each missing guard, trigger, and effect, we assign value 1 to the corresponding variable (E_{guard_k}, $E_{trigger\_k}$ or E_{effect_k}), otherwise 0.

Similarly, we calculate *CERS* as shown in Table 4, whereas Table 5 shows the measures needed for the calculation. Since state and transition are two main types of model elements of a UML state machine, the overall conformance error (*CERSM*) of the state machine is therefore calculated based on the conformance error of states and transitions, as shown in Table 4. A simpler way to do so is to just simply take average of *CERT* and *CERS*. However, the numbers of states and transitions in a

Table 4. Conformance error rate measures for a state machine diagram

Category	Measure	Formula	Formula
CERSM	CERS	E_S	$\dfrac{(N_{t\_r} * CERT + N_{s\_r} * CERS)}{N_{t\_r} + N_{s\_r}}$
	CERT	E_T	

N_{t_r} is the total number of the transitions in the reference model. N_{s_r} is the total number of the states in the reference model.

Table 5. Collected state machine diagram data

Measure	Specification
E_{Sname_k}	Missing name of the k_{th} state in a subject's state machine diagram
$E_{Sstereotype\_k}$	Missing stereotype of the k_{th} state in a subject's aspect state machine diagram
E_{guard_k}	Missing guard of the k_{th} transition in a subject's state machine diagram
$E_{trigger\_k}$	Missing trigger of the k_{th} transition in a subject's state machine diagram
E_{effect_k}	Missing effect of the k_{th} transition in a subject's state machine diagram
$E_{Tstereotype\_k}$	Missing stereotype of the k_{th} transition in a subject's aspect state machine diagram
E_S	For a standard state machine: $\dfrac{\sum_{k=1}^{n}(E_{Sname\_k})}{n}$
	For an aspect state machine: $\dfrac{\sum_{k=1}^{n}(E_{Sname\_k}+E_{Sstereotype\_k})/2}{n}$
E_T	For a standard state machine: $\dfrac{\sum_{k=1}^{n}(E_{Tguard\_k}+E_{Ttrigger\_k}+E_{Teffect\_k})/3}{n}$
	For an aspect state machine: $\dfrac{\sum_{k=1}^{n}(E_{Tguard\_k}+E_{Ttrigger\_k}+E_{Teffect\_k}+E_{Tstereotype\_k})/4}{n}$

E_{Sname_k}, $E_{Sstereotype\_k}$, E_{guard_k}, $E_{trigger\_k}$, E_{effect_k}, and $E_{Tstereotype\_k}$ are Boolean measures that take value 0 and 1 only. 'n' refers to the number of matched states or transitions.

Table 6. Statistical tests for measures

Round	Task	Measure	Approach	Mean difference	p-value (α = 0.05)
1	R1T1	ERID	ASM vs HSM	-0.56	**0.0011**
			ASM vs FSM	-0.62	**0.0001**
			HSM vs FSM	-0.06	0.8590
	R1T2	ERC	ASM vs HSM	2.17	**0.0419**
			ASM vs FSM	-1.89	0.0821
			HSM vs FSM	-4.06	**0.0038**
2	R2T1	CERT	ASM vs FSM	-0.05	**0.0237**
		CERS	ASM vs FSM	0.07	**0.0127**
		CERSM	ASM vs FSM	-0.14	**0.0368**

solution might be different, so taking average of them is unfair. So, to be fair in the calculation and considering each modeling element (state or transition) having same weight, we calculate the overall conformance error based on the proportions of states and transitions in a state machines. To achieve this, first we obtain the overall conformance error of transitions by multiplying *CERT* with the total number of the transitions in the reference model (N_{t_r}). Similarly, we calculate overall completeness of states by multiplying CERS with the total number of the states N_{s_r}. Finally, we take sum of both and divide it with the sum of the numbers of states and transitions in the reference state machine.

3.6 Procedure (Training)

The subjects were trained by the first author of this paper. Two three-hour sessions were given on the following topics: 1) Recap of UML state machines since subjects were already familiar with this topic preceding the training (Section 3.2), 2) Introduction to the Object Constraint Language (OCL), 3) Introduction to aspect-oriented software development (AOSD), and 4) Aspect-oriented modeling (AOM) using the AspectSM profile. Each topic was accompanied with several examples and interactive class assignments. As previously discussed, the subjects were given a home assignments after the training sessions to practice the three state machine modeling approaches and groups were later formed based on the grades of this assignment.

4. Results and Discussion

We analyze and present our experiment results in this section. Descriptive statistics and statistical tests are presented in Section 4.1 and Section 4.2, respectively. The discussion of results is provided in Section 4.3.

4.1 Descriptive Statistics

We report descriptive statistics for each dependent variable designed to answer each research question in Table 7. Descriptive statistics for each variable is characterized using their minimum, maximum, median, mean and standard deviation.

Recall from Section 3.5 that *ERID* aims to measure the percentage of defects not identified by the subjects in R1T1. We see that on average *ERID* for ASM is 19%, which is much lower than HSM and FSM, which are 74% and 81%, respectively. Regarding *ERC* (the variable that measures the error rate of answering the comprehensive questionnaire in R1T2), mean *ERC* for HSM is 1.44, which is lower than both ASM and FSM, which are 3.61 and 5.5, respectively.

To answer RQ2 and RQ3, variables *CERT*, *CERS*, and *CERSM* were designed to measure the conformance errors for ASM and FSM. As shown in Table 7, for R2T1, mean *CERT* for FSM (37%) is higher than ASM (23%). Mean *CERS* is 13% and 19% for FSM and ASM, respectively. Total conformance error rates (*CERSM*) for FSM and ASM are 36% and 22%, respectively. For R3T1, *CERT* for FSM is 31% and *CERS* is very low (i.e., 5%). Total mean conformance error (*CERSM*) is 29%.

4.2 Statistical Tests

In this section, we check whether the differences observed in the previous section are statistically significant to determine if we can reject the null hypotheses stated in Section 3.1. For all the statistical tests reported in this section, we used a significance level of α=0.05.

To check if, overall, there exist significant differences among the three approaches under investigation for round 1, we performed the Kruskal–Wallis one-way analysis of variance [22] on ERID and ERC. We performed this test since our samples are not normal as we checked with the Shapiro–Wilk W test [22]. We

Table 7. Descriptive statistics for measures

Round	Task	Measure	Approach	Min	Median	Max	Mean	Std
1	R1T1	ERID	ASM	0	0	1	0.19	0.32
			HSM	0	0.83	1	0.74	0.34
			FSM	0.1	0.9	1	0.81	0.25
	R1T2	ERC	ASM	1	3.5	6.25	3.61	2.08
			HSM	0	1.5	3.5	1.44	1.24
			FSM	2.25	6.13	8.5	5.5	2.45
2	R2T1	CERT	FSM	0	0.33	1	0.37	0.28
			ASM	0	0.13	1	0.23	0.30
		CERS	FSM	0	0	1	0.13	0.34
			ASM	0	0.25	0.5	0.19	0.18
		CERSM	FSM	0	0.33	0.89	0.36	0.24
			ASM	0	0.15	0.8	0.22	0.21
3	R3T1	CERT	FSM	0	0.34	0.84	0.31	0.28
		CERS	FSM	0	0	0.5	0.05	0.15
		CERSM	FSM	0	0.32	0.78	0.29	0.26

obtained p-values of 0.0001 and 0.0047 for ERID and ERC respectively, which are less than 0.05 hence are significant (Table 8). This encouraged us to perform a pairwise comparison of the distributions obtained for the three state machines using Mann–Whitney U for ERID and ERC. It doesn't assume normally distributed samples as it is our case as the results of the Shapiro–Wilk W test [22] showed. Pairwise p-values and mean differences across pairs for each measure are reported in Table 6. Bold p-values highlight statistically significant results. The mean differences between pairs of approaches indicate the direction in which the result is significant. For instance, in row 1, for measure ERID, between ASM vs HSM, the mean difference is negative and p-value is less than 0.05 (our selected significance level). This means that ERID for ASM is significantly lower than HSM.

For *CERT*, *CERS*, and *CERSM*, since we have two treatments, we performed the Wilcoxon signed-rank test [22], which is non-parametric equivalent of t-test. We performed this test because our samples are not normally distributed as we checked with the Shapiro–Wilk W test [22]. Again, bold values highlights that the results are significant and mean differences indicate the direction in which the results are significant.

4.3 Discussion

The above results showed that (Section 4.1 and Section 4.2), aspect state machines have significantly lower error rates than flat and hierarchical ones in terms of ERID given our selected α (0.05) and sample size (Table 3). This indicates that for the activity of identifying defects, the subjects given ASM made fewer errors than the subjects inspecting FSM and HSM. This can be explained from the fact that ASM is much simpler than HSM and FSM in terms of number of modeling elements (Table 1) and therefore the subjects with ASM had high possibility to identify defects. We did not observe significant difference between HSM and FSM in terms of ERID.

In terms of ERC, we observed that HSM achieved statistically lower error rate than ASM and FSM. The mean error rate of ASM is lower than FSM, though no significant differences were observed. Recall that, answering the comprehensive questionnaire requires the subjects to comprehensively comprehend the given state machines. For Aspect state machines, the subjects were required to understand for example Pointcut specifications (written in OCL) in order to correctly answer the comprehensive questions. A plausible explanation is that due to insufficient training given to the subjects on understanding OCL expressions (as part of the training given to AspectSM (Section 3.6)), the solutions of the subjects with ASM exhibit more errors as compared with HSM.

Recall that for the activity of modeling crosscutting behaviors using state machines (R2T1) we have only two treatments: ASM and FSM. For CERT (transitions), we found that ASM has significantly lower error rate than FSM, whereas for CERS (states), FSM has significantly lower error rate than ASM. The reason why significant differences were observed for transitions (CERT) (in favor of ASM) instead of states is that (as shown in Table 1) the aspect state machines contain comparable number of states as the flat state machines modeling the same set of crosscutting behaviors. Aspect state machines additionally require applying stereotypes, which is not the case for flat state machines. Therefore, more modeling effort is required to apply AspectSM and actually for this specific set of crosscutting behaviors, more states were required to be modeled in aspect state machines than flat state machines. Hence in such case, aspect state machines are more error-prone. Regarding CERT (transitions), ASM achieved

significantly lower error rate than FSM. This is because AspectSM helped to reduce the number of transitions in aspect state machines (Table 1) for the three crosscutting behaviors. It is worth noticing that with more complicated crosscutting behaviors, one can expect that AspectSM will reduce the number of states in aspect state machines and therefore lower error rate for states in aspect state machine can be expected. Total conformance error rate (CERSM) is significantly lower in ASM than FSM (Table 6). Again this is due to the fact that ASM are much simpler that FSM in terms of total number of modeling elements (states and transitions).

In round 3, recall that we didn't have multiple treatments as the subjects were required to weave aspect state machines into a base state machine. We observed that on average CERT (transitions) is 31%, CERS (states) is 5%, whereas CERSM is 29%, as shown in Table 7. Notice that CERT is much higher than CERS. This is due to the fact that the subjects had to weave more transitions in the base state machine than states (Table 1). We assume that more training will further reduce these percentages of weaving errors. However, it is important to note that the errors made by the subjects may be for example, accidentally missing modeling a transition and not due to the actual understandability of aspect state machines. This might happen during the weaving process when many model elements, especially transitions, have to be added to the base state machine. It is very important to notice that the subjects were asked to weave state machines, which is an indirect way to study how the subjects understand aspect state machines; weaving aspect state machines to their base state machines requires the subjects to understand both state machines and how their composition takes place. Of course, the weaving process can be automated but the objective of this task is to test the understandability of AspectSM. Using our automated weaver [1], a correct woven state machine can be automatically derived from aspect state machines and their base state machine.

5. Threats to Validity

Below, we discuss the threats to validity of our controlled experiment based on template in [20].

As with most controlled experiments in software engineering, our main conclusion validity threat is related to the sample size on which we base our analysis. We designed and conducted the experiment to maximize the number of observations within time constraints. For instance, in round 3, we combined observations from three different crosscutting behaviors.

Through our experiment design, we have tried to minimize the chances of other factors being confounded with our primary independent variable: the use of aspect state machines. For example, blocking was used based on assignment marks to form the groups of subjects. Furthermore, we used a between-subjects design, i.e., each subject is exposed to one type of approach once to counterbalance the learning effects [26], i.e., since each subject is exposed to just one type of treatment (e.g., the Aspect approach) and one task (e.g., one crosscutting behavior) and thus the performance of subjects is not influenced with the experience gained while working with other treatments with the same crosscutting behavior.

One possible construct validity threat in our experiment is that

Table 8. Kruskal–Wallis test results for ERID and ERC

Round	Task	Measure	p-value ($\alpha = 0.05$)
1	R1T1	ERID	**0.0001**
	R1T2	ERC	**0.0047**

we were not able to investigate all features of aspect-orientation (such as all types of basic advice) in this experiment due to the nature of our crosscutting concerns. The other concern is that the conformance error rate measures for a state machine (CERSM) can be interpreted in various ways, depending on the application domain or one's subjective opinion. However we made the effort to devise a set of objective metrics to measure conformance error rates by comparing with reference models, such that subjective perceptions and application specific measurement can be reduced to a minimum and hence the comparison of models across different case studies (perhaps with different application domains), derived by different subjects (e.g., experts, students) is possible. In addition, these metrics are general so that they are reusable and can be applied to multiple experiments. By doing so, we can therefore make sure that we don't introduce bias (beside the actual choice of those metrics) to the evaluation results which might be a threat to validity.

External validity threat is the most commonly found threat in any controlled experiment. Due to time constraints, case studies and tasks are usually small. As we see in Table 1, our models are of reasonable size. Such numbers are at least representatives of the state machines of classes and small components. However, because crosscutting concerns are expected to have an even higher impact on large models, we expect the use of AspectSM to be even more beneficial in such cases. One may also question the use of students as subjects for the experiment. Our motivation was to find a group of subjects with adequate background that could be trained to use AspectSM over a short period of time. Most practitioners have very little knowledge of AOP or AOM in general, and significant training would therefore be required. This is why relying on a group of experienced graduate students with the right educational background (Section 2) seemed to be the better option. In addition, some studies are reported in [23-25], where the performance of trained software engineering students for various tasks was compared with professional developers. The differences in performance were not statistically significant when compared to junior and intermediate developers, thus leading to the conclusion that there is no evidence that students trained for the tasks at hand may not be used as subjects in place of professionals.

6. Related Work

Most experimentation in Aspect-Oriented Software Development (AOSD) has been conducted to evaluate AOP when compared to Object-Oriented Programming (OOP) in terms of development time, errors in development, and performing maintenance tasks. An initial search on IEEE resulted in 169 papers on AOM; however, none of them reported any controlled experiment to evaluate AOM approaches. A controlled experiment [26] was performed in industry settings to measure effort and errors using aspect-oriented programming for applying different maintenance tasks related to the tracing crosscutting concern, i.e., the use of logging to record execution of a program. The results showed that aspect-orientation resulted in reducing both development effort and number of errors.

Another experiment is reported in [27], which compares aspect-orientation (AspectJ) with a more traditional approach (Java) in terms of development time for crosscutting concerns. A similar experiment is reported in [28] focusing on development time to perform debugging and change activities on object-oriented programs using AspectJ. Both of these experiments revealed mixed results, i.e., aspect-orientation has positive impact on development time only for certain tasks. For instance, AOP seems to be more beneficial when the crosscutting concern is more separable from the core behavior.

An exploratory study is reported in [29] to assess if AOP has any impact on software maintenance tasks. Eleven software professionals were asked to perform different maintenance tasks using Java and AspectJ. The results of the experiment revealed that AOP performed slightly better than OOP, but there were no statistically significant results observed. Another exploratory study is reported in [30] to measure fault-proneness with AOP. Three evolving AOP programs were used and data about different faults made during their development were collected. The experiment revealed two major findings: 1) Most of the faults were due to lack of compatibility between aspect and base code, 2) The presence of faults in AOP features such as Pointcuts, Advice, and inter-type declarations was as likely as for normal programming features. The results turned out to be statistically significant.

An experiment is reported in [31], where two software development processes based on a same aspect modeling approach (i.e., the Theme approach [32]) are compared to determine their impacts on maintenance tasks such as adding new functionality or improving existing functionality. The first process (aspectual process) involves generating AOP code in AspectJ from Theme models, whereas the second process (hybrid process) involves generating object-oriented code in Java from Theme models. Maintenance tasks are measured based on metrics such as size, coupling, cohesion, and separation of concerns. The results showed that on average the aspectual process took lesser time than the hybrid process.

An exploratory study is reported in [33], which aims to assess if aspects can help reducing effort on resolving conflicts that can occur during model compositions. To do so, they compared AOM with non-AOM in terms of effort to resolve conflicts and number of conflicts resolved on six releases of a software product line. The results of the study showed that aspects improved modularization and hence helped better localize conflicts, which in turn resulted in reducing the effort involved in resolving conflicts.

Our controlled experiment is different from the above experiments from several perspectives. First, our controlled experiment focused on the design of the software development life cycle and aspect-oriented modeling. Most of the experiments in the literature have focused on comparing AOP with OOP. We evaluated the errors in modeling made by subjects when doing different kinds of AOM tasks, i.e., defect identification, answering comprehension questionnaire, designing aspect state machines, and weaving aspect state machines.

7. Conclusion and Future Work

Aspect-oriented Modeling (AOM) has received lots of attention in the recent years, but unfortunately it lacks empirical evaluations to support its proclaimed benefits such as reduced modeling errors and reduced modeling effort. In this paper, we presented a controlled experiment, to assess conformance error rates of an AOM profile: AspectSM. This profile is developed to support state-based robustness testing at Cisco, Norway. However, it is general enough to be applied in any situation where state-based robustness testing is required. Using AspectSM, robustness crosscutting behaviors are modeled as stereotyped state machines termed as aspect state machines. Conformance error rates of applying AspectSM are assessed from four different perspectives by conducting four modeling activities: 1) identifying modeling defects, 2) comprehending state machines, 3) modeling crosscutting behaviors, and 4) weaving crosscutting behaviors. Results of the experiment show that for most of the activities, the subjects who were given treatment AspectSM achieved significantly lower error rates than the ones given standard UML state machines.

In the future, we are planning to conduct similar controlled experiments to assess if AspectSM supports other benefits declared by AOM such as higher maintainability and changeability of models. We also plan to empirically compare AspectSM with other similar AOM profiles that support modeling crosscutting behaviors on UML state machines. In addition, we plan to compare AspectSM with domain specific languages for AOM that can be used to achieve the similar objective as AspectSM.

8. References

[1] Ali, S., Briand, L. C. and Hemmati, H. Modeling Robustness Behavior Using Aspect-Oriented Modeling to Support Robustness Testing of Industrial Systems. *Systems and Software Modeling (SOSYM)*(2011).

[2] Weigert, T. and Reed, R. *Specifying Telecommunications Systems with UML*. Kluwer Academic Publishers, 2003.

[3] Drusinsky, D. *Modeling and Verification using UML Statecharts: A Working Guide to Reactive System Design, Runtime Monitoring and Execution-based Model Checking*. Newnes, 2006.

[4] *SmartState*, http://www.smartstatestudio.com/, 2010

[5] Utting, M. and Legeard, B. *Practical Model-Based Testing: A Tools Approach*. Morgan-Kaufmann, 2007.

[6] Binder, R. V. *Testing object-oriented systems: models, patterns, and tools*. Addison-Wesley Longman Publishing Co., Inc., 1999.

[7] Cavarra, R., Crichton, C., Davies, J., Hartman, A. and Mounier, L. Using UML for automatic test generation In *Proceedings of the International Symposium on Software Testing and Analysis (ISSTA '02)* (2002).

[8] Pender, T. *UML Bible*. Wiley, 2003.

[9] Yedduladoddi, R. *Aspect Oriented Software Development: An Approach to Composing UML Design Models*. VDM Verlag Dr. Müller, 2009.

[10] *IBM OCL Parser, IBM*, http://www-01.ibm.com/software/awdtools/library/standards/ocl-download.html, 2010

[11] *OCLE*, http://lci.cs.ubbcluj.ro/ocle/, 2010

[12] *EyeOCL Software*, http://maude.sip.ucm.es/eos/, 2010

[13] Zhang, G. Towards Aspect-Oriented State Machines. In *Proceedings of the 2nd Asian Workshop on Aspect-Oriented Software Development (AOASIA'06)* (Tokyo, 2006).

[14] Zhang, G. and Hölzl, M. HiLA: High-Level Aspects for UML-State Machines. In *Proceedings of the In Proceedings of the 14th Workshop on Aspect-Oriented Modeling (AOM@MoDELS'09)* (2009).

[15] Zhang, G., Hölzl, M. M. and Knapp, A. *Enhancing UML State Machines with Aspects*. 2007.

[16] Xu, D., Xu, W. and Nygard, K. A State-Based Approach to Testing Aspect-Oriented Programs. In *Proceedings of the 17th International Conference on Software Engineering and Knowledge Engineering* (Taiwan, 2005).

[17] Whittle, J., Moreira, A., Araújo, J., Jayaraman, P., Elkhodary, A. and Rabbi, R. *An Expressive Aspect Composition Language for UML State Diagrams*. 2007.

[18] Laddad, R. *AspectJ in Action: Practical Aspect-Oriented Programming*. Manning Publications, 2003.

[19] Gomaa, H. *Designing Concurrent, Distributed, and Real-Time Applications with UML*. Addison-Wesley Professional, 2000.

[20] Wohlin, C., Runeson, P. and Höst, M. *Experimentation in Software Engineering: An Introduction*. Springer, 1999.

[21] Ali, S., Yue, T., Briand, L. C. and Malik, Z. I. *Does Aspect-Oriented Modeling Help Improve the Readability of UML State Machines?* Simula Research Laboratory, Technical Report(2010-11), 2010.

[22] Sheskin, D. J. *Handbook of Parametric and Nonparametric Statistical Procedures*. Chapman and Hall/CRC, 2007.

[23] Höst, M., Regnell, B. and Wohlin, C. Using Students as Subjects—A Comparative Study of Students and Professionals in Lead-Time Impact Assessment. *Empirical Software Engineering*, 5, 3I (2000), pp. 201-214.

[24] Arisholm, E. and Sjoberg, D. I. K. Evaluating the Effect of a Delegated versus Centralized Control Style on the Maintainability of Object-Oriented Software. *IEEE Transactions on Software Engineering*, 30, 8I (2004), pp. 521-534.

[25] Holt, R. W., Boehm-Davis, D. A. and Shultz, A. C. *Mental Representations of Programs for Student and Professional Programmers*. Ablex Publishing Corp., 1987.

[26] Durr, P., Bergmans, L. and Aksit, M. *A Controlled Experiment for the Assessment of Aspects - Tracing in an Industrial Context*. University of Twente, CTIT, 2008.

[27] Hanenberg, S., Kleinschmager, S. and Josupeit-Walter, M. Does aspect-oriented programming increase the development speed for crosscutting code? An empirical study. In *Proceedings of the 2009 3rd International Symposium on Empirical Software Engineering and Measurement* (2009). IEEE Computer Society.

[28] Walker, R. J., Baniassad, E. L. A. and Murphy, G. C. An initial assessment of aspect-oriented programming. In *Proceedings of the 21st international conference on Software engineering* (Los Angeles, California, United States, 1999). ACM.

[29] Bartsch, M. and Harrison, R. An exploratory study of the effect of aspect-oriented programming on maintainability. *Software Quality Control*, 16, 1I (2008), pp. 23-44.

[30] Ferrari, F., Burrows, R., Lemos, v., Garcia, A., Figueiredo, E., Cacho, N., Lopes, F., Temudo, N., Silva, L., Soares, S., Rashid, A., Masiero, P., Batista, T. and Maldonado, J. An exploratory study of fault-proneness in evolving aspect-oriented programs. In *Proceedings of the Proceedings of the 32nd ACM/IEEE International Conference on Software Engineering - Volume 1* (Cape Town, South Africa, 2010). ACM.

[31] Farias, K., Garcia, A. and Whittle, J. Assessing the impact of aspects on model composition effort. In *Proceedings of the Proceedings of the 9th International Conference on Aspect-Oriented Software Development* (Rennes and Saint-Malo, France). ACM.

[32] Carton, A., Driver, C., Jackson, A. and Clarke, S. *Model-Driven Theme/UML*. Springer-Verlag, 2009.

[33] Hovsepyan, A., Scandariato, R., Baelen, S. V., Berbers, Y. and Joosen, W. From aspect-oriented models to aspect-oriented code?: the maintenance perspective. In *Proceedings of the Proceedings of the 9th International Conference on Aspect-Oriented Software Development* (Rennes and Saint-Malo, France). ACM.

Are Automatically-Detected Code Anomalies Relevant to Architectural Modularity?
An Exploratory Analysis of Evolving Systems

Isela Macia[1], Joshua Garcia[2], Daniel Popescu[2], Alessandro Garcia[1], Nenad Medvidovic[2], Arndt von Staa[1]

[1]Opus Group, LES, Informatics Department, PUC-Rio, RJ, Brazil
[2]University of Southern California, Los Angeles, CA, USA

{ibertran, afgarcia, arndt}@inf.puc-rio.br, {joshuaga, dpopescu, neno}@usc.edu

ABSTRACT

As software systems are maintained, their architecture modularity often degrades through architectural erosion and drift. More directly, however, the modularity of software implementations degrades through the introduction of code anomalies, informally known as code smells. A number of strategies have been developed for supporting the automatic identification of implementation anomalies when only the source code is available. However, it is still unknown how reliable these strategies are when revealing code anomalies related to erosion and drift processes. In this paper, we present an exploratory analysis that investigates to what extent the automatically-detected code anomalies are related to problems that occur with an evolving system's architecture. We analyzed code anomaly occurrences in 38 versions of 5 applications using existing detection strategies. The outcome of our evaluation suggests that many of the code anomalies detected by the employed strategies were not related to architectural problems. Even worse, over 50% of the anomalies not observed by the employed techniques (false negatives) were found to be correlated with architectural problems.

Categories and Subject Descriptors D.2.8 [Software Engineering]: Metrics; D.2.10 [Software Engineering]: Design; D.2.11 [Software Engineering]: Software Architectures.

General Terms: Measurement, Design.

Keywords: Code anomalies; architectural degradation symptoms; architectural violations; architectural anomalies.

1. Introduction

Code anomalies, also referred in the literature as "code smells" [13], emerge in programs structured with any kind of modularization technique, including object-oriented programming [31] and aspect-oriented programming [19]. Code anomalies are often considered as key indicators of architectural degradation [13]. Hence, if these code anomalies are not systematically removed, the system's architectures may degrade due to erosion or drift [16]. Architectural erosion occurs when architectural violations are introduced, whereas drift is the realization of unintended design decisions also known as architectural anomalies [39].

The detection of architecturally-relevant code anomalies is particularly challenging when architectural designs are absent or obsolete, which is a common situation in evolving software projects. A complicating factor is that, due to time constraints, developers often need to concentrate on the most relevant anomalies. In other words, they should focus on code anomalies that are actually contributing to architecture erosion or drift. Let's consider a simple example of code anomaly, such as *God Class* [27]. Occurrences of *God Class* only cause harm to the architectural modularity when their realization of multiple concerns introduce undesirable dependencies between architecture elements (e.g., multiple architecture layers). Therefore, such *God Class* instances require closer, more immediate attention than other instances [37].

Recent research has developed complementary ways to improve automatic detection of code anomalies. They are usually based on exploiting information that is extracted from the source code [21, 26, 28, 32, 40, 46] and rely on the combination of static code metrics. These mechanisms, known as *detection strategies* [27], have been the subject of recent studies reported in the literature. Several studies have reported acceptable accuracy rates (60% or higher) for such strategies used in anomaly detection processes [27]. Studies have also evaluated the impact of the code anomalies detected by these strategies on maintenance effort [18, 37, 38]. However, it is still unknown whether the code anomalies detected by current strategies could be also used for indicating more severe architectural problems.

The objective of this paper is to assess the usefulness of automated code anomaly detection strategies for uncovering architecture modularity problems. To this end, we carried out an exploratory study to analyze the influences of code anomaly on architectural designs in 38 versions of 5 applications from heterogeneous domains. These applications followed different architectural patterns and styles, such as Layers, Model-View-Controller and Aspectual Design [4]. The anomalies were detected in these systems using automated detection strategies [21, 27] which were the most effective to detect those anomalies in recent studies [18, 21, 23, 27, 44]. In addition, the original architects were consulted to reliably identify architectural problems in the studied systems. We explicitly selected systems for which architectural information was accessible so that we could correlate the architectural problems with the presence of code anomalies.

Our results confirmed that current automated strategies were not accurate to identify code anomalies that attempt against architectural modularity in the target systems. More specifically:

- More than 50% of the *automatically-detected code anomalies* were not correlated with architectural problems. This means that developers could spend most of the time reviewing code that might not represent threats to the system's architectural design.
- Even worse, more than 50% of the false negatives "generated" by automated strategies were found to be correlated with architectural modularity problems. This means that developers would lead to neglect code anomalies that are critical to architectural design.
- The inefficiency of detection strategies cannot be simply addressed by calibrating specific metric thresholds or determining different combinations of particular measures. It seems that their imperfection is largely due to their inability to exploit architectural concern's properties or architectural information in the source code.
- Certain recurring patterns of anomaly co-occurrences seem to be better indicators of architecture modularity problems than individual anomaly occurrences. These patterns usually cannot be directly specified and identified by existing detection strategies [21, 23, 32].

The rest of this paper is organized as follows. Section 2 presents the related work and its limitations in the context of this study. Section 3 introduces the different kinds code anomalies and of architectural modularity problems that are considered in our analysis. Section 4 describes our analysis procedures. Section 5 presents the obtained results, whereas Section 6 discusses their relevance and the main findings. Section 7 highlights the limitations of our study and, finally, Section 8 provides some concluding remarks.

2. Related Work

Our focus is on automatic detection of code anomalies as engineers usually do not have time and resources for carrying out a manual detection process. In this context, we divided the related work in two categories. First, we present current research aiming to support automatic detection of code anomalies. Second, we overview empirical studies that analyze the impact of automatically-detected code anomalies from different perspectives.

Automatic Detection of Code Anomalies. Emden and Moonen [9] describe *jCosmo*, an approach for detecting code anomalies based on the structural properties of code elements. Ratzinger et al. [41] detect code anomalies by examining change couplings. Strategies for detecting code anomalies [27] are the most common mechanism referenced and studied in the literature. The reason is that they generate a list of suspects; as a result, a wide range of static analysis tools, including visualization ones (e.g. [6, 49]), are based on such strategies. Marinescu [21, 27] introduced the concept of detection strategy, which consists of a logical expression composed by metrics to detect code anomalies. A concrete example is given in Section 3.1. Marinescu et al. [28] also presented *inCode*, a tool used to automate the application of certain detection strategies.

Other authors also proposed strategies and tools for anomaly detection in the literature. For instance, Munro [32] proposed some heuristics for detecting code anomalies. Alikacem and Sahraoui [1] proposed a language to detect code anomalies. This language allows the specification of rules using metrics and thresholds. Moha et al. [32] presented the *Decor*, a tool and a domain-specific language to automate the construction of anomaly detection strategies. However, none of these tools were used in the context of this work (Section 4.4) because they are neither available [1, 33] nor support the detection of all code anomalies that are considered in our analysis [28, 32].

Studies of Code Anomalies. The effectiveness of automatically-detected code anomalies using strategies have been recently studied under different perspectives. The authors have conducted empirical studies to investigate the negative effects of such automatically-detected anomalies. For instance, Mantyla and Lassensius investigate to what extent automatically-detected code anomalies can be used as a basis for subjective evaluation of code evolvability [25]. Olbrich et al. [37, 38] and Khomh et al. [18] investigate the evolution of automatically-detected code anomalies. The authors analyze whether the number of code anomalies increases over time, and the anomalies' influence on how often a code element changes. However, they did not study to what extent these phenomena are related to architectural modularity problems (Section 3). Certain classes (classified as "anomalous") might coincidently change more often because the associated requirements are naturally more volatile than others. In other words, the rate of individual class changes might not necessarily be an indicator of architecture modularity problems.

Other works investigate the impact of automatically-detected code anomalies on software defects (i.e. the need for corrective maintenance). For instance, D'Ambros et al. [6] found that, while some code anomalies are more frequent, none of them can be considered more harmful with respect to software defects. In the context of aspect-oriented systems, Macia et al. [23] analyzed the influence of code anomalies on corrective changes. They also analyzed their influence on perfective changes (i.e. refactoring effort).

However, none of these analyses investigate to what extent detection strategies accurately localize code anomalies that are related to architectural modularity problems. That is, they do not assess the impact of automatically-detected code anomalies on architectural designs.

3. Code Anomalies and Architectural Problems

This section introduces relevant concepts related to code anomalies (Section 3.1) and architectural modularity problems (Section 3.2). It also illustrates how they could be interrelated (Section 3.3) using a running example.

3.1 Code Anomalies and Detection Strategies

The modularity of system implementations degrades through the introduction of code anomalies. They affect different code units, such as classes and methods. For example, *God Class* is a code anomaly in which a class (i) realizes various concerns – i.e. it performs too much work on its own, delegating minor responsibilities to a set of simple classes, and (ii) uses data from many other classes, increasing its coupling. For instance, *MediaController* in Figure 1 was classified as a *God Class* instance.

Detection strategies interpret a set of code metrics that are extracted from a specific code element (e.g., class or method) by using a set of threshold filter rules [27]. Then, the results of these filters are combined and used to identify code anomalies. Below, we present the detection strategy used to identify *God Classes* in our study. This detection strategy and its thresholds were defined in [21] and have been used in other studies [37, 38]. The calibration of these thresholds (see Section 4.4) is required in some cases.

$$GodClass(C) = (WMC(C) \geq 47) \wedge (TCC(C) < 0.3) \wedge (ATFD(C) > 5)$$

where:

- C is the class being inspected;
- Weighted Method Count (WMC(C)) is the sum of the cyclomatic complexity of all methods in C [21];
- Tight Class Cohesion (TCC(C)) is the relative number of directly connected methods, i.e. methods that access the same instance variables, in C [30];
- Access To Foreign Data (ATFD(C)) is the number of attributes in foreign classes accessed by class C [21].

Table 1 summarizes the set of code anomalies that we have analyzed in this study. These anomalies were selected because they represent all the code anomalies identified by developers in the systems we analyzed (Section 4.3). In addition, their detection strategies have been widely studied (Section 2), with detection accuracy rates higher than 60%. The details governing the anomalies' definitions as well as their detection strategies can be found in [21, 23, 44]; we elide them here for brevity and space constraints.

3.2 Degradation: Architecture Modularity Problems

The phenomenon of architectural degradation was introduced by Hochstein and Lindvall [16] as aiming at

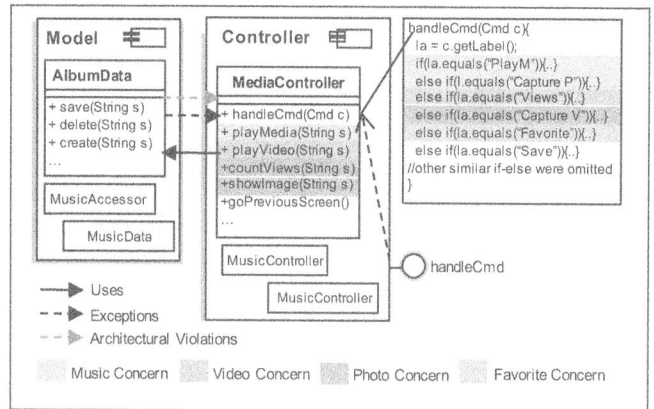

Figure 1. Relationship between code anomalies and architectural modularity problems

referring to the continuous decline of the architectural modularity. Architectural degradation encompasses architectural modularity problems caused by the processes of erosion and drift [39].

Architectural Erosion is the process of introducing decisions into a system architectural design that violates the system's intended architecture [39] and, therefore, attempt against the architectural modularity. As a result, architecture violations can only be observed if an explicit specification of the prescribed (i.e. intended) architectural design decisions is available.

Figure 1 depicts an example of architectural violation in the MobileMedia system. The problem is associated with the realization of the exception handling policy in this system. Most exceptions are propagated through component interfaces across the system layers, thereby going against the architects' original intent in some cases. For instance, the MediaController component invokes different services from the *AlbumData* component, which partially realizes the *Model* layer. *MediaController* ends up handling exceptions (e.g. *PersistentException*) signalized by *AlbumData*, including those that should be treated internally to the other component realizing the *Model* layer. This means that additional code couplings, between elements realizing the *Model* and *Controller* layers, are the sources of architecture violations.

Architectural Drift is the introduction of design decisions into a system's architecture that were not included in the intended architecture, albeit they do not violate any of the

Table 1. Code anomalies analyzed in our study

Aspect-Oriented Code Anomalies	Object-Oriented Code Anomalies
Composition Bloat [23]	Data Class [13, 21]
Duplicate Pointcut [44]	Divergent Change [13, 21]
Forced Join Point [23]	Feature Envy [13, 21]
God Aspect [23]	God Class [21, 29]
God Pointcut [23]	Large Class [13, 21]
Redundant Pointcut [23]	Long Method [13, 21]
	Long Parameter List [13, 21]
	Misplaced Class [13, 21]
	Shotgun Surgery [13, 21]
	Small Class [13, 21]

prescribed design decisions [39]. Some architectural drift symptoms are caused by applying a design decision that neglects or impairs one or more modularity principles. Each of these symptoms of architectural drift is often referred as an *architectural anomaly* [14, 22]. These anomalies comprise decisions that may negatively impact architectural modularity principles, such as narrow component interfaces and components realizing a single concern [14, 29].

In order to select a set of drift symptoms to be analyzed in our study, we considered catalogs of architectural anomalies explicitly documented in the literature [14, 29]. Our final subset of analyzed anomalies encompassed those that were identified by architects in the target systems of our study (Section 4.3). The types of architectural anomalies analyzed in our study are summarized in Table 2. Note that each architectural anomaly hinders different modularity principles. For instance, while *Component Concern Overload* anomaly does not adhere to the single responsibility principle, the *Ambiguous Interface* violates the simple interface principle [29].

Table 2. Architectural anomalies detected in our study

Architectural Anomalies	Definition
Ambiguous Interface	Interfaces that offer only a general entry-point into a component that handles more requests than it should actually process
Extraneous Connector	Connectors of different types are used to link a pair of components
Connector Envy	Components which realize functionality that should be assigned to a connector
Scattered Parasitic Functionality	Multiple components are responsible for realizing the same high-level concern and orthogonal ones
Component Concern Overload	Components responsible for realizing two or more unrelated architectural concerns

As an illustration, Figure 1 depicts an *Ambiguous Interface* anomaly in the context of the MobileMedia system used in our study [12]. The interface *handleCmd* of the component *Controller* is implemented by the class *MediaController*. However, the interface offers only one method, which receives all service requests and, therefore, it handles more types of commands than it should actually process; i.e. it receives the parameter *Cmd* with the generic type *Command*. This situation hinders the architecture modularity as over-generalized interfaces allow additional dependencies between components [14, 29]. Note that even though this situation is not necessarily a violation of prescribed design decisions (i.e. symptoms of architecture erosion), over-generalized interfaces might favor tight component coupling as the system evolves. Additional examples and a discussion of each architectural anomaly can be found in [14, 29] and is out of the scope of our work.

3.3 Code Anomalies as Indicators of Architecture Degradation Symptoms

Previous research [21, 32] departs from the following assumption: detection strategies (Section 3.1) accurately localize code anomalies related to architectural modularity problems (Section 3.2). Our study (Section 4) is aimed to analyze to what extent this assumption holds. A code anomaly C is related to an architecture modularity problem A when: (i) the code elements (e.g., methods or classes) affected by C are in charge of implementing the architectural elements (e.g., components, interfaces, connectors), and (ii) these architectural elements are affected by A. In this work we considered only those relationships for which the cause-effect was confirmed by architects (Section 4.4).

Figure 1 depicts an example of this cause-effect relationship. The *MediaController.handleCmd* method was considered as the source of two code anomalies and one architectural anomaly. First, this method was classified a *Long Method* (Table 1) as it contains many lines of code, presents high cyclomatic complexity, and realizes several architectural concerns. This method was also classified as *Divergent Change* because it is using information from several classes to deal with different services. In addition, its implementation is responsible for dealing with different exceptions propagated by the *Model* component; however, these exceptions are not related with the method's goal. Finally, this method is in charge of implementing the interface *handleCmd* of *Controller* classified as *Ambiguous Interface*.

4. Study Definition and Design

The relationship between code anomalies and architectural modularity problems has often been recognized by the literature [13, 16]. However, as software projects evolve, the source code is usually the only artifact available and the architectural design is not explicitly documented. Hence, the detection of code anomalies related to architectural problems is only viable if the available automated strategies (Section 3.1) are accurate. This study aims at analyzing whether detection strategies are accurate in localizing architecturally-relevant anomalies in the source code.

4.1 Hypotheses

In order to evaluate the accuracy of detection strategies for localizing architectural modularity problems (Section 3.2), we have divided the analysis into two perspectives by observing both architectural violations and architectural anomalies. These perspectives lead us to two null hypotheses H1 and H2 as defined below.

H1$_0$: *The accuracy of detection strategies to identify code anomalies related to architectural violations is high.*

H2$_0$: *The accuracy of detection strategies to identify code anomalies related to architectural anomalies is high.*

Strategies are considered accurate in the literature when their precision and recall rates are 60% or higher for detecting code anomalies [18, 27, 37, 38]. This threshold has been derived from empirical studies involving systems implemented using different programming languages [21].

As it is assumed that code anomalies are intrinsically related to architectural modularity problems [13, 16], we have used the same threshold in this study for assessing the strategies' accuracy to localize architecturally-relevant code anomalies. That is, we consider that their accuracy was 'high' if 60% of the code anomalies related to architectural modularity problems (Section 3.3) are automatically-detected.

4.2 Variable Selection

In order to test our hypotheses, we have defined the following independent and dependent variables.

Independent Variable. There are as many independent variables as there are kinds of automatically-detected code anomalies (Table 1). Each variable $C_{i,k,j}$ indicates the number of times that an entity i suffers from a code anomaly k in a version v_j. All code anomaly occurrences used in testing these hypotheses were confirmed by developers (Section 4.5).

Dependent Variable. Similar to the independent variables, there are many dependent variables as there are kinds of code anomalies. The dependent variables $V_{i,k,j}$ and $A_{i,k,j}$ for H1 and H2 indicate whether the entity i affected by the code anomaly k is introducing any violation or architectural anomaly in a version v_j, respectively. All instances of architectural degradation symptoms used in testing these hypotheses were confirmed by the original architects (Section 4.4).

4.3 Target Systems

In this study we decided to focus on investigating short-term architectural modularity problems because they can provide early symptoms of architectural degeneration. For this kind of study, it is important to select systems implemented with object-oriented programming and aspect-oriented programming. The goal is to make a broader analysis and identify whether there could be any influence of the modular programming technique on the results. However, the comparison between the strategies' accuracy rates for these two programming techniques is beyond the scope of our study. It is also important to select systems developed using different practices related to architectural rule enforcement in the source code as well as counting on the availability of their original architects and developers. Their availability is important to help us to validate the identified architectural modularity problems (Section 3.3). A complete list of criteria for supporting the system selection process is provided in [5].

Based on the aforementioned criteria, we chose 38 releases of 5 medium-sized applications. Table 3 summarizes the general characteristics of each target system. Two of these applications are Web-based information systems, which allow citizens to register complaints about health issues in public institutions. HealthWatcher (HW) [15] is based on the layers architecture style. AspectualWatcher (AW) also follows this style, but relies on aspect-oriented design [4] for modularizing concerns that crosscut the layers in the HW system. Note that in this table the token "/" is used to separate the data of the object-oriented (Java) version and its aspect-oriented (AspectJ) counterpart.

We have also selected two software product lines and a middleware. The third and fourth systems are product lines for deriving applications that manipulate media on mobile devices [12]. MobileMedia (MM), relies on the model-view-controller architectural pattern, while AspectualMedia (AM) was structured based on aspectual architecture design for modularizing features that crosscut the MM architecture. The fifth system is a lightweight middleware platform, called MIDAS, for distributed, event-based sensor applications [24]. The two selected versions are the before and after versions of a major architectural restructuring with the widest impact in this system history. A high number of changes of architectural elements took place in this transition and are realized by the latest version.

Table 3. Systems used in our study

	HW/AW	MIDAS	MM/AM
Application Type	Web-based system	Middleware	Software Product Line
Code Availability	Java/Aspect	C++	Java/Aspect
# of Versions	10/10	2	8/8
# of Selected Versions	10/10	2	8/8
Avg. # of CE	85/113	22	60/94
Avg. # of AE	34/41	14	48/61
Avg. KLOC	6	7	8

HW=HealthWatcher; AH=AspectualWatcher; MM=MobileMedia; AM=AspectualMedia; CE=Code Elements (classes and aspects); AE=Architectural Elements (components and connectors)

4.4 Procedures for Data Collection

In order to perform the data collection process we count on the help of two groups of architects: (i) those that defined the original intended architecture, and (ii) independent reviewers of the software architecture; and on a group of original developers. These three groups were involved in the main phases of our study, which are described next.

Recovering the Actual Architecture. This phase was based on a semi-automatic process. We have used Sonar [43] and Understand [47] to support the recovery of the actual architecture from the source code. These tools support architecture and code analyses in order to help developers to analyze and measure the modularity of the system's architecture and implementation. To make possible the architectural analysis, architects and original developers mapped code elements to architectural elements. These mappings allowed us to trace the influence of a code anomaly on the introduction of modularity problems in a system's architecture. These mappings also allowed us to identify how modularization of architectural concerns in the code were related to architecture modularity problems. An example of this mapping is showed in Figure 1 where the *MediaController.handleCmd* method is implementing *Music*, *Video*, *Photo* and *Favorite* concerns.

Identifying Architectural Degradation Symptoms. In order to identify symptoms of architectural erosion we used Software Reflexion Model [35]. As this technique demands the intended architecture was provided by architects. The comparison of the actual, extracted architecture (EA), and the intended architecture (IA) was supported by the two groups of architects. They were responsible for measuring the architecture conformance in terms of *convergence* (a component or relationship that is in both EA and IE), *divergence* (a component or relationship that is in EA but not in IA), and *absence* (a component or relationship that is in IA but not EA). For instance, all absence classifications were considered as violations. Although divergence classifications are natural suspects of possible violations, they can be related to unintended architectural decisions. Therefore, architects needed to validate their actual impact on architecture designs.

Furthermore, architectural anomalies were detected by architects based mainly on: (i) a visual inspection of the EA, and (ii) a careful analysis of the code elements mapped to architectural elements, due to the lack of tools. We also asked the architects to indicate other anomalies observed in the architecture design beyond those presented in Table 2. This helped us to better judge whether and which code anomalies are good indicators of architectural modularity problems.

As result of this stage, architects provided reports describing the architectural problems observed in each system's version. These reports described, for instance, the problem's type (e.g. violation, architectural anomaly), its location in the design, the architectural elements related to it and, in some cases, an explanation of the problem's cause.

Automatic Detection of Code Anomalies. Code anomalies were automatically identified using detection strategies. We selected metrics and thresholds that have shown high accuracy to identify code anomalies in previous studies [21, 23]. Sometimes, the thresholds suffered some minor adjustments in order to maximize the accuracy. For instance, certain thresholds were calibrated according to the specific programming styles and system characteristics [20]. When multiples detection strategies for a code anomaly were available in the literature, we analyzed which metrics and thresholds would be the most appropriate to reach the highest accuracy rates. The goal was to get the best possible results with the detection strategies at hand. If needed, the changes in the original detection strategies [21, 23, 44] were discussed with the systems' original developers. A complete list of the detection strategies used and their corresponding thresholds are available in a supplementary web site [5].

Furthermore, the metrics used in the detection strategies were mostly collected with existing tools such as: MuLATo [34], Together [45] and Understand [47]. These tools were chosen as they are complementary: MuLATo is a static analyzer for AspectJ programs whereas Together and Understand analyze Java programs. They have been used in previous studies reported in the literature [15, 21, 23] and,

more importantly, they collect a large number of metrics that were required for the detection strategies employed.

4.5 Analysis Method

We also asked the developers to identify all the code anomalies that influenced on the architectural design. The lists of code anomalies provided by developers included fine-grained and accurate details about the code anomaly facilitating our analysis. For instance, the lists describe the code anomaly's type, the code elements affected by it, and its correlation with the architectural problems previously identified by architects. Afterwards, a stage was dedicated to investigate the accuracy of the detection strategies [21, 23] when detecting the code anomalies previously identified by developers. Therefore, this investigation was based on both lists: (i) automatically-detected code anomalies using existing detection techniques and, (ii) code anomalies detected by developers through the code review stage. In particular, the lists provided by developers were useful to assess the impact of non-automatically-detected code anomalies on architectural decompositions.

In order to reject $H1_0$ and $H2_0$, we calculated the precision and recall of detection strategies using the following formulas:

$$precision = \frac{TP}{TP + FP} \qquad recall = \frac{TP}{TP + FN}$$

where, *True Positive* (TP) and *False Positive* (FP) encompass all automatically-detected code anomalies that respectively were or not confirmed as relevant by architects and developers. As we described previously developers performed a code review in order to detect code anomalies related to architectural problems that were not automatically identified by the detection strategies; i.e. *False Negative* (FN). Based on these criteria, a detection strategy achieves 100% of precision and 100% of recall if it only pinpoints the same set of architecturally-relevant code anomalies confirmed by developers.

5. Study Results

Before discussing the strategies' accuracy to identify architecturally-relevant code anomalies (Section 5.2), this section presents how often the code anomalies were actually related to architecture problems in the target systems. Tables 4 and 5 summarize the overall impact of code anomalies on architectural designs. The list of code anomalies (used to compute the table values) represents all the occurrences of anomalies (Section 3.2), whether automatically detected by the strategies or not. The tables present, for each of the target systems, the relationship between code anomalies and architectural violations (Table 4) or particular types of architectural anomalies (Table 5). The columns are headed with the acronym of each system. The rows x and S in both tables represent the mean and the standard deviation, respectively. Violations in Table 4 were related to divergent relationships (Section 4.4) as the system's implementation started based on its intended architecture. Data for MIDAS are not presented in Table 4 as no violation occurred in this system. This observation was expected as the development process in the MIDAS project strictly enforced architecture conformance [24].

Table 4. Code anomalies related to architectural violations

		AW	HW	AM	MM
Violations	X	134.9	207.2	43.5	46.7
	S	2.81	9.46	4.57	4.56
Non-related	X	24.7	51.8	10.87	7.8
	S	1.82	5.12	2.29	4.67
Total		**160**	**259**	**54**	**55**

Table 5. Code anomalies related to architectural anomalies

		AW	HW	AM	MM	MIDAS
Ambiguous Interface	X	8.6	6.4	9.25	12.16	2.5
	S	2.06	1.03	2.48	3.22	0
Connector Envy	X	5.6	5.6	7.25	8.63	2
	S	2.75	2.75	2.17	2.95	0
Component Concern Overload	X	-	3	1.41	2.73	1
	S	-	0	2.39	1.86	0
Extraneous Connector	X	3.8	-	1.38	-	14
	S	1.82	-	0.84	-	3.18
Scattered Parasitic Functionality	X	4.7	2.2	2.13	3.75	-
	S	1.85	1.01	1.18	1.3	-
Non-related	X	3.1	2.7	1.6	2.62	6
	S	1.44	1.91	1.52	1.78	4.5
Total		**26**	**20**	**22**	**30**	**29**

A first analysis of Tables 4 and 5 revealed that the architectural modularity problems were significantly related to code anomalies. The correlation was usually higher than 80% for both violations and architectural anomalies. This conclusion can be drawn by comparing the total number of architectural modularity problems (row "Total") and the mean of those problems unrelated to code anomalies (i.e. row "Non-related") in each table. Interestingly, around 15% of the architectural modularity problems were related to code anomalies that emerged in the first system's versions. On the other hand, less than 20% of the architectural problems were not related to code anomalies. From the opposite perspective, we observed that just about 10% of the architectural anomalies were not related to code anomalies.

The aforementioned results were particularly relevant as the high correlation coefficient was observed even in systems developed with modularity principles in mind. The developers tried to maximize such principles in both architecture design and implementation phases. These results confirm that code anomalies may be indicators of architectural modularity problems in the source code. It reinforces the motivation of using detection strategies as indicators of architectural modularity problems in the source code. On the other hand, the success of this approach largely depends on the accuracy of existing strategies to detect architecturally-relevant code anomalies.

5.1 Diverse Degradation Symptoms in the Systems

The individual analysis of the systems revealed that the HealthWatcher (HW) system presented the largest number of architectural violations of the five systems. The number of violations increased over time in this system, leading to the highest architecture erosion rate. According to its architects, the main reason for introducing violations was the incremental addition of classes in the *GUIElements* layer that illegally access information in the *DataManagement* layer.

On the other hand, the MobileMedia (MM) system presented the largest number of architectural modularity anomalies of the five systems. The majority of these architectural drift symptoms were related to code anomalies that emerged along the system evolution. In particular, they were mostly caused by the non-modular realization of new concerns progressively included in the latest system versions. They were often instances of the following architectural anomalies: *Connector Envy, Scattered Parasitic Functionality* and *Component Concern Overload*.

Interestingly, the results show that architecture problems also occurred in the evolution history of systems or packages where architecture conformance was more strictly enforced in the code. The MIDAS project is the best example. Most architectural anomalies in MIDAS occurred due to interfaces are underlying the event-based middleware and misuse of connectors provided by the middleware. These anomalies were mostly cases of *Extraneous Connector* and *Connector Envy* occurrences. In addition, single components in MIDAS were realizing multiple scattered concerns, including service discovery, the fault tolerance policy, and dynamic adaptation. As a consequence, these components suffered from occurrences of *Component Concern Overload* and *Scattered Parasitic Functionality* anomalies.

As we can observe from the discussion above, code anomalies tend to manifest in different ways according to the system's characteristics. The extent of their contribution to either architectural erosion or architectural drift was also diverse. Regardless of these variations, the results revealed that a considerable amount of architectural modularity problems were introduced in the first system versions of all the 5 systems. This was observed even in MobileMedia, in which most of the architecture problems were introduced along the system evolution as discussed above. We further elaborate the implications of this finding in Section 6.

5.2 Accuracy of Investigated Detection Strategies

The accuracy of automated strategies for detecting architecturally-relevant code anomalies is summarized in Table 6. The token '-' is used in this table to represent the cases where modularity problems did not occur or they were not related to architectural problems. The average of the strategies' accuracy rates is also presented for anomalies in both object-oriented and aspect-oriented code. For aspect-oriented systems, we concentrate on presenting the details related to the code anomaly occurrences. A detailed list of all code anomalies, false positives and false negatives in each one of the investigated systems can be found at [5].

In general, our analysis reveals that detection strategies are inaccurate in identifying architecturally-relevant code anomalies. Specifically, most of the automatically-detected code anomalies were not associated with architectural modularity problems, leading to many false positives. In general, the average of the automatically-detected code anomalies represented about 45% (or less) of the total number of code anomalies related to architectural modularity problems. MIDAS was the only exception, which will be discussed later. Consequently, these results might imply a problem to engineers who are interested in performing clean-up code revisions to avoid architecture degeneration. In these cases, developers are likely to devote most of their time analyzing code anomalies that do not represent a threat to the architecture modularity.

Even worse, many of the code anomalies harmful to architectural modularity problems were not automatically detected by strategies, leading to a high rate of false negatives. Developers will miss a wide range of architecture erosion and drift symptoms. In particular, many of the strategies exhibited recall rates close or much lower than 45%. That is, about 55% or more of the non automatically-detected code anomalies were related to architectural modularity problems. These results indicate that detection strategies seem to have a tendency to send developers in wrong directions when addressing code anomalies related to architectural modularity problem.

The next subsections discuss how accurate the strategies were when localizing code anomalies related to both violations (Section 5.2.1) and anomalies (Section 5.2.2).

5.2.1 Revealing Symptoms of Architecture Erosion

On average about 41% of the code anomalies related to violations were automatically-detected by strategies in the target systems. The results also show that code anomalies related to violations emerged in systems developed with both OO and AO modularity techniques. In OO systems, these violations were related to undesirable interdependencies between classes responsible for implementing different architectural elements. For instance, 69% of the violations in HealthWatcher were related to exception events propagated from the *DataManagement* layer to the *GUIElements* layer. Consequently, all interfaces between *DataManagement* and *GUIElements* layers propagated these exceptional events, even though the majority of these exceptions should be treated internally by classes defined in the *DataManagement* layer according to the designers. intent. The propagation of exception events introduced several occurrences of *Long Method*, *Misplaced Class*, *Divergent Change*, and *Shotgun Surgery*. However, just about 33% of these architecturally-relevant anomalies were automatically-detected by strategies.

Other kinds of violations emerged in AO systems as they follow a different architecture design. For instance 26% of the total number of architecturally-relevant anomalies was related to undesirable tight coupling between aspects and the base code. These relations were motivated by the fact that classes were exposing internal information just to be used by aspects. For instance, artificial methods had to be created in later system versions, aiming at allowing the expected composition between aspects. This situation leads to interface bloat occurrences and to the introduction of relevant *Long Parameter Lists* and *Forced Join Points*. However, detection strategies were able only to identify about 40% of these relevant occurrences.

5.2.2 Revealing Symptoms of Architecture Drift

Architectural anomalies were mostly related to the inappropriate modularization of architectural concerns in the target systems. *Exception Handling* for AspectualWatcher and *Connection* for AspectualMedia presented the strongest relationship with architectural modularity problems as they

Table 6. Results for the analyzed detection strategies

Code Smells	True Positives			False Positives			False Negatives			Precision			Recall		
	HW	MM	MIDAS	HW	MM	MIDAS	HW	MM	MIDAS	HW	MM	MIDAS	HW	MM	MIDAS
Divergent Change	7	1	4	14	2	43	19	2	2	0.33	0.33	0.09	0.27	0.33	0.67
Feature Envy	5	2	-	27	6	-	9	3	-	0.16	0.25	-	0.36	0.40	-
God Class	1	3	2	2	4	0	4	5	1	0.67	0.43	1.00	0.33	0.38	0.67
Large Class	1	1	2	2	0	4	4	1	0	0.43	1.00	0.30	0.38	0.50	1.00
Long	23	7	6	33	24	37	18	10	4	0.41	0.23	0.34	0.56	0.41	0.50
Long Parameter List	4	-	-	12	-	-	5	-	-	0.25	-	-	0.44	-	-
Misplaced Class	2	1	-	5	2	-	1	2	-	0.33	0.33	-	0.50	0.33	-
Shotgun Surgery	6	2	3	19	6	23	9	7	6	0.24	0.25	0.22	0.40	0.22	0.32
OO Avg. Rates										**0.35**	**0.40**	**0.33**	**0.41**	**0.38**	**0.63**
	AW	AM	MIDAS	AW	AM	MIDAS	AW	AM	MIDAS	AW	AM	MIDAS	AW	AM	MIDAS
OO Avg. Rates										**0.47**	**0.32**	**-**	**0.38**	**0.44**	**-**
Composition Bloat	2	3	-	4	1	-	3	4	-	0.33	0.50	-	0.40	0.43	-
Duplicate Pointcut	8	65	-	11	47	-	3	31	-	0.42	0.58	-	0.72	0.68	-
Forced Join Point	6	1	-	6	2	-	9	6	-	0.50	0.33	-	0.40	0.14	-
God Aspect	11	6	-	11	4	-	17	9	-	0.50	0.60	-	0.39	0.40	-
God Pointcut	10	8	-	20	7	-	14	11	-	0.33	0.53	-	0.42	0.42	-
Redundant Pointcut	52	3	-	17	3	-	32	2	-	0.75	0.50	-	0.62	0.60	-
AO Avg. Rates										**0.47**	**0.50**	**-**	**0.49**	**0.44**	**-**

are very context-specific with code. *Exception Handling*, for instance, was scattered among different architectural components and, therefore, it was related to *Scattered Parasitic Functionality* occurrences. On the other hand, the high tangling of *Connection* with *Persistence* and *Logging* led to the architectural components responsible for its modularization were classified as *Component Concern Overload*. The inappropriate modularization of these concerns was associated with several occurrences of *Long Method*, *God Aspect*, *God Class*, *Divergent Change*, *Shotgun Surgery* in the target systems. *Exception Handling* and *Connection* were responsible, respectively, for 53 % and 41% of the total of architecturally-relevant code anomalies in AspectualWatcher and AspectualMedia. However, just about 47% of these relevant anomalies was automatically detected by strategies.

5.2.3 Hypotheses and Overall Accuracy Results

Based on the aforementioned results, we can conclude that metrics-based strategies were not accurate in detecting architecturally-relevant code anomalies (Section 3.2). Therefore, we reject both null hypotheses $H1_0$ and $H2_0$ (Section 4.1) for all the systems, except MIDAS (Table 6). Several detection strategies presented recall rates greater than 60% in MIDAS. That is, more than a half of code anomalies related to architectural degradation symptoms were automatically identified by detection strategies in MIDAS. We also observed that the number architectural anomalies not related to code anomalies tend to increase compared with the other systems.

The MIDAS case confirmed our intuition that detection strategies are more effective in systems where architecture conformance is more strictly enforced in the code. The better the code modularity reflects the architecture decomposition, the fewer the number of code anomalies. This finding was not actually exclusive to MIDAS. Similar results were observed in packages of MobileMedia and HealthWatcher with highest adherence to the architectural rules. In these packages (e.g., Model for MobileMedia and Business for HealthWatcher) the detection strategies presented precision and recall rates higher than 60%. These packages also presented the lowest number of architecturally-relevant code anomalies.

Another relevant characteristic that is likely to favor the success of detection strategies (i.e., accuracy rates higher than 60%) is when the projection of architectural elements occurs in a few code units. In these cases, single code anomalies will exert a more direct impact on the architectural element that they are implementing. This phenomenon was observed in all target systems.

6. Analyzing Overlooked Code Anomalies

Once we have discussed the strategies' accuracy, we reflect upon the *key factors* that contributed to their failure in localizing architecturally-relevant code anomalies (Sections 6.1 and 6.2). This discussion can provide insights on how to improve the techniques to detect architecture degradation based on source code analysis.

6.1 Inability to Analyze Architectural Concerns' Properties in the Source Code

Code anomalies were often the source of architectural modularity problems when they were located in modules realizing various architectural concerns. We noticed that 62% of the total number of architecturally-relevant code anomalies exhibited this characteristic. This frequency reinforces that detection strategies should be more sensitive to the degree of concern scattering and tangling in the code. In fact, the employed strategies were not accurate when detecting anomalies associated with the inappropriate modularization of architectural concerns; they presented precision and recall rates around 43% and 48% respectively.

For instance, the class *BaseController* in MobileMedia was classified by developers as an architecturally-relevant occurrence of *God Class* since it is realizing different architectural concerns (e.g. *Photo*, *Music*, and *Persistence*). However, differently from *MediaController* (Figure 1), it was not automatically detected by the strategies. Even though this class was the source of highly tangled and scattered concerns, its methods present neither low cohesion nor high complexity (Section 3.1). However, changes associated with each of the architectural concerns were performed in this class, confirming its anomalous nature. This class was particularly related to two architectural anomalies, namely *Component Concern Overload* and *Scattered Parasitic Functionality*.

As a conclusion, the results reveal that conventional detection strategies are not accurate largely due to their lack of sensitivity to properties of architectural concerns in the code. Detection strategies are limited to metrics of structural properties (detected by static analysis tools) of modules in the code. Existing concern metrics [42] and concern tracing tools [10] should be leveraged to improve the accuracy of detection strategies used to assess architecture degradation.

6.2 Inability to Identify Architectural Information in the Source Code

Architecturally-relevant code anomalies often occurred in code elements responsible for implementing different architectural elements. Specifically, 49% of the architecturally-relevant code anomalies fell in this category. However, precision and recall rates of the strategies were 36% and 44%, respectively, when identifying these code anomalies.

For instance, the method *InsertEmployee.execute* in HealthWatcher represents an example of an architecturally-relevant code anomaly that was not automatically detected by our employed strategies. In particular, this method was classified as *Divergent Change* by developers since it accesses information and call methods of classes responsible for implementing different architectural elements. This method also introduces undesirable dependencies between

non-adjacent layers, condition to be classified as an architecturally-relevant occurrence. However, such *execute* method was not automatically detected by strategies because they focus on measuring method's strong coupling degree based on syntactic dependencies.

However, this method had instead a semantic dependency with other methods: the former changed together with other methods realizing different architectural components, which were not syntactically coupled to the former. Hence, we observed that strategies were not effective in detecting this kind of anomaly as they are not sensitive to which architectural elements a code anomaly is responsible for implementing. The key issue is that detection strategies cannot rely on information about how the code elements are associated with architectural modules and their inter-dependencies; this information cannot be extracted using code metrics. This might indicate the need for further investigating how detection strategies could exploit traces of architectural information in the code.

6.3 Patterns of Code Anomalies

It was observed that certain patterns of code anomalies tend to be better indicators of architectural degradation symptoms than single code anomalies. However, these patterns cannot be directly detected by strategies, which focus on identifying individual code anomalies. They do not capture, for instance, a chain of inter-related anomalies.

Co-occurrences of Code Anomalies. Certain recurring patterns of co-occurring code anomalies tend to be stronger indicators of architectural degradation symptoms. For instance, co-occurrences of *Long Method* and *Divergent Change* were associated with architectural problems in all the systems. That is, methods with either high cyclomatic complexity or many lines of code and, high coupling degree with different architectural elements were better indicators than single *Long Method* occurrences. More than 75% of these combined occurrences were associated with architectural problems while just about 43% of single *Long Method* occurrences were related to architectural problems.

It is important to point out that many of these relevant co-occurrences cannot be detected by simply combining multiple strategies using logical operators (Section 3.1). Aiming at identifying these co-occurrences, detection strategies must rely on some kind of architectural information (Section 6.2). For instance, it would be also useful to consider how many different architectural elements a method is accessing. Otherwise, strategies will just detect such relevant co-occurrences that present similar characteristics of non-relevant co-occurrences. That is, those co-occurrences that present tight coupling degree with several elements, disregarding their distribution on architectural decompositions.

Code Elements suffering from the Same Anomaly. Interesting findings emerged from analyzing *groups of code elements that suffer from the same code anomaly*. For instance, when a group of classes that suffer from *God Class* or *Large Class* are implementing the same architectural component *A* and realizing different concerns it may indicate that *A* suffers from *Component Concern Overload*. This assumption departs from the fact that *God Classes* and *Large Classes* are likely to be related to the inappropriate modularization of architectural concerns. Furthermore, when other architectural components and *God Classes* of *A* are sharing the same architectural concern, it may suggest that *A* is affected by *Scattered Parasitic Functionality*. This situation was observed in all the systems.

Propagation of Architectural Problems. It was also often observed the propagation of architectural problems from parents to children in the inheritance trees of all the systems. There are two main categories related to such *propagation of architectural problems*. The first is related to architectural problems that are propagated to all the children in the inheritance tree whereas in the second category the architectural problem is not propagated to all the children, i.e. some children are free of architectural problems. Examples of both categories were found in all systems. For instance, in HealthWatcher it was observed that several interfaces were introducing undesirable relationships via their parameter types. These interfaces were not identified by detection strategies because they had a well-defined interface (e.g. several members, without a high coupling degree). However, they had a considerable negative effect as these violations were propagated down through the class hierarchies. Usually these undesirable references are left in a system over a long period due to the ripple effects when refactorings are applied to remove them.

The limitations of detection strategies for localizing propagated relevant occurrences of code anomalies are the same for localizing single relevant occurrences. This is due to the propagation of code anomalies in the inheritance trees itself could be detected using static code analysis.

6.4 Architectural Design and Strategy Accuracy

There was a direct influence of the lack of modularity of certain concerns on the architecturally-relevant anomalies when analyzing different architectural decompositions. We observed that when the modularization of architectural concerns is more explicit in the source code the number of architecturally-relevant anomalies tend to decrease. For instance, OO systems presented a higher number of conventional code anomalies [13] than AO systems. We suspect this occurred due to most of the code anomalies were related to the inappropriate modularization of architectural concerns, which are more scattered in OO systems. As AOP mechanisms tend to improve the modularization of concerns in single aspects, they may remove relevant anomalies related to this factor. It is not our intention to compare the results in both decompositions, as we discussed in previous sections the inadequate use of AO mechanisms may introduce other kinds of architecturally-relevant code anomalies.

Even more interesting is the fact that we have observed how the strategies' accuracy for identifying architecturally-relevant anomalies seem to be similar in both kinds of architectural decompositions. This assumption is derived from results regarding to the "*average rows*" in Table 6. The strategies' accuracy rates are about 40% for detecting architecturally-relevant code anomalies in all AO and non-AO systems, except in MIDAS.

7. Threats to Validity

This section summarizes the main threats to validity and the mitigations considered; a detailed analysis of all the possible imperfections and mitigations for our study can be found at the supplementary website [5].

Construct Validity. Threats to construct validity are mainly related to possible errors introduced in the identification of code anomalies and architectural problems. There are different kinds of detection strategies documented in the literature. In particular, we opted for not selecting history-sensitive detection strategies as they tend to be less predictive and require multiple versions of the system [26, 40]. Consequently, they accurately reveal code anomalies just in later releases, when the system may have already achieved critical degradation stages.

We are aware that detection strategies, manual inspection and other mechanisms to identify code anomalies and architectural problems can introduce imprecision. However, we mitigated this threat by: (i) involving original developers and architects in this process, and (ii) using architectural models where architectural elements were mapped to different levels of granularity. That is, the relationships between code elements and architecture elements were often not 1-to-1. Furthermore, the architectural problems were identified by architects, who had previous experience on the detection of architectural violations and anomalies in other systems. The correlation analysis between code anomalies and architectural problems was also validated with the architects and developers.

Conclusion Validity. We have two issues that threaten the conclusion validity of our study: the number of evaluated systems and assessed anomalies. Two versions of MIDAS, eight versions of MobileMedia, eight versions of Aspectual-Media, ten versions of HealthWatcher and, ten versions of AspectualWatcher were used for the purposes of this study, totaling 38 versions. Of course, a higher number of systems is always desired. However, the analysis of a bigger sample in this study would be impracticable for different reasons.

First, the relationship between code anomalies and architectural problems needed to be confirmed by architects. Second, the number of systems with all the required information and stakeholders available to perform this study is rather scarce. Then, our sample can be seen as appropriate for a first exploratory investigation [20]. All the findings (for example, those discussed in Section 6) contribute with

more specific hypotheses that should be further tested in repetitions or more controlled replications of our study.

Related to the second issue (completeness of code anomalies and architectural problems), our analysis was concerned with a wide variety of code anomalies and problems that occur in system's architecture. We analyzed the accuracy of detection strategies for identifying all architecturally-relevant code anomalies that occurred in the target systems. In addition, certain code anomalies were not discussed (e.g. *Data Class*) since their occurrences did not influence on studied system architectures.

Internal and External Validity. The main threats to internal and external validity are the following. First, the level of experience of systems' programmers could be an issue. In order to mitigate this, we used systems that were developed by more than 20 programmers with different levels of software development skills. The main threat to external validity is related to the nature of the evaluated systems. In order to minimize this threat we have tried to use applications with different sizes, that suffer from a different set of code anomalies and that were implemented using different architectural styles and environments. However, we are aware that more studies involving a higher number of systems should be performed in the future.

8. Concluding Remarks

Our results suggest that state-of-the-art detection strategies were not able to identify and locate architecturally relevant code anomalies. Specifically, more than 60% of the automatically-detected code anomalies were not correlated with architectural problems (neither with other threats, such as faults in the code). This means that developers might be spending a lot of time reviewing code anomalies (and refactoring code) that do not represent architectural (or other) threats to the system. Even worse, many of the false negatives (i.e. about 50%) generated by automated anomaly detection are often correlated with architectural problems. This means that developers would not be informed by detection strategies of code anomalies that are critical to architecture sustainability. These findings are interesting because they question the effectiveness of existing strategies and tools in supporting "architecture revision" strictly based on the source code (which is commonly the case). Also, it is in such case where the current mechanisms for "architecture revision" [1][8] cannot be used since they rely on the existence of the intended architectural design.

We found that the imperfection of the detection strategies is not simply related to specific thresholds or combinations of particular measures. On the contrary, the false positives and false negatives often cannot be resolved if design decisions are not traced and mapped to the source code, and exploited by detection strategies (Section 6). For instance, detection strategies cannot decide whether (or not) relationships between two classes are introducing violations. They cannot decide either whether a class is accessing information from classes defined in different architectural elements. It was also found that certain recurring patterns of anomaly combinations or anomaly propagations are better indicators of architectural problems than individual anomaly occurrences. Therefore, developers should be warned about the harmful impact of these patterns and their existence in the source code in order to perform their early removal. However, these patterns usually cannot be specified or detected by existing techniques [21, 32], as they are intended to pick out individual anomaly occurrences.

9. Acknowledgements

This was sponsored by: I.Macia CNPq grant 579604/2008-0; A.Garcia FAPERJ grant E-26/102.211/2009, 111.152/2011 and CNPq grant 305526/2009-0; A.v.Staa CNPq grant 306802/2008-2; Projects: CNPq grants 483882/2009-7, 479344/2010-8 and 485348/2011-0. It was also sponsored by the US National Science Foundation under Grant number 1117593. Any opinions, findings, and conclusions expressed in this paper are those of the authors and do not necessarily reflect the views of the NSF.

References

[1] Aldrich, J. ArchJava: Connecting Software Architecture to Implementation. In Proc of the 24th ICSE, pp. 187-197, 2002.

[2] Alikacem, E.H and Sahraoui, H. Generic metric extraction framework. In Proc. of the 16th IWSM/MetriKon, 2006, pp. 383–390.

[3] Bieman, J.M. and Kang, B.K. Cohesion and Reuse in an Object Oriented System. In Proc of the ISSR, pp 259-262, 1995.

[4] Clements, P et al. Documenting Software Architectures: Views and Beyond. Addison-Wesley, 2nd Edition, 2010

[5] Code smells study: http://www.inf.puc-rio.br/~ibertran/aosd12.

[6] D'Ambros, M. et al. the Impact of Design Flaws on Software Defects. In Proc. of the 10th QSIC, pp. 23 - 31, 2010.

[7] Dhambri et al. Visual Detection of Design Anomalies. In Proc. of the 12th CSMR, pp. 279-283, 2008.

[8] Eichberg, M. et al. Defining and Continuous Checking of Structural Program Dependencies. In Proc. of the 30th ICSE, 2008.

[9] Emden, E. and Moonen, L. Java quality assurance by detecting code smells. In Proceedings of the 9th ICRE, 2002.

[10] FEAT tool, http://www.cs.mcgill.ca/~swevo/feat/

[11] Ferrari, F. et al. An exploratory study of error-proneness in evolving Aspect-Oriented Programs. In: Proc. of the 25th OOPSLA, USA, 2009.

[12] Figueiredo, E. et al. Evolving software product lines with aspects: An empirical study on design stability. In Proc of the 30th ICSE, 2008.

[13] Fowler, M. Refactoring: Improving the Design of Existing Code. Addison-Wesley, 1999.

[14] Garcia, J. et al. Identifying architectural bad smells. In Proc of the. 13th CSMR, pp 255–258, 2009.

[15] Greenwood, P. et al. On the impact of aspectual decompositions on design stability: An empirical study. In Proc. of the 21st ECOOP, 2007.

[16] Hochstein, L. and Lindvall, M. Combating architectural degeneration: A survey. Info. & Soft. Technology July, 2005.

[17] Hosmer, D. and Lemeshow, S. Applied Logistic Regression (2nd Edition). Wiley, 2000.

[18] Khomh, K. et al. An exploratory study of the impact of code smells on software change-proneness. In Proc of the 16th WCRE, 2009.

[19] Kiczales, G.,et al. Aspect-oriented programming. In Proc. of the 11th ECOOP. LNCS, vol. 1241. Springer, Heidelberg. pp. 220-242, 1997.

[20] Kitchenham, B. et al. Evaluating guidelines for empirical software engineering studies. ISESE pp 38-47, 2006

[21] Lanza, M. and Marinescu, R. Object-Oriented Metrics in Practice. Springer, 2006.

[22] Lippert, M. and Roock, S. Refactoring in Large Software Projects: Performing Complex Restructurings Successfully. Wiley. 2006.

[23] Macia, I. et al. A. An Exploratory Study of Code Smells in Evolving Aspect-Oriented Systems. In Proc of the 10th AOSD, 2011.

[24] Malek, S. et al. Reconceptualizing a family of heterogeneous embedded systems via explicit architectural support. In Proc. of the 29th ICSE. 2007.

[25] Mantyla, M.V. and Lassenius, C. Subjective evaluation of software evolvability using code smells: An empirical study. Empirical Software Enggineering, vol. 11, no. 3, pp. 395–431, 2006.

[26] Mara, L. et al. Hist-Inspect: A Tool for History-Sensitive Detection of Code Smells. In Proc. of the 10th AOSD, 2011

[27] Marinescu, R. Detection strategies: Metrics-based rules for detecting design flaws. In Proc. of the 20th ICSM, pp 350-359, 2004.

[28] Marinescu,R.; Ganea, G. and Veredi, I. inCode: Continuous Quality Assessment and Improvement. In Proc of the 14th CSMR, 2010.

[29] Martin, R. Agile Principles, Patterns, and Practices. Prentice Hall, 2002.

[30] McCabe, T.J. A Software Complexity Measure. IEEE Transactions on Software Engineering, 2 (4), pp 308-320, 1976.

[31] Meyer, B. Object-Oriented Software Construction. Prentice Hall Professional Technical 2nd edition, 2000.

[32] Moha, N. et al. DECOR: A Method for the Specification and Detection of Code and Design Smells. IEEE TSE, 2010.

[33] Munro, MJ. Product metrics for automatic identification of bad smell design problems in java source-code. In Proc of 11th METRICS, 2005

[34] MuLATo tool, http://sourceforge.net/projects/mulato/ (3/08/2009)

[35] Murphy, G.C., et al.. Software Reflexion Models: Bridging the Gap between Design and Implementation. IEEE TSE, pp 364–380, 2001.

[36] Murphy-Hill, E. Scalable, expressive, and context-sensitive code smell display. In Proc of the 23rd OPSLA, 2008.

[37] Olbrich, S.M. et al. Are all code smells harmful? A study of God Classes and Brain Classes in the evolution of three open source systems. In Proc of the 26th ICSM pp 1-10, 2010.

[38] Olbrich, S.M. et al. The evolution and impact of code smells: A case study of two open source systems. In Proc of the 3rd ESEM, 2009.

[39] Perry, D.E. and Wolf, A.L. Foundations for the study of software architecture, ACM Software. Eng. Notes 17 (4) pp 40–52, 1992.

[40] Ratiu, D. et al. Using History Information to Improve Design Flaws Detection. In Proc of the 8th CSMR, 2004.

[41] Ratzinger, J. et al. Improving evolvability through refactoring. In Proc of the 5th IEEE MSR, 2005.

[42] Sant'anna, C. et al. On the modularity of software architectures: A Concern-Driven measurement framework. In Proc. of ECSA, 2007.

[43] Sonar: http://docs.codehaus.org/display/SONAR/

[44] Srivisut, K. and Muenchaisri, P. Bad-smell Metrics for Aspect-Oriented Software. In Proc of the 6th ICIS, 2007.

[45] Together: http://www.borland.com/us/products/together/

[46] Tsantalis, N. and Chatzigeorgiou, A. Identification of move method refactoring opportunities. IEEE TSE, 35(3), pp 347–367, 2009.

[47] Understand: http://www.scitools.com/

[48] Wake, W.C. Refactoring Workbook. Boston, MA, USA: Addison-Wesley Longman Publishing Co., Inc., 2003.

[49] Wettel, R. and Lanza, M. Visually localizing design problems with disharmony maps. In Proc. of the 4th Softvis pp. 155–164, 2008.

LARA: An Aspect-Oriented Programming Language for Embedded Systems

João M. P. Cardoso,
Tiago Carvalho

Universidade do Porto,
Faculdade de Engenharia (FEUP),
Dep. de Engenharia Informática
Rua Dr. Roberto Frias, s/n
4200-465 Porto, Portugal

jmpc@acm.org,
tiago.diogo.carvalho@fe.up.pt

José G. F. Coutinho,
Wayne Luk

Department of Computing,
Imperial College London,
180 Queen's Gate,
London SW7 2BZ,
United Kingdom

gabriel.figueiredo@imperial.ac.uk,
w.luk@imperial.ac.uk

Ricardo Nobre,
Pedro C. Diniz

INESC-ID,
Rua Alves Redol 9
1000-029 Lisboa, Portugal

rjfnobre.disk@gmail.com,
pedro@esda.inesc-id.pt

Zlatko Petrov

Honeywell International s.r.o,
Turanka 100
627 00 Brno
Czech Republic

zlatko.petrov@honeywell.com

Abstract

The development of applications for high-performance embedded systems is typically a long and error-prone process. In addition to the required functions, developers must consider various and often conflicting non-functional application requirements such as performance and energy efficiency. The complexity of this process is exacerbated by the multitude of target architectures and the associated retargetable mapping tools. This paper introduces an Aspect-Oriented Programming (AOP) approach that conveys domain knowledge and non-functional requirements to optimizers and mapping tools. We describe a novel AOP language, LARA, which allows the specification of compilation strategies to enable efficient generation of software code and hardware cores for alternative target architectures. We illustrate the use of LARA for code instrumentation and analysis, and for guiding the application of compiler and hardware synthesis optimizations. An important LARA feature is its capability to deal with different join points, action models, and attributes, and to generate an aspect intermediate representation. We present examples of our aspect-oriented hardware/software design flow for mapping real-life application codes to embedded platforms based on Field Programmable Gate Array (FPGA) technology.

Categories and Subject Descriptors   D.3.3 [**Programming Languages**]: Language Constructs and Features – Frameworks. D.3.3 [**Programming Languages**]: Processors – Compilers, Retargetable Compilers, Optimization, Code Generation. C.3 [**Special-purpose and application-based systems**]: Real-time and embedded systems, Microprocessor/microcomputer applications. B.7.1 [**Integrated circuits**]: Types and Design Styles – Algorithms implemented in hardware.

General Terms   Design, Experimentation, Languages.

Keywords   Aspect-Oriented Programming; Compilers; Reconfigurable Computing; FPGAs; Embedded Systems; Domain-Specific Languages

1. Introduction

The development and mapping of applications to contemporary heterogeneous high-performance embedded systems requires tools with very sophisticated design-flows that are aware of critical applications requirements, both functional and non-functional (e.g., real-time performance and safety) while meeting target architecture's stringent resource constraints (e.g., storage capacity and computing capabilities).

This development and mapping process must consider a myriad of design choices. Typically, developers must partition the application code among the most suited system components – a process commonly known as hardware/software partitioning [1]. Subsequently, they have to deal with multiple compilation tools (sub-chains) that target each specific system component. These problems are exacerbated when dealing with FPGAs (Field-Programmable Gate Arrays), a popular technology which combines the performance of custom hardware with the flexibility of software [2][3]. As a consequence, developers must explore code and mapping transformations specific to each architecture so that the resulting solutions meet the overall requirements. As the complexity of emerging heterogeneous embedded systems continues to grow, the need to meet increasingly challenging design trade-offs (e.g., weight, size, energy efficiency, reliability and performance) will undoubtedly exacerbate the complexity of the mapping of sophisticated applications to these embedded systems.

In practice, this approach leads to code that is transformed beyond recognition and where developers have manually applied an extensive set of architecture-specific transformations and tool-specific directives. However, such practice leads to low developer productivity and, more importantly, limited application portability. For instance, when the underlying architecture changes developers may need to restart the design process.

This paper describes LARA, a novel aspect-oriented programming (AOP) [4] language for mapping applications to heterogeneous high-performance embedded systems. This language allows developers to capture non-functional requirements from applications in a structured way, leveraging high-level abstractions such as hardware/software design templates and flexible toolchain interfaces. Developers can thus benefit from retaining the original application source while exploiting the automation benefits of various domain-specific and target component-specific compilation/synthesis tools. In essence, LARA uses AOP mechanisms to offer in a unified framework (a) a vehicle for conveying application-specific requirements that cannot otherwise be specified in the original programming language for design capture, (b) using these requirements to guide the application of transformations and mapping choices, thus facilitating design-space-exploration (DSE), and (c) interfacing in an extensible fashion the various compilation/synthesis components in the toolchain. This paper makes the following specific contributions:

- Introduces LARA, an AOP language capable of capturing transversal (across multiple codes) and vertical concerns (across different stages of a design flow);

- Describes the LARA join point model that can include not only program execution points but also hardware system components and their properties;

- Extends the join point model with attributes used and defined in the aspects to codify complex strategies;

- Covers a programmable and systematic approach to control and guide different design flow actions and/or application of code transformations;

- Presents experimental results of the use of LARA for a set of real-life codes targeting a heterogeneous embedded architecture with both general-purpose processor (GPP) and FPGA technologies, using commercially available tools for compilation and hardware synthesis.

The results described in this paper reflect the development of the LARA language in the context of the RE-FLECT (REndering FPGAs to MuLti-Core Embedded CompuTing) research project [5][6][7]. The applications selected in our study and thus the corresponding requirements were drawn from two of this project's industrial partners, targeting the Avionics and Audio domains. Specifically, the LARA AOP approach has been designed to help developers to reach good design solutions with low programming effort. This experience of using aspects for hardware-oriented transformations reveals the benefits of AOP in: (a) application program portability across architectures and tools, and (b) productivity improvement of developers and programmers.

This paper is organized as follows. Section 2 describes a motivating example. Section 3 presents the design flow for our approach. Section 4 describes our AOP approach. Section 5 focuses on the LARA aspect language, providing a number of illustrative examples. Section 6 focuses on the practical impact of our approach. In Section 7, we summarize related work and Section 8 then concludes.

2. Compilation/Synthesis Example

We now present a motivational example that highlights some of the challenges faced by application developers when targeting embedded systems. In this example, we assume that the developer has already carried out a performance analysis study and has selected a set of computational kernels that can benefit from either hardware acceleration or source-level code transformations.

We consider a particular implementation of the MPEG-2 Audio Encoder (layers I and II) in C. One of the hot-spots is the polyphase filter bank function depicted in Figure 1. This function is structured as two doubly nested for-loops that manipulate four one- and two-dimensional array variables of 64-bit floating-point values. It processes 512 audio samples and outputs 32 equal-width frequency sub-

bands. The statically allocated m array holds the filter coefficients.

```
1.  void fsubband(double z[512], double s[32]){
2.    double y[64];
3.    int i,j;
4.    static const double m[32][64] = {...};
5.    for(i=0;i<64;i++) {    // loop1
6.      y[i] = 0;
7.      for(j=0;j<8;j++)     // loop2
8.        y[i] += z[i+64*j];
9.    }
10.   for(i=0;i<32;i++) {    // loop3
11.     s[i] = 0;
12.     for(j=0;j<64;j++)    // loop4
13.       s[i] += m[i][j] * y[j];
14.   }
15. }
```

Figure 1. C source code of the function *fsubband* in the MPEG-2 audio encoder application.

An implementation of this kernel for an embedded system with a GPP coupled to an FPGA (e.g., acting as a hardware accelerator) could explore two mapping scenarios, namely[1]: (1) the complete mapping of the code to the GPP leveraging software-only GPP compiler optimizations, and (2) the generation of an application-specific architecture implemented on the FPGA derived from partitioning the application between the GPP and the FPGA hardware.

Each of these mapping scenarios may require different strategies in terms of how the computation is partitioned between the target components (GPP vs. FPGA), and consequently how data manipulated by the sub-computations are organized and partitioned. Furthermore, as a multi-computing architecture, once the data and the computation have been partitioned, data communication between the components and their subsequent synchronization need to be considered and included in the mapped code.

Once the partition and mapping have been decided, each of the partitioned computations may still be subject to further transformations. The computations to be executed on the GPP can be subject to a wide variety of transformations offered by C compilers such as *gcc*. These include loop-based transformations (e.g., loop unrolling and/or software pipelining), data type conversions (double to float or double/float to fixed-point), and even array to memory mapping and caching in local scratch-pad memories.

With respect to computations mapped to the FPGA-based hardware accelerator, there is a wider range of compilation and synthesis options that can be exercised which further increase the complexity of this mapping process. For example, in the accumulation statements in lines 8 and 13 in Figure 1, one could cache (scalar replace) the values associated with the y array thus substantially reducing the number of load/store operations from/to external memories. In the presence of dual-ported on-chip memories, local arrays m and y could be mapped to distinct memories. Loop transformations could then be used to expose concurrent accesses to the m and y arrays. To achieve this mapping result, a developer would define a strategy to combine unroll-and-jam to *loop1* and unrolling to *loop4* followed by a specific mapping of array variables to internal FPGA storage (e.g., Block RAMs - Random Access Memories - in a Xilinx FPGA).

---

[1] A third scenario where the entire computation is mapped to the FPGA would, in practice, be infeasible.

These mapping strategies and the associated compiler and mapping transformations highlight the interplay between them and the complexity in assessing their potential performance and resource use. To address this complexity we developed the LARA AOP language. LARA allows developers to control the tools in a compilation toolchain and to apply a wide range of transformations and target architecture mapping choices in an automated fashion. We now illustrate how a developer could specify examples of these transformations using LARA.

The first of these aspects, depicted in Figure 2, instructs a weaver (Figure 5, see Section 3) to fully unroll all innermost for-type loops in which the number of iterations is known at compile-time and does not exceed 32. For instance, when this aspect is applied to function *fsubband*, the weaver will fully unroll *loop2* shown in Figure 1. This aspect is generic and can be reused for other functions/applications as part of an optimization strategy. The developer can even increase its potential reuse by defining the number of iterations (32 in this example) and the unrolling factor as two additional aspect input parameters.

```
aspectdef strategy1
  input functionName end
  select function{name==functionName}.
           loop{type=="for"} end
  apply optimize("loopunroll", "full"); end
  condition
      $loop.numIterIsConstant &&
      $loop.num_iter <= 32 &&
      $loop.is_innermost
  end
end
```

Figure 2. Aspect module that fully unrolls innermost loops with the number of iterations less than or equal to 32.

The second aspect, shown in Figure 3, focuses on the software/hardware partition problem where functions and code sections can be selected and mapped to hardware specified in a hardware description language such as Verilog or VHDL. This particular aspect also conveys to the compiler and synthesis tools that are part of the design flow (see Section 3), information about the interval range of variable "z", the maximum noise power allowed and the data type of argument "s". This information can be used by a word-length analysis engine (here identified as *datarepr*) to derive customized word-lengths by exploring acceptable precision and accuracy values. Lastly, in Figure 4, we present an aspect for the mapping of array variables to local storage for a specific target hardware architecture: an internal Block RAM in a Xilinx Virtex-5 FPGA device.

Regarding code generation, the weaver component included in our compilation infrastructure (see Section 3) creates two source code partitions: a software partition which is compiled by the native target GPP compiler, and a hardware partition which is processed by a target hardware architecture synthesis tool responsible for generating the corresponding bit-level device configuration, able to program the FPGA.

This example highlights a set of features of our combined hardware/software aspect-oriented mapping approach:

- It enables the specification and control of software- and hardware-related transformations with specific parameter values, such as the amount of unrolling.

- It supports the identification of code sections to be mapped to classes of computation nodes, such as traditional GPPs and hardware accelerators, facilitating the interface and interplay of diverse front-end and back-end tools such as source-to-source compilers, code generators, and hardware synthesis tools.

- By maintaining a single source code, the approach allows the composition of transformations and strategies, thus promoting code portability.

```
aspectdef maximizePerformance
  input funcName = "fsubband" end
  select
    function{name==funcName}.arg{name=="s"} end
  apply $arg.noise_power <= 1E-3;
        $arg.def type="float"; end
  select
    function{name==funcName}.arg{name=="z"} end
  apply $arg.range = "[-40..120]"; end
  select function{name==funcName} end
  apply
    $function.map(to: "hardware", id: "virtex5");
    call strategy2;
    optimize("datarepr");
    call map2BRAMs(funcName);
  end
end
```

Figure 3. Aspect module used to map to hardware and optimize the *fsubband* function using range values.

```
aspectdef map2BRAMs
  input func_name end
  var id=1;
  select function{name==func_name}.var end
  apply
    $var.map(to: "Memory", type:"BRAM",
             ports: 2, id: id++);
  end
  condition $var.isarray &&
            $var.scope == "local" &&
            $var.size <= 2048 &&
    ($var.parloads >=2 || $var.parstores >=2)
  end
end
```

Figure 4. An aspect module used to map specific array variables to local on-chip block RAM.

Although not highlighted in this example, our compilation and synthesis approach also enables the developer to engage in design space exploration (DSE). In this specific example, loop-unrolling exposes additional instruction-level parallelism (ILP) opportunities for the hardware-based solution, but may increase the amount of required hardware resources and the associated code as it expands the source program. Similarly, mapping variables to local storage (in effect caching them) may reduce the number of memory accesses at the expense of an increased amount of storage resources. As such, developers can repeatedly use the same aspect with a wide range of parameter values and modify the sequence of application of the aspects in search of a design that meets specific overall requirements.

We next describe the basic structure of the compilation and synthesis design flow we have developed, highlighting the ability of the aspect-oriented approach to control a wide range of transformations and tools.

3. Design Flow

LARA, the AOP language described in this paper, was developed in the context of the compilation and synthesis design flow for the REFLECT research project [6][7]. One of the goals of REFLECT is to map applications described in high-level programming languages such as C[2] to multi-core embedded architectures. This mapping, and subsequent compilation/synthesis, invariably makes use of a wide variety of tools with unique features and interfaces. LARA has been designed to capture non-functional requirements and to guide tools so that developers can quickly achieve design solutions that meet these requirements, which cannot be easily expressed using common programming languages such as C. In addition, LARA allows the definition of strategies specifying which aspects to apply and in what order. Ultimately, strategies can be seen as rules that implement specific design patterns.

We now describe in more detail the overall design flow, highlight its main components and explain how LARA enables their effective use in developing feasible embedded systems design solutions. A detailed description of LARA can be found in Sections 4 and 5.

As shown in Figure 5, our design flow accepts two types of source descriptions as inputs: **(1) Input Application**: The current implementation supports C sources (C99 std. compliant); **(2) LARA Description**: The LARA descriptions capture non-functional requirements in the form of aspects and strategies. They enable developers to define application characteristics such as precision representation, input data rates or even reliability requirements for the execution of specific code sections.

This design flow chain is structured as three major components, namely:

- **LARA Front-End:** The front-end converts LARA descriptions into Aspect-IR (Aspect Intermediate Representation) to be processed by the weavers. The Aspect-IR is a low-level representation of LARA in XML format, where information is structured in a way to facilitate the parsing of aspects and strategies.

- **Source-to-source transformer**: This stage, using the Harmonic tool (based on [9]), performs source-level transformations (C to C) which include: arbitrary code instrumentation and monitoring, hardware/software partitioning using cost estimation models, as well as insertion of primitives (such as remote procedure calls) to enable communication between software and hardware components. The results of this stage are source files reflecting the partitioning, and additional code generated to realize synchronization and communication between software and hardware partitions.

- **Compiler Tool Set:** This stage includes the front-end, middle-end and optimization phases, with the latter two common to both software and hardware partitions, which are target architecture independent. The CoSy [10] compilation framework is currently being used. The back-end includes assembly code generators for the GPP (software sections) and VHDL/Verilog generators for specific hardware cores.

The design flow includes several weavers at different levels of the toolchain. Each weaver receives as input: C source code or an IR and the Aspect-IR, and outputs: the transformed C code or the transformed IR and if required a modified Aspect-IR for the next weaver in the sequence.

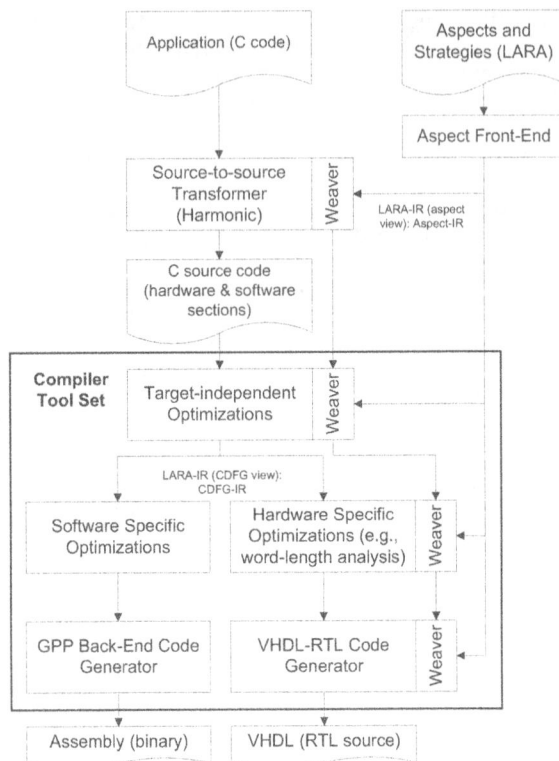

Figure 5. LARA based Design Flow.

4. The LARA Approach

A key innovation of our aspect-based approach lies in bringing together, in the same framework, various types of transformation and operational aspects in the mapping of computations to embedded systems. Specifically, LARA allows developers to specify the following types of aspects:

- **MONITORING:** Specification of which implementation features, such as current value of a variable or the number of items written to a specific data structure, provide insight for the refinement of other aspects;

- **SPECIALIZING:** Definition of specific properties for a particular input code when targeting a specific system (e.g. specializing data types, numeric precision and input/output data rates);

- **MAPPING AND GUIDING:** Specification of design patterns, which embody mapping actions to guide tools to perform specific implementation decisions (e.g. mapping array variables to memories; using FIFOs to communicate data between cores; leveraging dynamic reconfiguration techniques for performance or using temporal/spatial redundancy for fault-tolerance);

- **RETARGETING:** Specification of characteristics of the target system in order to make the tools adaptable and aware of those characteristics, as well as facilitating implementation on other systems.

LARA relies on the main concept of aspects, generically defined by the following statement:

"In programs P, whenever condition C arises, perform action A." [11]

Associated with AOP are usually the notions of pointcut and advice. A pointcut exposes points of interest (join

---

[2] Although our compilation framework is applicable to other imperative programming languages, due to the constraints imposed by the availability of the front-end we are only focusing on the C programming language. We have, nevertheless validated the same approach for MATLAB [8].

points) related to a program. Join points refer to points in the code and/or in the program execution. An advice refers to the actions to be performed for each join point exposed by the pointcut mechanism.

In addition, AOP defines the notion of a join point model, which defines the points of interest for a given programming language. A typical join point model includes program constructs and structures such as function calls, fields in a class, and functions. In our approach, we consider a join point model that captures most structures and constructs (e.g., loops, conditionals, variables, array accesses) found in C in order to specify actions that target complex applications containing such code artifacts.

Our approach also considers points of interest as points in the execution of a program as well as in the target physical system. These points may include components of the system, such as a microprocessor, and the system's parameters, such as its specific inputs. As such our AOP approach can be thought as:

> "In programs P and/or systems S, whenever condition C arises, perform action A."

The following are a few examples that can be captured by our AOP approach:

- For each variable of type double in function *f1*, change the type to float.
- Set noise power of parameter *s* of function *f1* to 1E-3.
- Set microprocessor clock frequency to 400 MHz.
- Map arrays of functions migrated to hardware, with size < N, to BRAMs (local memories).

Figure 6 illustrates the LARA front-end which converts a LARA aspect file into Aspect-IR. To perform this conversion, the front-end requires three specification files: (1) the join point model representing the points of interest in the input programming language and in the target architecture; (2) the join point attributes defining properties associated with each join point type; and (3) the action model describing each possible action that an aspect can perform on a join point. We describe each of these models next.

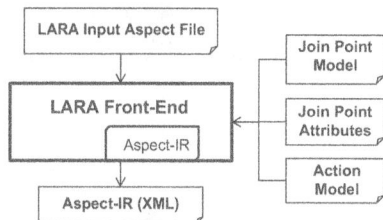

Figure 6. The LARA Front-End component.

4.1 Join Point Model

The points of interest in the program code and/or program execution are specified in the join point model, which is structured hierarchically in an XML file. Since the join point model specification describes join point types and their hierarchy, it can be used to validate pointcut expressions. Rather than hardcoding types in the grammar, this approach allows the model to be easily updated and expanded. Also, by accepting a join point model file externally to the front-end, it is possible to reuse the LARA front-end for other programming languages (see [8]) and with different system components and architectures.

Figure 7(a) shows an excerpt of the join point model currently used for C programs. In this case, the join point type *loop* has as its predecessor the *body* of a *function*, followed by the *file* it belongs to.

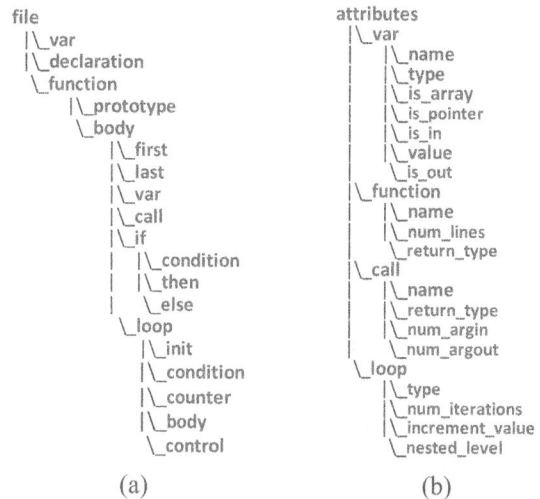

(a)   (b)

Figure 7. Excerpt of the input models: (a) join point model definition for C programs; (b) the attribute model.

In addition to the join points related to the C program (as illustrated in Figure 7(a)), our approach also considers join points related to system components. Examples of those join points are the GPP (General Purpose Processor), the CCU (Custom Computing Unit), and the Memory.

4.2 Join Point Attributes

The attributes associated with each join point type are specified in the join point attributes file. Figure 7(b) and Table 1 illustrate examples of attributes for some of the join points supported by our join point model. Attributes are properties in which values are either statically or dynamically known. These values can be used to filter join points (e.g., a `for` type loop is defined as a join point *loop* with attribute *type* with value "for") in conditions that trigger the use of a certain action on the aspect, and also as arguments for the apply sections of an aspect.

Table 1. Artifact list containing examples of join point attributes associated with system components.

Join point	Attributes	Examples of values
GPP (general purpose processor)	name	PowerPC
	family	P440
	clk_freq	400 MHz
CCU (custom computing unit)	id	1
	clk_freq	100 MHz
	max_slices	4,000
Memory	num_ports	1
	max_size	256 × 32-bit
	type	BRAM, DRAM, Distributed RAM

In addition, attributes expose information for each join point, and that information can be obtained by the weavers in the compilation flow and/or can influence the use of actions. For example, the join point type *var* has properties including the *name of the variable*, the *number of readings and writings*, and the *initialized value*. Another example is the information we can obtain about a loop. With the *num-*

183

ber of iterations it is possible to choose whether an aspect should perform loop unrolling or not. With the nested level attribute it is possible to select specific loops.

There are global attributes that are common for all join points in a program, such as the name of the file or the total number of array references. As with the join point model, the attributes specification file allows the aspect language to be updated and expanded more easily.

4.3 Action Model

The action model specifies all actions that can be applied to join points. For instance, when optimizing code by using the loop unrolling action, the tool should specify which stage and which engine can perform this optimization. In our current design flow we consider six types of actions:

- **INSERT** allows arbitrary code to be instrumented before, around or after a specific join point. This action is used mainly for monitoring-based aspects.

- **DEFINE** allows existing attributes to be modified, and new attributes to be created.

- **MAP** allows developers to associate computations and data structures to specific hardware components.

- **OPTIMIZE** allows a number of compiler transformations and optimizations (e.g., loop unrolling, function inlining/outlining, scalar replacement, loop fusion) to be performed on a specific set of join points.

- **REPORT** instructs the weaver to generate an aspect file with a set of attribute definitions (see above) with the values of attributes for selected join points. This action is particularly useful for sharing data across weavers, and to perform feedbacks in the design flow.

- **CALL** invokes an aspect, allowing input arguments to be passed, and output arguments to be accessed.

The action model is specific to a design flow and makes the LARA front-end aware of what tools and which arguments to use. The action model for each compiler optimization (related to the *optimize* action) defines the name of the compiler engine and the possible parameters. Example parameters are: *loopunroll* and unroll factor; *tiling* and size of the block; *loop-pipelining* and initiation interval (II); target clock frequency and function *inlining/outlining*. In summary, by having a join point model, join point attributes, and an action model independent of the LARA front-end, we improve flexibility and adaptability of different programming languages, target systems, and compilation/design flows.

5. LARA Language Description

In this section we provide details about the LARA language. The complete specification of LARA has been included in a report [12].

5.1 Aspect Definition

The current version of the LARA language is compliant with the grammar partially depicted in Figure 8. An aspect file is composed of three sections: the import declarations, the definitions of aspect modules, and code definitions. The import declaration section is optional and allows references to external aspects; the section with aspect definitions, on the other hand, specifies for each aspect the join points to be captured and the actions to be performed on them when

certain requirements are fulfilled; finally the code definition section, also optional, includes code to be injected into the source code.

An aspect definition is declared using the *aspectdef* keyword. Here, developers can define pointcut expressions and also the actions to take place on the selected join points. In the current version of the LARA language, an aspect definition can have *Select*, *Apply* and *Condition* sections. These sections have dependences between them. For instance, the *Apply* section can be associated with one or more pointcut expressions (*Selects*). Also, a *Condition* section is used to validate an *Apply*, i.e., to enable or disable an action over a join point. In general, we can have various applies to the same select, and an *Apply* associated with more than one select. Not all applies need to have a condition section.

Each aspect definition can start with the declaration of input and output parameters. These parameters are used to pass values to aspects and to program aspects to return values, respectively. Each aspect has four additional optional sections for: declaring variables, declaring functions, code to initiate (prolog) the execution (*initialize*) and for code to terminate (epilogue) the execution (*finalize*) of the aspect.

```
Start    = {Import}, AspDef, {AspDef}, {Code-
           Def};
Import   = 'import', Identifier, {'.', Iden-
           tifier} ';' ;
AspDef   = 'aspectdef', Identifier, Input,
           Output, {VarDecl}, {FunctionDecl},
           Initialize, AspBody, {AspBody}, Fi-
           nalize, 'end'
AspBody  = Select, {Select}, Apply, {Apply},
           {ConditionExpr} ;
CodeDef  = 'codedef', Code, 'end';
```

Figure 8. Excerpt of the LARA language grammar.

Figure 9 depicts an aspect definition that inserts a *printf()* statement immediately before each function call. To capture the intended join points a *Select* statement is used. The *Select* statement is identified by a label (in our example, `allFunctionCalls`) and referred by *Apply* statements, and includes a pointcut expression that defines the join points to be captured. The pointcut expression is validated by the front-end using the join point model specification (Section 3).

Developers do not need to specify in LARA the complete join point hierarchy in the pointcut expression, as the front-end auto-completes the entire hierarchy using the join point model specification as a reference. Also, the pointcut expression can use, for a specific selection, join point attributes to filter the selection according to specific attribute values. For instance, the pointcut expression in Figure 9(a) uses the attribute *name* to specify all function calls. As shown in this example, the code section (between tags %{ and }%) allows the use of parameters (between *[[* and *]]*) that will be replaced by the weaver with the corresponding values.

The corresponding Aspect-IR code is shown in Figure 9(b). LARA has been designed for code compactness, legibility and flexibility. Aspect-IR, on the other hand, was designed to facilitate the parsing and processing of aspect definitions by weavers. As explained before, the LARA front-end automatically generates the corresponding Aspect-IR from a LARA description that will be subsequently passed to the weavers in the design flow.

One type of action associated with a pointcut expression is the insertion of C code into the source code (Figure 9(a)) with the option to use values of join point attributes. This insertion can be done *before*, *after* or *around* the join point. Target code can be placed between brackets after the *insert* command, as depicted in Figure 9(a), or in a separated structure called *codedef*. The LARA front-end does not take actions over the code by itself and therefore the insertion action is passed to the Harmonic weaver.

```
aspectdef monitoringCall
  allFunctionCalls: select function.call end
  applyAllCalls: apply to allFunctionCalls
   insert before
    %{printf("call to [[$call.name]]\n");}%; end
end
```
(a)   LARA description

```
<aspects>
 <aspect name="monitoringCall">
  <pointcut name="allFunctionCalls"><file>
   <function>
     <body> <call name=".*"/> </body>
   </function></file></pointcut>
   <apply to="allFunctionCalls"><actions>
    <insert
     code="monitoringCall_applyAllCalls_0.txt"
     stage="harmonic" position="before">
      <parameter target="function"
        attribute ="name"
        replace="<$function.name>"/>
   </insert></actions></apply>
</aspect></aspects>
```
(b) Aspect-IR description

Figure 9. (a) Simple LARA code that performs instrumentation; (b) corresponding Aspect-IR.

Another supported action is *optimize* (Figure 2). This feature specifies compiler source-level transformations and optimizations, such as *loop unrolling* and *function inlining*. The *loopunroll* action triggers the unrolling of selected loops using a factor number specified by the developer. The *inline* option inserts the body of the function to inline on the location of the function call.

Besides the assignments to existing join point attributes without directing affect the representation of a program, our current action model also includes the *define* action (*def* keyword used in Figure 3). This leads, whenever possible, to modifications of the program representation (e.g., defining the type of a variable as in the aspect in Figure 3). Assigning values to join point attributes also provides a way to share information between different stages of the design flow. For example, specific stages can set values of certain attributes so that they can be used by subsequent stages of the design flow.

To limit *Apply* statements, developers can define conditions. Conditions can be regarded as logical expressions that define the triggering conditions for actions specified in an *Apply*. Join point attributes can also be used in conditions. Examples of actions dependent on specific conditions are: (a) apply *loop unrolling* only if the loop is of type "for" and has at most 8 iterations; (b) insert code before a function call if it returns a float; (c) *inline* a function if it does not contain loops. Additional examples of the use of conditions are illustrated in Figure 2 and Figure 4.

5.2   Join Point Chains

One novel feature of our approach is that pointcut expressions are written in a form that reflects the hierarchy de-

fined in the join point model (see Section 4.1). For instance, in Figure 10 the pointcut expression has 4 elements connected in a chain: the **file** which captures all files with names starting with *grid*, the **function** which includes all functions enclosed in those files, the **body** which reflects these functions definitions, and the **loop** which captures `for`-type loops in those functions. This hierarchical mechanism has similarities to the *within/within code* used in AspectJ.

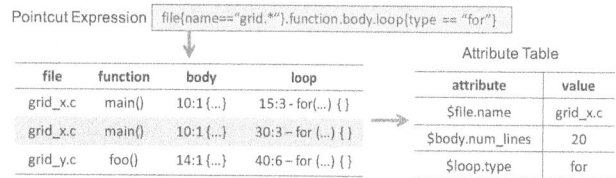

file	function	body	loop
grid_x.c	main()	10:1{...}	15:3 – for(...) {}
grid_x.c	main()	10:1{...}	30:3 – for (...) {}
grid_y.c	foo()	14:1{...}	40:6 – for (...) {}

Attribute Table

attribute	value
$file.name	grid_x.c
$body.num_lines	20
$loop.type	for

Figure 10. The evaluation of pointcut expression results in a table, where each row captures a chain of related join points, whose attributes can be used in actions and conditions.

To access the join points resultant from the evaluation of a pointcut expression, we simply attach the $ operator with the join point identifier. In our example, **$file**, **$function**, **$body** and **$loop** refer to chained join points. We can use these join points and their attributes as part of an action or a condition definition. Join point identifiers enable access to join point attributes, e.g., $file.name refers to the name of the file where a particular $loop join point can be found. In addition, an action can target any element associated with a join point chain, which by default is the last element of the pointcut expression. In the following example, the first action inserts code after the $loop join point, whereas the second inserts code after the $body join point.

```
select function{"main"}.body.loop end
apply
    insert after %{ ... }%;
    $body.insert before %{ ... }%
end
```

Furthermore, multiple pointcut expressions can be joined and associated with a single *apply*, allowing access to multiple branches in the join point hierarchy at once, thus reducing the size of the aspect definition. In particular, LARA supports the (::) operator which, when used in an apply definition, joins the results of two pointcut expressions. In particular, the (::) operator performs the natural join of two *select* statements. A natural join performs a set of combinations of two join point chains that are equal on their common point element identifiers. Consider the following example where the first pointcut expression (A) refers to all loops in function *f1*, and the second pointcut expression (B) refers to the first statement of the function.

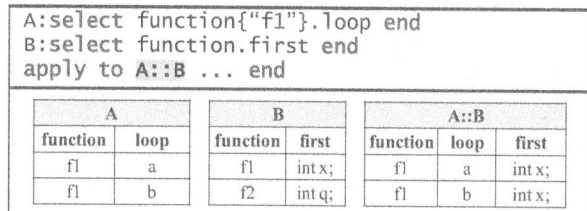

```
A:select function{"f1"}.loop end
B:select function.first end
apply to A::B ... end
```

A		B		A::B		
function	loop	function	first	function	loop	first
f1	a	f1	int x;	f1	a	int x;
f1	b	f2	int q;	f1	b	int x;

By using the natural join operator (::), we are able to apply actions and access attributes in join points that are found in different hierarchical branches (*$loop* and *$first*) of the join point model.

5.3 Examples of Instrumentation

The following two examples illustrate the practical support provided by the LARA aspects.

5.3.1 Timing an application

Developers often need to time their applications, which would require additional code to be inserted in the original application. One can describe this concern using LARA, so that the aspect can be reused in other applications, while reducing code pollution in the original source.

Figure 11(a) illustrates an aspect description which instruments the main function, and adds the necessary code to time the application (see Figure 11(b)). It contains three pointcut expressions. The first, *SF*, selects the first statement of every file. The second, *SM*, selects the first statement of the main function. The third, *SR*, selects the return statements found in the main function. We join all three pointcut expressions to access these join points in one apply section and insert the required code. Note that the pointcut expression identifier *$first* is renamed to *$fstmt* and *$bstmt* to ensure there is no conflict, and that the necessary join combinations are performed.

```
aspectdef timer
  SF: select file.($fstmt=first) end
  SM: select file.
         function{"main"}.($bstmt=first) end
  SR: select file.function{"main"}.return end
  apply to SF::SM::SR
    $fstmt.insert before %{#include <time.h>}%
    $bstmt.insert before %{
          time_t start,end;
          printf("starting timer!\n");
          time (&start);}%;
    $return.insert before %{
        time (&end);
        printf("elapsed time: %.2lfs\n",
        difftime(end,start));}%;
  end
end
```
(a)
```
#include <time.h>
int main() {
  time_t start,end;
  printf("starting timer!\n"); time(&start);
  ...
  f();
  ...
  time (&end);printf("elapsed time: %.2lfs\n",
  difftime(end,start));
  return 0;
}
```
(b)

Figure 11. Timing applications: (a) aspect that instruments the code to time the application; (b) code of the application after weaving (inserted code is highlighted).

5.3.2 Counting number of loop iterations

Loops can often induce hot-spots in the application, and finding the number of iterations can be useful to determine the applicability of specific transformations. Figure 12(a) illustrates an aspect which instruments every *for* loop using two pointcut expressions. The first pointcut expression selects the loop itself, in which two actions are applied, namely initializing the loop count before the loop and printing the count result after loop execution, respectively. The

second selection point selects the first statement of the loop body, where an increment loop count is inserted before that statement. The loop count *uid* attribute returns a unique identifier for every join point, and in this case ensures that every declared variable is unique. An example of the code after weaving is shown in Figure 12(b).

```
aspectdef loop_count
  select loop{type=="for"} end
  apply insert before
         %{int count_[[$loop.uid]] = 0;}%;
      insert after
         %{printf("loop [%s(), %d, %s]:
         %d\n", "[[$function.name]]",
         [[$loop.level]], "[[$loop.loc]]",
         count_[[$loop.uid]]);}%;
  end
  select loop{type=="for"}.body.first end
  apply insert after
         %{count_[[$loop.uid]]++;}%; end
end
```
(a)
```
...{
  int count_01 = 0;
  for (int i = 0; i < N; i++) {
    count_01++;
    int count_02 = 0;
    for (int j = 0; j < M; j++) {
      count_02++;
      ...
    }
    printf("loop [%s(), %d, %s]: %d\n",
          main, 1, "(10,5)", count_02) ;
  }
  printf("loop [%s(), %d, %s]: %d\n",
        main, 0, "(7,2)", count_01) ;
}
```
(b)

Figure 12. Adding loop count for every loop in the application: (a) aspect; (b) woven code.

6. Impact and Experimental Evaluation

In this section we present the experimental results using our compilation and synthesis design flow approach on four real-life applications which have been provided by two industrial partners in the REFLECT project. These applications consist of two audio domain codes, namely an MPEG-2 Audio encoder (MPEG) and a G729 Voice Encoder and two avionics applications, stereo navigation (SN) and 3D Path Planning (3DPP). Both partners have identified a set of concerns and application requirements (e.g., safety in the avionics 3D path planning code) from an industrial perspective which we translated to aspects using the LARA language.

These concerns relate to different stages of the development cycle including: monitoring, fine-tune optimizations, and efficiently mapping the application to the target architecture using schemes such as hardware/software partitioning. As an illustrative example we present in Table 2 a list of concerns for the MPEG Audio encoder application provided by one of the REFLECT industry partners. These concerns span the application development cycle from the analysis phase (with the use of instrumentation to log and monitor specific properties) to the mapping to the target architecture. This, we believe, demonstrates the flexibility and wide scope of our approach.

The monitoring capability enables us to understand runtime behavior, such as (a) the most executed paths in *if-then* constructs, (b) non-variant parameters in specific function calls which enable distinct specializations for the same function, and (c) data ranges and accuracy that can be used to guide word-length optimizations. The use of aspects related to (b) allowed us to identify opportunities for function specializations in all the four applications. For instance, in 3D Path Planning we evaluated three specialized versions of the *griditerate* function, and in the Stereo Navigation we have three possible specializations of a function. These specializations were important to achieve better performance as in most cases, they were related to loop iteration counts, enabling fully loop unrolling and operator strength reduction.

The use of hardware/software partitioning directives allows us to guide the toolchain to map specific functions or code sections to hardware-customized cores. This, in turn, enabled the definition of compilation sequences producing designs that met application requirements and target architecture features.

We next present experimental results using the AOP approach presented in this paper. These experimental results focus on examples of aspects used for application analysis for understanding their dynamic behavior, and on a number of aspects used for performance tuning considering both software and hardware implementations.

Table 2. Examples of aspects applied to the MPEG Audio encoder.

Type of Aspects	Examples
Monitoring (C code insertion)	Monitor range of the variables **z** and **m** in **fsubband** for word-length optimization.
	After word-length optimization, monitors the output variable **s** and variable **y** to validate deviations to their original values.
	Replicate the body of the **fsubband** function with different word-lengths. So, deviation analysis can be done internally.
Specializing	Variables defined as "double" (in functions **add_sub**, **fsubband** and **II_f_f_t**) should be analyzed by the word-length analysis tool to optimize their sizes.
	Convert "double" to "float" data-types in function **II_f_f_t**. A "Code Insertion" aspect is added to monitor the deviations introduced by this transformation.
Mapping and Guiding	Map to hardware functions **add_sub**, **fsubband** and **II_f_f_t**.
	Define specific hardware mapping strategies for **add_sub**, **fsubband** and **II_f_f_t** functions.
	FIFOs, as well as hardware cores for audio I/O, are the hardware blocks necessary in any audio system. These hardware blocks need to interface with the **read_samples** function in the specializing aspect. Aspects can be used to add these hardware blocks without modification of the original code.
	Binding the functions **pow** and **log10** in the **II_f_f_t** and **add_db** to hardware.
	Arrays in functions **fsubband** and **II_f_f_t** mapped to external memories.

6.1 Aspects for Application Code Analysis

Table 3 shows the impact of LARA on the four applications used in our experiments. We consider the following monitoring concerns: measuring branch frequencies, monitoring range (min and max) for variables in the program, monitoring function calls, and timing the application. To assess the impact, we use five metrics: LOC, CDLOC [13], aspectual bloat [14], tangling ratio [14], and the percentage of functions that are affected by the given aspect. We explain each of these metrics next.

The LOC metrics referred in Table 3 are: (a) the number of lines of code in the original application, (b) the number of lines of code in the woven application, and (c) the number of lines in the LARA descriptions. They provide us with a measure of size for both C and LARA descriptions. For instance, applications SN and MPEG are 9 times larger

than 3DPP. On the other hand the timing aspect description is 4 times larger than the call monitoring aspect.

The CDLOC (concern diffusion over LOC) metric indicates the number of switch points where concern-specific code transitions to functional code and vice-versa [13]. We report on the tangling ratio metric, as the ratio between the CDLOC count and the woven code LOC. The tangling ratio gives us a more accurate measure of intermingling. The higher the tangling ratio, the more intermixed is the concern code with the functional code. The lower the tangling ratio, the more localized the concern related code is. The four highlighted aspects (with names ending with 3DPP) in Table 3 target one specific function in the 3DPP application. As these aspects only focus on one code section, their tangling ratio is considerably lower than other wide scope aspects.

Table 3. Aspect metrics for several monitoring concerns: branch frequencies, variable range, function calls, and timing.

Aspect	App	LOC (original C)	LOC (woven C)	LOC (LARA)	CDLOC	Tangling Ratio (%)	Aspectual Bloat	% of affected functions
FrqBranches3DPP	3DPP	1152	1157	17	10	0.86	0.29	2.17
FrqBranches	3DPP	1152	1187	20	250	21.06	1.75	32.61
FrqBranches	SN	9394	9958	20	1128	11.33	28.20	57.43
FrqBranches	MPEG	8925	9312	20	774	8.31	19.35	56.05
FrqBranches	G729	5835	6094	20	518	8.50	12.95	48.65
RangeExec3DPP	3DPP	1152	1167	25	30	2.57	0.60	4.35
RangeExec	3DPP	1152	1374	23	444	32.31	9.65	39.13
RangeExec	SN	9394	11125	23	3462	31.12	75.26	89.19
RangeExec	MPEG	8925	10747	23	3644	33.91	79.22	84.71
RangeExec	G729	5835	7560	23	3450	45.63	75.00	90.99
CallExec3DPP	3DPP	1152	1159	18	12	1.04	0.39	13.04
CallExec	3DPP	1152	1340	12	188	14.03	15.67	63.04
CallExec	SN	9394	10006	12	612	6.12	51.00	41.22
CallExec	MPEG	8925	10109	12	1184	11.71	98.67	55.41
CallExec	G729	5835	6365	12	530	8.33	44.17	31.53
TimerPC3DPP	3DPP	1152	1185	40	34	2.87	0.83	4.35
TimerPC	3DPP	1152	1533	40	382	24.92	9.53	63.04
TimerPC	SN	9394	10623	40	1230	11.58	30.73	41.22
TimerPC	MPEG	8925	11299	40	2374	21.01	59.35	55.41
TimerPC	G729	5835	6900	40	1066	15.45	26.63	31.53
Average		5291.6	6010	24	1066	15.63	31.96	45.23

The aspect bloat measures the efficiency of an aspect with respect to the woven code generated. This metric is computed by dividing the number of lines of code that implement a concern by the aspect LOC. If the aspect bloat is less than 1, it means low aspect efficiency as more code was used to write the aspect than the code to implement the concern. In general, a higher aspect bloat means that the aspect has a higher impact factor in the application, and potentially higher reuse.

Table 4 shows the aspect metric results for the following hardware/software partitioning strategy:

```
import gprof_results;

aspectdef PartitionStrategy
  initialize call gprof_results; end
  select function{*} end
  apply map(to: "hardware", id: "virtex5"); end
  condition $function.time > 15 &&
            $function.name != "main" &&
            $function.is_synthesizable end
end
```

which states that all functions that contribute to more than 15% of the total application time and are synthesizable shall be mapped to the FPGA (hardware). The remaining functions are to execute in the PowerPC (software). The toolchain automatically converts to LARA the *gprof* profiling results associating attributes such as timing and number of calls to each function. The Harmonic weaver splits the application into two C sub-applications: one for the PowerPC and another for the FPGA. Each source contains the functions for each partition, in addition to global variables and type definitions that are shared by both partitions, and the code to implement the remote procedure calls. Note that the number of functions mapped to the FPGA, as shown in Table 4, includes not only the functions that run more than 15% of the total application time, but also includes all invoked functions which are part of their implementation.

These results indicate the potential of a LARA aspect to control the entire hardware/software partitioning process without developer intervention. With this approach other partitioning can easily be evaluated without the tedious and error prone manual efforts otherwise required.

Table 4. Aspect metrics extracted when applying LARA aspects for hardware/software partitioning.

App	LOC original C	LOC woven C	LOC LA-RA	total # functions	# functions mapped to FPGA	Aspectual Bloat	% of affected functions
3DPP	1,152	1,246	15	46	7	6.27	15.22
SN	9,394	9,646	15	148	102	16.80	68.92
MPEG	8,925	9,087	15	157	3	10.80	1.91
G729	5,835	5,998	15	111	2	10.87	1.80

6.2 Aspects for Performance Tuning

We now illustrate the use of performance tuning aspects for two specific hot-spot functions, respectively *fsubband* (from MPEG), and *griditerate* (from 3DPP). We report results for a Xilinx Virtex5 FPGA (xc5vfx130t-2ff1738) in terms of the number of FPGA slices and DSP blocks. The software implementations were derived using *ppc-gcc* as backend (w/ option -O3) whereas for the hardware results we used Catapult-C as high-level synthesis tool [15] and the Xilinx ISE 13.1 as back-end tool. For all the results we used fixed-point implementations of the functions and considered the baseline hardware and software implementation as the original untransformed C code.

Figure 13 and Figure 14 illustrate, respectively, the impact of the application of the hardware-oriented aspects on hardware resources[3] and on hardware and software speedups over baseline implementations for different implementations of functions *fsubband* and *griditerate*, using different strategies specified as aspects.

The strategies for *fsubband* included *loopscalar* (B1-B8), *loop-pipelining* (B2-B8), *unroll-and-jam* first nested loops (B3), *fully unroll* first innermost loop (B4), *fully unroll* first innermost loop + *unroll* 16 times of inner second nested loops (B5), *unroll+jam* first nested loops and *unroll* 2 times

---

[3] Xilinx's FPGAs are organized as arrays of programmable slices, interconnect resources, local memories, and DSP components that implement logic functions and local storage structures. For example, on a Virtex-5 FPGA, a 32-bit integer adder requires 5 slices whereas a 32-bit integer multiplier requires 3 DSP blocks. The Virtex-5 FX FPGA also includes two PowerPC processors.

of inner second nested loops (B6), *unroll+jam* first nested loops and *unroll* 2 times of inner second nested loops (with second index variables) (B7), and fully unrolling of all the 4 loops (B8). The best strategy allows us to achieve a speedup of 10 times over the baseline implementation with only an increase of 9% and 57% of hardware resources (number of slices and DSP blocks, respectively).

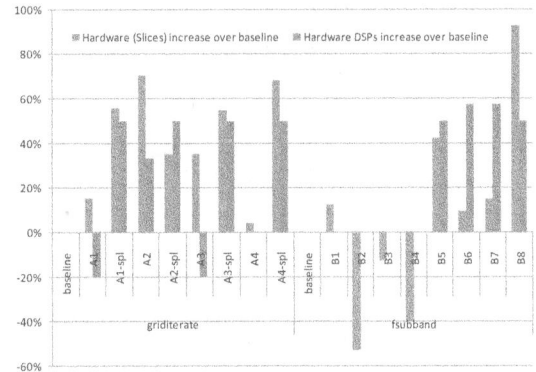

Figure 13. Hardware resources for *griditerate* and *fsubband* considering different strategies over baseline.

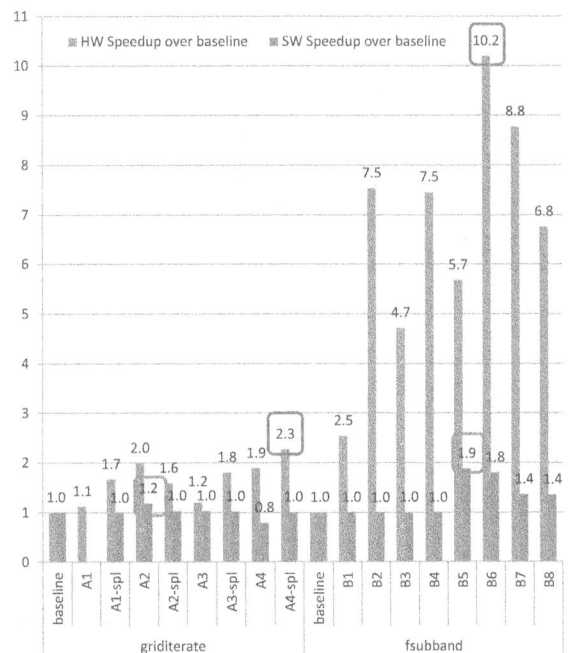

Figure 14. Hardware (HW) and software (SW) speedups over the respective baseline implementations for the *griditerate* and *fsubband* functions considering different strategies.

The strategies for *griditerate* included loop pipelining (A1), specialized versions (A*n*-spl), loop coalescing of the two inner loops (A2), loop unrolling of the innermost loop by two (A3), and data replication in 4 memories (A4). The strategies for *griditerate* result in performance improvements over the reference FPGA hardware implementation of a maximum speedup of 2.26 with an increase of 68% of slices and 50% of DSP blocks.

Our approach also allowed us to have two distinct strategies: one used for the best FPGA hardware implementation, and another one used for the best FPGA software implementation (i.e., for the code generated for the GPP). For the software implementation we use one of the PowerPC hardcores of the target FPGA. Figure 14 presents speedups obtained using different strategies. It is clear from the results that the two toolchain flow paths (software and hardware) require different strategies to obtain the best performance. For the *griditerate* function the best strategies are A4-spl and A2 for hardware and software implementation, respectively. For *fsuband*, the best strategies are B6 and B5, for hardware and software implementation, respectively.

6.3 Discussion

Regarding the aspect-related code transformation and analysis metrics, the results reveal high tangling and aspectual bloating ratios of, respectively, 15.6% and 31.9%. These are particularly encouraging as the percentage of affected functions is quite large.

With respect to the software- and hardware-oriented mapping and guiding transformations, the attained performance for the best compilation and synthesis strategy is also very good as the results exhibit very consistent speedups. Developers are able to leverage the compactness of aspect-based mapping strategies and back-end synthesis tools to quickly, and predictably, develop strategies to map applications to hardware/software target architectures.

While we have not yet focused on an evaluation of this aspect-based approach for DSE, these early experimental results do reinforce the claim of its usefulness in the mapping of real applications to complex target architectures.

7. Related Work

We now highlight related work in the areas of Aspect Oriented Programming (AOP) [4][16][17].

AOP has been the subject of intense research over the last decade. AspectJ [18], one of the most widely known AOP languages, is an AOP extension for Java aimed at providing better modularity for Java programs. AspectJ contributes to cleaner and better code by modularizing programs, providing solution for several cross-cutting concerns such as monitoring, logging, debugging, synchronization, and performance. Another example of an AOP language with noticeable success is AspectC++ [19][20], which is an AOP extension to the C++ programming language. Both AspectJ and AspectC++ do not consider join points related to local variables, statements, loops and conditional constructs. For instance, LoopsAJ [21] extends the join point model of AspectJ to allow the direct intervention over loops by adding a new *loop* pointcut (captured with different pointcut expressions), including contextual information used for loop parallelization. @AspectJ [22] is a refinement of AspectJ that allows the specification (using labels) of join points at level of individual statements such as *if* and *while* loops.

Reflecting AOP's growing acceptance, several AOP extensions have been proposed to other languages and domains of applicability. For instance, AspectMatlab [23] provides AOP extensions for MATLAB focusing on array variables and loops, as these are key constructs in scientific applications. AspectMatlab supports the AOP notion of pointcuts (called *patterns*) and advices (called *actions*).

Our AOP-based approach differs from related work in several ways. First, we extend the capabilities associated with types, such as their shapes and precision (as described in our previous work [24][25]). In addition, the join point model allows the specification of pointcuts in virtually all points in a program diminishing the need for labels.

LARA has been inspired by many AOP approaches, such as AspectJ and AspectC++. For instance, during the evolution of LARA we have adopted mechanisms similar to the ones used by AOP approaches based on functional queries [26]. In our approach, pointcut expressions allowed by select sections of the aspect modules are able to define composable select expressions (similar to composable queries) as in [26]. We can associate two or more pointcut expressions to the same advice (apply statement) along with an operator to specify the type of association thus enriching the semantics of the pointcut mechanisms.

We have defined a hardware/software join point model that reflects the need to interface with a potentially wide variety of tools and target embedded computing systems. Lastly, following the notion of patterns and actions in AspectMatlab, our approach also formalizes the concept of strategies as a way to capture and reuse a sequence of program transformations and application mapping choices.

The main drivers of our AOP approach have been the functional requirements elicited by the industrial partners of the REFLECT project [6]. Based on the requirements, LARA includes in the actions associated with join points not only code to be executed (as in AspectJ), but also compiler optimization directives and data and type information about variables. LARA allows powerful dynamic pointcut mechanisms to expose context information about join points.

One of the requirements we faced was the migration of code related to conditional compilation (#ifdef clauses in C) to aspects [27][28]. We have also faced the need of migrating to aspects toolchain directives implemented as C #pragmas. They spread around code artifacts and are commonly used to annotate code with directives for compiler optimizations and code transformations. As their use depends on the target architecture and on the toolchain being used, it is common to have variations for the same application. Aspects mitigate this problem.

In addition, this separation of concerns facilitates the manual exploration of certain compiler properties, as the changes to be evaluated are performed to concentrated code in aspects and not to pragmas spread along the application (as it seems to be a trend [29]). As an example, the Catapult-C version we use [15] allows at least 10 different pragmas. Annotations have severe limitations as they refer to static join points, pollute the code, impose code variations (possibly implemented using conditional compilation mechanisms), and do not allow compiler sequences, while our AOP approach allows semantic and dynamic join points, and join points exposed along compiler sequences.

One of the strengths of our approach is to use AOP to support portability and retargetability. By exposing to aspects concerns such as the ones related to safety and performance requirements, different aspects can lead to the generation of different hardware or hardware/software implementations. This can be conceptually thought as the implementation of portability addressed by Alves *et al.* [30] in the context of software product lines. By exposing to aspects the characteristics of the target architecture, we promote tool-flow adaptability for different architectures. Note that besides code variations we also support AOP-based strategies that allow different implementations by controlling key toolchain stages.

8. Conclusion

This paper presents a novel aspect-oriented programming language named LARA, which provides separation of concerns, including non-functional requirements and strategies, for the mapping of high-level applications to high-performance heterogeneous embedded systems. We described how LARA supports monitoring, specialization, hardware/software partitioning, and retargeting in the context of multiple programming languages and design flows. The LARA prototype is being evaluated with real-life industrial application C codes. The experimental results provide strong evidence of its usefulness and significance in the mapping of applications to heterogeneous embedded architectures.

We see the flexibility of aspect-oriented approaches, such as the one presented in LARA, as a key programming technology that will enable developers to meet increasingly demanding challenges in developing embedded systems.

Acknowledgments

This work was partially supported by the European Community's Framework Programme 7 (FP7) under contract No. 248976. Any opinions, findings, and conclusions or recommendations expressed in this material are those of the author(s) and do not necessarily reflect the views of the European Community. The authors are grateful to the members of the REFLECT project for their support. Carvalho and Cardoso also acknowledge the support of FCT through grant PTDC/EIA/70271/2006, and Coutinho and Luk acknowledge the support of UK EPSRC.

References

[1] Y. Lam, J. Coutinho, W. Luk, and P. Leong, *Integrated Hardware/Software Codesign for Heterogeneous Computing Systems*, in Proc. of the South. Programmable Logic Conf., 2008, pp. 217–220.

[2] K. Compton, and S. Hauck, *Reconfigurable Computing: a Survey of Systems and Software*, ACM Computing Surveys, 2002, 34(2), pp. 171–210.

[3] T. Todman, et al., *Reconfigurable Computing: Architectures and Design Methods*, IEE Proc. In Computing and Digital Techniques, Vol. 152, No. 2, March 2005, pp. 193-207.

[4] G. Kiczales, *Aspect-Oriented Programming*, in *ACM Computing Surveys (CSUR)*, 1996. 28(4es).

[5] REFLECT, FP7 EU Project: http://www.reflect-project.eu.

[6] J. M. P. Cardoso, *et al.*, *REFLECT: Rendering FPGAs to Multi-Core Embedded Computing*, book chapter in Reconfigurable Computing: From FPGAs to Hardware/Software Codesign, J. M. P. Cardoso and M. Huebner (eds.), Springer, Aug., 2011, pp. 261-289.

[7] J. M. P. Cardoso, *et al.*, *A New Approach to Control and Guide the Mapping of Computations to FPGAs*, in Proc. Int'l Conf. Engineering of Reconfigurable Systems and Algorithms (ERSA'11), July, 2011, CSREA Press, pp. 231-240.

[8] T. Carvalho, *A Meta-Language and Framework for Aspect-Oriented Programming*, Informatics and Computing Eng. MSc Thesis, Univ. of Porto, Faculty of Eng. (FEUP), Porto, Portugal, July 2011.

[9] W. Luk, *et al.*, *A High-Level Compilation Toolchain for Heterogeneous Systems*," in *Proc. IEEE Int'l SOC Conf. (SOCC'09)*, Sept. 2009, pp. 9-18.

[10] ACE CoSy Compiler Development System, http://www.ace.nl/compiler/cosy.html

[11] R. Filman, and D. Friedman, *Aspect-oriented programming is quantification and obliviousness*. In Workshop on Advanced Separation of Concerns at OOPSLA'00, Oct. 2000.

[12] REFLECT Consortium, *LARA Programming Language Specification*, version 1.0 defined as part of deliverable D4.2, Sept. 2011.

[13] E. Figueiredo, et al., *On the Maintainability of Aspect-Oriented Software: A Concern-Oriented Measurement Framework*, in Proc. 12th European Conf. on Software Maintenance and Reengineering, IEEE Computer Society, 2008, pp. 183-192.

[14] C. V. Lopes, *D: A Language Framework for Distributed Programming*. PhD thesis, College of Computer Science, Northeastern University, Nov. 1997.

[15] © Mentor Graphics, Catapult C Synthesis, http://www.mentor.com/esl/catapult

[16] T. Elrad, R. Filman, and A. Bader, *Aspect-Oriented Programming*, in Comm. of the ACM, 44(10), Oct. 2001, pp. 29-32.

[17] G. Kiczales, *et al.*, *Aspect Oriented Programming*, in *Proc. European Conf. on Object-Oriented Programming (ECOOP'97)*, Finland. Springer-Verlag LNCS 1241. June 1997.

[18] J. Gradecki and N. Lesiecki, *Mastering AspectJ: Aspect-Oriented Programming in Java*. 2003, J. Wiley & Sons, Inc..

[19] D. Lohmann, Olaf Spinczyk. *Aspect-Oriented Programming with C++ and AspectC++*. Tutorial, AOSD'2007, March 13, 2007.

[20] O. Spinczyk, A. Gal, W. Schröder-Preikschat. *AspectC++: An Aspect-Oriented Extension to the C++ Programming Language*. in Proc. 40th Int'l Conf. on Tools Pacific: Objects for internet, mobile and embedded applications, 2002, pp. 53-60.

[21] B. Harbulot, and J. R. Gurd. *A join point for loops in AspectJ*. In Proc. 5th Int'l Conf. on Aspect-Oriented Software Development (AOSD '06). ACM, NY, USA, 2006, pp. 63-74.

[22] M. Poggi. *@AspectJ - An Extension to the AspectJ Join Point Selection Mechanism to Support @Java Annotation Meta-Facility*. Master thesis (in Italian), Università di Genova, Oct. 2009.

[23] T. Aslam, J. Doherty, A. Dubrau, and L. Hendren. *AspectMatlab: An Aspect-Oriented Scientific Programming Language*, in Proc. 9th Int'l Conference on Aspect-Oriented Software Development (AOSD'10). ACM, New York, NY, USA, 2010, pp. 181-192.

[24] J. M. P. Cardoso, J. Fernandes, and M. Monteiro, *Adding Aspect-Oriented Features to MATLAB*, in SPLAT! 2006, Software Engineering Properties of Languages and Aspect Technologies, Workshop affiliated with AOSD 2006, March 2006. Germany.

[25] J. M. P. Cardoso, *et al.*, *A Domain-Specific Aspect Language for Transforming MATLAB Programs*, in Domain-Specific Aspect Language Workshop (DSAL'2010), part of AOSD'10, March 2010.

[26] M. Eichberg, M. Mezini, and K. Ostermann, *Pointcuts as Functional Queries*, in Programming Languages and Systems, W.-N. Chin (Ed.), Springer Berlin/Heidelberg, 2004, pp. 366-381.

[27] V. Alves, *et al.*, *From Conditional Compilation to Aspects: A Case Study in Software Product Lines Migration*, In: Aspect-Oriented Product Line Engineering (AOPLE'06), Workshop of the 5th Int'l Conf. on Generative Programming and Component Engineering (GPCE'06), ACM, 2006.

[28] B. Adams, W. Meuter, H. Tromp, and A. Hassan, *Can we refactor conditional compilation into aspects?*, in Proc. 8th ACM Int'l Conf. on Aspect-Oriented Soft. Development, 2009, pp. 243-254.

[29] R. Ferrer, *et al.*, *Optimizing the Exploitation of Multicore Processors and GPUs with OpenMP and OpenCL*, in Proc. LCPC, 2010, pp. 215-229.

[30] V. Alves, *et al.*, *Extracting and Evolving Code in Product Lines with Aspect-Oriented Programming*, in Trans. on Aspect-Oriented Software Development IV, A. Rashid, M. Aksit (Eds.), Springer Berlin / Heidelberg, 2007, pp. 117-142.

ContextErlang: Introducing Context-oriented Programming in the Actor Model *

Guido Salvaneschi, Carlo Ghezzi, Matteo Pradella

DEEPSE Group, DEI, Politecnico di Milano, Piazza L. Da Vinci, 32, Milano, Italy

{salvaneschi, ghezzi, pradella}@elet.polimi.it

Abstract

Self-adapting systems are becoming widespread in emerging fields such as autonomic, mobile and ubiquitous computing. Context-oriented programming (COP) is a promising language-level solution for the implementation of context-aware, self-adaptive software. However, current COP approaches struggle to effectively manage the asynchronous nature of context provisioning.

We argue that, to solve these issues, COP features should be designed to fit nicely in the concurrency model supported by the language. This work presents the design rationale of CONTEXTERLANG, which introduces COP in the Actor Model. We provide evidence that CONTEXTERLANG constitutes a viable solution to implement context-aware software in a highly concurrent and distributed setting. We discuss a case study and an evaluation of run-time performance.

Categories and Subject Descriptors D.1.3 [*Software*]: Programming Techniques—Concurrent Programming; D.3.3 [*Programming Languages*]: Language Constructs and Features

General Terms Languages, Design

Keywords Context-oriented programming, Self-adaptive software, Erlang, OTP platform

1. Introduction

Dynamic adaptation of a software system to a changing context has emerged as a common need in a wide range of scenarios. For example, autonomic computing is about providing a system the means to be self-managing in changing conditions. Mobile and ubiquitous computing often require applications to adapt to the external environment.

Since context-depending behaviors must be activated at run time and typically crosscut the system functionalities, managing context-dependent features in a systematic and effective way became a key software challenge. The context-oriented programming paradigm (COP) introduced by Costanza and Hirschfeld [9] has emerged as a viable approach and language-level support for context management. The key idea of COP is to provide specific language abstractions that enable context-adaptability through well engineered modularization of *behavioral variations*, whose dynamic activation and composition changes the basic program behavior to support context-aware adaptation [17].

The Actor Model – originally proposed by Hewitt [16] – is an alternative solution over traditional thread-and-lock concurrency approaches. There is growing interest around languages that are based on this paradigm, such as Erlang [1] and Scala [2] which easily allow to take advantage of increasing hardware parallelism. In this scenario, actors offer an interesting solution to the new challenges of self-adaptive and context-aware software. We argue that the Actor Model strongly fits the requirements of context awareness. Asynchronous message passing offers an intuitive representation for context provisioning and agents are a natural abstraction for context-adaptable units inside an application.

Hereafter, we briefly provide the motivations that lead to the development of CONTEXTERLANG, an extension we designed and developed for the Erlang programming language. Most COP languages implement a *programmatic* and *synchronous* variation activation model *on a specific control flow*. Variations are activated and composed through an explicit statement such as

```
with(variationList) { codeBlock }
```

and activation is scoped to the dynamic extent of the code block. This model has two shortcomings. On the one hand *all* the objects in the control flow are automatically adapted. This precludes fine-grain adaptation on single entities of the application. Fine-grain control is needed in many real-world applications where adaptation is required (see Section 2). On the other hand, dynamically scoped activation fails to

---

* This research has been funded by the European Community's IDEAS-ERC Programme, Project 227977 (SMSCom).

manage event-specific context changes, i.e. context changes that are asynchronously delivered to the application. Event-based context changes can impact several control flows and it is not possible to react to them through conventional COP with-driven activations occurring at fixed points in the code. Event-specific context changes have a prominent role in real world applications where the adaptation is driven by changes discovered via environmental monitoring, user interaction, or the insurgence of internal system conditions.

Our approach abandons the traditional per-control-flow dynamic scoped activation mechanism of thread-based COP languages. Because of the asynchronous nature of context-change notifications that generate event-specific context changes, we propose a solution that is tightly coupled with the adopted concurrency model.

Specifically, we leverage the agent-based model of Erlang to support context-adaptations. CONTEXTERLANG is based on the concept of context-aware reactive agents. Context-adaptable agents have a basic behavior which can be altered by *variations*, i.e. behavioral units that can be *activated* on the agent. Variations can be *composed* to produce the actual behavior of the agent. Variation activation and the other context-related operations are performed by sending *ad-hoc* messages to the agent. Therefore, in CONTEXTERLANG, asynchronous activation, as required by real-world adaptive systems, is the norm. Instead of the dynamically scoped activation model of COP languages, we adopt *per-agent* variation activation and composition. This gives the programmer full control over fine-grained adaptation of the application components.

CONTEXTERLANG also supports *variation transmission*. An agent on a remote Erlang node can be provided with a new behavior by sending a variation to the node and activating it on the agent. This introduces a very useful support for systems that must adapt to unforeseen situations. Since we wanted to rely on a robust implementation, compatible with existing Erlang applications, we developed CONTEXT-ERLANG as part of the OTP platform, on which practically any real-world Erlang application is based.

To summarize, the main contribution of this paper is the introduction of COP in the Actor Model, through the design and the implementation of CONTEXTERLANG. More precisely in our work we achieved the following results:

- Integration of COP concepts with the Actor concurrency model.

- Implementation as part of Erlang OTP, an industrial-strength language for distributed and concurrent applications.

- Experimental validation of our approach through prototypes of significant complexity and performance evaluation.

The paper is organized as follows. In Section 2 we discuss the motivation this work. In Section 3 we describe CONTEXT-ERLANG and its design. Section 4 discusses the validation of our approach. Section 5 discusses the related work. Section 6 draws some conclusions and presents future research.

2. Motivation

To motivate the design choices behind our work, we introduce a non-trivial example called ContextChat, our prototype of an instant messaging server. We discuss possible designs and implementations of ContextChat using existing COP languages and CONTEXTERLANG. More details of the implementation will be presented along the paper to illustrate CONTEXTERLANG's features.

In ContextChat, the connected clients can exchange messages in real time. The server also implements some advanced features, which can be dynamically activated. When users go offline, received messages are stored on the server and delivered later when the addressee connects. An optional backup can be enabled by the user to save both the received and sent messages on a remote server. Additionally, the system can activate a tracing functionality to collect information on client communications. In a distributed environment, this allows for self-adaptive behavior, moving users who often exchange messages on the same physical machine and reducing cross-node communications.

An abstract view of the application is sketched in Figure 1. For each user i an always-alive component U_i embodies the user even when he or she is offline (e.g. U_4). Border components B_i are created when clients C_i connect. Each border component is in charge of the network connection with the client and controls the always-alive component. Consider the scenario in which the client C_1 sends a message to the client C_2. C_1 communicates the message to the border component (e.g. via some protocol over HTTPS). The border component B_1 decodes the "send_msg" command and controls U_1. B_1 activates the *send message* functionality on U_1. U_1 forwards the message to U_2 and through B_2 the message reaches C_2.

Context-oriented programming. In ContextChat, the variations to the basic behavior are clearly identified, should be separated from the rest in the codebase, must be dynamically activated, and depend on the current *context* of the application – as we explain in a while. Therefore, COP looks like the natural solution for the requirements of ContextChat. While in traditional OO programming method dispatching is two-dimensional, depending on the message and on the receiver, COP adds a further dimension: methods may also be dispatched according to the current context [17]. In COP, the notion of context is abstract and general. *Every computationally accessible information* can be considered as context. The user condition (e.g., online/offline, enabled backup) can be considered its current *context*. To enable run time adaptation, COP supports dynamic context composition and its abstractions avoid cluttering the code with *if* statements to express context dependency. Therefore using COP to auto-

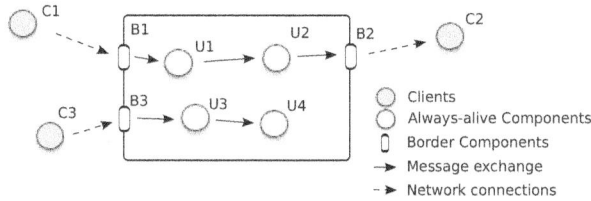

Figure 1. The ContextChat application.

matically select and combine the proper behaviors is an appealing solution.

Figure 2 shows a possible implementation of the `User` object implementing an U_i component in a COP language extension to Java, such as ContextJ [5]. For the benefit of the reader we use this example also to shortly introduce the typical COP features. A more conceptual analysis and an overview of COP can be found in [17]. COP provides language-level abstractions to modularize context-dependent behavioral variations and dynamically activate and combine them. In COP languages, behavioral variations are reified in *layers*[1], abstractions which group *partial method definitions*. For example, in Figure 2 the `tracing` layer contains a partial definition of the `receive_msg` and of the `send_msg` methods. When a method is called, the implementation to execute is chosen according to the active layers. The `proceed` keyword allows dynamic combination. It is similar to `proceed` in aspect-oriented programming and calls the partial definition in the next active layer or the basic definition. Layer activation has dynamic extent and it is done through the `with` statement: in the control flow all the method calls are dispatched according to the active layers.

Dynamic scope is a powerful mechanism for variations activation, since it allows remote effect, setting the active layers once and automatically adapting all the objects in the execution flow. This behavior has already proved useful in several application scenarios [5, 9, 26]. However, implementing ContextChat with the traditional COP dynamically scoped activation highlights some inconveniences. We argue that these problems are due to the asynchronous nature of context provisioning, to the concurrent nature of the application and to its non-trivial complexity. Therefore the issues analyzed in the rest are likely to be encountered in any sufficiently large self-adaptive application which needs to be organized in several functional modules, and are not specific of this example.

First, a context change is often an *asynchronous* event coming from *outside* the execution flow. Since layers are activated when the control flow reaches the statement, the `with` construct is inherently synchronous and is not suitable for these cases. For example, the `tracing` layer is ac-

```
public class User {
  layer offline {
    void receive_msg(User source,M msg){
      store_chats.store_message(source, msg);
  } }
  layer tracing { ...
    void receive_msg(User source,M msg){
      // send msg to the tracing listener
      proceed(source, msg);
    }
    void send_msg(User source,M msg){
      // send msg to the tracing listener
      proceed(source, msg);
  } }
  layer backup { ...
    void receive_msg(User source,M msg){
      // send msg to the remote server
      proceed(source, msg);
  } }
    ... // Other methods
  void receive_msg(User source,M msg){
    //forward msg to my border component
  }
  void send_msg(User dest,M msg){
    // forward to dest client
} }
```

Figure 2. An implementation of the chat server in ContextJ.

tivated by an external engine in charge of implementing the autonomic behavior. The same holds for the activation of the backup functionality which can be performed anytime by the client while `User` objects are exchanging messages with other users. A possible solution is to adopt inversion of control [22] and first class layers. For example, a `setActiveLayers` callback method can be implemented in the `User` class to notify the change of the active layers and store them locally. However, this solution increases the complexity the application making it less readable. Indeed, in this case, inversion of control does not capture the design intention. Conceptually, the programmer's intention is to cause an entity adaptation and not to notify an entity letting it perform the activation at the next `with` statement. In addition to that, in some applications, it is not possible to identify unique entry points for the control flow. As already noticed by COP researchers [6], in this cases, layer composition statements must be scattered and replicated across all the possible control flows, such as all the callback methods in a GUI application.

Second, in a highly concurrent environment, the control flow can follow complex paths. These paths hardly map on dynamically scoped program sections, i.e. contextual regions whose adaptation condition is known where the region is entered. For example, the `User` object (Figure 2) may be traversed by several control flows, and the information of which behavioral variation to activate is not directly available to all of them. The backup functionality is enabled by the client C_1 and therefore the associated border component B_1 can trigger the backup behavior by interacting with the `User` object U_1 in the dynamic scope of a `with` statement.

---

[1] For continuity with our previous work, ContextErlang keeps the name *variation* also to indicate the language abstraction. CONTEXTERLANG variations are quite similar to COP layers; a comparison between the two is in Section 5.

However, when the `User` object U_1 is called from another `User` object U_2 to receive a message, U_2 does not know if the `backup` layer should be activated on U_1.

A third issue is that in a complex application with several components, dynamic scope is difficult to control and can extend *too far*. For example, in case a border component B_1 delivers a message through the associated `User` object U_1 and the client C_1 activated the backup feature on U_1, the backup functionality is propagated along the flow to the other `User` object U_2.

COP researchers have already investigated the limitations of dynamically scoped variation activation. ContextJS [20] is an open implementation of COP which supports user-defined activation strategies, such as indefinite scope or per-object activation. Per-object activation is performed calling a `setWithLayer` method on the instance. Per-object activation solves the problem of the activation along the execution path, since objects identify the boundaries in which layer activation is constrained. This solution nicely fits in the OO model, resembling the way other design problems have been solved for objects. For example, in Java, concurrency is addressed at the language level by assigning a monitor to each object. Similarly, in per-object activation, a list of currently active layers is associated to each object.

EventCJ [29] is a Java COP extension which supports declarative layer transitions and implicit activation through pointcut-like predicates. The issue of asynchronous activation, discussed previously, is solved by AspectJ-like statements: when a pointcut-like event occurs, a layer transition is triggered. Layers are activated on per-object basis. Figure 3 shows a possible implementation of an `User` object in EventCJ. Events and layer transitions are declared inside `direction` modules. When the `onStatusChanged` method is called, the `StatusOffline` or the `StatusOnline` events are triggered, depending on the parameters. These events trigger layer `transitions` from `Online` to `Offline` and vice versa. The approach solves the problem of asynchronous activation by introducing points in the program execution which implicitly activate layers.

However, none of the existing COP languages leverages the concurrency model to easily support asynchronous context propagation. As a result, the layer activation mechanism can be quite complex (Figure 3).

As we have seen, the backup and the tracing functionalities in the example are activated by a different thread than the one actually affected by them. This aspect is not peculiar of our example, but is common to many self-adaptive applications. The MAPE-K model (*Monitor, Analyze, Plan, Execute-Knowledge*), conceived by the autonomic computing community, decouples the adaptive application in a managed element, which implements the application logic and an autonomic manager, which collects data from sensors and plans the adaptive behavior [18]. So, these subsystems are not only conceptually separated, but usually run in sep-

```
public class User {
  void onStatusChanged(Status s){...}
  ...
}
direction UserLayerActivations{
  declare event StatusOffline(User u)
    :after call(onStatusChanged(Status s)) && target(u)
        && args(s) && if(s==Status.OFFLINE) :sendTo(u);
  declare event StatusOnline(User u)
    :after call(onStatusChanged(Status s)) && target(u)
        && args(s) && if(s==Status.ONLINE) :sendTo(u);
  ... // Other events
  transition StatusOffline: Offline switchTo Online;
  transition StatusOnline: Online switchTo Offline;
  ... // Other transitions
}
```

Figure 3. ContextChat in EventCJ.

arate threads and communicate asynchronously. However, the relation between context-adaptation and the language concurrency model has not been investigated so far in COP research. Even more advanced COP languages are quite traditional in this sense. ContextJS is single-threaded, since it extends JavaScript, a single-threaded language; while EventCJ adopts the standard Java share-and-lock concurrency model. By leveraging the integration of COP with the Actor Model, CONTEXTERLANG directly addresses the issue of context propagation in concurrent systems, it allows asynchronous context provisioning directly in the language, without pointcut-like expressions, and solves in a natural way the problem of context confinement adopting actors as context boundaries.

ContextErlang. CONTEXTERLANG mainly differs from other COP languages in the way it supports the activation of context-specific functionalities. To address the issue of asynchronous context provisioning, variations are activated through messages. This approach nicely reflect the design intention and avoids the cluttering of control inversion. To cope with the complexity of a concurrent application organized in several behavioral units, in CONTEXTERLANG, variations are activated on *per-agent* basis, and each agent can be controlled individually. This also eliminates the risk of unintended adaptation propagation. After activation, variations are implicitly associated with the agent. They are managed transparently and do not need dedicated local variables or other boilerplate code.

To make the benefits of such design more concrete, hereafter we illustrate how ContextChat is designed in CONTEXTERLANG. Always-alive components are context-aware `user` agents exchanging Erlang messages. Border components are standard Erlang agents, since no special adaptation is required. The `offline`, `online`, `backup` and `tracing` variations implement the dynamically activatable features for the `user` agents. Other agents can directly control the adaptation state of a `user` agent. For example when a client C_i closes the connection, the border agent sends a context-related message to the associated agent U_i, which has the effect of

```
-module(cache).
-behavior(gen_server).
    ...
start() ->
  gen_server:start_link({local, ?MODULE},
                         ?MODULE, [], []).
get(Name) ->
  gen_server:call(?MODULE, {get, Name}).
add(Name, Item) ->
  gen_server:cast(?MODULE, {add, Name, Item}).

init([]) ->
    % ... initialization here
    {ok, State}.
handle_call({get, Name}, From, State) ->
    % ... retrieve Item from the state
    Reply = Item, {reply, Reply, State}.
handle_cast({add, Name, Item}, State) ->
    % ... add Item to the state
    {noreply, State}.
terminate(Reason, State) ->
    % ... manage shutdown here
    ok.
```

Figure 4. A callback module of an OTP `gen_server`.

activating the `offline` variation. In a similar way B_i activates the backup of the conversations and the autonomic engine activates the `tracing` variation. Active variations can be dynamically combined to allow coexisting multiple adaptations. For example, the `backup` variation proceeds to either the `online` or the `offline` variation to send a chat to a backup server and then either forward or store it locally.

In order to present a peculiar feature of CONTEXTERLANG, i.e. *variation transmission*, we augment the ContextChat application with an additional functionality. A client can apply a customizable filter to its outgoing messages such as capitalizing all the first letters of sentences or adding emoticons to each message. Despite its triviality, this feature is interesting because the type of filter cannot be forecast in advance. In CONTEXTERLANG this kind of situation is specifically addressed by variation transmission, which allows one to send a variation to a remote agent and dynamically load it. In this way the agent can react to unforeseen situations.

Further insights into the details of the ContextChat implementation in CONTEXTERLANG are provided in the following sections.

3. Design of ContextErlang

In this section, we describe and motivate the basic concepts and the language constructs introduced by CONTEXT-ERLANG. To achieve the high quality standards of Erlang applications, CONTEXTERLANG is built on the OTP platform – a library and a set of procedures for structuring fault-tolerant, large-scale, distributed applications. We provide a minimal description of the Erlang syntax and a short introduction to the OTP.

3.1 OTP in a Nutshell

While the language provides the basic functionalities for software development, practically any real-world Erlang application is based on the OTP platform. The concept of *behavior* is central in OTP and is based on the idea that, in an application, many processes enact similar patterns, such as serving requests, handling events, or monitoring other processes. OTP generalizes these common patterns, and gives a ready implementation of the generic structure (called the *behavior*), which provides features such as message passing, error handling and fault-tolerance. The user only needs to implement the specific part in a *callback* module, which exposes a predefined interface. This kind of code structuring makes programs easier to understand, and prescribes a general architecture that should be common to all OTP applications. In the paper we use the term *behavior* also to indicate the way an agent behaves with respect to the software system. To avoid confusion, we will use the term *OTP behavior* to disambiguate.

In Figure 4 we present a callback module for the most common OTP behavior, the `gen_server`, a process which stands waiting for requests from other processes. An Erlang module starts with attributes introduced by "-". They state the module name, the exported functions and other declarations. Functions implementation follows. A function body is started by "->". Curly braces indicate tuples of fixed length, square braces indicate lists. Variables start with an uppercase letter, other literals are atoms, i.e. literal constants. The `?MODULE` literal macroexpands to the module name. In the example, the process implements a cache that allows for adding and retrieving items. The `gen_server` process is spawned with the `start` function. It is common practice in OTP that the callback hides the interaction with the behavior, providing an API to the user. In this case, the callback exposes the `get` and the `add` functions that in turn interact with the spawned process. A call to the `get` function invokes `call` on the `gen_server` module, which causes a message to be sent to the created process. When the message is received, the corresponding callback function `handle_call({get, Name}, From, State)` is invoked (notice that this function is executed in a different process with respect to `call`). The returned result is sent back through a message and the `gen_server:call` function ends. All the machinery associated with message passing, possible message loss, timeout, and dispatching over callback functions, is hidden from the programmer. `call` functions are used for synchronous messages expecting a return value, `cast` functions are asynchronous and do not return a value to the caller.

3.2 CONTEXTERLANG **Basics**

To support fast development of self-adaptive applications, CONTEXTERLANG provides context-aware agents through the OTP `context_agent` behavior. According to the OTP conventions, the programmer only needs to define the callback

```
-module(user).
-behavior(context_agent).
-include("context_agent_api.hrl"). % contextual API
% API
receive(AgentId, Source, Msg) ->
context_agent:cast(AgentId, {receive_msg, Source, Msg}).
add(AgentId, Dest, Msg) ->
context_agent:cast(AgentId, {send_msg, Dest, Msg}).

handle_cast({receive_msg, Source, Msg}, State) ->
    % ... forward to my client
    {noreply, State}.
handle_cast({send_msg, Dest, Msg}, State) ->
    % ... forward to dest client
    {noreply, State}.
% startup, shutdown and other auxiliary functions
```

Figure 5. The callback for the user agents in ContextChat.

```
-module(offline).
-context_cast([receive_msg/2]). % Contextual dispatch
    ...
handle_cast({receive_msg, Source, Msg}, State) ->
    store_chats:store_message(Source, Msg),
    {noreply, State}.
```

Figure 6. The offline variation in ContextChat.

module containing the functions for the core functionalities. We refer to these functions as *handle* functions [2].

Behavioral adaptation of context-aware agents is performed in CONTEXTERLANG through *variations*. A variation encapsulates a set of changes that modify the way an agent reacts to messages. Variations are combined in a stack fashion through proceed. When the agent receives a request message, the function to execute is searched along the stack of *active* variations up to the callback. This design is substantially similar to the layer combination in other COP languages. It clearly separates the basic behavior of an agent from the variations, making the application easier to understand and maintain, and supports reuse through combination of variations.

Figure 5 shows the callback of the context-aware agents that implement user agents inside the ContextChat server. The callback declares a function for receiving messages and a function for sending them to a different agent. Based on this example, hereafter, we analyze how the programmer can interact with variations in CONTEXTERLANG. Then we discuss how variations are declared and activated and how they can be sent to another node, changing the behavior of remote agents.

Variation creation. A variation is an Erlang module defining a set of handle functions exposed to the contextual dispatching. Implementing variations as Erlang modules has

---

[2] In the OTP terminology, functions inside callback modules are commonly referred to as *callback functions*. Since in CONTEXTERLANG functions like handle_call and handle_cast appear both in callback and in variation modules, we indicate them uniformly with the term *handle* functions to avoid confusion.

```
-module(backup).
-context_cast([receive_msg/2]).
    ...
handle_cast({receive_msg, Source, Msg}, State) ->
    % send Msg to the remote server
        ...
    ?proceed_cast({receive_msg, Source, Msg}, State),
    {noreply, State}.
```

Figure 7. The backup variation in ContextChat.

several advantages. It makes their development invaluably simple. It does not require syntax extensions, increasing the chances of acceptance by the programmers and avoiding the risk of breaking tool compatibility. Finally improves extensibility, since new variations can be added by implementing new modules without modifying the existing code.

The offline variation (Figure 6) defines an asynchronous receive_msg function, which at the moment of the activation, overrides the corresponding function in the callback module. In Figure 7, the backup variation redefines the receive_msg function in order to forward the message to a remote server in charge of the backup. If the backup variation is activated on top of the user callback, a call to receive causes the implementation inside backup to be called. The proceed call resolves to the implementation of receive_msg inside the callback module.

Variations can require an initialization or a shutdown phase to work properly. For example, if the offline variation in ContextChat saves the conversations on disk, a file must be created and opened. CONTEXTERLANG allows a variation to declare the on_activation and the on_deactivation functions, which are guaranteed to be called when the variation is respectively made active or deactivated. Initialization and cleanup code is placed inside these functions.

Variation activation. To allow asynchronous contextual adaptation, variation activation is performed in an imperative way by a different agent (an exception is discussed in Section 3.4). A common pattern is that a single agent enacts the role of context manager, and activates variations on the other agents depending on the context conditions. We expect that with the development of agent-based context-aware applications, new patterns arise. For example, agents could be organized in communities sharing a *local* context manager, while global context managers supervise other managers, in a hierarchical fashion.

The modification of the behavior of context-aware agents is exposed by the API of the context_agent module. The activate_variations function activates a list of variations on a given agent. In this example, the offline variation is activated on the agent AgentId. Then the backup variation is activated on top of the offline variation:

```
context_agent:call(
    {activate_variations, AgentId, [offline]}),
    ...
context_agent:call(
    {activate_variations, AgentId, [backup, offline]}),
```

```
CONTEXT_SPEC  ::=  [ SLOT_SPEC* ]
SLOT_SPEC  ::=  { Slotname, SLOT }
SLOT  ::=  SWITCH_SLOT
        |  ACTIVATABLE_SLOT
        |  FREE_SLOT
SWITCH_SLOT  ::=
        [ (Varname1,)* { Varname2, active } (,Varname3)*]
ACTIVATABLE_SLOT  ::=
        { Varname, active } | { Varname }
FREE_SLOT  ::=  free_slot
```

Figure 8. The syntax specification of a context ADT.

The same updating mechanism can then be used for variations deactivation. We require the atoms in the list to be valid names of modules available to the Erlang virtual machine. Beside direct interaction with the `context_agent`, we adhere to the OTP convention of hiding the interaction with OTP behaviors inside the callback and referencing the agent with the callback name (Section 3.1). The following code equivalent to the first call in the previous example:

```
user:activate_variations(AgentId, [offline]),
```

This is achieved thanks to a `context_agent_api.hrl` module which makes the API is available when imported by the callback.

Variation transmission. Variation transmission is a powerful mechanism to implement software which reacts to unforeseen conditions. For example, our previous work [11] shows how this feature can be used to adapt PDA devices to support rescue operations in an emergency scenario.

To design variation transmission and variation dynamic loading we leveraged advanced Erlang VM features, such as run time code manipulation, dynamic module loading and remote procedure call. The `variation_code` module provides the API for the functionalities concerning variation transmission. The following call sends a variation `var` to a remote node `node2`, and loads `var` in the virtual machine of `node2`:

```
% on node1@machine1
variation_code:send_var(node2@machine2, var)
```

The `send_var` call requires the `var` module to be available to the `node1` virtual machine. In the case of the ContextChat server, variation transmission can be used to allow clients to create a filter variation that manipulates the characters of their messages. The variation is then dynamically loaded and activated on the `user` agent. To include the filter in a variation, on the fly compilation is obtained using the Erlang compiler API. After this process completes, the variation can be activated on an agent as usual:

```
user:activate_variations(AgentId, [text_effect])
```

Of course, loading a module created from a user-defined filter is potentially dangerous and proper input validation is required to avoid security flaws.

3.3 Coherence among variations: context ADT

COP behavioral variations are activated and combined while the application is running. As a result, the issue of the consistency among variations arises. For example, the `offline` and the `online` variations in the ContextChat example should not be active at the same time. COP researchers have already investigated this problem. For example, reflection [10] has been leveraged to dynamically check the constraints. Other solutions use domain specific languages (DSL) to express *declarative* constraints on layers [8], in a way similar to feature diagrams in software product lines. The violation of a constraint raises an error which must be interactively managed by the programmer, so the need for human intervention limits the applicability of this approach. Subjective-C [13] also introduces a DSL to express context dependencies. The system inspects all the user-defined relations, possibly triggering an activation if needed. Another approach is to employ formal verification to statically guarantee layer constraints [29].

Our solution starts from the observation that organizing adaptability concerns in an application, and mapping them to variations and meaningful variation combinations, always requires careful design. For this reason, in practice, the programmer defines in advance which variation combinations are required. To explicitly capture these design choices, CONTEXTERLANG introduces a context abstract data type (ADT). The context ADT encapsulates the variations that can be activated on an agent, organizing the possible variation combinations and enforcing constraints on their activation. In this way the user of the context ADT instance is forced by the interface to activate only valid combinations (i.e. those designed in advance by the ADT programmer). The creation of an unforeseen combination, required by remote variation transmission, is made explicit. Note that the context ADT solution is not specific to ContextErlang and in principle could be ported to layer-based COP languages.

The `context_ADT` module creates a context data type instance from a given specification. The context ADT is organized as a fixed-size stack. Each level of the stack, referred as a *slot*, has a name for direct access. Three types of slots are defined. *Activatable* slots contain a single variation which can be active or not. *Switch* slots contain one or more variations, only one of which can be active at a certain instant of time. *Free* slots contain a single variation which is left undefined and can be assigned later. Free slots are the way variations transmitted by remote nodes can be used. In the following example a context ADT is created for the variations of a `user` agent.

```
Spec = [{persistency, {backup, active}},
        {tracing, {trace, active}},
        {status, [{offline, active}, online]},
        {text_effect, free_slot},
        {base_behavior, {user, active}}],

Context = context_ADT:create(Spec),
```

```
user:start_link(AgentId, Context)
```

The specification required to create a context ADT must obey the rules in Figure 8.

To start an agent with a given context ADT, the ADT is passed to the `start_link` function which spawns a new agent. The management of the variations in the context ADT is performed through the API we provide. The following call performs a switch on the `status` slot, activating the `online` variation.

```
user:in_cur_context_switch(AgentId, online, status)
```

Similar functions are provided for activating and deactivating the variation in an activatable slot, and for filling a free slot with a variation sent from a remote agent. After filling, the variation in the free slot can be activated normally.

The introduction of a context ADT has some drawbacks. Most noticeably, ADT specifications require an extra effort to be designed. However, the impact on complexity is kept minimum by using a DSL. In addition to that, introducing a variation into an existing context ADT instance requires to change the specification, forcing the programmer to think how to combine variations in a coherent way. In any case, the effort required is similar to write a new set of layer transitions in EventCJ when a new layer is added. Another observation should be made about the choice of limiting the stack size and forcing variations to obey certain constrains, which possibly limits variation capabilities. This design choice advantages safety against flexibility. However, in our experience, more flexibility is not really required. For example, changing active variations by specifying the list of all the active ones (like we showed in the previous sections) is a highly dynamic and flexible mechanism, which gives the programmer more freedom than it is really needed in most scenarios. Even in the examples provided in COP literature, most activation schemas are quite simple and encompass only few variations often in mutual exclusion [5, 6, 17, 29]. Nonetheless, in the spirit of leaving open the exploration of more dynamic solutions, we decided to maintain both activation mechanisms.

The context ADT solution is different from other COP proposals essentially in that it limits the ADT user to correct configurations instead of allowing free interaction and *ex-post* constraints check. However, analogies in the kind of constraints the context ADT allows to express can be envisaged. The context ADT in CONTEXTERLANG resembles approaches based on feature diagrams to express constraints among layers such as the *one-of* or the *all-of* relations. E.g., the `switch` slot clearly allows to express a *one-of* constraint. Finally, note that none of the approaches proposed so far, including the context ADT, relies on some automatically inferred semantics to check variations configurations. Instead, they only ensure constraints determined by the programmer. Investigation in this direction is an open research problem.

3.4 Concurrency: consistency with context change

The combination of COP with concurrency is not easy. While Erlang offers invaluable support for concurrency, integrating actors with run time behavioral change requires careful comprehension of how these aspects interact. In this section we clarify some fundamental points.

A crucial requirement is that behavioral change is *safe*, i.e. a change of the active variations does not corrupt the task in execution. As we will explain shortly, this cannot be achieved by simply forbidding a context change in the middle of message-triggered computations. In fact, this functionality is sometimes required. Our solution is based on shaping CONTEXTERLANG around the following principles:

- **Non interference.** The context of a running computation cannot be altered by a contextual message.

- **Agent authority.** An agent retains ultimate authority on its current context.

The first rule states that if an agent A sends a message to an agent B, triggering a computation cmp on B, no agent (not even A) can change the context of B in the middle of cmp by sending a contextual message to B. This is achieved by processing context-related and other messages one at a time, picking them up from the agent mailbox. Therefore, it is not possible that context-related messages interfere with the execution activated by a standard message.

The second rule states that an agent can change its context arbitrarily during a computation. This principle reminds OO programming, where an object is ultimately responsible for how it responds to messages. The second rule is required in some practical scenarios with non-trivial concurrency patterns. For example, when a client connects to the ContextChat server, some data structures in the `user` agent can be required to be initialized. Examples are the source IP, the client version, or a status variable that must be set to *online*. In addition to these operations, since the client is now connected, the `online` variation must be activated and the `offline` one deactivated. Now consider the case in which these actions (state changes and variation activation) are performed by two subsequent calls from another agent. With an unlucky interleaving, a call coming form a third agent can fall between these two, and find the agent with the status set to *online* but still with the `offline` variation active.

In general, it is not possible, with the functions for variation management seen so far, to execute a variation manipulation atomically with a set of operations. Of course, agents can coordinate to enforce this constraint at higher level, implementing some synchronization mechanism. However this solution requires a lot of error-prone code even for trivial tasks. For this reason in CONTEXTERLANG all the functions like `in_cur_context_switch` have an *immediate* counterpart which has effect on the context-aware agent that calls them. For example when the `user` agent receives the `init` message, it atomically initializes its internal data structures and activates the `online` variation atomically.

```
—module(user).
  ...
  handle_cast({init, Data}, State) —>
    % ... initialize the data structure
    user:in_my_cur_context_switch(online, status),
    {noreply, State}.
```

While a message is served, other messages are queued and cannot interrupt it. So atomicity is guaranteed. Interestingly, immediate activation is more general than message-based activation, since context-related messages could be implemented as standard messages which triggers the execution of an immediate activation. To alleviate the programmer from this annoying task we maintain both versions.

4. Validation

In this section, we discuss how we validated CONTEXTER-LANG. To demonstrate that CONTEXTERLANG is effective in the development of real-world applications we implemented two prototypes: one is the ContextChat extensively presented in the previous sections, and the other is an autonomic storage server which will be analyzed in the rest. To prove that a language is usable, we studied the critical performance aspects of CONTEXTERLANG through a micro-benchmark and we compared its performance with other COP languages. Then we reimplemented the autonomic storage server in plain Erlang and we compared its performances with the CONTEXTERLANG version.

4.1 Case Study

The design of CONTEXTERLANG was done in conjunction with the development of the ContextChat prototype which has been an immediate testbed for our choices. This approach helped us to design CONTEXTERLANG with the concrete problems or run time adaptation in mind, however, further validation is required to avoid overfitting. Indeed, the instant messaging domain somehow puts a message-based approach in a position of possibly unfair advantage.

The development of the storage server allowed to gain better confidence that CONTEXTERLANG is effective in general. The storage server is an autonomic application which provides a space for generic resources such as web pages or serialized data structures. The application behaves like a key-value map: keys allow to retrieve resources or modify their value. Resources can be stored in memory or on disk. Autonomicity provides that the most requested entities are moved into memory to reduce service time. The disk is used for other resources to avoid excessive memory consumption.

Each resource is implemented as a context-aware agent which reacts to messages like `set_value` and `get_value`. These details are hidden from the user which interacts only with an API module. The implementation of each resource with an agent is normal in Erlang OTP due to the extremely lightweight Erlang processes [21]. This makes the application scalable by simply spawning agents on several machines, because Erlang manages remote messaging in a transparent way. The `on_disk` and the `in_memory` variations can be dynamically activated on each agent. An optional `logging` variation provides a trace of the system execution. Autonomic behavior is implemented in a decentralized fashion: each agent migrates the resource to memory depending on the frequency of the requests it receives.

The development of the application confirmed the design choices of CONTEXTERLANG. Since the `on_disk` and the `in_memory` variations are in mutual exclusion they were managed through a *switch* slot of the context ADT. The `logging` variation occupies an *activatable* slot. The support for initialization and shutting down of variations (Section 3.3) is required to automatically initialize the needed files when the `on_disk` variation is activated and to move the resource in memory when it is deactivated. Since each agent adapts autonomously, the `in_memory` variation activation is performed by the agent itself through the immediate API (see Section 3.3). Note that moving the autonomic capabilities to a centralized engine would require that the adaptation is driven by context-related messages.

As a final remark we observe that all the considerations that motivated our work (see Section 2) could be repeated almost unchanged for the storage server example.

4.2 Performance

Our implementation introduces a performance overhead, because a function call requires to be dispatched over possibly several active variations. CONTEXTERLANG is a prototype and a wide space for optimization is available, e.g. hashing the function lookup. However our evaluation shows that the approach is feasible and already usable. All tests were performed on a laptop equipped with an Intel Core 2 Duo T9500 2.60GHz, 4GB RAM, and GNU/Linux OS. Concerning the languages, the version numbers are: Erlang R13 hipe, Ruby 1.8.7, ContextR 1.0.2, JavaScript Chrome 16.0.912.63, ContextJS Lively Kernel 2, Python 2.7, ContextPy 1.1, PyContext 1.0, SBCL 1.0.45.0, ContextL 0.61.

Microbenchmark. We compare the overhead introduced by CONTEXTERLANG with respect to other COP implementations [4]. The purpose is to compare the message dispatching slowdown introduced by each COP extension. We decided to keep our methodology as simple as possible, following the approach elaborated in [15] for AOP micro-benchmarking: compare methods performance without aspects (i.e. a non-advised method) and with aspects deployed. To remove a source of variability, the comparison is limited to dynamically typed languages.

We assume a message delivery in a non-layered method, as a reference (Table 1, second column). Then we evaluate the time required to dispatch a layered method with 0 to 5 active proceeding layers/variations (columns from 3 to 8). Each method and each partial method increments a global

Language	Basic Call	0	1	2	3	4	5
ContextErlang	540.65 (OTP) / 90.58 (PA) / 9.38 (FC)	815.33	1071.14	1311.59	1531.77	1819.07	2074.73
ContextR	43.52 (Ruby)	768.58	1768.58	2768.58	3768.58	4768.58	5768.58
ContextJS	0.40 (JavaScript)	85.90	158.60	211.00	256.80	299.20	338.30
ContextPy	24.22 (Python)	406.85	661.01	873.50	1163.31	1397.62	1623.49
PyContext	24.48 (Python)	410.66	854.66	1265.21	1668.65	2073.56	2472.16
ContextL	2.2 (Common Lisp)	2.50	3.50	4.30	5.30	6.40	7.40

Table 1. Performance of COP languages in the microbenchmark. All values are in milliseconds.

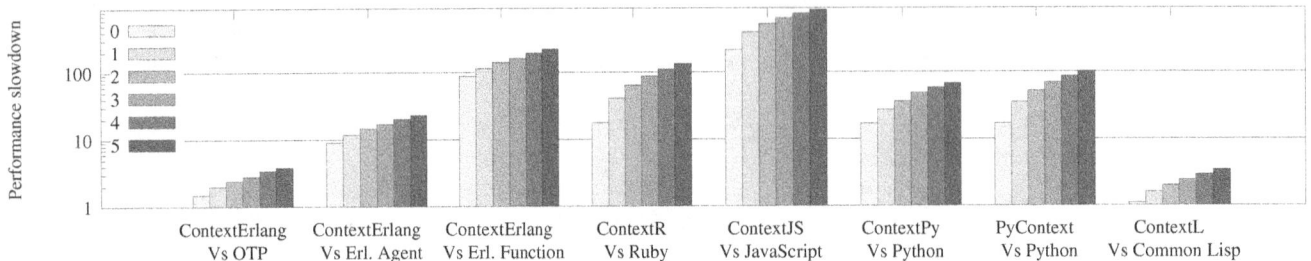

Figure 9. Performance of layered methods compared to the basic methods in various COP languages.

variable (in the CONTEXTERLANG benchmark we used an agent-local variable, since Erlang has no shared state by design). All benchmarks are executed 10^5 times taking the mean over 10 executions, with a complete dry run (therefore 10^6 executions) to achieve steady state of the runtime. Information about warm-up times for each implementation is not easy to find. However benchmarks are running for minutes, and we observed a x10 time factor from 10^5 to 10^6 executions, increasing our confidence on the steady state of the runtimes. In the case of CONTEXTERLANG, COP functionalities are implemented in the OTP library which adds many time-consuming operations due to the built-in fault-tolerance support. Therefore, it has scarce significance to compare message sending to a CONTEXTERLANG context-aware agent with a basic function call. For this reason, we compare it (Table 1, line 2, column 2) not only with a pure Erlang function call (FC), but also with a message to a pure Erlang agent (PA), and with a message to a standard `gen_server` OTP agent. Figure 9 shows the ratio between the time required to call a layered method and a basic method for various languages (note the logarithmic scale). For CONTEXTERLANG we report the comparison with all the three cases.

Previous work [4] highlighted a huge performance impact of COP and motivated research on possible optimizations [3]. Our evaluation confirms this result. Our results also show that CONTEXTERLANG introduces a non-negligible overhead, which, however, is not dissimilar from other COP languages. For example, a CONTEXTERLANG message to a context-aware agent is approximately 87 times slower than a function call in Erlang and 1.5 times slower than a message sent to a `gen_server` standard OTP agent. Note that Figure 9 should be read carefully. For example, results of ContextJS are due to the aggressive optimization of JavaScript compiler and VM which makes basic methods extremely effi-

cient [20]. This leads to the apparently poor performance of the ContextJS COP implementation compared to the basic language in Figure 9. Nevertheless, ContextJS is among the fastest COP extension in our test (Table 1).

Performance on the case study. To overcome the obvious limitations of micro-benchmarking, we estimated the overhead of CONTEXTERLANG in a complete application. We implemented the autonomic storage server in plain Erlang. Variations are simulated by `if` chains switching between different behaviors. Active behavioral variations are stored in each agent's state. Since the logging functionality introduces a uniform overhead, we left it off. The Erlang version resulted in 390 non-comment LOC instead of the 380 non-comment LOC of the CONTEXTERLANG version. While this value is not impressive, it is likely to significantly increase with the number of variations and variations combinations.

In the experiment, each resource is initially created, it is requested 10 times, and then deleted. This is equivalent to starting an agent, delivering 10 messages, and shutting down the agent. We tuned the autonomic behavior so that the resource is initially stored on disk and after the first 2 requests is moved to memory. The measures were taken by repeating this process on all the resources for a variable number of resources, from 1 up to 1000. For each run we took the mean among 10 executions. Figure 10 shows the results. To make the graph more readable we plot the trend of the two executions as the mean over 100 values. The analysis shows that the significant overhead detected by the micro-benchmark becomes almost negligible in a real application.

5. Related work

The problem of dynamic software adaptation to respond to context changes has been extensively tackled from a software architecture standpoint [23]. Over the years, however,

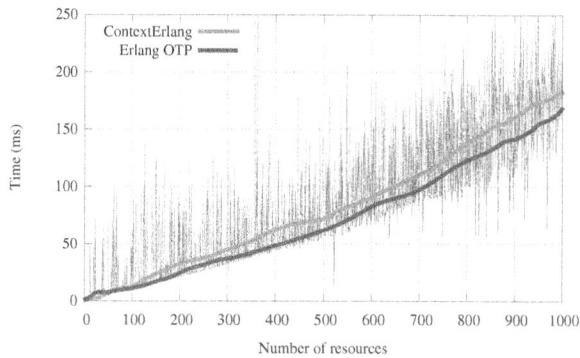

Figure 10. Performance comparison for the autonomic storage server.

language-centered techniques have been progressively investigated leading to the development of *ad-hoc* programming paradigms for context adaptation.

Context oriented programming. COP has been recently explored, starting from the pioneering work on ContextL [9, 10] based on the CLOS metaobject protocol. Over the time, many COP extensions have been developed for different languages such as Python, Smalltalk, Ruby, JavaScript and Groovy. This effort has been extended to less dynamic languages, in which COP extensions are more difficult to implement due to the limited reflective capabilities, such as Java [5, 6, 17, 27, 29]. A comparison of the existing COP languages with a performance evaluation of the available solutions can be found in [4].

CONTEXTERLANG is in the COP tradition since it supports modularization, dynamic activation, and combination of behavioral variations. It differentiates from most COP approaches, since behavioral variations are activated on per-agent bases through context-related messages rather than in a dynamic scope. CONTEXTERLANG *variations* are similar to COP *layers*. The difference is that layers usually contain partial definitions associated with different classes. While nothing prevents a CONTEXTERLANG variation from containing partial definitions referring to different agents, this is scarcely used in applications, since the variation must be activated singularly on each agent. Therefore a CONTEXT-ERLANG variation is usually associated with a specific agent and contains the partial definition for that agent.

Ambience is a COP language based on AmOS, an object system built on top of Common Lisp [14]. Ambience – designed simultaneously with ContextL – is alternative approach to layer-based COP languages, leveraging multi-methods dispatching and context objects. In [14] the authors recognize the need for variations activation by an external monitoring thread. In Ambience the context – and therefore the active variations – is global and shared among all the threads. A monitoring thread can asynchronously change the context of the whole application. In CONTEXTERLANG each agent can adapt individually, as we believe that in certain scenarios this feature is required. For example, in the Con-

textChat server, per-agent adaptation is crucial to adapt to each single client. As stated by the authors of Ambience, asynchronous activation exposes the system to the risk of behavioral inconsistency. CONTEXTERLANG enforces consistency by design, avoiding that variation activations conflict with other computations (Section 3.3).

Event-based COP. The need for event-based composition and activation has been recognized as an emerging need for COP in our previous work [12], in which we presented the initial implementation of CONTEXTERLANG as a promising solution. As already discussed (Section 2) Kamina et al. [29] also tackled this issue in the EventCJ Java COP extensions.

Jcop [6] is a Java COP extension which introduces two constructs. *Declarative layer composition* allows to express variation activation declaratively through joinpoint quantification. *Conditional composition* activates variations depending on a run time condition. So the developer is relieved from specifying variation activation programmatically in the code. Jcop allows the compact representation of otherwise scattered with activation statements, a problem that emerged in the development of ContextChat (Section 2). However, activation in Jcop is always dynamically scoped and can lead to the problem of excessive adaptation propagation.

Aspect oriented programming. COP has a certain degree of similarity with Aspect-Oriented Programming [19], which may be viewed as a general term indicating a family of approaches that support modularization of crosscutting concerns. The main contribution of COP with respect to AOP is to provide specific abstractions for context adaptation. AOP can be indirectly applied for the same purposes and some COP language implementations rely on AOP [6, 27, 29]. However, although AOP frameworks exist which support dynamic aspect activation, such as Prose [24], AOP focuses on compile time feature selection and combination, while the COP core concept is run time activation and combination of behavioral variations. A detailed comparison of the two approaches can be found in [6, 9, 17].

Event-based programming. Event-driven or event-based programming is a programming paradigm in which the flow of control is determined by events that can be triggered and listened according to the Observer pattern. This approach is a contribution to address the problem of concerns not amenable to modularization along the main dimension of decomposition. Implicit invocation (II) languages [22] offer a linguistic support for this mechanism, obtaining better encapsulation of crosscutting concerns and decoupling from other code. The Ptolemy language [25] combines ideas from AOP and II languages. In Ptolemy code blocks are bound to events as closures which can be executed inside the event handler. Since basic behavior can be written in the closure and observers can execute code *around* the execution of the closure, Ptolemy seems to be the II language that most resembles COP techniques.

Other language-level techniques. Subjective dispatch [28] adds a dimension to the receiver-based method dispatch of OO languages, considering also the sender in the dispatch mechanism. COP conceptually operates in a similar way, taking into account the context as a dispatching dimension. Feature oriented programming (FOP) targets crosscutting concerns with the goal of synthesizing programs in software product lines [7] from single units of functionality conventionally called *features*. Features are selected and combined at compile time while COP variations, due to the volatile nature of the context, are activated and combined dynamically.

6. Conclusions and Future Work

Model through the development of CONTEXTERLANG, a COP extension of the Erlang language based on the OTP platform. We discussed the mechanisms through which CONTEXTER-LANG supports dynamic software adaptation. We argue that due to the asynchronous nature of context provisioning, context adaptation should be designed taking into account the concurrency model of the language. CONTEXTERLANG constitutes a first contribution in this direction.

Our purposes for the future are twofold. On the one hand we plan to further improve the CONTEXTERLANG implementation, for example by optimizing the code in order to minimize the overhead introduced by the context management. On the other hand we are considering the option of exploiting the coupling between event-based context adaptability and concurrency model investigated in this paper in other agent-based languages, such as Scala.

References

[1] *http://erlang.org*. Reference website for Erlang.

[2] *http://www.scala-lang.org/*. Reference website for Scala.

[3] M. Appeltauer, M. Haupt, and R. Hirschfeld. Layered method dispatch with INVOKEDYNAMIC: an implementation study. COP '10, pages 4:1–4:6, 2010.

[4] M. Appeltauer, R. Hirschfeld, M. Haupt, J. Lincke, and M. Perscheid. A comparison of context-oriented programming languages. In *COP '09*, pages 1–6, 2009.

[5] M. Appeltauer, R. Hirschfeld, M. Haupt, and H. Masuhara. ContextJ: Context-oriented Programming with Java. *Information and Media Technologies*, 6(2):399–419, 2011.

[6] M. Appeltauer, R. Hirschfeld, H. Masuhara, M. Haupt, and K. Kawauchi. Event-specific software composition in context-oriented programming. In B. Baudry and E. Wohlstadter, editors, *Software Composition*, volume 6144 of *LNCS*. 2010.

[7] D. Batory, J. N. Sarvela, and A. Rauschmayer. Scaling step-wise refinement. In *Proceedings of the 25th International Conference on Software Engineering*, ICSE '03, Washington, DC, USA, 2003.

[8] P. Costanza and T. D'Hondt. Feature descriptions for context-oriented programming. In *Software Product Lines, 12th International Conference (SPLC)*, pages 9–14, September 2008.

[9] P. Costanza and R. Hirschfeld. Language constructs for context-oriented programming: an overview of ContextL. In *Proceedings of the 2005 symposium on Dynamic languages*, DLS '05, 2005.

[10] P. Costanza and R. Hirschfeld. Reflective layer activation in contextL. In *SAC '07: Proceedings of the 2007 ACM symposium on Applied computing*, 2007.

[11] C. Ghezzi, M. Pradella, and G. Salvaneschi. Programming language support to context-aware adaptation - a case-study with Erlang. *SEAMS: Software Engineering for Adaptive and Self-Managing Systems,International Workshop, ICSE 2010*.

[12] C. Ghezzi, M. Pradella, and G. Salvaneschi. Context-oriented programming in highly concurrent systems. In *Proceedings of the 2nd International Workshop on Context-Oriented Programming*, COP '10, New York, NY, USA, 2010. ACM.

[13] S. González, N. Cardozo, K. Mens, A. Cádiz, J.-C. Libbrecht, and J. Goffaux. Subjective-C: Bringing context to mobile platform programming. In *Proceedings of the International Conference on Software Language Engineering*, Eindhoven, The Netherlands, 2010.

[14] S. González, K. Mens, and P. Heymans. Highly dynamic behaviour adaptability through prototypes with subjective multimethods. In *Proceedings of the 2007 symposium on Dynamic languages*, DLS '07, pages 77–88, 2007.

[15] M. Haupt and M. Mezini. Micro-measurements for dynamic aspect-oriented systems. In M. Weske and P. Liggesmeyer, editors, *Object-Oriented and Internet-Based Technologies*, volume 3263 of *LNCS*. Springer Berlin / Heidelberg, 2004.

[16] C. Hewitt, P. Bishop, and R. Steiger. A universal modular ACTOR formalism for artificial intelligence. In *IJCAI'73: Proceedings of the 3rd international joint conference on Artificial intelligence*, pages 235–245, San Francisco, CA, USA, 1973. Morgan Kaufmann.

[17] R. Hirschfeld, P. Costanza, and O. Nierstrasz. Context-oriented programming. *Journal of Object Technology*, 7(3), Mar. 2008.

[18] J. O. Kephart and D. M. Chess. The vision of autonomic computing. *Computer*, 36:41–50, 2003.

[19] G. Kiczales, E. Hilsdale, J. Hugunin, M. Kersten, J. Palm, and W. Griswold. An overview of AspectJ. In J. Knudsen, editor, *ECOOP 2001 – Object-Oriented Programming*, volume 2072 of *LNCS*, pages 327–354. Springer Berlin / Heidelberg, 2001.

[20] J. Lincke, M. Appeltauer, B. Steinert, and R. Hirschfeld. An open implementation for context-oriented layer composition in ContextJS. *Sci. Comput. Program.*, 76:1194–1209, 2011.

[21] M. Logan, E. Merritt, and R. Carlsson. *Erlang and OTP in Action*. Manning Publications, 2010.

[22] D. Notkin, D. Garlan, W. G. Griswold, and K. Sullivan. Adding implicit invocation to languages: Three approaches. In *Object Technologies for Advanced Software, First JSSST International Symposium*, volume 742 of *LNCS*, 1993.

[23] P. Oreizy, N. Medvidovic, and R. N. Taylor. Architecture-based runtime software evolution. In *ICSE '98: Proceedings of the 20th international conference on Software engineering*, pages 177–186. IEEE Computer Society, 1998.

[24] A. Popovici, T. Gross, and G. Alonso. Dynamic weaving for aspect-oriented programming. In *Proceedings of the 1st international conference on Aspect-oriented software development*, AOSD '02, 2002.

[25] H. Rajan and G. T. Leavens. Ptolemy: A language with quantified, typed events. In J. Vitek, editor, *ECOOP 2008, Cyprus*, volume 5142 of *LNCS*, pages 155–179, Berlin, July 2008.

[26] G. Salvaneschi, C. Ghezzi, and M. Pradella. *Context-Oriented Programming: A Programming Paradigm for Autonomic Systems*. Technical Report, arXiv:1105.0069, 2011.

[27] G. Salvaneschi, C. Ghezzi, and M. Pradella. *JavaCtx: Seamless Toolchain Integration for Context-Oriented Programming*. COP '11. 2011.

[28] R. B. Smith and D. Ungar. A simple and unifying approach to subjective objects. *TAPOS*, 2(3):161–178, 1996.

[29] K. Tetsuo, A. Tomoyuki, and H. Masuhara. EventCJ: A context-oriented programming language with declarative event-based context transition. In *Proceedings of the 10nd international conference on Aspect-oriented software development*, AOSD '11, 2011.

Fine-Grained Modularity and Reuse of Virtual Machine Components

Christian Wimmer*   Stefan Brunthaler[†]   Per Larsen[†]   Michael Franz[†]

*Oracle Labs   [†]Department of Computer Science, University of California, Irvine

christian.wimmer@oracle.com   s.brunthaler@uci.edu   perl@uci.edu   franz@uci.edu

Abstract

Modularity is a key concept for large and complex applications and an important enabler for collaborative research. In comparison, virtual machines (VMs) are still mostly monolithic pieces of software. Our goal is to significantly reduce to the cost of extending VMs to efficiently host and execute multiple, dynamic languages. We are designing and implementing a VM following the "everything is extensible" paradigm. Among the novel use cases that will be enabled by our research are: VM extensions by third parties, support for multiple languages inside one VM, and a universal VM for mobile devices.

Our research will be based on the existing state of the art. We will reuse an existing metacircular Java™ VM and an existing dynamic language VM implemented in Java. We will split the VMs into fine-grained modules, define explicit interfaces and extension points for the modules, and finally re-connect them.

Performance is one of the most important concerns for VMs. Modularity improves flexibility but can introduce an unacceptable performance overhead at the module boundaries, e.g., for inter-module method calls. We will identify this overhead and address it with novel feedback-directed compiler optimizations. These optimizations will also improve the performance of modular applications running on top of our VM.

The expected results of our research will be not only new insights and a new design approach for VMs, but also a complete reference implementation of a modular VM where everything is extensible by third parties and that supports multiple languages.

Categories and Subject Descriptors   D.3.4 [*Programming Languages*]: Processors—Run-time environments, Compilers, Optimization

General Terms   Algorithms, Languages, Performance

Keywords   Maxine, languages, dynamic languages, Java, virtual machine, modularity, modular VM, metacircular VM, just-in-time compilation, optimization, performance

1. Introduction

Modularity enables developers to build increasingly large and complex applications. It is often not feasible to closely control the entire architecture of such applications. They are often developed by distributed teams or even multiple vendors, so it is necessary that individual modules are independent and have a well-defined interface to the rest of the application. The concept of a *module system*, i.e., a software layer that loads, unloads, and connects modules, is well understood in the field of software engineering [29]. It is used on a daily basis with industry standards like OSGi [24].

The complexity of virtual machines (VMs) is steadily increasing. This includes the development of more advanced just-in-time (JIT) compilers and garbage collectors, but also optimized run-time services such as thread synchronization. Additionally, the rise of dynamic languages has led to a plethora of new VMs, since a completely new VM is typically developed for every new language. VMs are still mostly monolithic pieces of software. They are developed in C or C++, the languages that they aim to replace. In summary, VMs offer a lot of benefits for applications running *on top* of them, but they mostly do not utilize these benefits for themselves.

The reason often cited for this is performance. Many subsystems are highly performance critical or have performance critical connection points with other subsystems. For example, when a garbage collector needs write barriers, the JIT compiler must efficiently embed them into the generated code. A callback into the garbage collector for every field access would be too slow. Using modularity and interfaces, it would be an even slower call that needs dynamic dispatch. Existing modular VMs therefore have carefully selected module boundaries to avoid the performance impact.

An important step towards true modularity for VMs are metacircular VMs, i.e., VMs written in the same language as they execute. The two most prominent examples for Java™ are the Jikes RVM [16] and the Maxine VM [20]. Maxine is designed with modularity in mind: the core subsystems are exchangeable using so-called "schemes". However, there is still no explicit concept of modules. Additionally, the modularity is on a coarse level. Individual modules are not designed with fine-grained extensibility in mind.

Most current VMs are designed to execute only a single input language. The monolithic design makes it difficult to adapt major parts when building a new VM for a new language. For example, Java VMs have been extensively optimized over the last decade, which has led to aggressively optimizing JIT compilers as well as parallel and concurrent garbage collectors. However, the dynamic language VMs that have become highly popular in recent years do not incorporate these implementation-intensive optimizations. The lack of modularity has prohibited the reuse of existing VM optimizations. With fine-grained modularity, implementing a VM for a new language requires only implementing the new language-specific parts, while the core runtime and optimization infrastructure remains unchanged.

The goal of our research is to investigate the impact of fine-grained modularity on VMs. We envision a VM following the "everything is extensible" paradigm, by combining best practices of existing VM design and existing module systems.

We expect our research to contribute along three axes.

- *Direct research results*: We will study the performance impact of fine-grained modularity in VMs, develop new optimizations to eliminate possible overhead, and generalize the results for the benefit of all modular applications.

- *Benefits for future research*: We will develop a VM research platform that is ideal for future research. It will make comparisons of different optimizations much easier than before.

- *Optimized VMs for many languages*: We will define a customizable family of VMs that can easily be configured for different languages (static and dynamic languages), different target systems (from embedded devices to servers), and different optimization strategies. For some of these configurations, no optimized VMs are available yet, e.g., we expect to contribute significantly to the performance of dynamic language VMs.

2. Vision of a Modular VM

While the performance and complexity of VMs have been greatly increased over the last decade, the internal structure of VMs still neglects the concepts of modern modular

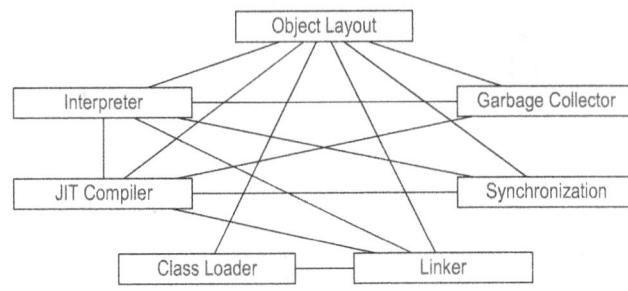

Figure 1. Structure of current VMs.

software development. Consequently, it is not possible to implement different VM optimizations independently from each other: all parts of a VM interdepend on each other. Figure 1 shows important subsystems of a current VM. There are multiple circular and bidirectional dependencies, e.g., between the JIT compiler and the garbage collector: the JIT compiler emits read and write barriers specifically for a garbage collector, while the garbage collector traverses stack frames and root pointers defined by the JIT compiler.

We want to disentangle the structure of the VM by introducing an explicit concept of modules and module dependencies. Modules provide well-specified extension points that are used by other modules. We outline the main features of the resulting system below.

- *No circular dependencies*: The module system prohibits circular dependencies, leading to an overall structure that is easier to understand.

- *Fine-grained modules*: Every subsystem is split into several modules with explicit dependencies and extension points in between.

- *Ubiquitous extensibility*: There is no distinction between "internal" modules that constitute the core runtime system, and "external" modules supplied by third-party vendors. All use the same extension points and have access to the same data and interfaces.

- *Metacircularity*: The VM is mostly written in one of the many managed languages that it can execute (we anticipate the VM to be written in Java). Modules that extend the VM are shipped in the same form as applications running on top of the VM. Therefore, all optimizations that improve the application speed also improve the VM speed, and it is possible to eliminate the overhead of modularity.

2.1 Performance

Performance is a key aspect for VMs because it affects all applications running on top of the VM. However, we believe that the current VM development process is too centered around performance, thereby sacrificing other important aspects such as maintainability, portability, and extensibility. Many optimizations are applied prematurely because there is

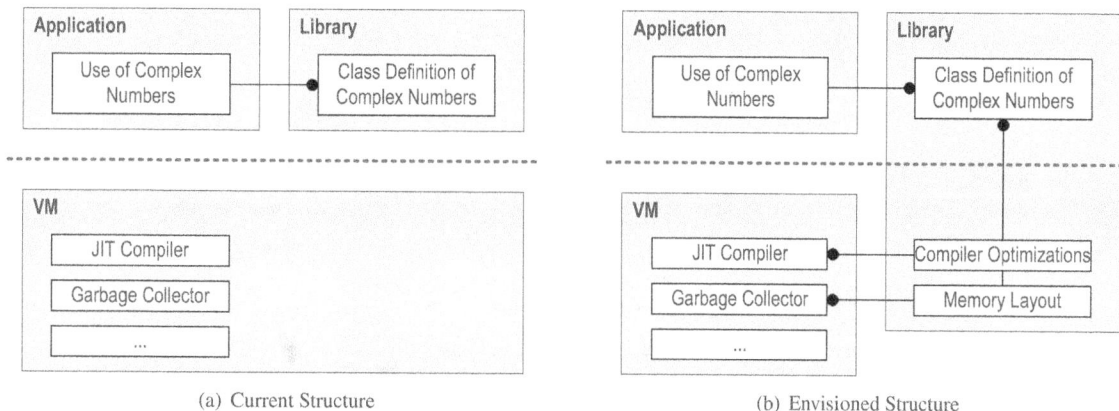

(a) Current Structure

(b) Envisioned Structure

Figure 2. Case study for the support of complex numbers inside the VM.

the common belief that they are indispensable. To overcome this, we will follow a three step process.

1. Define the module boundaries so that each module is a small, self-contained, and individually meaningful entity.

2. Measure the performance impact of modularity in various configurations to identify whether there are bottlenecks and where they are.

3. Implement optimizations that eliminate the bottlenecks. Since these optimizations can be implemented as independent modules themselves, they do not erode the overall system architecture.

The ability of a VM to "optimize itself" offers unique benefits compared to, e.g., a modular operating system (OS). In a modular OS, the module boundaries remain in effect at run time. Calls that cross method boundaries are expensive because they require a table lookup to find the current implementation of an interface, or at least an indirect method call using a function pointer. In our modular VM, run-time profiling and the JIT compiler can eliminate the overhead completely. Even in current VMs, interface calls are aggressively optimized when there is only one implementation of the interface available. Therefore, method inlining and other inter-procedural optimizations across module boundaries are feasible. We therefore argue that a modular VM has a vast performance advantage compared to a modular OS.

2.2 Case Study: Third-Party VM Extensions

Suppose that a third party vendor offers a library providing classes for computations with complex numbers. Figure 2(a) illustrates this structure. The library is centered around a class that combines two floating point numbers to one complex number. Therefore, every complex number is a separate object, leading to sub-optimal performance.

The library developer cannot solve this problem because modifications of the VM are not possible. The VM developer cannot solve the problem because implementing optimiza-

tions for a certain library is out of scope for a VM—only important methods of the standard library that ships with the VM are optimized by the VM.

Using our approach, the library vendor can also supply extension modules for the VM. Figure 2(b) shows this approach. One VM module can define the object layout for complex numbers, i.e., it defines that complex numbers are handled in the same way as floating point numbers and are not separate objects. Another module can define compiler optimizations for complex numbers, e.g., perform constant folding or use special processor instructions for complex numbers. These extension modules are loaded when the library for complex numbers is loaded, i.e., the modules have no impact on applications that do not use the library.

2.3 Case Study: Mixing of Languages

Figure 3 sketches the continuum of programming languages in a very coarse and superficial manner. At one end of the spectrum are statically typed languages such as *Java* and *C#* that provide type safety and highly optimized execution environments. On the other end are dynamic languages such as *Python, Ruby,* and *JavaScript.* These are more flexible and easier to use, especially for end users. In the middle range are programming languages such as *Visual Basic* that provide some (sometimes optional) static typing while being suitable for casual users. No single language can fulfill the needs for all kinds of programming tasks, so the combination and integration of languages is important.

To get the best of both worlds, a hybrid approach is increasingly used in which the *core* of an application is written by experienced developers in a statically typed language while domain experts and end-users write *extensions* in dynamically typed (and often domain-specific) languages. In many cases, the dynamic language is implemented on top of a static language that also uses a virtual machine environment for its execution (see for example [8, 15]), leading to a big overhead due to double interpretation and compilation.

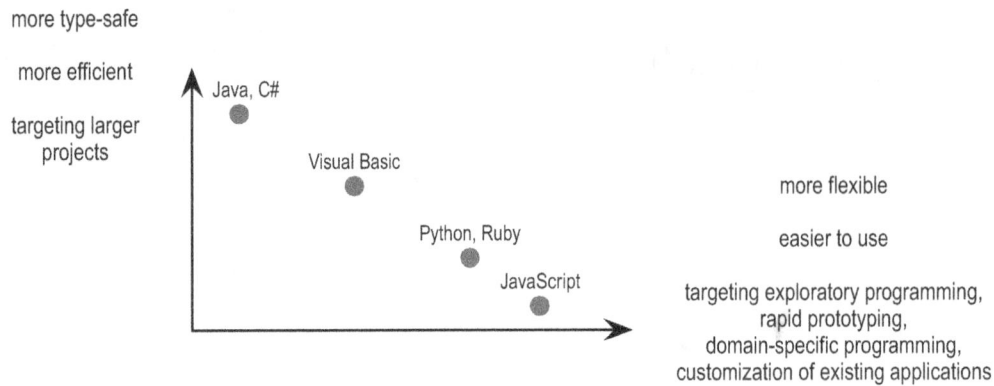

more type-safe

more efficient

targeting larger
projects

Java, C#

Visual Basic

Python, Ruby

JavaScript

more flexible

easier to use

targeting exploratory programming,
rapid prototyping,
domain-specific programming,
customization of existing applications

Figure 3. *A continuum of programming language characteristics.*

Our approach to handle multiple languages in one VM addresses the layering cost. All languages use the same implementation infrastructure, so data can be shared between the languages. There is no more need for conversion between different object models and wrapping or unwrapping of data. By leveraging VM extensibility, we also will support highly efficient ways to implement bytecode interpreters. Currently, all of these techniques require the use of unsafe, systems-oriented programming languages such as C and C++.

2.4 Case Study: One VM for Mobile Devices

Smartphones and other mobile or embedded devices have become ubiquitous. Although their computational power has increased, they are still much more limited than PCs. Nevertheless, users want to access web pages that use JavaScript, run Flash applications inside the browser, and execute their well-known rich-client Java applications. All these languages require a VM with the same core functionality, such as a garbage collector, an interpreter, and a JIT compiler. Figure 4(a) illustrates the current situation. It is a waste of resources to ship a mobile device with three completely separate VMs. From a security perspective, a larger code base means more potential vulnerabilities for attackers to exploit.

Using our approach, the core functionality is shared between all VMs, as shown in Figure 4(b). The language specific parts are added as additional modules to the language-independent set of core modules. No functionality is duplicated, saving valuable disk space. Additionally, the different applications can also be executed in one VM *at run time*, provided that the VM is shipped with the appropriate modules that provide isolation between multiple applications running inside one VM. This eliminates the duplication of data structures in the main memory at run time.

Having a fine-grained set of core module also simplifies customization of the VM for different device configurations. A small-scale device can be shipped with the bare minimum of modules, e.g., without a JIT compiler. The more powerful

a device is, the more optimizations can be added. This allows to support the full scale of devices and the full scale of languages with only one customizable VM.

2.5 Case Study: A Multi-Language VM-Based Web Browser to Increase Web Security

The web is one prominent case where the interaction between multiple languages currently poses significant problems. The core of current web browsers is implemented in C or C++, and they execute web applications written in JavaScript, Flash, and other dynamic languages. However, the boundary between the languages is not as clear as it seems at the first glance. JavaScript is also used for core browser components, for example the user interface of Mozilla's Firefox is written in JavaScript. And browser extensions can be implemented in JavaScript too. As a result, current browsers have much communication between parts written in different languages, which requires expensive conversion and duplication of data structures in these worlds.

Our solution allows a browser, where the main components are implemented in a static managed language like Java, to transparently communicate with extensions and web applications written in JavaScript, as well as web applications written in Flash. That enables seamless and combined optimization of the browser core, browser extensions, and web applications running inside the browser. The code handling a single mouse click on a web page button currently crosses the language boundary several times. We allow method inlining and other aggressive optimizations from the code that receives the mouse event to the JavaScript handler and then to the code that accesses and modifies the document object model (DOM) representing the page in memory.

An additional benefit of our approach that we want to highlight is the possibility for increased security. Attacks such as cross-site scripting and deficiencies of the same-origin policy that is currently used by most browsers can be solved by approaches such as fine grained information

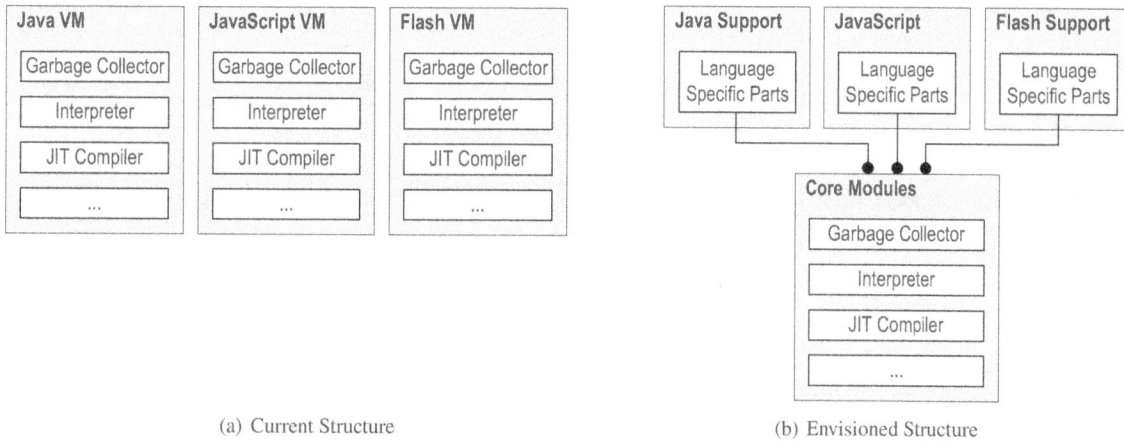

(a) Current Structure

(b) Envisioned Structure

Figure 4. Case study for the support of multiple languages in one VM on mobile devices.

flow tracking inside the JavaScript VM. From a conceptional point of view, every JavaScript value has a label with its origin attached. However, when the web page source code with the DOM is part of the browser core written in C or C++, DOM elements cannot be labeled and tracked by the JavaScript VM. Our envisioned VM allows end-to-end information flow tracking in the whole browser. A single implementation of information flow tracking secures the browser and web applications, so our VM is the ideal basis for future research in this area.

2.6 Metacircular VMs

As previously mentioned, traditional VMs are written in a language different from the one they execute. In many cases, the VM is implemented using a low-level or system oriented programming language like C or C++, while the VM itself executes a high-level programming language. The VM offers productivity advantages such as type safety, memory safety, garbage collection, and JIT compilation, but the VM itself does not benefit from these features.

In contrast, metacircular VMs [14, 16, 20, 28] are implemented in the same programming language they execute. Both the application and VM code are treated uniformly. There is no internal distinction between parts of the VM and parts of the application. Metacircular design is advantageous in terms of both performance and development time. For example, the JIT compiler of the VM optimizes both the VM and application code together in the same context. A VM with run-time profiling not only optimizes the running application, but also the VM itself. Similarly, a VM with run-time profiling makes no distinction between optimizing the VM itself and the application it runs.

Although there is no difference between VM and application code inside a metacircular VM, the outside view is still different. The VM requires a bootstrapping process that translates the VM to machine code ahead of time. This requires a second, non-metacircular VM for the language,

so that the JIT compiler can run the first time and compile itself. The result of the bootstrapping process is a machine code image of the VM that can be executed directly by the processor. For all VMs we are currently aware of, the image is a monolithic piece of machine code. We want to evaluate whether splitting the file into several smaller parts and preserving the module structure, i.e., a reduced image that covers only essential parts, is sufficient and beneficial.

2.7 Reliability

A modular VM design embraces and encourages extension from third-party vendors. That can raise concerns about the reliability of the VM. Code from different vendors, which is unlikely to have been tested together, must interact. Several parts of a modular VM are quite similar to ordinary modular applications. They do not need access to low-level data structures such as raw memory, threads, or synchronization primitives. For example, an optimization for the JIT compiler transforms high-level graph-based data structures and not raw memory. The dependency tracking of the module system enforces that such access does not happen. Additionally, modules that contribute optimizations are not critical for the overall functionality of the VM and can be disabled when they show erroneous behavior.

Still, the machine code generated by the JIT compiler operates on raw memory, so an erroneous optimization can lead to code that crashes the VM; and modules extending the garbage collector require arbitrary memory access to work. This problem can be tackled for example with integrity checks performed by the core modules or with module interfaces that encourage fault-tolerant programming.

We consider it an essential part of this research to evaluate reliability issues. This includes both a formal analysis of our prototype implementation, as well as field studies that combine our core modules with third-party extensions.

In addition to guaranteeing this low-level system integrity, we realize the danger of interference between third-

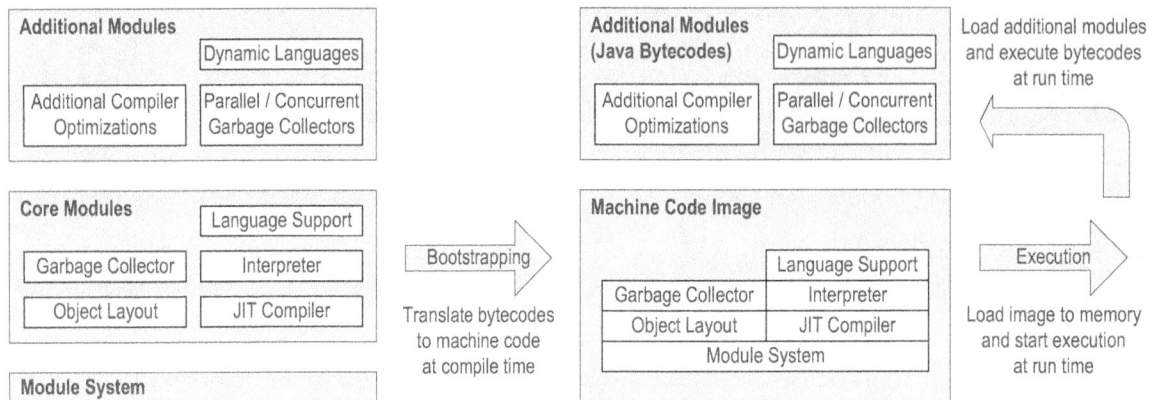

Figure 5. Architecture of the modular VM.

party modules. For example, our envisioned modular VM indicates a conflict, if there are two modules A and B, both altering the same code fragment, such as the same class, or method. In such a case, there are basically several ways to proceed. First, we resolve conflicts by restricting the access to the same piece of code such that we give permission to only one of the two conflicting modules. Next, we think that both modifications are permissible if both modules share a common namespace, similar to the same-origin-policy in web browsers. Finally, the conflict is analogous to conflicting compiler optimizations (corresponding to modules): before actually performing any transformation, each optimization ensures soundness by ensuring that its preconditions hold.

2.8 System Architecture

We envision a VM where all subsystems are split into small modules with well-defined module boundaries. On the lowest level, a module system manages the dependencies between the modules and allows module interactions in a controlled way. Figure 5 shows the overall structure. On top of the module system, a small set of core modules provides the basic runtime environment of the VM. During the bootstrapping process, this part must be compiled to machine code to get an initial running VM image. Additional modules with advanced optimizations are loaded on demand. These modules are shipped as bytecodes, so they are executed and optimized like any application running on top of the VM.

Modules are kept at the smallest feasible granularity to allow fine-grained configurability and extensibility. As an example, Figure 6 shows a possible structure of the optimizing JIT compiler. The intermediate representation and flow of compilation is defined in a central module. All other parts, especially the individual optimizations, are in separate modules that depend on the central module. Additionally, other subsystems contribute to the compilation process, such as the garbage collector, the run-time profiling, and the definition of language-specific semantics. It is also possible to integrate optimizations contributed by third-party vendors.

This breaks up the current paradigm that mandates the whole VM to be defined, maintained, and shipped by a single vendor.

Splitting up a VM into modules separates the classic subsystems such as the interpreter, JIT compiler, and garbage collector, from each other. It also separates the language-specific parts from language-independent parts on a fine-grained level. For example, the JIT compiler of a current Java VM contains many global optimizations that are applicable for any language, but also Java-specific parts such as method and field linking. Separating these parts into different modules allows for an easy re-use of language-independent VM parts.

When building the VM for a new language, it is consequently only necessary to define the language-dependent parts for the new language, which is most likely only a small subset of the whole VM. This reuse of modules is especially important in the context of emerging dynamic languages. Instead of building a whole new VM for every language, our approach requires only a small addition to the existing VM framework. To demonstrate this potential, we are in the process of adding support for an additional language to an existing VM.

3. Expected Outcomes

Our project is expected to yield new insights and a design rationale for modular VMs. We have no desire to re-invent the wheel. Hence, our work benefits intelligently from prior research and existing open-source projects. For example, we are using an existing Java VM—Maxine from Oracle Labs [20]—which is already clearly divided into independent subsystems as the basis for our host VM. Maxine is our VM of choice because it is a well-structured Java VM and it is available under an open source license.

Converting Maxine into a modular VM is non-trivial. While high-level components such as the garbage collection algorithm, the layout of objects, and the JIT compiler are exchangeable, it is currently not designed to be modular. Additionally, it is tailored towards the Java VM specification,

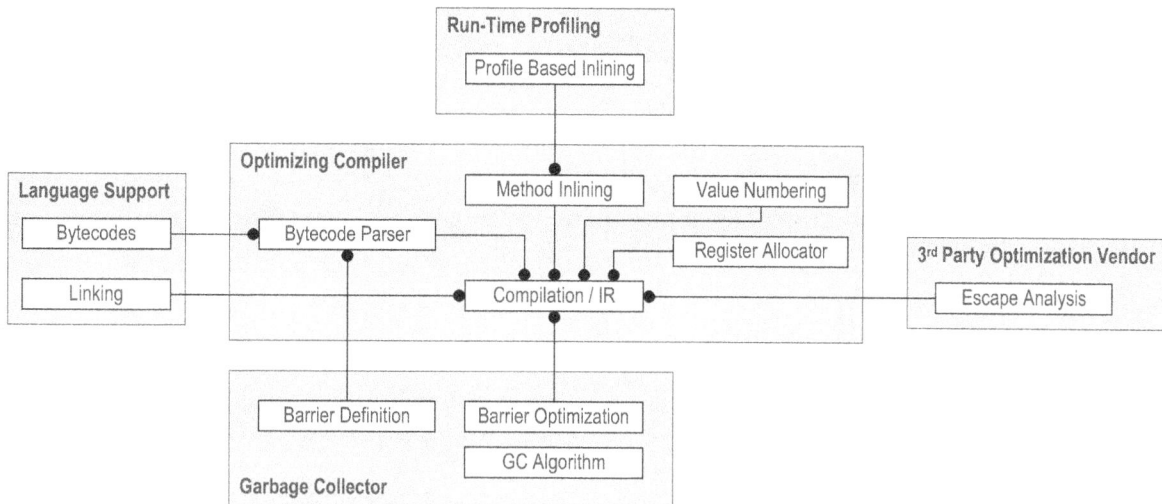

Figure 6. Examples of fine-grained modules for JIT compilation.

and not ready to support multiple languages. For example, the semantics and constraints of Java bytecodes are visible throughout the whole VM, from the class loader to the JIT compiler.

Even the recently added C1X JIT compiler provides no support for different input languages; it only provides an interface between the compiler and the rest of the VM using the intermediate language XIR [31]. We will use C1X as the starting point, but we need to open up the intermediate representation to support both static and dynamic typing, and we need to incorporate run-time type feedback in the compiler. Significant research is necessary throughout the whole VM to isolate the Java-specific parts from the language agnostic parts and re-connect them using a well-defined module interface.

There are many high-quality implementations of dynamic languages available as open-source projects. We want to support at least one dynamic language in addition to Java. For all major dynamic languages, VMs written in Java are available as open-source projects. Among applicable candidates are the Rhino JavaScript VM [27], the JRuby VM for Ruby [17], and the Jython VM for Python [18]. All these VMs currently run *on top* of a Java VM, i.e., from the point of view of the Java VM they are applications. This leads to double interpretation and compilation overhead, which is no longer present in our approach. Incorporating code from an existing VM not only saves development resources, but also allows direct comparison with the original VM. We expect our dynamic VM to be faster than the original because it leverages the optimization system designed to accommodate dynamic languages. However, our system is not limited to existing dynamic languages, but also simplifies and encourages the development of new domain-specific and simple end-user programming languages targeted for special limited programming tasks.

In summary, our research has four expected outcomes.

- The definition of a module system at the VM level. We believe this will significantly lower the cost of supporting new languages efficiently.

- A set of new optimizations that eliminate the possible overhead of modularity and layering of languages.

- Evaluations and experiments with different module configurations, especially with different amounts of code to be bootstrapped.

- A platform and baseline for other researchers that simplifies the development of new optimizations and the comparison of optimizations of different research groups.

4. Realizing the Vision

In previous work, we have experienced both the shortcomings of existing VM structures and the benefits of modular applications. Based on the insights and experience, we are confident that a broad and systematic research on this topic can revolutionize the implementation of VMs.

4.1 Enabling Modularization

The first and fundamental basic step is to define an explicit module structure for VMs. As we do not want to reinvent the wheel, we are using the existing Maxine VM.

The initial module structure is rather coarse-grained and matches the existing subsystem boundaries of Maxine. In future steps, we will then refine the modules and split them to get the desired fine-grained modularity. This process includes the definition of suitable extension points for all parts of the VM. Once all modules are present, we will investigate the minimum set of modules that are necessary to run a Java application.

To get a broader variety of modules and configurations, we will then add a trace-based JIT compiler as an alternative to the existing JIT compiler. This trace-based JIT compiler re-uses several of Maxine's compilation systems. Its integration in the existing system architecture is the first proof-of-concept that the module interfaces are useful to re-use parts of the existing compiler.

Finally, we will start to separate the Java-specific parts into separate modules. This is the first step towards a language-independent VM where special language features are supplied using additional modules.

4.2 Exploiting Modularity

In the second step, we want to add support for a dynamic language. Since all major dynamic languages (e.g., Python, Ruby, or JavaScript) have VMs available written in Java, a smooth integration is possible. We plan to modularize the dynamic language VM and strip away the parts that are already covered by Maxine. The challenge is to re-use as many modules as possible from the previous step. For example, the optimizing JIT compiler can be re-used immediately without larger changes, while the garbage collector needs to be opened to support dynamically growing objects. Therefore, the process of integrating the dynamic language also involves a broadening of the existing modules by providing even more extension points. The resulting dynamic language VM has the potential to outperform existing VMs because it leverages compiler and garbage collector optimizations that were not previously available for dynamic languages.

4.3 Eliminating Module Overhead

In the final stage, we will analyze and optimize inter-module calls in the VM. Following the spirit of feedback-directed dynamic optimizations, we will implement optimizations that specifically target frequently executed inter-module calls. Using profile information and dynamic code specialization, overhead introduced by modularization can be eliminated.

Additionally, we will develop inter-language optimizations. The modular VM approach enables support for multiple static and dynamic languages inside one VM. All code is optimized together, so we can study the commonalities and the differences in the respective optimization approaches. This will demonstrate the full power of our modular VM approach.

Finally, we will perform a quantitative and qualitative analysis of the module overhead. By studying different methods of bootstrapping, the full spectrum from the minimal set of modules to the whole VM can be bootstrapped, while the remaining modules are loaded on demand. This evaluation will answer our primary research question: which amount of modularity and bootstrapping is best for a VM.

5. Related Work

Most research and production quality VMs are internally designed in a fairly modular way. The different subsystems are separated in different packages, namespaces, directories, or other means offered by the language the respective VM is written in. The "modularity" is only expressed as different namespaces and directories and not in minimized dependencies and clear interfaces, and no explicit module system is present. Therefore, we do not consider these VMs to be modular in a fine-grained way. Additionally, these VMs are not extensible at run time. Only a small number of research projects explicitly target the VM structure and modularity.

Haupt et al. propose to disentangle VM architectures using an explicit architecture description language [12, 13]. They use the *VM Architecture Description Language* to describe the interface of a module. It is a mixture of declarative specifications and actual code that is merged into the VM source code. The merging is similar to code weaving of aspect oriented programming. All configuration is performed at compile time, so the resulting VM is not extensible at run time. They then define a product line of VMs using a standard product line modeling tool. Our approach does not require the definition of a separate architecture description language. Instead, we propose to embed the module definitions directly into the source code.

Thomas et al. introduce a *Micro Virtual Machine* (MVM) that is then extended to the JnJVM [30]. MVM is a minimal but nevertheless complete VM that consists of a code loader, an extensible JIT compiler, and I/O functionality. Additionally, it is extensible using aspect oriented programming techniques. For this, MVM includes an aspect weaver that can integrate new VM parts at run time. A small Lisp-like language is used to specify the extensions. JnJVM is a Java VM developed on top of MVM. It is written in the Lisp-like language, and the MVM compiles the JnJVM on the fly when it is loaded. This leads to a high run-time overhead. Our solution will perform all source code compilation at compile time, and provide the option to optimize and combine the modules either at compile time or run time.

Harris presents a prototype *eXtensible Virtual Machine* (XVM) [11] that allows application code to interact with the VM. Because of the inherent safety risk of untrusted application code modifying the VM, the interaction is limited. We do not plan to have direct interactions of applications with the VM (although such modules would be possible to implement), instead we focus on extensibility inside the VM.

Geoffray et al. present I-JVM [9], a Java virtual machine for component isolation in OSGi. They address problems of module isolation. One malicious module can accidentally or deliberately crash the complete application platform. I-JVM isolates the modules so that they can be reliably terminated without affecting other modules. The VM itself is not based on OSGi. However, their ideas on module isolation apply to our envisioned modular VM.

Metacircularity originates from LISP [21]. Its eval() function requires a LISP interpreter, which was defined in

LISP itself. Also, the first successful LISP compiler was already developed in LISP.

The idea was then applied to other languages. For example, the programming environments and compilers for Oberon [33] and Cecil [4] were written in the respective language. This leverages the benefits of the language for the language development itself, and also simplifies reflective access in the language. Modules could be loaded and unloaded on demand, and the use of a bootlinker was explored to manage VM images. However, these languages were statically compiled to machine code and not executed by a VM, so there were no metacircular runtime environments.

Similar ideas apply to Pascal p-Code, one of the predecessors of modern bytecodes [26]. In this case, even whole operating systems were written in the system, allowing the operating system and all applications to be ported easily to different platforms. On the lowest level, p-Code was still interpreted by a small runtime layer that remained separated from the code it executed.

In Smalltalk [7], large parts of the system were written in Smalltalk itself. Powerful reflective facilities allowed the access of class, method, and field metadata objects from within an application. Also, the modular programming style of Smalltalk could be applied to these reflective system parts. However, the core bytecode interpreter of most Smalltalk systems was still written in a statically compiled language. Only the "blue book" reference implementation was written in Smalltalk itself [10], but it was intended only for illustrative purposes.

Squeak [14] is a metacircular Smalltalk VM. It is written in a subset of Smalltalk: a non-object-oriented programming style is necessary to allow the interpreter to be translated to C code, which is then compiled to machine code. The reduced language limits the metacircular benefit because VM extensions have to be coded in a special way before they can be integrated with the VM.

SELF [5] is a language that offers even more dynamic reflective facilities. Every method dispatch is dynamic and can be changed a run time. The original VM was written in C++ and was the incubator for many dynamic and feedback-directed optimizations available in today's VMs.

The *Klein VM* [32] is a metacircular SELF VM written entirely in SELF. The dynamic nature and run-time configurability of this VM probably makes it the VM most closely related to the system we envision. According to its authors, the primary goal for Klein is to achieve feature parity with the existing SELF VM, while reducing the amount of source code by two thirds. Klein achieves a high degree of reuse by trading off performance for architectural simplicity and ease of development. Rather than minimizing the codebase, we seek to make a different set of tradeoffs. We will leverage metacircularity and modularity to support multiple languages while retaining high performance through new, feedback-directed optimizations.

PyPy [28] is a VM for Python, based on a framework useable for any dynamic language, written in Python. It is an example of a dynamic language VM written in a dynamic language itself. Run-time optimizations are performed by a trace-based JIT compiler. During bootstrapping, the VM code is either translated to C code or to the .NET common intermediate language. This requires an additional C compiler or .NET runtime environment for execution.

The two major metacircular research Java VMs are Jikes [2, 16], which was originally developed by IBM and is now used in many research projects, and Maxine [20], which is a novel research VM developed by Oracle. The execution environment of Jikes is fairly modular and provides different JIT compilers, and its *Memory Manager Toolkit* (MMTk) allows to integrate new garbage collection algorithms. However, there is no explicit concept of modules in the VM. Maxine provides modularity using the concepts of schemes and snippets. A scheme encapsulates the different subsystems, e.g., there is a scheme that specifies how fields are accessed. The code for the field access is then compiled to a snippet when the VM is started, and the JIT compiler uses the snippet when compiling field access bytecodes. Although this design disentangles different VM subsystems quite well, there is still no extensibility at run time and no fine-grained modularity.

The *Open Runtime Platform* (ORP) [6] developed by Intel is a research VM targeted not only towards multiple architectures, but also towards multiple languages. It can run either Java or Common Language Infrastructure (CLI) applications by applying the compile-only approach. It is available as open source from [23], but this version seems to be quite old and does not reflect the current development version of Intel. ORP offers a flexible compiler interface, and different JIT compilers were developed. An example is the *StarJIT* compiler [1].

The *Dynamic Runtime Layer Virtual Machine* (DRLVM) of Apache Harmony [3] is a Java VM written in C++. Modularity is a key feature of the VM: it is separated in a small number of coarse-grained modules with well-defined interfaces. Modules are compiled to separate libraries that are dynamically linked at run time. However, inter-module calls cannot be optimized at run time because the VM is written in C++. There is no fine-grained modularity.

The Java HotSpot™ VM of Oracle [22] is a production-quality open-source Java VM written in C++. The source code base contains two interpreters, two JIT compilers, and multiple different garbage collection algorithms (some of them being parallel or concurrent). However, these parts are not separated into modules, so it is sometimes difficult to identify the boundaries of and interfaces between these subsystems in the source code. Only the compiler interface, which separates the client compiler [19] and the server compiler [25] from the rest of the VM, is explicitly defined.

6. Conclusions

Modularity for virtual machines is a promising research area: our project has the ability to completely change the way production-quality virtual machines are built. When companies see that modular VMs are possible without performance overhead, they will quickly adapt this paradigm and use it when they design new VMs, or even retrofit their existing VMs.

Our preliminary work extends the Maxine VM and serves as a foundation towards addressing issues central to the three mentioned case studies. By doing so, we expect to validate our research hypotheses and in turn inspire further research on modular VM architectures.

Acknowledgments

Parts of this effort have been sponsored by the National Science Foundation under grant CCF-1117162 and by Samsung Telecommunications America under Agreement No. 51070. Any opinions, findings, and conclusions or recommendations expressed in this material are those of the authors and should not be interpreted as necessarily representing the official views, policies or endorsements, either expressed or implied, of the National Science Foundation (NSF), nor that of Samsung Telecommunications America. The authors also gratefully acknowledges gifts from Adobe and Google.

Oracle and Java are registered trademarks of Oracle and/or its affiliates. Other names may be trademarks of their respective owners.

References

[1] A.-R. Adl-Tabatabai, J. Bharadwaj, D.-Y. Chen, A. Ghuloum, V. Menon, B. Murphy, M. Serrano, and T. Shpeisman. The StarJIT compiler: A dynamic compiler for managed runtime environments. *Intel Technology Journal*, 7(1):19–31, 2003.

[2] B. Alpern, C. R. Attanasio, J. J. Barton, M. G. Burke, P.Cheng, J.-D. Choi, A. Cocchi, S. J. Fink, D. Grove, M. Hind, S. F. Hummel, D. Lieber, V. Litvinov, M. F. Mergen, T. Ngo, J. R. Russell, V. Sarkar, M. J. Serrano, J. C. Shepherd, S. E. Smith, V. C. Sreedhar, H. Srinivasan, and J. Whaley. The Jalapeño virtual machine. *IBM Systems Journal*, 39(1):211–238, 2000.

[3] Apache. *Apache Harmony, Dynamic Runtime Layer Virtual Machine*, 2010. http://harmony.apache.org/subcomponents/drlvm/.

[4] C. Chambers. The Cecil language specification and rationale, version 3.0. Technical report, Department of Computer Science and Engineering, University of Washington, 1998.

[5] C. Chambers, D. Ungar, and E. Lee. An efficient implementation of SELF, a dynamically-typed object-oriented language based on prototypes. In *Proceedings of the ACM SIGPLAN Conference on Object-Oriented Programming Systems, Languages, and Applications*, pages 49–70. ACM Press, 1989. doi: 10.1145/74878.74884.

[6] M. Cierniak, M. Eng, N. Glew, B. Lewis, and J. Stichnoth. The open runtime platform: a flexible high-performance managed runtime environment. *Concurrency and Computation:*

Practice and Experience, 17(5-6):617–637, 2005. doi: 10.1002/cpe.852.

[7] L. P. Deutsch and A. M. Schiffman. Efficient implementation of the Smalltalk-80 system. In *Proceedings of the ACM SIGACT-SIGPLAN Symposium on Principles of Programming Languages*, pages 297–302. ACM Press, 1984. doi: 10.1145/800017.800542.

[8] Dynamic Language Runtime. *Dynamic Language Runtime*, 2010. http://dlr.codeplex.com/.

[9] N. Geoffray, G. Thomas, G. Muller, P. Parrend, S. Frénot, and B. Folliot. I-JVM: a Java virtual machine for component isolation in OSGi. In *Proceedings of the International Conference on Dependable Systems and Networks*, pages 544–553. IEEE Computer Society, 2009. doi: 10.1109/DSN.2009.5270296.

[10] A. Goldberg and D. Robson. *Smalltalk-80: The Language and Its Implementation.* Addison-Wesley, 1983.

[11] T. L. Harris. *Extensible Virtual Machines.* PhD thesis, Computer Laboratory, University of Cambridge, UK, 2001.

[12] M. Haupt, B. Adams, S. Timbermont, C. Gibbs, Y. Coady, and R. Hirschfeld. Disentangling virtual machine architecture. *IET Software*, 3:201–218, 2009. doi: 10.1049/iet-sen.2007.0121.

[13] M. Haupt, S. Marr, and R. Hirschfeld. CSOM/PL - A virtual machine product line. *Journal of Object Technology*, 10:12:1–30, 2011. doi: 10.5381/jot.2011.10.1.a12.

[14] D. Ingalls, T. Kaehler, J. Maloney, S. Wallace, and A. Kay. Back to the future: the story of Squeak, a practical Smalltalk written in itself. In *Proceedings of the ACM SIGPLAN Conference on Object-Oriented Programming Systems, Languages, and Applications*, pages 318–326. ACM Press, 1997. doi: 10.1145/263698.263754.

[15] Java Specification Request 223. *Java Specification Request 223: Scripting for the Java^{TM} Platform*, 2006. http://www.jcp.org/en/jsr/detail?id=223.

[16] Jikes. *Jikes RVM*, 2010. http://www.jikesrvm.org/.

[17] JRuby. *JRuby*, 2010. http://www.jruby.org/.

[18] Jython. *Jython*, 2010. http://www.jython.org//.

[19] T. Kotzmann, C. Wimmer, H. Mössenböck, T. Rodriguez, K. Russell, and D. Cox. Design of the Java HotSpot^{TM} client compiler for Java 6. *ACM Transactions on Architecture and Code Optimization*, 5(1):Article 7, 2008. doi: 10.1145/1369396.1370017.

[20] Maxine. *Maxine Research Virtual Machine*, 2010. https://wikis.oracle.com/display/MaxineVM/.

[21] J. McCarthy. History of LISP. In *Proceedings of History of Programming Languages*, pages 173–185. ACM Press, 1978. doi: 10.1145/960118.808387.

[22] Oracle. *The Java HotSpot Performance Engine Architecture*, 2006. http://www.oracle.com/technetwork/java/whitepaper-135217.html.

[23] ORP. *Open Runtime Platform*, 2010. Intel Corp. http://sourceforge.net/projects/orp/.

[24] OSGi. *OSGi - The Dynamic Module System for Java*, 2010. http://www.osgi.org/.

[25] M. Paleczny, C. Vick, and C. Click. The Java HotSpot™ server compiler. In *Proceedings of the Java Virtual Machine Research and Technology Symposium*, pages 1–12. USENIX, 2001.

[26] S. Pemberton and M. Daniels. *Pascal Implementation: The P4 Compiler and Interpreter*. Ellis Horwood, 1983.

[27] Rhino. *Rhino: JavaScript for Java*, 2010. http://www.mozilla.org/rhino/.

[28] A. Rigo and S. Pedroni. PyPy's approach to virtual machine construction. In *Companion to the ACM SIGPLAN Conference on Object-Oriented Programming Systems, Languages, and Applications*, pages 944–953. ACM Press, 2006. doi: 10.1145/1176617.1176753.

[29] R. Strniša, P. Sewell, and M. Parkinson. The Java module system: core design and semantic definition. In *Proceedings of the ACM SIGPLAN Conference on Object-Oriented Programming Systems, Languages, and Applications*, pages 499–514. ACM Press, 2007. doi: 10.1145/1297027.1297064.

[30] G. Thomas, N. Geoffray, C. Clément, and B. Folliot. Designing highly flexible virtual machines: The JnJVM experience. *Software: Practice and Experience*, 38(15):1643–1675, 2008. doi: 10.1002/spe.887.

[31] B. L. Titzer, T. Würthinger, D. Simon, and M. Cintra. Improving compiler-runtime separation with XIR. In *Proceedings of the ACM/USENIX International Conference on Virtual Execution Environments*, pages 39–50. ACM Press, 2010. doi: 10.1145/1735997.1736005.

[32] D. Ungar, A. Spitz, and A. Ausch. Constructing a metacircular virtual machine in an exploratory programming environment. In *Companion to the ACM SIGPLAN Conference on Object-Oriented Programming Systems, Languages, and Applications*, pages 11–20. ACM Press, 2005. doi: 10.1145/1094855.1094865.

[33] N. Wirth and J. Gutknecht. *Project Oberon*. Addison-Wesley, 1992.

An Object-Oriented Framework for Aspect-Oriented Languages

Marko van Dooren *   Eric Steegmans   Wouter Joosen

IBBT-DistriNet, KU Leuven, 3001 Leuven, Belgium.

{marko,eric,wouter}@cs.kuleuven.be

Abstract

Aspect-orientation is a mechanism for modularizing cross-cutting concerns that has been added to many existing software engineering languages. The implementations of aspect-oriented language extensions, however, are typically tied to a specific base language. There is little or no code reuse between aspect-oriented extensions for different base languages, which makes these extensions difficult and expensive to build. In addition, existing software engineering tools do not work with the resulting aspect-oriented languages unless new plugins are developed.

We present Carpenter, an object-oriented framework for developing aspect-oriented language extensions. An aspect language is developed by reusing classes for generic language constructs from Carpenter, and writing subclasses of the abstractions in Carpenter to define new language constructs. An aspect weaver is created by implementing framework interfaces to weave language-specific constructs. The coordination of the weaving process is done by the Carpenter framework. Aspect languages developed with Carpenter get full IDE support with only a few lines of code. We have used our framework to create aspect weavers for Java, JLo, and AspectU.

Categories and Subject Descriptors D.3.3 [*Language Constructs and Features*]: Frameworks

General Terms Languages

Keywords Aspect, language, framework

1. Introduction

Aspect-orientation is an increasingly used technique to modularize cross-cutting concerns. Originally developed for programming languages, with AspectJ [20] as the main imple-

---

* Post-doctoral researcher of the Fund for Scientific Research - Flanders.

mentation, the technique is now being used in more and more languages in various stages of the software development process. Aspect-orientation has been added to use cases [17, 19, 33], to architectural description languages [10, 25, 27, 28], and to many programming languages such as C++ [34] and C# [32]. In addition to adding aspect-orientation to existing languages, there is also a need to add new aspect-oriented capabilities to existing aspect-oriented languages [13, 22, 24, 36].

The implementations of the aspect-oriented extensions of most languages, however, are typically written from scratch. This is an error-prone and costly way to create an aspect language. To make matters worse, advanced programming tools, which are essential in a modern software development process, do not work with the aspect-oriented versions of the languages they were designed for. Plugins must be developed to provide tool-support for the new aspect language.

Fradet and Südholt [8] already recognized in 1998 that aspect weaving can be performed using a general transformation framework because the mechanism is always the same. A cross-cutting concern is captured as an advice that is woven into the model at the places (join point shadows) specified by pointcut expressions.

A number of approaches exist to improve the development of aspect-oriented languages. SourceWeave.NET [18], Weave.NET [21], LOOM.NET [32], and Aspect.NET [30] exploit the common language infrastructure of the .NET platform to add aspect-orientation to a language. These approaches, however, are inherently limited to programming languages supporting .NET. In addition, they force programmers to write aspects using language constructs of the common intermediate language (CIL), which is not appropriate for logic or functional programming. The abc compiler [1] and Reflex AOP [35] simplify the development of aspect languages, but the host language is limited to Java, or an extension of Java. Roychoudhury et al. [29] present a model-driven approach for creating aspect languages. Their approach is generic, but the developer of an aspect language must work with multiple transformation languages, and transformations that generate other transformations.

The contribution of this paper is the development of an object-oriented framework for developing aspect-oriented languages, called Carpenter. In our approach, aspect languages are developed by implementing only the language-specific constructs and their accompanying weavers directly using standard object-oriented techniques. Common language constructs for aspect languages, and most of the infrastructure for aspect weavers are provided by Carpenter. To provide more specialized support for families of languages, paradigm-specific layers can be developed. The current Carpenter framework contains such a layer for object-oriented programming languages. We evaluated the Carpenter framework to develop aspect-oriented extensions of Java, JLo, and a language for use cases.

Outline

The remainder of the paper is structured as follows. In Section 2 we discuss the requirements for easily creating aspect-oriented languages. In Section 3 we give an overview of the Carpenter framework, which is discussed in more detail in Section 4. We discuss the creation of parsers in Section 5. We evaluate our approach in Section 6 by implementing a aspect-oriented extensions for Java, JLo, and a language for use cases. We discuss related work in Section 7, and conclude in Section 8.

2. Requirements

In this section, we discuss the requirements for simplifying the development of aspect-oriented languages.

In the process of developing aspect-oriented languages, we identify three main stakeholders: the developer of the base language, the developer of the aspect-oriented extension of a language, and the developer of an aspect weaver for an aspect-oriented language. Note that the second and third stakeholders are not necessarily the same. For example, multiple aspect weavers can be created for a single aspect-oriented language to perform different kinds of optimizations, such as maximizing the execution speed of the woven program, or minimizing its size.

To simplify the development of aspect-oriented languages, we identify the following main requirements for the different stakeholders. The involved stakeholders are shown between parentheses for each requirement.

1. **A language- and paradigm-independent approach:** *(all)* The approach must be applicable to all types of languages, from requirements engineering languages to domain specific programming languages.

2. **Modularity of aspect weavers:** *(aspect weaver developer)* Similarly, the aspect weaving mechanisms for many aspect-oriented languages have much functionality in common. Such common functionality should be provided in reusable modules that can be composed by the developer of an aspect-oriented language. For example, the high-level orchestration is always the same: find join point shadows, sort the advices per shadow, and perform the actual weaving. The developer for a particular

aspect-oriented language extension should not have to implement this process from scratch.

3. **Modularity of aspect-oriented language constructs:** *(aspect weaver developer, aspect language developer)* Multiple aspect-oriented languages can have language constructs in common, such as generic pointcut expressions and advice types. The developer of an aspect-oriented language extension must be able to reuse the implementations of the semantics of these language constructs in a modular way.

4. **Modularity of the base language:** *(all)* The semantics and the parser for the base language can be very complex. Therefore, their implementations should be reusable to build language extensions. The semantics of language extensions should be plugged into the semantics of the base language. In addition, if a base language is changed (for example in a new version) in a way that does not affect an extension of that language, then that extension should not require any changes to work with the new version of the base language.

Requirements 2 and 3 apply at multiple levels in the language hierarchy. For example, aspect-oriented extensions of languages that belong to a particular family, such as object-oriented programming languages, should be able to share common pointcut expressions and weaving functionality. Similarly, an aspect-oriented extension of JLo, which itself is an extension of Java, should be able to reuse the implementation of the aspect-oriented extension of Java.

For requirements 2, 3, and 4 the set of stakeholders becomes bigger with every step. This reflects the stack structure of the process. An aspect weaver is built for an aspect language, which is built for a base language. Reusing aspect weaving functionality across different aspect-oriented languages is very difficult if those languages cannot share language constructs. Reusing aspect-oriented language constructs and their semantics is very difficult if the base languages cannot share language constructs.

3. An Object-Oriented Approach

Our approach is based on the Chameleon framework, which is a generic object-oriented framework for language development. Figure 1 illustrates the architecture of our approach. Layers with a thick black border are part of Carpenter, while layers with a thick gray border are part of Chameleon. To keep the figure simple, arrows for *uses* relations are only drawn towards the most specific layer that is used by another layer. The *super* layers are used as well.

The top of the language hierarchy is the Chameleon layer for generic language constructs. Language constructs do not only contain the structure of a program – like AST nodes – but they also encapsulate the static semantics. For example, each language construct has a `verify` method to determine whether it is valid, such tool developers do not have

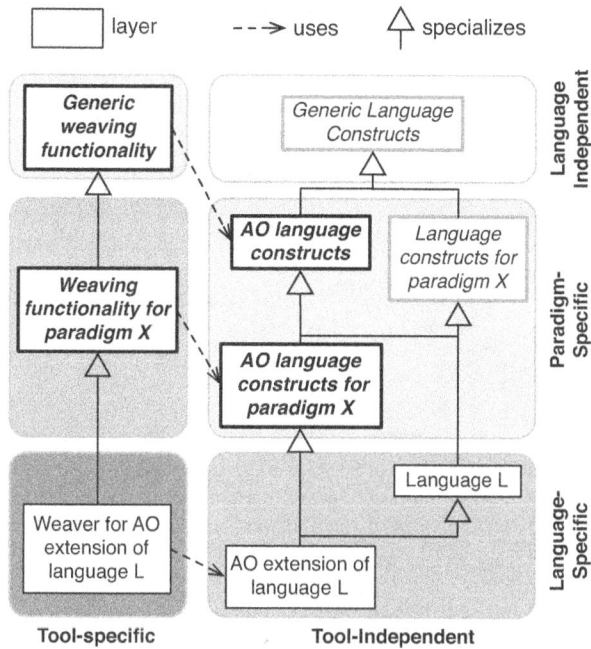

Figure 1. The architecture of Carpenter.

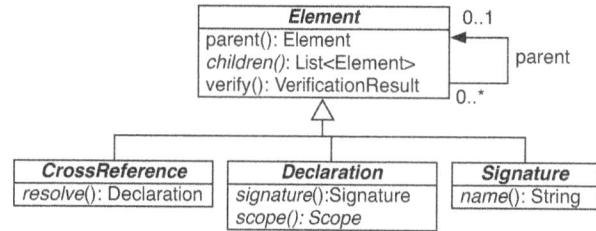

Figure 2. A few core abstractions of Chameleon.

The hierarchy for aspect weavers – or any other tool – follows the same layering structure. The language-independent weaving code is written in the top layer, while subsequent layers add support for weaving specific paradigms of language or specific languages. For example, the top layer of the aspect weaver of Carpenter contains the code to coordinate the weaving process. It uses abstractions such as `PointcutExpression` to find join point shadows without having to know which aspect-oriented language is used. The actual weaving is performed by lower layers since that requires paradigm-specific or language-specific knowledge.

3.1 Core Abstractions of Chameleon

Figure 2 shows a simplified class diagram of the most important classes of Chameleon that are used in Carpenter. Every language construct implements the top interface `Element`, which has methods for navigating the lexical structure of a model. The `verify` method checks whether or not an element is valid.

A `Declaration` is any element that has a signature (name). Examples of declarations are methods, class, aspects, use cases, and so forth. A `Signature` has at least a string that represents its name, but can also contain additional information such as parameter names and types.

A cross-reference is any element that references a declaration. Examples are method invocations, type names, and so forth. The `resolve` method encodes part of the semantics of the cross-reference by computing which declaration is referenced. The Chameleon IDE, for example, uses this method to support navigable hyperlinks without having to know which concrete language is used.

4. A Framework for Aspect Languages

In this section, we discuss the most important classes of the Carpenter framework. In section 4.1, we discuss the top layer for aspect-oriented languages. In section 4.2 we discuss the top layer for aspect weavers. In section 4.3 we discuss the layer for object-oriented languages.

Because of space concerns, the class diagrams that we use throughout the paper are *simplifications* of the real framework. As such, we omit all elements that are not required for explaining our approach.

to duplicate these semantics. The top layer also contains many abstractions for similar language constructs. For example, a `Declaration` is any language construct that has a `Signature`, such as a type, a method, or a use case. These abstractions greatly improve the language-independence of software engineering tools.

Below the top layer, there are paradigm-specific layers. Top layer of the Carpenter framework provides classes for generic aspect-oriented language constructs. Many pointcut expressions can implemented directly in this layer by using the abstractions provided by the top layer. The `within` pointcut expression, for example, matches any element that is lexically within a certain `Declaration`. As such, this pointcut expression can be reused directly in any aspect-oriented language. The top layer of Carpenter also provides abstractions to improve the language-independence of aspect-oriented tools.

Multi-paradigm layers provide additional language constructs for language that belong to a specific combination of paradigms. For example, we have implemented a layer in Carpenter for aspect-oriented extensions of object-oriented programming languages. This layer contains for example a pointcut expression for method invocations.

At the bottom of the hierarchy are the implementations of concrete languages. A concrete aspect-oriented language `AO-L` reuses both the implementation of the base language L, and the implementation of the aspect-oriented language constructs for the paradigm of L. Aspect-oriented language constructs that are specific for L are implemented in `AO-L`.

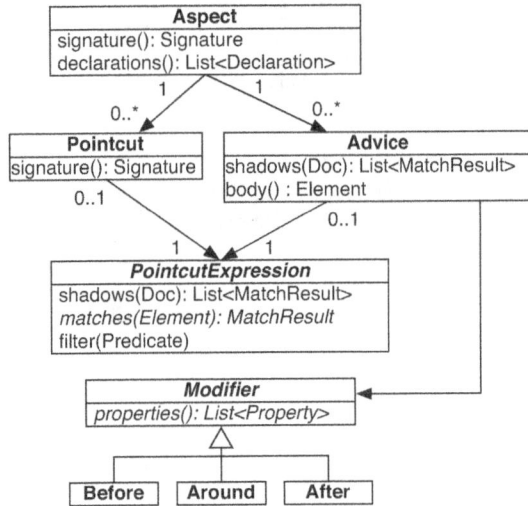

Figure 3. Aspects.

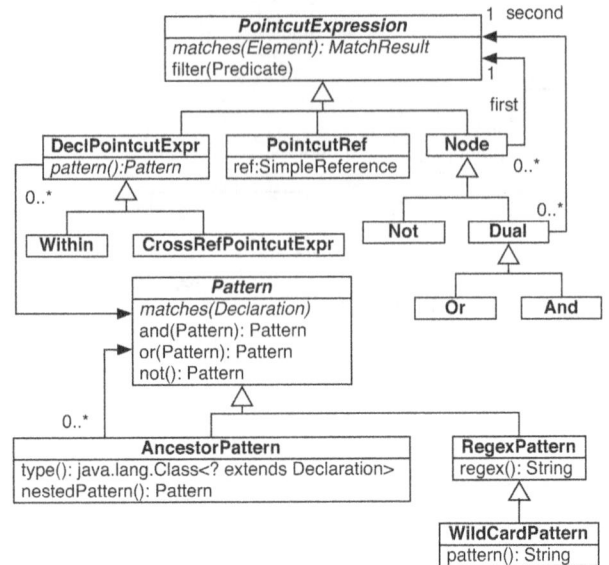

Figure 4. Pointcut expressions.

4.1 Abstractions For an Aspect-oriented Language

Figure 3 shows the generic classes to model aspects. An aspect has a name, pointcuts, and advices. A pointcut has a name and a pointcut expression. An advice has a body, which in general can be any kind of element, and a pointcut expression. The types of advice are modeled as modifiers and accompanying properties, which are omitted to save space. Neither a pointcut nor an advice can have formal parameters in the top layer of the framework, since they are not available in all languages. Support for parameters is added in the layer for object-oriented languages.

Figure 4 shows a number of language constructs of the generic pointcut language. The semantics of a pointcut expression is defined by its `matches` method, which determines whether the pointcut expression matches a potential join point shadow. Note that redefinitions of the `matches` methods are not shown to save space. The `filter` method is used to compute the pointcut residue, which is the dynamic subtree of a pointcut expression.

The generic pointcut language supports disjunction, conjunction, and negation, and provides classes for a number of concrete pointcuts. A pointcut expression (`PointcutRef`) delegates join point shadow matching to an existing pointcut. It matches each element that is matched by the referenced pointcut. The `CrossRefPointcutExpr` class selects join point shadows that are cross-references and that reference a declaration that satisfies a certain pattern. Similarly, the `Within` expression matches elements that are lexically defined within a declaration that satisfies a pattern. A number of typical patterns for aspect-oriented programming are provided by the framework. The regular expression and wildcard patterns constrain the signature of a declaration, while the container pattern puts a constraint on the nearest lexical parent declaration of a certain type. This can be used for example, to match references to a field name `f` of class `T`.

It is important to note that the leaf classes in Figure 4 are concrete and have only dependencies with classes from the top-level Chameleon layer. Therefore, the classes shown in Figure 4 can be used regardless of the language to which aspect-orientation is added. The developer of the aspect language must only add classes for new language constructs.

4.2 The Weaving Process

In this section, we present the generic weaving infrastructure of Carpenter. It is important to note, however, that whereas the generic aspect language of the previous section resembles a library due to the amount of concrete classes, the weaving infrastructure is more like a real framework with many abstract classes. This is because selection of join point shadows can be done easily based on high-level abstractions, but the actual weaving requires construction and manipulation of elements at the level of the concrete language.

Figure 5 shows the top classes of the aspect weaver infrastructure. The `AspectWeaver` class represents the entire aspect weaver. The actual weaving is delegated to a linked list of `Weaver` objects that implement the *Chain of Responsibility* design pattern [9]. To define the order in which multiple aspects are applied to a single join point shadow, the aspect weaver uses a sorting strategy. Each aspect language defines a concrete subclass of `AspectWeaver` that initializes the weaver chain and the sorting *Strategy*. Each subclass of `Weaver` is responsible for weaving one or more combinations of a type of advice and and type of join point shadow.

The weavers do not immediately perform the weaving because the order in which the aspects for a particular join point shadow must be woven does not correspond to the order in which advice objects are selected by the as-

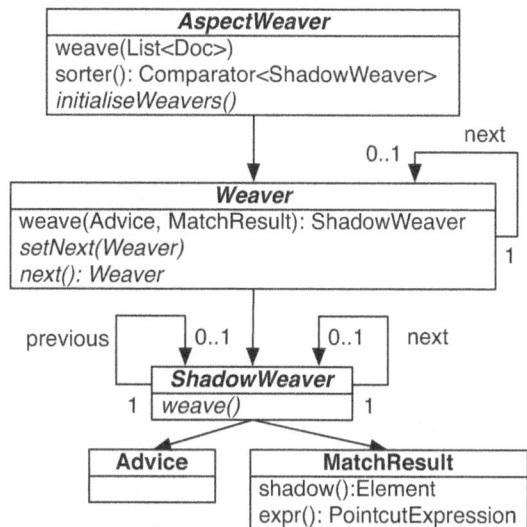

Figure 5. The aspect weaver infrastructure.

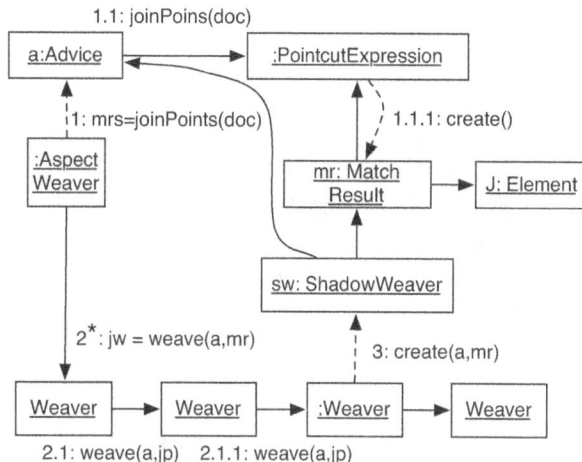

Figure 6. Phase 1: creating shadow weavers.

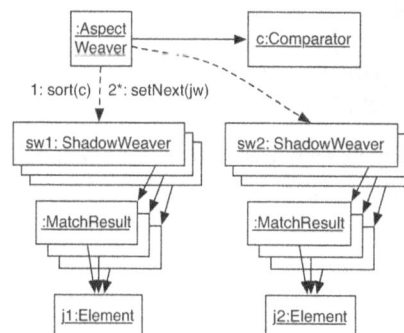

Figure 7. Phase 2: sorting the shadow weavers.

pect weaver. Instead, they create `ShadowWeaver` objects. A `ShadowWeaver` is responsible for weaving one particular advice for a particular join point shadow. A `ShadowWeaver` contains a reference to the advice that must be woven and a `MatchResult` object. A `MatchResult` object is created during selection of the join point shadows and keeps a reference to the shadow and the pointcut (sub)expression that matched the shadow. The reference to the pointcut (sub)expression is stored to allow support for dynamic pointcut expressions. For such pointcut expressions, it is necessary to know exactly which part of the pointcut expression of an advice matched the join point shadow such that the correct dynamic code can be inserted. For example, if pointcut expression `within(T) & if(f()) | within(S) & if(g())` matches within T, only code for evaluating `f()` should be inserted. The `ShadowWeaver` objects for a particular shadow will be connected to form a doubly linked list. This allows the various advices for a single join point shadow to be chained together correctly during the actual weaving.

Figures 6, 7, and 8 illustrate the weaving process. The solid arrows in collaboration diagrams denote references that are stored in fields, whereas the striped arrows denote references via local variables. Note that the messages in the collaboration diagrams are not exact representations of the code in the classes of Figure 5 since these classes are abstract. For example, the `create` call will be performed by a subclass of `Weaver`, and will create an object of a subclass of `ShadowWeaver`.

For each advice in the model, the aspect weaver asks the advice to which join point shadows it must be applied. The advice delegates this call to its pointcut expression, which encapsulates the semantics of join point shadow matching. The resulting `MatchResult` objects (mr in the figure) are then given to the chain of weavers, together with the advice.

In this figure, only the call for weaving a single combination of advice and match result is shown. In this case, the third weaver decides it is responsible for weaving this combination, and creates a shadow weaver that will perform the actual weaving.

After passing all join point shadows to the chain of weavers, the aspect weaver builds a map with the shadows as keys, and a collection of `ShadowWeaver` objects as the value. These collections are then sorted, and the shadow weavers are linked together.

Finally, the `weave` method is invoked on the first shadow weaver to start the actual weaving process. Each shadow weaver first passes control to the next one in the list, and then weaves its own advice. The actual weaving is performed in two steps. In the first step, any infrastructure is generated to store the advice. This can for example be a method. In the second step, the join point shadow is transformed to incorporate the advice, for example an expression can be replaced with an invocation of the method that contains the advice code. The second step is only performed by the first shadow weaver in the chain. Every shadow weaver N beyond the first one will instead return an element that allows the previous shadow weaver P in the chain to incorporate the

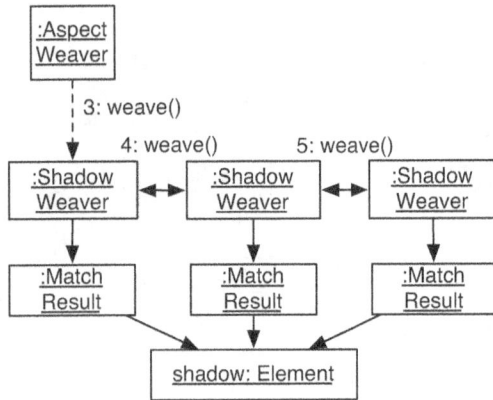

Figure 8. Phase 3: performing the weaving.

advice woven by N in the advice woven by P. Therefore, all shadow weavers restrict the kind of shadow weaver that they can be connected to, such that they know how to process the result of the next shadow weaver. We do not consider this to be a severe restriction since we do not know of a situation where this would be inappropriate

4.3 The Object-Oriented Layer of Carpenter

The OO layer of Carpenter provides additional support for adding aspects to object-oriented programming languages and for the corresponding weavers. The code in this layer assumes that the host language is an object-oriented programming language, and can therefore rely on abstractions defined in the OO layer of Chameleon.

4.3.1 A Pointcut Language for OO Languages

Figure 9 shows the support for exposing context information via parameters is provided. Both pointcuts and advice get a list of formal parameters, which are defined in the Chameleon OO layer. The pointcut expressions that expose parameters are taken from the AspectJ pointcut language. They are used within the shadow weavers to insert local variable in the generated code. In addition, a pointcut expression is added to reference a pointcut that has parameters.

Support for matching method and constructor invocations, and field reads is provided through new subclasses of `DeclarationPattern` that are similar to those of Figure 4. For reasons of space, we do not show a separate class diagram for the new patterns. These patterns can be used together with the pointcut expression for cross-references, which is defined in the top layer of Carpenter.

4.3.2 Advice Weaving for OO Languages

Support for advice weaving is limited to providing helper classes to perform the weaving. Generating the actual language specific code is the responsibility of the language module of the specific aspect language. The OO layer of Carpenter offers classes to facilitate weaving advice for expressions and statements. TO create language constructs that

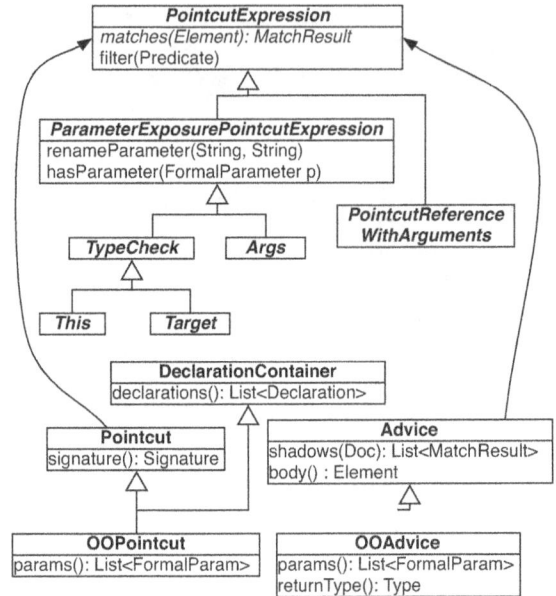

Figure 9. Exposing context in pointcuts and advice.

are represented differently in different object-oriented languages, such as `if-then-else` statements and exception handlers, factories are used.

The OO layer also contains classes for orchestrating the binding of context information in the form of parameters. Shadow weavers for pointcut expressions that support parameter exposure the `RuntimeContextProvider` interface. This interface is used by the parameter binder class of the OO layer to add parameters to the advice and bind them to the appropriate values in the context.

5. Creating Parsers for Aspect Languages

Gray et al. identify parser construction as one of the main challenges for constructing aspect weavers [11]. First, there is a need for a good parser for the base language. Second, the parser for the base language must be extended with a syntax for defining aspects.

In this section, we report on our experience with using the ANTLR [26] parser generator to construct parser for aspect-oriented languages. ANTLR supports composition of grammars, and grammar files are available for many existing languages. Other parsing technologies can be used, though, since Chameleon hides parsing behind a generic interface.

Figure 10 illustrates how a parser for an aspect-oriented extension of Java is created in ANTLR. In this figure, the double arrows denotes imports. The grammar of Java is defined in two files: one for the lexer (JavaL.g) and one for the parser (JavaP.g). The parser file contains the syntax rules for Java, along with semantics actions that create on object representation of the model. To construct an actual Java parser, both files are imported in a root parser file (Java.g). To add syntax definitions for aspect-oriented programming, both the

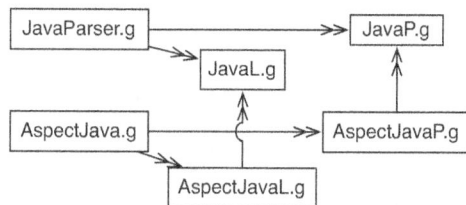

Figure 10. Extending a parser to support aspects.

lexer and parser are extended and the recombined into a new parser. Extending the lexer and parser of Java is done by importing them in the lexer and parser of AspectJava, and then overriding and adding syntax definitions.

Multiple inheritance in ANTLR should make it possible to reuse the grammar rules for generic aspect-oriented language constructs, but a bug in ANTLR prevented us from writing the required grammar compositions. In addition, ANTLR does not allow the addition of a case to a syntactic rule in a modular way. This is needed for example to add `proceed` to the existing Java expressions such that it can be used in advice code. Currently, either all existing cases of the rule for expressions must be duplicated in the overriding definition, or the original Java must be refactored. We plan to experiment with PPG [3] or Rats! [12] to reuse the grammar rules for generic aspect-oriented language constructs.

6. Evaluation

In this section we evaluate Carpenter by building a number of aspect oriented language extensions and measuring the amount of work that is required. We first discuss the evaluation approach in Section 6.1. We then discuss the three aspect-oriented languages that we developed in Sections 6.2, 6.3 and 6.4. Finally we summarize the results of the case studies by revisiting the requirements in Section 6.5.

6.1 Evaluation Approach

We have used the Carpenter framework by building aspect weavers for the Java and JLo, which is an extension of Java. We have also developed a weaver for the AspectU language, which adds aspect-orientation to use cases. The implementations of these languages and the Carpenter framework are available online [37].

We use the size of the code base for each extension as an indication of the amount of work that is required to create the extension. Therefore, the line counts do not include comments, generated code (such as imports), and lines that contain only braces or brackets. Figure 11 shows the size of the generic and object-oriented layers of Chameleon and Carpenter, along with the size of the Chameleon IDE. The bold rows in the tables in this section are used for code that is related to aspect-orientation.

The Chameleon Eclipse IDE is an Eclipse plugin that uses Chameleon for modeling the source of a project. The IDE uses only a few abstractions of Chameleon to support a number of essential features for modern IDEs. An outline shows a tree structure of the declarations in a file. Navigable hyperlinks allows a user to click on a cross-reference after which the IDE jumps to the definition of the referenced declaration. Errors in the model are reported by underlining the problem region in red and adding an entry to the *problem view* of Eclipse. Language-specific requirements of the IDE are hidden behind interfaces that must be implemented to provide support for a concrete language. This mostly concerns parsing, providing meta-information such as the positions of elements, and optionally custom visualizations.

6.2 An Aspect-oriented Extension of Java

We have implemented an aspect weaver for Java 1.5, which we call AspectJava in the remainder of this paper. The AspectJava weaver does not generate bytecode, but generates Java source code instead. The supported advice types are: *after*, *before*, *around*, *after returning*, and *after throwing*. AspectJava supports the following pointcut expressions: calls of methods based on their signature or annotation, field reads, catch clauses, delegation to pointcuts, elements within a certain type or method, class cast expressions, dynamic pointcut conditions (`if`), run-time condition based on the type of arguments, and the target or receiver of a message.

The advice infrastructure factories for all expressions generate static methods that contain the advice. Each shadow weaver provides support for weaving multiple advices into a single join point shadow by generating an invocation of the static method generated by the next shadow weaver in the chain. Passing of arguments and invoking the original method call (if the join point shadow is a method or constructor invocation) is done using reflection.

The motivation for using reflection was to make it easier to get the generated Java source code accepted by the Java type checker. The downside of using reflection in the generated advice infrastructure, however, is that the code of the shadow weavers becomes less reusable. The reflective capabilities of for example Java, Smalltalk, and C++ are too different to be able to extract much common code. The static structures of these languages, however, have much more in common. Implementing a factory to generate for example, a method that behaves like a static method in Java is much

	LOC
Top layer of Chameleon	4644
Chameleon Eclipse IDE	6989
Top layer for aspect-oriented Languages	**856**
Top layer for aspect weavers	**433**
OO layer of Chameleon	7640
OO layer for aspect-oriented languages	**895**
OO layer for aspect weavers	**234**

Figure 11. Line counts for Chameleon and Carpenter.

Java language	5183
Java grammar file	1170
Java plugin for Chameleon IDE	223
AspectJava language	**126**
AspectJava weaver	**1438**
AspectJava grammar file	**151**
AspectJava plugin for Chameleon IDE	**39**

Figure 12. Line counts for Java and AspectJava.

	LOC
JLo language	1663
JLo to Java compiler	1703
JLo grammar file	233
JLo plugin for Chameleon IDE	92
AspectJLo language	**9**
AspectJLo weaver	**267**
AspectJLo grammar file	**235 (86)**
AspectJLo plugin for Chameleon IDE	**37**

Figure 13. Line counts for JLo and AspectJLo.

easier. In addition, such factories are also reusable for creating other tools such as a refactoring tool. Having a refactoring tool that generates reflective code, even if it does so correctly, does not seem like a good idea. The use of reflective code also prevented us from implementing the functionality for exposing context information in Carpenter. The orchestration of the process is done in Carpenter, but since formal method parameters are part of the context information, the code mechanism for context information also suffers from our choice to generate reflective code. An additional problem is that the code for generating the reflective Java code in some of the shadow weavers for run-time pointcut expressions is hard to read.

The table in Figure 12 shows the line counts for AspectJava and the language module for Java. It is clear from these numbers that the framework approach works very well for the definition of the AspectJava language itself. Most aspect-oriented language constructs can be reused from CarpenterThe entire base language is reused from the Java language module. The code for Java specific aspect-oriented language constructs (126 LOC) is less than 7% of the total code for the aspect-oriented language constructs in AspectJava. Since AspectJava reuses virtually all code for aspect-oriented language constructs from the generic and OO layers of Carpenter, this total is 126+895+856=1877 LOC. In reality this number is even better since it does not yet include code that is reused from Chameleon, such as code for resolving cross-references. The precise amount of code that is reused from Chameleon, however, is hard to count.

For the aspect weaver, the percentage of reused code is significantly lower. Only about a third of the code for the AspectJ weaver could be reused – it uses virtually all code from the Carpenter weaving layers. While this is still a good result, we expect that reuse can be improved further by generating regular code instead of reflective code. We expect that generating regular code will allow more generic OO code to be moved to the OO layer of Carpenter.

The line count parser for the ANTLR grammar files is calculated in a similar way. Grammar reuse is very good, only two rules from the Java grammar had to be overridden: `compilationUnit` to add aspects, and `expression` to add `proceed`. As such, there is still some duplication, but it only concerns about 20 lines of code.

A remarkable result is that IDE support is virtually free. Plugin functionality that is specific for Java – mostly code for visualizing method signatures – is reused by extending the plugin for Java. The two classes in the AspectJava plugin take only 39 lines of code, 14 of which are methods for creating user interface strings such as the version number. The outline shows the aspects and pointcuts in a file, using a reference to a parameter of a pointcut or advice as a hyperlink make the cursor jump to its definition, and syntactic and semantic errors are reported. Not a single line of code was written for AspectJava to support these features.

It is hard to compare line counts of our approach with those of other approaches, but Avgustinov et al. report 167 lines of code to add support for matching and weaving cast join point to AspectJ with the abc compiler [1]. We need 176 lines for the cast join point, so the effort is similar. The advantage of abc is that is offers advanced optimization of the woven code for Java. The advantage of our approach is that it is much more generic.

6.3 An Aspect-Oriented Extension of JLo

To test the extensibility of AspectJava, we developed an aspect weaver for JLo, which adds a dedicated composition relation to Java [38]. It is not in the scope of this paper to discuss the benefits or full semantics of this composition relation. What is important is that JLo extends Java with new language constructs that have a significant influence on the lookup mechanism of the language. AspectJLo is implemented as a layer that specializes AspectJava, and can therefore reuse all functionality defined for AspectJava.

The aspect weaver for AspectJLo supports all of the advice types and pointcut expressions of AspectJava, but adds a pointcut expression for subobject reads. These are similar to field reads, but the AspectJava weaver cannot process them since it has no knowledge of subobjects.

The table in Figure 13 shows the size of the AspectJLo implementation. The sizes of the JLo components are included for reference. The AspectJLo language module contains only a subclass of `Language` to represent the AspectJLo language. No new language construct is needed for subobject reads because they can be modeled directly with the Carpenter classes of Figure 4.

	LOC
Use case language	2665
Use case grammar file	435
Use case plugin for Chameleon IDE	33
AspectU language	**72**
AspectU weaver	**125**
AspectU grammar file	**104 (64)**
AspectU plugin for Chameleon IDE	**39**

Figure 14. Line counts for use cases and AspectU.

For AspectJLo, the Carpenter framework allowed us to define an aspect weaver with very little work. Because JLo is a Java extension, the use of reflection in the generated code caused no problems, and we could reuse the complete AspectJava weaver. Only the code for matching and weaving subobject reads must be written. Everything else is reused from the AspectJava weaver.

The grammar definitions in AspectJava could not be reused because we could not get the multiple inheritance mechanism of ANTLR to work correctly, as mentioned in Section 5. Therefore, the AspectJLo grammar extends the JLo grammar, and the syntax definitions for aspects and pointcuts are copied from the AspectJava grammar. Otherwise, the grammar would only be 86 lines long.

As with AspectJava, obtaining support for the Chameleon IDE requires some trivial configuration code.

6.4 An Aspect-Oriented Extension of Use Cases

To study how well Carpenter works for a non-programming language, we implemented AspectU [33]. AspectU is an aspect-orientated extension of a language for use cases, and provides support for pointcut expressions for matching steps, use cases, and use case extensions. All use cases, steps, and extensions in the base language are annotated with a name that can be used in the pointcuts. Context information is exposed via the pointcut expression bind(var,val). An advice consists of a list of steps and a list of extensions that can be added to a use case. A special proceed step can be used in around advice.

The table in Figure 14 shows the size of the AspectU implementation. The base use case language is included for reference. Note that our base use case language is more advanced than that of AspectU. Both the implementations of the AspectU language and the AspectU weaver are very small. The fact that the semantics of the bind pointcut expression of AspectU can be expressed as simple text substitution makes it much easier to insert the context information than is the case for Java. As with AspectJLo, the grammar definition duplicates grammar rules for generic aspect-oriented language constructs. The line count between parenthesis shows the size of the grammar if we could reuse those definitions. Again, IDE support is virtually free.

6.5 Conclusion of the Case Studies

In this section, we revisit the requirements that we presented in Section 2, and summarize the results of the case studies.

1. **A language- and paradigm-independent approach:** By developing aspect-oriented extensions of two programming languages and a language for use cases, we have shown that the approach works for languages in two completely different paradigms. We found no indications that the approach would not work for other paradigms.

2. **Modularity of aspect weavers:** The framework approach worked well for the aspect weavers. All aspect weavers reuse the framework classes of Carpenter. In addition, the AspectJava weaver reuses functionality from the OO layer of Carpenter, and the AspectJLo weaver reuses the complete AspectJava weaver.

   The developed languages also revealed a number of limitations of our approach. First, the generation of reflective code in the AspectJava weaver prevents reusing that code for other object-oriented languages because the reflection mechanisms of these languages differ too much. An important research challenge is to study whether generating regular code can lead to reusable weaving code for object-oriented languages.

   Second, the current weavers insert the advice body in some form for every matched join point shadow, which is problematic for large programs. Such optimizations can be implemented in the language-specific weavers, but an important research challenge is to study how they can be supported by Carpenter.

3. **Modularity of aspect-oriented language constructs:** The framework approach worked very well for defining the aspect languages. Only a few language-specific elements had to be implemented for each language. The rest of the language could be used from Carpenter. AspectJLo completely reuses the language definition of AspectJava.

   ANTLR has proven helpful for creating parser for the aspect languages, but did not result in fully modular parsers. The inability to add cases to an extended grammar resulted in some duplicated cases. In addition, problems with multiple inheritance prevented the extraction of the common grammar rules for the generic aspect-oriented language constructs.

4. **Modularity of the base language:** Aspect-oriented language constructs were be added to the base language without modifying the latter. The base language semantics are completely reused. Even though the concrete aspect-oriented languages contain no code for name resolution, the lookup mechanisms of the base language still works within an advice body still works. In addition, variable names in the base language code resolve to a parameter of an advice block if the name matches, even though the base language has no knowledge of advice.

Carpenter significantly reduced to work to define aspect-oriented extensions of Java, JLo, and our use case language. Most of the aspect-oriented language constructs and the code to orchestrate the weaving process could be reused from Carpenter. For the aspect weavers, a significant amount of code could be reused but we think that the support for weavers can be further improved. The use of Chameleon in the aspect-oriented languages made it very easy to obtain IDE support. Only a few lines of code were needed for each language, giving support for syntax highlighting, an outline, navigable hyperlinks, and error-reporting.

The development of Carpenter also revealed a few short-comings in Chameleon. Carpenter revealed the need for a generic mechanism for modifying `Declarations`. This is needed to support for example inter-type declarations. Such a mechanism is implemented for particular elements, but is not yet available in general. In addition, the builder infrastructure had to be modified because the aspect weavers must know which parts of a model represent the user project in which aspects must be woven, and which parts (if any) represent unmodifiable elements such as the language library.

7. Related Work

Roychoudhury et al. present a model driven approach for construction of aspect weaver[29]. They identify four main challenges: 1) parser construction , 2) weaver construction , 3) accidental complexity of transformations, and 4) language-independent generalization of transformations. The authors address challenges 1 and 2 by using program transformation techniques. They address challenge 3 by defining an abstract layer for aspect-orientation (called GAspect), and using ATL transformations to generate RSL program transformation rules which incorporate low-level language details. This allows the aspect developer to focus on the language concepts without dealing with low-level details. Challenge 4 is addressed by using higher-order transformations, which allow reuse across multiple aspect languages. The authors construct aspect weavers for FORTRAN and Object Pascal. In our approach, challenge 1 is addressed by using a parser generator, challenge 2 by using Carpenter, and challenges 3 and 4 by using Chameleon. The main differences with our approach are the following. First, the metamodels in Carpenter encapsulate the language semantics instead of having them spread over data models, transformations, and program analyzers. Second, we implement the aspect languages and weavers directly using object-orientation instead of defining transformations to generate other transformation rules.

JastAdd [7] provides a DSL and accompanying tools for implementing languages. The AST structure is defined in an attribute grammar from which corresponding AST classes are generated. Additional functionality is implemented in inter-type declarations and woven into the AST classes. Similar to Chameleon, a language can reuse elements from other languages. But JastAdd does not provide a library of generic abstractions. As such, the implementation for Java and a use case language would share nothing. But even if such abstractions were defined, it would be impossible to develop a tool that works with multiple languages. The generated AST classes are never shared between languages, even if they share the definitions of the language constructs. Therefore, there are no interfaces that a generic tool could use. JastAdd would work well for defining AspectJava and AspectJLo, but there would be no IDE support. Defining AspectU would require more work because both the aspect weaver and the pointcut language would have to be reimplemented. In case of AspectU, this is a relatively large overhead.

Dinkelaker et al. present the POPART [5] meta-aspect protocol (MAP) on top of a meta-object protocol (MOP). The MAP extends the MOP such that it can intercept method calls, and adds support for aspect-orientation. Both POPART and Carpenter provide a generic aspect language that can be extended by creating subclasses, and both approach use a similar modularization of the weaving process. The key difference between both approaches is that POPART processes aspects at run-time, while Carpenter does that at compile-time. The MAP makes developing a language extension in POPART easier than in Carpenter, but the dependency on a MOP limits its applicability. Mainstream languages such Java, C#, and C++ do not natively support a MOP. To support JLo, its implementation would have to be rewritten as a dedicated virtual machine with MOP support instead a transformation to Java code. In addition, POPART cannot be used for the use case language, as it is not executable.

Dyer and Rajan [6] present *Nu*, an aspect-oriented intermediate language. The added *bind* and *remove* primitives add and destroy advising relations. The authors implemented *Nu* in the JVM and show that there is no significant performance impact, and demonstrate that *Nu* can model a wide range of aspect-oriented features. Similar to POPART, the approach is limited to executable languages, and requires modifications of the native implementations of mainstream languages. Because *Nu* reduces the gap between an aspect-oriented language and its execution environment, using *Nu* as a compilation target would significantly simplify our AspectJava weaver.

Haupt and Schippers [14] define a machine model for aspect-oriented programming. Aspect-oriented programming is modeled in a prototype based object-oriented language. Each object has a proxy that determines the identity of the object. Method calls are sent through a delegation chain with the proxy at the start and the object at the end. Class-based languages are supported by appending a shared class proxy to the chains for objects. Schippers et al. [31] demonstrate the expressiveness of the machine model by encoding four different languages. The machine model directly and elegantly models aspect-orientation instead of modifying join point shadows, which is the approach taken in Carpenter. The downside is that it would have to be implemented separately for each language run-time, which is not practical for mainstream languages. Carpenter does not depend on the implementation of a language run-time and is applicable to languages other than programming languages.

Tanter and Noyé propose Reflex, a kernel for multi-language aspect-oriented programming [35]. Their approach uses three layers. The first layer performs the actual weaving. The second layer manages aspect interactions. The third layer enables modular definitions of aspect languages. The authors use reified links to model the connection between advices and join point shadows. Interactions between aspects are resolved using link composition rules. To define an aspect language, a plugin is implemented which translates aspect programs written in that aspect language into a Reflex configuration. The authors implemented plugins for SOM and AspectJ. While Reflex AOP enables the definition of modular aspect languages, the host language is limited to Java. The principle is not Java-specific, but the kernel would have to be reimplemented for other host languages.

Heidenreich et al. present a model-driven approach to add modularization technique to a language [16]. They offer two ways of adding modularization to languages. The first approach is to extend the metamodel of the language by defining component interfaces. The second approach extracts those interfaces automatically. The latter technique has the advantage that existing tools keep working, but is sometimes more difficult to implement than a metamodel extension. They evaluate their approach by creating adding component capabilities to UML activity diagrams and the domain-specific language TaiPan. In earlier work, the authors have added aspect-orientation to Java [15]. The authors implemented the ReuseWare composition framework on top of the Eclipse Modeling Framework [4].

Weave.NET [21], Aspect.NET [30], and LOOM.NET [32] offer language-independent aspect-oriented programming by operating on the common language infrastructure (CLI) of the .NET platform. The use of CLI allows these aspect weavers to work with large collection of programming languages, and even support cross-language weaving. The latter is not supported by our framework, since there is no intermediate language that supports all possible languages. These approaches, however, reflect the object-oriented model behind the common intermediate language (CIL) in the aspect language that they define. While this is not a problem for object-oriented languages such as C# and Visual Basic, this is problematic for languages whose language constructs do not map well to object-oriented languages, such as functional and logical programming languages. The approach is also limited to programming languages.

SourceWeave.NET [18] uses an approach that is similar to that of the .NET approaches that operate on the CLI, but instead of operating on .NET assemblies, it operates on CodeDOM models. CodeDOM is the .NET standard for representing models of source code. Because CodeDOM is strongly related to CIL, SourceWeave.NET has the same limitations as the assembly based approaches.

Avgustinov et al. present abc, an extensible AspectJ compiler [1]. The abc compiler can use Polyglot [23] or JastAdd [7] for the front-end. A program is transformed to an intermediate representation called Jimple to perform the actual aspect weaving. The abc compiler uses a generic intermediate representation for pointcuts to simplify the development of new pointcut expressions. This representation is similar to the generic top layer of Carpenter. The abc compiler is limited to extensions of Java, but implements many optimizations to improve the performance of the woven program, which Carpenter does not do.

ALIA4J is an execution model for advanced-dispatching languages [2]. ALIA4J defines a language-independent metamodel for advanced-dispatching (LIAM), which is similar to the top layer of Carpenter. Concrete languages extend this model to define additional constructs. A plugin interacts with the JVM to ensure that the custom dispatching mechanism is used at run-time. An intermediate representation of a program is used to make the approach language-independent. The approach is not limited to building aspect-oriented extensions of languages, but because it uses run-time interception, it is limited to executable languages. The authors evaluate their approach by implementing language constructs from languages such as AspectJ and CaesarJ.

8. Conclusion

Aspect-orientation is added to ever more software engineering languages. Existing approaches to simplify the development of aspect-oriented language extensions are either limited in the types of supported host languages, or use complicated code generation techniques.

We defined Carpenter, an object-oriented framework for the development of aspect-oriented languages. Aspect-oriented languages constructs and the corresponding weavers are implemented directly in an object-oriented programming language. This approach enables the definition of abstractions that improve the language-independence of the aspect weavers without having to write a tool for generating weavers. Classes for generic aspect-oriented language constructs and generic weaving functionality can be reused from the Carpenter framework.

We used Carpenter to create aspect-oriented extensions of Java, JLo, and a language for use cases. This showed that a significant amount of work was saved by using Carpenter. Providing IDE support for aspect-oriented languages developed with Carpenter requires only a few lines of code.

Acknowledgements

We thank the reviewers for their insightful comments. We especially thank Eric Bodden for his support in the discussion of related work.

References

[1] P. Avgustinov, A. Christensen, L. Hendren, S. Kuzins, J. Lhoták, O. Lhoták, O. de Moor, D. Sereni, G. Sittampalam, and J. Tibble. abc: An extensible AspectJ compiler. *Transactions on Aspect-Oriented Software Development I*, pages 293–334, 2006.

[2] C. Bockisch, A. Sewe, M. Mezini, and M. Akşit. An overview of ALIA4J. *Objects, Models, Components, Patterns*, pages 131–146, 2011.

[3] M. Brukman and A. Myers. PPG: a parser generator for extensible grammars, 2003. http://www.cs.cornell.edu/Projects/polyglot/ppg.html.

[4] F. Budinsky, S. Brodsky, and E. Merks. *Eclipse modeling framework*. 2003.

[5] T. Dinkelaker, M. Mezini, and C. Bockisch. The art of the meta-aspect protocol. In *AOSD '09*, pages 51–62.

[6] R. Dyer and H. Rajan. Nu: a dynamic aspect-oriented intermediate language model and virtual machine for flexible runtime adaptation. In *AOSD '08*, pages 191–202, 2008.

[7] T. Ekman and G. Hedin. The JastAdd extensible Java compiler. In *OOPSLA '07*, pages 1–18.

[8] P. Fradet and M. Südholt. Towards a generic framework for aspect-oriented programming. In *Workshop on AOP '98, ECOOP*, pages 394–397, July 1998.

[9] E. Gamma, R. Helm, R. Johnson, and J. Vlissides. *Design Patterns*. January 1995. ISBN 0201633612.

[10] A. Garcia, C. Chavez, T. Batista, C. Sant'anna, U. Kulesza, A. Rashid, and C. Lucena. On the modular representation of architectural aspects. In *Software Architecture*, volume 4344 of *LNCS*, pages 82–97. 2006.

[11] J. Gray and S. Roychoudhury. A technique for constructing aspect weavers using a program transformation engine. In *AOSD '04*, pages 36–45, 2004.

[12] R. Grimm. Better extensibility through modular syntax. In *PLDI '06*, pages 38–51.

[13] K. Gybels and J. Brichau. Arranging language features for more robust pattern-based crosscuts. In *AOSD '03*, pages 60–69.

[14] M. Haupt and H. Schippers. A machine model for aspect-oriented programming. In *ECOOP '07*, pages 501–524.

[15] F. Heidenreich, J. Johannes, and S. Zschaler. Aspect orientation for your language of choice. In *AOM at MoDELS'07*.

[16] F. Heidenreich, J. Henriksson, J. Johannes, and S. Zschaler. On language-independent model modularisation. *Transactions on Aspect-Oriented Software Development VI*, pages 39–82, 2009.

[17] S. Herrmann, C. Hundt, and K. Mehner. Mapping use case level aspects to Object Teams/Java. In *OOPSLA Workshop on Early Aspects*, 2004.

[18] A. Jackson and S. Clarke. SourceWeave.NET: Cross-language aspect-oriented programming. In *GPCE '04*, pages 115–135, 2004.

[19] I. Jacobson. Use cases and aspects–working seamlessly together. *Journal of Object Technology*, 2(4):7–28, 2003.

[20] G. Kiczales, E. Hilsdale, J. Hugunin, M. Kersten, J. Palm, and W. Griswold. An overview of AspectJ. In *ECOOP '01*, pages 327–354.

[21] D. Lafferty and V. Cahill. Language-independent aspect-oriented programming. In *OOPSLA '03*, pages 1–12.

[22] H. Masuhara and K. Kawauchi. Dataflow pointcut in aspect-oriented programming. *Programming Languages and Systems*, pages 105–121, 2003.

[23] N. Nystrom, M. Clarkson, and A. Myers. Polyglot: An extensible compiler framework for Java. In *CC '03*, pages 138–152.

[24] K. Ostermann, M. Mezini, and C. Bockisch. Expressive pointcuts for increased modularity. *ECOOP '05*, pages 214–240.

[25] K. Palma, Y. Eterovic, and J. M. Murillo. Extending the rapide adl to specify aspect oriented software architectures. In *15th International Conference on Software Engineering and Data Engineering*, page 170, 2006.

[26] T. Parr and R. Quong. ANTLR: A predicated (k) parser generator, 1995.

[27] J. Perez, E. Navarro, P. Letelier, and I. Ramos. A modelling proposal for aspect-oriented software architectures. In *IEEE International Symposium and Workshop on Engineering of Computer Based Systems '06*, pages 32–41.

[28] M. Pinto and L. Fuentes. AO-ADL: An ADL for describing aspect-oriented architectures. In *Early Aspects: Current Challenges and Future Directions*, volume 4765 of *LNCS*, 2007.

[29] S. Roychoudhury, J. Gray, and F. Jouault. A model-driven framework for aspect weaver construction. *Transactions on aspect-oriented software development VIII*, pages 1–45, 2011.

[30] V. Safonov and D. Grigoryev. Aspect.NET: aspect-oriented programming for Microsoft .NET in practice. *NET Developers Journal*, 7, 2005.

[31] H. Schippers, D. Janssens, M. Haupt, and R. Hirschfeld. Delegation-based semantics for modularizing crosscutting concerns. In *OOPSLA '08*, pages 525–542, 2008.

[32] W. Schult, P. Tröger, and A. Polze. LOOM.NET-an aspect weaving tool. In *Workshop on AOP '03, ECOOP*.

[33] J. Sillito, C. Dutchyn, A. D. Eisenberg, and K. D. Volder. Use case level pointcuts. In *ECOOP '04*, 2004.

[34] O. Spinczyk, A. Gal, and W. Schröder-Preikschat. AspectC++: an aspect-oriented extension to the C++ programming language. In *Proceedings of the Fortieth International Conference on Tools Pacific: Objects for internet, mobile and embedded applications*, CRPIT '02, pages 53–60, 2002.

[35] É. Tanter and J. Noyé. A versatile kernel for multi-language aop. In *GPCE*, pages 173–188, 2005.

[36] É. Tanter, K. Gybels, M. Denker, and A. Bergel. Context-aware aspects. In *Software Composition*, pages 227–242, 2006.

[37] M. van Dooren. Carpenter, 2011. http://www.cs.kuleuven.be/~marko/carpenter.html.

[38] M. van Dooren and E. Steegmans. A higher abstraction level using first-class inheritance relations. In *ECOOP '07*, pages 425–449.

Reusing Non-Functional Concerns Across Languages

Myoungkyu Song and Eli Tilevich

Dept. of Computer Science
Virginia Tech
{mksong,tilevich}@cs.vt.edu

Abstract

Emerging languages are often source-to-source compiled to mainstream ones, which offer standardized, fine-tuned implementations of non-functional concerns (NFCs)—including persistence, security, transactions, and testing. Because these NFCs are specified through metadata such as XML configuration files, compiling an emerging language to a mainstream one does not include NFC implementations. Unable to access the mainstream language's NFC implementations, emerging language programmers waste development effort reimplementing NFCs. In this paper, we present a novel approach to reusing NFC implementations across languages by automatically translating metadata. To add an NFC to an emerging language program, the programmer declares metadata, which is then translated to reuse the specified NFC implementation in the source-to-source compiled mainstream target language program. By automatically translating metadata, our approach eliminates the need to reimplement NFCs in the emerging language. As a validation, we add unit testing and transparent persistence to X10 by reusing implementations of these NFCs in Java and C++, the X10 backend compilation targets. The reused persistence NFC is efficient and scalable, making it possible to checkpoint and migrate processes, as demonstrated through experiments with third-party X10 programs. These results indicate that our approach can effectively reuse NFC implementations across languages, thus saving development effort.

Categories and Subject Descriptors   D.2.3 [*Software Engineering*]: Coding Tools and Techniques—Object-oriented programming; D.2.5 [*Software Engineering*]: Testing and Debugging—Testing tools; D.3.3 [*Programming Languages*]: Language Constructs and Features—Frameworks; D.3.4

[*Programming Languages*]: Processors—Code generation, Interpreters, Parsing

General Terms   Languages, Design, Experimentation

Keywords   X10, Java, C++, source-to-source compilation, metadata, enterprise applications, non-functional concerns, transparent persistence, unit testing

1. Introduction

Modern industrial scale programming languages are much more than a grammar and syntactic rules for the programmer to follow. Mainstream enterprise languages feature complex and elaborate ecosystems of libraries and frameworks that provide standard application building blocks. In particular, many NFCs, including persistence, security, transactions, and testing, have been implemented in a standardized and reusable fashion. These implementations have become indispensable in modern enterprise applications. Examples abound: transparent persistence mechanisms facilitate data management; security frameworks provide access control and encryption; unit testing frameworks provide abstractions for implementing and executing unit tests, etc.

A common implementation strategy for emerging programming languages is to compile them to some existing language. Source-to-source compilation is more straightforward than providing a dedicated compiler backend. Additionally, because mainstream, commercial programming languages have been highly optimized, compiling an emerging language to a mainstream one can produce efficient execution without an extensive optimization effort. The emerging languages that compile to mainstream languages or bytecode include Scala [20], JRuby [2], Jython [11], and X10 [23].

Because a source-to-source compiler can only directly translate a program from the source language to the target language, the NFC implementations in the target language cannot be accessed from the source language. Provided as libraries and frameworks in the target language, these implementations can be accessed only by declaring appropriate metadata for target language programs. As a result, emerging languages must reimplement all the NFCs from scratch.

In this paper, we present a novel approach to reusing NFC implementations across languages. Rather than reimplement an NFC in an emerging language, the programmer can reuse the existing target language implementations. The approach enables the programmer to specify the needed NFC in a source language program by declaring metadata. The declared metadata is then automatically translated, so that the needed NFC implementation in the target language can be reused. If the source language compiles to multiple target languages, the NFC implementations can be reused for each target language.

The thesis behind our work is that it is possible to translate metadata alongside compiling the source language. Our approach requires expressive languages to specify metadata and how metadata is to be translated. We show how our Pattern Based Structural Expressions (PBSE) language [24] and its pattern-based implementation mechanism can play that role. For this work, we have extended PBSE to compile across languages, as specified by declarative translation strategies, to work with target language programs.

We validate the efficiency and expressiveness of our approach by adding unit testing and transparent persistence to X10, an emerging language being developed at IBM Research. The X10 compiler compiles an X10 program to both Java and C++, but does not implement unit testing or transparent persistence natively. We have reused well-known Java and C++ implementations of these NFCs in third-party X10 programs. X10 programmers express an NFC in PBSE, which is automatically translated to the metadata required for the NFC implementations in Java and C++.

Based on our results, this paper contributes:

- An approach to reusing NFC implementations of a mainstream language from an emerging language program, when the emerging language is compiled to the mainstream language;
- Automated cross-language metadata translation—a novel approach to translating metadata alongside compiling the source language;
- *Meta-metadata*, a domain-specific language that declaratively expresses how one metadata format can be translated into another metadata format;
- The ability to unit test and transparently persist X10 programs for both Java and C++ backends, the X10 compilation targets.

The remainder of this paper is structured as follows. Section 2 defines the problem and sketches our solution. Section 3 details our design and implementation. Section 4 presents our case studies. Section 5 compares this work to the existing state of the art, and Section 6 concludes.

2. Problem Definition and Solution Overview

The programming model for implementing NFCs is becoming increasingly declarative. To add persistence, security, or testing to an application, programmers rarely write code in a mainstream programming language. Instead, programmers declare metadata such as XML files, Java 5 annotations, or C/C++ pragmas. Such a metadata declaration configures a standardized NFC implementation, provided as a library or a framework. Because NFCs are expressed declaratively through metadata, a source-to-source compiler cannot emit code for their standardized implementations. Thus, to reuse NFC implementations, metadata translation must supplement source compilation.

To demonstrate the problem concretely, consider writing an X10 program. The X10 compiler translates X10 programs to either a C++ or Java backend. At some point, the programmer realizes that some portion of the program's state must be persisted. In other words, certain X10 object fields need to be mapped to the columns of a database table, managed by a Relational Database Management System (RDBMS). As the program is being developed, the persistent state may change with respect to both the included fields and their types. In terms of persistent storage, it is desirable for the C++ and Java backends to share the same RDBMS schema. This way, the state persisted by the Java backend can be used by the C++ backend and vice versa.

These requirements are quite common for modern software applications, and mainstream programming languages have well-defined solutions that satisfy these requirements. In particular, object-relational mapping (ORM) systems have been developed for all major languages, including Java and C++. Commercial ORM systems implement the NFC of transparent persistence. An ORM system persists language objects to a relational database based on some declarative metadata specification, so that the programmer does not have to deal with tables, columns, and SQL. However, because X10 is an emerging language, an ORM system has not been developed for it. Developing an ORM system is a challenging undertaking for any language, but for X10 it would be even more complicated. Because X10 is compiled to Java or C++, an X10 ORM solution must be compatible with both of these compilation target languages.

The approach we present here addresses the problem described above. For this example, our approach can add transparent persistence to X10 programs by leveraging existing ORM solutions developed for Java and C++. To demonstrate how our approach works from the programmer's perspective, consider the X10 code snippet in Figure 1.

This figure depicts the X10 class `FmmModel`[1] that contains fields of different types. The number of fields and their types are likely to change as the program is maintained and evolved. Furthermore, our compilation target changes repeatedly between the Java and C++ backends. We need to persist the `private` fields of this class to a relational database according to the following naming convention. The class and the table share the same name, while the columns have the same names as the fields, but capitalized.

---

[1] http://squirrel.anu.edu.au/hg/public/x10-apps/file/ 909f49fd95de/apps/fmm

```
1  package model;
2
3  public class FmmModel {
4    private var modelId:Long;
5    private var energy:Double;
6    // ...
7    public def this(modelId : Long,
8                    energy : Double, ..) {
9      this.modelId = modelId;
10     this.energy = energy;
11     // ...
12   }
13   // ...
14 }
```

Figure 1. An X10 class to be compiled to Java and C++.

```
1  Metadata PersistentModelClasses<Package p>
2    Class c in p
3    Where (public class *Model)
4      c += @table
5      @table.name = c.name
6      @table.class = c.name
7      Field<c>
8  Metadata Field<Class c>
9    Field f in c
10   Where (private var *:*)
11     f += @column
12     @column.name = (f.name=~s/[a-z]/[A-Z]/)
13
14 PersistentModelClasses <"model">
```

Figure 2. Metadata to persist the X10 class in Figure 1.

To that end, the programmer writes a metadata specification listed in Figure 2. We use Pattern-Based Structural Expressions (PBSE), a new metadata format we introduced recently [24] to improve the reusability, conciseness, and maintainability of metadata programming. PBSE leverages the correspondences between program constructs and metadata and uses queries on program structures to express how metadata should be applied. In Figure 2, the PBSE specification on the right expresses that all private fields of classes with suffix "Model" should be persisted. This PBSE specification constitutes all the manually written code that the programmer has to write to use our approach.

Based on a PBSE specification, our automated code generation tools produce all the necessary functionality to persist the fields of class FmmModel in an RDBMS for the Java and C++ backends. The automatically generated code artifacts include:

1. An X10 class called TP (short for **T**ransparent**P**ersistence) that provides an X10 API for saving and restoring the persistent fields. This class encapsulates all the low-level database interaction functionality such as transactions and can be further modified by expert programmers.

2. An XML deployment descriptor required by the Java Data Objects (JDO) ORM system. The descriptor specifies how JDO should persist the fields of the Java class emitted by the X10 compiler for the Java backend.

3. A C++ header file that contains #**pragma** declarations required by ODB,[2] an open source ORM system for C++ [3]. The **pragma** declarations specify how ODB should persist the fields of the C++ class emitted by the X10 compiler for the C++ backend.

When either the Java or C++ target of the X10 program executes, the fields in class FmmModel are transparently persisted to a database table. Our approach is highly customizable and configurable. Any Java or C++ ORM solution can be used by changing a configuration file. The code generated for the TP class can be easily modified by editing our code generation template. Finally, if the X10 compiler were to be

---
[2] Surprisingly, ODB is not an acronym.

extended for yet another cross language, our approach can be easily extended to transparently persist the target code, as long as the new target language has an ORM solution.

Our approach is intended to support the implementation of major NFCs that include security, transactions, and testing. Although we demonstrate our approach on the domain of unit testing and transparent persistence, our approach is general because of how NFCs are commonly implemented in modern languages. In particular, declarative approaches are common, with metadata being used as the preferred expression medium. Programmers use metadata, such as XML files, Java 5 annotations, C/C++ pragmas, macros, or C# attributes, to express how NFCs should be implemented in their programs.

For example, a C# security framework can provide special attributes for the programmer to restrict access to methods and fields. Once the programmer annotates the program, the framework will furnish the specified security functionality, thus implementing this NFC. If an emerging language compiled to C# needs to implement security, the methods and fields of the emerging language can be marked with the required access restrictions using any available metadata format. The resulting metadata specification in any format can then be translated to C# attributes that work with the C# code emitted by the source-to-source compiler.

3. Design and Implementation

In the following discussion, we first outline our requirements and design space considered, and then detail our implementation, including PBSE enhancements, metadata translation, and NFC API generation.

3.1 Design Objectives and General Approach

When designing our approach, we aimed at (1) providing a declarative programming interface, (2) maintaining generality, and (3) not imposing an unreasonable performance overhead. Specifically, our approach is designed to support those existing implementations of NFCs that expose a high level, declarative programming interface. Expressing major NFCs—including persistence, transactions, security, and testing—through metadata has become an industry practice.

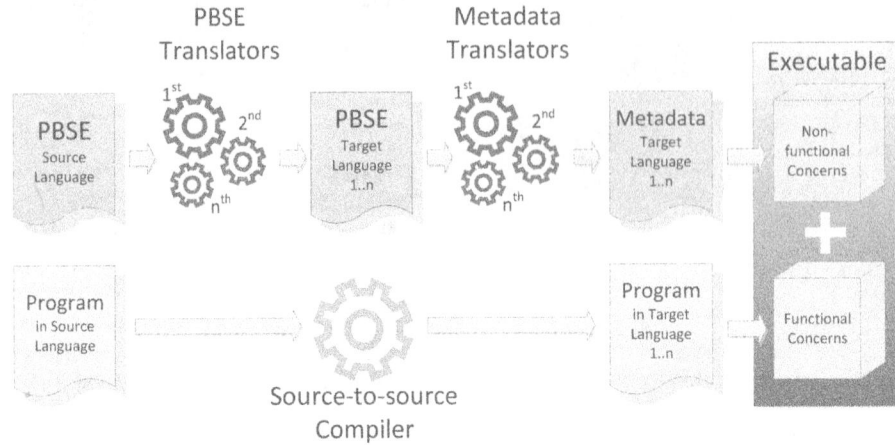

Figure 3. Generating Target Sources and Metadata formats.

Thus, our programming interface design goal was to enable the programmer to interface with our tool chain through declarative metadata specifications. We aimed at making our approach general with respect to both the NFCs it supports and the kinds of languages to which it applies. Finally, our approach should not impose an undue performance overhead on the target programs.

To support these design goals, we had to choose an appropriate metadata format that can be translated to the required metadata representations used by the existing NFC implementations in mainstream languages. To that end, we chose PBSE to support our goal of generality. PBSE is external to the source code and can work with any source languages, even if they do not provide built-in metadata constructs such as X10 annotations [19]. To fulfill this goal we could also have used XML files, but we found that XML is not a suitable format as a programmer written medium. PBSE provides conciseness, reusability, and maintainability advantages [24]. By capturing the naming correspondences between programming constructs and their metadata, PBSE is more expressive than mainstream metadata formats.

Because our approach hinges on the ability to effectively translate PBSE to existing metadata formats used with existing mainstream languages (e.g., annotations, pragmas, XML deployment descriptors, macros, etc.), we considered several choices with respect to designing our metadata translation infrastructure. Some emerging languages provide sophisticated facilities for systematically extending the core compiler. For example, the X10 compiler can be extended through plug-ins, but not all the emerging languages can be similarly extended. Striving for generality, we made our metadata translation infrastructure external to the source-to-source compiler, and ensured that the translation strategies are adaptable, customizable, and configurable.

In terms of the programming model, our approach requires that the source-to-source compilation mappings between the emerging and target languages be made available. NFC implementers (e.g., an ORM or a unit testing framework vendor) can then use these mappings to derive a simple declarative specification that expresses how to compile PBSE across languages. To that end, our approach provides a simple declarative Domain-Specific Language (DSL) that is derived from PBSE. The resulting PBSE mapping specification parameterizes a generator that synthesizes a PBSE cross-translator (Section 3.3). Finally, the emerging language programmers only need to declare PBSE to add any NFC implementation to their programs.

To increase flexibility without jeopardizing performance, we also automatically generate a special target language API for each supported NFC implementation rather than provide a pre-defined library. Automatically generating the API also makes it possible to introduce workarounds whenever an NFC implementation cannot be straightforwardly added to the target language programs. For example, Scala functional lists and maps translate to Java classes that cannot be directly persisted using mainstream Java persistence frameworks interfaces. They are translated to Java classes that do not implement the `java.util.List` and `java.util.Map`. Our code generator synthesizes mirror data structures compatible with Java persistence and copies the data back and forth during the saving and restoring operations.

3.2 Implementation Details

Figure 3 gives an overview of our approach. To add an implementation of an NFC to a program in the source language, the programmer writes a PBSE specification that refers to that program's constructs. For each concern to be added, the programmer needs to provide a separate PBSE specification. For example, if a program needs both persistence and security, the program must specify separate PBSE specifications for each of these two NFCs. PBSEs are then translated from the source to the target language specifications. Our approach supports PBSE for multiple languages, including Java, C++, X10, Scala, and C#. Then, the PBSE specifications in the target language are translated to the metadata format required by the NFC's target language implementations. Each implementation may use a different metadata format and sometimes use multiple formats simultaneously. For example, the Java Data Objects persistence system takes as input both XML files and Java 5 annotations. At the same time, the Security Annotation Framework (SAF)[15] requires that the programmer use Java 5 annotations. Our approach can translate a PBSE specification to all the major metadata formats, including XML files, annotations, pragmas, and macros. Once the translated metadata is added to the program emitted by the source-to-source compiler, the resulting executable artifact implements both functional and non-functional concerns. The functional concerns are implemented by translating the source program to the target one, while the NFCs are implemented by adding the appropriate metadata to the target program.

This process must be repeated for each of the supported source-to-source compilation targets. For example, the X10 compiler emits both Java and C++. Thus, if an NFC is needed in both backends, the appropriate metadata has to be generated for each of them. Because language ecosystems tend to implement the same NFC distinctly, the NFC implementations in each compiled language may require different metadata formats and content. For example, for the persistence NFC, a Java ORM may require XML configuration files, while a C++ ORM may require C/C++ pragmas.

3.3   Metadata Translation

Our design is based on the assumption that if a source language can be source-to-source compiled to a target language, then the metadata with which a source language program is tagged can be translated to tag the resulting target language program. Figure 4 demonstrates this assumption pictorially. We assume that (1) the program's source-to-source compiler is not aware of metadata, and (2) the metadata's compiler can be derived from the program's source-to-source compiler. This entails that metadata is external to the source language. If it were part of the language, such as in the case of Java 5 annotations, the program's source-to-source compiler would have to compile the metadata as well. If the format between the source and target metadata is not going to change (e.g., if it were an XML file for the source language

program, it will also be an XML file for the resulting target language program), then the metadata's compiler must mirror the program's source-to source compiler transformations for the program's constructs tagged with metadata.

In our approach, PBSE specifications can be translated across languages. In particular, a PBSE specification for X10 is translated to PBSE specifications for Java and C++, whenever an X10 program is compiled to these languages. We call this translation process *cross-language metadata transformation*. In addition, PBSE specifications can be translated to mainstream metadata formats, including XML, Java 5 annotations as well as C/C++ pragmas and macros.

Metadata translation framework   Since metadata translation is the cornerstone of our approach, one of the key design goals we pursued was to facilitate cross-language metadata transformation. Our solution is two-pronged: metadata translation is specified declaratively and implemented using a generative approach. That is, to express metadata translation rules, our approach features a declarative domain-specific language. In addition, we provide a PBSE translation framework that transforms a PBSE specification into an abstract syntax tree that can be operated on using visitors. Our code generator takes declarative metadata translation rules and synthesizes the translation visitors.

PBSE meta-metadata   Within the same language, different metadata formats for a given NFC tag the same program constructs. Across languages, the tagged source language constructs map to their source-to-source compilation targets. Because NFC metadata tags structural program constructs (i.e., classes, methods, and fields), one can express declaratively how metadata is to be translated both within and across languages.

To that end, our approach extends PBSE with *meta-metadata*—meta constructs that codify differences between metadata formats. In Figure 5, we show meta-metadata for translating between PBSE for X10 (Figure 2) and Java (Figure 20). Because metadata applies to structural program constructs (i.e., classes, methods, and fields), meta-metadata needs to express how these structural constructs map to each other between the source and target languages.[3]

The meta-metadata in Figure 6 expresses how to translate from PBSE to XML for the JDO ORM. Pattern matching expresses how different metadata variables, depicted as Java 5 annotations, should map to the corresponding XML tags.

Generative visitors   Based on the meta-metadata specification in Figure 6, our code generator synthesizes a visitor class in shown Figure 7. Because it would not be pragmatic to generate all code from scratch, the generated `PBSEVisitorJavaToXML` class references several classes provided as a library. In particular, it extends the `PBSEVisitor-`

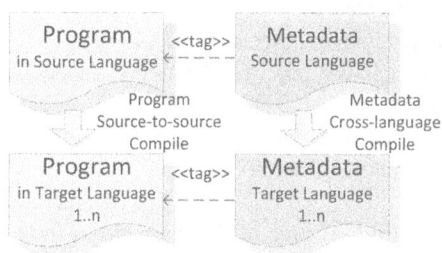

Figure 4.   Translating Metadata formats.

[3] Meta-metadata specifications are to be crafted by language compiler writers—intimately familiar with how their source language translates into the target language—who can easily declare the mapping.

```
1  MetaMetadata PBSEX10toJava<PBSE pbse>
2    Where (Class c in pbse)
3      Where (public struct *)
4        "struct" -> "class"
5    Where (Field f in pbse)
6      Where (private * ${temp1}:${temp2})
7        ${temp1} <-> ${temp2}
8      Where (private * *:*)
9        ":" -> "\s"
10     Where (private val *:*)
11       "val" -> "final"
12     Where (private var *:*)
13       "var" -> ""
14   Where (Method m in pbse)
15     Where (* def *:${returntype})
16       "def" -> ${returntype}
17   ...
```

Figure 5. Meta-metadata for translating PBSE from X10 to Java.

```
1  MetaMetadata PBSEJavaToXML<PBSE pbse>
2    Where (Class c in pbse)
3      @Table -> "<class/>"
4      @Table.name -> "<class name=" + c.name + "/>"
5      @Table.class -> "<class table=" + c.table + "/>"
6    Where (Field f in pbse)
7      @Field -> "<field/>"
8      @Field.name -> "<field name=" + f.name + "/>"
9      @Column -> "<column/>"
10     @Column.name -> "<column name==" + f.column + "/>"
11   ...
```

Figure 6. Meta-metadata for translating PBSE for Java to XML used by the JDO system.

```
1  class PBSEVisitorJavaToXML extends PBSEVisitorAdater {
2    void visit(PBSEElementClass elem){
3      if(elem.tagWith("@Table")){
4        out.write(JavaToXML.
5        translate("@Table","<class/>"));
6      } else
7      if(elem.tagWith("@Table.name")){
8        out.write(JavaToXML.translate
9        ("@Table.name","<class table=${value}/>"));
10     } else
11     if(elem.tagWith("@Class.table")){
12       out.write(JavaToXML.translate
13       ("@Table.class","<class name=${value}/>"));
14   }}
15
16   void visit(PBSEElementField elem){ /*..*/ }
17   // other visit methods go here.
18 }}
```

Figure 7. A generated visitor.

Adaptor class and manipulates various PBSE AST element classes such as `PBSEElementClass` and `PBSEElementField`. It also uses a utility class `JavaToXML` that encapsulates low-level translation functionality. The XML in Figure 8 was produced by one of the generated visitors.

Figure 9 presents a UML diagram of the visitors used in the examples discussed throughout the paper. All the core pieces of our translation framework have been implemented. Some of the code generation functionality is provided by code templates. Future work will refine our code generation infrastructure and explore whether some library pieces can be generated from scratch instead.

Generating client APIs Since not all NFC functionality can be expressed via metadata, some client API must sup-

```
1  <jdo><package name="ssca1">
2  <class name="SSCA1Model"
3      table="SSCA1"
4      identity-type="application">
5      <field name="modelId" persistence-modifier=
6        "persistent" primary-key="true">
7        <column name="MODELID"/>
8      </field>
9      <field name="winningScore"
10       persistence-modifier="persistent">
11       <column name="WINNINGSCORE"/>
12     </field>
13     <field name="shorterLast"
14       persistence-modifier="persistent">
15       <column name="SHORTERLAST"/>
16     </field>
17     <field name="longerLast"
18       persistence-modifier="persistent">
19       <column name="LONGERLAST"/>
20     </field>
21     <field name="longOffset"
22       persistence-modifier="persistent">
23       <column name="LONGOFFSET"/>
24     </field>
25     ...
26 </class></package></jdo>
```

Figure 8. Translated XML metadata for the JDO system.

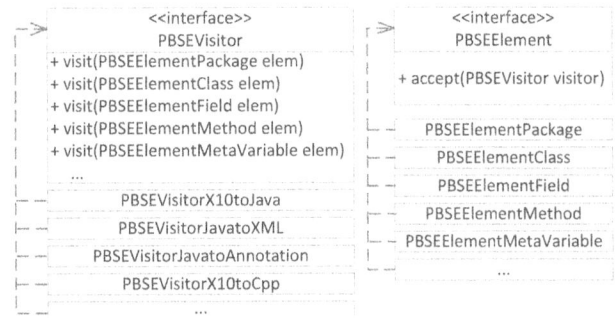

Figure 9. PBSE visitors translating metadata format.

plement the automatically translated metadata process described above. To that end, our infrastructure features NFC-specific client APIs. These APIs are invoked to access certain NFC functionalities explicitly. For example, persistent objects may need to be stored and retrieved from stable storage within a transactional context. In lieu of a transaction framework based on metadata, one may provide a code template to easily add transactional context to the persistence operations performed on any object. Figure 10 shows our code templates that can be used to add transactional support to persisting objects in Java and C++, shown in the upper and lower parts of the figure, respectively. The code templates are parameterized with the needed program construct names. The parameters are distinguished by their names, with the $ sign prefixing each parameter. For example, \$[Class.name] expresses that this parameter should be substituted with the value of this variable in the configuration file, composed of key-value pairs. The $iterator[..] metavariable iterates over all fields or methods of a class.

```
1  $[Class.name] getPersistentObj ($[Class.name] param) {
2      PersistenceManager pm = getPersistenceManager();
3      $[Class.name] pobj = getObj(pm,"$[Class.name].class",param);
4      Transaction tx = pm.currentTransaction();
5      tx.begin();
6      ...
7      if (pobj == null) {
8        pobj = new $[Class.name]($iterator
9                    [param.$[Class.field.name]]);
10       pm.makePersistent(pobj);
11     }
12     tx.commit();
13     return pobj;
14 }

1  ref<$[Class.name]> getPersistentObj (ref<$[Class.name]> param) {
2      auto_ptr < database > db (create_database (argc, argv));
3      $[Class.name]* pobj = param._val;
4      transaction t(db->begin());
5      ...
6      if (checkNull(pobj)) {
7        db->persist(*pobj);
8      }
9      t.commit();
10     return param;
11 }
```

Figure 10. The code template for generating database transaction API for the Java (top) and C++ (bottom) backend.

3.4 Discussion

Our approach leverages the prevalence of declarative abstractions for expressing NFCs in modern enterprise applications. In particular, the programmer expresses these concerns by declaring metadata. The expressed functionality is provided by libraries and frameworks, which heavily rely on code generation and transformation both at source or bytecode levels. For example, a specialized compiler or a bytecode enhancer can add persistence to an application as specified by a metadata declaration. Due to their conciseness and simplicity, declarative specifications are particularly amenable to automatic transformation, a property exploited by our approach.

Our approach would be inapplicable if NFCs were implemented through custom coding in mainstream languages. In fact, when reusing unit testing functionality, our approach addresses the issue of reusing test drivers and harnesses, facilities that execute programmer-written unit tests and report the results. Programmers still have to write their unit tests in X10, albeit using a provided assertion library.

Declarative approaches are widely used to implement the majority of NFCs. One reason for this is because Aspect-oriented programming has entered the mainstream of industrial software development. Another reason is because metadata has been integrated into programming languages, such as Java 5 annotations and C# attributes. As declarative approaches become even more dominant, more functionality will become reusable through approaches similar to ours.

When applied to the same codebase, NFC implementations may harmfully interfere with each other. Although our approach does not change how NFCs are implemented, but only how they are expressed, we plan to explore whether PBSE be extended with constructs that specify the order in which NFCs should be applied. When multiple NFCs influence the same program element, ensuring a specific order can help avoid some harmful interferences. Notice that mainstream metadata formats provide no such constructs.

So far, declarative abstractions have been used primarily to express NFCs. However, if portions of core functionality become expressible declaratively, the potential benefits of our approach will also increase. If metadata can be used to express certain core functionalities, metadata translation can supplement or, in some instances, replace compilation.

4. Case Studies

To validate our approach, we applied it to reuse four NFC implementations across two domains and two languages. We reused the JUnit and CppUnit testing frameworks, thereby adding unit testing capabilities to X10. We also reused Java Data Objects (JDO) and ODB, Java and C++ ORM systems, thereby adding transparent persistence to X10 programs. In the following description, we detail our experiences with reusing these NFC implementations in X10.

4.1 Unit Testing X10 Programs

As is true for many emerging languages, no unit testing framework has yet been developed for X10. Although unit testing is an NFC, it is an integral part of widely used software development methodologies such as test-driven development (TDD) and extreme programming (XP). As a result, programmers following these methodologies in other languages are likely to miss unit testing support when programming in X10.

Although testing has not been explicitly identified as an NFC in the literature, unit testing is indeed an NFC. Unit tests help ensure that a program does what it is expected to do, but they do not affect the program's core functionality. Adding unit testing to a program does not change the program's semantics. Furthermore, unit testing frameworks heavily rely on metadata used by the programmer to declare how a framework should run unit tests.

Consider the X10 class `Integrate` in Figure 11 that uses Gaussian quadrature to numerically integrate between two input parameters—the left and the right values. This class comes from a standard IBM X10 benchmark.[4] An area is computed by integrating its partial parts. For example, when computing the area with the start of a and the end of b, $\int_a^b f(x)dx$ computes partial results through integration. The application then sums up the partial integration results— $\int_a^b f(x)dx = \frac{b-a}{2} \int_{-1}^{1} f(\frac{b-a}{2}x + \frac{b+a}{2})dx$.

Gaussian quadrature is non-trivial to implement correctly, but this implementation is even more complex as it involves parallel processing. X10 `async` and `finish` constructs spawn and join parallel tasks, respectively. Even a testing skeptic would want to carefully verify a method whose logic is that

---

[4] http://x10.svn.sourceforge.net/viewvc/x10/benchmarks/trunk/microbenchmarks/Integrate/

233

```
1  public class Integrate {
2    static def computeArea(left:double, right:double) {
3      return recEval(left, (left*left + 1.0) * left,
4        right, (right*right + 1.0) * right, 0);
5    }
6
7    static def recEval(l:double,.. r:double,..) {
8      // ..
9      finish {
10       async { expr1 = recEval(c, fc, r, fr, ar); };
11       expr2 = recEval(l, fl, c, fc, al);
12     }   return expr1 + expr2;
13  }}
```

Figure 11. An X10 Integrate class to be unit tested.

complex. The irony of the situation is that both of the X10 compilation targets—Java and C++—have mature unit testing frameworks developed for them (e.g., JUnit and CppUnit [8]). The programmer should be able to write unit tests in an X10 program, and depending on the compilation target, compile these tests to be run by JUnit or CppUnit.

Our approach makes it possible to reuse the implementations of this NFC. To implement and run unit tests in X10, the programmer first implements the needed unit tests in an X10 class. For example, the unit tests for class Integrate in Figure 11 is shown in Figure 12.

```
1  public class IntegrateTest {
2    var parm : double;
3    var expt : double;
4    var integrate : Integrate;
5
6    def init() {integrate = new Integrate();}
7
8    def finish() {integrate = null;}
9
10   def this(parm : double, expt : double) {
11     this.parm = parm;
12     this.expt = expt;
13   }
14
15   public def testComputeArea() {
16     val result = integrate.computeArea(0, this.parm);
17     TUnit.assertEquals(this.expt, result);
18   }
19
20   public static def data() {
21     val parm = new Array[double](0..1*0..2);
22     parm(0, 0) = 2;
23     parm(0, 1) = 6.000000262757339;
24     parm(1, 0) = 4;
25     parm(1, 1) = 72.000000629253464;
26     parm(2, 0) = 6;
27     parm(2, 1) = 342.000001284044629;
28     return parm;
29  }}
```

Figure 12. The unit testing class for the X10 Integrate class.

This class implements a typical test harness required by major unit testing frameworks. In particular, methods init and finish initialize and cleanup the test data, respectively. Method testComputeArea tests method computeArea in class Integrate by asserting that the method's result is what is expected. Method data provides the parameters for different instantiations of class IntegrateTest as a multi-dimensional array, in which each row contains a parameter/expected value pair, located in first and second columns, respectively.

To translate this code to work with unit testing implementations in Java and C++ as shown in Figure 13, the programmer also has to declare a simple metadata specification shown in Figure 14. This specification establishes a coding convention as the one used in class IntegrateTest. The main advantage of PBSE as compared to annotations is that this metadata specification can be *reused* with all the classes ending with suffix "Test" in a given package.

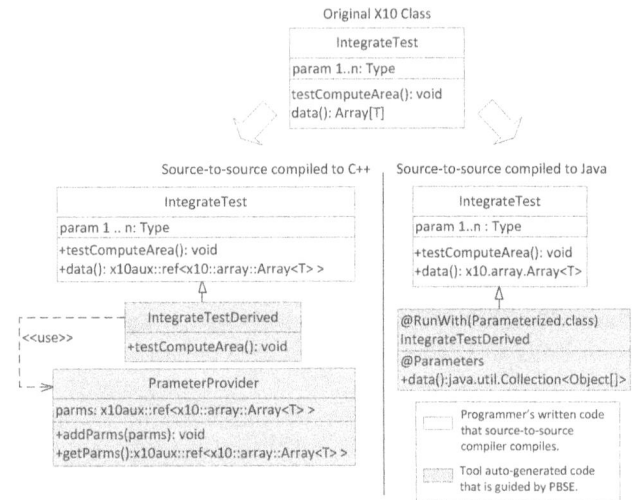

Figure 13. The class diagram for unit testing X10 programs with JUnit and CppUnit.

```
1  Metadata UnitTest<Package p>
2    Class c in p
3    Where(public class *Test)
4      c += @RunWith
5      @RunWith.value = "Parameterized"
6      TestMethod<c>
7  Metadata TestMethod<Class c>
8    Method m in c
9    Where (public def init ())
10     m += @Before
11   Where (public def finish ())
12     m += @After
13   Where (public def test* ())
14     m += @Test
15   Where (public static def data ())
16     m += @Parameters
17 UnitTest<"integrate">
```

Figure 14. The PBSE for unit testing the X10 program.

Given this PBSE specification as input, our approach then generates the Java or C++ code required to run the translated test harness of the unit testing framework at hand. A key advantage of our approach is that it addresses the incongruity of features in different NFC implementations through code generation. While parameterized unit tests are supported by JUnit in the form of the @RunWith(value=Parameterized. class) annotation, CppUnit has no corresponding feature to implement this functionality (the left part of Figure 13). In addition, JUnit requires that the method providing the parameters for unit test instantiations return java.util.Collection (the right part of Figure 13). Because x10.array.Array, the return type of the emitted Java method data, does not extend java.util.Collection, the auxiliary code generator uses the the Adaptor design pattern. To ensure that the `data` methods return the required `java.util.Collection`, an adaptor method wraps the returned type to an instance of `java.util.ArrayList`, thus satisfying this JUnit convention (Figure 15).

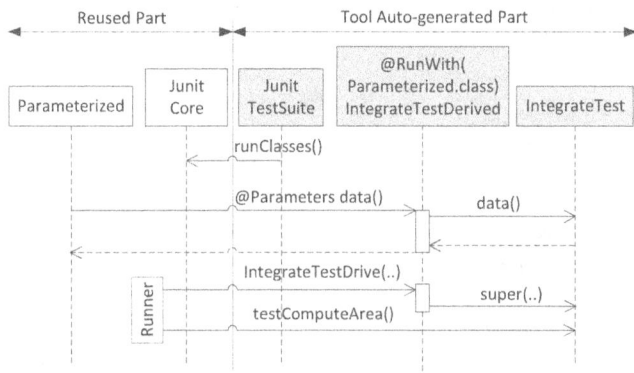

Figure 15. The sequence diagram for unit testing X10 programs with JUnit.

Supporting parameterized unit test execution in CppUnit requires more elaborate code generation. In particular, CppUnit features special macros to designate test classes and methods. We argue that such C++ macros serve as predecessors of modern metadata formats such as XML files and annotations. The defining characteristic of enterprise metadata is the ability to express functionality declaratively, describing *what* needs to take place rather than *how* it should be accomplished. In that regard, C/C++ macros are commonly used to define a DSL for expressing functionality at a higher abstraction level.

The macros in Figure 16 play the role of metadata that specifies how the CppUnit test harness should execute the tests defined in class `IntegrateTest`. To simplify the required metadata translation, we extended the built-in set of CppUnit macros to support parameterized unit tests.[5] The CppUnit macros express declarative metadata directives to initialize the framework, instantiate parameterized unit test classes, add them to a test harness, and run the added test methods (Figure 17).

```
1  void cppUnitMainTestSuite() {
2    INIT_TEST();
3    INIT_PARAMETER(ParameterProvider);
4    PARM_ITERATOR(SIZE()) {
5      ADD_TEST(IntegrateTest, /* a test class. */
6              testComputeArea); /* a test method. */
7    }
8    RUN_TEST();
9  }
```

Figure 16. Extended macros based on CppUnit.

Standard implementations of NFCs in richer languages expectedly provide more features and capabilities. In the

---

5 These macros are regenerated from scratch for every PBSE translation.

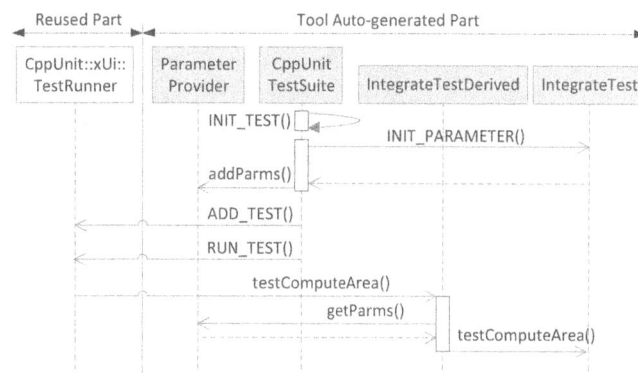

Figure 17. The sequence diagram for unit testing X10 programs with CppUnit.

case of unit testing, JUnit has built-in support for parameterized unit testing. As a result, adapting the X10 Java backend to work with JUnit is more straightforward than adapting the C++ backend for CppUnit. In particular, the `@RunWith` annotation is natively supported by JUnit. Thus, to annotate the Java methods returning the parameterized test parameters with `@RunWith`, they simply need to be adapted to return `java.util.Collection`, as discussed above.

4.2 Transparently Persisting X10 Programs

Next we describe how we applied our approach to enhance X10 programs with transparent persistence capabilities.

```
1  public class Fmm3d{
2  def getDirectEnergy() : Double{
3    val model = new FmmModel();
4    val directEnergy = finish (SumReducer()){
5    ateach (p1 in locallyEssentialTrees) {
6    var thisPlaceEnergy : Double = 0.0;
7    for ([x1,y1,z1] in lowestLevelBoxes.dist(here)){
8      val box1 = lowestLevelBoxes(x1,y1,z1) as FmmLeafBox;
9      for ([atomIndex1] in 0..(box1.atoms.size()-1)){
10     for (p in uList){
11       for ([otherBoxAtomIndex] in 0..(boxAtoms.size-1)){
12       thisPlaceEnergy +=
13         atom1.charge * atom2Packed.charge /
14         atom1.centre.distance(atom2Packed.centre);
15   }}}
16   model.setModelId(id(box1.x,box1.y,box1.z));
17   model.setEnergy(thisPlaceEnergy);
18   // other setter methods go here.
19   TP.setFmmModelObj(model);
20   }
21   offer thisPlaceEnergy;
22   }};
23   return directEnergy;
24   }}
```

Figure 18. A persisting class `Fmm3d` (simplified version) for the X10 `FmmModel` class in Figure 1.

Both compilation targets of X10—Java and C++—use ORM engines to implement transparent persistence. Our approach makes it possible to reuse these implementations, thereby making X10 programs transparently persistent.

Figure 18 shows an X10 class `Fmm3d` [17] that implements the Fast Multipole Method for electrostatic calculations with

```
 1  <jdo>
 2  <package name="au.edu.anu.mm">
 3  <class name="FmmModel"
 4       table="Fmm"
 5       identity-type="application">
 6      <field name="modelId" persistence-modifier=
 7           "persistent" primary-key="true">
 8           <column name="MODELID"/>
 9      </field>
10      <field name="energy" persistence-modifier=
11           "persistent">
12           <column name="ENERGY"/>
13      </field>
14      ...
15  </class>
16  </package>
17  </jdo>
```

Figure 19. Translated XML for the JDO system.

```
 1  Metadata PersistentJava<Package p>
 2    Class c in p
 3    Where (public class *Model)
 4      c += @Table
 5      @Table.name = (c.name=~s/Model$//)
 6      Column<c>
 7  Metadata Column<Class c>
 8    Field f in c
 9    Where (private * *)
10      Method m in c
11      Where((get+(f.name=~s/^[a-z]/[A-Z]/))==m.name)
12        m += @Column
13        @Column.name = (f.name=~s/[a-z]/[A-Z]/)
14      Where (public * *Id ())
15        @Column.primaryKey = true
16        m += @Id
17  PersistentJava <"sscal">
```

Figure 20. PBSE for transparent persistence in Java.

```
 1  #ifndef ODB_MAPPING_H
 2  #define ODB_MAPPING_H
 3
 4  #include <x10/lang/Runtime.h>
 5  #include <x10aux/bootstrap.h>
 6  #include <x10/lang/Runtime.h>
 7  #include <x10aux/bootstrap.h>
 8  #include "FmmModel.h"
 9
10  #pragma db object(FmmModel) table("Fmm")
11
12  #pragma db member(FmmModel::FMGL(modelId)) id
13       column("MODELID")
14
15  #pragma db member(FmmModel::FMGL(energy))
16       column("ENERGY")
17  ...
18  #endif
```

Figure 21. Translated C++ pragmas for the ODB system.

```
 1  Metadata PersistentCpp<Package p>
 2    Class c in p
 3    Where(class *Model)
 4      c += #pragma
 5      #pragma.object = c.name
 6      #pragma.table = (c.name=~s/Model$//)
 7      Field<c>
 8  Metadata Field<Class c>
 9    Field f in c
10    Where (* *)
11      Method m in c
12      Where((get+(f.name=~s/^[a-z]/[A-Z]/))==m.name)
13        f += #pragma
14        #pragma.member = c.name + "::FMGL(" + f.name + ")"
15        #pragma.column = (f.name=~s/[a-z]/[A-Z]/)
16      Where (* *Id ())
17        #pragma.id = true
18  PersistentCpp<"model">
```

Figure 22. PBSE for transparent persistence in C++.

analytic expansions. The implementation is real and current: it follows the strategy outlined by White and Head-Gordon [25] which was recently enhanced by Lashuk et al. [14]. The getDirectEnergy method sums the value of direct energy—directEnergy—on line 4 for all pairs of atoms. This operation requires only that atoms be already assigned to boxes, and can be executed in parallel with the other steps of the algorithm.

The ability to transparently persist a program's data can be used in multiple scenarios. For class Fmm3d, a programmer may want to optimize the execution by keeping a persistent cache of known values of thisPlaceEnergy. The cache must be persistent if different processes invoking the algorithm are to take advantage of it. The required functionality can be added to the program by using the PBSE specification from the motivating example (Figure 2). Based on this specification, our approach generates all the required metadata for the ORM system at hand, for either the Java or C++ backend, as well as X10 API through which the programmer can explicitly save and retrieve the persisted state. The generated X10 Application Programming Interface (API) that provides various platform-independent convenience methods for interfacing with the platform-specific implementations. The API is represented as a single X10 class, TP (short for TransparentPersistence). For example, to restart a program from a saved state, the X10 programmer can use the

provided TP API class as follows:
`val pobj = TP.getModel().getModelObj(latestCheckID).`
Therefore, our approach shields the programmer from the idiosyncrasies of platform-specific NFC implementations.

In this case study, we reused two mainstream, commercial ORM systems for Java and C++, JDO and ODB. While JDO uses XML files or Java annotations as its metadata format, ODB uses C/C++ pragmas. Nevertheless, our approach was able to seamlessly support these disparate metadata formats. Furthermore, the metadata specifications for both Java and C++ backends were automatically generated from the same PBSE X10 specification.

Figure 19 depicts a segment of the generated JDO XML deployment descriptor. To generate this deployment descriptor, our approach uses the PBSE depicted in Figure 20. Parameterized with this descriptor, the JDO runtime can transparently persist the specified X10 fields when the program is compiled to Java. Figure 21 depicts a segment of the generated ODB pragma definitions. To generate these pragmas, our approach uses the PBSE depicted in Figure 22. Parameterized with a file containing these pragmas, the ODB compiler generates the functionality required to transparently persist the specified X10 fields when the program is compiled to C++. Both JDO and ODB can create a relational database table to store the transparently persistent state. Furthermore, both backends share the same database schema. In other words, if an X10 program is compiled to both Java and C++ backends, both of them will share a database schema and thus can interoperate with respect to their persistent state. If the Java backend persists its state, it can then be read by the C++ backend and vice versa.

5. Related Work

Our approach to reusing NFCs across languages is rooted in metadata translation, expressing NFCs via AOP, and code generation—an extensive body of related work. Thus, next we discuss only the closely related state of the art.

Metadata Translation   Similarly to our approach, several prior approaches also leverage metadata translation, albeit not across languages. Godby et al. [6] translate among the common metadata schemas by using syntactic transformation and semantic mapping to retrieve and create heterogeneous databases in the digital library's web service. Mining-Mart [18] presents a metadata compiler for preprocessing their metadata *M4* to generate SQL code while providing high-level query descriptions for very large databases.

Ruotsalo et al. [22] transform across different metadata formats to achieve knowledge representation compatibility in different domains by means of domain knowledge. Hernández et al. [9] translate their custom metadata specifications for database mapping and queries.

Popa et al. [21] generate a set of logical mappings between source and target metadata formats, as well as translation queries while preserving semantic relationships and consistent translations, focusing on capturing the relationship between data/metadata and metadata/data translations.

These metadata translation approaches are quite powerful and can avoid inconsistencies when translating metadata. Our approach follows similar design principles but focuses on cross-language metadata and provides meta-metadata to encode the translation rules. The objective of our approach is to bring the power of metadata translation to emerging source-to-source compiled languages, enabling the programmer to reuse complex NFC implementations declaratively.

Reusing Non-Functional Concerns with AOP   Aspect-oriented Programming [12] is the foremost programming discipline for implementing NFCs. It has been debated which NFCs can be treated separately [13]. However, our approach reuses only those NFCs that have already been expressed separately in target languages. Even though our approach does not use any mainstream AOP tools, it follows the general AOP design philosophy of treating cross-cutting concerns separately and modularly.

AOP tools, including AspectJ 5 [1] and JBoss AOP [10], can introduce metadata to programs (e.g., `declare annotation` and `annotation introduction`), thereby implementing NFCs. However, these means of introducing metadata are not easily reusable as they are not parameterizable. As compared to AspectJ 5 and JBoss AOP, PBSE captures the

structural correspondences between program constructs and metadata, and as a function of the program constructs can be reused across multiple programs.

Code Generation   Much of the effectiveness of our approach is due to its heavy reliance on automatic code generation. The benefits of this technique are well-known in different domains.

Milosavljević et al. [16] map Java classes to database schemas by generating database code given an XML descriptor. XML schema elements translate to Java classes, fields, and methods. Our approach relies on standardized, mainstream implementations of NFCs. Instead of generating database code directly, our approach generates metadata that enables the target program to interface with platform-specific ORM systems.

DART [7] is an automated testing technique that uses program analysis to generate test harness code, test drivers, and test input to dynamically analyze programs executing along alternative program paths. Based on an external description, the generated test harness systematically explores all feasible program paths by using path constraints. Our approach to reusing unit testing is similar in employing an external specification to describe tests. However, the X10 programmer still writes test harness code by hand. As future work, we may explore whether our approach can be integrated with a unit test generator such as JCrasher [4].

Devadithya et al. [5] add reflection to C++ by adding metadata to the compiled C++ binaries. Metadata classes are generated by parsing input C++ class and traversing the resulting syntax trees. Our approach can be thought of as a cross-platform reflection mechanism, albeit limited to the program constructs interfacing with NFC implementations. Although our reflective capabilities are not as powerful and general, we support both Java and C++ as our source-to-source compilation platforms.

6. Conclusions

In this paper, we have presented a novel approach to reusing NFC implementations across languages. Our approach enables emerging language programmers to take advantage of such implementations in the target languages of a source-to-source compilation process. As a specific application of our approach, we added unit testing and transparent persistence to X10 programs, thereby reusing four existing, mainstream, NFCs implementations in Java and C++.

This paper contributes an approach to reusing NFCs implemented in a mainstream language from an emerging language program, when the emerging language is source-to-source compiled to the mainstream one; automated cross-language metadata translation—a novel approach to translating metadata alongside compiling the source language; meta-metadata that declaratively specify mappings between metadata formats; and the ability to unit test and transparently persist X10 programs for both Java and C++ backends.

The ongoing quest to bridge programmer imagination and computing capabilities motivates the continuous emergence of new programming languages. When an emerging language is source-to-source compiled to a mainstream one, the NFC implementations of the mainstream language remain inaccessible to the emerging language programmers. The presented novel approach reuses NFCs in mainstream languages by automatically translating metadata alongside compiling the source language. By eliminating the need to reimplement NFCs in emerging languages, our approach saves development effort.

Acknowledgments

This research was sponsored through an IBM X10 Innovation Award. The IBM Research X10 team patiently answered our questions about the X10 language, compiler, and benchmarks. Fruitful discussions with our IBM liaison, Igor Peshansky, helped crystallize many of this paper's ideas. Boris Kolpackov helpfully guided us through our experiences with ODB. Yannis Smaragdakis, Wesley Tansey, Ben Wiedermann, and the AOSD anonymous reviewers provided valuable feedback that helped improve the paper.

Availability

All the software described in the paper is available from: http://research.cs.vt.edu/vtspaces/x10pbse/.

References

[1] AspectJ Team. The AspectJ 5 development kit developer's notebook. http://eclipse.org/aspectj/doc/next/adk15notebook/.

[2] Charles Nutter, Thomas Enebo, Ola Bini and Nick Sieger. JRuby. http://www.jruby.org/.

[3] CodeSynthesis. ODB: C++ Object-Relational Mapping. http://www.codesynthesis.com/products/odb/.

[4] C. Csallner and Y. Smaragdakis. JCrasher: An automatic robustness tester for Java. *Softw. Pract. Exper.*, 2004.

[5] T. Devadithya, K. Chiu, and W. Lu. C++ reflection for high performance problem solving environments. In *Proceedings of the spring simulation multiconference*, 2007.

[6] C. J. Godby, D. Smith, and E. Childress. Two paths to interoperable metadata. In *DCMI: Proceedings of the international conference on Dublin Core and metadata applications*, 2003.

[7] P. Godefroid, N. Klarlund, and K. Sen. Dart: directed automated random testing. In *PLDI: Proceedings of the ACM SIGPLAN conference on Programming language design and implementation*, 2005.

[8] P. Hamill. *Unit test frameworks*. O'Reilly, first edition, 2004.

[9] M. A. Hernández, P. Papotti, and W. C. Tan. Data exchange with data-metadata translations. *Proc. VLDB Endow.*, 2008.

[10] JBoss. JBoss AOP. http://www.jboss.org/jbossaop/.

[11] Jython Project. Jython: Python for the Java Platform. http://www.jython.org/.

[12] G. Kiczales, J. Lamping, A. Mendhekar, C. Maeda, C. Lopes, J. M. Loingtier, and J. Irwing. Aspect-oriented programming. In *ECOOP: Proceedings of the 11th European Conference on Object-Oriented Programming*, 1997.

[13] J. Kienzle and R. Guerraoui. AOP: Does It Make Sense? The Case of Concurrency and Failures. In *ECOOP: Proceedings of the 16th European Conference on Object-Oriented Programming*, 2002.

[14] I. Lashuk, A. Chandramowlishwaran, H. Langston, T.-A. Nguyen, R. Sampath, A. Shringarpure, R. Vuduc, L. Ying, D. Zorin, and G. Biros. A massively parallel adaptive fast-multipole method on heterogeneous architectures. In *Proceedings of the Conference on High Performance Computing Networking, Storage and Analysis*, 2009.

[15] Maven. Security Annotation Framework. http://safr.sourceforge.net/.

[16] B. Milosavljević, M. Vidaković, and Z. Konjović. Automatic code generation for database-oriented web applications. In *Proceedings of the second workshop on Intermediate representation engineering for virtual machines*, 2002.

[17] J. Milthorpe, V. Ganesh, A. P. Rendell, and D. Grove. X10 as a parallel language for scientific computation: Practice and experience. In *IPDPS: Proceedings of the IEEE International Parallel & Distributed Processing Symposium*, 2011.

[18] K. Morik and M. Scholz. The miningmart approach to knowledge discovery in databases. In *Intelligent Technologies for Information Analysis*, 2003.

[19] N. Nystrom and V. Saraswat. An annotation and compiler plugin system for X10. Technical report, IBM TJ Watson Research Center, 2007.

[20] M. Odersky, P. Altherr, V. Cremet, B. Emir, S. Maneth, S. Micheloud, N. Mihaylov, M. Schinz, E. Stenman, and M. Zenger. An overview of the Scala programming language. Technical report, EPFL.

[21] L. Popa, Y. Velegrakis, M. A. Hernández, R. J. Miller, and R. Fagin. Translating web data. In *VLDB: Proceedings of the international conference on Very Large Data Bases*, 2002.

[22] T. Ruotsalo and E. Hyvönen. An event-based approach for semantic metadata interoperability. In *Proceedings of the 6th international semantic web conference*, 2007.

[23] V. Saraswat, B. Bloom, I. Peshansky, O. Tardieu, and D. Grove. X10 Language Specification Version 2.1. Technical report, IBM TJ Watson Research Center, 2011.

[24] E. Tilevich and M. Song. Reusable enterprise metadata with pattern-based structural expressions. In *AOSD: Proceedings of the 9th International Conference on Aspect-Oriented Software Development*, 2010.

[25] C. A. White and M. Head-Gordon. Derivation and efficient implementation of the fast multipole method. *The Journal of Chemical Physics*, 1994.

DiSL: A Domain-Specific Language for Bytecode Instrumentation

Lukáš Marek

Charles University, Czech Republic
lukas.marek@d3s.mff.cuni.cz

Alex Villazón

Universidad Privada Boliviana, Bolivia
avillazon@upb.edu

Yudi Zheng

Shanghai Jiao Tong University, China
zheng.yudi@sjtu.edu.cn

Danilo Ansaloni   Walter Binder

University of Lugano, Switzerland
{danilo.ansaloni, walter.binder}@usi.ch

Zhengwei Qi

Shanghai Jiao Tong University, China
qizhwei@sjtu.edu.cn

Abstract

Many dynamic analysis tools for programs written in managed languages such as Java rely on bytecode instrumentation. Tool development is often tedious because of the use of low-level bytecode manipulation libraries. While aspect-oriented programming (AOP) offers high-level abstractions to concisely express certain dynamic analyses, the join point model of mainstream AOP languages such as AspectJ is not well suited for many analysis tasks and the code generated by weavers in support of certain language features incurs high overhead. In this paper we introduce DiSL (domain-specific language for instrumentation), a new language especially designed for dynamic program analysis. DiSL offers an open join point model where any region of bytecodes can be a shadow, synthetic local variables for efficient data passing, efficient access to comprehensive static and dynamic context information, and weave-time execution of user-defined static analysis code. We demonstrate the benefits of DiSL with a case study, recasting an existing dynamic analysis tool originally implemented in AspectJ. We show that the DiSL version offers better code coverage, incurs significantly less overhead, and eases the integration of new analysis features that could not be expressed in AspectJ.

Categories and Subject Descriptors D.3.3 [*Programming Languages*]: Language Constructs and Features—Frameworks

General Terms Languages, Measurement, Performance

Keywords Bytecode instrumentation, dynamic program analysis, aspect-oriented programming, JVM

1. Introduction

Dynamic program analysis tools support numerous software engineering tasks, including profiling, debugging, testing, program comprehension, and reverse engineering. Despite of the importance of dynamic analysis, prevailing techniques for building dynamic analysis tools are based on low-level abstractions that make tool development, maintenance, and customization tedious, error-prone, and hence expensive. For example, many dynamic analysis tools for the Java Virtual Machine (JVM) rely on bytecode instrumentation, supported by a variety of bytecode engineering libraries that offer low-level APIs resulting in verbose implementation code.

In an attempt to simplify the development of dynamic analysis tools, researchers have explored the use of aspect-oriented programming (AOP) languages, such as AspectJ [16]. Examples of aspect-based dynamic analysis tools are the DJProf profilers [20], the RacerAJ data-race detector [10], and the Senseo Eclipse plugin for augmenting static source code views with dynamic information [21]. However, as neither mainstream AOP languages nor the corresponding weavers have been designed to meet the requirements of dynamic program analysis, the success of using AOP for dynamic analysis remains limited. For example, in AspectJ, join points that are important for dynamic program analysis (e.g., the execution of bytecodes or basic blocks) are missing, access to reflective dynamic join point information is expensive, data passing between woven advice in local variables is not supported, and the mixing of low-level bytecode instrumentation and high-level AOP code is not foreseen.

In this paper, we introduce DiSL, a new domain-specific language for bytecode instrumentation. DiSL relies on AOP principles for concisely expressing efficient dynamic analysis tools. The language provides an open join point model defined by an extensible set of bytecode markers, efficient access to static and dynamic context information, optimized processing of method[1] arguments, and synthetic local vari-

---

[1] In this paper, "method" stands for "method or constructor".

ables for efficient data passing. While DiSL significantly raises the abstraction level when compared to prevailing bytecode manipulation libraries, it also exposes a low-level API to implement new bytecode markers. The DiSL weaver guarantees complete bytecode coverage to ensure that analysis results represent overall program execution. DiSL follows similar design principles as @J [8], an AOP language for dynamic analysis, which however lacks an open join point model and efficient access to method arguments.

Compared to high-level dynamic analysis frameworks such as RoadRunner [13] or jchord[2] that restrict the locations that can be instrumented, DiSL offers the developer fine-grained control over the inserted bytecode; that is, DiSL is not tailored for any specify dynamic analysis task, but provides constructs for concisely expressing any bytecode instrumentation. Instrumentation sites can be specified with a combination of bytecode markers, scoping expressions, and guards; guards represent static analyses executed at weave-time. Instrumentation code is provided in the form of snippets, that is, code templates that are instantiated for each selected instrumentation site and inlined. Snippets may access synthetic local variables to pass data from one instrumentation site to another. Snippets may access any static or dynamic context information; they may also process an arbitrary number of method arguments in a custom way.

The scientific contributions of this paper are twofold:

1. We present our design goals, the DiSL language constructs, and the implementation of the DiSL weaver.

2. We present a case study to illustrate the benefits of DiSL. We recast Senseo [21, 22] in DiSL; Senseo is an AspectJ-based profiling tool that supports various software maintenance tasks. In contrast to the former AspectJ implementation, the DiSL version of the tool features complete bytecode coverage, introduces significantly less overhead, and can be easily extended to collect additional dynamic metrics on the intra-procedural control flow.

This paper is structured as follows: Section 2 describes the design goals underlying DiSL. Section 3 gives a detailed overview of the DiSL language constructs. The software architecture of the DiSL weaver and its implementation are discussed in Section 4. Our case study is introduced in Section 5 and evaluated in Section 6. Section 7 discusses related work, Section 8 summarizes the strengths and limitations of DiSL, and Section 9 concludes.

2. Design of DiSL

Designing a good language for instrumentation-based dynamic program analysis is challenging, because we need to reconcile three conflicting design goals: (1) high expressiveness of the language, (2) a convenient, high-level programming model, and (3) high efficiency of the developed

analysis tools. On the one hand, existing bytecode manipulation libraries meet the first and the third goal, but provide only low-level abstractions that make tool development cumbersome. On the other hand, mainstream AOP languages achieve the second goal, but lack expressiveness (e.g., lack of join points that would allow tracing the intra-procedural control flow) and suffer from inefficiencies (e.g., access to dynamic reflective join point information may require the allocation of unnecessary objects). The design of DiSL aims at bridging the gap between low-level bytecode manipulation frameworks and high-level AOP. Below, we motivate the main design choices underlying DiSL.

Open join point model. DiSL allows any region of bytecodes to be used as a join point, thus following an open join point model. That is, the set of supported join point *shadows* [15] is not hard-coded. To enable the definition of new join points, DiSL provides an extensible mechanism for marking user-defined bytecode regions (i.e., shadows).

Compatibility with Java and the JVM. DiSL is a domain-specific embedded language which has Java as its host language. DiSL instrumentations are implemented in Java, and annotations are used to express where programs are to be instrumented. Dynamic analysis tools written in DiSL can be compiled with any Java compiler and executed on any JVM.

Advice inlining and data passing in synthetic local variables. Advice in DiSL are expressed in the form of code *snippets* that are inlined, giving the developer fine-grained control over the inserted code. DiSL *instrumentations* (corresponding to aspects in AOP) describe where snippets are to be inserted into the base program. Thanks to inlining, snippets woven into the same method are able to efficiently communicate data through *synthetic local variables* [6].

Efficient access to complete static and dynamic context information. In DiSL, all static context information is exposed to the developer. This feature is similar to AspectJ's static reflective join point information (offering class and method properties), but exposes additional information at the basic block and bytecode level. DiSL also supports user-defined static analysis to compute further static context information at weave-time. In addition, DiSL provides a simple, yet powerful reflective API to gather dynamic context information which gives access to local variables and to the operand stack, supporting also efficient access to an arbitrary number of method arguments.

No support for around advice. Mainstream AOP languages support advice execution *before*, *after*, and *around* join points. Three common use cases of around advice are (1) passing data around a join point, (2) skipping a join point, and (3) executing a join point multiple times. As we assume that instrumentations do not alter the control flow in the base program, only the first use is relevant for us. However, for the first use case, the same behavior can be achieved with before and after advice using synthetic local variables [6].

[2] http://code.google.com/p/jchord/

240

Hence, DiSL only supports before and after advice, which helps keep the weaver simple.

Complete bytecode coverage. DiSL is designed for weaving with complete bytecode coverage. That is, the DiSL weaver ensures that all methods that have a bytecode representation can be woven, including methods in the standard Java class library. To this end, the DiSL weaver relies on implementation techniques developed in previous work [19].

3. Language Features

In this section we give an overview of the language features of DiSL. In Section 3.1 we introduce DiSL instrumentations specified in the form of snippets; markers determine where snippets are woven in the bytecode. The mechanism to control the inlining order of snippets is explained in Section 3.2. Synthetic local variables for efficiently passing data between woven snippets are presented in Section 3.3, and efficient access to thread-local variables is discussed in Section 3.4. In Section 3.5 we introduce static context to provide static reflective information, and we present the reflective API for obtaining dynamic context information in Section 3.6. In Section 3.7 we explain DiSL's support for method arguments processing. In Section 3.8 we introduce guards that enable the evaluation of conditionals at weave-time to decide whether a join point is to be captured, as well as a scoping construct to restrict weaving.

3.1 Instrumentations, Snippets, and Markers

DiSL *instrumentations* are Java classes. An instrumentation can only have *snippets* that are static methods annotated with `@Before`, `@After`, `@AfterReturning`, or `@AfterThrowing`. Snippets are defined as static methods, because their body is used as a template that is instantiated and inlined at the matching join points in the base program. Snippets do not return any value and must not throw any exception (that is not caught by a handler in the snippet).

Because of DiSL's open join point model, pointcuts are not hardcoded in the language but defined by an extensible library of *markers*. Markers are standard Java classes implementing a special interface for join point selection. DiSL provides a rich library of markers including those for method body, basic block, individual bytecode, and exception handler. In addition, the developer may extend existing markers or implement new markers from scratch.

The marker class is specified in the `marker` attribute in the snippet annotation. The weaver takes care of instantiating the selected marker, matching the corresponding join points, and weaving the snippets.

In addition to the predefined markers, DiSL offers join point extensibility by exposing the internal representation of method bodies to the developer, who has to implement code to *mark* the bytecode regions defining the shadows for the new join points.

3.2 Control of Snippet Order

It is common that several shadows coincide in the starting instruction, that is, several snippets may apply to the same join point. Similar to AspectJ's *advice precedence* resolution, DiSL provides a simple mechanism to control snippet ordering through the `order` attribute in the snippet annotation. The order is specified as a non-negative integer value. For `@Before`, snippets with higher order are inlined before snippets with lower order. For `@After`, `@AfterReturning`, and `@AfterThrowing`, snippets with lower order are inlined before snippets with higher order. Thus, the order indicates "how close" to the shadow the snippet shall be inlined.

3.3 Synthetic Local Variables

DiSL provides an efficient communication mechanism to pass arbitrary data between snippets. The mechanism relies on inlining so as to store the data in a local variable, which is therefore visible in the scope of the woven method body. DiSL provides the `@SyntheticLocal` annotation to specify the holder variable. Synthetic local variables must be declared as static fields and can be used in any snippet. The weaver takes care of translating the static field declared in the instrumentation into a local variable in each instrumented method, and of replacing the bytecodes that access the static field with bytecodes that access the introduced local variable. For details, we refer to [6].

3.4 Thread-local Variables

DiSL supports thread-local variables with the `@ThreadLocal` annotation. This mechanism extends `java.lang.Thread` by inserting the annotated field. While the inserted fields are instance fields, thread-local variables must be declared as static fields in the instrumentation class, similar to synthetic local variables. These fields must be initialized to the default value of the field's type.[3] The DiSL weaver translates all access to thread-local variables in snippets into bytecodes that access the corresponding field of the currently executing thread. An `inheritable` flag can be set in the `@ThreadLocal` annotation such that new threads "inherit" the value of a thread-local variable from the creating thread. Note that the standard Java class library offers classes with similar semantics (`java.lang.ThreadLocal` and `java.lang.InheritableThreadLocal`). However, accessing fields directly inserted into `java.lang.Thread` results in more efficient code.

3.5 Static Context Information

Accessing static context information is essential for dynamic analyses, for example, gathering information about

---

[3] During JVM bootstrapping, in general, inserted code cannot be executed because it may introduce class dependencies that can violate JVM assumptions concerning the class initialization order. Hence, threads created during bootstrapping could not initialize inserted thread-local fields in the beginning.

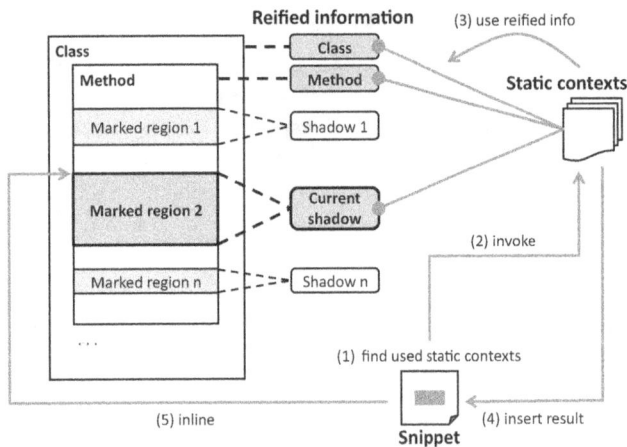

Figure 1. Gathering static context information at weave-time

```
public class CallingContextBBAnalysis {
  @ThreadLocal
  static CCTNode currentNode;

  @SyntheticLocal
  static CCTNode callerNode;

  @Before(marker = BodyMarker.class, order = 1)
  static void onMethodEntry(MethodStaticContext msc) {
    if ((callerNode = currentNode) == null)
      callerNode = CCTNode.getRoot();
    currentNode =
      callerNode.profileCall(msc.thisMethodFullName());
  }

  @After(marker = BodyMarker.class)
  static void onMethodCompletion() {
    currentNode = callerNode;
  }

  @Before(marker = BasicBlockMarker.class, order = 0)
  static void onBasicBlock(BasicBlockStaticContext bbsc) {
    currentNode.profileBB(bbsc.getBBIndex());
  }
}
```

Figure 2. Sample instrumentation for calling context-aware basic block profiling (class CCTNode is not shown)

the method, basic block, or bytecode instruction that is executed. Because of the open join point model of DiSL, there is no bound static part of a join point as in AspectJ. In DiSL, the programmer can gather reflective static information at weave-time by using various *static contexts*. DiSL provides a library of commonly used static contexts such as MethodStaticContext, BasicBlockStaticContext, and BytecodeStaticContext. The developer may also implement custom static context classes.

For every snippet, the programmer can specify any number of static contexts as argument. Each static context class implements the StaticContext interface and provides methods without argument that must return a value of a Java primitive type or a string. The reason for this restriction is that DiSL stores the results of static context methods directly in the constant pool of the woven class. Static contexts receive read-only access to the shadow containing the following reflective information: the class and method under instrumentation, the snippet, and the beginning and ending positions of the current shadow.

Figure 1 depicts the reflective approach for gathering static context information. After shadow marking according to the selected marker, the snippet is parsed to locate invocations to static context methods (step 1). Static contexts are then instantiated by the weaver and the corresponding methods are invoked for every shadow (step 2). Static context methods access the exposed reflective data to compute the static information to be returned (step 3). The weaver replaces the invocation of the static context methods in the snippet with bytecodes to access the computed static information (step 4). The snippet code is inlined before or after the matching shadows (step 5).

Figure 2 shows how static contexts are used in an instrumentation for calling context-aware basic block analysis. The goal is to help developers find hotspots in their programs taking both the inter- and intra-procedural control flow into

account. The presented instrumentation collects statistics on basic block execution for each calling context.

For storing inter-procedural calling context information, a Calling Context Tree (CCT) [3] is used. For each thread, the current CCT node is kept in the thread-local variable currentNode that is updated upon method entry and completion (onMethodEntry(...) and onMethodCompletion() snippets using the BodyMarker). The synthetic local variable callerNode is used to store the CCT node corresponding to the caller. The CCTNode.getRoot() method returns the root node of the CCT. The method profileCall(...) takes a method identifier as argument and returns the corresponding callee node in the CCT. The method identifier is obtained from the MethodStaticContext; it is inserted as a string in the constant pool of the woven class.[4]

The onBasicBlock() snippet captures all basic block join points using the BasicBlockMarker. The idea is to count how many times each basic block is executed, so as to detect hot basic blocks. To this end, the snippet uses the BasicBlockStaticContext for gathering the index of the captured basic block. This value is used to increment the corresponding counter in the CCT node (not shown). Note that the order of the @Before snippets ensures that the initialization of the synthetic local variable callerNode and the update of the thread-local variable currentNode are done at the very beginning of the method body, before they are accessed in the first basic block.

3.6 Dynamic Context Information

Access to dynamic join point information (e.g., getThis(), getTarget(), and getArgs() in AspectJ) requires gathering data from *local variables* and from the *operand*

---

[4] This is similar to the use of JoinPoint.StaticPart in AspectJ. While AspectJ inserts static fields in the woven class to hold reflective static join point information, DiSL avoids structural modifications of the woven class.

```
public interface DynamicContext {
  <T> T getLocalVariableValue(int index,
                              Class<T> valueType);
  <T> T getStackValue(int distance, Class<T> valueType);
  Object getThis();
}
```

Figure 3. DynamicContext interface

```
public class ArrayAccessAnalysis {
  @Before(marker = BytecodeMarker.class, args = "aastore")
  static void beforeArrayStore(DynamicContext dc) {
    Object array = dc.getStackValue(2, Object.class);
    int index = dc.getStackValue(1, int.class);
    Object stored = dc.getStackValue(0, Object.class);
    Analysis.process(array, index, stored); // not shown
  }
}
```

Figure 4. Profiling array access

stack [15]. DiSL provides an API to explicitly access this information. Figure 3 shows the DynamicContext API which provides reflective information through the getLocalVariableValue(...) to access a local variable, getStackValue(...) to access a stack value, and getThis() returning this object or null in the case of a static method. Similar to static contexts, the DynamicContext can be passed to snippets as an argument. The programmer must provide the index and the type of the data to access. Note that the use of DynamicContext is not restricted to any particular marker. The developer must know how to access the correct data from local variables or from the operand stack. The weaver takes care of translating calls to the API methods into bytecode sequences to retrieve the desired values.

An example of the use of DynamicContext is access to the return value of a method, which is on top of the stack upon normal method completion. The programmer may implement an @AfterReturning snippet with the BytecodeMarker (for different return bytecodes) and use getStackValue(0,...) to retrieve the return value. The index zero indicates the top of the stack.

The combination of DynamicContext with the BytecodeMarker provides a powerful mechanism to gather join point information for implementing dynamic analysis tools, such as memory profilers. For example, Figure 4 shows how to capture array accesses, which is not possible in AspectJ. The beforeArrayStore(...) snippet captures all objects being stored in arrays, where the element type is a reference type. The profiler can keep track which object has been stored at which position of an array. Before every aastore bytecode, the snippet gets the array, the index[5] where the element will be stored, and the object to be stored from the operand stack (at positions 2, 1, and 0, respectively). The process(...) method processes the collected information (not shown).

---

[5] The use of Java generics in the API results in autoboxing of primitive values (e.g., index) in the compiled snippet. The DiSL weaver removes the unnecessary boxing code before inlining.

```
public interface ArgumentProcessorContext {
  Object getReceiver(ArgumentProcessorMode mode);
  Object[] getArgs(ArgumentProcessorMode mode);
  void apply(Class<?> argumentProcessor,
             ArgumentProcessorMode mode);
}
```

```
public enum ArgumentProcessorMode {
  METHOD_ARGS, CALLSITE_ARGS
}
```

Figure 5. Argument processor API

3.7 Argument Processors

Method arguments are retrieved from local variables or, in the case of call sites, from the operand stack. DiSL's DynamicContext can be used to access these values when the argument index and type are known, which is not always the case. DiSL also provides a reflective mechanism, called *argument processor*, to process all arguments by their types.

The ArgumentProcessorContext interface (see Figure 5) can be used within snippets to access method arguments; it is to be passed to snippets as an argument, similar to static contexts or DynamicContext. Two modes can be specified, to process either arguments of the method where the snippet is inlined (METHOD_ARGS), or arguments of a method invocation (CALLSITE_ARGS). The getReceiver(...) method returns the receiver, or null for static methods. The getArgs(...) method returns all arguments in an object array, similar to JoinPoint.getArgs() in AspectJ for execution respectively call pointcuts. However, if the programmer needs to selectively access arguments, or does not want them to be wrapped in an object array (e.g., for performance reasons or to preserve the original type for arguments of primitive types), the API provides the apply(...) method, where the programmer can specify an argument processor class that handles the generation of code to access the arguments.

Argument processors are classes annotated with @ArgumentProcessor. At weave-time, DiSL checks which argument processor is selected in the snippet, and for each matching join point, generates the code to process the arguments according to their types.

Argument processors must implement static void methods, where the first parameter is required and additional (optional) parameters may be passed. The type of the first parameter selects the type of argument to be captured. The first parameter's type can only be java.lang.Object or a primitive type. For each argument of the woven method, the weaver checks whether the selected argument processor has a method where the first parameter type matches the current method argument type. In this case, the weaver generates the code to access the corresponding argument, which is eventually inlined within the snippet. As additional parameters, the argument processor method can take any static context, DynamicContext, or ArgumentContext. ArgumentContext is an interface to access argument type, argument position, and the total number of arguments.

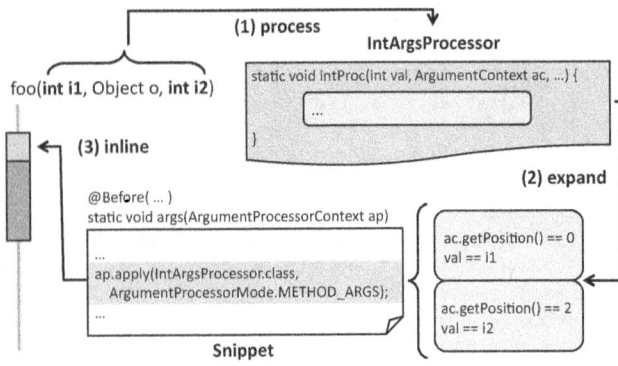

Figure 6. Processing of integer arguments

```
public class ArgumentAnalysis {
  @Before(marker = BodyMarker.class,
          guard = MethodReturnsRef.class)
  static void onMethodEntry {
    ... // inlined only if the method returns an object
  }
}

public class MethodReturnsRef {
  @GuardMethod
  static boolean evalGuard(ReturnTypeStaticContext rtsc) {
    return !rtsc.isPrimitive();
  }
}
```

Figure 7. Snippet guard restricting weaving to methods that return objects

Figure 6 illustrates the weaving of a snippet before a join point in method foo(...). In this example, the developer only wants to process arguments of type int. For method foo(...), only two of the arguments will match the intProc(...) processor method (i1 and i2). First, the weaver finds out which argument processor and mode should be applied to the snippet (step 1). Then, the invocation to apply(...) in the snippet is replaced with the expanded method bodies of the processor for each matching argument (step 2). In the example, the generated code will give access to the two integer arguments, i.e., the snippet will contain expanded processor code to access the values i1 and i2. Finally, the expanded snippet is inlined (step 3). For METHOD_ARGS, the generated code retrieves the arguments from local variables; for CALLSITE_ARGS, the arguments are taken from the operand stack. The use of CALLSITE_ARGS throws a weave-time error if the snippet is not woven before a method invocation bytecode.

There are several advantages of using argument processors compared to, for example, JoinPoint.getArgs() in AspectJ. Firstly, there is no need for creating objects that hold dynamic join point information. DiSL efficiently takes the correct values directly from local variables or from the stack. Secondly, argument types are preserved. The values of primitive types are not boxed as in AspectJ. Finally, it is straightforward to apply argument processors to a subset of arguments, without requiring complex pointcuts to be written. We will illustrate these advantages in more detail with our case study and evaluation in Sections 5 and 6.

3.8 Guards and Scope

DiSL provides two complementary mechanisms for restricting the application of snippets. The first one, *guard*, is based on weave-time evaluation of conditionals. The second one, *scope*, is based on method signature matching.

Guards allow us to evaluate complex weave-time restrictions for individual join points. A guard has to implement a static method annotated with @GuardMethod. The guard method may take any number of static contexts as arguments. The guard method returns a boolean value indicating whether the current joint point is to be instrumented. Static

contexts can be used to expose reflective weave-time information to the guard. The guard has to be specified with the guard attribute of the snippet annotation.

In contrast to AspectJ's if pointcut, the evaluation of guards is done for each join point at weave-time. This avoids runtime overhead due to the evaluation of statically known conditionals. To illustrate this point, let's consider the example shown in Figure 7. The programmer wants to restrict weaving only to methods returning objects; methods returning values of primitive types (or void, which we consider a primitive type here) shall not be woven. The evalGuard(...) method of the MethodReturnsRef guard uses ReturnTypeStaticContext to determine whether the return type of the instrumented method is primitive. Because this evaluation is performed at weave-time, the onMethodEntry(...) snippet will be inlined only in methods that return objects.

Another interesting example of weave-time conditional evaluation is the use of data flow analysis within guards. This feature helps avoid inlining snippets that would otherwise access uninitialized objects (passing an uninitialized object to another method as argument would be illegal and cause a verification failure). For example, the programmer may capture all putfield bytecodes in constructors, where the target is a properly initialized object. Consequently, putfield bytecodes that write to the object under initialization before invocation of the superclass constructor will not be captured.

Even though guards are expressive, in many common cases, a more concise scoping expression is sufficient. In DiSL, scope is a simplified signature pattern matching pointcut designator. The scope attribute of the snippet annotation specifies which methods shall be instrumented. Scope expressions specify method, class, or package names and may contain wildcards (e.g., scope = "* java.io.*(..)"). Typically, scope evaluation is faster than guard evaluation, as it is done only once for each method. In contrary, a guard has to be invoked (using reflection) for each join point in the method. The best combination is the usage of scope expressions for fast method filtering and of guards for fine-grained joint point selection.

4. Implementation

DiSL is implemented in Java using the ASM[6] bytecode manipulation library in about 100 classes and 8000 lines of code. The DiSL weaver[7] runs on top of jBORAT[8], a lightweight toolkit providing support for instrumentation with complete bytecode coverage [19]. jBORAT uses two JVMs: an *instrumentation JVM* where bytecode instrumentation is performed and an *application JVM* that executes the instrumented application. This separation of the instrumentation logic from the instrumented application reduces perturbations in the application JVM (e.g., class loading and initialization triggered by jBORAT or by the DiSL weaver do not happen within the application JVM). DiSL simplifies deployment with scripts, hiding the complex JVM setup from the user.

Figure 8 gives an overview of the DiSL weaver running on top of jBORAT. During initialization, DiSL parses all instrumentation classes (step 1). Then it creates an internal representation for snippets and initializes the used markers, guards, static contexts, and argument processors. When DiSL receives a class from jBORAT (step 2), the weaving process starts with the snippet selection. The selection is done in two phases, starting with scope matching (step 3) and followed by shadow creation and selection. Shadows are created using the markers associated with the snippets selected in the previous scope matching phase. Shadows are evaluated by guards and only snippets with at least one valid shadow are selected (step 4). At this point, all snippets that will be used for weaving are known. Static contexts are used to compute the static information required by snippets (step 5). Argument processors are evaluated for snippets, and argument processor methods that match method arguments are selected (step 6). All the collected information is finally used for weaving (step 7). Argument processors are applied, and calls to static contexts are replaced with the computed static information. The weaver also generates the bytecodes to access dynamic context information. Finally, the woven class is emitted and passed back to jBORAT (step 8).

5. Case Study: Senseo

In this section, we illustrate the benefits of DiSL by recasting *Senseo* [21], a dynamic analysis tool for code comprehension and profiling. Senseo uses an aspect written in AspectJ for collecting calling context-sensitive dynamic information for each invoked method, including statistics on the runtime types of method arguments and return values, the number of method invocations, and the number of allocated objects. These metrics are visualized by an Eclipse plugin[9] that en-

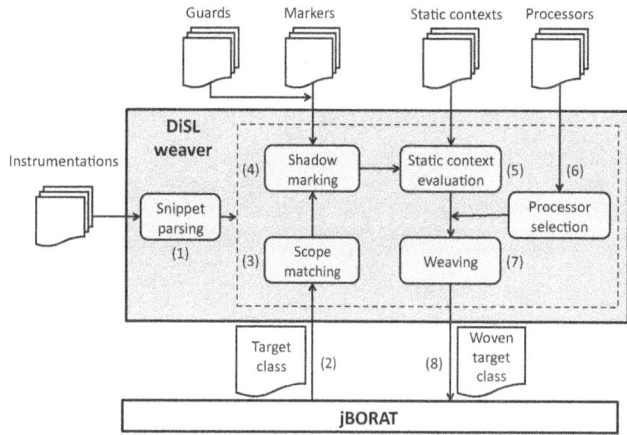

Figure 8. Overview of DiSL weaving process

riches the static source code views with the collected dynamic information. Senseo helps developers understand the dynamic behavior of applications and locate performance problems.

The original version of Senseo has two main limitations: (1) lack of intra-procedural profiling and (2) high overhead for metrics collection. Both limitations stem from the use of AspectJ to express the instrumentation. Because of the absence of join points at the level of basic blocks, dynamic metrics on the intra-procedural control flow are missing, making it difficult for the developer to locate hot methods with complex intra-procedural control flow that are not invoked frequently. Moreover, access to dynamic join point information is inefficient due to the boxing of primitive values and because of the allocation of object arrays, notably for processing method arguments. For example, although only the first argument of method `paint(Object o, int x, int y)` could receive objects of different runtime types, the AspectJ implementation of Senseo collects the runtime types of all three arguments upon each invocation, because `JoinPoint.getArgs()` returns all arguments in a newly created object array, boxing values of primitive types.

Figure 9 shows the (simplified) DiSL instrumentation `Senseo2` that overcomes the limitations of the previous AspectJ implementation. To collect dynamic metrics for each calling context, the `onMethodEntry(...)` and `onMethodCompletion()` snippets reify the calling context in a similar way as explained in Section 3.5 (Figure 2). Each CCT node stores the dynamic information collected within the corresponding calling context, as explained below.

Number of method executions. The counting of method executions is subsumed in the `onMethodEntry(...)` snippet and performed in the `profileCall(...)` method by incrementing a counter. This information is used to compute the number of method calls for each calling context.

Number of allocated objects and arrays. To count the number of allocated objects and arrays, the `onAllocation()`

[6] http://asm.ow2.org/

[7] http://disl.origo.ethz.ch/

[8] jBORAT stands for Java Bytecode Overall Rewriting and Analysis Toolkit.

[9] http://scg.unibe.ch/research/senseo

```java
public class Senseo2 {
  @ThreadLocal
  static CCTNode currentNode;

  @SyntheticLocal
  static CCTNode callerNode;

  @Before(marker = BodyMarker.class, order = 1)
  static void onMethodEntry(MethodStaticContext msc,
      ArgumentProcessorContext proc) {
    if ((callerNode = currentNode) == null)
      callerNode = CCTNode.getRoot();
    currentNode =
      callerNode.profileCall(msc.thisMethodFullName());

    proc.apply(ReferenceProcessor.class,
            ProcessorMode.METHOD_ARGS);
  }

  @After(marker = BodyMarker.class, order = 2)
  static void onMethodCompletion() {
    currentNode = callerNode;
  }

  @AfterReturning(marker = BodyMarker.class, order = 1,
            guard = MethodReturnsRef.class)
  static void onReturnRef(DynamicContext dc) {
    Object obj = dc.getStackValue(0, Object.class);
    currentNode.profileReturn(obj);
  }

  @AfterReturning(marker=BytecodeMarker.class, order=0,
      args = "new,newarray,anewarray,multianewarray")
  static void onAllocation() {
    currentNode.profileAllocation();
  }

  @Before(marker = BasicBlockMarker.class, order = 0)
  static void onBasicBlock(BasicBlockStaticContext bbsc){
    currentNode.profileBB(bbsc.getBBIndex());
  }
}

@ArgumentProcessor
public class ReferenceProcessor {
  static void objProc(Object obj, ArgumentContext ac) {
    Senseo2.currentNode.profileArgument(ac.getPosition(),
                                  obj);
  }
}
```

Figure 9. DiSL instrumentation for collecting runtime information for Senseo

snippet uses the `BytecodeMarker` to capture allocation bytecodes for both objects (`new`) and arrays (`newarray`, `anewarray`, and `multianewarray`). The `profileAllocation()` method updates an allocation counter in the current CCT node.

Runtime argument and return types. To collect runtime type information only for arguments of reference types, the `onMethodEntry(...)` snippet uses the argument processor `ReferenceProcessor`. Since this argument processor only defines the `objProc(...)` method to process arguments of reference types, all arguments with primitive types are automatically skipped. The `objProc(...)` method invokes the `profileArgument(...)` method of the current CCT node, passing the position of the argument and the reference.

For collecting runtime return types, the `onReturnRef(...)` snippet uses the `MethodReturnsRef` guard (see Figure 7 in Section 3.8) to ensure that the

	DiSL	AspectJ	ASM
Physical lines-of-code	74	44	489
Logical lines-of-code	44	19	338

Table 1. Lines-of-code for three implementations of Senseo

return type of a woven method is a reference type. Because the returned object reference is on top of the operand stack upon method completion, it is accessed with the `DynamicContext` API.

Basic-block metrics. As the execution of basic blocks cannot be captured with AspectJ, the following information is collected only by the DiSL version of Senseo. The `onBasicBlock(...)` snippet captures every basic block using the `BasicBlockMarker`; the `BasicBlockStaticContext` provides the index of the captured basic block (`getBBIndex()`). This allows us to keep track how many times a basic block is executed in each calling context.

Comparing different Senseo implementations. For a comparison of DiSL with low-level bytecode manipulation libraries and with AOP, it is interesting to consider the lines-of-code (LOC) used in the different implementations of the same tool. Hence, we implemented a third version of Senseo with the ASM bytecode manipulation library and compared the source code of the DiSL, AspectJ, and ASM versions. In contrast to the DiSL and ASM versions, the AspectJ version lacks basic block profiling, that is, it offers less functionality.

Table 1 summarizes the physical and logical LOC metrics of the three implementations, considering only the code related to the actual instrumentation logic (and disregarding the Java code for analysis at runtime, which is common to all three implementations). Compared to ASM, the DiSL and AspectJ versions are significantly smaller, as the direct manipulation of bytecodes requires much more development effort than relying on the high-level pointcut/advice mechanism of AspectJ and DiSL. The higher LOC number of the DiSL implementation compared to the AspectJ version is mainly due to the separation of the code that is evaluated at weave-time (guards) from the instrumentation code (snippets). However, weave-time evaluation brings significant performance gains as we will show in Section 6.

In summary, our case study illustrates how DiSL enables the concise implementation of a practical dynamic analysis tool, thanks to DiSL's open join point model, efficient access to both static and dynamic context information, weave-time evaluation of conditionals, and argument processors. Dynamic analysis tools written in DiSL are much more concise than equivalent tools developed with bytecode manipulation libraries.

6. Performance Evaluation

In this section, we evaluate the runtime performance of the DiSL instrumentation presented in the Senseo case study.

	Reference	SenseoAJ application only		SenseoDiSL application only		SenseoDiSL full coverage		Senseo2 application only		Senseo2 full coverage	
	[s]	[s]	ovh.	[s]	ovh.	[s]	ovh.	[s]	ovh.	[s]	ovh.
avrora	5.11	30.96	6.06	12.61	2.47	12.41	2.43	13.66	2.67	14.62	2.86
batik	1.28	2.70	2.11	1.78	1.39	2.47	1.93	2.14	1.67	3.09	2.41
eclipse	16.16	152.92	9.46	70.73	4.38	81.52	5.04	152.41	9.43	163.36	10.11
fop	0.35	3.36	9.60	1.68	4.80	3.09	8.83	2.07	5.91	3.93	11.23
h2	5.84	63.25	10.83	25.27	4.33	31.78	5.44	29.55	5.06	41.81	7.16
jython	2.67	5.70	2.13	3.89	1.46	28.28	10.59	4.29	1.61	34.21	12.81
luindex	0.90	7.06	7.84	2.71	3.01	3.31	3.68	3.45	3.83	4.30	4.78
lusearch	1.98	13.09	6.61	5.49	2.77	6.57	3.32	6.19	3.13	8.85	4.47
pmd	2.05	10.09	4.92	5.10	2.49	7.60	3.71	6.54	3.19	10.31	5.03
sunflow	3.45	57.24	16.59	21.44	6.21	20.49	5.94	24.57	7.12	25.37	7.35
tomcat	1.97	4.46	2.26	3.16	1.60	6.70	3.40	3.87	1.96	9.32	4.73
tradebeans	5.56	71.48	12.86	30.76	5.53	76.43	13.75	42.90	7.72	117.40	21.12
tradesoap	6.77	25.40	3.75	12.80	1.89	53.60	7.92	17.30	2.56	76.12	11.24
xalan	1.11	20.39	18.37	8.15	7.34	11.38	10.25	10.08	9.08	17.33	15.61
geo. mean			6.47		3.09		5.26		3.91		7.19

Table 2. Execution times and overhead factors for `SenseoAJ`, `SenseoDiSL`, and `Senseo2`

First, we compare the previous AspectJ implementation with an equivalent DiSL instrumentation (i.e., without basic block metrics). In addition, we evaluate our DiSL instrumentation with full bytecode coverage, collecting also basic block metrics. Second, we explore the different sources of the measured overhead. Third, we investigate the differences in the collected profiles, considering the number of intercepted join points, when weaving only application code, respectively when weaving with full bytecode coverage. Fourth, we study weaving time and overall class loading latency due to jBORAT and DiSL.

For our measurements, both the DiSL weaver and the AspectJ weaver run on top of jBORAT. This ensures exactly the same weaving coverage for application code (otherwise, the AspectJ load-time weaver would exclude some application classes from weaving). Both the instrumentation JVM and the application JVM run on the same host. We use the benchmarks in the DaCapo suite (dacapo-9.12-bach)[10] as base programs in our evaluation. All measurements correspond to the median of 15 benchmark runs within the same application JVM. The measurement machine is an Intel Core2 Quad Q9650 (3.0 GHz, 8 GB RAM) that runs Ubuntu GNU/Linux 10.04 64-bit. We use AspectJ 1.6.11[11], DiSL pre-release version 0.9, and Oracle's JDK 1.6.0_27 Hotspot Server VM (64-bit) with 7 GB maximum heap size.

Table 2 reports the runtime overhead for the original AspectJ version of Senseo (`SenseoAJ`), for the equivalent instrumentation in DiSL, that is, without basic block metrics (`SenseoDiSL`), and for the DiSL instrumentation including basic block metrics (`Senseo2`). On average (geometric mean for DaCapo), the overhead factor introduced by `SenseoAJ` is 6.47, while for `SenseoDiSL`, with the same code coverage, the overhead is only a factor of 3.09. With full bytecode coverage, the average overhead of `SenseoDiSL` is a factor of 5.26; surprisingly, the overhead is still lower than for `SenseoAJ` covering only application code. Finally, the average overhead introduced by `Senseo2` is a factor of 7.19.

[10] http://www.dacapobench.org/
[11] http://eclipse.org/aspectj/

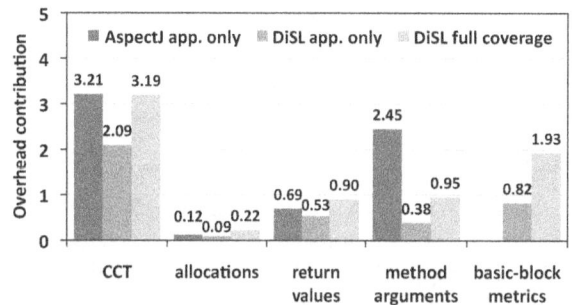

Figure 10. Contributions to the average overhead factor for different versions of Senseo

	application only	full coverage	increase [%]
Method bodies	5.60E+09	8.84E+09	57.75
Methods returning a ref.	1.76E+08	3.44E+08	95.28
Methods with ref. arg.	1.78E+09	2.57E+09	44.56
Object and array alloc.	1.14E+09	2.00E+09	76.11
Basic blocks	2.21E+10	3.34E+10	51.26

Table 3. Total number of intercepted join points for a single iteration of the whole DaCapo suite

Figure 10 quantifies the different overhead contributions. For CCT reification, the DiSL implementation benefits from efficient access to static context information, from data passing in synthetic local variables, and from the use of an `@ThreadLocal` variable (compared to a `java.lang.ThreadLocal` variable in `SenseoAJ`). The overheads for capturing allocations and runtime types of return values are relatively small for both implementations. The biggest difference between the two implementations is observed for the processing of method arguments; the DiSL instrumentation leverages an argument processor, whereas the AspectJ implementation relies on `JoinPoint.getArgs()`. As shown in Figure 10, argument processing in the AspectJ version introduces more than 6 times the overhead of the equivalent DiSL instrumentation.

Table 3 summarizes the number of intercepted join points for a single iteration of each considered benchmark, weaving only application code, respectively weaving with full byte-

	SenseoAJ app. only	SenseoDiSL app. only	SenseoDiSL full cov.	Senseo2 app. only	Senseo2 full cov.
Weaving [s]	54.97	43.28	134.17	65.61	174.73
Latency [s]	66.42	53.86	155.25	75.06	213.71

Table 4. Total weaving time and latency for a single iteration of the whole DaCapo suite

code coverage. For all kinds of join points, full bytecode coverage results in an increase of 45–95% in the number of intercepted join points. These results confirm that supporting weaving with full bytecode coverage is essential in the context of dynamic program analysis.

Finally, we compare the total time required to weave the complete benchmark suite. Table 4 reports (a) the total weaving time measured in the instrumentation JVM, and (b) the total weaving latency observed by the application JVM. This allows us to know the latency introduced by jBORAT. Overall, for application only, SenseoAJ is woven in 54.97s, whereas SenseoDiSL requires only 43.28s. The DiSL weaver outperforms the AspectJ weaver by a factor 1.27. With full coverage, SenseoDiSL requires 134.17s, and adding basic block metrics with Senseo2 increases the weaving time to 65.61s for application code, and to 174.73s with full coverage. The latency contribution of jBORAT is between 14% and 24%, due to client-server communication.

Our evaluation confirms that DiSL enables the development of efficient dynamic analysis tools, which often cannot be achieved with general-purpose AOP languages. For our case study, the DiSL instrumentation reduces the overhead by more than factor 2 in comparison with the previous AspectJ version. Even with full bytecode coverage, the DiSL instrumentation still outperforms the AspectJ version.

7. Related Work

In previous work, we presented @J [8], a Java annotation-based AOP language for simplifying dynamic analysis. Similar to DiSL, @J uses snippet inlining and provides constructs for basic block analysis. However, @J lacks the open join point model of DiSL (i.e., @J does not support custom join point definitions), reflective access to weave-time information, and support for efficient access to reflective dynamic join point information (i.e., @J lacks argument processors). @J supports staged advice where weave-time evaluation of advice yields runtime residues that are woven. While this feature can be used to emulate guards in DiSL, it requires the use of additional synthetic local variables and more complex composition of snippets.

In [7] we discussed some early ideas on a high-level declarative domain-specific aspect language (DSAL) for dynamic analysis. DiSL provides all necessary language constructs to express the dynamic analyses that could be specified in the DSAL. That is, in the future, DiSL can serve as an intermediate language to which the higher-level DSAL programs are compiled.

High-level dynamic analysis frameworks such as RoadRunner [13] or jchord[12] ease composition of a set of common dynamic analyses. In contrast, DiSL is not tailored for any specify dynamic analysis task and offers the developer fine-grained control over the inserted bytecode.

The use of AOP for dynamic analysis [10, 20–22] has revealed some limitations in general-purpose AOP languages for that particular domain. In [1], a meta-aspect protocol (MAP) for dynamic analysis is proposed to overcome these limitations. Similar to our approach, the authors propose a flexible join point model where shadows are accessible in advice. Code snippets are used to inject callbacks to advice. MAP uses a meta object to reify context at runtime. While MAP allows fast prototyping of dynamic analyses, it does not focus on high efficiency of the developed analysis tools. In contrast, DiSL avoids any indirections to efficiently access static and dynamic context information.

The AspectBench Compiler (*abc*) [5] eases the implementation of AspectJ extensions. As intermediate representation, *abc* uses Jimple to define shadows. Jimple has no information where blocks, statements and control structures start and end, thus requiring extensions to support new pointcuts for dynamic analysis. In contrast, DiSL provides an extensible library of markers without requiring extensions of the intermediate representation.

Prevailing AspectJ weavers lack support for embedding custom static analysis in the weaving process. In [18] compile-time statically executable advice is proposed, which is similar to static context in DiSL. SCoPE [4] is an AspectJ extension that allows analysis-based conditional pointcuts. However, advice code together with the evaluated conditional is always inserted, relying on the just-in-time compiler to remove dead code. DiSL's guards together with static context allows weave-time conditional evaluation and can prevent the insertion of dead code.

In [2], the notion of region pointcut is introduced. Because a region pointcut potentially refers to several combined but spread join points, an external object shared between the join points holds the values to be passed between them. DiSL's markers provide a similar mechanism, and synthetic local variables help avoid passing data through an external object. In addition, region pointcuts are implicitly bound to the block structure of the program. In contrast, DiSL allows arbitrary regions to be marked.

Javassist [11] is a load-time bytecode manipulation library allowing definition of classes at runtime. The API allows two different levels of abstraction: source-level and bytecode-level. In particular, the source-level abstraction does not require any knowledge of the Java bytecode structure and allows insertion of code fragments given as source text. Compared to DiSL, Javassist does not follow a pointcut/advice model and does not provide built-in support for synthetic local variables.

---

[12] http://code.google.com/p/jchord/

Josh [12] is an AspectJ-like language that allows developers to define domain-specific extensions to the pointcut language. Similar to guards, Josh provides static pointcut designators that can access reflective static information at weave-time. However, the join point model of Josh does not include arbitrary bytecodes and basic blocks as in DiSL.

The approach described in [17] enables customized pointcuts that are partially evaluated at weave-time. It uses a declarative language to synthesize shadows. Because only a subset of bytecodes is converted to the declarative language, it is not possible to define basic block pointcuts as in DiSL.

Steamloom [9, 14] provides AOP support at the JVM level and improves performance of advice execution by optimizing dynamic pointcut evaluation. In DiSL, performance gains stem from static contexts combined with efficient access to dynamic context information. No JVM support is needed.

8. Discussion

In this section we discuss the strengths and limitations of DiSL for implementing dynamic analysis tools, comparing DiSL with the mainstream AOP language AspectJ [16] and with the low-level bytecode manipulation library ASM.

Expressiveness. AspectJ lacks certain join points that are important for some dynamic analysis tasks (e.g., bytecode-level and basic block-level join points). Thus, it is not possible to implement analysis tools that trace the intra-procedural control flow. In DiSL, any bytecode region can be a shadow, thanks to the support for custom markers. Likewise, with ASM, any bytecode location can be instrumented.

In AspectJ, the programmer has no control over the inserted bytecode. The AspectJ weaver inserts invocations to advice methods; inlining of advice is not foreseen. In contrast, the DiSL programmer writes snippets that are always inlined. If desired, it is trivial to mimic the behavior of the AspectJ weaver by writing snippet code that invokes "advice" methods. Still, if DiSL code is written in Java and compiled with a Java compiler, the snippets cannot contain arbitrary bytecode sequences. For example, it is not possible to write a snippet in Java that yields a single dup bytecode when inlined. Using ASM, there are no restrictions concerning the inserted bytecode.

Level of abstraction. In comparison with AspectJ, DiSL offers a lower abstraction level. The DiSL programmer needs to be aware of bytecode semantics, whereas AspectJ does not expose any bytecode-level details to the programmer. Nonetheless, DiSL relieves the developer from dealing with low-level bytecode manipulations such as producing specific bytecode sequences, introducing local variables, copying data from the operand stack, etc. Using ASM, the programmer also needs to deal with such low-level details, resulting in verbose tool implementations.

Compliance of the generated bytecode with the JVM specification. Weaving any aspect written in AspectJ results in valid bytecode that passes verification. In contrast, woven DiSL code may fail bytecode verification; it is up to the programmer to ensure that the inserted code is valid. For instance, synthetic local variables must be initialized before they are read, and the stack locations and local variables accessed through DynamicContext must be valid. Similarly, bytecode instrumented with tools written in ASM may fail verification.

While it is usually desirable that woven code passes verification, violating certain constraints on bytecode sometimes simplifies analysis tasks. For example, if the analysis needs to keep track of objects that are currently being initialized by a thread, the programmer may want to store uninitialized objects in a data structure on the heap, although the resulting bytecode would be illegal. Nonetheless, the analysis can be successfully executed by explicitly disabling bytecode verification. With AspectJ, such tricks are not possible.

Interference of inserted code with the base program. With ASM, local variables or data on the operand stack belonging to the base program may be unintentionally altered by inserted code. In contrast, AspectJ and DiSL guarantee that instrumentations cannot modify local variables or stack locations of the base program.

Bytecode coverage. For many analysis tasks, it is essential that the overall execution of the base program can be analyzed. However, prevailing AspectJ weavers do not support weaving the Java class library. In contrast, DiSL has been designed for weaving with complete bytecode coverage, which does not introduce any extra effort for the developer. With ASM, it is possible to develop tools that support complete bytecode coverage. However, the ASM programmer has to manually deal with the intricacies of bootstrapping the JVM with a modified class library and preventing infinite regression when inserted bytecode calls methods in the instrumented class library.

9. Conclusion

In this paper we presented DiSL, a new domain-specific language for bytecode instrumentation. The language is embedded in Java and makes use of annotations. DiSL allows the programmer to express a wide range of dynamic program analysis tasks in a concise manner. DiSL has been inspired by the pointcut/advice mechanism of mainstream AOP languages such as AspectJ. On the one hand, DiSL omits certain AOP language features that are not needed for expressing instrumentations (e.g., around advice and explicit structural modifications of classes). On the other hand, DiSL offers an open join point model, synthetic local variables, comprehensive and efficient access to static and dynamic context information, and support for weave-time execution of static analyses. These language features allow expressing bytecode transformations in the form of code snippets that are inlined before or after bytecode shadows as indicated by (custom) markers, if user-defined constraints specified as guards are satisfied. As case study, we recasted the dynamic analysis tool Senseo in DiSL and compared it with the previous implementation in AspectJ. In contrast to the AspectJ version, the DiSL implementation ensures complete bytecode coverage, reduces overhead, and allows us to gather additional intra-procedural execution statistics.

In an ongoing research project, we are working on advanced static checkers for DiSL instrumentations to help detect errors before weaving, on partial evaluation of instantiated snippets before inlining, and on general techniques to split overlong methods that exceed the maximum method size imposed by the JVM. In addition, we are exploring the use of higher-level, declarative domain-specific languages for dynamic program analysis. We plan to compile such higher-level languages to DiSL, which will serve us as a convenient intermediate language.

Acknowledgments

The research presented here was conducted while L. Marek, A. Villazón, and Y. Zheng were with the University of Lugano. It was supported by the Scientific Exchange Programme NMS–CH (project code 10.165), by a Sino-Swiss Science and Technology Cooperation (SSSTC) Exchange Grant (project no. EG26–032010) and Institutional Partnership (project no. IP04–092010), by the Swiss National Science Foundation (project CRSII2_136225), and by the Czech Science Foundation (project GACR P202/10/J042). The authors thank Aibek Sarimbekov and Achille Peternier for their help with jBORAT, and Andreas Sewe for testing DiSL and providing detailed feedback.

References

[1] M. Achenbach and K. Ostermann. A meta-aspect protocol for developing dynamic analyses. In *Proceedings of the First International Conference on Runtime Verification*, RV'10, pages 153–167. Springer-Verlag, 2010.

[2] S. Akai, S. Chiba, and M. Nishizawa. Region pointcut for AspectJ. In *ACP4IS '09: Proceedings of the 8th Workshop on Aspects, Components, and Patterns for Infrastructure Software*, pages 43–48. ACM, 2009.

[3] G. Ammons, T. Ball, and J. R. Larus. Exploiting hardware performance counters with flow and context sensitive profiling. In *PLDI '97: Proceedings of the ACM SIGPLAN 1997 conference on Programming language design and implementation*, pages 85–96. ACM, 1997.

[4] T. Aotani and H. Masuhara. SCoPE: an AspectJ compiler for supporting user-defined analysis-based pointcuts. In *AOSD '07: Proceedings of the 6th international conference on Aspect-oriented software development*, pages 161–172. ACM, 2007.

[5] P. Avgustinov, A. S. Christensen, L. J. Hendren, S. Kuzins, J. Lhoták, O. Lhoták, O. de Moor, D. Sereni, G. Sittampalam, and J. Tibble. abc: An extensible AspectJ compiler. In *AOSD '05: Proceedings of the 4th International Conference on Aspect-Oriented Software Development*, pages 87–98. ACM, 2005.

[6] W. Binder, D. Ansaloni, A. Villazón, and P. Moret. Flexible and efficient profiling with aspect-oriented programming. *Concurrency and Computation: Practice and Experience*, 23(15):1749–1773, 2011.

[7] W. Binder, P. Moret, D. Ansaloni, A. Sarimbekov, A. Yokokawa, and E. Tanter. Towards a domain-specific aspect language for dynamic program analysis: position paper. In *Proceedings of the sixth annual workshop on Domain-specific aspect languages*, DSAL '11, pages 9–11. ACM, 2011.

[8] W. Binder, A. Villazón, D. Ansaloni, and P. Moret. @J - Towards rapid development of dynamic analysis tools for the Java Virtual Machine. In *VMIL '09: Proceedings of the 3th Workshop on Virtual Machines and Intermediate Languages*, pages 1–9. ACM, 2009.

[9] C. Bockisch, M. Haupt, M. Mezini, and K. Ostermann. Virtual machine support for dynamic join points. In *AOSD '04: Proceedings of the 3rd international conference on Aspect-oriented software development*, pages 83–92. ACM, 2004.

[10] E. Bodden and K. Havelund. Aspect-oriented Race Detection in Java. *IEEE Transactions on Software Engineering*, 36(4):509–527, 2010.

[11] S. Chiba. Load-time structural reflection in Java. In *Proceedings of the 14th European Conference on Object-Oriented Programming (ECOOP'2000)*, volume 1850 of *Lecture Notes in Computer Science*, pages 313–336. Springer Verlag, Cannes, France, June 2000.

[12] S. Chiba and K. Nakagawa. Josh: An open AspectJ-like language. In *AOSD '04: Proceedings of the 3rd International Conference on Aspect-Oriented Software Development*, pages 102–111. ACM, 2004.

[13] C. Flanagan and S. N. Freund. The RoadRunner dynamic analysis framework for concurrent programs. In *Proceedings of the 9th ACM SIGPLAN-SIGSOFT Workshop on Program Analysis for Software Tools and Engineering*, PASTE '10, pages 1–8. ACM, 2010.

[14] M. Haupt, M. Mezini, C. Bockisch, T. Dinkelaker, M. Eichberg, and M. Krebs. An execution layer for aspect-oriented programming languages. In *VEE '05: Proceedings of the 1st ACM/USENIX international conference on Virtual execution environments*, pages 142–152. ACM, 2005.

[15] E. Hilsdale and J. Hugunin. Advice weaving in AspectJ. In *AOSD '04: Proceedings of the 3rd International Conference on Aspect-Oriented Software Development*, pages 26–35. ACM, 2004.

[16] G. Kiczales, E. Hilsdale, J. Hugunin, M. Kersten, J. Palm, and W. G. Griswold. An overview of AspectJ. In *Proceedings of the 15th European Conference on Object-Oriented Programming*, ECOOP '01, pages 327–353. Springer-Verlag, 2001.

[17] K. Klose, K. Ostermann, and M. Leuschel. Partial evaluation of pointcuts. In *Practical Aspects of Declarative Languages*, volume 4354 of *Lecture Notes in Computer Science*, pages 320–334. Springer-Verlag, 2007.

[18] K. Lieberherr, D. H. Lorenz, and P. Wu. A case for statically executable advice: Checking the law of Demeter with AspectJ. In *Proceedings of the 2nd International Conference on Aspect-Oriented Software Development*, AOSD '03, pages 40–49. ACM, 2003.

[19] P. Moret, W. Binder, and É. Tanter. Polymorphic bytecode instrumentation. In *AOSD '11: Proceedings of the 10th International Conference on Aspect-Oriented Software Development*, pages 129–140. ACM, Mar. 2011.

[20] D. J. Pearce, M. Webster, R. Berry, and P. H. J. Kelly. Profiling with AspectJ. *Software: Practice and Experience*, 37(7):747–777, June 2007.

[21] D. Röthlisberger, M. Härry, W. Binder, P. Moret, D. Ansaloni, A. Villazón, and O. Nierstrasz. Exploiting dynamic information in IDEs improves speed and correctness of software maintenance tasks. *IEEE Transactions on Software Engineering*, PrePrint, 2011.

[22] D. Röthlisberger, M. Härry, A. Villazón, D. Ansaloni, W. Binder, O. Nierstrasz, and P. Moret. Augmenting static source views in IDEs with dynamic metrics. In *ICSM '09: Proceedings of the 25th IEEE International Conference on Software Maintenance*, pages 253–262, Edmonton, Alberta, Canada, 2009. IEEE Computer Society.

Multi-View Refinement of AO-Connectors in Distributed Software Systems

Steven Op de beeck, Marko van Dooren, Bert Lagaisse, Wouter Joosen

IBBT-Distrinet, KU Leuven, 3001 Leuven, Belgium.

{steven.opdebeeck, marko.vandooren, bert.lagaisse, wouter.joosen}@cs.kuleuven.be

Abstract

This paper presents MView, a technique that enables the separation of various developer stakeholder views on an architectural connector in distributed software systems.

While state-of-the-art AO-ADLs focus on describing compositions using aspect-based connectors, there is no support for describing a connector across multiple architectural views. This is, however, essential for distributed systems, where run-time and distribution characteristics are not represented in a single view. The result is connectors that suffer from monolithic descriptions, where the views of different stakeholders are tangled.

MView untangles these stakeholder views by defining them in separate modules and specifying refinement relations between these modules. We have integrated MView in a prototypical ADL, which allows code generation for multiple AO-middleware platforms.

We evaluate MView in terms of stakeholder effort in a content distribution system for e-Media. We have created an Eclipse-plugin that supports the ADL, and performs code generation to the JBoss and Spring middleware platforms.

Categories and Subject Descriptors C.2.4 [*Distributed Systems*]: Distributed Applications; C.2.11 [*Software Engineering*]: Software Architectures

1. Introduction

Distributed software systems consist of *complex compositions* of components and third-party subsystems. This complexity is inherent to the growing need to take into account the run-time and distribution characteristics of compositions, as well as their crosscutting nature. This is a trend that is gaining support from AO-Middleware platforms (AOM)

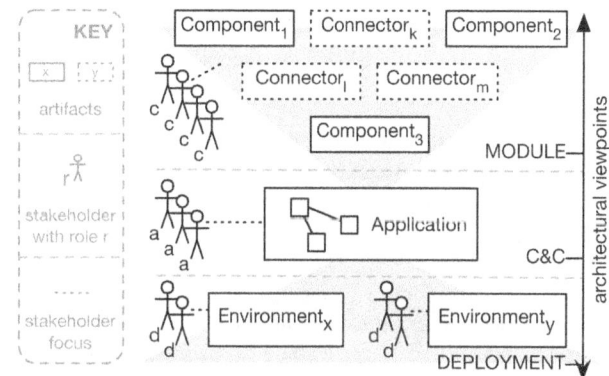

Figure 1. The development process in terms of stakeholder roles and architectural viewpoints.

such as ReflexD, DyMAC, and AWED [21, 23, 36], which offer direct support for such complex compositions.

In software architecture, a *view* captures the concerns of a *stakeholder* on the basis of a *viewpoint*, while a viewpoint defines the language for describing a specific facet of the system [20]. Distributed software systems are described based on the views of multiple developer stakeholders with varying expertise and development roles: e.g. component developers, application assemblers, and deployers. Their views are specified in accordance with at least the architectural viewpoints of module, component-and-connector and deployment, respectively [9]. Figure 1 outlines how stakeholder roles match viewpoints in the development process.

To describe components and their compositions, several Architectural Description Languages [6, 14, 17] (ADL) have been proposed. More recently, various AO-ADLs [15, 16, 24, 26, 28, 31–34] have been defined that capture the crosscutting compositions of software systems in AO-connectors.

The goal of these AO-ADLs differs from ours: they aim to separate the crosscutting concerns of stakeholders with role c (see Figure 1) by means of AO-connectors k, l, and m. However, they do not separate the various views of stakeholders c, a, and d, involved in such an AO-connector throughout the development process. Here, c, a, and d stand for *component developer*, *assembler*, and *deployer*.

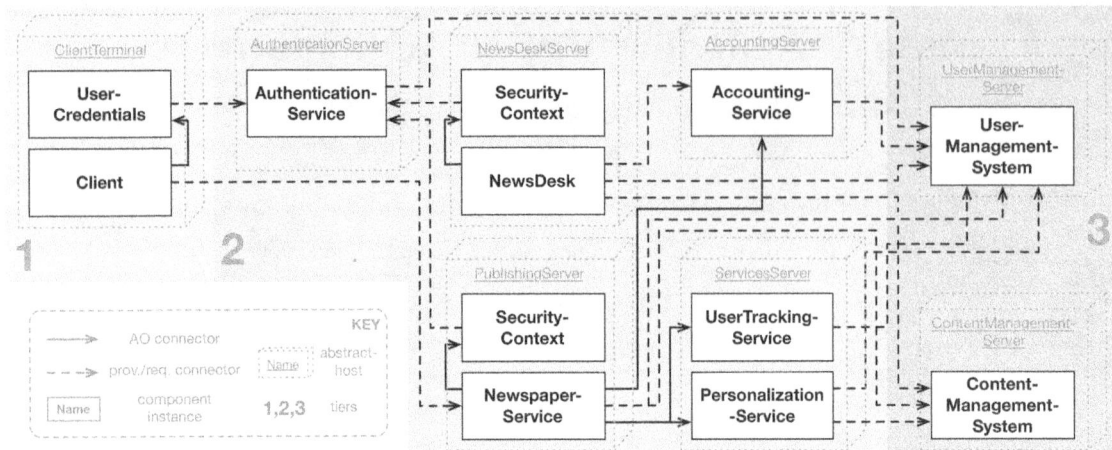

Figure 2. A component-and-connector view on the publishing architecture.

Consider for example the composition of the *accounting* and *news delivery* services in a content distribution system for e-Media. Informally, the composition is described as follows:

> "<u>Call</u> the *chargeForService* method, <u>whenever</u> these conditions hold: the *execution* of *method* fetchArticle of the NewsRemote *interface*, <u>and</u> on the NewspaperService *component instance*, <u>and</u> located on the PublishingServer *host*."

This complex composition suffers from a monolithic description, where the views of different stakeholders are tangled. We discern the following expert stakeholders: a component developer (*execution of a method of an interface*), an application assembler (*of a component instance*), a deployer (*located on a remote host*). Since the views of these stakeholders are not all available or even relevant at one time during architecture, a single artifact should not capture this entire composition. Furthermore, because of low-level details like *host* conditions, adapting the composition for use in another deployment environment is error-prone.

We propose MView to achieve the desired modularity of stakeholder views in the development process. MView is a technique for *multi-view refinement* of connector descriptions, that builds on inheritance and step-wise refinement. In MView, a complex composition is modularized across multiple connectors, where each one deals with the composition in the context of the view of a *single* stakeholder. For example, a module view adds module related constraints: *method M on interface I*. MView enables one connector view to refine another connector view. So, as the architecture is further developed, a connector can be refined by an additional view, for example by a deployment view that adds deployment related constraints: *must be running on host R*. As a result, the complex composition is specified through a process of multi-view refinement of connectors. Each connector view is constructed separately, by the right stakeholder for the job, at the appropriate time during development.

We have integrated MView in a prototypical ADL, called MViewADL, that we support with an Eclipse plugin [2]. This plugin supports code generation to multiple distributed middleware platforms, JBoss [1] and Spring [3].

We have applied MView in a case study on e-Media [38] where we compare its stakeholder effort with other techniques. The case study has a detailed architecture that is based on industry requirements and it serves as the running example throughout this paper.

The remainder of the paper is structured as follows. Section 2 introduces the e-Media case study, followed by an illustration of the problem. In Section 3, we analyze the requirements for MView refinement in ADLs and we discuss the support in existing approaches. Section 4 introduces and illustrates the MViewADL, followed by a detailed explanation of MView refinement. Section 5 discusses automatic code generation to JBoss. Section 6 evaluates MView in terms of stakeholder effort, and revisits the requirements for MView. Section 7 presents the related work, and Section 8 concludes.

2. Case Study and Problem Illustration

In this section, we define the case study that we use throughout the paper, followed by a detailed problem illustration.

The subject of our case study is a content distribution system for e-Media. A digital newspaper offers news in different media formats and sizes, to be delivered through different communication channels. It supports various additional services, like flexible accounting, tracking user-interest and content personalization. A consumer can browse recent headlines and read article summaries for free. However, to have access to the full content and additional services, a consumer is required to sign up. The system charges a signed-up consumer for paid services by means of micropayments. User-tracking, personalization, authorization and accounting are examples of services that are integrated using complex composition.

This case study was developed throughout a number of research projects in the e-Media space, in close collaboration with actual industrial news publishers. The architecture and implementation were performed for an AOSD Industry Demonstrator [38].

Figure 2 shows a component-and-connector view of a relevant subset of the publishing software architecture, consisting of component instances, their compositions and abstract host allocation. The architecture is deployed along three tiers: (1) Client, (2) Business and (3) Storage.

The Business tier consists of a number of subsystems: the Newspaper, NewsDesk and Auxiliary services. The NEWSPAPERSERVICE component is externally accessible by the CLIENT. It supplies the services to browse and read articles.

Authentication and Authorization are supplied by the AUTHENTICATIONSERVICE, USERCREDENTIALS and SECURITYCONTEXT components. The additional services USERTRACKINGSERVICE and PERSONALIZATIONSERVICE can be activated on a per-user basis. User tracking keeps track of the reading behavior of the consumer, while personalization uses this to personalize the view of the consumer on the news.

The ACCOUNTINGSERVICE component is responsible for doing the accounting of *Service Usage* behavior of the consumer. The methods that belong to this *Service Usage* category are fetchArticle, listNewestArticles, listArticlesForTag, and listArticlesForCategory —a part of the main interface of the NEWSPAPERSERVICE. The complex composition between the NEWSPAPERSERVICE and ACCOUNTINGSERVICE components is modeled, in our component-and-connector view, by means of a full line arrow. The accounting composition is tangled by the following stakeholder views: Accounting must only interact with (a) the specific *service usage* methods of (b) the NEWSREMOTE interface, implemented by any component instance that is (c) deployed on the PUBLISHINGSERVER abstract host.

Problem Illustration. We illustrate the problem of tangling further with an example in an existing ADL: Fractal-ADL [32]. Figure 3 shows a complex composition description that realizes *Accounting*.

The example shows two component declarations, ACCOUNTINGSERVICE and NEWSPAPERSERVICE with their provided interfaces (*role="server"*). The part of the composition we are interested in, is the *weave* XML element (line 12–18). The *root* attribute indicates the application scope of the aspect, and the *acName* attribute indicates the component that supplies the additional behavior (advice). The *pointcutExp* attribute contains the *conditions* for composition, and must conform to the following template:

"(client | server | both) component; interface; method:type"

Client and *Server* indicate an expected outgoing or incoming call respectively, followed by a *component* name, *interface* name, and *method* name, and return *type*.

```
1  <definition name="NewspaperApp">
2    <component name="AccountingService">
3      <interface name="AccountingRemote" role="server"
4          signature="org.objectweb.....AspectComponent"/>
5    </component>
6    <component> name="NewspaperService">
7      <interface name="NewsRemote" role="server"
8          signature="Service"/>
9    </component>
10   <binding client="NewspaperService.NewsRemote"
11     server="AccountingService.AccountingRemote"/>
12   <weave root="this" acName="AccountingService"
13     aDomain="ServiceAccounting"
14     pointcutExp="
15   <!-- PublishingServer; (unsupported informal description) -->
16       SERVER *;
17       NewsRemote;
18       fetchArticle(ContentItemId):ContentItem" />
19 </definition>
```

Figure 3. The complex SERVICEACCOUNTING weave combines contribution from three stakeholders into a single description.

This *pointcutExp* representation is tangled with the views of multiple stakeholders, as indicated by the different gray areas. The first one from the bottom (line 17–18) is a module-viewpoint description that focusses on interfaces and their methods. It describes a pointcut that matches calls of the fetchArticle method, of the NEWSREMOTE interface. This is the responsibility of a module developer familiar with the newspaper service and the *Accounting* requirements. The next view (line 16) further specifies the pointcut in terms of the Component-and-connector viewpoint: only incoming calls are allowed for any (indicated with *) component instance. This is the job of an application assembler. Finally, the called component is required to be allocated on the *PublishingServer* abstract host (line 15). This is the job of an application deployer. This last condition, however, is not supported in Fractal-ADL. We had no choice other than to specify it informally in the architectural description.

This example shows how the views of different stakeholders w.r.t. a single composition are tangled in a monolithic connector description. Furthermore, it shows that the rigid structure of this particular description is difficult to refine across multiple connectors.

3. Requirements Analysis

In this section, we present four requirements for ADL features that are necessary in order to support multi-view refinement. We apply these requirements in a study of the related work.

3.1 Requirements

It is our goal to enable the stakeholders, that are involved with a composition, to specify their views on that composition separately and at the appropriate time during development—*the right stakeholder at the right time*. This requires the monolithic connector to be split up into multiple explicitly related connectors, that are no longer tangled with respect to the concerns of the involved stakeholders.

We break this goal down into four requirements for ADL features that we deem necessary. We use these requirements in a study of the related work to determine for each approach what is missing in order to achieve our goal. These requirements are, in part, based on the Classification and Comparison Framework for ADLs by Medvidovic, et al. [22], but applied in the context of distributed middleware systems.

1. *Open Connector.* First, the specification of a connector is defined as the high-level model of its composition behavior. In order to consistently refine this specification across the levels of architectural abstraction (the architectural process), the ADL must support connector specification and it must be in a form that is open for customization. To contrast, a black-box connector does not convey its meaning and cannot be further refined. Second, it is required for the connector to support composition that is sufficiently expressive to support complex composition, as detailed in Section 2. This requirement is based on the *Semantics* and *Evolution* features of the Classification Framework [22].

2. *Multi-Platform Support.* First, the ADL is highly independent of the details of a specific run-time platform. It facilitates generic specifications in the face of heterogeneous component models. This avoids postponing important decisions until such a platform is chosen, e.g. the specification of complex compositions. Additionally, it avoids the risk of architects building architectures for one specific platform or make the wrong trade-offs because of it. Second, in the face of this heterogeneity, it is desirable for an ADL to come with the tools required to assist in the generation of implementation code, preferably to multiple platforms, that is consistent with the software architecture [22].

3. *Multiple Views and Viewpoints.* The description of the architecture occurs in terms of multiple views and viewpoints. Each view describes the architecture from the perspective of a particular stakeholder concern (or a set thereof). Each view is constructed according to an architectural viewpoint that matches the expertise of the stakeholder. Support for this requirement means a clear multi-view description across a set of architectural viewpoints. For distributed systems such a set would have to include at least the viewpoints of module, component-and-connector and deployment [9]. Examples of views can be seen in Figure 2, which shows a graphical representation of a component-and-connector view, but also the composition in Figure 3 is considered a view. We build on the *Multiple Views* feature in [22].

4. *View and Viewpoint Relations.* First, the views in an architectural description of a system are always related but often only implicitly, in part because they describe different perspectives of the same system. But some views are related more closely and elicit explication. An example is the *unification* of identical elements in different views. Explicit descriptions of relations between views has many uses [12], some of which are essential to our goal, such as composition

and model transformation. Second, this requirement encompasses support for explicit relations between views of different viewpoints.

3.2 Existing Approaches

Table 1 shows the features that are supported by various approaches in the related work. For each requirement we discuss the most important observations.

	1. Open Connector	2. Multi-Platform Support	3. Multiple View(point)s	4. View(point) Relations
[33] DAOP-ADL (a)	○			
[34] AO-ADL (b)	○	●		
[32] Fractal-ADL (c)	○	○		
[24] AspectLEDA (d)	○	○	○	
[15] AspectualACME (e)	○	○		
[27] π-ADL^{ARL} (f)	○	○	○	○
[31] Prisma (g)	○	●		
[11] View Composition (h)		○	●	○
[19] Multi Perspective (i)		●	●	○
[8] Stratified Frameworks (j)		○	○	○
[25] Viewpoints Framework (k)		○	●	○

○ – limited support   ● – support

Table 1. Feature matrix for requirements.

1. *Open Connector.* ADLs a–g support a connector that is open for customization. However, the connector often has semantics that are constrained to a specific composition model that, for instance, does not support deployment context (see problem illustration in Section 2). The approaches h–k have connectors —which act as black boxes— with pre-defined semantics, that do not allow customization. Approach j makes abstraction of the connector altogether.

2. *Multi-Platform Support.* ADLs b–g have not been created for use in a single platform. Fractal, AspectLEDA and π-ADL support generation to a single platform (FAC, and twice Java, respectively). Only AO-ADL and Prisma support code generation to multiple platforms. DAOP-ADL was specifically designed for the DAO-Platform. Approaches h–k support more generic descriptions by design, when compared to a typical ADL. Only the Multi Perspective approach supports generation to multiple platforms.

3. *Multiple Views and Viewpoints.* π-ADL^{ARL} and AspectLEDA support a structural and behavioral viewpoint. Stratified frameworks supports only a structural viewpoint. Approaches h, i and k, on the other hand, support an arbitrary number of views and viewpoints.

4. *View and Viewpoint Relations.* π-ADL^{ARL} supports a refinement relation between intermediate architectural

views, however, limited to a single viewpoint (component-and-connector). The ADL does not support refinement in terms of hosts, for example. The generic view approaches h–k support relations between views as well. Specific cross-viewpoint relations are considered feasible but are not detailed.

4. MView

MView is a technique for multi-view refinement of architectural connector descriptions. It facilitates the decomposition of a complex monolithic connector into connector descriptions that are no longer tangled with stakeholder views. To apply and validate MView, we have integrated it in the MViewADL prototypical ADL.

First, we explain and illustrate the core concepts of MViewADL, without going into the refinement details. Then we provide a detailed explanation of refinement. We end with an overview of the available tool support.

4.1 Introducing MViewADL

MViewADL is an ADL for component-based distributed systems, that supports aspect-oriented composition. The running example of this section is a refinement scenario of the compositions of both the *Accounting* and *Authorization* services from the e-Media system.

```
1 component NewspaperService {
2   provide { NewsRemote, ManagementRemote }
3   require { UserProfileRemote, ContentBrowseRemote }
4 }
5
6 abstract connector ServiceUsageCn {
7   abstract ao-composition ServiceUsage {
8     pointcut {
9       kind: execution;
10      signature:  ContentItem fetchArticle(ContentItemId),
11                  List listNewestArticles(int),
12                  List listArticlesForTag(Tag),
13                  List listArticlesForCategory(Cat);
14      callee { interface: NewsRemote; }
15    }
16  }
17 }
```

Figure 4. The *component*, *connector* and *AO-composition* declarations.

MViewADL has two kinds of *module* declarations: the *component* and the *connector*. Both modules are shown in an example in Figure 4. A component has a name and it contains a *provide* and optional *require* element as its only members. These describe the dependencies of the component in terms of the *interface* declarations that it provides and requires, respectively. The example shows the NEWSPAPERSER-VICE component with its dependencies (line 1).

The connector describes the composition between components. A connector has a name and the following members: the optional *require* and *provide* elements, and zero or more *AO-composition* (AOC) declarations. The AOC consists of a single *pointcut* and a single *advice* member. Either

member is optional. Without both present, the AOC is abstract. A connector that contains at least one abstract member, is abstract itself. We show in the next section that refinement is used to introduce missing or abstract members.

A *pointcut* has a *kind* member, which can be call or execution, and a signature member. The signature is a comma-separated list of method patterns, supporting negations and wildcards to define the set of join points for composition. A pointcut supports further constraining in terms of the caller and callee join point context of the composition. The kind, signature, caller, and callee members of the pointcut are related through conjunction.

The caller and callee element can constrain the pointcut further in terms of the following join point context properties: the *interface*, the *component*, the *host*, the *instance* and the *application*. Each property accepts a comma-separated list of definitions from its respective type, and it supports negation, like the signature does.

The *advice* has a *type* (before, around, or after) and a *service* member that references a method that acts as the advice. The specific method is resolved through the interfaces in the *require*-member of the connector.

The connector in the example is SERVICEUSAGECN. It has a single AOC member called SERVICEUSAGE. The AOC is abstract because it is incompletely specified, as it contains only a pointcut element (lines 8–15) and no advice. The pointcut is of kind *execution* (line 9). This means that interception needs to takes place at the callee side. The pointcut has a signature comprising the four *Service Usage* methods (lines 10–13). The pointcut is further constrained in terms of the callee context: the called component must provide the NEWSREMOTE interface (line 14).

```
1 abstract application NewspaperApp {
2   host PublishingServer; host ContentManagementServer; host
          ServicesServer;
3   ContentManagementSystem cms on ContentManagementServer;
4   NewspaperService    ns on PublishingServer;
5   // other host and instance declarations cut
6 }
```

Figure 5. The *application* declaration.

Figure 5 shows a basic example of an application declaration. An application consists of zero or more members of each of the following declarations: the *host*, the *module instantiation*, and the *inline module*. An application is abstract if it contains a member that is abstract, it has no hosts, or it has no instances.

A host declaration has a name, and, optionally, a mapping to a real-world host (host NS is "news.com";). Host declarations are used to represent host deployment topologies. A module instantiation has a name, a type that refers to a component or connector declaration, and a host on which the instance must be allocated, prefixed with the on keyword. An inline module declaration is a component or connector declaration that is specified inline, as a part of the application description.

The application declaration in the example is called NEWS-PAPERAPP. It declares a number of abstract hosts: PUBLISHINGSERVER, SERVICESSERVER, etc. (line 2), and a number of instances: *cms* and *ns*. *ns* is an instance of the NEWSPAPERSERVICE component that is allocated on the PUBLISHINGSERVER host. This application does not specify any inline module declarations. Subsection 4.2 on refinement contains more elaborate examples of the application type.

4.2 Multi-view Refinement

In this subsection we provide a detailed explanation of multi-view refinement (MView) of architectural descriptions.

A key feature of MView is explicit support for the step-wise refinement [7] and redefinition of pointcuts in AO-connectors. Pointcuts are refined based on context information specific to the role of the stakeholder: e.g. the allocation of components on host, new components that provide additional join points. Another MView feature is the refinement of application deployment topologies. This enables the definition of additional context for composition in terms of instances, hosts, etc.

First, we introduce the general concept of MView refinement and provide more context for the running example. Then we explain the refinement of declarations, followed by an explanation on how inherited elements can be redefined.

4.2.1 The MView Concept

In Section 3, we illustrated the problem of *view tangling in connector description* by means of the Accounting composition in Fractal-ADL. Now, we introduce some more context for the example from the requirements of the case study:

"Any consumer can view the headlines and summaries for the newest articles, free of charge. However, only a signed-up consumer can browse and access full-content articles. Whenever a consumer makes use of paid services, both Authorization and Accounting apply. Authorization regulates consumer access to these services, while Accounting needs to keep track of consumers using these services."

After analyzing this further, we conclude that the compositions of Authorization and Accounting intersect at the same four methods: *fetchArticle*, *listNewestArticles*, *listArticlesForTag*, and *listArticlesForCategory*. We summarize composition at these methods as *Service Usage*.

Figure 6 illustrates the untangled views and the possibility for hierarchical reuse between the Authorization and Accounting compositions. The SERVICEUSAGECN connector (at the top) captures the composition with the *Service Usage* methods. Both the Authorization and Accounting compositions share this view. The connectors for both compositions reuse the SERVICEUSAGECN connector description by refining it. The figure shows that the untangling of stakeholder views in compositions is achieved by means of step-wise refinement of connector descriptions. Each connector —possibly a refinement of the previous— captures the concerns of a

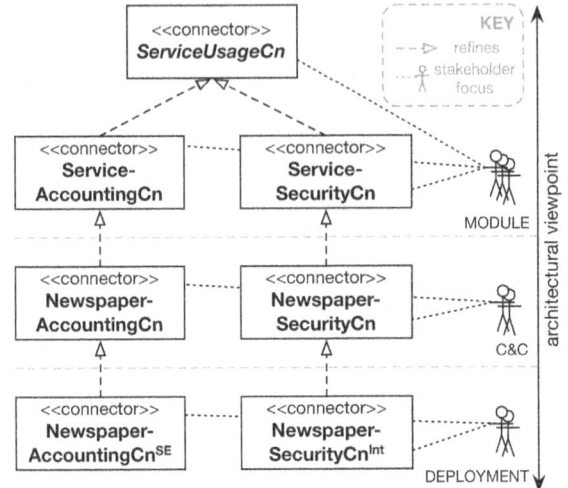

Figure 6. Eliminating tangling using refinement.

particular stakeholder as a *view* on the composition. A stakeholder expresses his view in terms of the knowledge associated with the *architectural viewpoint* that matches his expertise.

Only the availability of context knowledge imposes constraints on the order in which the views can be defined. In this paper we apply the scenario that is typical for the development of distributed middleware applications. There, development adheres to a structure that consists of three stages and developer roles [5]: *(a)* development of components and connectors by a module developer, *(b)* composition of components into applications by an application assembler, and *(c)* deployment of applications by a deployer. We start at the module development stage. In this stage, the description of compositions, in connectors, is limited to the knowledge of the module viewpoint (components, interfaces, methods, etc.). Then, in the application assembly stage, connectors can be created, and existing connectors can be refined, in terms of previous, and additional context (instances, host allocation, etc.). Finally, the deployment stage makes hosts explicit and allows connector refinement in this context. MView supports alternative scenarios where one starts at the application assembly stage with an abstract application that is further refined as development progresses with components, connectors, hosts and instances.

4.2.2 Refinement of Declarations

We start the running example at the top of Figure 6 and move through it one refinement at a time. We limit the explanation to the composition of Accounting, as Authorization employs refinement in a similar manner.

The first connector, SERVICEUSAGECN, was explained in our discussion on MViewADL in Section 4.1 (see Figure 4).

Figure 7 shows two examples of refinement: the SERVICEACCOUNTINGCN connector that refines SERVICEUSAGECN,

```
1  connector ServiceAccountingCn refines ServiceUsageCn {
2    require { AccountingRemote }
3
4    ao-composition ServiceUsage refines
            ServiceUsageCn.ServiceUsage {
5      advice {
6        service: chargeForService();
7        type: after;
8      }
9    }
10 }
```

Figure 7. Refinement of a Connector and an AO-composition with an *advice* member.

and the SERVICEUSAGE AO-composition that refines its parent by the same name.

Multi-view refinement of declarations is similar to the familiar technique of inheritance in object-orientation, but it differs in the kinds of members that can be *inherited*, and in the way these members can be *redefined*. For instance, by default, pointcut members (elements without a name) will be merged under refinement, instead of overridden.

If declaration A refines declaration B, A has a *refines*-part that starts with the `refines` keyword (line 1), followed by the name of declaration B. The refinements that A can perform are: *(1)* redefine members inherited from B (*merge* or *override*), *(2)* introduce members that are missing from B, if B is abstract, or *(3)* add new members. In addition, A inherits all members of B that are not redefined in the body of A. In this relationship B is the parent and A the child. Refinement is only supported between declarations of the same declaration type, and it is not allowed to create loops in the refinement graph.

In MViewADL, the declarations that are refinable are: the AO-composition, the connector, and the application.

The AOC refinement in Figure 7 (line 4) results in SER-VICEUSAGE inheriting all members of its parent by the same name (line 7 in Figure 4), without redefinition. Additionally, refinement adds an *advice* element to the AOC. The new advice element declares the *chargeForService()* method as advice of type *after*. *chargeForService* is a method from the ACCOUNTINGREMOTE interface that plays the roll of advice for this composition. The AOC does not further refine the inherited pointcut element.

The SERVICEACCOUNTINGCN connector on line 1 refines the SERVICEUSAGECN connector of Figure 4. The connector inherits the SERVICEUSAGE AOC from its parent. However, because both the newly defined AOC and the inherited AOC share the same name, the inherited one is overridden. It is also necessary to supply the fully qualified name of the AOC that is being refined, because the SERVICEUSAGE name now points to the local one in this context (line 4). Additionally, the connector defines the *require* element (line 2). This dependency on the ACCOUNTINGREMOTE interface is required by the *advice* element in the SERVICEUSAGE AOC, as ACCOUNTINGRE-MOTE provides the *chargeForService()* method.

The goal of this SERVICEACCOUNTINGCN connector is to compose the *Accounting* service. It does this by reusing a pointcut that was defined in a parent connector, SER-VICEUSAGECN, and by then refining it with the accounting advice specified here. Similarly, the SERVICESECURITYCN connector (Figure 6) composes the *Authorization* service by refining the same parent connector with advice that handles authorization.

The connector and AOC descriptions in figures 4 and 7 are all done in the context of the Module viewpoint.

4.2.3   Redefinition of Members

The child in a refinement relation inherits all members from its parent, except for the ones that it redefines. The semantics of the redefinition depend on the kind of the member that is redefined.

When a child inherits a member that is a declaration and that already exists locally, redefinition always implies *override*.

Overriding an inherited declaration   happens when the child in a refinement relation has a local declaration that has the same name as the declaration that is inherited. As a result, only the local declaration is accessible.

Because override is the only possible behavior between declarations, emphasizing it by adding the `override` modifier to a declaration means that override is the only desirable outcome. In MViewADL, these declarations are: the *component*, the *connector*, the *AOC*, the *host*, and the *instantiation*.

When a child inherits a member that is not a declaration (member without a name) and that already exists locally, redefinition defaults to the *merge* technique.

Merging elements K and M   is a structurally recursive operation. First, it is verified whether the locally declared element has the `override` modifier, or if it is a declaration. This turns the *merge* behavior into *override*, which result in choosing the locally declared element over the inherited element. Second, if it *is* a merge, all members of K will be merged, type by type, with members of element M, according to the merge semantics of that type. This is repeated until an element is reached that does not have a body, that is a declaration, or that demands override semantics.

In MViewADL, the elements without a name, that support merge are the *require*, the *provide*, the *pointcut*, its *signature*, the *caller* and *callee*, and their context properties: *interface, component, host, instance* and *application*, and finally, the *advice*. There are three elements that do not support merge, because they can hold only a single value: the pointcut *kind* (Figure 4), and the advice *type* and *service* (Figure 7).

We have previously discussed the refinement of the connector and the AO-composition. Now we consider the refinement of an *application* declaration (Figure 8). In the example, the ACCOUNTEDNEWSPAPERAPP application refines NEWS-PAPERAPP (Figure 5). The ACCOUNTEDNEWSPAPERAPP applica-

```
1  abstract application AccountedNewspaperApp refines NewspaperApp{
2    host AccountingServer;
3
4    AccountingService accServs  on AccountingServer;
5    NewspaperAccountingCn accConn on PublishingServer;
6
7    connector NewspaperAccountingCn refines ServiceAccountingCn {
8      ao-composition ServiceUsage refines
             ServiceAccountingCn.ServiceUsage {
9        merge pointcut {
10         merge callee {
11           override component: NewspaperService;
12         }
13       }
14     }
15   }
```

Figure 8. The NewsAccounting connector refining the Ser-viceAccounting connector with a component condition; in the context of the AccountedNewspaperApp.

```
1  application NewspaperAppDeployment refines
         AccountedNewspaperApp, SecuredNewspaperApp, ... {
2    host PublishingServer is "pub0.news.com";
3    host StagingServer    is "stage.internal.news.com";
4    // other host declarations cut
5    NewspaperService   stagingNS on StagingServer;
6    NewspaperAccountingCn accConn on PublishingServer;
7
8    connector NewspaperAccountingCn refines
         AccountedNewspaperApp.NewspaperAccountingCn {
9      ao-composition ServiceUsage refines AccountedNewspaperApp.
           ...NewspaperAccountingCn.ServiceUsage {
10       pointcut { callee { host: ! StagingServer; } }
11     }
12   } // security connector refinement cut
13 }
```

Figure 9. The NewsAccountingCn connector refining its parent with a host condition; in the context of the Newspa-perAppDeployment.

tion inherits all of its members, and adds a host declaration (line 2), a component and a connector instantiation (line 4–5), and a connector declaration (line 7).

The NewspaperAccountingCn connector, in this application, refines the ServiceAccountingCn connector from the previous example (Figure 7). The connector adds one member: the ServiceUsage AOC. This AOC is a refinement as well. It refines the pointcut that it inherits from its parent. In this scenario, the composition is further constrained by limiting interception to the those callee components that are of type NewspaperService. In other words, only those join points remain where the callee is of component type Newspa-perService. Because the refining AOC shares the same name as its parent, the parent is overridden instead of inherited.

We have explicitly added the superfluous merge modifier to the pointcut and callee elements to illustrate the contrast with the override component element. In this example, a stakeholder has specified that all prior definitions of *compo-nent* are to be ignored for the callee.

Next, the signature is merged with the signature of the parent by concatenating their lists of members. This con-forms to an implicit disjunction with *super*, if both elements define a signature. Merging the caller (or callee) element means merging each of the context properties of the same type (interface, instance, etc.). Merging these is similar to merging the signature element.

Finally, when merging a pointcut (line 9 in Figure 8), the *kind* of the child overrides the *kind* of the parent, if both elements define a kind. This is because the kind can only hold a single definition (either execution or call). In addition, at any point in this explanation, the override keyword may force an override. Similarly, when merging the advice, the *type* (and *service*) member of the child overrides that of the parent, if both child and parent define it.

The application descriptions and connector refinements are all done in the context of the Component-and-Connector viewpoint.

Finally, the non-abstract application specification in Fig-ure 9 refines the previous application specifications (line 1)

in the context of the Deployment viewpoint. Every inherited abstract host declaration is overridden with a host that de-fines a physical system (lines 2–4). Connectors are refined in terms of deployment concerns as well. In this case, the deployer set up a *staging environment* where employees can perfect layout and editing before publishing to the produc-tion server. The StagingServer hosts a NewspaperService in-stance (line 5) that serves up the online newspaper for inter-nal review. As the *accounting* service is not required for the instance on this host, the NewspaperAccountingCn connector is refined to exclude the StagingServer host (line 10).

4.3 Tool-support and Implementation

We have implemented and validated MView in an Eclipse plugin [2]. The reusable core of this plugin is a parser for the MViewADL, which supports multi-view refinement. The parser has been developed using ANTLR [29]. The lan-guage meta-model is built on top of Chameleon [37] —an in-house meta-framework for programming language con-struction. We support automatic code generation for partic-ular middleware systems, which is further detailed in Sec-tion 5.

5. Code Generation for Middleware Systems

In this section we discuss automatic code generation for dis-tributed middleware systems. We currently support gener-ation to two of the more industry-ready application middle-ware platforms, JBoss [1] and Spring [3]. Because JBoss and Spring are related to some extend, we limit our discussion to JBoss.

We continue the running example and discuss the result of the automatic generation of the Accounting connector into an implementation artifact for JBoss. Figure 10 shows the result of this generation: a JBoss aspect class (line 3). The aspect is called NewspaperAccounting. This name is taken from the connector type that is instantiated in our refinement scenario in the previous section (Figure 8, line 5).

The MViewADL language model supports resolving the refinement relations between the different ao-composition

```
 1  package accounting;
 2  import accounting.AccountingRemote; // other imports cut
 3  @Aspect  public class NewspaperAccounting {
 4    public static String[] VALID_HOSTS = {};
 5    public static String[] INVALID_HOSTS = {"unit.."};
 6    /* the pointcut definition */
 7    @PointcutDef(
 8    "execution(ContentItem *-> fetchArticle(Co..Id))" +
 9    "OR execution(List *-> listNewestArticles(int))" +
10    "OR execution(List *-> listArticlesForTag(Tag))" +
11    "OR execution(List *-> listArticlesForCat..(Cat))" +
12    "AND class($instanceof(NewsRemote))" )
13    public static Pointcut newspaperAccounting;
14    /* required for advice */
15    @EJB private AccountingRemote accountingRemote;
16    /* advice method /*
17    @Bind(
18      pointcut="newspaperAccounting",
19      type=AdviceType.AFTER,
20      cflow="NpAccountingHostConditions")
21    public void chargeForService() {
22      accountingRemote.chargeForService();
23    }
24  }
```

Figure 10. A JBoss aspect class generated from the NEWS-PAPERACCOUNTING connector.

descriptions of the NEWSPAPERACCOUNTING connector. This results in a complete specification for that particular composition. The generator uses this specification to output the JBoss pointcut (line 13) and advice (line 21) in Figure 10.

The pointcut is configured by means of the PointcutDef annotation (line 7). It is described in the JBoss pointcut language, but we can clearly recognize the *execution* of the four *service usage* methods on a component implementing the NEWSREMOTE interface.

The advice body (line 21) denotes a call to a business method on an instance of a component implementing the ACCOUNTINGREMOTE interface. To retrieve such an instance, JBoss uses dependency injection (line 15). The advice is linked to its pointcut using the @Bind (line 17) annotation. It references the name of the pointcut and includes the type of advice: after.

The host-conditions on the composition with a callee component are shown on lines 4 and 5. A callee component conforms if it is deployed on a host in the valid list, but not in the invalid list.

Additionally, Figure 10 shows the various concerns of multiple stakeholders in this composition by means of the gray areas. The three shades of gray retain the same meaning as in the motivating example in Section 3 (the roles of module developer, assembler, and deployer).

Verifying Host Conditions via Dynamic CFlow The generation to JBoss is seldom a one-to-one mapping from source to target model. JBoss has some limitations that require specific techniques to solve. One of these is the verification of host conditions.

JBoss does not support reasoning about host allocation in the pointcut. Alternatively, we use a dynamic control flow,

or cflow, statement that determines at runtime whether the advice should execute or not.

Whenever a pointcut specifies host-conditions, we generate a cflow class that verifies whether the callee is not allocated on the testing host "UNIT.NEWS.COM", every time after the pointcut matches, but before the advice is executed.

The cflow class in this example is called NPACCOUNTINGHOSTCONDITIONS, and it is coupled to the aspect by means of the cflow-attribute of the Bind annotation (Figure 10, line 17) of the advice.

6. Evaluation

In this section we evaluate how MView refinement affects the development effort for the different stakeholders in comparison with other architectural techniques. We conclude by revisiting the four requirements from Section 3.

6.1 Stakeholder Effort

We used the MViewADL to specify the architectural structure of the e-Media case study. The case has four architectural concerns that are composed through AO techniques, namely *accounting, user tracking, personalization,* and *authorization*. This amounts to 11 connectors and a total of 24 *refinements*, distributed evenly across the four architectural concerns.

In this evaluation we compare the effort, that is required of stakeholders to define such views, between MView refinement and two other, less systematic, techniques for architectural description.

To estimate the effort, we use the Lines of Code metric (LOC) in an absolute as well as a relative comparison. The two other techniques we compare MView to are (a) the *import of unchanged descriptions* and (b) *manual specification*. We use the MViewADL syntax in each of these cases to avoid representational differences from skewing the measurements.

Technique (a), called *Import*, is that of the import of unchanged specifications between two artifacts. Just like with refinement, all elements within the parent are imported, unless they are overridden. However, *Import* does not support connector refinement. Each connector that requires refinement must be manually copied and locally adjusted. An approach that applies this technique is Fractal-ADL [32].

Technique (b), called *Flatten*, is that of manual copy and local adjustment. Stakeholders put all their descriptions, belonging to a single stage in the process (e.g. Module), into a single artifact. Instead of refinement, stakeholders in a later stage manually copy the specification before adding the necessary changes. Approaches that apply this technique are DAOP-ADL, AO-ADL, and AspectualACME [15, 33, 34].

For both techniques, we only count the lines of code after adjustment is completed. Replaced or removed lines are disregarded. The results of our evaluation are presented in Table 2. The numbers in the row named *Total* represent the to-

	MView	%	Import	%	Flatten	%
Components	150		150		150	
Interfaces	74		74		74	
sum (x)	224		224		224	
Module	90	21	123	21	105	17
Assembly	80	19	162	28	149	24
Deployment	38	9	75	13	156	25
sum (y)	208	49	360	62	410	66
Total (x + y)	432		584		634	

Table 2. Stakeholder effort in terms of codebase size (LOC)

tal size of the architectural description codebase for the three techniques. From these LOCs numbers we conclude that the total effort to construct the application is considerably less with MView (432 vs. 584 and 634 LOC, respectively 26% and 32% less LOC). This total consists of the sums of the sizes of components and interfaces (sum x); and the sizes of connector descriptions in Module, Assembly and Deployment (sum y).

The effort for the components and the interfaces is the same in each approach (224 LOC) —their syntax is identical. Therefore, this reduction in effort can be completely attributed to the connector descriptions in Module, Assembly and Deployment (208 vs 360 and 410 LOC, respectively 42% and 49% less LOC to compose and deploy the application). The relative effort of the connector descriptions, in comparison with the total effort of a certain technique, also decreases: MView requires 208 out of 432 LOC for this process (or 49% of the total effort), while the other approaches require 62% (Import) and 66% (Flatten).

We now focus on the effort for the assembler and deployer. These are the stakeholders that are responsible for the descriptions in *Assembly* and *Deployment*.

It is the job of a deployer to refine the descriptions with physical host allocations and deployment-level connector refinements. Their effort when applying each of the three techniques, is considerably less with MView: 38 vs 75 and 156 LOC. The relative effort for MView is 9%, vs 13% and 25% for *Import* and *Flatten* respectively. Flatten requires the most effort, as the deployers need to copy the entire application assembly description, before carefully adding changes. Import does a lot better, as the adjustments of the deployers are limited to the host allocations and the changes to the full copies of a small number of connector descriptions. MView performs best, as refinement allows the changes to connectors to be done in terms of the smaller delta.

A similar conclusion applies to the *application assembler* stakeholder in the assembly stage: 80 LOC for MView vs 149 LOC and 162 LOC for the other techniques. The relative effort is respectively 19%, vs 28% and 24%, for *Import* and *Flatten* respectively. A lot more connector refinements are performed at this stage which explains the bad performance of Import.

The composition effort in *Module* is 90 LOC for MView vs 123 and 105 for the other techniques. The relative effort for these tasks is 21% for MView, vs 21% and 17% for *Import* and *Flatten* respectively. For MView, a relatively big size of the descriptions is pushed to the connectors in *Module* as the reusable bits are defined in these connectors (see Figure 4), while the other stages can be described as a delta. However, MView can still express this in lesser LOC in comparison to the other techniques. This is because of internal reuse in *Module* connectors.

In summary, MView does not only reduce the development effort in absolute numbers, it also reduces the effort for the assembler and the deployer relatively to the total specification size. This is because more of the composition workload is pushed towards the stakeholders in the earlier development stages, and can be easily reused.

6.2 Revisiting the Requirements

MViewADL builds strongly on each of the requirements from Section 3 to reach our goal of allowing different stakeholders to separately specify their views on the architectural descriptions. MViewADL allows views of different viewpoints to be related together in a way that is generic enough to be supported by multiple relevant technologies.

Open Connector. MViewADL supports connector specifications that are customizable through *refinement*. Currently, refinement has complete access to a parent's description. This may not always be desirable. The study of accessibility modifiers like *private* and *final* is left to future work.

Multi-Platform Support. MViewADL focusses on distributed AO-Middleware. Our toolchain already supports generation to JBoss and Spring.

Multiple Views and Viewpoints. MViewADL currently has support for the three important viewpoints in distributed systems design: *module*, *C&C*, and *deployment*. While *refinement* is broadly applicable, the syntax and semantics of the ADL need to be extended to support additional viewpoints.

View and Viewpoint Relations. View relations in multi-viewpoint representations are challenging [25]. While MView supports refinement between views of different viewpoints, this is only possible if the viewpoints share a clear goal —the description of distributed systems. Adding arbitrary viewpoints might prove challenging as well.

Discussion. The validation of MView and the ADL is limited to an application case study in the e-media domain. However, our ADL is applicable beyond this specific application and this specific domain, to typical distributed component-based architectures. To further validate this, it is part of future work to apply MView in additional case studies. As stated in the introduction, architectures for distributed systems are the focus of MView. This strong focus, however, limits its applicability in software systems with different architectural styles, such as embedded systems, or the internal structures of compilers [9].

7. Related Work

The typical AO-ADLs, that have also been considered in the analysis in Section 3: *DAOP-ADL* [33], *AO-ADL* [34], *Fractal-ADL* [32], *AspectLEDA* [24], *AspectualACME* [15], *π-ADL* [27], *Prisma* [31], all use some form of AO-Connector. While these connectors capture complex composition to a certain degree, they do not support the distribution context in distributed software systems, nor stepwise refinement. While inheritance could be used, instead of refinement, to achieve a similar separation (without the *merge* operation) of stakeholder concerns in a complex composition, it is not supported by default in these AO-ADLs. As it would require some restructuring of the composition specifications in some, if not all, of these languages. Finally, with the exception of *AO-ADL* and *Prisma*, tool-support for the generation to multiple platforms is missing.

AO-middleware technologies such as JBoss, Spring, GlueQoS [40], CAM/DAOP [33], DADO [39], FAC [32] and Prose [35] do not support the evaluation of distributed context properties. Supporting those platforms in the code generation thus needs a similar approach as presented in the generation to JBoss. On the other hand, platforms such as JAC [30], AWED [23], ReflexD [36] and DyMAC/M-Stage [21] do support the evaluation of distributed context properties, greatly simplifying the generation to these platforms.

MStage is an extension to the DyMAC platform to develop DyMAC applications over different stages using refinement. The refinement is limited to a fixed set of context properties of DyMAC components such as interfaces, component names, hosts and applications. MView ADL, however, offers a middleware-independent multi-platform ADL that supports refinement at the level of architectural views and over an open set of properties.

ArchJava [4] brings user-defined connectors to an OO-programming language. The connectors are customizable and the strong presence of inheritance should allow stakeholder separation. *ArchJava*, however, does not support AO-Connectors. While MView does not focus on implementation specifications, connectors at this level would simplify code-generation.

Batory et al. present a software composition model and associated tool set, called AHEAD [10], that supports large-scale refinement of aspect-like modules in a product family. There are important differences between AHEAD and MView. First, MView has a more focused goal, it supports stepwise refinement of interaction, not behavior. Second, MView supports stepwise refinement across multiple views and viewpoints at the architecture level, while AHEAD supports multiple levels of abstraction in the design of a software system. Finally, the AHEAD tool set does not target AO middleware.

Model-driven development of distributed software systems partially targets a similar goal as MView: a higher-level system description based on abstractions above platform-specific artifacts and implementation details. In model-driven middleware (e.g. [13, 18, 41]), multiple design models of aspects and applications can be specified, composed and possibly verified. Once composed, these models can be automatically synthesized to deployment descriptors for a specific (non-AO) middleware platform of choice [13] or to middleware implementations itself [41].

8. Conclusion and Future Work

In software architecture, AO-Connectors capture complex compositions between components. But state-of-the art AO-ADLs do not allow the separation of the various stakeholder views involved in such connectors. This results in monolithic descriptions in which these stakeholder views are tangled.

MView is a technique that enables multi-view refinement of architectural connector descriptions. Complex composition is specified through a process of multi-view refinement of connectors, each in the context of a specific stakeholder view.

We have integrated MView in a prototypical ADL and constructed an Eclipse-based tool to support MView and the ADL. The tool supports automatic code generation to specific middleware frameworks (currently JBoss and Spring).

Our evaluation of MView in the e-Media case study showed that MView reduces the overall stakeholder effort (in LOC), and the relative effort of assemblers and deployers with respect to the total specification size.

It is part of our ongoing work to further enhance the transformation framework and to validate the benefits of interaction untangling and reuse on additional case studies.

Acknowledgments

This research is partially funded by the Interuniversity Attraction Poles Programme Belgian State, Belgian Science Policy, the Fund for Scientific Research (FWO) in Flanders and by the Research Fund KU Leuven.

References

[1] Redhat inc., http://labs.jboss.com/jbossaop.

[2] Mview tool, http://distrinet.cs.kuleuven.be/software/mview.

[3] The spring enterprise platform http://www.springsource.com/products/enterprise.

[4] J. Aldrich, V. Sazawal, C. Chambers, and D. Notkin. Language support for connector abstractions. In *Object-Oriented Programming*, 2003.

[5] P. Allen and S. Frost. *Planning team roles for CBD*. Addison-Wesley Longman Publishing Co., Inc., 2001.

[6] R. Allen. *A Formal Approach to Software Architecture*. PhD thesis, Carnegie Mellon, School of Computer Science, January 1997.

[7] S. Apel, C. Kästner, T. Leich, and G. Saake. Aspect refinement-unifying aop and stepwise refinement. *Journal of Object Technology*, 6(9):13–33, 2007.

[8] C. Atkinson and T. Kühne. Aspect-oriented development with stratified frameworks. *IEEE Software*, 20(1):81–89, 2003.

[9] L. Bass, P. Clements, and R. Kazman. *Software Architecture in Practice*. Addison-Wesley, second edition, 2003.

[10] D. Batory, J. N. Sarvela, A. Rauschmayer, S. Member, and S. Member. Scaling step-wise refinement. *IEEE Transactions on Software Engineering*, 30, 2003.

[11] N. Boucké. *Composition and Relations of Architectural Models Supported by an Architectural Description Language*. PhD thesis, October 2009.

[12] N. Boucké, D. Weyns, R. Hilliard, T. Holvoet, and A. Helleboogh. Characterizing relations between architectural views. In *LNCS*, volume 5292. Springer, September 2008.

[13] G. Deng. Resolving component deployment & configuration challenges for enterprise dre systems via frameworks & generative techniques. In *International Conference on Software Engineering*. ACM, 2006.

[14] P. Feiler, B. Lewis, S. Vestal, and E. Colbert. An overview of the sae architecture analysis & design language (aadl) standard. In *Architecture Description Languages*, volume 176. Springer Boston, 2005.

[15] A. Garcia, C. Chavez, T. Batista, C. Sant'anna, U. Kulesza, A. Rashid, and C. Lucena. On the modular representation of architectural aspects. In *Software Architecture*, volume 4344 of *LNCS*. Springer Berlin / Heidelberg, 2006.

[16] A. F. Garcia, E. M. L. Figueiredo, C. N. Sant'Anna, M. Pinto, and L. Fuentes. Representing architectural aspects with a symmetric approach. In *Early Aspects '09*. ACM, 2009.

[17] D. Garlan, R. T. Monroe, and D. Wile. Acme: An architecture description interchange language. In *CASCON'97*, 1997.

[18] J. Gray, T. Bapty, S. Neema, D. C. Schmidt, A. Gokhale, and B. Natarajan. An approach for supporting aspect-oriented domain modeling. In *International Conference on Generative Programming and Component Engineering*. Springer-Verlag New York, Inc., 2003.

[19] J. Grundy. Multi-perspective specification, design and implementation of components using aspects. *International Journal of Software Engineering and Knowledge Engineering*, 10(6), December 2000.

[20] ISO/IEC. Systems and software engineering - architecture description. *ISO/IEC standard, draft D8*, August 2010.

[21] B. Lagaisse. *A Comprehensive Integration of AOSD and CBSD Concepts in Middleware*. PhD thesis, K.U.Leuven, Dec. 2009.

[22] N. Medvidovic and R. N. Taylor. A classification and comparison framework for software architecture description languages. *IEEE Transactions on Software Engineering*, 26(1), Jan 2000.

[23] L. D. B. Navarro, M. Südholt, W. Vanderperren, B. De Fraine, and D. Suvée. Explicitly distributed aop using awed. In *AOSD'06*. ACM, 2006.

[24] A. Navasa, M. A. Pérez-Toledano, and J. M. Murillo. An adl dealing with aspects at software architecture stage. *Inf. Softw. Technol.*, 51(2), 2009.

[25] B. Nuseibeh, J. Kramer, and A. Finkelstein. Viewpoints: meaningful relationships are difficult! In *International Conference on Software Engineering*. IEEE Computer Society, 2003.

[26] F. Oquendo. π-arl: an architecture refinement language for formally modelling the stepwise refinement of software architectures. *SIGSOFT Softw. Eng. Notes*, 29, September 2004.

[27] F. Oquendo. pi-adl: an architecture description language based on the higher-order typed pi-calculus for specifying dynamic and mobile software architectures. *ACM SIGSOFT Software Engineering Notes*, 29(3), 2004.

[28] K. Palma, Y. Eterovic, and J. M. Murillo. Extending the rapide adl to specify aspect oriented software architectures. In *15th International Conference on Software Engineering and Data Engineering*, page 170. ISCA, 2006.

[29] T. Parr and R. Quong. Antlr: A predicated (k) parser generator, 1995.

[30] R. Pawlak, L. Seinturier, L. Duchien, and G. Florin. Jac: A flexible solution for aspect-oriented programming in java. In *Reflection*, 2001.

[31] J. Pérez, I. Ramos, J. J. Martínez, P. Letelier, and E. Navarro. Prisma: Towards quality, aspect oriented and dynamic software architectures. In *International Conference on Quality Software*, 2003.

[32] N. Pessemier, L. Seinturier, L. Duchien, and T. Coupaye. A component-based and aspect-oriented model for software evolution. *Int. J. Comput. Appl. Technol.*, 31(1/2), 2008.

[33] M. Pinto, L. Fuentes, and J. M. Troya. A dynamic component and aspect-oriented platform. *Computer Journal*, 48(4), 2005.

[34] M. Pinto, L. Fuentes, and J. M. Troya. Specifying aspect-oriented architectures in ao-adl. In *Information and Software Technology*. Elsevier, 2011.

[35] A. Popovici, T. Gross, and G. Alonso. Dynamic weaving for aspect-oriented programming. In *AOSD'02*. ACM, 2002.

[36] E. Tanter and J. Noyé. A versatile kernel for multi-language aop. In *Generative Programming and Component Engineering*, LNCS. Springer Berlin / Heidelberg, 2005.

[37] M. van Dooren. *Abstractions for improving, creating, and reusing object-oriented programming languages*. PhD thesis, Department of Computer Science, K.U.Leuven, Leuven, Belgium, June 2007.

[38] D. Van Landuyt, S. Op de beeck, E. Truyen, and P. Verbaeten. Building a digital publishing platform using aosd. In *LNCS Transactions on Aspect-Oriented Software Development*, volume 8, December 2010.

[39] E. Wohlstadter, S. Jackson, and P. T. Devanbu. Dado: Enhancing middleware to support crosscutting features in distributed, heterogeneous systems. In *ICSE*, 2003.

[40] E. Wohlstadter, S. Tai, T. Mikalsen, I. Rouvellou, and P. Devanbu. Glueqos: Middleware to sweeten quality-of-service policy interactions. In *26th International Conference on Software Engineering*. IEEE Computer Society, 2004.

[41] C. Zhang, D. Gao, and H.-A. Jacobsen. Generic middleware substrate through modelware. In *Middleware*, 2005.

Weaving Semantic Aspects in HiLA

Gefei Zhang

arvato Systems Technologies GmbH
gefei.zhang@pst.ifi.lmu.de

Matthias Hölzl

Ludwig-Maximilians-Universität München
matthias.hoelzl@pst.ifi.lmu.de

Abstract

UML state machines are widely used for modeling software behavior. Due to the low-level character of the language, UML state machines are often poorly modularized and hard to use. High-Level Aspects (HiLA) is an aspect-oriented extension of UML state machines which provides high-level language constructs for behavior modeling. HiLA considerably improves the modularity of UML state machines by extending them by semantic aspects. This paper presents the weaving process for HiLA that we have shown to be sound with respect to the transition-system semantics of HiLA. In particular, we show how our weaving process deals with implicit state activation (and deactivation), maps semantic pointcuts to syntactic elements, and resolves potential conflicts between different aspects. The process has been implemented in an extension of the Hugo/RT UML translator and model checker, the correctness of our weaving is validated by model checking.

Categories and Subject Descriptors D2.2 [*Software Engineering*]: Design Tools and Techniques—State diagrams

Keywords Aspect-Oriented Modeling, UML, Algorithms

1. Introduction

UML state machines [15] are widely used for modeling software behavior. They are considered as simple and intuitive, and are even deemed to be "the most popular modeling language for reactive components" [7]. However, UML state machines exhibit modularity problems, and even some simple behaviors may be hard to model, see [17] for examples.

Proposals have been made [3, 5, 12, 14] to use aspect-oriented modeling to tackle the modularity problems of UML state machines. In the prevalent proposals, aspects define model transformations, most commonly graph transformations: an aspect specifies in its pointcut a fragment of the base model, and defines in its advice a graph to replace the parts of the base model matched by the pointcut. The weaving is then the process of actually performing the transformation.

Aspects in these proposals are therefore syntactic constructs: they define how to modify (the syntax tree of) the base model. While these approaches provide a means for modeling parts of the system separately, they hardly help to reduce the complexity of the model, because, even though the factorization provided by the match-and-replace semantics might eliminate some redundancy, the modeler still has to define the system behavior in every little detail. Moreover, the aspects (which are in fact model transformations) are defined in syntactic terms, and do not have a behavioral semantics. When they are applied to behavioral models like state machines, the semantics of the overall system can therefore be only obtained by carefully studying the weaving result.

Our approach, High-Level Aspects (HiLA), in contrast, extends UML state machines by semantic aspects. In HiLA, a pointcut defines specific points of time in the execution of the base machine, and the advice defines some additional or alternative behavior to execute at these points of time. The behavior of HiLA aspects can therefore be understood independently of any weaving process, and indeed the semantics of HiLA is defined by a transition-system model rather than by a graph transformation that weaves aspects into the base state machine, see [17]. State machines using HiLA aspects are therefore easier to read and also easier to construct than their graph-transformation-based counterparts, since the modeler only has to define what to do instead of how to do it.

To implement HiLA aspects it would therefore be possible to develop an interpreter that directly implements the semantics of HiLA. In order to leverage the sophisticated possibilities for formal analysis and code generation offered by the Hugo/RT system[1], and to avoid the overhead of evaluating the dynamic activation and deactivation of aspects specified by the semantics of HiLA at run time, we have opted to implement HiLA by weaving aspects and base state machine together. Given the nature of HiLA aspects, this weaving process is more elaborate than the one required by

AOSD'12, March 25–30, 2012, Potsdam, Germany.

---

[1] http://www.pst.ifi.lmu.de/projekte/hugo

graph-transformation-based aspect systems: The modeler no longer directly specifies the elements that have to be modified by the weaver; instead the weaver has to determine which model elements are modified by HILA aspects. This is rather challenging, as even a simple aspect may touch many model elements that are scattered throughout the state machine.

In this paper, we present the weaving algorithms of HILA aspects. In particular, we show how we handle syntax variations of UML state machines, how the semantic pointcuts are mapped to syntactic elements, and how we resolve conflicts between aspects. The presented algorithms have been implemented as an extension of the model checker Hugo/RT, model checking HILA aspects is thus an easy task. Many of the issues encountered by weaving aspects for HILA also apply to the implementation of semantic aspect systems for concurrent, state-based languages in general. Therefore, the techniques presented in this paper are not only a description of the implementation strategy we have used for our current HILA system, they can also serve as guideline for implementors of other aspect-oriented languages. We will address one example of this in Sect. 6.

The rest of this paper is structured as follows: In the next two sections we give short introductions to UML state machines and HILA. The fourth section, the core of this paper, details the weaving algorithm; it is followed by a discussion of the implementation in Hugo/RT and some remarks on formal validation of the weaving results. Finally, we present related work and conclude.

2. UML State Machines

A UML state machine provides a model for the behavior of an object or component. Figure 1(a) shows a state machine modeling (in a highly simplified manner) the behavior of a player during a part of a game. The player—a magician—starts in a state where she has to chose a NewLevel. Upon completion of the preparations she is transferred into the Play state which contains two concurrent regions, corresponding to two parallel threads of execution. The upper region describes the possible movements of the player, the lower region specifies her behaviors. After completing the current level, the player can go to the next level which has the same topology and general gameplay.

In each level the player initially starts in an entrance hall (Hall), from there she can move to a room in which magic crystals are stored (CrystalRoom) and on to a room containing a Ladder. From this room the player can either move back to the hall or, after excavating a treasure consisting of gold coins, exit the level. After starting the level, the player first has to acquire enough magical power (PowerUp), then cast a Spell that, make here invisible, or transforms her into an Enchanted state. Once she is in this enchanted state, the player may either try to fight the guard of the treasure (Fight), collect the treasure (CollectTreasure) and then exit the level

via the ladder, or she may use her magical power to exit the current level without fighting the guard and collecting the gold (in which case she may encounter the guard again later on in the game). The player may lose the fight against the guard in which case she is transferred back to one of the previous states, depending on the severity of the defeat.

2.1 Syntax and Informal Semantics

We briefly review the syntax and semantics of UML state machines according to the UML specification [15] by means of Fig. 1(a). A UML state machine consists of *regions* which contain *vertices* and *transitions* between vertices. We require every state machine to have a top-level region called top.[2] A vertex is either a *state*, where the state machine may dwell in and which may show hierarchically contained regions; or a *pseudo state* regulating how transitions are compound in execution. Transitions are triggered by *events* and describe, by leaving and entering states, the possible state changes of the state machine. The events are drawn from an *event pool* associated with the state machine, which receives events from its own or from different state machines.

A state of a state machine is *simple*, if it contains no regions (such as NewLevel in Fig. 1(a)); a state is *composite*, if it contains at least one region; a composite state is said to be *orthogonal* if it contains more than one region, visually separated by dashed lines (such as Play). Each state may show an *entry* behavior (like spellHex in Spell), an *exit* behavior (like takeCrystal in CrystalRoom), which are executed on activating and deactivating the state, respectively; a state may also show a *do activity* (like in NewLevel) which is executed while the state machine sojourns in this state. Transitions are triggered by events (toCrystalRoom, fight), show guards (fightLost), and specify effects to be executed when a transition is fired (losePower). Completion transitions (e.g., the transition leaving NewLevel) are triggered by an implicit *completion event* emitted when a state completes all its internal activities. Events may be *deferred* (e.g., fight and hide in NewLevel), that is, put back into the event pool if they are not to be handled currently. By executing a transition its source state is left and its target state entered; transitions may also be declared to be *internal* (not shown in this example), thus skipping the activation-deactivation scheme. An *initial* pseudo state, depicted as a filled circle, represents the starting point for the execution of a region. A *final* state, depicted as a circle with a filled circle inside, represents the completion of its containing region; if the region top of a state machine is completed the state machine terminates. *Junction* pseudo states, also depicted as filled circles (see lower region of Play), allow for case distinctions. Transitions to and from different regions of an orthogonal composite state can be synchronized by *fork* (not shown here) and *join* pseudo

---

[2] This was required by UML 1.x. In UML 2.x, this restriction was dropped. However, we can always put a top-level region around a state machine without changing its semantics.

(a) Movement and basic actions

(b) Mutual exclusion: player cannot be in crystal room while enchanted

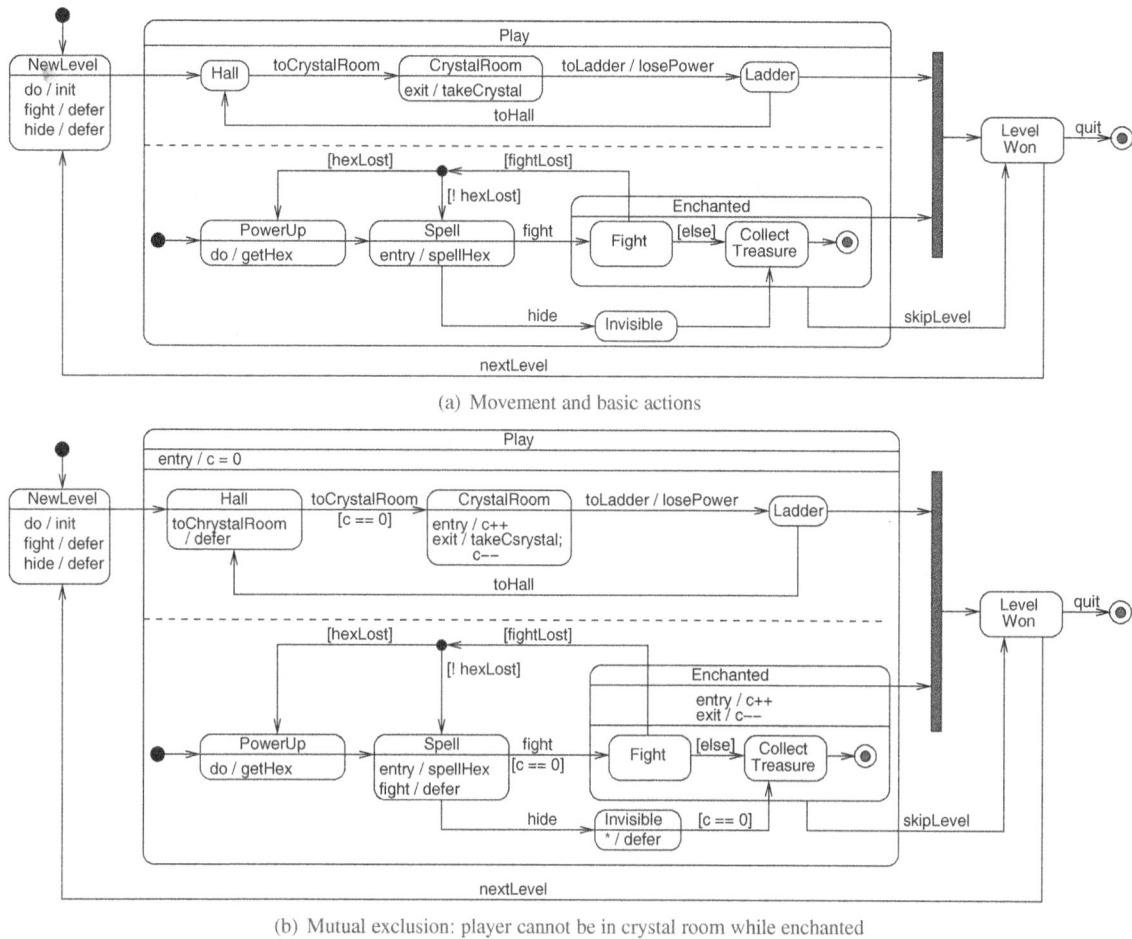

Figure 1. UML state machine for a magician in a computer game

states, presented as bars. For simplicity, we omit the other pseudo state kinds (entry and exit points, shallow and deep history, choice, and terminate).

At run time, states get activated and deactivated as a consequence of transitions being fired. The active states at a stable step in the execution of the state machine form the active *state configuration*. Active state configurations are hierarchical: when a composite state is active, then exactly one state in each of its regions is also active; when a substate of a composite state is active, so is the containing state too. The execution of the state machine can be viewed as different active state configurations getting active or inactive upon the state machine receiving events.

For example, an execution trace, given in terms of active state configurations, of the state machine in Fig. 1(a) might be (NewLevel), (Play, Hall, PowerUp), (Play, Hall, Spell), (Play, Hall, Enchanted, Fight), (LevelWon), followed by the final state, which terminates the execution.

2.2 Modularity Problems

Models of plain UML state machines may exhibit modularity problems, in particular when modeling synchroniza-

tion of parallel regions or history-based behaviors, see [17, 18]. For simplicity, we show only an example of modeling mutual-exclusion.

Assume in the example above an additional rule that the player cannot enter the crystal room while she is enchanted (because, for instance, she might damage the room). That is, in Fig. 1(a) the states CrystalRoom and Enchanted must not be simultaneously active. In plain UML, this rule has to be modeled *imperatively*. An example is given in Fig. 1(b), where a variable c is introduced and used to control the access to the two critical states: it is initialized as 0 in the entry action of Play, increased whenever CrystalRoom or Enchanted is activated, and decreased whenever one of the two states is deactivated. The three transitions that activate the two states (from Hall to CrystalRoom, from Spell to Fight, and from Spell to CollectTreasure) are extended by a guard, such that they are only fired when c equals 0, which means that the other critical state is currently inactive and the mutual exclusion rule is satisfied. A subtle point is that we have to declare the events toCrystalRoom and fight to be deferrable in the states Hall and Spell, respectively, and we also have to declare the completion event of state Invisible to be de-

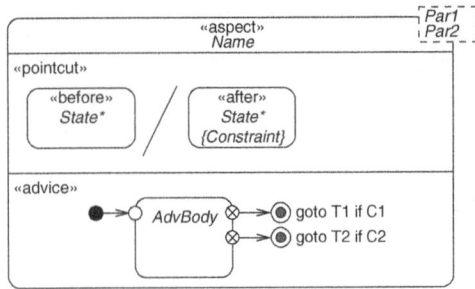

Figure 2. HiLA: concrete syntax

(a) «after»

(b) «before»

(c) Mutex

Figure 3. HiLA aspects

ferrable (we use the notation */defer for deferring the completion event; UML provides no standard syntax for this). In this way the transitions are only postponed if the other critical state is active, and will be automatically resumed without requiring the events to be sent again. Otherwise the events would be lost in case exactly one of the critical states were active, since the event would then be taken from the event pool without firing a transition.

It is obviously unsatisfactory that modeling even such a simple mutual exclusion rule requires modification of many model elements, which are scattered over the state machine. Furthermore, it is easy to introduce errors which are hard to find, as evidenced by the need to defer events. Such modeling makes maintenance difficult, the models are complex and prone to errors.

3. HiLA in a Nutshell

As a possible solution of UML state machines' modularity problems, the language High-Level Aspects (HiLA, [17]) was defined as an aspect-oriented extension for UML state machines. HiLA provides high-level constructs for declarative behavior modeling. The concrete syntax of a HiLA aspect is shown in Fig. 2 and explained in the following.

Syntactically, a HiLA aspect is a UML template containing at least a name, a pointcut and an advice. The template parameters allow easy customization, so that aspects for functionalities such as logging, transactions or mutual exclusions can easily be reused in many places.

An aspect is applied to a UML state machine, which is called the *base machine*. An aspect defines some additional or alternative behavior of the base machine at some points in time during the base machine's execution. The behavior is defined in the *advice* of the aspect; the points in time to execute the advice are defined in the *pointcut*. The advice (stereotype «advice» in Fig. 2) also has the form of a state machine, except that the final states may carry a label. The "body" of the advice, i.e. the part without the initial vertex, the final states, and the connecting transitions, models the behavior to carry out. A label on a final state names the state that should be activated when the advice is finished and the execution of the base machine should be resumed. We refer to this state as the *resumption state* of the final

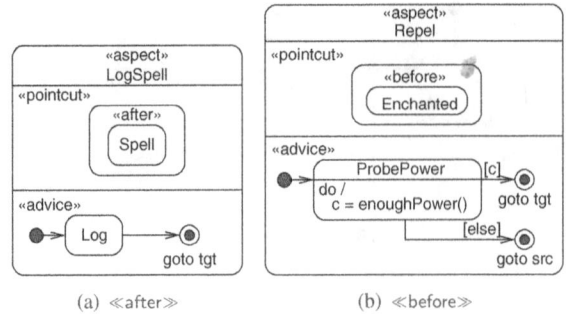

state. The label may optionally be guarded by a *resumption constraint*, which is indicated by the keyword if and has the form (like|nlike) StateName* where StateName is the set of qualified names of the base machine's states. like S is true iff after the resumption all states contained in S will be active, otherwise nlike S is true.

The pointcut («pointcut») specifies the points in time when the advice is executed. These points in time may be 1) when a certain state of the base machine is just about to become active or 2) a set of states has just been left.[3] The semantics of a pointcut can be regarded as a selection function of the base machine's transitions: a pointcut «before» s selects all transitions in the base machine whose firing makes state s active, and a pointcut «after» S selects those transitions whose firing deactivates S. Note this does not mean "a pointcut «before» s selects all transitions whose target is s" or "a pointcut «after» S selects all transitions whose source is a state contained in S". The semantics of UML state machines is actually more involved, which makes the weaving more complex, see Sect. 4.

Overall, an aspect is a graphical model element stating that at the points in time specified by the pointcut the advice should be executed, and after the execution of the advice the base machine should resume execution by activating the state given by the label of the advice's final state, when the conditions given there are satisfied. For «before» and «after» pointcuts, this "point in time" is always the firing of a transition; we say that this transition is *advised* by the advice.

---

[3] Actually there is still another kind of pointcut, «whilst», which defines the time spans during which certain states are active, see [17]. For simplicity, «whilst» pointcut is not discussed in this paper.

For example, aspect LogSpell in Fig. 3(a) states that a log message is written whenever the player has just cast a spell, i.e., when state Spell has just turned inactive («after»). At such points of time, i.e., whenever the transition from Spell to Enchanted should be fired, the advice of the aspect LogSpell is executed: the state Log is activated and writes a log message, then the final state of the advice is activated, and the base machine continues the advised transition and goes to the original target state. Since no constraint is specified for the label of the final state, the original transition will be resumed as soon as the advice is finished.

To show a more involved example, we now consider an additional behavior of the magician. Suppose the magician is not always allowed to be enchanted by casting a spell, he also need a certain amount of power (we abstract from details of the magician gaining or losing power). This feature is realized by the aspect Repel in Fig. 3(b). Aspect Repel activates state ProbePower whenever state Enchanted is just about to turn active. This state sets the boolean variable c to true when the player is more powerful than the guard and to false otherwise. The aspect then either proceeds to Enchanted (goto tgt) if c is true, or it returns to the source of the advised transition (label goto src).

An even more complex feature involves mutual exclusion, as discussed in Sect. 2.2. That is, the magician should not be able to enter CrystalRoom while being Enchanted. Since mutual exclusion is a very common requirement in parallel systems, we define a HiLA template to model it, see Fig. 3(c). The template takes two State parameters, S and T. The pointcut is a shortcut of "«before» S or «before» T", and specifies all the points in time when either S or T is just about to get active. In such moments the advice is executed, which contains an empty body and simply conducts the base machine to resume the advised transition (by going to its target), when after the resumption the states S and T would not be both active (condition nlike S, T). Compared with the UML solution, the imperative details of mutual exclusion are now transparent for the modeler, the modeling is non-intrusive, the semantics of the aspect (template) is much easier to understand hence less error-prone. Instantiating the template by binding S to Enchanted and T to CrystalRoom elegantly prevents our magician from entering the crystal room while being enchanted and also from becoming enchanted while in the CrystalRoom.

4. Weaving

Weaving is the process of transforming the base machine to incorporate the behaviors defined in aspects. It includes determining (according to the pointcut) which transitions are advised, and to advise these transitions correctly (so that the behavior of the advice is executed and then the base machine is resumed correctly).

Due to the semantic nature of HiLA aspects, the final check whether a transition is actually advised by some as-

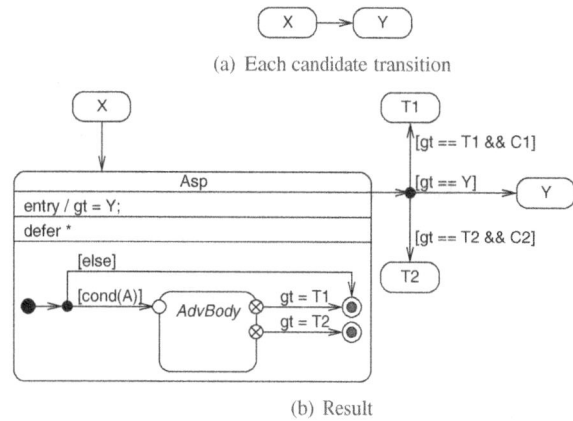

(a) Each candidate transition

(b) Result

Figure 4. Weaving a single aspect A

pect, and therefore if the advice should be executed, can only be performed at run time. However, given an aspect A, we can statically determine the set $C(A)$ of *candidate transitions* that may be advised by A. Our weaving process actually applies a transformation to each candidate transition to implement the run-time logic that checks dynamically whether the transition is advised and, if so, executes the advice and returns to the base machine according to the label of the final state.

In the following, we first define in Sect. 4.1 some notation that we need for the discussion. Then, in Sect. 4.2, we consider the case that there is only one aspect to weave. Even on this simplistic stage, some rather elaborate techniques are required to calculate $C(A)$, implement the check whether a transition is actually advised, and resume the base machine by activating the states demanded by the label. These techniques will be extended in Sect. 4.3 to handle the more realistic situation of a multitude of aspects being applied simultaneously. In particular, our weaving is designed in such a way that minimizes possible conflicts between aspects, and remaining conflicts at least can be detected at run time. To keep the size of the examples manageable we use a simplified excerpt from the state machine in Fig. 1(a) to demonstrate the weaving process. In this excerpt, shown in Fig. 7(a), we have removed some transitions which are not essential to show features of the normalization and weaving process.

4.1 Notation

The abstract syntax of UML state machines and HiLA is defined in Fig. 5. When discussing the weaving algorithms, we use the usual UML convention and write prop(el) to refer to the property prop of el. In order to better focus on the weaving process, we use a simplified metamodel of UML and do not consider entry and exit points, history, choice and terminate vertices. History and choice vertices can be simulated using other model elements, and terminate vertices can be included by a simple extension of our weaving, see [17].

(a) UML

(b) HiLA

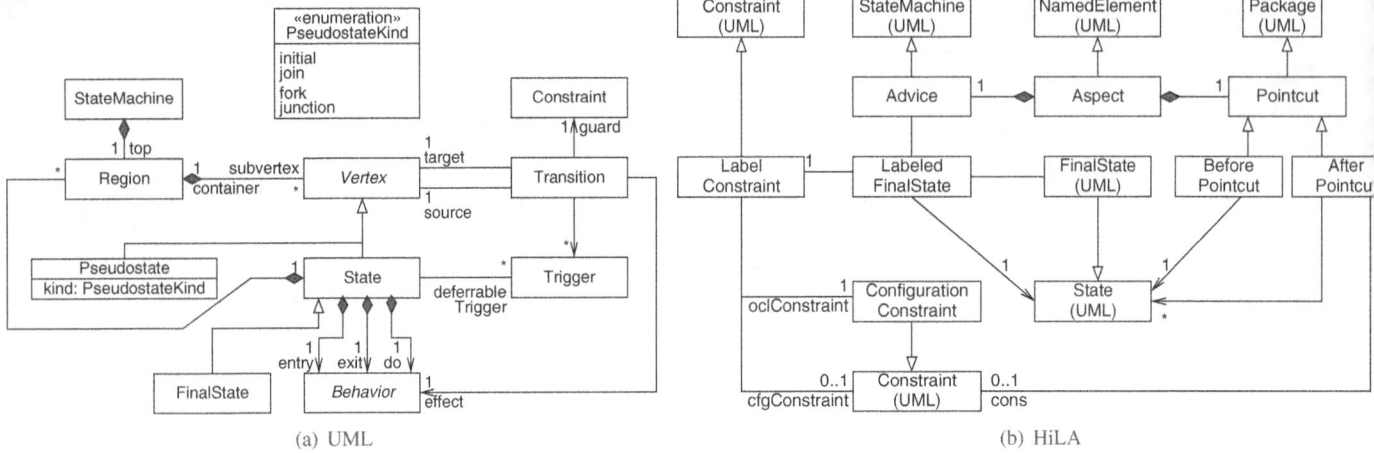

Figure 5. Metamodel (simplified)

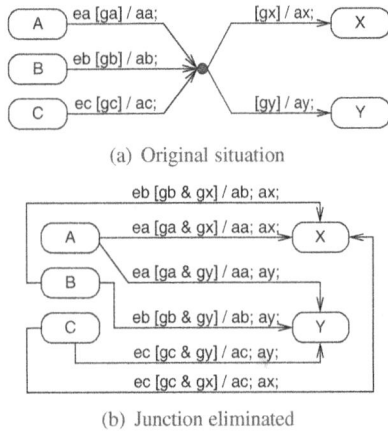

(a) Original situation

(b) Junction eliminated

Figure 6. Elimination of junction vertices

Moreover, we require the base machine to be free of junction vertices,[4] which can be achieved performing the transformation shown in Fig. 6 to eliminate undesired junctions.

Given states s and z, and transition t, we write $\mathrm{src}(t)$ for $\mathrm{source}(t)$, $\mathrm{tgt}(t)$ for $\mathrm{target}(t)$, $\mathrm{LCR}(s, z)$ for the least region containing both s and z. Given region r, we write $\mathrm{substate}^+(r)$ to represent all states (directly or recursively) contained in r. For a state s, we write $\mathrm{substate}^+(s)$ to represent $\bigcup_{r \in \mathrm{region}(s)} \mathrm{substate}^+(r)$ and write $\mathrm{substate}^*(s)$ for $\mathrm{substate}^+(s) \cup \{s\}$.

4.2 Weaving A Single HiLA Aspect

The transformation applied to the candidate transitions in the case of weaving one single aspect is described in Fig. 4. Given an aspect A, where we assume it has the very general advice as given in Fig. 2, we introduce for each transition in the candidate set $C(\mathsf{A})$ (we call its source state X and its target state Y) a composite state, which we call Asp here

---

[4] Except the targets of the transitions leaving initial vertices, if these are junctions. Note that every region may contain an initial vertex.

and in actual weaving is assigned a unique name. The state Asp contains a slightly modified copy of the advice where: 1) labels of final states are removed (in plain UML state machines there are no labels), 2) gotos are implemented by storing the state that should be activated in the *resumption variable* gt, and 3) an additional case distinction is added, which is carried out when Asp is activated and ensures that the advice body is only executed when the transition is really advised. The construction of the condition to check here, cond(A), will be explained in Sect. 4.2.2. After the execution of Asp, the transition to fire is selected depending on the value of gt. The transition from the junction to the final state in Fig.4(b) is called the *bypass transition* of aspect A. It ensures that the advice body is skipped if cond is not satisfied.

In the following, we show in detail how we implement 1) the selection defined by the pointcut and 2) the resumption conditions. For both tasks, we first need to introduce *trace variables* into the base machine to trace its execution.

4.2.1 Trace Variables

In plain UML state machines, no information is provided on which states (in different regions) are currently active or on which states have just turned inactive. Since HiLA aspects may define behaviors to be executed just after a multitude of states have been active, we must make such information explicit by introducing additional variables.

For each state s of the base machine, we introduce a variable a_s, and set it to true in the entry action of s, and to false in the exit action. We initialize all variables a_s with false. Obviously, a_s is true iff state s is active.

The basic idea of tracking states that have just turned inactive is also to introduce for each state s a variable l_s. l_s is set to true by the exit action of s and set to false by the exit action of the state activated after s. Since there may be several transitions leaving s, and we cannot determine statically which one will actually be fired (and therefore

268

(a) Original situation

(b) Normalized

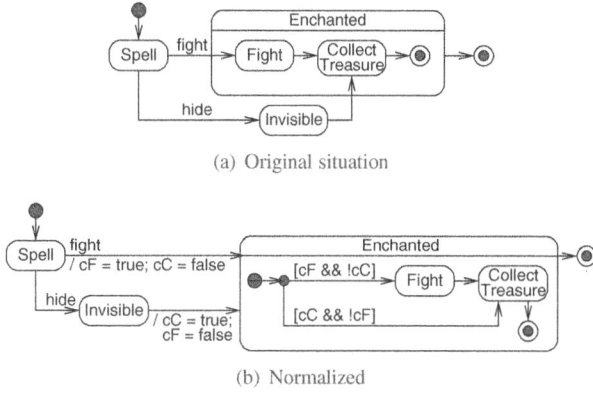

Figure 7. Transformation: before

(a) Original situation   (b) Normalized (does not conform to [15]!)

(c) Fork and assignments of false removed

Figure 8. Normalization of fork vertices

which state will be the next active one), we set l_s to false in the exit action of each state that may turn active after s. Seen from the target's point of view: for all states z and x, we set the variable l_x to false in the exit action of z if x may have been active just before z turns active.

Note, however, that generally states may be composite and contain several orthogonal regions. State x, which "may have been active just before z", is not necessarily the source of some transition leading to z. Instead, for each state z, we set in its exit action variable l_x to false, for each state x such that there is a transition entering z from x, from an ancestor state of x, or from any state contained in any ancestor state of x.

For example, we introduce for the state LevelWon in Fig. 1 the entry action $a_{\mathsf{LevelWon}} = \mathsf{true}$, setting variable a_{LevelWon} to true to indicate that state LevelWon is currently active.

The exit action of LevelWon is more complex:

$$l_{\mathsf{LevelWon}} = \mathsf{true}$$
$$l_{\mathsf{Ladder}} = \mathsf{false}; \qquad l_{\mathsf{Enchanted}} = \mathsf{false};$$
$$l_{\mathsf{Fight}} = \mathsf{false}; \qquad l_{\mathsf{CollectTreasure}} = \mathsf{false};$$
$$l_{\mathsf{Play}} = \mathsf{false}; \qquad l_{\mathsf{Hall}} = \mathsf{false};$$
$$l_{\mathsf{CrystalRoom}} = \mathsf{false}; \qquad l_{\mathsf{Ladder}} = \mathsf{false};$$

The first line indicates that after the execution of the exit action LevelWon is the state (more generally, one of the states) that has just turned inactive; the second line indicates that Ladder and Enchanted are no longer such states (these are the states from which—via a join vertex—LevelWon is directly reached); the other three lines indicate that the substates of Enchanted, as well as the states contained in the other region of Play are no longer such states either. It is not necessary to set l_{PowerUp} or l_{Spell} to be false, because they cannot have been the last active states before LevelWon turned active.

4.2.2 Pointcut

Equipped with trace variables, we are now in the position to implement pointcuts.

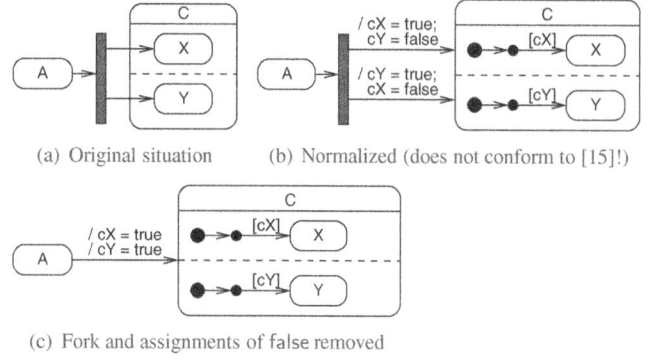

«**before**» A pointcut of the form «before» s advises all transitions which activate the state s. In UML, a transition t may active a state s iff one of the two following cases is true:

1. $\mathsf{tgt}(t) = \mathsf{s}$, (for example, in Fig. 1, the transition T from NewLevel to Hall activates state Hall),

2. (recall s may be a composite state) $\mathsf{tgt}(t) \in \mathsf{substate}^*(\mathsf{s})$, (transition T also activates Play).

To solve the problem of capturing both transitions (in particular the second one), we first transform the base machine to eliminate the second form of state activation. The transformation is straightforward. For each transition t "goes into" (see below) some state, we "redirect" t to the container state of $\mathsf{tgt}(t)$ by setting $\mathsf{tgt}(t) \leftarrow \mathsf{state}(\mathsf{container}(\mathsf{tgt}(t)))$, and setting a fresh variable to indicate what to do when the container state of $\mathsf{tgt}(t)$ turns active. This variable is called an *initial variable* and will be checked by the initial transition to determine the (first) state to activate after the container's activation. We say that a transition t "goes into" a state s iff $s = \mathsf{state}(\mathsf{container}(\mathsf{tgt}(t)))$ and s is contained in $\mathsf{LCR}(\mathsf{src}(t), \mathsf{tgt}(t))$. When a transition t of this kind is fired, it activates not only $\mathsf{tgt}(t)$, but also the container state s. Our transformation above removes such transitions.

After this transformation, every state is activated iff a transition leading to the state is fired. Since a pointcut «before» s does not contain any other constraints, we set $\mathsf{cond}(\mathsf{s})$ simply to be true. That is, the aspect advises exactly all the transitions leading to s. Therefore we do not need a bypass transition for «before» aspects.

For example, if an aspect with pointcut «before» Enchanted is applied to Fig. 7(a), the base machine is first transformed to Fig. 7(b), and the aspect advises the transitions from Spell and Invisible to Enchanted. The variables cF and cC are used to indicate whether to activate Fight or CollectTreasure when Enchanted gets active.

Forks Note that the normalization step described above has to be extended if the source of the transition going into state s is a fork. For example, when Fig. 8(a) is normalized, the result (Fig. 8(b)) will be violating the constraint that "all

269

transitions outgoing a fork vertex must target states in different regions of an orthogonal state" [15, p.556]. Therefore, to all such transitions, we apply an additional transformation to remove the fork as well as those assignments where initial variables are set to false. The final result is given in Fig. 8(c).

«after» Differently than in the case of «before», a pointcut of the form «after» S selects all transitions that are fired just after the *configuration* S gets inactive.[5] Obviously, we have to check if any state contained in S is deactivated. In UML, a state s can be deactivated by any one of the following transitions

1. all transitions t, such that $\mathsf{src}(t) = \mathsf{s}$ (for example, in Fig. 1, when the Transition $\mathcal{T}$ from Enchanted to LevelWon is fired, Enchanted is deactivated),

2. all transitions t, such that $\mathsf{src}(t) \in \mathsf{substate}^+(\mathsf{s})$ and $\mathsf{tgt}(t) \notin \mathsf{substate}^+(\mathsf{s})$ ($\mathcal{T}$ also deactivates Play),

3. all transitions t, such that $\exists S \in \mathsf{subvertex}(L), L = \mathsf{LCR}(\mathsf{src}(t), \mathsf{tgt}(t)), \mathsf{tgt}(t) \notin \mathsf{substate}^*(S) \cdot s, \mathsf{src}(t) \in \mathsf{substate}^+(S)$ ($\mathcal{T}$ also deactivates all states in the upper region of Play).

Given an «after» S aspect, its candidate set is therefore $T = \bigcup_{s \in S}(T_1(s) \cup T_2(s) \cup T_3(s))$, where $T_1(s) = \{t \mid \mathsf{src}(t) = s\}$, $T_2(s) = \{t \mid \mathsf{src}(t) \in \mathsf{substate}^+(s) \wedge \mathsf{tgt}(t) \notin \mathsf{substate}^+(\mathsf{s})\}$, $T_3(s) = \{t \mid s, \mathsf{src}(t) \in S \text{ for some } S \in \mathsf{subvertex}(\mathsf{LCR}(\mathsf{src}(t), \mathsf{tgt}(t)))\}$ such that $t \notin \mathsf{substate}^*(S)$.

On each transition t contained in the candidate set, we still need to implement the run-time check whether t is actually advised by a pointcut «after» S. When t is fired, we know that *one of* the states contained in S has just turned inactive, we still have to check whether *all* states in S were active before the transition was fired. This is the case iff (at run time) $z = \bigwedge_{s \in S} a_s \vee l_s$ is true, i.e. for each state s contained in S, either s is active, or s has just turned inactive. Recall that when this check is performed, i.e. when any transition $t \in T$ is fired, it is not possible that all states in S are active.

Finally, the constraint of the pointcut is also integrated (by conjunction) into $\mathsf{cond}(\mathsf{A})$ to ensure the aspect is only executed when the condition was satisfied. We therefore set condition c in Fig. 4(b) to be $\mathsf{cond}(\mathsf{A}) = z \wedge \mathsf{cons}(\mathsf{A})$. Recall $\mathsf{cons}(\mathsf{A})$ is the OCL constraint of the «after» pointcut, see Fig. 5(b).

Joins The above definition of T works fine if the base machine does not contain any join vertex. In order to include joins as well, we extend the definition of the candidate to $\{t \in T \mid \mathsf{tgt}(t) \text{ is not join}\} \cup T'$, where T is defined above, and T' contains all transitions such that $\mathsf{src}(t)$ is a join and for which t' and X exist, such that $\mathsf{tgt}(t') = \mathsf{src}(t)$, $X \in \mathsf{subvertex}(\mathsf{LCR}(\mathsf{src}(t), \mathsf{tgt}(t)))$, $\mathsf{src}(t') \in \mathsf{substate}^+(X)$ and $\exists s \in \mathsf{S} \cdot s \in \mathsf{substate}^+(X)$.

The basic idea here is that if a transition's target is not a join, then the definition above works fine, and if the target is a join, then we select the section leaving the join.

For example, let the base machine be given by Fig. 1(a), an aspect «after» Enchanted would advise the transitions from Enchanted and the join to LevelWon, as well as from Fight to Spell and PowerUp. Recall that since no constraint of the pointcut is explicitly given, the default is true.

4.2.3 Resumption

When the execution of the aspect is finished (at a final state of the advice), control is given back to the base machine by activating the state specified in the label of the final state, provided that the condition of the goto label is satisfied.

This is implemented as follows: we store in a *resumption variable* the state to activate, introduce transitions from the aspect state to all possible states (i.e. all states indicated by all the final states in the advice), and decide where to go by checking the value of the resumption variable at run time.

On every transition leading to a final state f of the aspect a (except the bypass $b(a)$, see the introduction part of Sect. 4.2), we assign the state of $\mathsf{label}(f)$ to the resumption variable. If a final state does not contain a label, the resumption variable is set to be the target of the advised transition. This variable will be used to determine the control flow of the base machine when the advice is finished. The bypass transition $b(a)$ does not carry an effect, so that the default value of the resumption variable is the target of the advised transition.

We also have to make sure the condition of the final state is satisfied before control is given back to the base machine. To this end, we guard the transitions leaving the aspect state by the condition $\mathsf{cond}(f)$. The oclConstraint part of the condition can be copied into the guard. The other part, cfgConstraint, which ensures that after the resumption a certain state configuration is (or is not) active, is implemented by checking if all states contained in the given configuration are active except for the target of the transition. In the implementation this amounts to checking the trace variables that were introduced in Sect. 4.2.1.

Note that we also declare the completion event of the aspect state to be deferrable[6], to make sure that this event is not lost even if the condition is not satisfied when the execution of the aspect state is finished.

For example, Fig. 9 shows the result of weaving Fig. 3(b) to the base machine Fig. 7(b). Note that both transitions from Spell and Invisible to Enchanted are advised, and that the resumption variables in the different aspect states are given unique names (by the weaver).

4.3 Multiple Aspects

Obviously, in any non-trivial system multiple aspects are needed to model the different features. For this reason, it is

---

[5] Actually, S getting inactive is caused by the transitions being fired.

[6] Using the syntax */defer, as before.

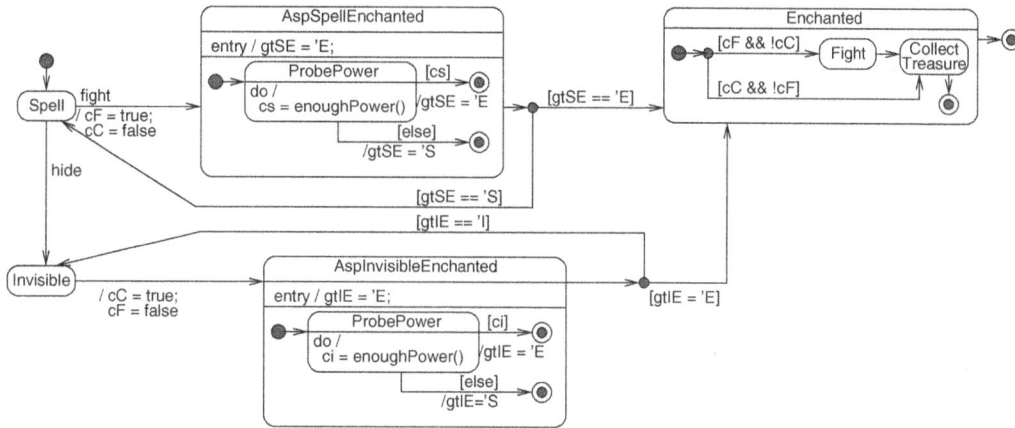

Figure 9. Weaving result of Fig. 3(b) to Fig. 7(b)

essential to design the weaving in a *confluent* way, i.e. the result is independent of the order of the individual aspects being woven. Particular care has to be taken for two kinds of conflicts: created joinpoints and shared joinpoints.

4.3.1 Created Joinpoints

After the execution of an aspect, if state x should be activated, the HILA semantics considers this also as a situation to execute the «before» x aspects, if any. Our weaving algorithm should ensure that in such cases, after the execution of the aspect and before state x is actually activated, all «before» x aspects are really executed.

For the implementation, we introduce another normalization step: before any weaving, we first "unify" the transitions leading to the same states. That is, we introduce for each state s a junction, which we call b4(s), introduce a transition tb(s) from b4(s) to s with no trigger, no guard and no effect, and make all transitions entering s lead to b4(s). In other words, we replace every transition from state x to s by two transitions: one from x to b4(s), as well as tb(s). Given an aspect with «before» s, the set of candidate transitions $T(s)$ contains then only tb(s). We also implement goto s by a transition from the aspect state to b4(s).[7] This way, when an aspect is finished with goto s, the transition tb(s), and therefore «before» s aspects do get executed.

Note that a prerequisite for this normalization is, in the effect of the transition from x to b4(s), to store the source state of the original transition in a variable, otherwise the label goto src of the advice could not be implemented correctly.

For example, applying this idea to Fig. 7(a), and then weaving Fig. 3(b) to it, the result is shown in Fig. 10. Variable s is used to indicate the (source of the) transition actually leading to the junction and then to AspEnchanted. The value is then read in AspEnchanted for the implementation of goto src.

---

[7] Except s is the target of the advised transition. In this case goto s is implemented by a transition leading to s.

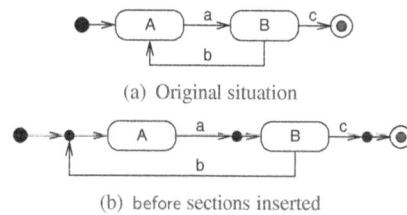

(a) Original situation

(b) before sections inserted

Figure 11. Weaving: unifying transitions leading to the same state

4.3.2 Shared Joinpoints

In non-trivial systems, joinpoints selected by (the pointcuts of) two or more aspects are generally not disjoint. In the context of HILA, this happens when at a certain point in time in the execution of the base machine, two or more aspects are all supposed to run. In aspect-oriented approaches, it is important yet challenging to make sure that the weaving result does not (semantically) depend on the order in which the aspects with shared joinpoints are woven, and that possible conflicts between the aspects are minimized, see [1].

In HILA, we benefit from the concurrent nature of UML state machines, and weave aspects with shared joinpoints into orthogonal regions of the aspect state. At run time, the aspects (that is, their advices) will be executed in parallel, and no goto is executed until all of the aspects are finished. This weaving is beneficial in that

- the weaving result is semantically independent of the order in which the individual aspects are woven, since different weaving orders only result in permutations of the regions of the aspect state. At run time, all the regions are, independently of their relative position, executed in parallel,

- and possible conflicting gotos of different aspects can be detected at latest at run time.

271

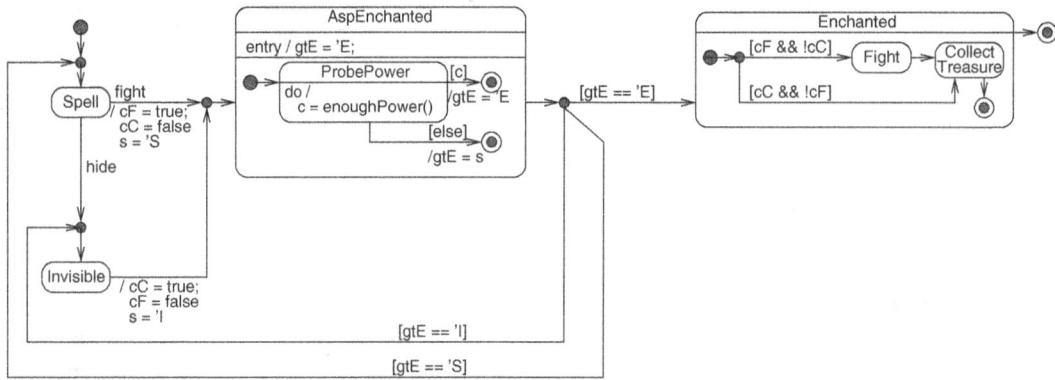

Figure 10. Normalization: before-section

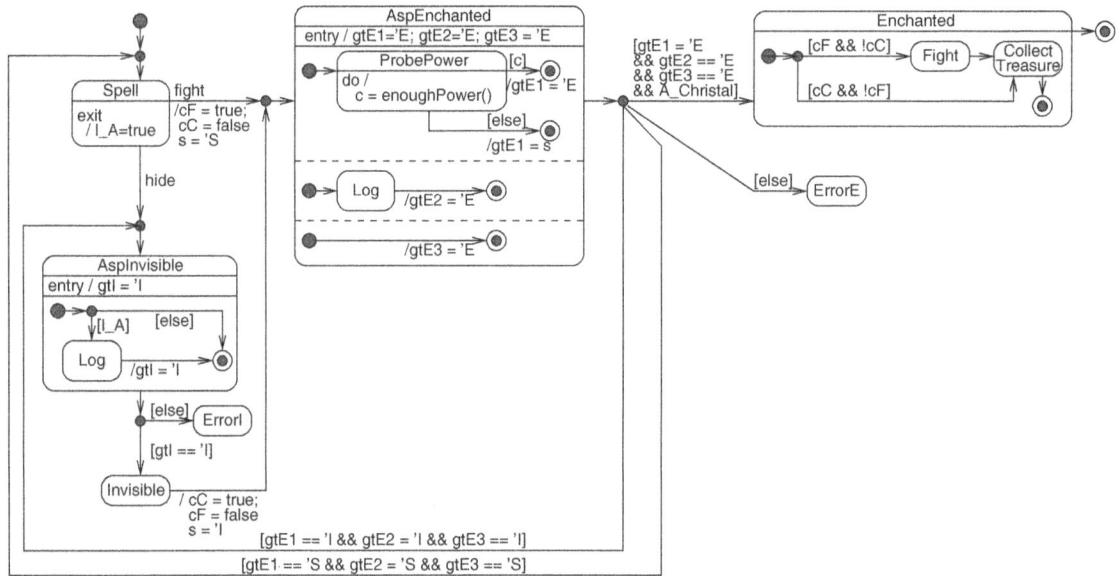

Figure 12. Weaving: shared joinpoints

For example, the result of weaving all three aspects defined in Fig. 3, with (S, T) bound to (Enchanted, CrystalRoom), to Fig. 7(a) is given in Fig. 12.

The idea of parallel execution of aspects is also valuable in other transition systems, beyond UML state machines. An example if given in Sect. 6.

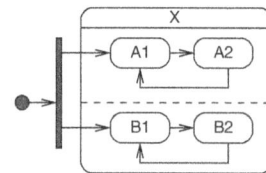

Figure 13. Base machine

5. Implementation and Validation

As a proof of concept, the above weaving process has been implemented in Hugo/HɪLA, an extension of the UML translator and model checker Hugo/RT. The case studies described in [10, 19], as well as several smaller examples have been translated and model checked using this implementation. Model checking the weaving result has helped validate our weaving algorithms: we discovered some subtle errors in earlier definitions of weaving and our implementation of the weaver when model checking did not produce the expected results. Having used our weaver in these small to medium

scale projects demonstrated not only the advantages of applying aspect-oriented techniques to state-machine models, but also that the implementation approach described in this paper can be applied to non-trivial examples.

Currently Hugo/HɪLA does not support the graphical notation of HɪLA. Instead, we have extended ute, the textual input format of Hugo/RT, to accept aspects as well. As an example, the ute definition of the simple base machine in Fig. 13 is shown in Fig. 14, and the ute presentation of the (instantiated) mutual-exclusion aspect in Fig. 3(c) is given

```
statemachine M1 {
  states {                transitions {
    initial INIT;           INIT -> FORK{}
    fork FORK;              FORK -> X.a.A1{}
    state X {               FORK -> X.b.B1{}
      region a {            X.a.A1 -> X.a.A2 {}
        state A1{}          X.a.A2 -> X.a.A1 {}
        state A2{}          X.b.B1 -> X.b.B2 {}
      }                     X.b.B2 -> X.b.B1 {}
      region b {          }
        state B1{}      }
        state B2{}
      }
    }
  }
}
```

Figure 14. UTE: base machine

```
aspect BeforeAspect {
  before config {           advice {
    state X.a.A2;             states {
    state X.b.B2;               initial AI;
  }                             labeledfinal AaF {
                                  goto tgt
                                    f nlike {A2, B2}
                                }
                              }
                              transitions {
                                AI -> AaF{}
                              }
                            }
                          }
```

Figure 15. UTE: instantiated aspect

in Fig. 15, with S and T being bound to A2 and B2. That is, we implement a mutual-exclusion rule to prevent A2 and B2 from being active simultaneously.

After weaving, we ask Hugo/HiLA if in the weaving result it is still possible for the states A2 and B2 to be active simultaneously, i.e. whether or not the states are really mutually excluded. This is expressed by the following formula in linear temporal logic (LTL):

```
F (inState(X.a.A2) and inState(X.b.B2))
```

The operator F (finally) states that the formula given as its argument will eventually hold, in this case that the states A2 and B2 will be active simultaneously at some point in time during the execution of the state machine. Hugo/HiLA answers that this is no longer possible, which confirms that the mutual-exclusion aspect performs its intended function.

On the other hand, we also want to be sure that the aspect does not break other properties of the base machine. For example, we can also ask Hugo/HiLA if it is still possible for the states A1 and B2 to be simultaneously active in the weaving result. This is expressed by the formula

```
F (inState(X.a.A1) and inState(X.b.B2))
```

and Hugo/HiLA answers that this result is indeed still possible.

6. Related Work

Prevalent approaches of incorporating aspect-orientation into UML state machines, such as [3, 5, 12, 14], are mainly syntactic: their semantics are typically defined by graph transformation systems, such as Attributed Graph Grammar (AGG, [16]). In contrast, HiLA has a transition-system semantics that is independent of any particular implementation strategy. We can therefore define the semantics of aspects in a purely behavioral manner and show that the weaving process described in this paper is sound with respect to the semantics; see [17] for details. Similar considerations apply to weaving processes for systems like Mealy-automata [4] or UML activity diagrams.

In static approaches, consistency checks are supported by a confluence check of the underlying graph transformation, see e.g. [12]. Due to the syntactic character of the aspects, this check is also syntactic: there may be false alarms if different weaving orders lead to syntactically different but semantically equivalent results. In contrast, in our approach described in Sect. 4.3.2, the error state is only entered when the resumption variables are really conflicting.

The pointcut language JPDD [9] also allows the modeler to define "stateful" pointcuts. Compared with HiLA, a weaving process is not defined. State-based aspects in reactive systems are also supported by the Motorola WEAVR tool [6, 20]. Their aspects can be applied to the modeling approach Rational TAU[8], which supports flat, "transition-centric" state machines. In comparison, HiLA is also applicable to UML state machines, that in general include concurrency. Moreover, HiLA also considers hierarchical states and comes up with a more elaborate weaving process.

Ge et al. [8] give an overview of an aspect system for UML state machines. They do not give enough details for a thorough comparison, but it appears that the HiLA language is significantly stronger the theirs, and that the issues presented in this paper are not addressed by their solution.

The position of HiLA in a model-driven software development process is described in [2]. HiLA has been successfully applied to model a crisis management system [10] and in the area of Web Engineering [19].

7. Conclusions and Future Work

We have presented HiLA, a high-level aspect language for UML state machines, and in particular the weaving process underlying the HiLA implementation in Hugo/RT. By eschewing a purely graph-transformation based approach in favor of a semantic one, HiLA provides powerful, reusable abstractions that can greatly increase the modularity of state-machine models. Therefore HiLA serves as an example of how a carefully designed aspect system can improve the expressive power and modularity of the base language. By basing our implementation on Hugo/RT it becomes possible to

[8] http://ibm.com/software/awdtools/tau/

validate the desired properties of model and aspects as well as the correctness of the weaving process.

The normalization step presented in this paper is heavily dependent on the semantics of UML state machines. It converts them into a form that is well-suited to static analysis since it clarifies the relationship between transitions and the states they activate and deactivate. Therefore this work may also be useful for static analysis of UML state machines.

Meanwhile, the issues addressed by the weaving process described in this paper are generally applicable to languages that support concurrency and hierarchical states. For example, we are involved in the development of the POEM language [11], an aspect-oriented modeling language for self-aware, autonomic ensembles. Aspects in POEM pose similar semantic challenges as aspects in HiLA, and we expect that the implementation of POEM will utilize the mechanisms described in this paper.

Currently, a graphical editor for HiLA aspects is under development [13] which will automate the translation step from graphical models to the textual ute notation, and therefore make HiLA easier to use in software development.

Acknowledgments

This work has been partially sponsored by the EU project ASCENS, 257414.

References

[1] M. Aksit, A. Rensink, and T. Staijen. A Graph-Transformation-Based Simulation Approach for Analysing Aspect Interference on Shared Join Points. In K. J. Sullivan, A. Moreira, C. Schwanninger, and J. Gray, editors, *Proc. 8th Int. Conf. Aspect-Oriented Software Development (AOSD'09)*, pages 39–50. ACM, 2009.

[2] M. Alférez, N. Amálio, S. Ciraci, F. Fleurey, J. Kienzle, J. Klein, M. E. Kramer, S. Mosser, G. Mussbacher, E. E. Roubtsova, and G. Zhang. Aspect-Oriented Model Development at Different Levels of Abstraction. In R. B. France, J. M. Küster, B. Bordbar, and R. F. Paige, editors, *Proc. 7th Eur. Conf. Modelling Foundations and Applications (ECMFA'11)*, volume 6698 of *Lect. Notes Comp. Sci.*, pages 361–376. Springer, 2011.

[3] S. Ali, L. Briand, and H. Hemmati. Modeling Robustness Behavior Using Aspect-Oriented Modeling to Support Robustness Testing of Industrial Systems. *Software and Systems Modeling (SoSyM)*, 2011. To appear.

[4] K. Altisen, F. Maraninchi, and D. Stauch. Aspect-Oriented Programming for Reactive Systems: Larissa, a Proposal in the Synchronous Framework. *Sci. Comp. Prog.*, 63(3):297–320, 2006.

[5] S. Clarke and E. Baniassad. *Aspect-Oriented Analysis and Design: the Theme Approach*. Addison-Wesley, 2005.

[6] T. Cottenier, A. van den Berg, and T. Elrad. Joinpoint Inference from Behavioral Specification to Implementation. In E. Ernst, editor, *Proc. 21st Eur. Conf. Oriented Programming*

[7] D. Drusinsky. *Modeling and Verification Using UML State-charts*. Elsevier, 2006.

[8] J.-w. Ge, J. Xiao, Y.-q. Fang, and G.-d. Wang. Incorporating Aspects into UML State Machine. In *Proc. Advanced Computer Theory and Engineering (ICACTE'10)*. IEEE, 2010.

[9] S. Hanenberg, D. Stein, and R. Unland. From Aspect-Oriented Design to Aspect-Oriented Programs: Tool-Supported Translation of JPDDs into Code. In B. M. Barry and O. de Moor, editors, *Proc 6th Int. Conf. Aspect-Oriented Software Development, (AOSD'07)*, pages 49–62. ACM, 2007.

[10] M. M. Hölzl, A. Knapp, and G. Zhang. Modeling the Car Crash Crisis Management System with HiLA. *Trans. Aspect-Oriented Software Development (TAOSD)*, 7:234–271, 2010.

[11] M. M. Hölzl, M. Wirsing, A. Klarl, N. Koch, S. Reiter, M. Tribastone, R. D. Nicola, D. Latella, M. Massink, U. Montanari, R. Bruni, F. Plasil, J. Kofron, J. Sifakis, S. Bensalem, J. Combaz, E. Vassev, and F. Zambonelli. ASCENS White Paper, 2011. http://www.ascens-ist.eu/.

[12] P. K. Jayaraman, J. Whittle, A. M. Elkhodary, and H. Gomaa. Model Composition in Product Lines and Feature Interaction Detection Using Critical Pair Analysis. In G. Engels, B. Opdyke, D. C. Schmidt, and F. Weil, editors, *Proc. 10th Model Driven Engineering Languages and Systems (MoDELS'07)*, volume 4735 of *Lect. Notes Comp. Sci.*, pages 151–165. Springer, 2007.

[13] A. M. Kourtessi. Entwicklung eines Modellierungswerkzeugs für aspekt-orientierte Zustandsmaschinen. Diplomarbeit, Ludwig-Maximilians-Universität München, 2011. In German.

[14] M. Mahoney, A. Bader, T. Elrad, and O. Aldawud. Using Aspects to Abstract and Modularize Statecharts. In *Proc. 5th Int. Wsh. Aspect-Oriented Modeling*, Lisboa, 2004.

[15] OMG. UML 2.3 Superstructure. Specification, Object Management Group, 2010. http://www.omg.org/spec/UML/2.3/Superstructure/PDF/.

[16] G. Taentzer. AGG: A Graph Transformation Environment for Modeling and Validation of Software. In J. L. Pfaltz, M. Nagl, and B. Böhlen, editors, *Rev. Sel. Papers 2nd Int. Wsh. Applications of Graph Transformations with Industrial Relevance (AGTIVE'03)*, volume 3062 of *Lect. Notes Comp. Sci.*, pages 446–453. Springer, 2003.

[17] G. Zhang. *Aspect-Oriented State Machines*. PhD thesis, Ludwig-Maximilians-Universität München, 2010.

[18] G. Zhang and M. M. Hölzl. HiLA: High-Level Aspects for UML State Machines. In S. Ghosh, editor, *Rep. & Rev. Sel. Papers Wshs at MODELS'09*, volume 6002 of *Lect. Notes Comp. Sci.*, pages 104–118. Springer, 2009.

[19] G. Zhang and M. M. Hölzl. Aspect-Oriented Modeling of Web Applications with HiLA. In A. Harth and N. Koch, editors, *Rev. Sel. Papers Wshs. at ICWE'11*, Lect. Notes Comp. Sci. Springer, 2011. To appear.

[20] J. Zhang, T. Cottenier, A. van den Berg, and J. Gray. Aspect Composition in the Motorola Aspect-Oriented Modeling Weaver. *Journal of Object Technology*, 6(7):89–108, 2007.

(ECOOP'07), volume 4609 of *Lect. Notes Comp. Sci.*, pages 476–500. Springer, 2007.

Author Index

www.ingramcontent.com/pod-product-compliance
Lightning Source LLC
Chambersburg PA
CBHW061349210326
41598CB00035B/5927